The Giants of The Polo Grounds

{111118}

Critical Praise for

The Giants of The Polo Grounds

"A compelling and comprehensive history of an extraordinary ballclub."

New York Times

"The owners, stars like Mathewson and Mays, various eccentric players are all here in this vivid history by *Sports Illustrated* contributor Hynd."

Publishers' Weekly

"Fans of all ages will treasure the crazy quilt text for its stylish recall of the game's summer roots."

Kirkus Library Journal

"Just plain enjoyable as baseball is supposed to be."

The Pennsylvania Gazette

The Giants of The Polo Grounds

Second printing – November 2018

Red Cat Tales Publishing LLC
PO Box 34313
Los Angeles, California 90034

TYPOS: Creating an expanded second edition of this book was an enormous undertaking. The original manuscript was created on a typewriter in 1986-7. No digital edition existed. Hence, a copy of the original book needed to be scanned to a pdf, adapted into a Word document, then OCR programs run relentlessly. Then the original text of 135,000 words was expanded by the author to 215,000 and new photos added. Four proofreaders each went over the final document at least twice. Bottom line: we hate typos as much as the reader. Maybe more. But you may find a tiny number. There are more than 1,500,000 million characters, commands and spaces in this volume. We hope we got everything correct. If you spot anything we missed, no matter how tiny, please let us know at the contact e-mail below, with TYPO in the subject heading. Corrections will be made for future editions on the day we are alerted.

Contact for typos and all other issues: Red.Cat.Tales.Publishing@gmail.com

© Noel Hynd 2018

THE GIANTS OF THE POLO GROUNDS

The Glorious Times of Baseball's New York Giants

By Noel Hynd

(Revised and expanded 2019 Edition)

The Giants of The Polo Grounds

A Giant thank you to some new friends and some longtime friends who contributed to the creation of this book, either with written contributions, editing or moral support, or all of these. I'm thinking of you, Gary Mintz, Steve Rothchild, Wally Exman, Dave Baines, Doug Cooper, Gordon Taylor, Eddie Logan., Jr., Jeroen ten Berge, Gary Bedingfield, Bart Bramley, John Thorn, Tom Yankus, George Vecsey, Rich Rodgers, Don Scheck, Patricia White, Robert Schwartz, David Lippman, Seth Jonas, Rich Tatum, H. Scott Peck, August Menchini and Barry Mednick.

A special posthumous thank you to my late friend Art Rust, Jr., author, sports historian and talk show guy, who was a great advocate of this book in its first edition and had me on his WABC radio show from Macy's basement in New York along with Ira Berkow and Ed Kranepool.

A special thank you also to Ira Sadoff, who allowed me again to use his wonderful poem, *Autumn Elegy for The Giants* and to provide some insight into how this work was conceived. Thanks also to Steven Williams at the Indiana University Press for facilitating the use of *Polo Grounds* by the late Rolfe Humphries.

This edition of ***The Giants of The Polo Grounds*** is dedicated to those former New York Giants who were still with us as this revised edition began in January of 2018.

They are… Joe Amalfitano, Johnny Antonelli, Jackie Brandt, Ed Bressoud, Pete Burnside, Foster Castleman, Gil Coan, Ray Crone, Billy Gardner, Harvey Gentry, Joe Margoneri, Willie Mays, Mike McCormick, Ron Samford, Red Schoendienst, Wayne Terwilliger, Ozzie Virgil, Sr., Bill White, Al Worthington, and Roy Wright….

And it is also for those men who played for our respected adversaries from Ebbets Field, The Brooklyn Dodgers, and who remain with us.

They are… Bob Aspromonte, Eddie Basinski, Tommy Brown, Roger Craig, Don Demeter, Carl Erskine, Jim Gentile, Chris Haughey, Randy Jackson, Fred Kipp, Sandy Koufax, Joe Landrum, Tommy Lasorda, Glenn Mickens, Bobby Morgan, Ron Negray, Don Newcombe, Joe Pignatano, Marv Rackley, Ed Roebuck, Wayne Terwilliger, and Tim Thompson.

Thank you, gentlemen, for enhancing our love of baseball and enriching our lives.

The Giants of The Polo Grounds

The Giants of The Polo Grounds

AUTUMN ELEGY FOR THE GIANTS

For those of us who remember
the Alley at Coogan's Bluff,
the famous overhead catch, the home run
that left the Dodgers stunned
in '51, for those who can't forget
the dream outfield they gave away -
as if God asked for charity
from the poor - the present
seems a tiny scar above the eye
that hurts in the humidity,
that no one notices,
that gives us character
when character's not required.

How did it get there? The child
in us remembers. We recall the hour
and the day of every error,
the way we remember Willie's number,
the way we still wonder
how Joey Amalfitano
had even one good day.

So today, as we wrap ourselves
in the chilled and foggy air
of another era, another park,
it shouldn't bother us,
the complacent and the aging,
the newly lost, to watch
the hitless, to count the empty seats.
We think ourselves beyond defeat.

But each seat radiates
its ghostly presence: the fan
who gave it up for alcohol,
for TV, for the daily
stroll through Golden Gate Park,
where he hoped to be mugged. It hurts
like history, the way pleasure fades
so quickly like the double play
that cut short a possibly wonderful inning.

The Giants of The Polo Grounds

It hurts like the strike they should have swung at
thirty years ago in a ballpark in Manhattan,
where thousands gather in their apartments now
not watching the Giants, enjoying themselves.

                    IRA SADOFF - 1983

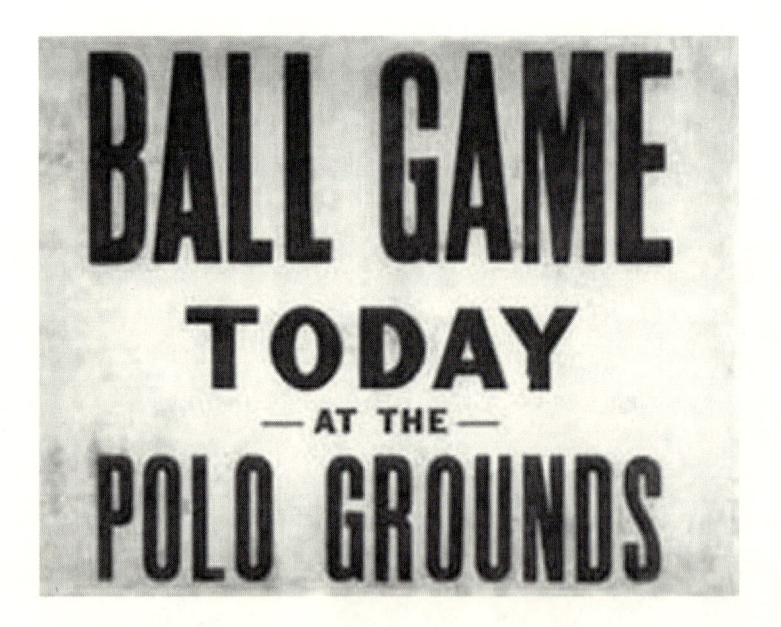

The Giants of The Polo Grounds

The Final Day...

September 29, 1957 was a sunny humid afternoon in upper Manhattan.

The New York Giants hosted their last home game at the rambling old stadium known as The Polo Grounds. Now the old place was an aging green ball park able to seat fifty-five thousand. Once it had been a horse-shoe shaped wooden grandstand with a carriage drive that enclosed the outfield. Yet, it seemed so recently that Dusty Rhodes had tortured the Cleveland Indians in the 1954 World Series, or that Bobby Thomson had lined a home run into the lower stands in left field to cap the greatest pennant race of all time.

All of the past screamed out and seemed so recent. But it was all gone and what was happening seemed to be plain wrong. On the right field grandstand there was a banner. "STAY TEAM STAY!" it begged. That same morning, head groundskeeper Matty Schwab had loaded a square of the center-field sod into a box for shipment to San Francisco. Photographers recorded the moment. The camera brigade also found Bobby Thomson, who had returned to the Giants mid-season in a trade. They posed him pointing to the spot in left-field where he had hit the most famous home run in baseball history. Thomson was a modest man who never would have stood there and pointed. But the camera guys posed him anyway. It was that sort of day.

Johnny Antonelli would pitch this day. Bobby Thomson was in the line-up at third base. Whitey Lockman had returned also. He was at first. For old times' sake, the final manager of the New

The Giants of The Polo Grounds

York Giants, Bill Rigney, who had once been a deft infielder for the club, had placed the final links to recent glory in the starting lineup. Dusty Rhodes started, too, as did Willie Mays and Wes Westrum. But the sad truth was that the New York Giants were once again mired in sixth place, a position they had occupied a good deal of the time for the past three seasons.

Fewer than twelve thousand fans attended, proving something that Horace Stoneham had been insinuating: people weren't coming to the ball park. In response, Horace was taking his fabled team to San Francisco.

It was unbelievable. New York's oldest team was leaving for a new life and new existence three thousand miles away. After eight decades of baseball at a place known as the Polo Grounds, there would be no baseball here the following April. For the New York Giants, winter would be forever.

Do you believe in ghosts? A few were on hand that day. You could have seen them in the Giants' locker room before the game. Now they were on the field as Russ Hodges, the affable television and radio commentator for the team these last few years, conducted a ceremony drenched in sadness.

Rube Marquard, the star pitcher of the pre-World War One era was there, visiting the players, taking a last glance at the old park. He looked to be in good health, despite his sixty-eight years. His face was weathered, but he was lean and erect. Rube told a few of the vintage stories, like the way McGraw had paid eleven thousand bucks for him, only to watch him get shelled in his first outing. He was joined by George Burns, McGraw's left fielder from the World War I era. When Russ Hodges introduced them, older fans remembered and gave them applause.

Larry Doyle was there, too. He was no longer young and no longer a Giant, except in his heart, where he was both. He talked about coming to the club in 1904. McGraw took him out for a beer and Doyle was too scared to order anything but ginger ale.

Moose McCormick, who had played against the Red Sox and A's in the World Series of 1912 and 1913, was there, too. So was Rosy Ryan, who had struck out the great Babe Ruth more than a few times in the World Series in the 1920's. Carl Hubbell attended also, as did Mrs. Blanche McGraw, John's widow. Mrs. Jane Mathewson, Christy's widow, was invited but declined to attend. She said it would be too painful.

Many of the fans who showed up had been following the Giants

The Giants of The Polo Grounds

since the turn of the century. In the poignant pre-game ceremony, they were happy to once again see Jack Doyle, Hook Wiltse, and other heroes of a bygone era. Jack Doyle, at age 86, was the oldest living ex-Giant. No relation to Larry, he was a native of Ireland who had played first base in the 1890s and managed in 1895. There also were Rosy Ryan, George (Kiddo) Davis, George Burns, Hans Lobert, Red Murray, Frank Frisch, and Moose McCormick, players who went back many decades. They had all played for John McGraw in the first third of the Twentieth Century.

Hal Schumacher, Carl Hubbell, Blondie Ryan, Billy Jurges, Buddy Kerr, Babe Young, Willard Marshall and Sid Gordon were there, too. They were from the Bill Terry era.

Finally, from Leo Durocher's two pennant winning clubs, there were Sal Maglie, Monte Irvin and Hank Thompson, in addition to Mays, Bobby Thomson and Rhodes who were still active. The loudest applause was for pitchers Hubbell and Maglie, a lefty and a righty.

Maglie had gone on to play for other teams, including the cross-borough Yankees and Dodgers. Today, all was forgiven.

"If you had one game you had to win," said one fan, "you'd want Maglie on the mound."

No one disagreed.

The sense of loss and the specters of the past were painful. Carl Hubbell couldn't bear to think what might become of the Polo Grounds. "I'd feel mighty bad to come back here and see a housing project," he said. "New York without the Giants just won't be the same."

Larry Doyle commented, "If you had told me a year ago that they would be going to San Francisco, I would have thought you were crazy."

Eddie Brannick, the Giants' long-time secretary who had worked for the team for more than fifty years, concurred. "It's a sad day. From 1905 is a long time," he added. "But, like the song, I guess it's best just to say, 'Que Sera Sera, whatever will be, will be.'"

Before the game, Bill Rigney walked around the center field clubhouse, constantly singing *Bon Voyage*." He said he couldn't keep it out of his head.

"I guess I'm a little nostalgic," Rigney said. "I'm going to miss this place. I like San Francisco, but this place here was our big goal when we were kids. Coming up through the minors, we were just hoping to get to the Polo Grounds. Now we're leaving it."

The Giants of The Polo Grounds

Russ Hodges valiantly continued the ceremony at home plate. At that time, the fans in attendance had their chance to transmit their sentiments to Horace Stoneham, the owner who was moving the team. The fans, who felt as if they had been disowned, reacted predictably at the one mention of the club owner's name in pre-game ceremonies.

"Mr. Stoneham," said Hodges to an avalanche of long loud boos, "asked me to express his thanks for your being here with him and the Giants today." Hodges continued. "He wishes to thank you for your generous support through the years." He was greeted with an even louder chorus of derisive laughter, inventive profanity and more boos. "All the Giants will remember," Hodges finished.

The club owner was on the other side of a closed window in his upstairs office in the clubhouse, far from his customers.

One by one, as Hodges presided near home plate, every old-timer stepped up for his special moment. Hodges gave each a laminated picture of the Polo Grounds. The picture had been taken at least a decade earlier when there still were elevated tracks where the housing project now was, adjacent to the Giants' home.

Present but not introduced were Baseball Commissioner Ford Frick and National League President Warren Giles. To more than a few fans, they looked like honorary undertakers. Even Coogan's Bluff in the background looked forlorn.

Bill Rigney placed an arm of comfort around Mrs. Blanche McGraw, John's widow for more than two decades. When Rigney kissed Mrs. McGraw, for the benefit of the newsreels, she shed so many tears that someone had to find a handkerchief. Rigney later presented her a bouquet of American Beauty roses, per the day's script. Mrs. McGraw was challenged to smile.

"I still can't believe I'll never see the Polo Grounds again," she said. "New York can never be the same for me."

The Giants even brought back one of the original voices of the Polo Grounds, a gentleman named George Levy, now eighty-one. He announced the day's batteries through a megaphone, exactly as he had done it 50 years ago, before the advent of public address systems. He had the old megaphone with him today and made the final call, walking the aisles as he had done decades earlier, booming it out for all the ages and to all the corners of the grand old ballpark.

"The baaaaatttereeees for today's gaaaaaaame...."

The ceremony ended. But along with the move of the Dodgers to

12

The Giants of The Polo Grounds

Los Angeles, which would not be "official" for another two weeks, nothing would ever be the same. The Giants and The Polo Grounds had once been the most famous names in baseball.

But not anymore.

Yes, a game of baseball would be played that day. But at the same moment something vital was being ripped out of the heart and soul of New York City.

The managers, Bill Rigney of the Giants and Danny Murtaugh of the Pittsburgh Pirates, met at home plate for the cursory mention of ground rules. They exchanged the starting line-ups. The umpires were Vic Delmore at home plate, Augie Donatelli at first, Vinnie Smith at second and Ed Sudol at third.

Johnny Antonelli (12-17) would pitch for the New York Giants. Bob Friend (13-18) would be on the mound for the Pirates. By a strange quirk of fate, the Giants would end New York's oldest baseball dynasty as they had begun it under Coogan's Bluff seven decades earlier, on July 8, 1889, when they had beaten the Pirates on this same field. Oddly enough, the Pirates had also closed out Ebbets Field, another icon in baseball history, five days earlier.

At a few minutes after two p.m., the New York Giants took the field for the final time.

The game began. Antonelli gave up a single to Gene Freese in the top of the first, then a triple to Bob Skinner. Willie Mays, much in his prime, retrieved the ball and threw to the plate, nailing Skinner who had tried for an inside the park home run.

Then, for a few minutes, some of the old Giants magic was back in the bottom of the first.

Don Mueller singled with one out. Mays followed with a single, sending Mueller to third.

Dusty Rhodes batted and lofted a short fly to the outfield. Mueller broke for home and scored on a close play at the plate, evading a tag by a rookie catcher.

The Giants were tied 1-1 after one inning.

For a final time, the Giants fans settled into a game. The Pirates came to bat in the second inning.

It was difficult to fathom that this game was the end of the Giants in New York. Just three years after a World Championship, the Giants were a second division club and dead last in the National League in attendance.

But one could daydream. One could recollect.

Memories were everywhere....

The Giants of The Polo Grounds

PART ONE:

THE EARLY YEARS

The Giants of The Polo Grounds

Chapter 1   In the beginning…

**"I see great things in baseball.
It's our game, the American game."**

Walt Whitman

Much New York baseball history could be traced to a misshapen shortstop named Davy Force and a jowly Chicago businessman named William A. Hulbert.

Hulbert was a shrewd, portly Midwesterner, an alumnus of Beloit College and very much a product of his times. Chicago of the 1870s was a bustling young city, recovering from the Great Fire of 1871 and rife with aspirations and opportunity. Hulbert saw plenty of opportunity in baseball, but not in the way the game was currently conducted. The sport's popularity had grown rapidly in the years since the Civil War. Local amateur "nines" frequently filled village greens with spectators. But in the larger metropolitan areas, professionalism had crept in. Although team loyalties remained vague, by the late 1860s some men were receiving a few dollars a head to participate in important games.

The year 1871 saw the first attempt to organize the sport. A league called the National Association of Professional Base Ball Players had been founded on St. Patrick's Day in New York, appropriately enough in a saloon. There were ten teams represented at that meeting, although only nine teams started the season. The team from New York was called the Mutuals and home games were played in Brooklyn. Another team called the White Stockings were from Chicago. William Hulbert, who had already made a fortune in the coal business, owned the latter. Proprietorship allowed Hulbert to see everything that was wrong with organized baseball.

Alcohol, for example, was a major problem. At every professional ball field, beer and whiskey were consumed liberally by players and fans - or "cranks" as the fans were then called. The result was much as it would be today. Rowdyism in the grandstands and something which might generously be termed impaired judgment on the field. But this wasn't the worst of it.

Two practices of the time, commonly known as "hippodroming" and "revolving," were diminishing the public's faith in the game's integrity.

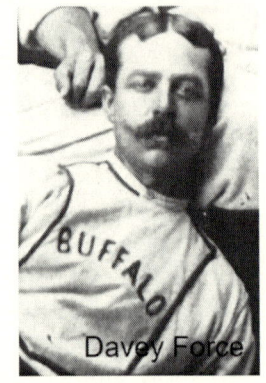

Revolving was the custom of jumping from one team to another as soon as a better monetary offer came along. As there was no reserve rule and frequently players competed without contracts, moving from one club to another was a relatively uncomplicated procedure. Then there was hippodroming, the practice of a ballplayer giving something less than 100 percent of his best efforts to win a game. More succinctly stated, ball games were frequently tanked in collusion with the professional bookmakers who worked the ball fields. Here was a problem that sent William Hulbert's blood boiling. Nothing, he reasoned, would poison the public against baseball more than gambling and rigged matches. As the seasons passed in the early 1870s, he was proven correct. Hippodroming became flagrant. Attendance at National Association games plummeted in response.

Enter Davy Force, looking out for no one other than himself.

Force was a freakish, bowlegged chunky little character, standing marginally higher than five feet, but weighing in at 160 pounds. He was reputed to be the best shortstop of his day, perhaps due to his proximity to the ground. In any case, the end of the 1874 season found Mr. Force in the employ of the Chicago White Stockings, Hulbert's team.

Hulbert, anxious to solidify his club for the following campaign, offered Force a contract. Davy read the terms and liked them. Then the Athletics of Philadelphia also made Force a good offer. So the shortstop signed with both teams.

Hulbert appealed to the league, maintaining that he had been first to sign Force, hence owned the rights to little Davy for the 1875 season. A league judiciary committee ruled in Hulbert's favor. But

The Giants of The Polo Grounds

not long afterward, in Philadelphia, some of the eastern club owners convened another judiciary meeting and reheard the case. Hulbert attended. Not surprisingly, the deck was stacked. This was Star Wars of the 1870s and the Force was awarded to Philadelphia. Hulbert stormed out of the meeting and returned to Chicago.

The Force case was another in a series of incidents where the more powerful eastern clubs (notably New York, Boston, and Philadelphia) had swiped players from western teams, particularly Chicago. Hulbert fumed. Then he did what any earnest American entrepreneur of his time would have done. He set out to destroy his competitors and their inept league, using any means at his disposal.

Hulbert began with two premises: The best team would quickly control the league and draw the best crowds. And similarly, as baseball was very much a pitcher's game, the best pitcher would control a club's fortunes. Hulbert's attention quickly settled upon one Albert Goodwill Spalding, currently of the Boston Red Stockings.

Spalding was the premier player in the game. He pitched Boston to 57 victories in 1875, against only 5 defeats. On his days off from hurling, he had batted .318 as a combination outfielder and first baseman. He was a big, strapping, intelligent man, standing just short of six-two (a veritable giant for his day) and often approaching 200 pounds. Fortunately for William Hulbert, Spalding was also a native of Illinois. Hulbert met with Spalding, then played neatly upon the Illini connection.

"You've no business playing in Boston," Hulbert said to A.G. "You're a western boy. You belong right here."

"Here" meant the Windy City. And to make sure that Spalding felt like he belonged, Hulbert offered his potential recruit a salary of $2000 a year, plus a quarter of the White Stockings' gate receipts, and the combined post of manager and captain of the team.

Spalding, no one's fool, quickly agreed. Then, to make sure that he would have something respectable to manage, he helped Hulbert pirate three other Boston stars for the following season: Ross Barnes, James (Deacon) White, and Cal McVey. They and Spalding became known as the "Big Four" when word of the arrangements leaked out during the 1875 season.

But Hulbert still had a score to settle with the Philadelphia club. So he and Spalding, on a day off from the Red Stockings' schedule, took a train to Philadelphia and secured the services of Adrian Constantine (Cap) Anson for Chicago in the 1876 season. Then, satisfied that he now had stars at five of nine positions for the following season, and confident that current personnel could round out the other four positions, Hulbert folded away his checkbook and went home.

There was much hostile press, particularly in New England, over Hulbert's moves. But the Big Four bore down and finished their commitment to Boston with poise and ability. The Red Stockings won 71 of 79 games in 1875, routing all opposition for the league championship.

Hulbert, of course, had transgressed the very league rules that he had wanted enforced. But so what? The eastern teams had done it to him time and time again. He had returned the favor in spades. But as the city of Boston celebrated their fourth consecutive title, other visions danced before Hulbert's eyes. What if, he mused, the governing eastern owners in the National Association retaliated by suspending the five jumping players?

This prospect must have cost Hulbert some sleep. But he had the angle covered by midwinter when Spalding brought up the subject.

"They can't suspend you," Hulbert answered. "They wouldn't dare."

"No?" Spalding asked.

"No," Hulbert answered. His reasoning was straightforward. The five players involved were some of the brightest stars of the National Association. No stars, no attendance around the league. No attendance, no gate receipts. Hulbert was probably correct, but he was taking no chances. He invited Spalding to move into Hulbert's Chicago home in December 1875. Together, the two men wrote a constitution for a new league. By New Year's, they had a finished document.

The new constitution addressed the self-destructive practices of the National Association. First, the new league would be an organization of baseball clubs, not players, a significant shift of power. New bylaws would add the proper professionalism and respect to the sport. Gambling on games, as well as drunken and disorderly behavior on club grounds, was to be prohibited. So was the sale of alcohol. In respect of the Sabbath, Sunday baseball was banned. Contracts would be strict. The practice of 'revolving' would

The Giants of The Polo Grounds

not to be tolerated. Umpires would be paid professionals. Ticket prices, a steep 50¢, would be uniform around the league. And, hippodroming would be dealt with harshly.

As far as the schedule was concerned, all games were to be played. It had been the practice of some of the weaker clubs in the National Association to fail to make expensive road trips at the end of a season, leaving the burden of completing pennant competition upon the contenders. With all this completed, Hulbert formulated a name for his new organization: the National League of Professional Base Ball Clubs.

Next, Hulbert traveled to Louisville, Kentucky, where he met with owners of the top semiprofessional clubs from St. Louis, Cincinnati, and Louisville. Appealing to their anti-East, anti-Association sentiments, he soon had their commitment to join his new league. They were, in fact, eager.

Hulbert returned to Chicago with a four-team league in his pocket. But he knew that to get his new league off the ground, he needed the cooperation of the very men he was trying to outflank. So in mid-winter, he journeyed to New York and registered at the Grand Central Hotel on Broadway between 8th and 9th streets, just east of Washington Square. He invited the presidents of the National Association's four strongest eastern teams to talk to him, first individually, then as a group.

The date was recorded: February 2, 1876. Representatives of the Philadelphia Athletics, the Boston Red Stockings, the Hartford Dark Blues, and the New York Mutuals met in Hulbert's hotel room. Lost in the shuffle was any discussion of Hulbert's pirating of the five players from Boston and Philadelphia. The owners listened to Hulbert's convincing plans for making professional baseball a profitable enterprise. When Hulbert left New York, the National League of Professional Base Ball Clubs was a reality. Not by coincidence, it had wonderful geographical balance: Chicago, St. Louis, Louisville, and Cincinnati in the West. Hartford, Boston, Philadelphia, and New York in the East.

Perfecto!

But there was one quirk to the proceedings which would have profound repercussions. One of Hulbert's primary goals was to eliminate such improprieties as drunkenness, unkept schedules, and fixed matches. Yet prominent among his guests at the Grand Central Hotel had been one William H. Cammeyer, president of the New York Mutuals.

The Giants of The Polo Grounds

In the old National Association days, the Mutuals had been among the most frequently guilty of the practices Hulbert loathed. And therein lay his problem.

Even in 1876 the Mutuals and the city they represented were too big to ignore. Baseball thrived in New York. The Mutuals had a strong following and, obviously, had the nation's largest metropolitan area to draw upon. To exclude the Mutuals would be to allow a heartbeat in the old National Association. To include them, would be to invite trouble. Hulbert chose the latter course…with predictable results.

A measure of how anxious Hulbert was for the Mutuals to break with their murky past can perhaps be seen in the team's attire. In the old National Association days, the club alternately wore green leggings or brown leggings and were known, alternately, as the Green Stockings or Chocolate Stockings. This year, going along with a charade concocted by Hulbert, they wore crisp white uniforms with red leggings. And since games were played again at the Union Grounds in Brooklyn, the team became known as the Brooklyn Mutuals.

It was as if the team were in disguise. This fooled no one.

As the infant league teetered through its inaugural season, the Chicago White Stockings supplanted Boston as the class of the circuit, with Hulbert's cash register happily ringing along the way. Boston, its best personnel gone, gave futile chase. The Mutuals and the Athletics, the two most tainted teams from the old days, merrily tainted themselves some more. Several contests were laughably suspicious. So attendance in New York and Philadelphia dwindled, just as William Hulbert had prophesized.

Toward the end of the season, the Mutuals' president, Bill Cammeyer, found himself pressed financially. With his home turnstiles quiet, he was unwilling to take his team on its final western swing. He figured Hulbert would understand. Cammeyer sent his regrets west, but no team.

In Philadelphia, the Athletics had a similar problem. The nation's Centennial Exposition of 1876 was staged in the Quaker City. It drew enormous crowds to Philadelphia. The crowds stayed away from the ball field almost in unison. So the Athletics joined the Mutuals in playing hooky from their final road trip.

But William Hulbert *didn't* understand. Not after all his hard work. And Bill Cammeyer, believing that Hulbert would turn into a softie in enforcing league rules, was mistaken.

On December 7, 1876, the league convened a meeting at the Kinnard House Hotel in Cleveland. Team executives congratulated each other on completing their first season. Of 280 games scheduled, 260 had been played. But in the next order of business, the Philadelphia Athletics were expelled from major league baseball. So were the Mutuals.

Hulbert's new circuit was one year old. And New York, the biggest city in the United States and arguably the most enthusiastic baseball city in the world, was without a franchise in the National League.

Chapter 2   The National League

"Baseball is the very symbol, the outward and visible push and rush and struggle of the raging, tearing, booming nineteenth century."

Mark Twain

i

One of William Hulbert's wisest moves in founding the National League was to not ask for the presidency for himself. Instead, the post went to one Morgan G. Bulkeley, president of the Hartford Dark Blues. Bulkeley was an Easterner, acceptable to all the owners, and a man who would lend prestige to the new operation. He was a successful businessman who had served as a private with the 13th New York Volunteer Heavy Artillery in the American Civil War. He had served from May 28, 1862 until September 28, 1862 under General George B. McClellan in the Peninsula Campaign and later under General Joseph K. Mansfield.

Bulkeley had agreed to serve for only one year. After leaving the game, Bulkeley would become the mayor of Hartford, governor of Connecticut, and eventually a U.S. senator. In 1877, though, when Bulkeley resigned his post, William Hulbert became the second president of the National League.

Problems beset him immediately. Cincinnati was, for example, a fertile ground for headaches. The Red Stockings were owned by a meat packer named Josiah Keck whose company was named Porkopolis. He also owned an enterprise known as the Cincinnati Fertilizing Company whose main asset was a contract with the city to remove all vegetable and animal offal from public places. The remains were carted to the suburb of Riverside where they were incinerated at a plant known colloquially as "Si Keck's Stink Factory."

Here's where things got nasty. The Red Stockings, in their maiden voyage through the National League, had won only 9 of 65 decisions. Local wags suggested that the baseball enterprise and the plant that cooked the offal were one and the same.

Keck had had enough of this by June of 1877. With the baseball team losing money, he walked into the clubhouse one afternoon and announced that he was resigning his ownership. In other words, no one owned the team.

"If you go east and complete your schedule," he told his players, "you will have to do so at your own expense."

This early twist upon free agency was not received with universal glee. Several players repaired to a local drinking establishment to discuss the situation and of these, one, a left-handed infielder-outfielder named Jimmy Hallinan, was in jail the next morning when a representative of the William Hulbert's Chicago White Stockings arrived to bail him out and sign him and a lumbering Cincinnati outfielder named Charley Jones. (Much later, Jones would be the first big leaguer to hit two home runs in the same inning: both in 1890 off the same lucky pitcher, the appropriately named Tom Poorman of the Buffalo Bisons.)

Two weeks later a local ice merchant by the name of J. Wayne Neff assumed Si Keck's assets and liabilities. Two of his new assets, however, were now playing for Chicago and an employer who had inveighed against the practice of "revolving" for years.

When Neff restored temporary stability to the Cincinnati franchise, Hulbert must have been relieved. He said little as Jones, the better of the two players, packed up in early July and returned to the Reds. Hallinan stayed with Chicago until the middle of the 1878 season before moving on to Indianapolis. Neff didn't want him back. Perhaps Neff knew something. Hallinan played modestly for only one more season, retired, became a bartender, then in late October 1879, dropped dead from gastritis at the age of thirty.

But Cincinnati, this time combined with St. Louis, presented Hulbert with an even more challenging problem. Both cities were

The Giants of The Polo Grounds

heavily populated by the families of German immigrants who had fled the European revolutions of 1848. They liked their beer. They liked their beer at the ballpark, where Hulbert didn't want them to have it. Worse, they wanted their beer at the ballpark on Sundays when Hulbert didn't even want games played. And to make it all complete, these crowds wanted their brew and their ball *cheap* on Sundays. Hulbert's 50¢ admission charge was a moral outrage to fans in these western cities.

What to do? Hulbert refused to budge. So the two clubs, particularly Cincinnati, continued with their Sunday traditions, hoping the league president would ignore them. He was, after all, occupied elsewhere. Louisville, for example.

Albert Spalding had shifted himself from pitching to first base in 1877 and Deacon White returned to Boston, where he became the batting champion that season. All of this weakened Chicago and allowed Boston to make a late drive for the pennant. They won the pennant by seven games, but not without the help of four players on the Louisville team, Boston's main competition.

When the four players were spotted making the rounds of the Louisville saloons, flush with cash and sporting enough new gold rings and diamond stickpins to open a small jewelry concession, Hulbert investigated. He found that three games in particular had been tanked. Hulbert brought the four guilty players before him: pitcher Jim Devlin, shortstop Bill Craver, infielder Al Nichols, and outfielder George Hall.

Nichols, Craver, and Hall denied their guilt (though Hall had previously confessed to a sportswriter). Devlin made a halfhearted confession, feebly explaining that he had needed some extra money to support his family. A hundred dollars had found its way into his pocket from gamblers who bet against Louisville. Accordingly, all four were banned from baseball for life.

Nichols, Craver, and Hall promptly disappeared from professional baseball. Devlin, however, did not. In the years that followed, he often hung around National League offices looking for either handouts or reinstatement. Hulbert remained adamant about the lifetime suspension, but, because he liked Devlin personally, was known to slip him as much as fifty bucks just out of sympathy. Eventually Devlin, his reputation for dishonesty intact, found employment as a police officer in Philadelphia. (There he died in 1883 at the age of thirty-four.)

William Hulbert had hoped that the expulsion of the

The Giants of The Polo Grounds

"Louisville Four" would bolster public confidence in the integrity of baseball. Long term, it did. Short term, the incident boomeranged, calling attention to the fact that games had been fixed. Appropriately, two old New York Mutuals on the Louisville roster had been the chief culprits.

All of which circled things back to the New York and Philadelphia problem. The National League barely completed its 1877 season. Only six clubs had survived. The Mutuals and the Athletics had spun off into their own little association, something called the League Alliance. It was barely a league. There were twelve loosely confederated teams and hardly an alliance. There was no schedule. Added to this was the fact that William Cammeyer, formerly manager of the Mutuals, had cajoled the Hartford team into playing their home games at the Union Grounds in Brooklyn, where the Mutuals had formerly toiled.

Hartford, then, was actually Brooklyn, though New York, which had formerly been Brooklyn, was out of the league. None of this was to be put over on the good burghers of Brooklyn, however, who from the outset of the season almost unanimously knew better than to support a team with a Connecticut label. That in itself was enough to doom the franchise.

Thus, when the 1878 season got off to a wobbly start, the closest National League team to New York was a new entry in Providence, Rhode Island. That franchise was competitive only because it had happened upon the league's best new pitcher that year. His name was John Montgomery Ward and his time with the Providence Grays would prove to be limited. But this season he was one of the league's most effective hurlers. He was eighteen years old.

ii

In the 1870s and '80s, professional baseball was becoming a city game, with avid followings in all the major urban centers. Yet the game was not long out of the farms and backwoods, either.

Consider, for example, the 1877 batting champion, James (Deacon) White, one of the original "Boston Four" who had jumped with Albert Spalding to Chicago. White was normally a catcher or a third baseman. So, things being as they were, White spent the 1877 season shuttling back and forth between first base and the outfield. He was *so* adversely affected that he batted a ringing .387.

The Giants of The Polo Grounds

Deacon had a long distinguished career, which eventually included managing the Cincinnati club. In the first game ever played in a professional baseball league, Deacon White was the first man to hit safely. He went on to play for another two decades. Deacon White invented the wind-up for pitchers and popularized the catcher's mask. In the off season he was a gentleman farmer and a Sunday school teacher. The pillar of propriety, the Protestant ethic, and progressive thinking?

Well, yes and no. By all accounts he was a man of great integrity and manners. He was also "a fire and brimstone Christian, a sinners-in-the-hands-of-an-angry-God Puritan," according to his great grandson, James B. Jackson, writing in *Slate* in 2013, on the occasion of White's long overdue entry into the Baseball Hall of Fame in 2013.

He did not drink, smoke, curse, or gamble, which was just short of shocking for a ball player of the era.

In addition to all of the above, Deacon White was also one of the last serious proselytizers of the Flat Earth theory. "He very much believed that the world is flat, based on the Biblical passage about how Jesus 'will send the angels out to the four corners of the earth to gather God's chosen people from one end of the world to the other,'" Jackson wrote. If the earth were spherical like a baseball and revolving on an axis, White used to ask other players in the locker room, "Why does a pop fly come back down onto the playing field?"

Good question! Many of us have often wondered.

Deacon reasoned that if the world were really spinning, a pop fly should spin off into oblivion. Several players ridiculed White's beliefs, their minds having been poisoned by Copernicus and Galileo. But as Deacon White passed through the National League, won converts.

In the latter years of his life, White sat on a rocking chair on his back porch, facing west. He was waiting for Jesus to return, which he was convinced would happen in his lifetime. He believed that was the direction The Lord would come from. White rocked. And waited. He lived till he was 91. It would be another seventy years before he was admitted to the Hall Of Fame, where his catcher's mask is on display to this day.

Then, speaking of Jesus, there was one William Ashley Sunday, the fourth outfielder on the Chicago White Stockings from 1883 through 1887. At a baseball clinic in Marshalltown, Iowa, Sunday had been discovered by Cap Anson, who had by the late 1880s taken over from Spalding as manager of the Chicago club. Sunday was never more than a spot player with the White Stockings, but he *was* fast. According to Anson, Sunday was the fastest man in the National League.

By William Sunday's estimation, however, he was not alone in the outfield. For years he pinpointed a moment in a game against the Detroit Wolverines in the closing days of the 1886 season. With the White Stockings ahead, Sunday recalled, Detroit put two men on base.

Then the Wolverines' catcher, Charlie Bennett, walloped a fly ball to deep center. Sunday gave chase, his glove extended in the air and his mouth raised in prayer, imploring the Almighty that he might catch the ball. Suddenly, Sunday found himself leaping over the spectators' benches that littered the far reaches of the outfield. "As though wings were carrying" him, he said, he caught the ball, winning the game in the process.

"I am sure the Lord helped me catch that ball," Billy Sunday later told millions of Americans during his nationally famous evangelistic crusades of the early 1900s, "and it was my first experience in prayer." Nonetheless, Sunday had much more success spreading the word of Christ than Deacon White had in refuting Columbus.

Converting to evangelical Christianity in the 1880s, Sunday gave up pro baseball for the Christian ministry. He gradually developed his skills as a pulpit preacher in the Midwest and then, during the early 20th century, he became the nation's most famous evangelist with his colloquial sermons and fiery delivery. "Going to church doesn't make you a Christian any more than going to a garage makes you an automobile," he told those who came to hear him. With electrifying sermons, he would move about the stage like a man possessed, a gifted orator and athlete as a preacher. If one were cynical, one might think of him as the Jimmy Swaggart of his day.

Sunday held hugely popular revival campaigns for Christ in America's largest cities. He drew the largest crowds of any evangelist before the advent of radio and television. He was a strong supporter of Prohibition.

"I am the sworn, eternal and uncompromising enemy of the Liquor Traffic. I have been, and will go on, fighting that damnable, dirty, rotten business with all the power at my command," he would say in sermons.

His preaching played a significant role in the adoption of the Eighteenth Amendment in 1919. It thus gave rise to the great criminal empires of the 1920s. He also made a ton of money, mostly off small donations of the millions of Americans who came to see and hear him preach. Among those who weren't entirely convinced of his sincerity was author Sinclair Lewis, who drew generously upon Billy Sunday when creating the character of Elmer Gantry in the novel of the same name.

'Sunday preaching' by George Bellows, Metropolitan Magazine, May 1915

No one, however, had to create the character of Old Hoss Radbourn. Radbourn existed by himself, and as a fiction, he would have defied credibility.

His real name was Charles Gardner Radbourn, and he was a man blessed with a burning desire to spend his life hunting and fishing. Yet, the fates intervened. In 1880, at age twenty-five, Radbourn played in six games with Buffalo in the National League as an infielder-outfielder. He didn't much care for the life of a ballplayer and went home to Bloomington, Illinois, that fall to be a butcher's apprentice. In his free time, when the weather permitted, he pitched for a local nine.

The Providence Grays, the following spring, were looking for warm, capable bodies to fill out their roster. Their star, Johnny Ward (or Monte Ward, as John Montgomery Ward was alternately known), was being groomed for a shift from pitching to playing right

The Giants of The Polo Grounds

field. That meant that there was a spot available for a player who could fill in at two or three spots. A player such as Radbourn.

Providence management wired Radbourn, asking what his terms would be. Radbourn considered himself finished with baseball and didn't intend to reply. But a friend somehow came across the telegram and answered it in Radbourn's name, asking wages of $750 for the season. Providence wired back their agreement. The friend cajoled Radbourn into reporting.

What a piece of work was Old Hoss. All he did next was win 191 games for Providence during the next five years. Gradually assuming more of his pitching duties, he won 25, 31, and 49 games in his first three seasons. Yet he hadn't hit stride. His most memorable season was 1884.

It was in that year that Radbourn and Providence's other pitcher, one Charlie Sweeney, became personal antagonists. Each was jealous of the other's role on the club. There were other factors, too: Sweeney had a preponderantly belligerent nature and was one of baseball's all-time great drunks.

The trouble began in June. Up until that month, Sweeney and Radbourn had alternated evenly in pitching assignments. Then Sweeney struck out nineteen batters in a game and claimed the pitching job as his. Radbourn's role was reduced to that of a utility infielder and a sorehead sitting on the end of the bench. Occasionally, Radbourn was asked to pitch. But by this time he was so angry that he routinely discarded the signs of his catcher and fired the ball as hard as he could wherever he wished. Eventually, he was suspended.

No doubt he was a crusty soul. In the team picture of 1886, he can be seen on the far left in the second row flipping the finger at…. Well, at everyone, included us, across a century and a quarter.

The team, however, did well. They closed in on Boston and fought for first place. But simultaneously, Sweeney's appetite for booze knew no limits. The crisis arrived in August. Sweeney went on a colossal binge, then turned up to pitch while still drunk. Somehow, he nursed a 6-2 lead through seven innings. Manager Frank Bancroft then suggested that Sweeney move to right field to "rest his arm" for future pitches. Sweeney did not take kindly to the suggestion. He marched off the field, dressed, and bolted the team, never to return. (He turned up a week later with St. Louis of the outlaw Union Association.) That left the pitching duties to Radbourn.

All of them.

Legend has it that Radbourn pitched and won all the remaining games of the season. Legend has it wrong, but not by much. What he did do was pitch 36 of the next 39 games, including the last 27 in a row. Of these, he won 26. He did this with an arm that was too sore to hold a comb or a toothbrush each morning, but which was miraculously unkinked and loose daily by game time. He finished the season with a record of 60 wins and 12 losses. And most of the losses had been during the early season. In addition, his ERA of 1.38 and 441 strikeouts led the league.

Thus a career followed that sent Radbourn into the Hall of Fame in 1939, one of the first old-timers elected. Radbourn pitched for 11 seasons, winning 308 games and losing 191. Old Hoss still holds the record for career innings pitched without giving up a grand slam.

Much later, when his career was over, he reverted to his old ways. He retired to Bloomington and used the money he had earned in baseball to purchase a pool hall. In 1895 a hunting accident blinded him in one eye. Shortly thereafter, a form of slow blood poisoning set in and sight began to fail in his other eye. He further retreated from the world and spent much of his remaining time sitting in a dark room behind his pool hall waiting to die.

On February 5, 1897, a broken, bitter man, he accomplished just that.

Chapter 3   Miss Maggie & The King

"In our sundown perambulations of late, through the outer parts of Brooklyn, we have observed youngsters playing 'base', a certain game of ball... A game of ball is glorious."

Walt Whitman, 1846

The 1879 season saw three National League entries in the state of New York: Syracuse, Buffalo, and Troy. None was near Manhattan or Brooklyn. Only the Troy team, the Haymakers, would have any lasting significance. In their second year, 1880, they would develop two outstanding pitchers: Mickey Welch and Tim Keefe. Welch and Keefe would propel the Haymakers as high as fourth in 1880. More significant, however, were the events which transpired in the Palace Hotel in Buffalo on September 29, 1879.

There the owners of the eight National League teams met to eat, drink and congratulate each other for surviving another season, then eat and drink some more. The eight owners quickly found that they agreed over the one issue that moved them most: their belief that players were paid too much, a notion that has been close to the hearts to almost all owners in professional sports. The root of this evil, they further concluded, was the unregulated competition between clubs for the top players.

What to do?

The moguls made speeches, then adjourned after lunch to attend the afternoon game between the Buffalo Bisons and the White Stockings. In the evening they met again, ate some more, drank some more and issued an ominous document to the press stating that salaries had to be held down.

Secretly, however, the owners had hatched out a scheme which, like the racially-exclusive campaigning of Cap Anson a few years in the future, would bedevil baseball for the next century.

Not a word was uttered to the press on the subject, but the eight owners each submitted to the others a "reserve list" of five players.

The club owners agreed that those on the reserve list of an individual club would be off limits to any other club owner. Collusion, anyone? A team, in other words, could now keep its nucleus intact from one year to the next.

In subsequent years, the number of names on the list would increase to nine, then eleven, then the entire roster. Thus was born the reserve rule. Its most immediate result was the reemergence of the Chicago White Stockings as the royalty of baseball. Chicago locked up its established stars and then added one that the Cincinnati club, the one holdout against the reserve rule, refused to sign: Mike (King) Kelly.

Mike "King" Kelly - circa 1888

Kelly was the game's first superstar. He was an outfielder and a catcher, a slugger and a demon on the base paths. But he was also a *persona,* a world-class skirt chaser, horseplayer, and drinker. He played the vaudeville halls in the offseason and was immortalized by the song, *Slide, Kelly, Slide!* sung by a sultry music hall star named Maggie Cline.

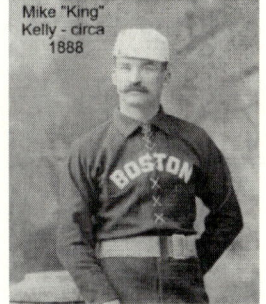

Like Kelly, Maggie was a star. She was a first-line American vaudeville singer, known across the country as "The Irish Queen." In New York, where she appeared most frequently and most lucratively, she was known as, "The Bowery Brunhilde."

Oh, what pipes this lady had.

Maggie's repertoire was a set of rough-and-tumble two-fisted Irish-themed songs and skits, belted out with a deep Gaelic brogue. She was the daughter of immigrants but had been born in Haverhill, Massachusetts, where she worked in a shoe factory as a girl in the era before child labor laws. She acted out her songs with boundless energy and ferocity for the beer swigging whiskey guzzling patrons who paid top dollar to see her. "The daughter of Hercules and descendant of Stentor," she billed herself, Stenor, in case you've forgotten, being the name of a remote herald in *The Iliad* who had a booming piercing voice.

Maggie sang such two-fisted Irish songs as *How McNulty Carved*

the Duck and *Nothing's Too Good for the Irish*. Now, what would be wrong with a few rounds of that? With beer of course! Maggie's first trademark song was *Mary Ann Kehoe*, a risqué ditty about a pretty young Irish lass pursued by two would-be lovers. "I have a daughter, Mary Ann, Mary Ann, my daughter, She fell in love with hump-back Dan."

Her second signature song was one called *Throw Him Down, McCloskey*, about a 47-round bareknuckle prize fight.

They fought like two hyenas 'till the forty-seventh round,
They scattered blood enough around, by gosh, to paint the town.
McCloskey got a mouthful of poor McCracken's jowl,
McCracken hollered 'murthur' and his seconds hollered "foul"!...
The friends of both the fighters that instant did begin
To fight, and ate each other—the whole party started in.
You couldn't tell the dif'rence in fighters if you'd try,
McCracken lost his upper lip. McCloskey lost an eye.

The Sporting News once took time out from baseball to enthusiastically describe Miss Cline to their readers as, "a buxom young lady." She was a lot more than that.

Cline was tall, tough, pretty and athletic. She would perform for more than 40 years, not retiring until she was sixty. *McCloskey* proved to Maggie's greatest hit. She once estimated that she sang it several thousand times. Whenever she performed the song it was as much a reenactment of the fight as it was a performance, typically involving furniture and other items being thrown about the stage and stage hands punctuating the chorus with the sounds of a struggle. It was quite a spectacle. You had to be there!

So *Slide, Kelly, Slide* was a natural for Maggie. It became a staple of her act, also. In between gigs in New York City and across the country, Maggie warbled "*Slide, Kelly, Slide!*" onto a phonograph record. The early recording became a national hit.

Think some of today's pop lyrics are a trifle banal? See if this sticks in your mind all day:

Slide, Kelly, slide!
Your running's a disgrace! Slide, Kelly, slide!
Stay there, hold your base!
If someone doesn't steal you,

The Giants of The Polo Grounds

*And if your batting doesn't fail you,
They'll take you to Australia.
Slide, Kelly, slide!*

Ms. Cline's hit was a chartbuster in 1888. Fans serenaded Kelly with it whenever he reached first base. He would then steal second and third as often as he could. The famous slide was a hook slide, with which Kelly would catch the edge of a base by a toe while his body swept away from the bag.

There was probably not enough mustard in the New World to cover King Kelly. Long before the Baltimore Orioles of the 1890s perfected the hit-and-run play, Kelly originated it. He also had a few pet plays of his own. Like going from first to third on a single. That is, *directly* from first to third, without the nuisance of stopping at second. This deft bit of base running was possible and indeed, not uncommon in the days of one umpire. Then there was the custom of announcing himself into the game at key moments. The rule of the day - subsequently changed due to abuses by Kelly among others - allowed a player into the game simply by loudly announcing himself to the umpire.

Once, according to contemporary observers, Kelly was sitting at the end of the Chicago bench with the White Stockings ahead and the opponents down to their final out. The batter lofted a pop foul in Kelly's direction, out of reach of any fielder. Off the bench sprang King Kelly.

"Kelly in the game at first base!" he bellowed, catching the ball and ending the contest. Not an entirely humble man, he also wrote a book about himself and his exploits, in that order of importance.

So Cap Anson provided the field leadership for the White Stockings. Kelly supplied the showmanship. The frontline pitching came courtesy of one Larry Corcoran. Corcoran was a hard throwing right-hander, Brooklyn born, who signed with Chicago at the age of twenty-one in 1880. Inadvertently, he became the first professional pitcher to work out a series of signals with his catchers. Corcoran was rarely without a massive chew of tobacco sloshing around his mouth. Lee Allen, the longtime historian at the Baseball Hall of Fame, in Cooperstown, New York, once described the movement of the tobacco around Corcoran's mouth as resembling "an elephant begging for peanuts from a crowd."

Corcoran's catchers, Frank (Silver) Flint and King Kelly, who spent a good deal of their working time watching Corcoran, thought

The Giants of The Polo Grounds

the motion was amusing, also. They suggested that Corcoran indicate the type of pitch he was about to throw by shifting his chaw around his mouth. Left cheek for a fastball, for example. Right cheek for a curve. And so on. Thus, amid much saliva, was born the system of catcher-to-pitcher signals. Over five seasons, Corcoran compiled a lofty won loss record of 170-84. Three of the wins were no-hitters and Corcoran's cumulative ERA was barely more than two runs per game. The next five years were less favorable to Corcoran, as he gradually wasted away of Bright's disease, the general term used for a severe kidney disorder and dissipation. By 1891, at the age of thirty-two, he was dead. But meanwhile, through the 1880s, the White Stockings were the team to beat in the National League.

The White Stockings were so relentless in their supremacy that they entered a new verb into the popular vernacular. To be shut out or badly thrashed in a ball game was to be "Chicagoed." The term passed into general usage. A man beaten up in a barroom brawl was said to have been Chicagoed. At least one writer suggested that General Custer, at Little Big Horn during the previous decade, had been Chicagoed by the Sioux. And after the 1880 season, the Cincinnati franchise got Chicagoed by the powers of the National League, the second immediate result of the reserve agreement.

Through the 1880 season, Cincinnati had continued to cater to the Germanic tastes of its fans. Hawkers peddled beer and whiskey in liberal quantities on club grounds. At the end of the season, William Hulbert prevailed upon the other owners to expel Cincinnati for this practice. Detroit joined the league in Cincinnati's place.

The move incensed the thirsty populace of the Queen City. Now they had beer and baseball on Sundays but no league in which to play. Cincinnati newspapers were filled with angry suggestions of what Hulbert and the National League could go do. One indignant writer maintained that as long as the league bigwigs were in the business of legislating morality, they might next turn their attention to Hulbert's Chicago, where, it was reliably reported, some of the Windy City's yummiest prostitutes plied a profitable trade in the right field grandstand.

If Hulbert winced at this suggestion, no one heard him. The truth was that he wanted Cincinnati out of the league due to its opposition to the reserve rule. He wanted a tight, workable agreement between club owners on certain basic rules.

In the end, Hulbert got his way.

The National League proceeded into the 1881 season with eight clubs: Chicago, Providence, Buffalo, Detroit, Troy, Boston, Cleveland, and Worcester, in that order of finish. It was the smoothest, most profitable season to date.

But it was the last year that William Hulbert was able to enjoy. His health was failing. Over the winter, much against his wishes, he was reelected president of the league. In January, when the 1882 schedule was being drawn, Hulbert was too ill to participate. Sensing the end, he sought to leave his work in good hands. Arthur Soden, the architect of the reserve rule, was appointed temporary president of the National League, entrusted to serve out Hulbert's term.

On April 10, 1882, William Hulbert died in his Chicago home. Had he been asked on his deathbed what his greatest bit of unfinished business had been, there is little doubt of how he might have replied. A major league, after all, was hardly a bigtime affair with America's two largest cities, Philadelphia and New York still absent.

Chapter 4   Deacon, Mutrie & Day

"Baseball was mighty and exciting to me, but there is no blinking at the fact that at the time the game was thought, by solid sensible people, to be only one degree above grand larceny, arson, and mayhem."

Connie Mack on baseball in the 1880s

William Hulbert died just in time.

In 1882 several teams had been cast off by the established National League St. Louis, Philadelphia, Cincinnati, and Louisville combined with new clubs from Pittsburgh and Baltimore to form the American Association. The new circuit was established to compete with the National League. At first it had trouble keeping its own gates open, as it was distinctly inferior.

The Giants of The Polo Grounds

But a few National League castoffs kept up fan interest, notably Will (Whoop La) White. Will was Deacon's brother, seen here, and an outstanding pitcher for Cincinnati. He had no use for his brother's flat earth theories and was the first player to wear eyeglasses during a game. But the owners knew how to sell the American Association brand of baseball to their fans. The new baseball moguls were aggressive businessmen (four of the six were brewers) who merrily raided National League rosters. Then they dressed their players in gaudy silk uniforms, creating a much more colorful field image than the staid flannels of the established circuit. They sold tickets for half the National League price, peddled beer from their own breweries at the ballpark and joyously played ball on the Sabbath

This was trouble. And here again arose the question of a franchise for New York. The National League and the American Association might be able to go head-to-head for a few seasons, but only one would eventually survive as a major league. Then, as in later years, financial survival was closely linked to dominating the major market areas. So who owned New York? The answer to that question was determined by the chance remark of a bootblack.

In the late 1870s, professional teams formed all over the eastern United States and Canada. Some were touring clubs. Others joined minor leagues. One such, as already mentioned, the League Alliance, took in the New York Mutuals and the Philadelphia Athletics after they had been expelled from the National League.

At about the same time, there was a prosperous young tobacco merchant named John B. Day, on view formally here. He lived in Manhattan. He fancied himself an athlete.

Day organized a ball club in Orange, New Jersey, purchased equipment, paid his players, and announced that he was the pitcher. On one momentous afternoon, Day and his team traveled to Brooklyn to play one of the local nines. Day pitched. The results were much the same as if one of today's owners, let's say a latter-day George Steinbrenner or a Ted Turner, decided to pitch. A short time later, Day found himself sitting in the grandstand, watching the game.

38

The Giants of The Polo Grounds

A stranger named James Mutrie settled into the next seat. Mutrie had just pedaled his way to New York on a bicycle from New Bedford, Massachusetts. He had a keen interest in baseball, high ambition, and no money. Like Day, he was in his mid-twenties. Mutrie had just seen Day get trashed by the Brooklyn club.

"Want to get a team that will beat those people who just knocked your brains out?" Mutrie asked at length.

Day laughed. *"Do* I?" he answered. "I'd give a thousand dollars if I could get one."

Mutrie began to talk. He was no stranger to trying to hustle wealthy men, as he had recently tried without success to interest industrialist August Belmont into bankrolling a ball club. But now Mutrie unfurled a wildly speculative plan to organize and field a good team. Day asked what sort of experience Mutrie had in baseball. Mutrie cited teams that he had managed in Massachusetts. But now, Mutrie concluded, he was ready for the big time.

Mutrie must have been quite a talker that day because the two men left together. A few weeks later, they jointly formed an enterprise known as the Metropolitan Exhibition Company. Day would provide the bankroll and Mutrie the expertise. Together, they decided, they would conquer New York baseball. So brash they were, so self-assured and full of themselves, that when they organized a baseball team they called their new club the Metropolitans, the same name as the outfit that had sent Day prematurely to the grandstand on the day when Mutrie had buttonholed him. But Metropolitans was a long name.

They quickly became the Mets.

The team opened in early 1880 as an independent club, playing whatever games could be arranged. They played some of their home games on a field in New Jersey, but most in Brooklyn at the Union Grounds (in present-day Williamsburg) and the nearby Capitoline Grounds, where both the Mutuals and the Hartford team had once toiled, seen here in the 1880s.

The Giants of The Polo Grounds

This site was the worst aspect of the Metropolitans' operations. The field was ragged and out of the way. The Great East River Bridge from Manhattan to Brooklyn was still under construction. The only ways to get to a ball game in Brooklyn were to take the ferry or be born there. In short, Day had difficulty drawing fans from Manhattan, fans he needed.

One morning, near his office on Maiden Lane near Wall Street, Day stopped to have his shoes shined. The bootblack knew Day had organized a baseball club. But he also couldn't understand why Day's team practically played in a foreign country.

"Mr. Day?" the shoeshine boy asked. "Why do you go all the way to Brooklyn to play your games?"

Day shrugged. He explained that the New Jersey field was even less accessible, and he knew of nowhere in Manhattan.

"I know a place," said the bootblack, finishing the shine. "The polo grounds at 110th Street and Sixth Avenue."

Day had never heard of the place, but he was shrewd enough to investigate. The location, he learned, was owned by James Gordon Bennett, Jr., son of the founder and owner of the New York *Herald*. Bennett, like many newspaper publishers, was both a millionaire and an egomaniac, whose newspaper and ego took turns inflating each other. On these grounds at 110th Street, John Day discovered, Bennett and his wealthy friends played polo. Day quickly leased the polo grounds from Bennett. He readied the field for baseball and drew up a brief autumn schedule. (In those days, baseball was played until snow and ice stopped it.) Then he invited the Manhattan public to travel up to 110th Street and, if one can excuse the expression, meet the Mets.

The team was an instant success, winning 16 games, tying 1, and losing only 7 of their 24 game fall card. It was a fine pace for any club. But Messieurs Mutrie and Day were businessmen, after all. What warmed their hearts were the large, curious, enthusiastic crowds that the Mets drew. Baseball in Manhattan was high concept for 1880, an idea whose time had come. When the brief season ended, Mutrie and Day knew they had a hit on their hands.

The two men set diligently to work over the winter, improving player personnel and drawing up a full schedule of 151 games for the following spring and summer. Opponents were easy to find. Other independents clamored to play in the big town. So did local college and university nines. Yale, Columbia, Seton Hall, and Pennsylvania all fielded fine teams. They were often quite good, as well as anxious to compete against professionals. Sixty exhibition games were even arranged against National League teams. The National League in 1881 was still under William Hulbert's leadership, and was eager to make any reasonable New York appearance.

The Mets won 81 of their games in their first full season in Manhattan, not a bad showing. Most important, however, were the five dozen games against the top professionals of the National League. There were two ways of looking at the results. Of these 60 contests, the Mets lost 42. Not good. But the Mets also won 18, including 3 in a six-game series with the talented Troy Haymakers. Looking at it from this angle, the Mets proved they could play ball with the big guys. Word circulated that they were the best independent team outside the National League. So naturally, when the American Association assembled members for their own first season of 1882, the Mets were invited to join.

Day and Mutrie declined. To them, the American Association, with its brewers, gaudy uniforms and rowdy fans, wasn't quite a real, dignified major league. Instead, Day and Mutrie were content to recreate the old League Alliance. Together with a Philadelphia club, the Mets were one of two teams in the Alliance that year, meaning neither team could finish lower than second. The Mets and the Philadelphians took turns playing each other and the usual assortment of college, independent, and professional teams. Meanwhile, Day took to dropping broad hints in public, picked up obediently by the press, that Philadelphia and New York belonged in the National League. It was New York bombast at its worst.

The Giants of The Polo Grounds

Nonetheless, the National League took the hint. On December 6, 1882, winter meetings were held in an appropriately snowy Providence, Rhode Island. Worcester and Troy (having finished eighth and seventh, respectively, in 1882) bowed to intense pressure from the other owners and "resigned" from the league. (The case of the Troy Haymakers was particularly poignant. Despite the nucleus of a good ball club, they had drawn only twenty-five fans to their final game. The previous year, they had closed the season with twelve. But at least no one remarked that attendance was on an upswing.)

The National League awarded "honorary membership" to both cities. No team, no special privileges, just honorary membership. Minutes later, John Day and Alfred J. Reach, proprietors of baseball clubs in New York and Philadelphia, respectively, applied for membership on behalf of their franchises. Next, moving swiftly along, the owners elected Abraham Gilbert Mills, a highly personable law school graduate and Civil War veteran, the league's new president.

Then Day and Mutrie stunned everyone anew. Expectation had been that the Mets would move directly into the National League. They didn't. John Day entered the Mets in the American Association for the following season and announced that he would field an entirely new team in the National League.

Day, frankly, was on a roll. So no one interfered. He hired a veteran catcher named John Clapp to manage the new club. Mutrie would remain manager of the Mets. But then there was the question of how to stock the new franchise. No problem. With the Troy club conveniently disbanded, those players under "reserve" were free to be signed. Day promptly signed the best of them.

Down the Hudson to New York went Roger Connor, a big brawny slugging first baseman, William (Buck) Ewing, one of the premier catchers of the day; and Mickey (Smilin' Mickey) Welch.

Welch was developing into one of the top righthanded pitchers in the game. He was also developing into one of the most prolific beer drinkers of the nineteenth century, one reason he was always said to be smiling. Welch loved his suds so dearly that he was even given to writing rhymes and jingles about them, then setting the verses to

The Giants of The Polo Grounds

music. A sample, which slyly refers to some of the other stimulants available from the trainer's room in that era:

Pure elixir or malt and hops
Beats all the drugs and all the drops.

   To the dismay of many parents, the jingle was known to most metropolitan schoolboys of the day. William Hulbert must have been spinning in his grave.
   The other star pitcher from Troy, Tim Keefe, went to Day's Mets. So did catcher Bill Holbert, so that Keefe's throws wouldn't land at the backstop. Manhattan, which had had no teams in any league for five years, now had two.
   Next, Day hedged his bets completely. Owning the New York entries in the two most competitive leagues, and having access to only one playing field, he began a strange definition of the two clubs. He might easily have arranged his schedules to need only one baseball diamond. But Day had the happy faculty of always doing the unexpected.
   The Polo Grounds was on a rectangle of land from 110th Street to 112th Street, bordered by the long block from Fifth to Sixth avenues. Day gave his National League team the existing diamond on the more desirable Fifth Avenue end. Then he built a new diamond for the Mets on the Sixth Avenue side.
   Economics and social awareness next worked into the equation. National League fans payed half a dollar and liked some civility as they watched a game. American Association fans entered the park for a quarter and guzzled as much beer as they could stand up and pay for. Perish the thought that the middle class and the working class should intermingle!
   So John Day had a solution for this, too. Down the center of James Gordon Bennett's pony field went a disgraceful, shabby canvas fence that effectively segregated his two teams. On the east were the New York Nationals with a green playing field and a fine grandstand, a first-class operation all the way. On the west were the Mets, a no-frills, steerage operation, complete with habitually drunken fans. When sections of the Mets' playing field proved uneven, Day used raw garbage as a landfill. To paraphrase a popular saying of the players, it was like the difference between the penthouse and the outhouse.

The Giants of The Polo Grounds

Not surprisingly, the "penthouse" was packed on May 1, 1883, when the New York Nationals played their first game in the National League. The finest grandstand in the country, a point that Day never tired of boasting about, overflowed with as many standees as seated fans. Attendance was more than twelve thousand, quite an assemblage to see young men play a boy's game. New York fielded an impressive starting lineup.

Buck Ewing, C
Roger Connor, 1B
John Montgomery Ward, CF
Pat Gillespie, LF
Mike Dorgan, RF
Mickey Welch, P
Ed Gaskin, 2B
John Troy, SS
Frank Hankinson, 3B

No fewer than four - Ewing, Connor, Gillespie, and Welch, whose name was misspelled on his tobacco card seen here, were refugees from Troy. The first three names in the lineup were future Hall of Famers, as was the pitcher. Then there were the quirks, perceived with a modern eye. The leadoff man was a catcher. The pitcher batted sixth. Ewing, batting first for most of the year, would also be the home run champion with the prodigious number of 10. And to make things complete, the player named Troy had been obtained from Providence. As for Mickey's misspelled name, he wasn't the luckiest guy when it came to people getting his name right. He had been born Michael Francis *Walsh* to Irish immigrants John and Mary Walsh. He later adopted the last name Welch, most likely from a sportswriter's mistaken entry of the name in a box score.

New York won the opener, 7-5, a successful debut both on the diamond and at the gates. According to witnesses, the crowd, which included former President U.S. Grant, left happy.

Smilin' Mickey Welch, whose endless pursuit of both women and beer greatly endeared him to New York's sporting public, won 27 games that year. Monte Ward, despite having pitched a perfect game for Providence against Buffalo in 1880, was still undergoing a permanent shift to position player. Nonetheless, he still won 12 games. Young Tip O'Neill handled the rest of the pitching. Roger

The Giants of The Polo Grounds

Connor was second in the league in batting average and hits in 1883, with .357 and 146, and Monte Ward finished fourth in home runs with 7. The team, however, could only muster a sixth-place finish, far behind a rejuvenated Boston club that won the pennant.

Yet it was a successful start, particularly compared with that of the Philadelphia team, originally called the Quakers but now known as the Phillies. (The Athletics were currently wandering around the American Association with the Mets.)

The Philadelphia team had picked the carcass of the Worcester team for players but had come up with none of the caliber of those cut loose by Troy. The results were predictable.

The Phils lost on Opening Day, 4-3, to Old Hoss Radbourn and the Providence Grays. There were twelve hundred witnesses to the event at a wooden tinderbox of a field called Recreation Park at 24th Street and Ridge Pike in Philadelphia. But the season was all downhill from there.

Following the first western trip, on which the team won 4 of 17 games, manager Bob Ferguson was replaced. Little did anyone know that in winning 4 out of 17, the Phillies were actually on a hot streak. Pitcher John Coleman, who did most of the hurling that year, started 61 games and lost 48. The team itself finished the season at 17-81, .173. No doubt, the good folks of the Quaker City were already booing lustily. There are, of course, two ways to look at the Phillies' opening season. One could say that it set the tone for dismal Phillies baseball for the several decades. Conversely, one could make the case that after a debut at .173, things have been looking up ever since.

In truth, the team did improve rapidly, rising all the way to sixth place in 1884, But the Phillies' surge was overshadowed. The following year was a magical one, and it belonged to New York. John Day owned two teams, but it was the "other" one that got hot.

Chapter 5   A Hall of Fame Line-up

"When I began playing the game, baseball was about as gentlemanly as a kick in the crotch."

Ty Cobb

The years 1884 and 1885 served as a watershed period for New York baseball. The Brooklyn Bridge was finally complete and open, making travel far easier between the two cities. Not entirely by coincidence, one of the high minor leagues, the Interstate Association, folded and its most capable entry, Brooklyn, survived and joined the American Association. The metropolitan area now had three teams, a condition which would prove familiar to future generations. The two New York clubs played at the Polo Grounds, while the Brooklyn team played at Washington Park at 3rd Street and Fourth Avenue in Brooklyn. It was a cozy, uneven stretch of land surrounded by low grandstands and bleachers, so named because it stood upon the soil where George Washington and his Continental Army had fought (and lost) the Battle of Long Island.

John Day's stepchildren, the Mets, played their American Association opponents competitively all summer, battling strong Louisville and Columbus clubs for league supremacy. They also split ten exhibition games against their co-tenants in the Polo Grounds. But as Brooklyn drifted to ninth, the Mets went into first place. They won the pennant by six and a half games, finishing with a record of 75-32.

Mutrie, the Mets' manager, was not given to ignoring profitable situations. During the season, for example, he hired the heavyweight boxing champion John L. Sullivan to pitch a few exhibition games. Sullivan wasn't much of a pitcher but was a fine drawing card. One suspects that no batters who had been hit by Sullivan's pitches charged the mound to settle things with the bareknuckle champ.

Then, with the season concluded, another vision danced before Mutrie's eyes: a playoff with the National League champions, the

The Giants of The Polo Grounds

Providence Grays. "Three out of five games," challenged Mutrie, "for the championship of the United States." The Providence manager, Frank Bancroft, quickly accepted. Post-season play became a reality.

Not only were the crowds lackluster for the championship series, but so were the Mets, who had shot their wad to finish first. Now they ran up against Old Hoss Radbourn, who was, it will be recalled, coming off a season in which he had won 60 games.

The series opened at the Polo Grounds, as the area was now called, Tim Keefe pitching for the Mets. Keefe, rattled by the absence of his regular catcher, Bill Holbert, hit two batters in the first inning. Both came around to score, courtesy of two wild pitches and a passed ball. The Grays amassed four more runs over the course of the game. Meanwhile, Old Hoss was unhittable. Providence won, 6-0.

The second game was much closer. Keefe had Holbert back and matched Radbourn pitch for pitch over the first four innings. Then he was a victim of bad luck. When a Providence runner tried to steal second, Holbert threw him out by five feet. Or so everyone thought. The umpire missed the play and called the runner safe, extending the inning. A walk followed, then a home run. Again, it was all Radbourn needed. Providence won, 3-1.

The third game was also played in New York. It was a cold, wet October 25 and only three hundred loyalists turned up at the Polo Grounds to watch. Then the Providence players, seeing the sparse turnout, refused to play.

The refusal, while probably sincere, was a terrific ploy. It undermined any chance the Mets had to creep back into the series. Mutrie was finally able to coax the Grays out onto the field on one condition: that they could choose the umpire.

They picked Tim Keefe, successfully removing the Mets' best hurler from the game. Mutrie countered with an unproven pitcher named Buck Becannon. Buck proved no mystery to Providence, who hit him early and often. By the sixth inning the Grays led, 12-2. Both teams then agreed that it was too dark to continue the agony any longer. So everyone, including the hundred or so fans still around, went home.

Ironically, the success of the Mets in 1884 sealed their fate. Despite their success, attendance had been dismal, largely due to the shabby playing conditions at the west end of the Polo Grounds. Simultaneously Day's National League team was catching the attention of the city. (Here was a case of William Hulbert's insistence upon the middle-class values of honesty, order, and dignity paying off.) So Day came to a singular conclusion: Bankrolling the Mets was eating into the profits of his more prestigious New York team.

Thus, he could strengthen the Mets, dignify their operation, and support them. Or he could unload them. By spring of 1885 it became clear which path he had chosen.

The Mets' two best players, Tim Keefe and third baseman Thomas (Dude) Esterbrook, were at the ends of their contracts. Under American Association rules, they could not sign with another club until ten days after their current contracts expired. But during these ten days, they were perfectly free to listen to offers from anyone.

Day was having none of this self-styled free agency. He had plans for his stars.

When the contracts of Keefe and Esterbrook had almost expired, Day packed up his boys and sent them by steamship to Bermuda, where they would be far away from the enticements of other team owners. When the ten days expired, he brought them back and quickly signed them to contracts with his New York National League team. Similarly, Jim Mutrie was invited in from sleazy western expanses of the Polo Grounds. Mutrie would manage the New York Nationals in 1885.

It was the start of a glorious era, a time when professionalism finally won respectability in New York and overtook amateur sports. Until this time, John L. Sullivan was the great professional athlete of the day. It was an era of athletic clubs that played "baseball without pay," as it was called on the sports pages. Track meets were popular, as were crew meets. As writer Joe King of the New York *World Telegram and Sun* once described it, on any weekend the waters of the Harlem River, the Passaic River, the Arthur Kill, and the Kill van Kull were swarming with amateur oarsmen and scullers. Bicycled "scorchers," with their tall, newfangled two-wheelers, whizzed over the bumpy streets of Manhattan and cricket leagues flourished in the parks, particularly on Staten Island.

Horse racing was both popular and professional. Run by aristocrats, it was also the bane of reformers, moralists, and whatever honest law enforcement officials could be found. The craze to wager on the ponies, said New York Superintendent of Police Thomas Byrnes, was "spreading and demoralizing all

The Giants of The Polo Grounds

classes. It begets poverty, unfits men for steady occupation, leads to drunkenness and often to crime." There were ten tracks in the metropolitan area, and all were packed.

Boxing news was all over the sports pages, too. John L. Sullivan fought when he needed the dough, but rarely more than twice a year. This was the punishing, bareknuckle stuff, don't forget. It took a lot out of a man. Yet amateur fights filled the papers each day. Consider an item from the 1883 New York *Herald:*

Pat Killion of the First Ward and George Lovell of the Fourth Ward, two youths who work in a packing box factory, met in a loft near the Post Office last night to settle a grudge, with friends contributing a purse of eighty dollars. An impartial referee was brought in from Jersey City. They fought with kid gloves and Killion scored a knockout in the forty-sixth round.

Forty-six rounds of mano-a-mano fist fighting. Ouch! The life of a ballplayer was cushy in comparison.

New York was in some ways much the same as it is today: tough, cynical, and charmingly corrupt. It was a city of immeasurable wealth and pitiable poverty. An observer who stood on Fifth Avenue in the fashionable Thirties to watch the Easter Parade could probably have counted most of Ward McAllister's "400." Many of them built extraordinary mansions farther up Fifth Avenue and ate off solid gold plates. They lived behind the chaste sedate fronts of their brownstones on quiet streets that were as yet unpolluted by the internal combustion engine. After dark, little was heard other than the *clip clop* of a horse-drawn coach. Their social mecca was the spectacular new sixteen story Waldorf Hotel at Fifth and 33rd. Their redoubt was the Union League Club, six blocks up Fifth on 39th Street. The League had declared publicly that Democrats were not welcome, never mind Jews, Catholics, or just about anyone else.

The symbol of the city was the spire of Trinity Church, overlooking the downtown waterfront. But the bustle of the young country had given rise to new engineering marvels: first, the Brooklyn Bridge, then the Statue of Liberty in 1886. Farther uptown, past the square-riggers that were tied up all along the East River, there was the elevated steam railway above Third Avenue. The curve in the tracks at 110th Street, where it shot off hot cinders upon anyone walking below, was a sightseeing attraction.

And yet, then as always, there was another city hidden from the

The Giants of The Polo Grounds

first. Manhattan in the 1880s had approximately one and a half million residents crammed onto the tiny island the same population as a hundred years later, but without any high-rise housing. More than a million of these inhabitants were immigrants or first-generation children. There were only so many means for these people to support themselves. Peddling from pushcarts was one. Working in "sweaters" or sweatshops (which the powerless state factory inspector denounced as "a disgrace to civilization") was another. Crime was a very popular third. Thus, much of the Tenderloin District and the narrow strip of luxury along Fifth Avenue was patrolled by private guards.

Slums, littered with garbage and ridden with cholera and tuberculosis, were a few minutes' walk from the finest mansions. Here there was little police presence at all, the only street authority being gangs of Irish-born toughs who fought each other for sections of city turf. Alcoholism and drunkenness was so much a part of everyday life that it is easy to comprehend how the Prohibition movement gained credibility in the years that followed. There were, in 1885, a combined total of eight thousand bakeries, butcher shops, and grocery stores in Manhattan. There were ten thousand saloons. It was easier, in other words, to partake of some liquid lightning than it was to buy a healthy meal.

Yet, into this setting John Day's new team dug in, created a base of fans and flourished. Having relegated his Mets to the standing of a modern-day farm club, Day was now putting together a lineup for his big club. And the 1885 edition was downright impressive.

The first six men in New York's starting lineup were future Hall of Famers. Buck Ewing was the field leader. He would catch or play first. John Montgomery Ward, now a law student in the off-season would play shortstop. Then there was one Orator Jim O'Rourke, also nicknamed "The Counselor" by his teammates.

O'Rourke was, like Ward, a law student when he wasn't playing baseball. (Ward would eventually earn a law degree from Columbia University. O'Rourke earned his from Yale.) He was by nature a grand, flowery speaker, given to dramatic pronouncements and overblown statements. Back in 1881 he had been the player manager of the Buffalo club. An infielder named John Peters asked O'Rourke about the possibilities of a pay raise.

The Giants of The Polo Grounds

"I'm sorry," O'Rourke answered, "but the exigencies of the occasion and the condition of our exchequer will not permit anything of the sort at this period of our existence. Subsequent developments in the field of finance may remove the present gloom and we may emerge into a condition where we may see fit to reply in the affirmative to your exceedingly modest request."

No, in other words. And O'Rourke hadn't even felt compelled to mention Peters' batting average of .214, which was also exceedingly modest.

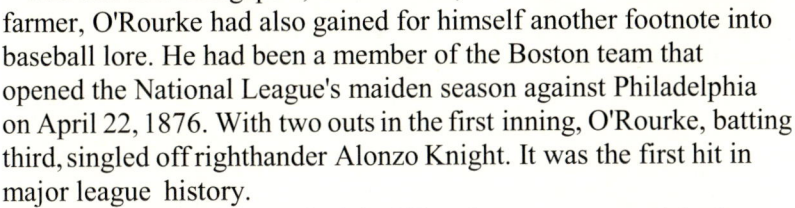

The son of a Bridgeport, Connecticut, farmer, O'Rourke had also gained for himself another footnote into baseball lore. He had been a member of the Boston team that opened the National League's maiden season against Philadelphia on April 22, 1876. With two outs in the first inning, O'Rourke, batting third, singled off righthander Alonzo Knight. It was the first hit in major league history.

Playing for the New York club, O'Rourke was, not surprisingly, disinclined to keep his mouth shut. He quickly became well known for a series of hot, running debates with Mutrie, the manager. O'Rourke also possessed a haughty, dignified stance at bat, and a powerful, effortless swing. For some reason, his uniform was always crisp and clean. O'Rourke played the outfield and occasionally filled in at catcher for Buck Ewing.

There were two good reasons why Mutrie had the luxury of moving Ward, a perfect game pitcher, to shortstop: Mickey Welch and Tim Keefe. Keefe, in his previous two years with the Mets, had been one of the most dominant pitchers in the American Association. He had won 78 games, had finished all but 1 of the 126 games he had started, and had hurled more than 1,100 innings. Now, however, he was getting better. Opposition batters respectfully referred to Keefe as "Sir Timothy." Off the field, he was a sober, thoughtful, introspective man. But that wasn't what lent Sir Timothy his aura of royalty. Keefe had a snappy fastball and a sly curve, but he also had a weapon in his arsenal that was previously unknown: the change of pace. Keefe was the first major league hurler to give hitters the big motion, then toss a softie across the plate. Think the changeup might have been baffling to batters in

The Giants of The Polo Grounds

the 1880s? Sir Timothy would fan 540 batters in 1886. Thus, along with Smilin' Mickey, he of the prodigious beer consumption, pitching was well taken care of.

Meanwhile, Roger Connor, the team's broad-shouldered slugger from exotic Waterbury, Connecticut, was at first base. The team started the season well and took aim on the Chicago White Stockings for the league lead. Chicago, surprised to be chased that closely, played superbly. But so did New York. Welch pitched at a pace that earned him 44 victories. Keefe would win 32 and Roger Connor would lead the league in hits with 169 and win the batting title. Over a Fourth of July weekend, Chicago visited New York. Mutrie's team, with Ward as its star, took three out of four games and pulled to within a game and a half of first place. The crowds at the Polo Grounds, counted between five and ten thousand for each of the contests, were delirious. A pennant race was on and the New York Nationals were, for the first time ever, the rage of the big town.

What a giddy season it was! Track meets, bareknuckle boxing, horse racing, and rowing on the rivers took a backseat to baseball. The average working man put in a ten-hour day, six days a week. Since baseball wasn't played on Sundays in the National League, newspapers followed the lead of Joseph Pulitzer and expanded their sports columns to keep pace with public interest. There was also plenty for the gossip columnists.

Monte Ward was one of the city's heartthrobs. Tall, articulate, handsome, and single, Ward was in the midst of a torrid romance with Miss Helen Dauvray (nee Ida Louise Gibson), a Broadway actress and one of the great beauties of her time.

Dauvray had begun her career in San Francisco as a child actress under the stage name "Little Nell, the California Diamond." She later invested in Comstock Mining in what is now Nevada but what was then western Utah Territory. When the vast lode of silver ore was discovered under the eastern slope of Mount Davidson, Dauvray became financially independent. She went to Paris to study and performed at the Folies Dramatique in 1884.

In 1885 she came to New York and started producing her own stage vehicles, including *Mona* at the (now demolished) Star Theatre on Broadway at Thirteenth Street. There, Ward would be waiting in the gas lit wings of the theater waiting for Helen to finish her performance. Then the couple would be out on the town, sometimes till 5 A.M. But new, impassioned love knows no bounds

The Giants of The Polo Grounds

for absence or, in this case, abstinence. Since the couple lived apart, Ward felt the need to communicate with his paramour, particularly before games. The chosen vehicle was a ten-year-old boy named Freddy Engel.

Before most New York home games that marvelous summer, Ward would scribble a steamy epistle to Helen, seal it in an envelope, and hand it to young Engel. Freddy was the official team mascot, ball boy, bat boy, and go-between. He was also the son of Nick Engel, the owner of a restaurant that flourished at 16 West 27th Street and that was popular with ballplayers, theater people, and assorted other 1880s glitterati. Nick Engel's place was among the most popular beaneries in town and, mixing the baseball metaphor with one of simple, hearty cuisine, was appropriately named The Old Home Plate.

"Deliver this to the goddess, will you, Freddy?" Ward would ask after scribbling and sealing one of his hot notes to Helen. Then the boy would be off like a shot.

Helen would wait for the pregame note at Roberts' Road House, which despite its name was a fancy restaurant on the corner of 110th Street and Fifth Avenue. Right across the street from the Polo Grounds, in other words, on the fashionable side of the avenue. Over the course of the season, Freddy Engel's role expanded until he had sometimes deliver six to a dozen messages a day from ballplayers to beautiful women.

"I'm the only one they trust," he often remarked, probably quite accurately.

Many of the players, including Ward, lived downtown at the Grand Central Hotel. There the National League had been founded in a snow storm nine year earlier. But now it was headquarters for Mutrie's marauders. From there, they would travel up to the playing field in horse drawn carriages. Fans would line the streets to watch and cheer them. This, naturally, gave Mickey Welch an audience. Welch, like Monte Ward, was a prince of the city and would seize the opportunity to serenade his fans. For example,

53

The Giants of The Polo Grounds

The rarebit served at Nick Engel's place
Would please the taste of any man...
A mug of ale without a question
When drunk on top would aid digestion.

What Welch lacked in potential as a poet laureate, he more than made up for as a pitchman for his friend Nick Engel. Traffic would make way and the crowds lining the streets would cheer. Often the carriages were so overcrowded that some players rode sidesaddle upon the two-horse team. It was a rowdy, raucous scene whenever the team set out for the Polo Grounds, yet it was great entertainment, a chance for New Yorkers to see their heroes up close. In 1885 it was part of the cityscape.

There was plenty of action at the ball field, too.

New York chased Chicago with the tenacity of a guard dog who had sunk his teeth into the seat of a burglar's pants. Into September went the pennant race. There were great sidelights.

Once, after a tough loss, Orator Jim O'Rourke, the genteel, dignified "Counselor" fell into a long, heated discussion with Jim Mutrie over responsibility for the defeat. O'Rourke finally eschewed a Socratic dialogue with his manager and winged a baseball cleat at him across the locker room. The press duly reported the incident.

On another occasion, Buck Ewing singled in the tenth inning of a scoreless game at the Polo Grounds. Ewing was also a highly popular player, a showman, and a crowd pleaser. And he was fast.

He promptly stole second and third. Then, in a scene that would have been cloyingly melodramatic in a dime novel, he turned and addressed the crowd behind third base. "It's getting late," he shouted. "I'm going to steal home and we can then all have dinner."

And he did, a few pitches later. An artist of the day set to work immediately and made a dramatic lithograph of the play and entitled it *Ewing's Famous Slide.* Soon rip-offs of it hung behind the bar in many of New York's saloons. The creator of the lithograph, which was originally in *Harper's Weekly*, most likely had spent little time at the ballpark researching

54

The Giants of The Polo Grounds

his subject. In the print, Ewing is depicted diving into third base headfirst, and there seemed to be a dirt path between the mound and third, which was more the custom between the mound and the plate. But, hey? What are a few details?

As for Jim Mutrie, who was greatly responsible for much of this, he rarely took a seat in the dugout. Buck Ewing functioned as both the team captain and manager, in the modern sense, and directed the offense and defense as he saw fit. Mutrie, meanwhile, was busy elsewhere.

He counted the receipts and managed the team's business. He was more equivalent to what we now know as a general manager than a manager. But he was also the chief cheerleader. On game days, Mutrie would turn up at the ballpark looking like the prototype of ZZ Top's *Sharp Dressed Man*: clean shirt, new shoes, black top hat, spats, gloves, formal black coat and cravat, and waxed saber mustache. "In the lobby of the Fifth Avenue Hotel," Lee Allen once wrote, "he was indistinguishable from a drummer of cigars." But at the ballpark, he was a blurry whirl of perpetual noise and motion.

Tirelessly, he would hustle up and down the aisles. *"Who are the people?"* he would yell. *"We are the people!"* would come the refrain from the stands. It sounded like something a century too late for the French Revolution. What it was, instead, was the cue for the team's followers from Jim Mutrie all the way down to the lowliest ticket holder to launch into a rousing rendition of the club's battle anthem. In case you've forgotten the w o r d s :

> We have fought all the fights to be fit,
> We have won all the games to be won,
> We have taken the. rag off the bush,
> And have yanked the traditional bun,
> Then who are the *people? We* are!
> I say *who* are the people? We are!
> We may dance and may sing,
> But odds, bodds, and by Jing,
> You can bet we're the people.
> We are!

The Giants of The Polo Grounds

Rag off the bush? Traditional bun? Bodds? Exactly what sport was this? On and on it went. One can only imagine a modern-day general manager, a Brian Cashman or Theo Epstein, for example, racing through the grandstand in formal attire, exhorting the paying customers, to appreciate Mutrie's performance.

Ah, but there were some magnificent performances *on* the field in 1885, also. Roger Connor, the strapping first baseman, led the team and the league in hitting with a sharp .371. Mike Dorgan, the New York right fielder, was third in the league at .326. But what carried the team was pitching: again, the tandem of Smilin' Mickey Welch and Sir Timothy Keefe.

Keefe was 32-13 with a league leading ERA of 1.58 and was only the number two man on the staff. Welch carried the day with 44 wins in 55 decisions. During the pennant run, however, he was virtually unbeatable. Not possessed of the dazzling speed of, say, Old Hoss Radbourn, Welch was something of a primeval junkman on the mound. He had a good curve, a change of pace similar to that of Sir Timothy, and a curve that broke the wrong way, an early version of the screwball. It was enough to baffle the league.

Starting on July 18, as Chicago and New York pulled away from the rest of the league, Welch won 17 straight games. The streak ended on September 5 with a 3-1 loss to Philadelphia. At the end of the season, Welch would be asked to what he attributed his 44-win year.

"To drinking beer," he answered.

Naturally. He probably had Nick Engle's place in mind.

But the final glory of the 1885 season was to elude New York this year.

Late in September, Jim Mutrie's New Yorkers went into Chicago for a four-game series at Lake Front Park. The flag was up for grabs. New York drew on youth and enthusiasm. Chicago drew on experience. Before noisy, capacity crowds of ten thousand fans, the White Stockings took three of the four games, clinching the pennant. New York finished the season two games behind, despite an 85-27 record, a winning percentage of .759. The third-place team, the Phillies, were twenty-eight games behind New York.

But the season had been, needless to say, an enormous success. That left one pressing order of business to John Day: the disposal of the Mets. With the best Met players transferred to Day's other New York team, the Mets, finished seventh in an eight-team league. Even the Brooklyn team, a stalwartly mediocre outfit, finished higher.

The Giants of The Polo Grounds

That did it.

Toward the end of the calendar year, Day peddled his team to a murky amusement park operator with the unlikely name of Erasmus Wiman. Erasmus was a jolly soul who also managed an animal menagerie known as Forepaugh's Circus (Get it? Forepaugh's? Forepaws? Animals?), concerts, fountain displays, an amusement park, and the Buffalo Bill Wild West Show (which advertised "real bloodthirsty Indians") on its annual swing through New York. Almost all of Wiman's productions took place on Staten Island. The Mets would, too. They would play at the St. George's fairgrounds on New York harbor, with a grandstand along the first base line and tall ships passing on the other side of the short fence behind third base.

Wiman, however, was up to something when he acquired the Mets. The wealthy Baltimore & Ohio Railroad had its eye upon Staten Island as the future site of its New York terminal. To this end, the railroad had already entered into an agreement to pay Wiman a set sum of money in exchange for the use of his ferries and terminal facilities. But the price was to be calculated from a formula that used as a factor the sum of passengers traveling by ferry from New York to Staten Island within a certain number of years. Wiman wanted ferryboats packed with customers. Putting the American Association Mets on Staten Island where the Mets played two final dismal years was an attempt to boost ferry traffic.

Aside from the disposal of the Mets, however, there was one other event of 1885 that would carry lasting significance. Popular teams were picking up nicknames in this era, and the nicknames were sticking. It happened officially and otherwise. The Brooklyn team which would endure many names over the ensuing decades became known as the Trolley Dodgers, a reference to the fact that Brooklyn residents spent a good deal of time in their trolley tangled city diving for the safety of sidewalks.

Two years later, in 1887, Pittsburgh would enter the league. Although the team's official name was the Alleghenies, the players wore such gaudy blue and black striped uniforms that fans and reporters dubbed them alternately the Smoked Italians, the Zulus, or the Potato Bugs. Only when the outrageous uniforms were discarded,

57

and they began to raid players from other teams did the nickname of Pirates manage to stick.

But back to Jim Mutrie. The man was obsessed with size. Bigger was better, a common attitude in the America of Mutrie's day. He liked to refer to his team as his "big fellows."

Well, Roger Connor was a legitimate hunk at six three, 220, and Pat Gillespie, at six feet one and a half inches, was not to be confused with a dwarf. But most of the rest of the players on the seventeen-man squad were five feet ten or shorter. They weren't elfin, but they weren't imposing, either, even for the 1880s.

But Jim Mutrie *loved* the idea. "My Giants!" he finally called them. "Come on, you *Giants!*"

A sportswriter named P. Jay Donohue of the New York *World* started using the nickname at about the same time. But Mutrie incorporated the tag into his cheers as he raced through the grandstand whipping up excitement. It all coalesced at once: the pennant race, the attention of the city, and the nickname.

The Metropolitans were gone. The Dodgers were Brooklyn's team. And the New York Giants, who played uptown at the Polo Grounds, were now poised for their first run at greatness.

Chapter 6 Racial Exclusion

"A new trouble has just arisen in the affairs of certain baseball associations [which] has done more damage to the International League than to any other we know of. We refer to the importation of colored players into the ranks of that body."

The Sporting News, July 11, 1887

No star of baseball's early years did more to harm the future of professional baseball in the United States than Cap Anson, a Radbourn adversary for many years and Billy Sunday's onetime mentor. And yet the ominous facets of Anson stemmed from his very respectability. They would also afflict professional baseball for many years to come.

Anson became the captain manager of the White Stockings in 1879. He also became, in a strange sort of way, one of the most influential men in America. He was a big handsome swaggering man from the heartland of the country, Iowa, at a time when the heartland was still very much frontier. He played in the majors for twenty-two seasons, hitting .343 his first year and .302 his last. He was the first player to amass 3,000 base hits and guided the Chicago club to five championships. He was a hero both to small boys, who treasured Anson model bats, and to adults, who admired his success, his athletic ability, and what was perceived as his "forthright integrity." This was the era of tainted baseball contests, don't forget, and Anson was the Joe DiMaggio, the Connie Mack and the Derek Jeter of his day, all combined. So, in some ways, it is difficult to understand benighted Anson's attitude toward one Moses Fleetwood Walker of Steubenville, Ohio, a catcher for the Toledo Blue Stockings of the American Association.

Walker was a college man who had studied first at Oberlin College in Ohio, then at the University of Michigan. His grades were more than adequate and, the son of a physician himself, he no doubt would have finished his education had baseball not beckoned. In 1883 he joined the Toledo team of the Northwestern League. The following year, Toledo joined the American Association. It was at that point that Anson's attention focused upon Walker. Walker was African-American. There is no other way to put it: Cap Anson was an overt racist and proud of it. And their two respective teams had scheduled an exhibition match on July 20, 1884 in Toledo.

When arrangements for the game were reaching a final stage, the management of the White Stockings sent a letter to the Toledo club reminding Charlie Morton, the Toledo manager, of an alleged earlier promise to "keep the colored man off the field." Accounts of what followed differ to this day, the accepted version maintaining that Toledo agreed rather than have Chicago not play and yet still be entitled to keep the $100 already paid to them. The incident is frequently cited as the first time the color line was successfully drawn in professional baseball.

The truth, as it often is, is murkier and more complicated. Anson was behind the letter. But the letter backfired. Charlie Morton called Anson's bluff, replying that Walker would play or there would be no game. Anson gave in, rather than lose his own share of what promised to be a good gate. The irony was that Toledo originally had no intention of using Walker. Their catcher was injured with a broken hand. But when Chicago attempted to intimidate Toledo, the players on the Toledo team stood by their teammate. Anson is alleged to have said, "We'll play this here game, but won't play never no more with the nigger in." Under these ugly conditions the game went on.

Six weeks later, Fleetwood Walker's younger brother, Welday Walker joined him on the team. Fleetwood played in 42 games for Toledo that year. Welday played in 5.

But sadly, the nasty ramifications would last for decades.

Anson continued his campaign to segregate baseball and *did* manage to intimate a handful of other teams that were already integrated. Soon the International League and the Ohio State League, fearing a repeat of the Anson-Walker incident in Toledo, had passed ordinances barring black athletes on their teams. Other minor leagues followed.

Although some ordinances were eventually repealed, Anson's prestige had lent credibility and acceptance to the segregation of the sport. Gradually, black players went into their own teams in "colored" leagues.

In March of 1888, obviously still seething over the treatment that black athletes were receiving and prompted by the repeal of laws that would have allowed "colored" to play professional ball, Welday Walker sent an articulate impassioned letter to *The Sporting Life*. The latter was a weekly sports paper published from 1883 to 1917 (and again from 1922 to 1924) which focused on baseball.

"Why discriminate?" Walker asked. "The law is a disgrace.... There should be some broader cause – such as want of ability, behavior and intelligence – for barring a player than his color."

The Sporting Life printed the letter. But the discrimination, as we all know, continued until Jackie Robinson broke the color barrier in 1947. No doubt Cap Anson, who lived until 1922, was pleased, though his plaque in the Hall of Fame makes no mention of this, his most infamous legacy.

The Giants of The Polo Grounds

Anson was known for his racial attitudes off the field, also. In his autobiography, *A Ball Player's Career*, first published in 1900, Anson wrote of Clarence Duval, Chicago's black team mascot. "Clarence was a little darkey that I had met some time before while in Philadelphia, a singer and dancer of no mean ability, and a little coon whose skill in handling the baton would have put to the blush many a bandmaster of national reputation."

It then gets worse. Anson describes Duval as "no account" and then throws in the reprehensible N-word.

What accounts for Anson's attitude? Anson was a successful white male. He enjoyed a place of privilege and prominence. He had grown up on the frontier in Iowa where Native Americans were not treated as people. Perhaps Anson's exposure to whites exploiting the Pottawattamie tribe Native Americans created his sense of white superiority. Equally, it was possible that Anson was adamant about excluding African Americans from the game because as the acknowledged superstar of the day, he did not want any competition to his throne from the many talented non-white players of the day. It was obvious to anyone with two eyes and a non-poisoned mind that there were many non-white black players with major league talent.

Racial intolerance, especially the sort that would be aimed at an educated black man, frequently found the Walker brothers, one way or another in their years after baseball. On April 9, 1891 in Syracuse, New York, four white men exiting a saloon began

The Giants of The Polo Grounds

taunting Fleetwood Walker. One of them, a redneck bricklayer named "Curly" Murray, threw a stone at Walker, hitting him in the head. Walker drew a pocket knife and fatally stabbed Murray, an act that might have been viewed as a civic improvement. Walker surrendered to police, claiming self-defense, but was charged with second-degree murder.

On the third of June 3, 1891, an all-white jury found Walker not guilty, much to the delight of spectators in the courthouse. He returned to Steubenville to work for the postal service.

As the years went by, Walker stayed in contact with a former Syracuse University professor, a man named Dr. Joel Gibert Justin. Justin was an inventor who had been experimenting with firing artillery shells with gunpowder rather than compressed air. He had an invention named the "Justin Gun" which only had one problem: it didn't work. Walker became involved. He designed and patented an outer casing in 1891 that improved Justin's design. It was the first of first four patents he achieved in his lifetime.

Fleetwood and Welday Walker later were co-owners of the Union Hotel in Steubenville. Fleetwood also managed a theatre which was host to silent movies, opera, live drama, vaudeville, and minstrel shows at the Opera House. He became a successful entrepreneur. He patented inventions that improved film reels when nickelodeons were popularized.

In 1902, the Walker Brothers explored philosophies of Black nationalism as editors for a publication they founded named *The Equator*. Walker expanded his ideas about race in a book titled *Our Home Colony*, which put forth Walker's thesis on the victimization of the black race in America and a proposal for African-Americans to emigrate back to Africa.

In 1897, Welday Walker served on the Executive Committee of the Negro Protective Party, a newly formed political party established in Ohio in protest of the failure of the Republican governor to investigate the lynching of an African American named Charles "Click" Mitchell in June 1897 at Urbana, Ohio, an ugly event that included a race riot, a celebration of the lynching by the townspeople, two celebrants shot dead by a local militia, and the sheriff fleeing town. Together, the brothers became active in the Back-to-Africa movement and promoted emigration to Liberia. According to Fleetwood biographer, David Zang, in *Fleet Walker's Divided Heart: The Life of Baseball's First Black Major Leaguer,* Welday's entrepreneurial spirit also led him into bootlegging during

Prohibition. More recently, however, they have also been viewed as early civil rights pioneers.

On May 11, 1924, Fleetwood Walker died of lobar pneumonia at the age of 67. Welday died on November 23, 1937 at the age of 77.

Thanks to the efforts of SABR member Craig Brown and the Negro Leagues Grave Marker Project, Welday's resting place finally received a grave marker in 2016 at Union Cemetery in Steubenville, Ohio, where several members of the Walker family are buried.

Brown spearheaded the fundraising effort to raise about $1,400 to purchase the grave marker. "It would be one thing if they were just baseball players, but Welday and his brother were extraordinary people at the same time," Brown told the *Toledo Blade*. "They are some of the earliest civil rights pioneers post-Civil War. They were both very active."

Although Jackie Robinson is credited with being the first African-American to play major league baseball in the *modern* era, and taking nothing away from Robinson's ability and courage, the Walker brothers held the honor among baseball historians for decades of actually being the first *ever*.

In 2007, however, the distinguished baseball researcher Peter Morris - best known for a two-volume book on the history of innovations in baseball entitled *A Game of Inches* as well as for *Baseball Fever*, a history of baseball in Michigan - discovered that another African-American played a single game for the Providence Grays five years before Walker debuted for the Toledo club.

The player's name was William Edward White. According to the research, White was born into slavery in 1860 in Georgia. He was one of three children born to his mother Hannah White and fathered by a prosperous plantation owner named A.J. White.

A.J. White named all of these children in a will dated in 1877. A. J. White stipulated that his children be educated in the North. Any wonder why? Hence, in 1879, when William Edward White was a student at Brown University at age 19, he played for the Brown University team.

On June 21 of that same year, the Providence team invited him to he replace a regular player, Joe Start, for one game when the latter was injured. White went 1-for-4 and scored a run in a 5-3 Providence victory. It is unknown why White did not play for the Grays again, but one has one's suspicions. He was replaced in the next game by future Hall of Famer "Orator Jim" O'Rourke who was

The Giants of The Polo Grounds

working toward his law degree from Yale at the time, but who would later join the New York Giants in the 1880's and 1890's.

If SABR's research is accurate, and invariably it is, the William Edward White who took the field that day was of African-American blood, half of it, anyway. Or maybe a quarter, if one wishes to parse such things, since his mother was said to be of mixed races. (White is seen here seated, 4th from right, with other members of the Brown baseball team.) After Brown University, he moved to Chicago and became an accountant.

There he lived for several decades until his death in 1937, oddly enough within a few months of Welday Walker. White, however, lived life as a white man and played baseball as one. So despite these findings, baseball historians still credit Fleetwood Walker with being the first in the major leagues to play openly as a black man, and his brother Welday the second.

Walker preceded Robinson in the major leagues, but without doubt they both suffered from the racism of their era, as well as the attitudes set in motion by Cap Anson in the 1880s.

Chapter 7   Bratwurst, Baseball, Booze and More Booze

"The strongest thing baseball has going for it today is its yesterdays."

Lawrence Ritter, 1982

The scourge of the American Association in the late 1880's was the so-called "beer and whiskey boys" from St. Louis, known more formally as the St. Louis Browns. The dominant team of the decade, they finished first, first, first, first, and second from the years 1885 through 1889. No one in baseball liked them, aside from in the city of St. Louis which was still very much of a frontier city. There, they were dearly loved.

The Browns were led by Charlie Comiskey, the first baseman and team captain, and a colorful character named Christian Frederick Wilhelm Von Der Ahe, a native of Hille, Germany, who found fame, fortune, and eventually notoriety in the bustling American Midwest of the mid-Nineteenth Century. Chris Von Der Ahe was the team's mentor, owner, guiding light and public persona.

Von Der Ahe was the delight of baseball scribes of the day. He was a wealthy self-made brewer and meat packer whose prominent, bulbous, incarnadine nose gave him the look of an early W. C. Fields. Often, he was much funnier than Fields would ever be, particularly when he wasn't trying. He was a shrewd businessman, a clever promoter, and a genius at the art of the malapropism.

He dressed garishly, spent freely and crashed amiably through life. Two Great Danes – Snoozer and Schnauzer - usually accompanied him. His accent in English, Lee Allen once wrote, "was thick as a prize knockwurst in the butcher's window." But Von Der Ahe was incomprehensible in any language, including his native one. Once he took his fellow owners in the American Association to task for scheduling the Browns to play so many games at home on days when it eventually rained.

Another time, before dozens of witnesses, he boasted that he had the biggest baseball diamond in the world. Charlie Comiskey, standing nearby, attempted to extricate Von Der Abe from this one by taking the owner aside and explaining that *all* baseball diamonds were the same size. Von Der Abe then shoved his foot a little deeper into his mouth by explaining that what he actually had meant was that his *infield* was bigger and better than anyone else's.

One day in September 1886, Von der Ahe, looking for ways to turn some extra bucks, put on his thinking cap. He already had a postseason series scheduled against the St. Louis Maroons of the Union Association for the "championship of St. Louis." But Von Der Ahe was also concerned with the championship of the world. Chris was incapable of writing a coherent letter in the English language himself, but apparently someone in his office was. Accordingly, a written proposal was sent to Albert Spalding, owner of the Chicago club, challenging the pennant bound Chicago White Stockings to contest a "world's championship series."

Spalding, cocky as ever, accepted, insisting on two unusual provisions: The series would be the best of nine games. And the winner would keep *all the* gate receipts.

Von Der Ahe accepted the second provision easily. He was just as headstrong about his guys as Spalding. But then Von Der Ahe brought up the matter of the St. Louis championship and claimed his club might not have time for a nine-game series. Could they play best of seven, Von Der Ahe countered. Spalding accepted and the framework for the modern World Series was born,

Beyond the personae of Von Der Ahe and Charlie Comiskey, St. Louis was carried on the field by Bill Gleason at shortstop, Curt Welch in center field, Walter Arlington (Arlie) Latham at third base, and Albert (Doc) Bushong at catcher. Latham, as a player, was known as "The Freshest Man on Earth," thanks to his endless sense of humor. From time to time, he would walk behind von der Ahe wearing a fake clown's nose that looked like von der Ahe's not-so-fake nose. Latham later played for the Giants of the NL in 1909, at which times he became the oldest man in Major League history to steal a

The Giants of The Polo Grounds

base, at age of 49, a record that still stands today. Later still, he became the colorful press box attendant at the Polo Grounds and Yankee Stadium, a post he held for many years. In the 1920's he owned a popular delicatessen on Saint Nicholas Avenue in Manhattan.

Bushong, an intelligent, cultivated man who somehow had gotten mixed up with the boozy boys from St. Louis, became a dentist after his retirement from baseball. Meanwhile, as a Brown, he caught two pitchers of astonishing consistency: Dave (Scissors) Foutz and Robert (Parisian Bob) Caruthers.

"Parisian Bob" may have spoken French, but he hailed from Memphis, Tennessee. In the winter months, Caruthers lived in France and negotiated his next year's contract via the trans-Atlantic cable, earning the nickname Parisian Bob, whether he was actually in Paris or not. Many baseball historians consider Carruthers one of the most deserving candidates for the Baseball Hall of Fame who remains unelected, along with players like Gil Hodges and Jim Katt. Reliable statistics credit him as having compiled 218 wins and 99 losses, giving him an amazing .688 winning percentage, third all-time behind only Whitey Ford, and Dave Foutz, his St. Louis teammate for eight seasons, among pitchers with at least 200 major league decisions.

Foutz and Caruthers would each win 99 games over the Browns' first three pennant years. Remember those names: Bushong, Foutz, and Caruthers. They will resurface.

The first three games of the series were played in Chicago. The White Stockings won two. The teams traveled to St. Louis and the Browns won the next two games to take a 3-2 lead in the series.

The next game became part of the folklore of the early days of baseball. Chicago, behind future Hall of Famer John Clarkson, led 3-0 in the eighth inning. The Browns rallied to tie the game, a two-run triple by "The Freshest Man on Earth" sparking the outburst. Then the Browns won the game and the series in the bottom of the tenth on a bizarre play that went down in history as "Curt Welch's $15,000 Slide."

Here's what happened.

Curtis Benton Welch, fishing for a way to get on base, stuck his shoulder in front of a John Clarkson pitch. He started for first base. (King) Kelly, the catcher, complained that Welch had moved in front of the ball intentionally. Umpire Gracie Pearce (yes, a man named Gracie) agreed, calling Welch back to the plate.

The Giants of The Polo Grounds

"I'll show that lusher Kelly!" Welch then boasted to the crowd. He followed his words with a sharp single to center.

Dave Foutz then grounded to short, but the infield booted a double play ball. William (Yank) Robinson, the second baseman, sacrificed successfully, putting Welch on third and Foutz on second with one out.

Doc Bushong was the next hitter. On the second pitch, Welch broke for the plate, attempting to end the game with a steal. Your grandmother could have scored. The ball sailed high and inside on the right-handed hitter, glanced off King Kelly's mitt, and rolled all the way to the grandstand. There was no play at the plate and the game was over. If Welch slid at all, it was a pure conceit.

Von Der Ahe tried to slap the label, "Curt Welch's $15,000 Slide," on the play to hype the game and the Browns. But The *Missouri Republican* said Welch "trotted home." The St. Louis *Globe-Democrat* reported that "Kelly made no effort to get the ball, and … in a dazed manner stood and watched Welch come in."

Nonetheless, the 1886 St. Louis Browns were "World Champions," the only American Association team with an undisputed claim to that title. Estimates at the time claimed that more than $100,000 changed hands on the results.

The "$15,000 Slide" made a good headline, but the actual receipts were $13,920.10 for a series attendance of 42,466 paying customers. Twelve members of the Browns pocketed $580 apiece.

The Chicago players went away worse than emptyhanded. Many were personally wiped out by losing side bets they had made on their own team. The arrogant White Stockings were left to float personal loans in an alien city in order to finance their trips home.

As for Chris Von Der Ahe, the victory put him in clover. The owner's share of the gate was 50 percent, almost $7,000. In an understandably expansive mood, the beer baron commissioned brightly colored horse blankets to be woven, bearing the legend: ST, LOUIS BROWNS, CHAMPIONS OF THE WORLD as well as a poster depicting a godlike St. Louis Brown standing astride the planet earth above the flowery legend: THE MONACHS OF THE SPHERE. The poster was a familiar sight around the Mound City for the next year.

But, with some money obviously left over, Von Der Ahe finally outdid himself when he had a statue carved in his own likeness. He erected it near the ballpark, a temptation that every other owner has been able to resist. There it would remain for many years until, following Von Der Ahe's mortal demise at age sixty-two in 1913, it was removed and used to mark his grave.

***

The St. Louis Browns repeated as American Association champions the following year, 1887, but found themselves unexpectedly facing an upstart team from Detroit, the Wolverines, in postseason play. The Detroit club was owned by a pharmaceutical wholesaler named Fred Stearns, who dispensed $25,000 out of his own pocket into the National League club, trying to dethrone the White Stockings. When the Detroit team pulled ahead of the fabled White Stockings and came home a pennant winner in 1887, Stearns hired a local lumberman to produce the tallest flagpole ever created, from which Detroit would fly their league pennant. The lumberman responded with a Bunyonesque pole 125 feet high. He delivered it to Detroit and way up there the pennant did fly.

Stearns was thinking big on the ground, too. No wimpy seven game postseason series for him! The drug kingpin had in mind a sprawling fifteen game affair, with three games in St. Louis, two in Detroit, and the rest spread around the cities of the East Coast. Von Der Ahe, who by this time was being referred to in print as "The Lucky Dutchman" by The Sporting News, loved the idea and pegged the admission for series games at $1 for a top seat.

Was this enough?

Hell, no.

The Giants of The Polo Grounds

Remember Helen Dauvray, fiancée of Monte Ward of the Giants? Now living life in the fast lane as a New York stage actress, Helen became an unexpected participant in the 1887 championship series.

La Dauvray had taken a legitimate interest in baseball since first meeting Monte Ward. Later that same year of 1887, the couple would finally be married at the fashionable Arch Street Presbyterian Church in Philadelphia, a lovely redbrick and marble edifice that still stands at 1724 Arch Street.

Helen got it into her head that it was shameful that no trophy was awarded to the winners of such a prestigious sporting event. So she enlisted Stearns and Von Der Ahe to open their checkbooks. Then she hired the Gorham Silver Company to design an elaborate trophy. Not surprisingly, it was called the Dauvray Cup. It was also not to be confused with the Hall Cup, sponsored that same year for the same purpose by a businessman named - you guessed it! – Thomas Hall.

The Dauvray Cup traveled with its own guard upon the special train hired by the St. Louis and Detroit clubs to move the players from one game location to the next, without them getting lost in the saloons along the way. The cup was an immediate symbol of postseason success and, naturally, elicited much publicity for the actress, a turn of events which didn't bother La Dauvray or her husband. There was only one catch to the cup. A team had to win the championship three years in a row to take permanent possession of the Dauvray Cup.

Baseball scholars love to debate the merits of each particular World Series as "Most Exciting," "Most Dramatic," or whatever. There can be little doubt, however, that the 1887 precursor may last forever as "Most Drawn Out" and "Most Cumbersome." Fifteen games were scheduled and, by God, all fifteen would be played.

Detroit ambushed St. Louis as soon as the series began, quickly winning seven of the first nine games. Anyone who has done a modern "motor coach" tour of Europe ("Twenty-three fabulous foreign cities in seventeen breathtaking days!") knows how this series was paced. The two teams arrived in Washington on October 20 to play the tenth and possibly deciding game.

It rained. Then it rained some more. It never stopped raining on October 20. So the teams sat tight and, in a procedure that mercifully has never been repeated, played two championship series games the next day, the first in Washington in the morning and the second in Baltimore in the afternoon. The latter installment resulted in a

The Giants of The Polo Grounds

sloppy 13-3 Detroit victory that gave the championship to the Wolverines. Then the final four games, the sheerest of anticlimax, were played anyway before sparse uncaring crowds in Brooklyn, Chicago, and Detroit.

As for the Giants in 1887, the team stayed in the pennant race until late in the season, before falling back to finish a respectable fourth. Monte Ward stole 111 bases to lead the league and Roger Connor finished second in home runs (17), triples (22), and RBIs (104). Tim Keefe won 35 games. Keefe might easily have won more had he not in September hit Boston second baseman Jack Burdock in the head with a fastball, ending Burdock's career.

Keefe, a sensitive, decent man, suffered a nervous breakdown after the accident and was lost to the team for the final weeks of the season. But what was happening off the field would have an even more lasting effect on the Giants and upon professional baseball.

Monte Ward had obtained his law degree from Columbia by now and, like most new graduates in the legal profession, wasted no time starting trouble. Ward was without question one of the most thoughtful, complex men in baseball. He was an outstanding pitcher, hitter, fielder, and base runner. He would become an excellent manager, a labor organizer, president of the Boston Braves in the 1910s, and eventually the attorney for the National League. He was also a visionary, as two events from 1887 will illustrate.

Ward saw that with the expanded National League schedule that the Giants now played - more than 120 games in 1887, as opposed to fewer than 100 in 1883 - the day of the two man pitching staff had already passed. Most teams in the league still relied on one mainstay hurler. Or, as in the Giants' case with Welch and Keefe, they split the chores in two. But when the regular arm or arms were weary, most teams fell back on unreliable third or fourth string pitchers.

Ward wanted to change that. Ward, looking for the best pitcher available not under contract to a National League or American Association team, settled his attention upon one George Stovey, who pitched for Newark of the International League. Stovey was a big, rugged left-hander with a cheerfully wild fastball, one that kept hitters fearing for their lives. Stovey led the International League in wins in 1887 with 33 and had the second lowest ratio of hits per nine innings. He was also black. Ward wanted to sign

The Giants of The Polo Grounds

him and use him with Welch and Keefe to create an overpowering three-man rotation.

Robert Peterson, author of *Only the Ball Was White,* described Stovey as "the first great Negro pitcher," a Don Newcombe lost in an 1887 time warp. Apparently, Day and Mutrie, enlightened men, particularly on matters that could help their franchise, went along with Ward. Preparations were made to acquire Stovey and move him to the Giants.

Then someone changed his mind. Exactly who is not known, but the temper of the times on racial issues reared its deplorable head in two other events that were almost simultaneous to the prospective sale of Stovey to the Giants.

First, the white players in the International League had begun a campaign of nasty grumbling against the handful of black players in their midst. As the season progressed, the complaints got angrier until, at a meeting of the International League's board of directors on July 14, the league owners capitulated and announced they would "approve no more contracts with colored men." Implicit in that pronouncement was the intention to rid clubs of the stars already under contract. (The league was lily white by Opening Day of the 1888 season.)

By curious coincidence, on the same day that the International League directors were putting the color line down on paper for the first time, the Newark *Evening News*, obviously unaware of what was transpiring at Buffalo, announced that George Stovey would be pitching for Newark in an exhibition game against Cap Anson's Chicago White Stockings at Newark on July 19.

Stovey, as you might imagine, never pitched that game. The excuse at the time was that Stovey had "complained of sickness" and was unable to play. The truth was that Cap Anson had refused to field a team against him. Succeeding now where he had failed against Fleetwood Walker in 1883, Anson now had the triumph of racial prejudice that would set other events in motion such as forcing Day and Mutrie to reconsider their purchase of Stovey. What good was a star pitcher, they easily could have reasoned, if other National League teams might refuse to play against him?

That fear was quite real, as can be demonstrated by a second event later that same season. In September of 1887, the St. Louis Browns were scheduled to play an exhibition game at West Farm, New York, against the Cuban Giants, an "All Negro" team based in

The Giants of The Polo Grounds

Havana. The game was well advertised. Upwards of seven thousand spectators were on hand on the day of the game. Then Chris Von Der Ahe claimed his team was hobbled by injuries and couldn't play. The true reason was that eight members of his twelve-man squad had informed him the night before that they would refuse to play. Had Von Der Ahe forced the issue, the game might have gone on. But he didn't. By the end of the season the yahoos were ascendant. Mutrie or Day, or perhaps both of them, must have taken the hint.

Which brings us back to Monte Ward. Not content to challenge baseball's racial attitudes sixty years before Jackie Robinson, Ward took aim on the sport's labor relations as well.

Two years earlier, in 1885, a Philadelphia sportswriter named William Voltz had tried to form a protective association of baseball players, ostensibly with the purpose of establishing a fund for injured or sick players. Most of the players were suspicious of Voltz's purposes and little came of his plan. But later that same year nine members of the Giants, with Ward as the central figure, picked up on the idea that Voltz had put into the air. The players formed a local chapter of something they called the Brotherhood of Professional Base Ball Players. Coinciding with the rise of the labor movement in the United States, the Brotherhood was the first serious attempt to unionize professional athletes.

John Montgomery Ward, Tim Keefe, Roger Connor, Buck Ewing, second baseman Joe Gerhardt, Mickey Welch, right fielder Mike Dorgan, utility infielder-outfielder Danny Richardson, and Jim O'Rourke all signed with the Brotherhood. Ward was chosen as the chapter's president and Tim Keefe was selected as secretary. In the season that followed, 1886, Ward established other chapters of the Brotherhood in Detroit, Philadelphia, Boston, Chicago, Washington, and Kansas City. By the autumn, when the Browns and the White Stockings were having at each other in the winner-take-all championship series, Ward had most of the game's stars signed with the Brotherhood.

Then, in February of 1887, Albert Spalding made a move that inadvertently gave the Brotherhood the impetus it needed. With an eye to his ledger's bottom line, and considering Silver Flint his catcher of the future, Spalding sold King Kelly, the most popular player in Chicago, to Boston for $10,000, an incomprehensible

The Giants of The Polo Grounds

sum of money in 1887. Despite the fact that other noteworthy players had been sold for thousands of dollars, even within recent weeks, this figure, combined with the popularity of Kelly, was what headlines were made of.

For the first time there was a true realization of what a player's contract could be worth in terms of cash. Coupled with the smelly image of "selling" the services of one human being by another (this was a mere twenty-five years after the Emancipation Proclamation), the King Kelly deal provided Ward and his Brotherhood instant credibility. Ward promptly formed a committee consisting of himself, Dan Brouthers, and Ned Hanlon, both stars of the Detroit club, to attend the National League meetings in March.

The property owners would not have entertained the revolutionaries at all had it not been, ironically, again for Spalding. Despite the fact that he had done as much as any owner to spark the players' labor movement, he had been a player himself. He understood their complaints. So Spalding talked the other owners into allowing Ward to air the players' grievances.

Ward did just that. But when he brought up the recurrent subject of the reserve clause which was effectively preventing players from capitalizing on the value of their own contracts the owners challenged him to devise a more workable system. He could not. And so the matter rested for several months.

In the midst of the 1887 season, Ward gave the matter more thought. He published a magazine article attacking the reserve clause. This was not a concept to warm the owners' hearts. Ward, articulate, well educated, respected by both the public and the other players, and now armed with a law degree, was serving notice that there was trouble to come.

But it would be another three years before the owners would push the situation far enough so that their worst fears could be realized. And first, John Montgomery Ward, having won the heart of the fair Helen Dauvray, now merited the chance to win her cup as well.

Chapter 8   Crazy Eights

"Ninety feet between bases is the closest thing to perfection that man has yet achieved."

Red Smith

The New York Giants lurched to an uneven start of the 1888 season, but Roger Connor provided one hint of the fireworks to come in a game on May 9.

Playing against Indianapolis, the big first baseman smashed three home runs in a single game. This was a mega feat for the time, equivalent to hitting seven in a game today. This was, after all, the height of the dead ball era of the 1880s. A home run was seen by many fans as a crude and vulgar intrusion to the leisurely pace of a game. Nonetheless, big strapping Roger was a bona fide slugger in a day when sluggers barely existed. (Pick up a bat sometime and try to hit modern croquet ball three hundred feet in the air. Then you'll get the idea.) So Roger or "Dear Old Roger" as the fans called him, was embraced with affection.

Connor hit so many home runs (137 in a career that spanned from 1880 through 1897) that he was the all-time career home run leader until the advent of one George Herman Ruth. That this was, and still is, a little-known fact is a testament to the low esteem in which the round tripper was long held. But Polo Grounds fans were different even back then, and Connor provided the faithful with many memorable shots.

One stands out. Connor, playing in the old park at 110th Street and Fifth Avenue, launched a ball that landed on 112th Street on the other side of the right field wall. Several members of the New York Stock Exchange were present at the game and took a particular liking to the blast. So, honoring their hero in a manner they deemed appropriate, they passed around a black top hat and took up a collection for Dear Old Rog. Not that he needed it. But when the money was tallied, there was enough for the brokers to stop by Tiffany & Company a few days later, purchase a $500 gold watch for their man, and present it to him before a subsequent game.

The Giants of The Polo Grounds

"Those Dear Old Stockbrokers," Dear Old Roger was probably thinking.

In July, the rest of the club caught fire, winning 18 of 23 games. Instrumental to the team's surge was the almost unhittable pitching of Mickey Welch and Tim Keefe. Keefe pitched so well that he and Buck Ewing, the catcher, inadvertently gave rise to a controversy that lasted far into the Twentieth Century.

On July 16, Keefe had won 8 straight games. In the second inning on a hot afternoon at the Polo Grounds, the Giants were already pummeling the White Stockings by a score of 9-zip. The field manager, Buck Ewing, was having no part of wasting his best pitcher. Ewing moved Keefe to right field and a substitute pitcher finished the game. Keefe followed with 10 more victories until the same White Stockings broke his streak with a 4-2 triumph before ten thousand fans in New York.

Under Twentieth Century rules, a pitcher must work five innings to get credit for the win. But no such provision was in effect in 1888, so Keefe was awarded 19 straight wins. The point was academic until 1912, when Rube Marquard of the Giants also was credited with 19 straight. Most authorities give Keefe a piece of the record for consecutive wins during a season, as he attained his 19 under the existing rules at that time. Another Giant, Carl Hubbell, would set the record for consecutive victories (24) over two seasons, 1936 and 1937.

The story of the Giants in 1888 was pitching, pitching, and more pitching. Keefe (35-12, 1.74) and Welch (26-19, 1.93) were so overwhelming that the Giants could even add a pair of occasional starters to their roster: Ed Crane and Ledell Titcomb.

Ever notice how the New York Mets of the 1970s and 1980s always seemed to have a few players named Ron? The Giants in 1888 had half their four man pitching staff nicknamed Cannonball: Cannonball Crane, who threw from the right side, and Cannonball Titcomb, who threw from the left.

The two Cannonballs would have short careers with the Giants and, for that matter, short careers in major league baseball. But the time they spent in Manhattan was eventful.

Crane had been around the Union Association and the National League for three previous years, time spent mostly as a substitute outfielder. In 1886 Washington manager Mike Scanlon had tried to make a pitcher out of him, but with meager success. Cannonball had only 1 win in 8 decisions. But Mutrie and Ewing had brought him along. In spot duty he had 5 wins and 6 losses. His real talent, however, was eating, an activity which with an eye to his adipose laden frame of five ten, 204 pounds earned him his nickname.

Cannonball didn't just eat; he gorged. His legendary snack was - hold your breath now - two dozen raw eggs in a soup bowl with a dozen raw clams swimming on top of the eggs.

Cannonball Titcomb acquired his name in a different manner. The allusion here was the velocity of the ball leaving his left arm, remarkable for a dude who only stood five feet six inches. Cannonball was dangerous. He walked a lot, struck out a lot, and sent a lot of batters diving for the proverbial storm cellars. A tobacco card of the day depicts him in the pitcher's box, something long gone, aside from the expression of being knocked out of said box. He was a rough-edged Sandy Koufax or Nolan Ryan without the brilliant future. But he had his days, such as one in 1890 when he pitched a no-hitter for Rochester of the American Association.

Titcomb had something else in common with Sandy Koufax. He was one of the most ill-equipped men of his generation to find his way up to home plate and escape alive. Over the course of 63 games lifetime, Titcomb would hit a robust .098. (Koufax hit .097.) But, hey, in 1888, everything was going the Giants' way and even Cannonball Titcomb had his best year swinging lumber, batting a fearsome .122, with nine singles and somehow a double. Throw out 1888 and Titcomb hit .047, a number more accurately in line with his batting skills. A perfect modern-day parallel? Onetime Yankee reliever Ryne Duren, who had seven hits in ten years for an .061 average.

(Duren, who pitched in the 1960's for the Yankees and Angels was known for his blazing fastball and his very poor vision, a dangerous daily double. He wore thick "Coke bottle" eye glasses. Few hitters were willing to crowd the plate. And who could blame them? Casey Stengel once said, "I would not admire hitting against Ryne Duren. If he ever hit you in the head, you might be in the past tense.")

The Giants of The Polo Grounds

But, we digress. Pitching was the Giants' game in 1888 and the two Cannonballs combined for 19 wins while spotting Keefe and Welch. The Giants coasted home a comfy nine games in front of the deposed White Stockings. The team, especially the pitching, was rested and in perfect health to start the autumn road show with the St. Louis Browns.

This year a modicum of common sense prevailed, and the championship series was set for ten games. Four in New York, one in Brooklyn, one in Philadelphia, and four in St. Louis. If the teams were tied 5 to 5 after ten games, further arrangements would be made.

The Browns, however, had made some arrangements of their own, mostly in regard to player personnel. The team had a different face than the one that had lost to Detroit the previous year.

Chris Von Der Ahe, demonstrating a churlish streak that would resurface at many such moments in his life, had sought to attribute blame for the "embarrassment" of losing to the Wolverines. He also had an eye to cashing in some of his star players, much as the saintly Albert Spalding had cashed in King Kelly and in a much quieter transaction John Clarkson by selling them to Boston. Von Der Ahe, following Spalding's lead, peddled his two star pitchers, Parisian Bob Caruthers and Dave Foutz, to Brooklyn. He also dispatched his best catcher, Doc Bushong, in the same deal. Then he sent Bill Gleason, a fan favorite and the star shortstop, to Philadelphia for a journeyman catcher to replace Bushong. And Curt Welch, he of the unnecessary $15,000 but-for-you $13,920.10 slide, went to Philadelphia for a lousy $3,000.

How then did the Browns ever manage to repeat and win their fourth straight American Association title? The answer is: Not by much.

Von Der Ahe still had one brilliant pitcher, Charles (Silver) King. Silver shined like sterling that year. Charlie Comiskey worked him to death and King responded by pitching 586 innings, winning 45 games, and compiling a 1.64 ERA to lead the league in all three categories. From Louisville, Comiskey also found a pitcher named Elton (Icebox) Chamberlain, so named for his coolness on the playing field as well as the billiard halls, who relieved the beleaguered Silver King when the latter wasn't icing down his arm. He also picked up a journeyman infielder named Bill White, who had been released by the same Louisville club. It was unfortunate, as it turned out, for White, as the infielder later became Von Der Abe's whipping boy.

Now, was there competition for the Browns this year? Yes. In Brooklyn, of all places. Earlier in the year, when four members of the Brooklyn club had taken marriage vows within a few weeks of each other, the team's nickname became the Bridegrooms, a nickname which would, over the long haul, prove less alluring than the Dodgers. But the team got off to a lackluster start, perhaps due to conjugal duties away from the 2,000 seat Washington Park.

By June the honeymoon was over, so to speak, and the boys were putting it together. Manager Bill (Gunner) McGunnigle whipped his legions into shape and, with a nod to the contemporary industrial age, announced that the Grooms were now working together like "well-oiled machinery."

And so they were. In July, while the Giants were pulling away from Chicago in the National League, the Grooms were in a dogfight for first place with the Browns. Then came a hot August and the Grooms, the only threat to the Browns, wilted, going 8-12 for the month. The club recovered in September and October, but the damage was done. St. Louis won the pennant by six and a half games. But the Bridegrooms had gained twenty-eight games in the standings, serving notice that they would be reckoned with in the future.

Meanwhile, however, the Browns would oppose the Giants in the 1888 championship series. Immediately, there was a hassle.

Von Der Ahe and John Day, salivating over the prospect of a "big" series, announced that general admission to the game would be $1.00. Such widespread revolt ensued that the plan was immediately disowned and modified. A record $1.50 was charged for a choice reserved seat, but the unwashed masses could still cram themselves into the grandstand for half a buck and guzzle beer. The two umpires from the previous series, Honest John Kelly and John Gaffney, were retained and on went the show.

Well, sort of. It went on without the Browns' number two pitcher, Nat Hudson. Hudson was that rarest of major league players in the 1880s, a man of independent wealth *before* playing ball. Hudson came and went from his club at his own volition. During the season he had spent enough time with the Browns to amass a creditable total of 25 wins. But during October, Hudson had a longing to immerse his tired arm, and the rest of his body as well, in the soothing natural baths of Hot Springs, Arkansas. So off he went, postseason series or not.

The Giants of The Polo Grounds

Hudson wasn't all that was wet. On the morning that the series began, a downpour drenched the field at the Polo Grounds. A grounds crew then went to work with wheelbarrows filled with sawdust and, before a packed house, the series began. Tim Keefe opposed Silver King and the fans saw a memorable if slightly unusual game.

In the bottom of the third inning, with the score tied one to one and with two outs, Silent Mike Tiernan, the New York right fielder, drew a walk. He then made a dash for second. The Browns' catcher, Honest Jack Boyle, the not so sensational replacement for ailing Doc Bushong, fired the ball toward second base. Not only did it sail past the second base, but it also rocketed past Harry Lyons, the St. Louis center fielder. Tiernan scored from first on the events set in motion by the stolen base attempt. There was no further scoring in the game and the Giants led the series one to nothing.

Enter Icebox Chamberlain, ninety-eight years before Refrigerator Perry.

Game Two looked like a mismatch, with Chamberlain pitching against Mickey Welch, the venerable drinking man. The Icebox had earned his nickname not through any dietary habits or physical attributes. Rather, they called him Icebox because he was cool under pressure, and so he was on this day. Icebox frosted the Giants, 3-0, and the series was tied.

Then the Giants took charge. Keefe beat King a second time. The series moved to Washington Park in Brooklyn. Cannonball Crane outpitched Chamberlain. Next, Keefe, starting for the third time, defeated King again and Welch won game six against Chamberlain, 12-5, in Philadelphia.

The Giants, in a workmanlike championship series, suddenly led five games to one. They needed only one more win and they would be a third of the way to the Dauvray Cup. The teams boarded a special train that would take them to St. Louis. And now the fun started.

When the train stopped in Pittsburgh, several players got off to stretch and get some air. Scores of fans crowded the platform to catch a glimpse of the baseballers. There were several local sports writers present, also, but beyond that there was a familiar face. Nestled among the fans was one Curt Welch, the former Brown and perpetrator of the famous $15,000 slide.

Welch was not in the best shape. He had, according to what he told friends on the St. Louis club, bet large sums of money on his former teammates and had lost it. Looking for a scapegoat, he singled out John Kelly, the umpire, and accused Honest John of a blatantly pro-Giant bias.

Kelly studied Welch for a moment, then decided not to take the bait. He walked back aboard the train. The incident would have been forgotten. Welch's charges had no credibility at all except that the jackass streak within Chris Van Der Ahe found that moment to bubble over again.

Von Der Ahe assembled the writers present and, apparently on the spur of the moment, told them that Welch was absolutely right. Kelly and Gaffney, he alleged, had wagered on the New York club and now favored them with every close call.

The charge was, of course, patently asinine, and it takes a thorough understanding of Von Der Abe's idiot quotient to understand why he would bother to amplify Welch's scurrilous remarks. Whatever else Von Der Abe's better character points may have been, the man was a world class sorehead when he was losing. But once he had spoken, his words were out. The charges were splashed across the nation's sports pages within a day.

Incredibly, there was another tainted story circulating from the same Pittsburgh train station. There was a writer for the Pittsburgh *Press,* who might otherwise have been truly gifted as either a novelist, a writer of pulp fiction, or some mixture of both. Instead, he wrote sports for the *Press* and made a comfortable living by never letting facts ruin a good story. Similarly, he conjured up many amusing tales that had no factual basis whatsoever. No one really seemed to mind.

For example, while Von Der Ahe was popping off about Gaffney and Kelly, the scribe filed a story to the effect that hulking Roger Connor had saved the life of the gorgeous La Dauvray right there on that eventful train platform.

A huge steel girder had tumbled from a construction platform overhead where men were working, the story went. Helen would have been crushed like a bug had not the brawny superman Roger Connor raised a hammy forearm to deflect the errant girder away from La Dauvray's fair head. "My hero!" swooned La Belle Dauvray.

And so on.

Such stories originating with this writer found their way into other newspapers around the country but were consumed primarily for their amusement value. Think of it as the 'space alien' story of the

The Giants of The Polo Grounds

day, or the Elvis sighting. There was a wink between the lines, intentional or not. In this specific case, both Roger Connor and Helen Dauvray freely admitted the story was a hoax. Yet they were amused by it.

The writer, however, also filed the story about Von Der Ahe's allegations of dishonest umpiring. In many places the two stories ran right next to each other, which meant that both were taken with equal seriousness. But then other writers started to file their own accounts of Von Der Ahe's allegations. When the train arrived in St. Louis, Von Der Ahe was stuck with his own quote.

This is perhaps the place to note that in the long history of major league baseball in the United States, not once has an umpire been found to have dishonestly influenced a game. Mistakes, yes, over the course of a century. But corruption, no. That should indicate something about how sensitive umpires would naturally be about their reputations . . . both then and now.

Von Der Ahe was asked to either retract or stand by his statement. When he was unwilling to eat his words, the umpires took the allegations seriously.

"I don't care about anyone's opinion of my work," John Gaffney told the press. "But I do object to being called crooked. And I will quit baseball before taking any more of that."

Honest John Kelly supported his associate. "If Gaffney won't umpire any more games," Kelly said, "I won't, either."

Now baseball had a championship series fully in progress and the umpires had just quit.

For several hours it appeared as though the series would end right there, with the Giants one game shy of victory. Eventually, Von Der Ahe backed off his charges, claiming now that he had been "misquoted." That was enough to get the series going again.

Silver King and the Browns won the seventh game, 7-5, with Cannonball Crane the losing pitcher. But the Browns' win at home only postponed the inevitable. Tim Keefe, blazing hot now and presumably anxious to end things, came out throwing fire the next afternoon. The Giants battered the Browns, 11-3, and clinched the series. But because ten games had been scheduled, ten were played. Hardly anyone cared.

Buck Ewing gave most of his regulars an early break for the winter. With both lineups watered down with substitutes, the Browns won two final tilts by what sounded more like football scores, 14-11 and 18-7. The play in both games was uniformly sloppy.

The Giants of The Polo Grounds

"The games played after the series had been won were mere farces," Jim Mutrie proclaimed just before leaving St. Louis for New York. "If I ever engage in another World Series, the ball will stop rolling just as soon as the series is decided."

NEW YORK BALL CLUB, 1888.

Mutrie's words would serve him well. Not only did they hold forth for every series ever after, but they also served as a vindication. The original championship series, that between the Mets and Providence five years earlier had been an act of Mutrie's instigation. Now, "Handsome Jeems," as the penny tabloids called him, had won a series of his own.

He had also done a bit more, though he didn't know it at the time. The defeat at the hands of the Giants served as the death knell for the fading St. Louis Browns. It would be another fifty-six years before a team bearing that name would appear in a World Series. And with the decline in the midwestern dynasty, Brooklyn was the heir apparent in the American Association. The pieces were now in place for one of the great sports rivalries of all time.

As for the Hall Cup itself, "baseball's oldest existing World Championship trophy," remains on display to this day at the Baseball Hall of Fame, in Cooperstown, New York, while the Dauvray Cup disappeared around 1893, never to be seen again, except by whoever it probably melted it down many years ago.

83

The Giants of The Polo Grounds

A Sportswriter's Reminiscence – George Vecsey

My introduction to the Polo Grounds came on July 11, 1948.

I had just turned nine, a Brooklyn Dodger fan, hopeful and innocent.

My life would never be the same.

I was taken to the game by three family friends who were like uncles to me -- Jim McGuinness and his younger brother Joe, and their dad whom I remember as Grandpa McGuinness. They were good men, whose only flaw was rooting for the New York Giants.

We sat in the upper-left-field stands, just below Coogan's Bluff, with a skewed view of the oval ball park.

My Dodgers were defending National League champions, their lineup filled with what Roger Kahn would later call "The Boys of Summer" – Reese, Robinson, Hodges, Furillo, Campanella, Roe, plus, George Shuba, one of the most sociable players in Kahn's book, who was playing left field that day, although you couldn't see him from where we sat.

I have downloaded the New York *Times* article from that day. There were 47,768 paying fans for that intra-city rivalry. I remember the day as warm and sunny. The memory of a former nine-year-old is blurred by time and people and multiple sensations, plus the odd angle and distance of our seats. Willard Marshall hit a homer for the Giants, and Shuba and Carl Furillo hit homers for the Dodgers, who were ahead, 2-1, in the eighth. Then a Dodger reliever named Willie (The Knuck) Ramsdell – he threw a knuckleball – relieved Preacher Roe and walked in the tying run.

With all the lineup machinations, I'm sure I was not aware that a marginal infielder named Jack Conway had gone in to play third base for the Giants in the eighth. No reason to know who he was – nearly 30, barely 100 games in the majors.

Conway came up for the first time to lead off the ninth. Far, far away, something happened. We lost sight of the ball. Then the three McGuinness men were lighting up cigars and pounding me on the back and informing me that Conway had hit a home run and the game was over. But how?

People with portable radios informed us that Conway's high popup had drifted, just barely ticking the upper left-field stands -- 274 feet or so. I was a broken child as my three hosts, my protectors, my surrogate uncles, celebrated and perhaps even gloated on the long subway trip to Queens. I suffered and whined all the way home. I have never forgotten, as you can tell.

In my retelling over the years, I have imagined Red Barber, on Dodger radio, making the call, describing how shortstop Pee Wee Reese "going back-back-back – and it hits the stands for a home run!" But I don't know that really happened.

I have found the article in the *Times* by Louis Effrat, who blamed "a sudden gust of wind" for blowing the ball into the upper deck, but I don't remember any breeze. Effrat, whom I later knew as a young reporter, called it "one of the most anemic home runs ever hit in a park noted for 'cheap' circuit swats." (That's how sports pages sounded back then.)

Only recently have I discovered that George Shuba was in left field, waiting for the ball to come down. In the 1980s and 90s, when I was a sports columnist for the Times, I became friendly with Shuba, who lived in his home town in Youngstown, Ohio, and visited New York for baseball events, and was indeed as gregarious and intelligent as Roger Kahn had depicted him. How I would have loved to hear Shuba's recollections about waiting for that ball to come down.

(Baseball box scores are treasure troves. This one reveals Dodger manager Leo (The Lip) Durocher, making all sorts of certified-genius lineup moves: broken-down Pete Reiser pinch-hitting for a new Dodger catcher named Roy Campanella – a future Hall of Famer; Gil Hodges moving from first base, where he would become one of the greatest players not to be in the Hall of Fame, to his old position of catcher; and Jackie Robinson moving from second base to his first major-league position of first base. The Lip himself would be making a switch, five days later, going from the Dodgers to the Giants, where he would win two pennants after the arrival of Willie Mays.

(One of those pennants would be won in the 1951 playoff by a more robust home run to the lower left-field stands by another Giant, Bobby Thomson, over another Dodger left fielder, Andy Pafko. This event would be immortalized in the epic *Pafko at the Wall*, by Don DeLillo, later used as the first, and best, chapter in his novel, *Underworld*.)

But this piece is, ultimately, about Jack Conway. Many years later, I discovered that the cheesy home run was the first and last in his major-league career. He would be sent back to the minors a few weeks later, never to re-emerge. He would finish with 128 games and a .223 batting average. He died on June 11, 1993, and is buried in Waco, Tex.

The Giants of The Polo Grounds

The photo in the *Times* the next day shows a man with *GIANTS* across his home-white jersey, and a smile on his face, as Bill Rigney, Buddy Kerr and manager Mel Ott - soon to be exiled to the front office - prepare to pummel him. I hope Conway remembered that moment the rest of his life.

As a young reporter, I would get back to the Polo Grounds when the Mets were formed in 1962-63, and I delighted in that rusting, resurrected ballpark, with all its imperfections. Other players would hit cheap home runs to left and right fields, but none would compare to the "anemic" shot I witnessed on my first trip to that strange ball park.

Rest in Peace, Jack Conway.

George Vecsey
New York, April 2018

Author's note: George Vecsey is a retired sports columnist for The *New York Times* and author of many books, including, *Stan Musial: An American Life*, *The Rivals*, *Maguire and Sosa* and *Joy In Mudville: Being a Complete Account of the Unparalleled History of the New York Mets From Their Most Perturbed Beginnings to Their Amazing Rise to Glory and Renown*. His *Baseball: A History of America's Favorite Game* is a concise history of the game of professional baseball. If asked, he will also admit having authored a chapter of the 1969 literary hoax *Naked Came the Stranger*.

Chapter 9 New York vs. Brooklyn

"The rivalry between New York and Brooklyn as regards baseball is unparalleled in the history of the national game."

New York *Times*, 1889

Thirty-five ballplayers circled the globe on Albert Spalding's world tour in the winter of 1888-89, a grand trek by boat and by land which took players from San Francisco, to Australia, to Ceylon, up through the Middle East, Europe and finally to Ireland. They returned by steamship to New York from Dublin immediately prior to the 1889 season. There was a massive banquet at Delmonico's in early April, attended by National League president Abraham G. Mills, Mark Twain, and, in the midst of an unsuccessful campaign for mayor of New York City, Theodore Roosevelt. There's a good chance that John Montgomery Ward didn't enjoy the meal.

In his absence, the owners had been busy. John T. Brush, a wealthy Indianapolis clothing manufacturer, had purchased the National League club of that city. Brush's experience in baseball was limited. He was usually a fair, sensible man, but he was also, upon occasion, given to some monumentally bad ideas. One of his worst was upon him while Spalding's All Stars were safely in Asia.

In the absence of Ward, Brush, brandishing influence proportionate to his bankroll, had secured league approval of an asinine scheme called the Classification Plan. Simply stated, all professional ballplayers would be graded on a scale of A to E. Gradings were to be based not just on ability and performance but also upon "morality" and off the field deportment. A player, in other words, who tended to be sober and uninvolved in paternity suits would thus have a higher mark than an equal player who was tainted by either. And so on. Get it? Once graded, with A being a high grade and E being low, salaries were to be uniform. An A player would pull in $2,500 per season. An E man would have to get by on $1,500.

Naturally, the owners set themselves up as the sole arbiters of

The Giants of The Polo Grounds

who was A material and who was E. And just as naturally, the owners were the first to violate their own rules: Boston found a way to pay King Kelly a $3,000 "signing bonus" and Keefe, Connor, and Crane of the Giants all drew salaries in excess of the limit. But John Montgomery Ward took the Classification Plan for what it was: a patronizing slap in the face. Ward demanded an immediate hearing of a Brotherhood committee before the National League. The owners, led by Brush, refused.

Ward simmered. Strike talk spread among dissatisfied players, but most players had signed their contracts for 1889. Ward feared that the players would lose the support of the public if they walked out on legal agreements. That left the players in the position of trying to negotiate a settlement with the owners during a season in progress.

In June the committee from the Brotherhood petitioned Nick Young, the new president of the National League, to end the Classification Plan and terminate the practice of selling players. Young took no action. Strike talk was everywhere, yet the owners only scoffed. John Day of the Giants, who owned Ward's contract, called the possibility of a strike "nonsense." Arthur Soden, Boston's president, went one better, saying it was "absurd" and threatened to use strikebreakers from the minor leagues if necessary to keep his ballpark open. To the end, the owners vowed to stick with their reserve clause and the Classification Plan. Tim Keefe, secretary of the Brotherhood, announced ominously, "The league will not classify as many as they think."

Still, the owners twiddled their thumbs.

In July of 1889, representatives of the various Brotherhood chapters met in New York at the Fifth Avenue Hotel. Ward told the Brotherhood reps that they, the players, would have to return to their respective cities to secure capital for one purpose, formation of a new Brotherhood League in which players and owners would share in profits.

Ward quickly found an early ally in one Albert L. Johnson, brother of Mayor Thomas L. Johnson of Cleveland. The Johnson brothers owned a network of streetcars. They were interested in financing a Cleveland franchise in a new league and putting the team's playing grounds at one end of one of their lines. Thus, they would have two businesses profiting off each other or so they reasoned. Johnson gave financial credibility to the plan for a new league and helped draw in other investors in other cities. By the end of the summer, the groundwork for a new league was in place.

The Giants of The Polo Grounds

The end of the summer traditionally brings with it the conclusion of a baseball season. Even in this tumultuous year the season was a good one. For the champion Giants, the year was in some ways as chaotic on the field as off.

For many years, the municipal government of New York had been telling John Day that the section of the Polo Grounds that enclosed 111th Street would have to be opened as a public street. Day managed to put the moment off for as long as possible, but the time had finally come. Day had little choice but to move his team farther uptown, escaping the clog of Manhattan. He settled upon a strip of land at the northern tip of Manhattan by the Harlem River. The land itself, New York City Plot 2006, Lot 100, was all that remained of a section of farmland granted in the early 1700s by King George I to an Englishman named John Lion Gardiner. A Gardiner descendant eventually married one James J. Coogan. Coogan was an undistinguished furniture dealer and upholsterer who, Manhattan politics being what it is, would suddenly become Manhattan's first borough president in 1890. His remaining area of farmland was called Coogan's Hollow. A rocky series of cliffs that overlooked it was known as Coogan's Bluff.

To the extent that there were any streets running through the land, the address was determined as being 155th Street and Eighth Avenue. To avoid confusion, John Day christened the area as the "New" Polo Grounds. Trees were cleared and a grassy meadow, where sheep and cows had once grazed, was converted into a playing field. A construction company built a horseshoe-shaped wooden grandstand. Target date for completion was the first day of the 1889 season. This being New York, nothing was ready on time. The Giants began defending their league title by alternating games between Jersey City and Staten Island. But on July 8 the team finally moved into its new 15,000 seat park.

The Giants had much the same winning combination in 1889 as they'd had the previous year. Mike Slattery, the center fielder, broke a finger in midseason and was replaced by George Gore, who hit .305. Roger Connor again carried the biggest bat on the squad with a .317 average and a league leading 130 RBIs. Silent Mike Tiernan spoke with his bat, finishing tops on the team and third in the league in batting with a .335 average. Buck Ewing wasn't far behind at .327.

The Giants of The Polo Grounds

Pitching again was excellent. Welch and Keefe teamed for 55 wins. Cannonball Titcomb faded to 12 while the other Cannonball, Ed Crane, won 14 games. Yet there was another pitching star. A twenty-six-year-old righthander named Hank O'Day joined the team in mid-season from Washington. He had an uneven 11-11 record for the year: 2-10 with Washington and 9-1 with the Giants.

Yet with all this, the Giants were pursued all season by the strongest Boston club since 1883-84. Boston, which had now changed their name from the Red Stockings to the Beaneaters, featured the ever-popular King Kelly in right field. (A hard-drinking Irishman, was Kelly ever a crowd favorite in the Hub!) The pitching staff consisted almost entirely of John Clarkson who started 72 games, finished 68 of them, and won 49.

Pitching behind Clarkson was Old Hoss Radbourn, who had his third worst season in the major leagues with a shabby 20 wins. Clarkson and Radbourn (who between them would amass a total of 637 major league wins) carried the Boston club through the season. On the morning of the season's final day, the Giants and the Beaneaters were tied for first place.

Then fifth place Pittsburgh knocked off Boston, 6-1, while Tim Keefe was defeating Cleveland, 5-3. The Giants won the pennant by one game, setting the stage perfectly for a memorable postseason series.

In the American Association, Chris Von Der Ahe's Browns were hanging on for survival against the very players they had cut loose: Foutz, Caruthers, and Bushong. In the end, Brooklyn won the American Association pennant on the final day of the season. Now, as would happen frequently for decades to come, Brooklyn and the Giants would square off.

The championship series of 1889 would go on as scheduled, but it would be played beneath a cloud. On October 11, a week before Game One, John Montgomery Ward met with John Day. Day was one owner whom the players liked and whom the players least wished to harm. When Ward met with him, it was to inform him that he and most of his players would be starting their own New York club the following season. Ward had financial backing in eight cities, he explained, and had also leased a tract of land for a ballpark in New York.

The new field, which didn't have a diamond or a grandstand yet, was right under Coogan's Bluff on the lot adjoining the Polo

The Giants of The Polo Grounds

Grounds. Ward finished his meeting with Day by offering the Giants' owner an executive job in the Brotherhood League. Day, loyal to the National League, declined.

Then the series started. True to his wishes from previous autumns, Jim Mutrie, who set up the rules for the series, ordained that the first team to win six games would be the champion, and that no unnecessary games would be played.

Game One was a wild one. Tim Keefe was uncharacteristically off the mark and Brooklyn touched him for five runs in the first inning. Sir Timothy's changeup was floating like a balloon that afternoon.

The Giants, however, rallied. Before eight thousand fans, Brooklyn added a run but barely maintained the lead. At the end of six innings, the score was 6-5, Brooklyn.

In the seventh, the Giants scored five runs. A four-run lead, however, was fragile on a day like this. New York pounded Adonis Terry for five runs, bringing a Brooklyn relief pitcher into the game. Brooklyn responded with two runs of their own in the bottom of the seventh and another four off Cannonball Crane in the bottom of the eighth.

Then, with the sky darkening, Brooklyn began to stall. Brooklyn's pitcher held the ball without throwing for several minutes. Other players took turns tying shoes or discussing points of procedure with umpire John Gaffney. Eventually, the fans became angered by the delays and started wandering across the field, further delaying the play.

Washington Park, Brooklyn. Circa 1888

Ultimately, Brooklyn got what it wanted: a game called on account of darkness and a 12-10 victory. This was 1880s baseball, after all. With no commissioner, anything went.

Hey, did the crowds in Brooklyn like knocking off the Giants? Sixteen thousand people swarmed into Washington Park the next day, a gargantuan attendance for a small park that only seated two

The Giants of The Polo Grounds

thousand. The crowd stood before the grandstands along the foul lines and was roped back by police at the fringes of the outfield.

Parisian Bob Caruthers pitched for Brooklyn. Joe Visner caught. Caruthers threw the ball better than Visner caught it. Visner had trouble finding second base with his throws. The Giants stole the base at will, then racked up runs with singles. At the end of nine innings, the score was 6-2, Giants. The series was even.

The series crossed the river to the Polo Grounds where, in the budding tradition of bizarre Giants-Brooklyn entanglements, the weird events continued.

By the ninth inning, the Bridegrooms had racked Mickey Welch for eight runs and held an 8-7 lead. But the Giants loaded the bases in the last of the ninth with Roger Connor at the plate. Just then John Gaffney raised his hands and called the game on account of darkness. The call set off a wild display among Polo Grounds fans as Gaffney hustled off to the umpire's dressing room. Several of the Giant players followed, arguing vehemently that Connor deserved to take his cuts even if it were pitch black.

Gaffney refused. Then the next day he showed he wasn't intimidated, either. The Bridegrooms worked over Cannonball Crane and built a 10-7 lead. This time Gaffney called the game after six innings.

On behalf of his team, John Day was apoplectic. "Three times we have lost in this series through trickery and we shall do so no more," Day proclaimed. "I don't mind losing games on their merits, but I do mind being robbed."

Jim Mutrie attempted to rally his men. He made a public pronouncement that the Giants would bounce back to win the series. No one believed him. But the Giants' bats came alive in Game Five and they blasted Bob Caruthers, 11-3. Brooklyn lost more than the game. Bob Clark, who had taken over the regular catching duties late in the season, sprained his ankle running the bases. That left the catching duties to Doc Bushong, who was fading badly at age thirty-three, and Joe Visner, who couldn't locate second base. Clark's injury would affect the rest of the series.

Adonis Terry and Hank O'Day hooked up in a brilliant pitchers' duel in Game Six. It went to the bottom of the ninth with Brooklyn leading, 1-0.

With two out, Monte Ward singled.

Ward stole second on the first pitch to Roger Connor and stole third on the second pitch. Next, Connor whacked the ball directly

The Giants of The Polo Grounds

through shortstop, scoring Ward. There the score remained at 1-1 until the eleventh. Then Ward singled through the same left side of the infield, scoring Mike Slattery from second. Just that quickly, the series was tied. And just as would happen in many future Octobers when Brooklyn relinquished a series lead, "dem Bums was dead."

New York scored eight times in the second inning of the seventh game and ran away with a sloppy 11-7 win behind Tim Keefe. Then, seizing the same strategy of scoring early and often, they bombarded Brooklyn's Bob Caruthers with nine runs in the first two innings of Game Eight.

Now the Giants had won four straight and led in games, 5 to 3. Somehow the Brooklyn team and their fans sensed the inevitable. The final game of the series was played on a miserably cold wet day at Coogan's Bluff. Adonis Terry went to the mound for the visiting Bridegrooms and Hank O'Day pitched for the Giants.

Brooklyn scored two runs in the top of the first, but the early rally would be their last hurrah of 1889. The Giants came back with a run in the bottom of the same inning. Both pitchers bore down. No one scored again until the Giants scraped together a run on a walk and two singles in the sixth. Then in seventh, with Connor on first base, Doc Bushong, whose career in dentistry was approaching ever faster, misplayed Buck Ewing's roller and fired it into left field. Dear Old Roger came all the way around to score what proved to be the winning run in a 4-2 Giant victory.

The three thousand Giant fans who had attended in the cold autumn gloom surged onto the field after the game. They chanted, "We are the people!" with linked arms and sang the Giants song like so many British soccer fans on a march through Amsterdam. They mobbed their heroes and tried to carry some from the field to the clubhouse. Order was restored only when the Giants disappeared from view.

Then the fans gathered around a victory gong at the Polo Grounds and cheered a peal that resounded through the neighborhood. The Giants had won their second championship in a row. They were just a year away, fans told each other, from taking permanent possession of the Dauvray Cup.

There was also an additional social note. For the past two years Tim Keefe had greatly admired what John Montgomery Ward was going home to each night, i.e., Helen Dauvray. Tim finally took the hint and married Helen's younger sister.

Chapter 10   **Workers of The World Unite!**

"Who killed baseball?"

A popular question in 1890.

i

Convening in Manhattan in early November of 1889 with three dozen members of the Brotherhood, John Montgomery Ward formally announced his union's intention of forming a new league. "Players have been bought, sold, or exchanged as though they were sheep, instead of American citizens," Ward proclaimed.

Arrangements in the new Players' League, he maintained, would be different. In truth, they would be. Ward had financial backers ready to bankroll franchises in eight cities: Boston, Brooklyn, Buffalo, Chicago, Cleveland, New York, Philadelphia, and Pittsburgh. The hated reserve rule was gone, three-year contracts at 1888 salary levels would be in effect, and club profits would be divided between owners and players. Inexpensive land had already been obtained at eight sites and wooden grandstands would rise before Opening Day the following April.

It was along about this time that the owners of the eight National League clubs began to panic. They threatened lawsuits and court injunctions against any player still under contract who played with the new league. And, at their own league meeting later that same month, they formed a "war committee" to combat the Brotherhood. There were three men on it: John I. Rogers, an attorney and owner of the Phillies; Albert G. Spalding, the most influential man in the baseball industry; and by surprise John B. Day of the New York Giants. Day's inclusion was an indication of where the war was shaping up. Obviously, New York was the key arena. If the Brotherhood could be defeated in the largest market area, the league would crumble.

Ward, of course, had already recognized this himself. Defecting from the Giants were all the stars, except for Smilin' Mickey Welch

The Giants of The Polo Grounds

and Silent Mike Tiernan, both of whom felt personally loyal to John Day.

Tempers ran high. Opinions were sharply divided.

Henry Chadwick, editor of *The Spalding Guide* (1889), was firmly on the side of management, accusing the players of - gasp! – a "revolutionary manifesto." The Cincinnati *Enquirer,* another royalist publication, changed John Montgomery Ward's name to "John Much Advertised Ward," and accused him of instigating labor problems in baseball to serve his own purposes as an attorney.

The Sporting News came down on the side of the players, a courageous act, considering how much advertising they carried from National League owners. Indeed, *The Sporting News* was soon grinding an ax with old Albert Spalding himself in almost every issue. Spalding had withdrawn his advertising as soon as the paper had sided with the insurgents. In return, *The Sporting News* gleefully reminded the public that as a player Spalding had jumped his Boston contract at the inception of the National League. Further, they reminded the public, Spalding had repeatedly "skinned" his loyal Chicago clientele with extortionate charges for cushions and scorecards once patrons were within his ballpark. Naturally, all of organized labor supported the Brotherhood. The American Federation of Labor invited them to join their ranks, but the players' union never responded to the invitation.

On other levels, there was no end to the sly methods Ward employed to battle the National League. One marvelous strategy involved the playing fields already in use. Where possible, the Brotherhood made bids to rent those fields for the 1890 season. In many cases, the Brotherhood had no intention of actually playing there. But their bids forced the price up for National League owners, thereby increasing the financial pressure upon the league.

Ward also attempted to keep the American Association neutral by promising not to raid any of its franchises for players. The Association owners listened with interest, then couldn't bring themselves to align with labor. By failing to side with one of the two combatants, the Association was soon at war with both the Brotherhood and the National League. The Players' League raided it for players. Then the National League, seeking to bolster its own ranks, dumped its weak Washington and Indianapolis franchises and invited the two strongest Association teams, Cincinnati and Brooklyn, to join the National League. Cincinnati and Brooklyn, tired of an amateurish "beer and whiskey" league dominated by the

The Giants of The Polo Grounds

mercurial boor Chris Von Der Ahe, bolted at the first invitation.

The real trench warfare, however, was reserved for the services of key players. Here Ward was of inestimable value to the Brotherhood. In the winter of 1889-90, he traveled the United States, keeping potential franchises in line. He personally devastated the Pittsburgh franchise with a visit to that city, leaving the National League entry within the words of Frank Brunel, the secretary of the Brotherhood, "a crowd of stiffs, and only four [real] ball players among them."

Naturally, the League responded with lawsuits. The New York Giants had sought an injunction against Ward playing in the Brotherhood League. The Giants and the National League lost when Justice John J. O'Brien found that Ward's 1889 contract had not fixed the time and conditions contemplated by the reserve clause.

O'Brien ruled that a specific performance, in this case Ward's playing of baseball, could not be ordered when the terms of the next agreement were so vague. The court went further to find that Ward's contract lacked fairness and equity, as it bound a player to a team for life, while a ball club could terminate its obligation to the player upon ten days' notice. A similar case, brought by the Giants against Buck Ewing, failed on similar grounds, as did a case brought against infielder Bill Hallman of the Phillies. It was probably only at this point, when lawsuits began to fail, that the owners fully realized that most of their key players would not be returning for the 1890 season.

John Day's franchise was the hardest hit in terms of personnel lost. And with New York considered the key area in terms of success or failure of the Brotherhood movement, the National League took take drastic measures to make Day's New York Giants competitive in 1890. Accordingly, the league instigated a complicated deal in which John T. Brush sold his entire Indianapolis roster to New York. The "Indians," as they were called colloquially, were now the New York Giants, in addition to Welch and Tiernan. Or at least John Day said they were.

Thus, with the battle lines drawn, the war began in earnest on April 19, 1890. Both the Players' League and the National League opened their seasons on the same day.

As foreseen, nowhere was the competition more savage than New York. The Brooklyn Bridegrooms of owner Charlie Byrne and manager Bill McGunnigle were now in the National League, while Monte Ward himself was now manager of the Brooklyn entry in the Players' League.

The Giants of The Polo Grounds

Yet a third Brooklyn club had materialized in the American Association, though it would fail in midseason and move to Baltimore. Over in Manhattan, there was a situation vaguely reminiscent of the Middle Ages when there was a Pope in Rome and a Pope in Avignon. In upper Manhattan, there were two versions of the New York Giants. To make things even more confusing, they both played at Coogan's Hollow in identical parks built right next to each other. And damned if both squads didn't look like and call themselves the Giants.

Fans traveled to upper Manhattan by carriage or steam railroad on Opening Day, and then they could take their pick. Hawkers and hustlers lined the route to the ball fields, pitching tickets for either "Jim Mutrie and the real Giants" in the National League, or "Buck Ewing and the Big Giants" in the Players' League. *Big* Giants? The renegade bunch featured such stars as Roger Connor, Tim Keefe, Hank O'Day, Orator Jim O'Rourke, George Gore, Mike Slattery, Cannonball Crane, and Danny Richardson, in addition to Ewing, who played and managed. The ersatz product, in other words, looked more legitimate than Jim Mutrie's "real thing."

Yet the crowds that flocked to the two Opening Day games broke down largely along social lines, as it would throughout the season. The established actors, capitalists, businessmen, and socialites were in the "old" New Polo Grounds to watch Jim Mutrie's team. The segment of the press that was sympathetic to Day and Mutrie reported that never had so many "prominent" citizens attended a ball game as were on hand to see Handsome Jeems' team open the season. Ladies "by the hundred," it was reported, "were in the upper story of Mutrie's grandstand," creating a "veritable garden" with lace and flower Easter bonnets. The observation of so many females in attendance was not an idle notation. Mutrie loyalists were telling their readers that the playing grounds of the "real" Giants remained a safe and decent place to go. By implication, the rebel joint across the street which bore the vaguely Marxist sounding name of Brotherhood Park was not.

Of course, patrons of the Players' League had their own sympathies, also, and probably wouldn't have been caught dead in the establishment place. Anyone with any kind of working class affiliation headed for the Brotherhood park and cheered on Buck Ewing's squad. Some unions had given their workers a day off with instructions to head for the ballpark to show sympathy with the unionized athletes. Samuel Gompers himself, the John the Baptist of

The Giants of The Polo Grounds

the American Labor Movement, had even put in several strong words in support of the Brotherhood during a rally of unionized carpenters at Manhattan's Webster Hall the previous evening. So the rebel stands were packed. Reasonable observers estimated the crowd at twelve thousand. Jim Mutrie's Giants drew approximately forty-five hundred, meaning there were plenty of seats available at game time. As far as the ledgers went, the Players' League seemed to be winning the first skirmish.

On the actual playing fields, the two organizations offered vague parodies of each other. The two grandstands both faced south from opposite ends of Coogan's Hollow but were angled in such a way that the two parks faced each other just slightly. The outfields were contiguous, separated only by a double fence. All of this created a situation where fans in one park could actually see some of the activities in the other. On Opening Day the spectators who were afforded this view must have had a strange sense of double vision.

At the Polo Grounds, for example, the tweedy band of the fashionable Seventh Regiment struck up a few popular songs. Almost simultaneously, the more plebian Sixty-ninth Regiment band struck up some music at Brotherhood Park. Jim Mutrie and John Day then raised their World Championship pennant. Across the Hollow, the Brotherhood team raised their own World Championship pennant. There they were, two "undisputed" world champs, right across the meadow from each other. Then the real Giants and the Big Giants both went out and lost.

Making his first start as a New York Giant, eighteen-year-old Amos Rusie lost to William (Kid) Gleason and the Philadelphia Phillies, 4-0. Across the way, Tim Keefe of the Players' League Giants struggled with a hopped-up baseball that the Brotherhood had introduced to inject more scoring (and theoretically excitement) into their version of the game. These Giants lost a squeaker, 12-11, to Philadelphia's Brotherhood team. The latter, as you might expect, was comprised primarily of the Phillies' stars of the preceding year. Opening Day set just the proper tone for the rest of the 1890 season: Everyone involved was destined to come out a loser.

Buck Ewing's Giants in the Players' League had a respectable season on the field, finishing third, eight games behind the pennant winning Boston club that featured King Kelly, Old Hoss Radbourn, and Dan Brouthers. Ewing's squad also scored the incomprehensible total of 1,018 runs in 131 games, meaning the

The Giants of The Polo Grounds

jackrabbit Players' League baseball had the fans on their feet a lot, watching runners circle the bases. Roger Connor, not surprisingly, was the league's Big Bopper with 13 home runs.

In Brooklyn, the Bridegrooms, with a lineup undamaged by player raids, were the class of the league. Bill McGunnigle's squad won the pennant by six games over Cap Anson's Chicago White Stockings, making Brooklyn the only club to have won a pennant two year in a row in two different leagues. John Montgomery Ward managed the Brooklyn team in the Players' League to a second-place finish, one rung above Buck Ewing's club. The Brooklyn club of the American Association finished the year in Baltimore, as previously noted, and in sixth place. A watered-down edition of the championship series was played between the Brooklyn Bridegrooms and the Louisville team of the American Association. The affair was so tepid and received so little fan support that it was halted after six games and declared a 3-3 tie.

The National League Giants of 1890? The situation was a catastrophe from which the franchise would not recover until well into the next century.

The team finished sixth in an eight-team league, a testament to how bad the squads from Cleveland (44-88) and Pittsburgh (23-113) were. Welch and Tiernan did nothing on the field to disgrace themselves, and two players from Indianapolis bloomed. One was a wiry shortstop from Wheeling, West Virginia, named John (Pebbly Jack) Glasscock. Pebbly Jack, who enjoyed a seventeen-year major league career, picked 1890 to have his finest season, hitting .336 and becoming the batting champion of the National League. The other bloomer was Amos Rusie.

Rusie was the prototype of the fire balling farm boy, a big (six one, 200 pounds) strapping kid from Mooresville, Indiana, Rusie had attracted scant attention when he won 13 games for Indianapolis in 1889. With the National League Giants of 1890, however, Rusie started 63 games, and had the third lowest ERA in an offense-minded year. He won 29 and lost 30.

He struck out 345 batters, more than the entire pitching staff of three other major league teams that year, but he walked 289, which also led the league. He turned nineteen years old in 1890 and was a prodigy.

How fast was Rusie?

Rusie threw the ball at a velocity that had not yet been seen in major league baseball. The first few batters to face him in 1890

The Giants of The Polo Grounds

claimed they couldn't see the baseball as it crossed the plate. Mickey Welch, who lived well into the Twentieth Century, claimed that of all the pitchers he ever saw, Rusie and Walter Johnson were the two fastest, in that order. When he came to New York in 1890, the press immediately dubbed him "The Hoosier Thunderbolt." What a fantastic name! That's exactly what he was.

A game played on May 12, 1890, captured the public imagination and launched Rusie to stardom. Press accounts at the time suggested it was the greatest game ever pitched. More than a hundred years later, some baseball historians maintain that it may have been.

The game took place between Boston and the Giants at the Polo Grounds, with Rusie, not yet nineteen, opposing Boston's Charles (Kid) Nichols, a rookie at age twenty. Inning by inning, Rusie and Nichols set down opposing batters with little more than whimpers. Rusie would limit Boston to three singles and two walks while striking out eleven. Nichols would allow four hits and one walk while fanning ten. Nichols was so overpowering that as the game proceeded with no scoring into the ninth, tenth, eleventh, and finally twelfth innings, John Day's Giants had only hit the ball out of the infield three times.

As the suspense mounted in the game, spectators from a game between New York and Boston in the Players' League began stationing themselves in the Brotherhood Park grandstand at places where the Polo Grounds game could also be watched. Other fans deserted the Brotherhood game and peered over the center field fence that separated the two operations. As the game went into the thirteenth inning, the Polo Grounds rocked with every out.

Rusie retired Boston in order in the top of the thirteenth. Then Nichols retired the first Giant he faced in the bottom of the inning. That brought Silent Mike Tiernan, one of the two Giants who were loyal to John Day, to the plate.

Tiernan fouled off the first pitch he saw. Umpire Phil Powers tossed a new ball to Nichols. But seconds later, the first baseball was tossed back onto the field. (Yes, baseball had some weird customs in the 1890s and returning baseballs was one of them.)

Nichols picked up the ball that had been returned. "This one is all right, isn't it?" he asked Powers.

"No. The new ball was in play already," Powers answered.

Little did young, innocent Kid Nichols know he was dealing with demons. He would remember the next pitch for the rest of his life.

"Oh, all right," he said. Nichols delivered a shoulder high fastball to Tiernan. The Giant outfielder was sitting on the pitch. According to newspaper accounts, Tiernan smacked a long line drive that was never more than thirty to thirty-five feet off the ground. But it was deep. Boston center fielder Walter (Steve) Brodie, a lifetime .300 hitter who would later find fame as a Baltimore Oriole and right fielder Al Schellhasse retreated for it. But the ball cleared the center field fence at the Polo Grounds and bounded up against the rear wall of Brotherhood Park. As Tiernan rounded the bases, and as Rusie had a 1-0, thirteen inning victories, a roar went up from both ballparks. The New York *Times,* humble as ever, the next day pronounced the game, "the finest contest ever played between two professional teams and will go down on record as such."

If only the rest of the season had matched it.

As might be expected, with five professional ball clubs vying for the Manhattan and Brooklyn baseball dollar over the summer of 1890, all lost money. John Day's situation, however, was the first of the established teams to become desperate. By July, with the old Giant stars gone and playing next door, and with his current club dropping out of the National League pennant race, the New York Giants were on the brink of bankruptcy.

Pressed from every direction, John Day first started tapping the profits from his tobacco business to keep his team afloat. When the profits were gone, Day started selling off his company's assets. When the assets were gone, he turned to the National League for help.

Day told Albert Spalding that the Giants needed $80,000 of fresh capital, otherwise Day would have to sell out his remaining interests to the Brotherhood. No one had to tell Spalding or any other National League owner what that move would do. A victory in New York for the Brotherhood could turn the tide of the war. So Spalding, ostensibly in New York on business from his sporting goods firm, arranged a meeting that included himself, Day, and owners Arthur H. Soden (Boston), Alfred J. Reach (Philadelphia), and Ferdinand A. Abell, a gambling hall owner who was a principal stockholder of the Brooklyn Bridegrooms. The owners, Spalding wrote years later, were "dazed" to learn that the Giants would have to be bailed out. But bailed out temporarily, at least they were. Spalding and Soden each lent $25,000 to Day. Reach and Abell plunged for $6,250 apiece. John T. Brush, meanwhile, was jawboned by Spalding into canceling a $25,000 debt from New York's purchase of players from Indianapolis. In return, each of these other men now owned stock in the Giants.

The salvation, like any good money thrown after bad, was short-lived. The grandstands at the Polo Grounds were virtually empty on most game days. *That* was the problem. Day was now a minority stockholder in the team that had brought him to glory, that had made him a celebrity, and that had been the toast of the Tenderloin in the 1880s. It was a rude, cruel turn of events. And it would get worse.

ii

One of the many casualties of the 1890 baseball season was any truthful reporting of attendance figures. Both sides of the struggle were desperate to appear to be winning and not a single team in any of the three major leagues was drawing enough fans to turn a profit. How was a franchise to look good?

Albert Spalding pulled the old theatrical trick of papering the house. Spalding gave out so many freebies to his sporting goods customers that his own business manager complained that free passes were "more plentiful than water" in Chicago. Spalding then had the temerity to post his own sentries outside the gates of the Chicago Brotherhood team to count their paid admissions. Using friendly press contacts, Spalding then had this count published in an attempt to show that the opposition wasn't being entirely honest with their attendance figures.

Even Spalding was embarrassed years later about these tactics. "If either party [in the Brotherhood dispute] ever furnished to the press one solitary truthful statement [about attendance]," Albert G. wrote in his memoirs in 1913, "a monument should be erected to his memory." In putting those words on paper, Spalding may very well have had in mind his own club secretary, Jonathan Brown.

If there is ever a special Sean Spicer Award created for overt mendacity toward reporters, and if such an award can be made retroactively, Brown is in line to be the 1890 winner. Once, as Spalding described the incident years later, a Chicago reporter approached Brown during a White Stockings game in midsummer of 1890. The writer asked for the day's paid attendance.

"Twenty-four eighteen," responded Brown, who was seated in the grandstand next to Spalding.

The reporter never raised his eyes to the nearly deserted grandstand. Instead, he hustled off to file his story. When the writer was out of sight, Spalding asked Brown how he had arrived at such a figure.

"Why, don't you see?" Brown asked. "There are twenty-four fans on one side of the grandstand and eighteen on the other. If he reports twenty-four hundred eighteen, that's on *his* conscience, not mine."

The end of the great player revolt of 1890 came not with a bang or a resolution of key issues, but rather with several whimpers of capitulation. Millions of dollars had been lost over the course of the season, the product before the public had been watered down, and baseball had again projected a negative image. Not surprisingly, several owners in all three leagues were looking to cut their losses and get out. The capitulation occurred where the disaster had been at its worst: in New York.

There appeared in that city in October one Allan W. Thurman, a director of the Columbus club in the American Association. Thurman was a genial man who had friends in all three major leagues. Now that a catastrophic season was complete, Thurman had worked out details for a peace. All sides were ready to listen. The press, getting wind of the story and given to the usual hyperbole of the late nineteenth century, promptly dubbed Thurman, "The White Winged Angel of Peace." Or, in the penny dailies, "White Wings" for short.

White Wings had a plan that would reduce major league baseball to two eight team leagues, with larger cities having teams in each. The plan was a farsighted one, considering that the structure of what Thurman proposed is what eventually worked for the first half of the Twentieth Century. Knowing what was about to be proposed, several owners "happened" to be in New York at the time. The mere invocation of the word "peace" had the owners churning the water like sharks during a feeding frenzy. Soon the specifics of Thurman's plan were lost as the owners sought to cut their own deals.

Wendell Goodwin of Brooklyn and Eddie Talcott of New York, both of the Players' League, approached the National League, in the persons of Spalding and John Day, with an offer to merge their squads into the Bridegrooms and the Giants. Immediately,

The Giants of The Polo Grounds

Spalding sensed that the other side was about to fold. Despite the fragile state of the National League, Cincinnati had sold out to its Brotherhood counterpart earlier in the month. Spalding was thus able to hang tough and dictate the terms of the merger. Soon Pittsburgh and Chicago were talking peace between the warring clubs. By December, the rest of the warring franchises had fallen into order and the Players' League was history.

The collapse would have far reaching effects, first in New York and Brooklyn, and then upon the structure of organized baseball.

In Brooklyn, George Chauncey, the principal stockholder in Brooklyn's Brotherhood team, agreed to put money into the Brooklyn Bridegrooms, but only upon two stipulations. He wanted the team transferred from Washington Park to the Brotherhood playing grounds, Eastern Park, which had a capacity of twelve thousand fans. Second, he wanted John Montgomery Ward named manager.

Charlie Byrne, who had owned the Brooklyn club since its Trolley Dodger days in the American Association, had no problems with the move to Eastern Park, even though it was in East New York, one of the far reaches of Brooklyn. Firing Bill McGunnigle was another matter, however. McGunnigle had been a faithful employee and was a proven winner in every league in which he had managed. Chauncey reminded Byrne that the latter was facing bankruptcy if he didn't see it Chauncey's way. McGunnigle was promptly sacked.

In Manhattan, John Day was having his tail twisted every bit as painfully. Eddie Talcott was an astute financier with a strong love for money and not much feeling for baseball. Talcott also knew that Day was desperate. Although Spalding could protect National League owners from the labor demands that the players had made, business deals involving the individual teams were another matter. Thus, Talcott, brandishing a bankroll, forced himself upon Day. A hostile takeover, in modern terms. Day sold Talcott a large block of stock and promptly became a minor stockholder in his own club. Talcott immediately dictated that Jim Mutrie, Day's old friend, with whom he had brought the Giants into being would have to be dismissed as a manager. Somehow Day talked Talcott out of this, at least for the 1891 season. Perhaps both men had their eyes on larger things, such as where the Giants would play in 1891.

By the terms of the treaty between the Players' League and the National League, the New York Giants took possession of

The Giants of The Polo Grounds

Brotherhood Park. They also retained use of the name the Polo Grounds and applied it to the field where the rebels had set up shop. Thus, the third and final playing field of the New York Giants bore that famous name. The grandstand used in 1890 was torn down.

By March of 1891, players from both Giants teams of 1890 began drifting back into the fold. It was a strange but exciting collection of players. Welch and Tiernan, loyal Giants throughout, were back. So were Rusie, Glasscock, Charley Bassett, and Lew Whistler, the best of the "Indian" Giants. But also returning were some of the familiar old names: Connor, Richardson, Keefe, Gore, and O'Rourke. On March 24, the team began their spring workouts at the Polo Grounds.

Players ran wind sprints and did calisthenics in the outfield. They ran laps around the inner contours of the park and then repaired indoors where, in front of a wood fire in the clubhouse, they sat sweating in heavy clothing. The gates to the park were left open and curious fans were allowed to drift in and watch the athletes get back into shape. Occasionally, as the weather warmed toward April, varsity nines from nearby universities, most notably Columbia, came by to play exhibition games. All told, the Polo Grounds had a sense of rebirth, even relief, from the horrors of 1890.

Before Opening Day, the park was freshened with paint and new sod. There was now a suggestion of how the park would look for many decades to come: a grandstand in the shape of a horseshoe stretched from third around to first base. There were open stands down toward the foul lines and a second level, rising halfway up the rocks of Coogan's Bluff, was built to accommodate the wealthy fans who bought books of season's tickets.

Opening Day gave John Day cause to be optimistic. More than seventeen thousand fans turned out, more than the combined attendance of the two Opening Day crowds of the previous year. A band played *Annie Rooney* and a popular fight song called *Throw Him Down, McCloskey*. Then the players took the field. Buck Ewing gathered his Brotherhood Giants with him and led them down the left field foul line. Mutrie walked down the right field line with his loyal Giants plus the new talent from Indiana. The band was silent for a moment, then struck up *Hard Times Come Again No More*.

From the two foul lines, players rushed toward each other, shook hands, and embraced. In the right field corner of the park, from the second story of the clubhouse, a banner was unfurled. It read:

The Giants of The Polo Grounds

UNITED, GREATER, AND STRONGER THAN EVER! A cheer went up and the team was back in business. Amos Rusie pitched that day, but Boston took the measure of the Hoosier Thunderbolt, 4-3.

Yet, if 1890 had been the year of the earthquake, 1891 was the year of the aftershocks. Tim Keefe played in only eight games for the Giants before being sold to Philadelphia. Buck Ewing injured his throwing arm and was displaced by Dick Buckley, the Indianapolis catcher. Ewing played in only fourteen games that year. By 1893 he had moved on to Cleveland, primarily as an outfielder first baseman. Amos Rusie pitched the first New York Giant no-hitter, 60, against Brooklyn on July 31, but the Giants finished 1891 in third place, thirteen games behind Boston. Mike Tiernan was one bright spot, leading the league in home runs with 17.

By the end of the calendar year, however, two other events had transpired, both of lasting significance for the Giants and their loyal followers.

First, the American Association had collapsed, unable to recover from its financial losses during the Brotherhood war. Its four remaining strong franchises - Baltimore, Louisville, St. Louis, and Washington - joined the National League, bringing the total number of clubs in the league to twelve. It was a cumbersome arrangement, closely resembling a horse race of maiden three-year-olds.

Second and more poignantly, Eddie Talcott struck up an alliance with John T. Brush, another minority stockholder in the Giants. Together, they prevailed upon John Day to fire his old friend Jim Mutrie. Surely, Day felt badly about it. But within another year, he also knew how it felt. Unable to reverse his own financial misfortunes, Day was forced out himself by Talcott and Brush in 1892. By that time, with Day and Mutrie gone, new names were ascendant both within baseball and within the New York Giants organization. And the era of the Giants' inception, as well as their first taste of glory, was at an end.

The Giants of The Polo Grounds

A Poet's Reminiscence   -   Ira Sadoff

After all these years, after watching so many games on old black and white tv's, I can't separate that experience from actually being at the Polo Grounds. I was between the ages of five and nine at the time. To this day I feel as if I were there for the Vic Wertz catch though I'm reasonably sure I was thrilled my father could get us in to another game in the series.

In 1986 I'd spent my sabbatical year in Berkeley. A generous friend's father who worked for the A's gave us great free tickets to many games. These were the Candlestick Park days when going to a Giants' game was like a visit to the Arctic. When I asked my friend how I could ever repay his father's generosity, he said, "Write a poem for him about the Giants." It turns out his father was an ex-New Yorker and lifetime Giant fan. Well, I never write occasional poems but as a life-long baseball fan whose own father took him to the Polo Grounds a number of times, I took up the challenge. In 1985 The Giants had just had a terrible last place year: a hundred losses, no starter hitting over .272 (Chili Davis), no starting pitcher winning over eight games. Many of my Giants friends began losing interest in baseball. At the same time, and this is where things got personal, I was a middle-aged man who felt he was up against his limits (in a bad marriage and in a writing slump to boot): I became nostalgic about happier times, those iconic moments in Giants history when I was growing up and I wanted to memorialize them. The poem was meant to be a personal gift, not a poem for publication. But at the last minute when I was about to send to *The New Yorker* three or four more "serious" poems, a friend suggested I add the Giants' elegy. How surprised I was, as well as gratified for my friend and his father, when they accepted the poem and many Giants fans wrote to me notes of encouragement.

Ira Sadoff
Stone Ridge, NY
April 2018

(Editor's note: Ira Sadoff is a distinguished American poet. In addition to *Autumn Elegy For The Giants*, which appears at the front of this edition, he is the author of seven collections of poetry, a novel, O. Henry prize-winning short stories, and The *Ira Sadoff Reader*, a collection of stories, poems, and essays about contemporary poetry. He is the recipient of a Creative Arts Fellowship from the National Endowment of the Arts and a Fellowship from the Guggenheim foundation. His work has been published *The New Yorker, Poetry, Antaeus, American Poetry Review, Boulevard, The Hudson Review, The New Republic, Esquire, New American Review, The Paris Review* and dozens of other literary journals.)

Chapter 11   Oriole Baseball

"Oriole baseball, as it flourished in 1894, was a combination of hostility, imagination, speed, and piracy."

Joseph Durso, 1969

i

When the American Association went belly up after the 1891 season, the National League was left with no postseason opponent for its champion. Whatever the shortcoming of previous autumn meetings, the contests had provided an important source of possible revenue for pennant-winning teams. What, then, was the National League to do?

In times of difficulty, baseball's club owners have always been able to come up with really bad ideas that will makes things worse. The year 1892 was no exception. Blessed with a clumsy association of twelve clubs, the league scheduled a split season, a hokey unpopular gimmick that was also seen during the strike disrupted 1981 major league season. Whoever won the pennant race for the

The Giants of The Polo Grounds

first half of the season would play whoever won for the second half. If the same team won both, that team would play the club with the next best record.

The Cleveland Spiders won the first half pennant in 1892 and the Boston Beaneaters won the second half. The first game of the playoff was a legendary eleven innings 0-0 tie, which, for decades, has been part of baseball folklore. The game, it has widely been reported, was a matchup between Denton (Cy) Young of Cleveland and Kid Nichols of Boston, two of the great pitchers of the decade. Some of the accounts of the matchup have been quite detailed over the years, making up in enthusiasm what they've lacked in accuracy. True, Cy Young pitched an eleven-inning shutout. But so did a young man by the name of Jack Stivetts, who had been 35-16 for Boston that year (the same won-lost totals Nichols posted). Nichols never pitched that day. So much for an otherwise wonderful story.

After the scoreless tie, Boston settled down and disposed of Cleveland in five of the next six undistinguished games. But the ersatz pennant race and then ensuing series was a bust with the paying customers.

In 1893 the split season format was dropped. Enter one William Chase Temple, a coal and lumber merchant who was also making serious money in Florida citrus. with what passed for a good idea. A former president of the Pittsburgh franchise and still part owner of the club, coal, Temple revised the system that had been in effect in 1892. Instead of a double pennant race, however, Temple proposed that a seven game postseason series should be held between the best two teams in the National League.

Temple presented his idea to the winter meeting of owners held between the 1893 and 1894 seasons. The symbol of baseball success, he proposed, would be an ornate $800 silver loving cup mounted upon a foot-high onyx pedestal. The trophy, thirty inches tall, which would be designed by the A. E. Thrall Company of New York, would be known as the Temple Cup, in honor, not surprisingly, of its generous donor. On the front of the Temple Cup, in bold relief, was a pitcher throwing a ball. The upper area of the cup, plus the two wide handles, were iced with silver filigree. More to the point were the financial arrangements for the series.

The second-place club from the next season's final standings, Temple proposed, would challenge the first-place team, who, theoretically, would have the cup to defend. If the first-place team should refuse to play, the second-place club would have to defend a

The Giants of The Polo Grounds

challenge from the third-place squad. And so on. Temple felt that existence of the series - the receipts of which would be split between winners and losers - with the winners getting two thirds and the losers getting one third would enliven the pennant race far into September. The other owners agreed. Temple Cup Competition, as it was officially known, was scheduled for the autumn of 1894.

Bad timing. The offering of the Temple Cup coincided perfectly with the advent of the Baltimore Orioles. Unless you've recently arrived from outer space, you probably already know all about the "old Orioles."

The franchise came into the National League in 1892, an unpromising collection of fringe players, minor leaguers, and refugees from the collapsed American Association. They promptly lost 14 of their first 15 National League games - shades of the 1962 Mets - and took up residence in the basement.

The owner of the team was Harry Vonderhorst, a bearded local brewer who knew enough about baseball to realize that no one was going to go to his ballpark to see a team that won 7 percent of their games. Thus, he relieved outfielder manager George Van Haltren of his managerial duties and installed a salesman from the brewery, one James Waltz, as "temporary manager."

Temporary, indeed.

Waltz only lost two games as the new Baltimore skipper. Then again, Waltz only managed two games. The appointment was made to allow Van Haltren to get back to the outfield to rededicate his efforts to hitting and catching flies. It also allowed Vonderhorst to travel to Pittsburgh to speak with a Ned Hanlon.

Hanlon had been an outstanding center fielder and sparkplug for the powerful Detroit team that had defeated the St. Louis Browns in 1887. More recently, he had been the player manager of Pittsburgh in the Players' League and then player-manager of the Pirates in the National League in 1891. He was still a center fielder and a good one. He was noted for his speed and range, though at age thirty-three he was slowing down.

Midway through the 1891 season, having compiled a 31-47 record as player-manager of the Pirates, and with the club mired in eighth place, Hanlon was fired as manager and replaced by Bill McGunnigle. Hanlon went back to playing the outfield. Then, on Opening Day in 1892, he ruptured a tendon in his left leg chasing a fly ball in center field. He limped along, but his career as a player was over. A few days later, Vonderhorst strutted into Pittsburgh and

The Giants of The Polo Grounds

asked Hanlon if he would come to Baltimore and manage the hopeless Orioles. Hanlon said yes.

Hanlon took one look at the demoralized 3-16 club that he found on arrival and began making changes. He found a scrawny but fiery nineteen-year-old from Truxton, New York, riding the bench. Hanlon liked the boy's pugnacious attitude and thus inserted the young John J. McGraw into the lineup. The team began to win occasionally. Then in September, Hanlon unloaded Van Haltren, the center fielder and former manager, to Pittsburgh in a deal that seemed ridiculous on the surface. Pittsburgh received the steady .300 hitting Van Haltren plus $2,000 for a vain, untested twenty-year-old rookie outfielder named Joe Kelley. Van Haltren stayed in Pittsburgh for a single season. Kelley, who used to carry a comb and pocket mirror to freshen up in left field between pitches, would become the greatest of all Oriole hitters, posting a .360 average during his glory years in Baltimore.

"Joe had no prominent weakness," John McGraw would later say of his teammate. "He was fast on the bases, could hit the ball hard and was as graceful an outfielder as one would care to see." He would eventually be elected to the Baseball Hall of Fame in 1971.

The 1892 Orioles finished last, exactly where Hanlon had found them. But improvement was already evident.

In the offseason, Hanlon found a Chicago-born infielder named Henry (Heinie) Reitz, who had no major league experience at all. Hanlon liked him, signed him to an Oriole contract, and penciled him in at second base for the following year, shifting McGraw to shortstop. (McGraw, who had once made nine errors in a single game, was nothing special with a glove.) Then, midway into the 1893 season, Hanlon took a shine to the Louisville shortstop, a thin, sickly kid named Hughie Jennings, who had hit a whopping .222 while playing every day the previous season. But again, Hanlon saw the future where other men saw failure. The Oriole manager traded away a steady infielder-outfielder named Tim O'Rourke to pry Jennings loose from Louisville.

Toward September of the same year, Hanlon found something else he was looking for. The St. Louis Browns had a "problem" outfielder named Walter Brodie, who was more colloquially called "Steve" Brodie after a daredevil of the same name who had been the first man crazy enough to jump off the Brooklyn Bridge. Chris Von Der Ahe was having attendance problems in St. Louis and subsequently was locked in salary disputes with several players,

The Giants of The Polo Grounds

including Brodie. (Von Der Ahe had partially converted his ball park into "The Coney Island of the West" when the Browns weren't playing. Fans could ride a roller coaster, watch a horse race, take in an all-female brass band, and watch a Wild West show before staggering into one of Von Der Ahe's nearby saloons. He was also having his problems with the press, who now referred to him alternately as "Der Poss President," "J. Christ Von Der Ahe," and "Chris Von Der Ha-ha.") So Brodie was obtained from St. Louis for cash.

Harry Vonderhorst had by this time been shoved out the back door of his own house. From the moment he arrived, Hanlon was never in doubt as to what he wanted and seldom wrong in what he did. Vonderhorst gave Hanlon free reign. Before he knew it, Hanlon was a minority partner in the club, as well as acting president. Vonderhorst was so nonplussed by the way Hanlon had seized control that he had taken to walking around his ballpark wearing a button that said: ASK HANLON.

The Orioles moved up four notches to eighth place in 1893. Hanlon knew that his younger players - Jennings, McGraw, Kelley, and Reitz - would take time to jell. He also recognized that his equation was not yet complete.

Hanlon soon became known as "Foxy Ned." He was credited with inventing a new strategy that ever after would be known as "inside" baseball. Teamwork, speed and execution were the elements. Hanlon refined and perfected the hit and run play, the squeeze play, the sacrifice bunt, the double steal, and - most aggravating of all - the Baltimore chop, the act of slapping the ball down on the plate so hard that a runner could get to first before a fielder could make a play.

"It occurred to Hanlon," wrote a baseball scribbler for *The Baltimore Sun*, "that a run gained by strategy counted as big as a run gained by slugging. Accordingly, Hanlon evolved an offensive technique that made baseball into something of an art."

Hanlon's pitching was adequate. His main arm was Sadie McMahon, and the catching, mostly by Wilbert Robinson, was steadily improving. But Hanlon was looking for more hitting.

He found it in Brooklyn. The Bridegrooms had a young man and an old man who Hanlon wanted. The young one was named Wee Willie Keeler, a Brooklyn native whose father drove a horse-drawn streetcar for a living, while Willie, who had originally been signed and released by the Giants, played for the Grooms. The old man was

The Giants of The Polo Grounds

Dan Brouthers, Hanlon's former teammate in Detroit. Brouthers was a big hulking slugger in the mold of Roger Connor. So Hanlon, in January of 1894, pulled off one of the greatest thefts in baseball history: Keeler and Brouthers to Baltimore for third baseman Bill Shindle and right fielder George Treadway, two expendable regulars.

Now Hanlon had what he desired, just in time for the 1894 season, the year that William C. Temple had decided to put up his silver cup. Mr. Temple would soon regret his generosity.

ii

The Orioles opened the 1894 season against Amos Rusie of the Giants, who was coming off a 29-victory season the year before. Rusie would long remember the day, as the Orioles would showcase their new style of baseball.

Hanlon had been working since the previous season on various new theories and strategies of the game. On this particular day, his Orioles, worked them to perfection.

McGraw laid down a bunt in the first inning, a ball that rolled perfectly dead in the high grass that head groundskeeper Tom Murphy, yet another right-thinking Irishman, had built up near the foul lines.

Wee Willie Keeler batted next. He took the first pitch. McGraw faked a steal of second but stopped as soon as he saw that shortstop Shorty Fuller would be taking the throw from the catcher. On the next pitch, McGraw started again toward second. Keeler whacked the ball through the gap vacated by Fuller.

Rusie and the Giants also got a glimpse of two other Oriole strategies.

Tom Murphy had also created an infield that was, in front of the plate, as hard as alabaster. When the Orioles weren't hitting and running, they were slapping down on the ball, causing it to bounce high in the air off, either home plate or the hard dirt of the infield. Thus was born the Baltimore chop. And on defense, the first known "cutoff" play, an Oriole invention, snuffed a Giant rally.

"This isn't baseball they're playing," complained the New York manager Monte Ward. "It's an entirely different game."

Yes, it was. And the Orioles opened the 1894 campaign with 5 victories in 6 games against Boston and the Giants, the two teams considered to be the class of the league. They continued, going 24-

The Giants of The Polo Grounds

10 at the start of the season. Ned Hanlon finally had his house in order. On one memorable afternoon, the Orioles dispatched Boston with a twelve run ninth inning. From that day on, the rest of the league was off balance.

Tricks? Of course.

The Orioles were by their very nature a raucous, pugnacious crew, sort of an Irish street gang wearing baseball uniforms. But they'd also resort to trickery to win ball games on days when intimidation wasn't working.

Joe Kelley devised a hidden ball trick unlike any other. A regular in left field, Kelley told the groundkeeper to keep the grass high in the far reaches of the outfield. The groundskeeper laughed and obeyed. Then Kelley stashed extra baseballs at strategic spots in the grass. For months he was able to miraculously come up with balls that, to a bewildered observer, would have seemed to have bounced past him. Center fielder Steve Brodie admired the trick so much that he started doing it, too. Kelley and Brodie had balls stashed in pockets of high grass all over the outfield until, one day during a game with the St. Louis Browns, Buttermilk Tommy Dowd lined a gapper to left center. Dowd was thrown out at second by Kelley. A few seconds later, Brodie heaved the original ball in to McGraw at third base.

Not only did the outfield look like amber waves of grain in certain areas, but groundkeeper Murphy also had the infield neatly tailored to the specifications of Hanlon and McGraw. The ground between the third base line and the infield grass was actually uphill slightly, so that the speedy Oriole batsmen could drop bunted balls down third that had to roll uphill to go foul. Similarly, the base path to first base was actually downhill, making sure that a dash to first after a bunt or a chop would be the easiest trip possible.

This was, as you might imagine, sort of an early version of "The Bowery Boys Play Baseball." Legend has it that "old Orioles" never sat out with injuries. This isn't quite the case, though it did take a significant blood loss for an Oriole to leave a game, and the standard medical intervention for a broken finger was to rub it in some mud.

Symptomatic of the Baltimore system was a play made by Willie Keeler in right field that concluded a game against Washington. Keeler raced back to the outfield fence chasing a long fly. When he ran out of room, he stuck his arm through a coil of barbed wire atop the fence. All in the same motion, he

The Giants of The Polo Grounds

snared the ball with his bare hand, saved the game, and slashed his arm from the base of the palm to the elbow. Naturally, he played the next day.

Dull moments? Ha! Never.

Outfielder Joe Kelley hid a vanity mirror inside his cap, the better to comb his hair between pitches. Hughie Jennings deliberately leaned into pitches to get hit in the head, which he did at a then-record pace. Third baseman John McGraw spewed tobacco juice in umpires' faces and ground his spikes into their shoes. But their antics paled beside those of the flashy but loopy center fielder. Brodie talked to baseballs, caught fly balls behind his back and once snared a line drive that had ricocheted off his head. He mumbled to himself in the outfield, passing time by reciting soliloquies from Shakespeare.

Once, Brodie loudly chastised himself for committing an error. Then, according to the next day's Baltimore *Sun*, "...as further punishment, he refused to talk to himself for the rest of the game." A solid fielder, he cut a hole in the pocket of his glove, believing he could better grasp the ball with his bare palm. Off season, the fun continued. He stayed fit by donning a catcher's mask and chest protector and wrestled with a muzzled black bear he kept in his backyard.

It will surprise no one that this sort of dirty tricks baseball, combined with slashing spikes, and contempt for decorum made many enemies. Many games featured brawls, sort of an early version of the National Hockey League in the 1970s. A team picture of the era, shows Steve Brodie on the far left of the middle row. "Wee Willie" Keeler is in the front row, to the right of club manager Ned Hanlon who wears business suit and almost looks respectable.

The Giants of The Polo Grounds

Keeler's elbow is on Hanlon's knee. John McGraw is second from the left in the same row.

By midseason, it occurred to Hanlon that the team could use a little extra "punch," something to see the team through their many donnybrooks. Accordingly, Hanlon attempted to sign Gentleman Jim Corbett, the reigning U.S. heavyweight boxing champion, as a pitcher.

Hanlon offered him $10,000 to travel with the Orioles for two months during midsummer, as both an extra hurler and a form of life insurance. An outcry from the rest of organized baseball stopped Hanlon. Two seasons later, however, Baltimore *did* sign Joe Corbett, the champ's younger brother.

Joe won two dozen games for the Orioles in 1897, despite having missed spring training by serving as a sparring partner for Big Jim. It was around that time that the champ, after walloping Little Joe around the ring all winter and attempting to exercise some form of fraternal discretion, suggested that young Joe give up the idea of playing for the Orioles.

"You might get seriously injured," the champ warned.

McGraw, even at his tender age, was also the acknowledged author of a few tricks. Shifted to his natural position of third base when shortstop Hughie Jennings joined the club, McGraw's masterwork was holding a runner's belt as he rounded third base or attempted to tag and score on a long fly. These were the one umpire days, except in postseason play. McGraw got away with his belt trick dozens of times until, inevitably, a runner on third one day, Pete Browning of the Louisville Colonels, loosened his belt, dashed for the plate after a long fly, and left a red-faced McGraw standing on third with leather dangling from his hand. McGraw had another pet play that he was also able to pull off until word got around the league. Coaching third base with a runner on first, McGraw would hold his hands aloft and ask to examine the baseball. But he wouldn't call time. When an unsuspecting pitcher or fielder would throw him the ball, McGraw would duck out of the way and wave his runner around the bases.

The Orioles jumped into first place early in the year, stayed there until July, then hit a slump when Reitz, McGraw, and Robinson were injured and out of the lineup. In late July, the fire-balling New York Giant Amos Rusie blanked the O's, 1-0, to allow Boston to pass them. At the end of the month, Baltimore was five games off the pace.

Then the injured returned to action and back roared the Orioles.

The Giants of The Polo Grounds

Playing what *The Sporting News* described as "the dirtiest ball ever seen in this country," Baltimore won 24 of their final 25 games in September. "We would have won all twenty-five," McGraw growled at the time, "if Robbie [Wilbert Robinson] hadn't tripped going after a foul fly. The clumsy ox!"

But Baltimore won the pennant, an unprecedented leap in the standings from twelfth to first in two years. Demoralized, the reigning champions, the Boston Beaneaters, dropped back to third place.

Brooklyn remained a team in transition. The cutesy nickname of the Bridegrooms had worn thin by this time and the franchise was in search of a new identity. For a short time, the team was unofficially known as Ward's Wonders, after their manager, the well-known labor insurgent.

This name fell flat by 1893, however. Ward had tired of the bucolic life in Brooklyn and had headed back to Manhattan as the manager of the New York Giants. The Brooklyn job, meanwhile, had been inherited by Dave Foutz, who was now playing left field. For a while the club was unofficially known as "Foutz's Fillies." Eventually, reason prevailed, and Brooklyn reclaimed its old name. By 1894, they were the Trolley Dodgers again. Soon it was just plain Dodgers. In 1893 and 1894, however, it was also just plain second division.

The return of John Montgomery Ward to Manhattan, however, sparked the stagnating Giants. Ward installed himself at second base and gradually the team began to win.

In mid-July, however, Ward made his most important decision as a manager. Ward pitched either Amos Rusie or Jouett Meekin, another Indiana native, in every game the Giants played. That was enough to bring the Giants up from the second division to finish second, putting the Giants straight up against the nasty young Orioles for possession of the Temple Cup. No one cared much for the Giants' chances.

From the start, there was trouble. The salaries of the Oriole players ran only until the end of the baseball season. The Orioles, with McGraw making most of the noise, were reluctant to enter into a series in which the loser's share would only be a third of the gate receipts. McGraw called this unseemly and unfair, arguing that a team that had won the pennant should be guaranteed a better cut. McGraw threatened to convince his teammates not to play the Temple Cup series unless better guarantees were made.

The Giants of The Polo Grounds

Well, what would a labor dispute have been without the presence of John Montgomery Ward?

Ward contacted McGraw and, seeing that his Giants were clear underdogs in the series anyway, readily agreed to split fifty-fifty, no matter who won. Preparations were under way to get the series started when word of the compromise reached William Temple. The cup's donor was apoplectic. What motivation did a team have to win, he screamed, if players would collect the same amount by losing? A day later, the fuming Temple threatened to withdraw his cup and send it back to the jeweler, A. E. Thrall.

Now the players faced the darkest prospect of all: no postseason series. So publicly the players agreed to compete under the original payment scheme. Yet behind the scenes, many Orioles cut private fifty-fifty deals with members of the New York squad. So on went the games. In many ways, it was the final hurrah for the first generation of great Giants. Connor, Ewing, Welch, Keefe, and O'Rourke were gone by now, but Mike Tiernan was still a strong hitter and good outfielder. Monte Ward was in his final year as a player and still had his moments. And again Giant pitching carried the day, even though the old Keefe-Welch tandem had now been replaced by the duo from Indiana.

The Orioles, who had scratched, clawed, and spiked their way to the pennant, had stunningly little fight left in October. The no-name Giants, however, brimmed with the quiet confidence of an underdog.

The Giants traveled to Baltimore, took up residence at a hotel, then rode in open carriages to the ball field singing, *Mamie! Come Kiss Your Honey Boy*, a chartbuster of the day, ripped off from black performers. Then they went out and knocked off the Orioles, 4-1, behind the Hoosier Thunderbolt in the first game of the series. The next day Jouett Meekin pitched and the Giants were again victorious, this time by a score of 9-6.

The Giants of The Polo Grounds

From that point on, Baltimore seemed interested in nothing other than getting the series finished. Playing torpidly, the Orioles were easily beaten in New York by the Giants, the scores being 4-1, again behind Rusie, and 16-3, behind Meekin. Around the country, the Giants were the toast of the sporting world. The defeated Orioles were that unpopular.

A somber note marked the conclusion of 1893. King Kelly, the heartthrob of the 1880s and a part-time player with the Giants as recently as 1893, had finally retired. No longer wanted as a player, Kelly caught on as manager of the minor league team in Allentown, Pennsylvania. Yet he was still much in demand on the vaudeville and celebrity circuits, particularly in the offseason. Inevitably, he would appear onstage, tell some amusing baseball stories, charm his devoted fans, and then step aside as a bosomy house soprano warbled an interpretation of *Slide, Kelly, Slide!*

It was a living; the money was good and there was no heavy lifting. Kelly's appearances were well attended and took place at the better vaudeville houses.

In November of 1894, for example, the King was booked at the Palace Theatre in Boston. He took a steamship to the Hub from New York and apparently spent too much time out on the windswept decks. Arriving in Boston, the King was ill.

The owner of the Plymouth Hotel, where Kelly was registered, was an old crony. He put Mike to bed and ordered that he not be disturbed. But soon the illness developed into pneumonia and the ravages of liquor, women, and the other joys of life in the 1880s fast lane took their aggregate toll. Kelly's condition deteriorated quickly. On November 8, he died.

Kelly's widow and friends were summoned to Boston. Funeral preparations were made. Plans were to lay the King to rest in his best dress suit. But along the route from New York the suit had

The Giants of The Polo Grounds

mysteriously vanished, prompting an investigation. Meanwhile, the King was put on ice.

As it turned out, a young stowaway had been arrested aboard the steamship. Kelly, a man whose sympathies and generosity matched his appetites, put his dress suit up as security for the young stranger. When the steamship company learned of the King's untimely demise in Boston, management returned the suit. Only then, six weeks before his thirty-seventh birthday and exiting in grand formal style, was baseball's first superstar laid to rest.

Chapter 12   Worst. Owner. Ever.

> "Mr. Freedman is a clever businessman . . .
> I hope he makes a lot of money."
>
> —A. G. Spalding, 1895

If one were a young business student and wanted a textbook example of how a profitable business could be run into the ground, one might settle upon the New York Giants, under the management of Andrew C. Freedman.

Andrew Freedman was a man of breathtaking arrogance, appalling miserliness, and uncompromising dishonesty. The best thing that can be said for him, now in the 21st Century, is that currently he's dead and likely to remain so. On January 17, 1895, however, the day he "officially" purchased the New York Giants, he was very much alive.

Freedman was not just an unscrupulous real estate lawyer, he was an unscrupulous real estate lawyer *par excellence*. It has been noted from time to time that the one problem with lawyers is that once they pass through law school they have no natural predators. Freedman in his day did nothing to diminish this theory.

Freedman was closely associated with the Tammany Hall ring of out-and-out crooks who controlled most municipal business in New York for several decades, starting off with Boss Tweed, who led the institutionalized banditry in the 1860s and 70s. It speaks volumes to recall that, under William Marcy Tweed, City

The Giants of The Polo Grounds

Comptroller Richard Connolly — that representative of the public welfare who holds the municipal wallet — was known as "Slippery Dick" to friends and foes alike. The City Council was known as "The Forty Thieves."

After Boss Tweed's demise, the mantle of the New York City Democratic Organization, Tammany Hall, in other words, was passed along to his worthy descendants, such as Richard C. Croker or "Boss" Croker, as he was called. Croker was a youthful protégé of Tweed and, having learned from the master, didn't do a bad job at raiding the city's coffers himself.

Naturally, he couldn't do it alone. *No one* could carry away all that cash alone. So on trips to Europe, on junkets around the United States, or when he was just hanging out at the comptroller's office to see what was going down, Croker was frequently accompanied by his organization's secretary, the intimate crony who had been the best man at Croker's wedding. That individual was Andrew C. Freedman.

Even Freedman's acquisition of the New York Giants was tainted. Freedman used his familiarity with the way things were done in New York to begin acquiring pieces of Giants stock for James A. Bailey, the circus promoter who later merged with P. T. Barnum. Freedman had represented Bailey in certain previous business transactions. Bailey had no idea he was buying part of a ball club for the simple reason that he wasn't. Freedman was. Freedman was using Bailey's name as a respectable cover . . . as respectable, that is, as the entrepreneur behind a caged animal, acrobat, and freak show could ever be. But in January of 1895, Freedman managed to buy out the interests of Edward Talcott. It was estimated at the time that Freedman paid $50,000 for an enterprise that was worth a quarter of a million dollars. Then, to show what sort of class act he was planning to run, Freedman fired John Montgomery Ward as manager.

Thereupon, the carnival began.

Freedman anointed George Davis, the third baseman, as the new field manager. Then he began "reorganizing" a franchise that had just won the championship series in four straight games. The first thing he did was to take away complimentary passes that had been enjoyed by former players and friends of the ball club. Then he suggested, before a game was even played in his regime, that Charlie Byrne, the president of the Brooklyn club, should move his team out of town or place it in a high minor league. Freedman wanted the entire New York metropolitan area for himself.

A little of this went a long way. Soon the fans were grumbling. Then the newspapers were taking potshots. Freedman — aggressive, belligerent, and pugnacious, even in the best of times — snapped back.

Sam Crane, a distinguished baseball writer in the New York *Commercial Advertiser*, was one of the first to get the full Freedman treatment. Crane was a rarity among sportswriters: he had actually played baseball professionally. He had been a so-so infielder over the course of seven seasons in three different major leagues and a manager twice. He had even played four games for the National League Giants during the misbegotten 1890 campaign.

Crane used his newspaper space to wax upon the many ways that Freedman was destroying a once proud franchise. Freedman responded by lifting Crane's Polo Grounds press credentials. When Crane paid his way into the park and filed his stories anyway, Freedman provided Crane's picture to his ticket sellers and ordered that he not be sold an admission. Other writers came to Crane's defense, both in person and in print. Freedman peevishly declared war on them also. Soon he was not barring writers individually, but as *units*. No one from the Cincinnati *Enquirer*, for example. Then no one from Joseph Pulitzer's New York *Sun*, a distinguished paper that exposed and fought corruption and municipal chicanery of all sorts.

The *Sun* was a particular Freedman target. Within the first five years of the Freedman reign, the Giants owner had filed almost two dozen libel suits against the paper, none of which he won. Eventually, Freedman fulfilled the fantasy of many malefactors in the New York region by punching out The New York *Times* reporter assigned to his beat. The *Times* writer had had the temerity to blame Freedman in person for the Giants' poor showing on the field.

Another target was Henry Chadwick, the Oxford-born baseball writer who originated the box score, wrote for three decades for the Brooklyn *Eagle*, and was the first baseball journalist in the Hall of Fame. When Chadwick, who covered the Giants, became an articulate Freedman critic in print (and by this time almost everyone was getting his licks in), Freedman took aim at the $500-a-year pension that the National League had awarded Chadwick, the seventy-year-old retired member of its Rules Committee.

Freedman wrote Chadwick a letter accusing him of "biting the

The Giants of The Polo Grounds

hand that fed" him. Chadwick retaliated by boycotting the Polo Grounds and urging true Giant fans to do the same. Freedman's relations with the press, however, were exemplary compared to his relations with his employees. The New York *World*, given to understatement in its editorial pages, once commented that Freedman had "an astonishing faculty for making enemies." Managers and players were included.

George Davis was fired after two months as manager. Dirty Jack Doyle, the Giants' first baseman, replaced him. Doyle couldn't stand Freedman and let him know it. Doyle was sacked five weeks later. Then Freedman, to finish off the season, hired the most unqualified manager in major league history, one Harvey Watkins. Watkins was an actor who frequently lurked in the background of Tammany Hall operations. When he was elevated to the position of manager of the New York Giants, he had most recently been employed in the offices of James A. Bailey's circus, where, it was rumored, his most visible activity was feeding the goldfish in the circus offices

All of this, it should be noted, was within the first nine months of Freedman's rule. Meanwhile, the Giants had plummeted to ninth place in a twelve-team league. An example of what things had come to could be viewed on June 1, 1895. On that day Roger Connor, who had escaped New York and was now happily playing for St. Louis, went six-for-six with two doubles and a triple, during a merry 23–6 rout of the Giants. It is a measure of the guidance the Giants received daily from management that Jouett Meekin pitched the entire game . . . and gave up all 23 runs.

Freedman didn't rest in the off season, either. With no fans or writers to fight with, he trumped up a couple of charges against Amos Rusie, who had just won 22 games for a ninth-place team and led the league in strikeouts. Freedman alleged that Rusie had broken unspecified training rules and had pitched "indifferently" in his final outing. Accordingly, Freedman deducted $200 from the Hoosier Thunderbolt's final paycheck of the year.

Rusie was furious, figuring correctly that the "fines" were nothing more than a crude attempt to cut his salary after the fact. Rusie, home in Indiana, insisted that the $200 be restored and further requested a $5,000 salary for 1896. Freedman ridiculed the requests. When Freedman mailed Rusie an 1896 contract for $2,400, Rusie announced that he would sit out the season.

The Giants of The Polo Grounds

In locking horns with Rusie, Freedman had once again demonstrated his unique gift for antagonizing the public. Rusie may have been a farm kid of twenty-four, but he had pitched faithfully for the Giants and had been the workhorse of the staff since 1890. He was seen as a model athlete trying to get a justified salary from a petulant owner.

Rusie was one of the few popular stars who remained with the Giants. The vaudeville team of Weber and Fields wrote a popular skit in his honor, actress Lillian Russell begged for an introduction to him, and the Waldorf named a cocktail after him.

A ghostwriter churned out a bestselling book with the short, pithy title of *Secrets of Amos Rusie, the World's Greatest Pitcher: How He Obtained His Incredible Speed on the Ball*. So when Rusie announced that he had sit out the season, and then proceeded to do it, Freedman's popularity rating dropped below zero. Previously, New York fans had hated Freedman. Now they were ready to lynch him. That simple statement is barely an exaggeration. During the 1896 season, a group of stockbrokers on Wall Street hung a sign out of their office windows urging a boycott of Giants' games until Rusie was paid and restored. A huge crowd gathered, shouting its approval and suggesting violence upon Freedman. Police had to forcibly break up a near riot. And who said New Yorkers don't take baseball seriously?

Enter John Montgomery Ward again, whom Rusie retained as his personal attorney. Ward was only too happy to file a suit against Freedman. Ward also presented Rusie's case to the league board, which quickly ruled that the $200 in fines were unjustified. When Freedman refused to go along with the board ruling, Ward pursued the case in civil court.

It should be remembered that the National League traditionally had not done well in courts. The presence of Rusie's suit on the trial dockets made much of the league nervous. There was no telling what sort of ruling Rusie and Ward might come away with which could open up new economic vistas for ballplayers.

A group of other owners cornered Freedman early in 1897 and suggested a settlement. They offered to put up much of the money themselves. Freedman, they recognized, was running baseball into the ground in the city in which it should have been most profitable. No more lucrative road trips to the Big Apple. The owners wanted "L'Affaire Rusie" settled. Freedman answered that the big dumb farm boy would have to drop his case first. The big dumb farm boy

The Giants of The Polo Grounds

told Freedman to go to hell.

Eventually, reason prevailed. The owners offered to reimburse Rusie for Freedman's fines, pay him for the season he sat out, and make up the difference in his 1897 salary between what Rusie wanted and what Freedman was willing to pay. Feeling vindicated, Rusie signed and came back to pitch for the Giants in 1897, winning 29 games (second in the league) for new manager Bill Joyce. Yet another manager, Arthur Irwin, a former Philadelphia shortstop, had come and gone in the season Rusie missed.

The press and personnel antagonisms continued unabated into 1898, but in that year, as the Giants headed for another second division finish, Freedman again outdid himself. This time the adversary was an opposing player named James (Ducky) Holmes, an outfielder with the Baltimore Orioles, who had played for the Giants in 1897.

In the fourth inning of a game on July 25, Holmes struck out with the bases loaded. He ambled back to the Oriole bench, the head of his bat clenched in his fist. A taunting Manhattan fan stood up, cupped his hands, and howled at him.

"Hey, Ducky!" the fan yelled. "You're a lobster! That's why you don't play for New York anymore." Lobster? Well, that was what the sanitized version in the newspapers claimed the fan said. One can use one's imagination to arrive it what actually was shouted.

Holmes raised his eyes, narrowed them, seized the moment, and shouted back, "But I'm glad I don't have to work for no Sheeny no more." The quote appeared in The New York *Times*. Lest you miss Holmes' now-obscure reference, "Sheeny" was a pejorative term for a Jewish person. The term arose in 19th-Century London, but was now common on the sidewalks of New York, east side, west side, all around the town, wherever verbal brickbats were tossed around.

Group sensitivity to racial slurs was not particularly pronounced in 1898. Slurs were commonplace and sometimes even fashionable. Whether Freedman actually heard the slur personally is unclear. He probably didn't: he often wasn't paying attention to what was happening on the field. But if not, someone conveyed the news of it to him.

As the teams switched sides, Freedman, now deeply offended, sent one of his lackeys toward the Baltimore bench with the demand that Manager Hanlon remove Holmes from the game. Hanlon laughed and refused, referring the Freedman shill to home plate umpire Tom Lynch. Lynch shrugged.

The Giants of The Polo Grounds

As the teams changed sides, Freedman charged down the aisle with a group of private "policemen." He came onto the field and tried to physically remove Holmes from the game. The rest of the Orioles blocked his path. Several hundred fans in attendance stood, then some climbed over the wooden barriers and inched closer to the foul lines.

The single umpire, Thomas Lynch, stood between the Orioles, bats in hand, on one side and Freedman, his truncheon-wielding private cops, and an increasingly surly mob on the other.

Freedman demanded an apology. Holmes spat at him. Freedman again demanded that Lynch remove Holmes from the game, but Lynch informed Freedman that he hadn't heard the insult and the game would be forfeited if the Giants' owner didn't clear his field.

Holmes remained in left field, grinning at Freedman. It should be noted that Holmes had the best smirking grin of the day. World class, by anyone's standards. So with the Giants due to bat, an incensed Freedman had had enough. He ordered Giants player-manager Bill Joyce to keep New York batsmen on the bench. Seeing no way beyond the impasse, umpire Lynch thereupon forfeited the game to Baltimore, 9–0. Lynch then joined the Orioles in racing toward the dressing room and locking the door behind him. Then, as now, being an umpire was not the smoothest way to make a living.

Ducky Holmes: Fair use image from Chicago Daily News. Chicago History Museum.

The National League had few rules in those days, but Freedman had violated two of them. He had interfered with play. And he had deliberately forfeited a game. These alone were enough to earn him a reprimand from the league, the condemnation of ten New York daily newspapers out of eleven published, and complete vilification in the other cities of the league. But he wasn't finished.

When the incident with Ducky Holmes began, the Orioles club had received a check for its share of gate receipts. After the forfeit, Freedman reimbursed his local spectators, who had been deprived of seeing a complete game. Then he turned to officials of the Baltimore club, which had done nothing to cause the forfeit, and

The Giants of The Polo Grounds

asked them to return their receipts. They refused. So Freedman stopped payment on their check. In turn, the Baltimore club petitioned Nick Young, the president of the league to fine the Giants $1,000 for the deliberate forfeit. He further demanded the payment of their receipts.

Freedman deposited the receipts with the league office, pending disposition of the case. Then he quickly got out of town, boarding a liner for Europe. In his absence, the league's board of directors met and ruled that the forfeit and the fine against the Giants should stand. But as a gesture to Freedman and his Tammany connections, since the league office was in New York they suspended Holmes for the rest of the season.

End of dispute? Not by a long shot.

The incident left National League officials with a mess. Freedman, citing Holmes' remark as not only personally offensive but "an insult to the Jewish people and the Hebrew patrons of the game," asked for Ducky Holmes to be suspended. Simultaneously, Foxy Ned Hanlon of the Oriole demanded punitive sanctions against Freedman for causing the game forfeiture and for withholding Baltimore's share of the gate.

The National League board of discipline tried to appease both sides and in doing so made both sides even angrier. The $1,000 game forfeiture fine imposed on the Giants enraged Freedman. An ensuing season-long suspension of Holmes infuriated not just Baltimore, but players throughout the league.

The press, the public, and the players of the league vociferously condemned Young and his board as lackeys of both Freedman and the Tammany Tiger. There were rumblings about another players' strike. Holmes went to court in Baltimore, found a judge who was an Oriole fan, and obtained an injunction permitting him to play.

Fearful of further court interference in baseball, Young's board reversed itself. Holmes was reinstated. The New York-Baltimore games were rescheduled. Freedman protested every game in which Holmes appeared. Here, as usual, Freedman was pitching his own version of a perfect game: He lost every protest.

Freedman's irascibility and unpopularity can be measured by the ardor with which his enemies were lining up against him. *The Sporting Life*, which was not otherwise known for taking racial or ethnic potshots, suggested that it was a miscarriage of justice for Ducky Holmes to have been disciplined "for the trifling offense" of "insulting the Hebrew race."

The Giants of The Polo Grounds

Meanwhile, Freedman smoldered and intentionally ran his ball club further into the ground in a spiteful attempt to hurt the league. Middle class patrons deserted the Polo Grounds and women no longer felt safe coming to the ballpark. The revolving door managerial system continued. Bill Joyce was fired after 44 games in 1898 and Cap Anson (as a favor to friends elsewhere in the league) came to New York and managed for 22 games. When he could no longer tolerate Freedman, Anson quit.

Bill Joyce returned. The team finished seventh. The following year Freedman hired a greatly aged John Day to lead the troops. Day, a broken, dispirited man by this time, was fired after 70 games and replaced by Fred Hoey, a thoroughly unqualified Freedman crony who had never managed before and never would again. The team finished tenth. Buck Ewing was lured back in 1900, managed for 62 games, and was fired. Freedman then made the comical cycle complete by replacing Ewing with shortstop George Davis, for whom Ewing had been traded in 1892 and who had started all this off by being Freedman's first manager in 1895.

Ah, the unending geometry of baseball! By this time, 1900, Freedman had accomplished the mission ordained for him: The Giants were dead last. They had few quality players and no fans. In six tempestuous years, Freedman had brought the franchise to ruin.

But he wasn't finished. While the National League remained a twelve-club circuit in the 1890s, Freedman maintained that this cumbersome league alignment was causing woes for the Giants. "I will not attempt to improve the New York club until the circuit is reduced," Freedman told anyone who would listen. What he really wanted, of course, what he wanted more than anything, was the Brooklyn team out of town.

What he wanted he wasn't getting. Things were happening quickly in Brooklyn now, and whenever the New York situation deteriorated, the Brooklyn situation shined a little brighter.

Chapter 13   The Merciful End of the 19ᵗʰ Century

"Mr. Freedman is the incarnation of selfishness supreme."

A. G. Spalding, 1901

Late in 1897, a young man named Charlie Ebbets, formerly an office boy but now the secretary of the Brooklyn franchise, acquired stock in the club from Ferdinand A. Abell and George Chauncey. Not long afterward, Charlie Byrne, the principal owner, died. Ebbets suddenly catapulted to president of the team.

Ebbets was what was desperately needed by most franchises at the time: a good, clear-headed baseball man, exactly what Andrew Freedman wasn't. Though prone to mistakes (attempting to manage team himself in 1898, for example) his intention was clear. He wanted a top ball club. Brooklyn, now part of Greater New York, had a vast, rabid audience for baseball. A winning team, he felt, could capitalize.

Ebbets moved the team's playing location from East New York to a "New" Washington Park at 1st Street and Third Avenue. "The ball season is on in Brooklyn!" rejoiced the Brooklyn *Eagle* on opening day as the new grounds in South Brooklyn drew a healthy crowd of 15,000. Unfortunately, the next day the same *Eagle* also reported that, "The heart of the fan today is heavy as lead," as the Brooklyn nine had lost an ugly game to the Philadelphia Phillies, 6–4.

During that 1898 season, he was also the manager for 106 games, compiling a miserable 38–68 record. The team finished tenth out of twelve teams and featured a wonderfully named outfielder named "Candy" LaChance. The latter was so nicknamed because he preferred to chew on peppermints rather than chewing tobacco. LaChance would later go on to greater things with Boston in 1903 as a member of the first World Champion team in major league history.

Ebbets was a resourceful fellow, however. He found help from an unexpected source: Harry Vonderhorst, owner of the Orioles.

Baltimore was still a league power. They had finished several light years in front of Brooklyn during the 1898 season. Their fans, however, had deserted them. Vonderhorst claimed to be making up

The Giants of The Polo Grounds

the team's financial losses with profits from his brewery, an arrangement that didn't particularly thrill him. But Vonderhorst, too, had been eyeing that keen clientele in the Borough of Churches.

The deal that was struck illustrates the type of overt conflict of interest that marked 1890s baseball. Vonderhorst swapped manager Ned Hanlon, Wee Willie Keeler, Joe Kelley, and Hugh Jennings, along with 10 percent of the Baltimore stock, to Brooklyn for 10 percent ownership of the Dodgers. In addition, seven expendable Brooklyn players were also shipped to Baltimore.

Originally, John McGraw and Wilbert Robinson were part of the package to go to Brooklyn. McGraw and Robinson, however, were partners in a bustling Baltimore saloon called the Diamond Cafe. They were in no mood to give up a profitable enterprise like that in hard-drinking, blue-collar Baltimore. So McGraw was elevated to manager of the Orioles, with Robinson as his chief coach. Meanwhile, the heart of the Orioles had been sent to Brooklyn. Years later, in his memoirs, McGraw summarized the deal in one sentence.

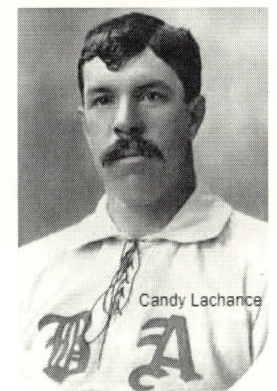

"The main point of the deal," he said, "was to make Brooklyn the dominating power in New York baseball, and we sure did."

They sure did, indeed. Brooklyn produced pennant winners in 1899 and 1900. It bothered no one that Ned Hanlon, for example, owned 10 percent of Brooklyn and was their manager while still owning 10 percent of the Orioles. Across the river, however, Andrew Freedman seethed. Not only had Brooklyn preempted the Giants as the power ball club in New York, but there was another invasion rumored as well. The American League, formerly the Western League, planned to set up shop as a major league in 1901. They were signing key players and intended to invade such National League markets as Chicago, Boston, and Philadelphia. New York was rumored to be next. Ban Johnson, the moving force of the new league, wanted a franchise in America's largest city.

The National League had dropped four clubs at the end of the 1899 season. Three of them - Baltimore, Cleveland, and Washington - would join Chicago, Boston, Detroit, Philadelphia, and Milwaukee in forming the new league. The reduction of the

The Giants of The Polo Grounds

National League to eight clubs had long been a Freedman demand. But now that it had come into reality, Freedman wasn't mollified. Further, the National League had given credibility to its new competitor by providing three key Eastern cities.

Needing just one more indecent, dishonorable act to cap his career, Freedman had one ready. He conceived a plan to operate the National League as a gigantic trust. "Syndicate baseball" it was called, and no doubt was inspired by the strange network of interlocking ownerships that already existed: John T. Brush, for example, owned Cincinnati and part of the Giants. Arthur H. Soden owned a third of the Boston National League club, plus part of the Giants. Ferdinand A. Abell owned 40 percent of Brooklyn, 40 percent of Baltimore, and about 10 percent of New York.

Freedman enlisted the support of Brush, Soden, and Frank Robison (who now owned the St. Louis franchise with his brother Stanley). If things went according to plan, the American League would collapse, and the National League would control a baseball monopoly. Players would be owned by a central league office and assigned to an individual team year to year. The owners would fix prices around the league and control all stock.

Sound farfetched? It nearly happened.

The New York *Sun*, the longtime Freedman nemesis, got wind of Freedman's idea and broke the story. The advance warning allowed the other National League owners to galvanize an anti-Freedman strategy at the National League meeting in New York in December of 1901.

The key issue became the presidency of the League. The Freedman forces lined up behind current president Nick Young. The anti-Freedman, anti-syndicate forces (Barney Dreyfuss of Pittsburgh, Ebbets of Brooklyn, Alfred J. Reach of Philadelphia, and John A. Hart of Chicago) magically came up with the only name in baseball who, as their candidate, might be able to block Young: Albert Spalding.

Follow this closely: When the league owners met, twenty-five ballots were taken for the election of the next league president. Twenty-five times the count was deadlocked at 4-4. Late in the evening, however, the Freedman faction left the room and the anti-syndicate faction stayed behind.

Ebbets, Reach, Hart, and Dreyfuss must have stared at each other in disbelief, then all shared the same idea. Illegally, they called a quorum and elected Spalding president, 4-0. Before dawn, Spalding called at Nick Young's hotel room and physically seized a trunk containing all league records. Spalding, acting much like Oliver Cromwell at a rump session of Parliament, declared himself president of the National League and proceeded to act as such. He might not have had legality on his side, Freedman sued within a day, but he did have the momentum . . . plus possession of league records.

Freedman won a small victory against Spalding when a New York court enjoined Spalding from even discussing baseball in the state of New York. But Spalding had plenty of pronouncements to make in other states. The press printed them and the fans, who justifiably felt that Spalding had saved them from yet another monopoly, supported him.

Throughout the winter, the war of words continued. The logjam was only broken in the spring with a compromise. Henry Clay Pulliam, formerly an official of the Pittsburgh club, would become league president. Spalding would relinquish the post he never legally held. And Andrew Freedman, finally realizing that he was surrounded on all sides, agreed to sell the New York Giants to John T. Brush, once the price and other details of the sale could be arranged.

Only one significant act remained in Andrew Freedman's ownership of the Giants: By mid-1902, having already changed managers twelve times in eight years, he was ready to do it again. As usual, there was a devious edge to his action.

It was widely rumored that when the American League invaded New York, it would be the Baltimore franchise that would be shifted there. So far, Tammany Hall had kept the league out by shooting public streets through any section of land that Ban Johnson's league considered as a playing field.

Freedman knew, however, that with the momentum the new league was now gaining, the arrival of a team, the Baltimore club, was probably inevitable. So Freedman, seeking to find a competent manager for the Giants (and thus boost his sale price to Brush), selected the man he wanted to take over his last place ball club.

Freedman's selection was currently the Baltimore manager, but was disenchanted with the American League, at war with Ban Johnson, and at odds with the Hanlon-Ebbets Baltimore management. He was ready to come to New York and bring as many Orioles with him as he could. It is doubtful that Freedman could have ever grasped the momentousness of what he was doing.

The Giants of The Polo Grounds

In changing managers for the thirteenth time, in trying to undercut the American League, Freedman unwittingly shaped baseball for the next half century. The man he selected was John J. McGraw, the accomplished umpire-baiter, ruffian, firebrand, and player-manager, the heart and soul of the nasty old Orioles.

On June 27, 1902, McGraw reached an agreement with the most despised man in baseball. On July 2 he took a train from Baltimore to New York and took over the helm of the New York Giants. There he would remain for the next thirty years.

With the advent of John McGraw, the Giants were on the verge of entering the Twentieth Century, two years after the rest of the world. It is noteworthy to take a final glance, however, at a few of the men who were so integrally involved in the Giants' first magnificent era. Some of these names will reappear briefly in the pages that follow.

Others won't. In alphabetical order:

Roger Connor retired from the National League in 1897 and bought the Waterbury club in the Connecticut League. There he managed and played first base. His adopted daughter sold tickets and his wife, as happens in the best of marriages, kept track of the money. Connor stayed in Connecticut for much of the rest of his life, serving as a school inspector for the city of Waterbury after his retirement from baseball. On one of the Connor family's homes in that city, there was a weather vane constructed from two bats that the slugger had used during his days with the Giants. Long after the Connors had moved from the home, and long after Dear Old Roger had died at age seventy-three in 1931, the vane remained a Waterbury landmark.

Buck Ewing left major league baseball after his final clash with Andrew Freedman in 1900. He parlayed the money he had earned playing ball into a small fortune by investing in real estate in his native Ohio. He was well-to-do when he left the game. Many years later, Connie Mack, a catcher himself and a man who managed Mickey Cochrane and managed against Bill Dickey, stated unequivocally that Buck Ewing was the game's greatest catcher ever. The accolade did Ewing no honor that he was ever able to enjoy: He died of diabetes and paralysis in 1906, three days after his forty-seventh birthday.

The Giants of The Polo Grounds

The name of Tim Keefe still appears in the sports pages whenever a modern pitcher approaches 300 wins. Keefe, at 344, ranks tenth in the "300 Win Club," having been passed in the Twenty-First Century by Greg Maddux and Roger Clemens. He had been second only to Pud Galvin when he retired in 1890.

What is little-known about his career in baseball is that he also served as an umpire in the 1890s. Calm, dignified Sir Timothy rarely questioned an umpire's call himself, but in the 1890s made some dramatically unpopular calls at of all places the Polo Grounds. The crowd turned on the old Giant, pelted him with pebbles, rocks, and bottles, and drove him from the field, escorted by city police. That evening he wired his resignation to the league office. It was a wise move.

He returned to his native Cambridge, Massachusetts, made money in real estate, coached baseball at Princeton, Tufts, and Harvard, and, during most of what remained of a long, comfortable life, was a regular spectator at Braves Field and Fenway Park. He died in 1933 at age seventy-seven.

Orator Jim O'Rourke, like teammate Roger Connor, tried his hand at administering minor league baseball in Connecticut and, like Tim Keefe, took a spin at being an umpire. His results in both were the same as his teammates'. Then Orator Jim turned his mind to, well, orating. Armed with his law degree from Yale, O'Rourke spent many prosperous years as an attorney and a public servant. During the winter of 1919, O'Rourke called upon a client on a very cold, very icy day in his native Bridgeport, Connecticut. O'Rourke, who played all nine positions at one point or another in his 1,774-game career, contracted pneumonia. At the time of his death seven days later, he was sixty-six years old.

John Montgomery Ward served baseball in almost every conceivable capacity, from perfect game pitcher to All Star shortstop to manager to legal counsel to team president (of the Boston Braves in 1912). Sadly, he and Helen Dauvray divorced after eleven years of marriage, but Ward remained close to baseball as an attorney and a member of the Rules Committee for most of his life. A mortal enemy of the reserve clause as a young man, he defended it in his later years, unable to conceive of any reasonable alternative. The court rulings in the cases of Curt Flood, Andy Messersmith, and Dave McNally later in the Twentieth Century

The Giants of The Polo Grounds

probably would have astonished him. On March 4, 1925, one day after his sixty-fifth birthday, he died of pneumonia.

Smilin' Mickey Welch, retired with 311 career wins — a total that was officially readjusted down to 307. But his name has surfaced like Keefe's in recent years. Gaylord Perry (314), Greg Maddux (355), Steve Carlton (329), Phil Niekro (318), Don Sutton (324), and Tom Seaver (311) have all edged past him as distinguished members of the "300 Win Club." Tom Glavine (305) and Randy Johnson (303) finished just behind him.

Welch, as a young man, was a legendary drinker and carouser. Apparently, Mickey knew how to do it and get away with it. Born during the administration of President James Buchanan two years before the Civil War, Welch lived to see World War II's outbreak and died during the third term of Franklin Roosevelt. He was eighty-two when he passed away in Nashua, New Hampshire, in 1941, the last of the first generation of Giants to pass from the scene. He was, in his later years, of infinite value to baseball historians with his sterling reminiscences about the old days at the Polo Grounds before the turn of the century. Like his five teammates, Connor, Ewing, Keefe, O'Rourke, and Ward, he was installed in baseball's Hall of Fame in the years after his death.

One early Giant upon whom fortune definitely did not smile was John B. Day. The Brotherhood war of 1890 ruined him for life. He lost not only his team, but the tobacco business that had once been his livelihood. As the years passed and as Day drifted into oblivion, the memory of his fateful partnership with Jim Mutrie in the 1880s must have carried with it a bittersweet poignancy.

Four decades later, in 1923, Day surfaced again. He was found destitute in a furnished tenement room on the Bowery, paralyzed and gravely ill. His wife was dying of cancer in the same room. "He doesn't look like a great man now," Agnes said to reporters who visited them, "but he was. A tobacco man when he came here to New York in the Eighties. He was worth nearly a million dollars. When he used to visit his cigar factory in Middletown, Connecticut . . . whistles blew, and work was suspended to greet him."

According to press reports, Day was unable to buy food or care for himself or his wife. Simultaneously, Jim Mutrie, the one-time sharp-dressed man who had helped create the Giants, was discovered living near destitution on Staten Island. Life before

Social Security and Medicare could be cruel beyond description. So Giant management arranged a benefit game which would be played for them by the Giants at the Polo Grounds.

The game, between the defending World Series champion Giants and a minor-league Baltimore team featured Baltimore alumnus Babe Ruth. It attracted a meager crowd of only 5,000. Contributions from Charles Comiskey, Garry Herrmann, and other baseball dignitaries boosted the disappointing gate receipts. The National League also granted Day a small pension. Before the game, Ruth posed with McGraw in an odd photo op in which Ruth wears a New York Giants uniform. The babe suited up with McGraw's team that day, perhaps for the only time in his life. The two men put aside their personal antagonisms for the day.

But when he died eighteen months later on January 25, 1925 at age seventy-seven in Cliffside, New Jersey, the man who had founded the New York Giants was a ward of the state.

Mutrie would linger for another thirteen years, almost to the day, before passing away in Staten Island in January of 1938 at age 86. In the latter part of his life he operated a small newsstand. Sic Transit Gloria. His living conditions at the end, were no better than Day's.

The Giants of The Polo Grounds

A baseball historian's reminiscence – John Thorn

"Remember your first time in a big-league ballpark? How dark and cool and secret it felt to prowl the caverns under the grandstand, and how dazzling was that first view of the great green field when you emerged from the tunneled aisle? I can recall my first visit, to the Polo Grounds on May 12, 1957, not as if it were yesterday, which at my age I can only hazily recall, but sharply. My beloved Brooklyn Dodgers, behind lefthander Johnny Podres, shut out the New York Giants 5–0, and my idol, Duke Snider, hit a home run. My father, who knew nothing about baseball except that I was crazy about it, did not let on that I was imposing upon his bounteous good will, and — just like an American, which he had only recently become — even hollered vigorously for the peanut vendor to throw a bag our way. Yet for all the pleasures of that sun-splashed Sunday, the feeling that I can summon up most vividly today is transcendent awe before the great green field."

John Thorn
May 2018

{Editor's note: John Thorn has been the Official Baseball Historian for Major League Baseball since 2011. Born in Germany, he is a notable American author, sports historian, publisher, and cultural commentator. He probably knows more about the history of the particularly American game than you or I combined. Special thanks to Mr. Thorn also for permission to reference his on-line material on Ida Schnall and the New York Female Giants.}

PART TWO:

THE McGRAW DECADES

Chapter 14   Muggsy Takes Charge

"The best player on my team is Johnny McGraw."

—Alfred William Lawson

Sure. But who was John McGraw?

In 1881, John McGraw Sr., a widower with one daughter, was a maintenance worker for the Elmira, Cortland & Northern Railroad. McGraw Sr. fell in love with a woman named Ellen Comerfort. He courted and married her. They had eight children, the third of which was John Joseph McGraw, born on April 7, 1873. Two sisters, Ellen and Margaret, grew to adulthood. A brother, James Michael, did also. During the winter of 1884–85, however, a diphtheria epidemic claimed four other siblings plus Ellen Comerfort McGraw, John's mother. Disease had cut the family in half, not unusual for the day. McGraw Sr., according to friends, never recovered emotionally.

John Jr.'s surviving brother and sisters went to live with Comerfort relatives. John stayed with his father, a relationship that was uneven at best. Eventually, he went to work in the Truxton House Hotel, which provided food and a warm place to stay. It also allowed him an opportunity to indulge his passion: playing baseball with the Truxton Grays, the local nine. McGraw was sixteen by this time and undernourished — a runt weighing barely more than a hundred pounds. He was also a pitcher and the best player on the team.

There was town thirteen miles away with the ballgame name of East Homer. The manager of the team had seen young Jack McGraw pitch and was impressed. He offered five dollars a game. McGraw accepted.

We are in the year 1889 now, a year in which the fabled New York Giants were winning their second consecutive pennant in the bright lights of New York City, 180 miles to the southeast. But young McGraw was enjoying a good year too. He pitched for East Homer for a few weeks, then was offered a position with the Olean team in the New York-Pennsylvania League. The pay was good: $40 a month. McGraw, age sixteen, cut his ties with Truxton and went off to Olean, where the team's owner, Bert Kenny, took a shine to McGraw and made a third baseman of him, a move not entirely to his liking. McGraw, while possessed of a pretty good wing in the pitcher's box, had what was known as a "scattershot" arm once he had knocked down a batted ball down in the field. "Scattershot" meant that his throws aimed at first base often landed somewhere else.

"I was quite a bust in my start as a third baseman," McGraw wrote in his memoirs years later. "I started six games there and we lost every one of them."

True. But he worked hard at the position, learned it, and trained his arm. By 1890 he had progressed to the Wellsville team of the Western New York League. There McGraw pitched, played third, got into fights, and hit .365. He lived in a local hotel and became the sparkplug of a popular team. His chest swelled with pride when people pointed to him or stopped him in the street. In Wellsville, for the first time in his life, he was known as "Johnny McGraw, the ball player."

The Wellsville club was owned and managed by a man named Alfred William Lawson, who became a friend, mentor and memorable soul in his own right.

Lawson was an Englishman by birth who had moved to Canada and then the United States. As a pitcher, he had made one start for the Boston Beaneaters and two for the Pittsburgh Alleghenys during the 1890 season. Now, in the winter of 1890–91, Lawson arranged to take his baseball players on a winter tour to the South. Lawson asked McGraw if he wished to go. The pay was $60 a month, plus travel fare. Hotel lodging was provided. Again, McGraw accepted. En route, the team stopped in New York City, where McGraw got his first look at the big town. Years later he would recall liking what he saw: the bustle, the pace, the excitement, and the endless intrigue.

The Wellsville team played a whistle-stop exhibition schedule across Florida, then traveled to Cuba, where they won 14 out of 17 games against other groups of minor leaguers who were also following the winter sunshine. Lawson, no one's fool, had sprinkled a few former major leaguers among his own ranks to make sure no one blew him off the field. No one did. But the greatest impression was made on the Cubans by the aggressive, nimble kid at shortstop — McGraw.

Lawson's invaders played in yellow uniforms, or at least they were yellow by the time the Cuban games rolled around. The

The Giants of The Polo Grounds

Cuban press dubbed McGraw *El Mono Amarillo* — "The Yellow Monkey." Despite what you might think, the term was a compliment.

The Wellsville contingent made their way back to Tampa in March 1891. "The best player on my team," Lawson told reporters, "is Johnny McGraw. He is a hard, left-handed batsman, a fine shortstop, a fine base runner, and last, but not least, a gentleman. He is one of the coming stars of the profession."

The quote found its way in print in more than one journal. McGraw's name was before the public. Instead of foolishly rushing back to icy New York State, Lawson decided to continue on the barnstorming tour through Florida and up to northern Georgia. The boys played for meal money and lodging and had a good time. Then another lucky star twinkled upon McGraw.

On March 26, 1891, the Wellsville wanderers happened upon the Cleveland Spiders, a bellicose squad that prowled the lower regions of the National League. They were looking for either a spring warmup or a gang rumble, whichever came first. The team featured the ill-tempered Patsy Tebeau, the manager-third baseman, and a right-handed pitcher named Cy Young, who would soon celebrate his twenty-fourth birthday. Also on the squad were Dirty Jack Doyle and George Davis, names that would surface later with the New York Giants.

Lawson arranged a game that day in Gainesville. In a fit of hyperbole, he called his own team, the "Champions of Florida." Local excitement mounted, and in the spring sunshine, 650 paying customers watched a historic game.

Leon Viau, a young but experienced major leaguer, pitched for Cleveland. Lawson himself pitched for Wellsville, limiting the Cleveland squad to just five hits. But his own team contributed eleven errors to help the Cleveland cause. Final score: Cleveland 9, "Champions of Florida" 6.

McGraw, however, had made the most of the opportunity. He played errorless ball, tagged Viau for three doubles in five at-bats and found a way to score each time, bringing across half his team's runs.

Within a few days, as newspaper accounts of the game spread through the United States, "John McGraw of Gainesville, Florida," began receiving offers via telegraph from high minor league teams. He received twenty-eight in all. Eventually, he accepted — and honored — an offer from Cedar Rapids of the Iowa-Illinois League, the predecessor of the Three-I League. So off went McGraw, far from Truxton now, to play baseball in the sprawling American Midwest during the presidency of Benjamin Harrison.

Lawson went in another direction but didn't disappear. He played in the minors through 1895. He later managed in the minors from 1905 to 1907, then shifted gears and became a pioneer in the American aircraft industry. Lawson published two early journals on flight, including a magazine called *Fly*, which was goofy, quixotic and far before its time. It had to do with flight, not an insect.

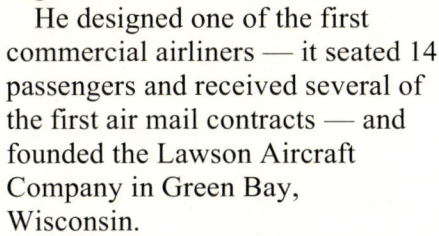

He designed one of the first commercial airliners — it seated 14 passengers and received several of the first air mail contracts — and founded the Lawson Aircraft Company in Green Bay, Wisconsin.

In the 1920s, Lawson morphed into personal philosophy, promoting health practices that were seen as unusual for the day, including vegetarianism. He maintained — and here it gets a trifle kooky — to have found the secret extending one's life to 200. (Lawson died at 85.) He conceived his own philosophy, Lawsonomy, and the Lawsonian religion, drawing thousands to his lectures and radio broadcasts in the early 1930s, mainly in the upper Midwest. His ideas are still around. Until the first years of the 21st Century, thousands of motorists who traveled I-94 between Milwaukee and Chicago see a sign reading "University of Lawsonomy" in Racine County, an institution that was never built.

Nonetheless, returning to young John McGraw out there in corn county, a couple of bits of baseball history intersected.

First, the Chicago White Stockings came to Cedar Rapids one day to play the locals. Cap Anson, the condescending old racist, led the Chicago club. At age forty, he could still rock National League pitching pretty well. Early in the game, Anson launched a bullet toward third base. McGraw caught it. As the teams were changing sides, the five-foot-seven, 140-pound McGraw saw fit to exchange insults with the six-foot, 227-pound star.

The Giants of The Polo Grounds

"Say, old-timer," McGraw said as he trotted by, "is that what you call big league hitting?"

Anson stopped and stared. McGraw trotted away. By the end of the day, McGraw had instigated three arguments with Anson. But Cap was apparently amused by the youth's truculence and no blows were exchanged. Chicago won the game, but only by 2–0.

The second incident occurred in August, after McGraw had hit .275 in 68 games for Cedar Rapids. In the league at that time, holding down a job as a shortstop for Rockport, was the same Bill Gleason who had played for Chris Von Der Ahe's rollicking St. Louis Browns in the 1880s. Gleason was on his way toward baseball oblivion, but still had some friends. He approached McGraw in mid-August 1891. "I have a letter from Billy Barnie, the manager of the Baltimore Orioles," Gleason said to McGraw. "He wants to know how good you are."

McGraw reached down for all the humility the young man could muster. "You can tell him," said McGraw, "that I'm as good as they come."

Gleason smiled. He wrote back to Barnie and relayed McGraw's words.

McGraw had no written contract with Cedar Rapids. He made two good friends on the club, players Henry Fabian and Dick Kinsella. But the league was teetering on the brink of collapse. (Then it teetered over the brink in September.) So a few days later, when Gleason informed McGraw that a train ticket to Baltimore had arrived, McGraw left Cedar Rapids. He arrived in Baltimore in another forty-eight hours.

Upon McGraw's arrival, manager Bill Barnie couldn't believe his eyes. Baltimore was a struggling American Association franchise that year and Barnie wasn't impressed with the little squirt who stood before him. To make matters more absurd, McGraw had to wear the only uniform available, one formerly owned by a husky five-foot-eleven infielder named Sam Wise.

"This is the ballplayer I've been writing to Gleason about?" Barnie gasped, observing the long and short of things. "Why, you're just a kid! Can you play ball?"

"If you don't think so," McGraw answered, "get me out on the field. I'm bigger than I look."

Barnie inserted McGraw into the line-up against the Columbus Senators. Phil Knell, who would win 27 games for Columbus that year, was the pitcher.

The Giants of The Polo Grounds

Playing second base, McGraw booted the first fielding chance to come his way. Batting for the first time, he struck out with the bases loaded. But before the end of the day, Baltimore had won, 6–5, McGraw had hit safely, scored a run, executed a perfect sacrifice, and flawlessly handled his next five fielding chances. At eighteen, just twenty-four months after leaving Truxton, McGraw was in Baltimore to stay.

Within the next few months, the American Association would fail. Baltimore would join the National League. Barnie would be gone and George Van Haltren, who succeeded Barnie as manager, would be back in the outfield. Ned Hanlon would arrive and McGraw, already on the roster, would develop into the first key player for the famous Baltimore Orioles of the 1890s.

Over the eight years from 1891 to 1898, the Orioles would win league championships only three times to Boston's five, but their aggressive style of play would catch the headlines, draw the crowds, and alter the future of baseball. During this time, McGraw assumed the captaincy of the team, became well known throughout organized baseball, and blossomed into a local hero in Baltimore. Yet all of this occurred with astonishing suddenness. By the time of the Temple Cup Competition with the Giants in 1895, when McGraw was an established star, he was only twenty-two years old.

His proprietorship of the Diamond Cafe sank his local roots even deeper. It had long been the desire of Wilbert Robinson, the likeable and memorably profane Oriole catcher and now McGraw's best friend on the team, to open a "hash house or beanery" to cater to the appetites and thirsts of Baltimore's workingmen. Robinson was an easygoing, pleasantly coarse man of plebian tastes. McGraw took his idea and elaborated upon it. They took their savings from baseball, as well as their Temple Cup bonuses, and in late 1896 leased three floors of a large building at 519 North Howard Street, across from where the Academy of Music was then located. At the front of the first floor they placed a dining room, and at the rear they installed a small bowling alley.

On the second floor was a reading room and gathering place, decorated with portraits of boxers, ballplayers, and some of the American athletes who had won medals at the 1896 Olympics in Greece. (A Baltimore native, Bob Garrett, had won medals in the shot put and discus throw.) On the third floor were rooms for club meetings and private functions. The joint was popular from the start, particularly among the sports crowd.

The Giants of The Polo Grounds

There was a strange footnote to McGraw's bowling enterprise. When the pins in McGraw's alley were chipped and worn down from the beating they took from the sixteen-ounce bowling ball, Frank Vansant, manager of the cafe, took them to a wood turner for repairs.

The wood turner placed the pins on a lathe and eventually evened them out, but not before sanding them down so severely that they were grossly undersized.

Robinson and McGraw returned from a hunting trip and saw them. The little pins flew wildly when hit with a bowling ball. McGraw roared with laughter. "Robbie, the pins look like the little ducks we've been chasing down the bay."

A reporter named William Clarke from the Baltimore *American* was on hand and joined the laughter. Vansant then produced a couple of eight-ounce balls used for summer lawn bowling. The smaller balls seemed ideal for the smaller "duckpins." Clarke wrote up the incident in the *American* and crowds flocked to the Diamond Cafe to try the new activity.

Thus was born duckpin bowling in the United States. And thus, with a thriving business in Baltimore, as well as a new wife — he married Minnie Doyle, daughter of Mike Doyle, a Baltimore printer, in February 1897 — John McGraw was reluctant to report to Brooklyn when Ned Hanlon tried to transfer all the Orioles to Brooklyn in early 1898.

It wasn't easy, but as noted earlier, McGraw convinced Hanlon to let him stay in Baltimore as the team's manager. Wilbert Robinson was his affable lieutenant, sort of a Basil Rathbone-Nigel Bruce situation.

McGraw then demonstrated again his ability to lash back at adversity. Left with a roster bereft of baseball talent, McGraw found a twenty-eight-year-old rookie in camp during spring training named Joe McGinnity. Big Joe threw a wide, sweeping pitch called a "Nickle Rocket" curve, a totally different pitch than the sharp, concise curveballs that most pitchers threw. McGinnity was a former iron foundry worker from the Indian Territory, which would later become part of Oklahoma. McGraw managed to keep Hanlon from taking McGinnity to Brooklyn for one more season.

In 1899, despite the exodus of stars to Brooklyn, the Orioles gasped their last as the greatest road show in baseball. McGraw got his charges fired up, hit .391 himself, stole 73 bases, and scored 140 runs. McGinnity won 28 games to lead the league in victories. Attendance boomed.

Even at home, the Orioles outdrew Brooklyn, which was now known as Hanlon's Superbas after a vaudeville troupe of the same name. For a while, McGraw's life seemed placid.

Then on Friday, August 25, McGraw was in Louisville with the team. He received a telegram saying that his wife Minnie, back in Baltimore, was suffering from an inflamed appendix. She was being moved by doctors from the McGraw home at 312 St. Paul Street to Maryland General Hospital. A second telegram arrived a few hours later, urging him to return home at once.

McGraw did. Connections took hours, however, and when the young Oriole leader arrived at the hospital, he found his wife barely conscious. Her appendix had ruptured. Three days later, after McGraw conducted a bedside vigil, she was dead. McGraw had not yet recovered from that shock when he received a second one. The National League was contracting from twelve teams to eight. One of the franchises to be dropped was the Baltimore Orioles.

Chapter 15   McGraw Hits Gotham

"McGraw's very walk across the field in a hostile town was a challenge to the multitude."

—Grantland Rice

Baltimore, or what remained of it, traded McGraw and Robinson to St. Louis of the National League in the off-season. Initially reluctant to go, both eventually reported, but only after striking the reserve clause out of their contracts. They played indifferently for St. Louis, getting bounced from enough games to attend the racetrack across the street from the ballpark. In June, McGraw traveled to Chicago, where plans were being laid by Byron Bancroft (Ban) Johnson to transform the Western League into the American League. This was a baseball war again, this time with a vengeance.

McGraw invested $7,000 in a block of stock in the Baltimore Orioles. Robinson acquired a smaller block. The money went to pay the club's debts. Thereupon, McGraw started raiding the National League of players he wanted to take to the Orioles.

He swiped Joe McGinnity back from Brooklyn, signing him to a handwritten contract for the 1901 season on a sheet of scrap paper. He lured outfielder Mike Donlin away from St. Louis, plied infielder Jimmy Williams from Pittsburgh, and spirited outfielder-catcher Roger Bresnahan away from Chicago.

McGraw's activities were nothing out of the ordinary. The American League was not honoring the National League reserve clause and had already run off with Napoleon (Nap) Lajoie, Cy Young, and Ed Delahanty, among others. By the following April, with Charlie Comiskey setting up shop with a team known as the Chicago White Sox and with Connie Mack installed as manager of the Philadelphia Athletics, the new league was stocked about 85 percent with National League refugees.

There was general consternation in the National League that McGraw had defected to the "enemy." It was openly recognized that McGraw was on the verge of an excellent career as a manager. In the war between the National League and the American League, the Senior Circuit wanted him on their side.

They soon would have him. One of the features of Ban Johnson's league was the curtailment of rowdyism on the field and increased authority for his umpires. McGraw found it difficult to live with this situation for more than a few minutes. He was soon fined by Johnson, then found himself engaged in increasingly bitter public disputes with him. This went on for all of 1901.

Tempers barely cooled over the winter, even though McGraw had lost his heart to a young woman named Blanche Sindall, the daughter of a prosperous Baltimore builder. Blanche was one of the most eligible young women in Baltimore and had scores of suitors. All of them vanished when McGraw arrived.

Here again were the many contradictions of John McGraw. A hell-raiser on the field, a truculent street-fighting man in locker rooms, he was a gentle, affectionate suitor who cherished Sunday evenings at the Sindall household when he and her family would gather around the piano and have a singing bee. Eventually, McGraw married his second wife on January 8, 1902, at St. Ann's Roman Catholic Church in Baltimore. Great crowds turned out in the streets, hoping to catch a glimpse of the many old Orioles — Keeler, Robinson, Jennings, and Kelley — who were present.

But it was also at this time that McGraw had a serious suitor himself: Andrew Freedman, who was intensifying his efforts to bring McGraw to New York.

The breaking point, as far as McGraw and the American League was concerned, came that same spring.

On Friday, May 23, Baltimore was in Detroit for the first of a two-game series. McGinnity was pitching for the Orioles and had taken a particular disliking to Tiger outfielder Dick Harley, who was the runner on third. McGinnity kept throwing to third, trying to pick Harley off. Third, of course, was McGraw's position.

After each throw, safely back on the bag, Harley would shout an insult at the Baltimore pitcher. McGraw finally concluded that he had heard enough from Harley, walked over, and stamped his spikes on Harley's foot.

Mr. Harley apparently did a lot of thinking about this overnight, presumably as he soaked his foot. The next day fans had rarely seen a man so anxious to reach third base. Harley singled and stole second immediately. Then, on the next pitch, he made a sprint for third. Well, actually, the sprint was toward the third baseman.

Roger Bresnahan fired the ball to third. Harley came at McGraw with his spikes sharpened and aloft, ripping into McGraw's right knee, gashing it, and sending a rush of blood through the leggings of McGraw's uniform. McGraw dropped the ball and went for Harley's throat. Both benches emptied, and four thousand fans went wild.

This was exactly what Ban Johnson wanted out of the American League. Both players were disciplined. But for once in his life, McGraw had gotten the worst of the fracas. He was out of the lineup until late June, an absence that caused Baltimore to wobble in the standings. Worse, when he attempted to come back, his knee kept slipping in and out of the socket. He could put full weight on it only with considerable pain. John McGraw, at age twenty-nine, did not need to be a genius to know that his playing days were numbered.

McGraw finally did get back into the Oriole lineup on June 25 as a pinch hitter. He played third again three days later and got into a vicious argument with an umpire over whether he had successfully made a tag during a rundown play. The ump bounced him. When McGraw refused to leave the field, the game was declared a forfeit. This earned McGraw an indefinite suspension from league president Ban Johnson.

It also was the breaking point. Ban Johnson wanted "clean ball" and by now it was clear that such would not be forthcoming from John McGraw. McGraw saw the writing on the wall: There was no way that he would ever be allowed to carry the mantle of the American League into New York.

Freedman and John T. Brush, of course, knew it was time to act. Enticements by the Giants to McGraw had been going on for a long time, but finally McGraw would have to make a move.

Brush helped force the issue. Brush and Ban Johnson had been adversaries for well over a decade, dating back to the times when Johnson was a sportswriter for the Cincinnati *Commercial Gazette* and Brush owned the Cincinnati ball club. Johnson used to add spice to his $25-a-week job by taking potshots at Johnson's management of the ball club. Now, in 1902, Brush welcomed the opportunity to zap Johnson in return by rustling one of the stars of the American League.

Freedman was anxious to get out of baseball by this time, and baseball was anxious to get rid of him. So Johnson allowed Brush to direct the traffic. McGraw was promised a "free hand" as manager if he came to the Giants. Freedman made the offer all the more attractive by reasserting his own intention to sell the club to Brush. All that was then blocking McGraw's exit from Baltimore was his American League contract.

Fortunately, he had an excellent way out. Not only had McGraw paid $7,000 of Oriole bills out of his own pocket, but he had also been paying players' salaries to keep the franchise afloat. Now he called a meeting of the team's board of directors and asked for his money to be repaid. The owners, as McGraw well knew, were insolvent. Then he made a counteroffer. If they would release him, he would go away and not ask for repayment.

They agreed. On July 9, McGraw was back in New York — much to the shock and delight of the New York sporting public — to sign a four-year contract as manager of the New York Giants.

The salary was a healthy $11,000 per year.

That, however, was just the beginning. On July 16 McGraw returned to Baltimore, intent on retrieving a few choice items left behind: players.

Follow this one: Back in Baltimore, McGraw huddled with Wilbert Robinson and swapped his share in the Diamond Cafe for Robinson's stock in the Orioles. Then McGraw peddled his own stock, plus the stock he had just obtained from Robinson, to another minority stockholder named John J. Mahon. Enter one of God's messengers here on earth, one Father John G. Boland.

Father Boland was one of the pastors of St. Vincent de Paul's Roman Catholic Church on Front Street. Baltimore politics being what they were, Father Boland and his parish were also stockholders in the Orioles. But not for much longer. Before evening vespers on July 16, Father Boland had also sold his interests to Mahon.

By a curious circumstance, Mahon happened to be the father-in-law of outfielder Joe Kelley. But by an even more curious turn of events, Mahon now held 201 shares of the 400 outstanding shares of stock in the Baltimore Orioles. These he signed over to an attorney named Joseph C. France, who was Andrew Freedman's mouthpiece in Baltimore.

France immediately passed the control of the 201 shares to John T. Brush, who remained on his estate in Indiana, awaiting the outcome of events back East. When Brush received word from France that he now controlled 201 shares in the Baltimore Orioles, the palace coup was complete. New York of the National League now had a controlling interest in Baltimore of the American League. When the story broke in the morning newspapers on July 19, it's a good bet that Ban Johnson didn't swallow his breakfast.

As the Giant manager, McGraw now transferred the players he wanted to New York: pitchers Joe McGinnity and Jack Cronin, center fielder Steve Brodie (the dude who used to talk to baseballs and catch fly balls behind his back), outfielder-catcher Roger Bresnahan, first baseman Dan McGann, and second baseman Billy Gilbert.

Two other players, Cy Seymour and Joe Kelley, went to Cincinnati, a franchise also owned by Brush. Kelley became manager, part of the deal that father-in-law Mahon worked out for him.

So back to New York went McGraw with his kidnapped (but ecstatic) ex-Orioles. Here was the most successful raid on Baltimore since the War of 1812. It created considerable excitement in New York as well as in the American League office. Back in Crab Cake City, of course, the citizenry was less enthusiastic. A particular downer came the next day, July 17, when the Orioles no longer had enough players on their roster to field a team against St. Louis. Ban Johnson hurriedly declared the game a forfeit and leaned on other owners to lend Baltimore enough players to finish the season.

As for John McGraw, he was now safely ensconced in New York. He and Blanche moved into a comfortable suite at the Victoria Hotel at Broadway and 27th Street and reported to the Polo Grounds. The team he took charge of on July 17, 1902, had a record of 23 wins and 50 losses. They were 33.5 games behind first-place Pittsburgh, the defending league champion. Even Philadelphia (with its usual haphazard entry in the National League) in seventh place appeared so far away as to be in a different time zone. The last-place Giants were a defeated, demoralized outfit.

McGraw's first act is part of baseball legend. He asked Freedman for a list of the players on the roster. Freedman produced twenty-three names. McGraw went down the list with a pencil and crossed off nine names. "You can begin by releasing these," he said.

Freedman screamed. Freedman howled. The nine, he protested, had cost Freedman $14,000.

"They'll cost you more if you keep them," said McGraw. "You're in last place, aren't you? I've brought some real ballplayers with me and I'll get some more."

Now Freedman knew what was meant by the "free hand" that McGraw had been promised. The nine players took a hike.

On July 19 McGraw and his contingent of ex-Orioles suited up as New York Giants for the first time. Yes, this was a last-place team, but the extensive newspaper coverage of the previous week's events had sparked the city's interest again. Hanlon's Superbas — the Trolly Dodgers, in other words — were in third place and playing good ball, but New York was a two-team city again.

The largest crowd of the season arrived at the Polo Grounds to watch Joe McGinnity of the Giants pitch against Herman (Ham) Iburg of the Phillies, pitching in his lone National League season in which he established a modern NL record for most losses by a pitcher in a single major league season.

The New York *World* estimated the attendance at ten thousand souls. The New York *Times* said the number was closer to sixteen thousand. What was uncontested, however, was that the Giants played like a new team. McGraw had a single in three at-bats and handled three fielding chances at shortstop without error, even though his knee still troubled him. Steve Brodie delivered a double late in the game, but a Philadelphia uprising in the second inning carried the day. The Phillies won, 4–3.

Joe "Iron Man" McGinnity

The fans, however, left the Polo Grounds that day feeling as if they'd received their money's worth, a dramatic change from recent years. And McGraw was not without a philosophical perspective. "The pennant," he announced, acknowledging the mathematics of his eighth-place location midway through July, "is out of our reach, of course. But look out for us next year."

The statement was pure McGraw. It sounded like a conceit, yet upon scrutiny conveyed promise, menace, and truth. So did the next two games the Giants played, across the East River in Brooklyn. The Superbas had been league champions as recently as 1899 and 1900. They were still one of the league's stronger entries, as well as the established team in New York. Ned Hanlon, for whom McGraw had played in Baltimore, was the manager. So there was a moral victory at stake.

McGraw won it. Behind a deaf mute from Kansas named Luther (Dummy) Taylor, the Giants beat the Superbas, 4–1, on July 23. It was the first of McGraw's 2,658 regular season managerial victories as a New York Giant. One day later he had his second, a crafty 2–0, five-hit shutout pitched by an unpolished right-hander named Christy Mathewson.

The team played respectable ball for the rest of the year, though McGraw was unable to win more than 40 percent of the games he managed. Significant, however, was the fact that Freedman was drifting out of the Giants' picture and the fans were slowly coming back.

A powerful (103–36, .741) Pittsburgh club dominated the National League that year, 1903. The Giants finished eighth, exactly where McGraw had found them. McGraw played in only 35 games, mostly at shortstop. He hit .234 as a Giant (a full hundred points below his eventual career average) and .253 for the year, a personal embarrassment. But he stationed himself in the third base coach's box and made himself a factor in almost every game with his noisy, aggressive tactics.

Though the Giants only won 40 percent of the games managed by McGraw, they were some definite improvement over recent years. On the closing day of the 1902 baseball season, the New York Giants were 53.5 games-and several light-years-away from first place. Yet, to any casual observer, it was also clear that finally there was a man on the scene — twenty-nine-year-old John Joseph McGraw — who would be able to lead the team out of the wilderness.

Chapter 16   **The Natural**

"Matty was the master of them all."

**—From Christy Mathewson's plaque
at Baseball's Hall of Fame**

It is difficult to imagine quite the degree to which chaos reigned at the Polo Grounds immediately before John McGraw's arrival.

Horace Solomon Fogel had begun the season as the Giants manager. Fogel had been a sportswriter in Philadelphia. He had always dreamed of being a manager, then president of a ball club. Unfortunately for everyone, his friendship with John T. Brush helped him realize his dream.

He had first become a manager at age 48 with the Indianapolis Hoosiers on July 11, 1887 and promptly ran the team into the ground. He then managed the New York Giants from the start of the 1902 season.

Young Christy Mathewson, who had signaled his potential as a pitcher by throwing a no-hitter and by winning 20 games for a seventh-place team in 1901, was undergoing a shift to first base. This had been Horace Solomon Fogel's idea.

Forty-one games into the season, Freedman, for reasons apparent only to himself, fired Fogel as manager and appointed George (Heinie) Smith, the second baseman, as manager. Smith had it in mind to try Mathewson at shortstop, and both Fogel and Smith liked to see Mathewson in the outfield occasionally. Or the infield. Anywhere except on the mound, where he belonged. The situation was made all the murkier by the fact that, even after Fogel had been relieved of duties as manager, he continued with the club in an unofficial capacity and gave Smith instructions how to manage, even popping into the dugout now and then. He sometimes he skipped Smith completely and ran the team by himself. Under such guidance, the Giants lost 27 of 32 games. This was where McGraw found them.

"You can get rid of Fogel, too," McGraw told Freedman in July of 1901, after indicating the nine players to be released. "Anybody that doesn't know any more about ballplayers than he does has no

155

place with a big-league ball club. Mathewson has as fine a pitching motion as any kid who's come up in a long time."

Freedman didn't necessarily agree, but he obeyed. Fogel was toast. Smith remained with the club till the end of the season, playing second base and wisely keeping his mouth shut.

McGraw, of course, already knew what he had: the beginnings of a fine pitching staff. McGinnity was a proven winner. He was a big, red-haired strongman who had led the National League in innings pitched (347) and wins (29) with Ned Hanlon's champion Brooklyn team in 1900.

Contrary to present-day legend, McGinnity did not obtain his nickname of "Iron Man" through the durability of his arm. Rather, when he first came to pitch in New York he already had the nickname. It was a relic of his minor league days with Kansas City, where a writer had asked him what he did in the off-season.

"I work in a foundry," McGinnity had replied. "I'm an iron man." There it was. Iron Man Joe. As simple as that. There was nothing simple at all, however, about the other half of the pitching staff: Christy Mathewson.

Mathewson was a glaring contradiction to what a baseball player was expected to be in 1900. In an age when the game was dominated by rough-hewn, hard-driven, working-class Irishmen, such as McGraw and McGinnity, Mathewson was an educated middle-class boy from a comfortable Pennsylvania home. His mother was affluent — if not actually wealthy — and his father was a gentleman farmer. Both parents had been born in England. While the rest of Mathewson's generation was learning the fundamentals of baseball in rock-and-bottle-strewn sandlots or on remote farms in the Midwest, Mathewson was sharpening his skills, both pitching and academic, at Keystone Academy, a polished private school for boys. Then, while other young men were scratching their way up the minor league ladder, Mathewson matriculated at Bucknell University, where he became a star at football, basketball, and baseball.

Fate had a way of smiling on Mathewson, then deserting him. One of the times it smiled was the summer of 1899. Mathewson had taken leave of Bucknell to play minor league hardball against the kids coming up the tough way. He signed with a team in Taunton, Massachusetts, where he was 5–2. There Matty met a pitcher named Virgil (Ned) Garvin.

Garvin was six years older than Mathewson and had knocked

around the minor leagues for several years. Garvin, who had pitched in two games for Philadelphia in 1896, was looking for a ticket back to the big time. He knew what the ticket could be: a trick pitch he was working on. The pitch was a reverse curve, thrown by snapping the wrist to the left instead of the right when the ball was released. Thrown by Garvin, when the pitch worked, the ball would break *in* on a right-handed hitter and *away* from a left-hander, just the opposite of a traditional curveball. (Years later, perfected by left-handed pitchers from Carl Hubbell to Tug McGraw and Fernando Valenzuela, the pitch would be known as a "screwball.")

It was at Taunton that summer that Mathewson first saw the pitch and first started working on it. Garvin did ride a so-so version of the pitch back to the major leagues for six undistinguished seasons. Mathewson, however, coupled a snappy fastball and a respectable sweeping curve with his new weapon, known as "the fadeaway." The next summer Mathewson pitched for Norfolk of the Virginia League. There the fadeaway caused batters to do exactly that. The ball would approach the plate in key situations and then fade away from where it was expected to go. Mathewson was so out of his class that Andrew Freedman purchased his contract for the Giants.

Straight to stardom from here? Well, no.

In the minor leagues Mathewson had depended as much on his other pitches as the fadeaway, which still didn't always behave. When he joined the Giants in mid-1900, his curve was hit hard. He pitched thirty-four innings in six games, mostly in mop-up relief. His ERA was 4.76 and his won-loss mark was 0–3.

There followed one of the murkier and more memorable player transactions of that or any other era. Mathewson was returned to Norfolk during the 1900 season. Within a few days, he was purchased by Cincinnati, then owned by John T. Brush. Brush held Mathewson's contract for six months, then traded him back to the Giants for Amos Rusie.

Looked at from either angle, the deal appeared queer. Rusie, the workhorse of the Giant staff in the 1890s, had 243 career wins. Why peddle him for a kid who had barely gotten anyone out in six games? The answer to that was that Brush thought Mathewson had great stuff. Rusie, on the other hand, was at loggerheads with Andrew Freedman again and had held out for both the 1899 and 1900 seasons. He had also pitched 3,747 innings over his last nine seasons, throwing mostly fastballs — and a lot of them each game. Rusie, rumor had it, was "pitched out."

The Giants of The Polo Grounds

Why, then, did Brush want Rusie? He didn't.

Brush already knew he was on his way to New York and *that* was where he wanted Mathewson. In the meantime, however, he wished to safeguard his contract before Andrew Freedman could double-cross him.

That brought Mathewson back to New York for the 1901 season, where he won 20 games in spite of everything. Mathewson already knew how to throw. When John J. McGraw took over the club, one of his top priorities was to show Matty how to pitch. Mathewson, of course, from the very start was more than the sum of his pitching parts. Mentally, he was as sharp a young man as ever came to the game. He was, it was widely believed, the possessor of a photographic memory and could prove it at checkers, playing and winning up to eight games simultaneously against worthy opponents. He was equally proficient at chess and cards and was an avid reader. In a day of boorish, almost brutish behavior on the professional ball field, Matty didn't swear, rarely smoked or drank, and — *gasp!* — didn't beef with umpires. He was a devout Methodist and announced early in his career that he preferred not to pitch on Sundays, a wish that John McGraw (who, not surprisingly, was a religious man in his own way) would always respect. In time, he would become exactly what the image-conscious National League most needed: a stellar athlete of impeccable personal behavior, an example to be put before the adults and children of the nation.

In the meantime, however, he was an integral part of John McGraw's plans for 1903.

Chapter 17   Down and Out With The Tammany Tiger

"As a Chief of Police, [Bill Devery] is a disgrace,
but as a character, he is a work of art."

Lincoln Steffens

Over the winter, Andrew Freedman finally completed the sale of the New York Giants to John T. Brush. Freedman's influence in the city was on the decline. Tammany Hall's candidate for mayor, the incumbent Robert A. Van Wyck — for whom the ever-cluttered present-day expressway is named — had accidentally lost the election to an earnest reform man named Seth Low. Even worse from the Tammany standpoint was the election of a reform district attorney named William Travers Jerome, formerly a fine trial lawyer and an avowed enemy of the Tammany crooks. With this unappealing vision at City Hall, Boss Croker took an extended vacation in Europe (his first since the last reform mayor was elected) and Freedman decided to retreat to his Red Bank, New Jersey, estate, a less convenient address for process servers.

Freedman never ceased being a contrarian, however. As years passed, the horror seized him that during the financial panic of 1907, he had almost lost his entire fortune. Thinking things over, he developed a charitable trust to build a home for older individuals who had lost their fortunes, a comfy place where they could enjoy their dotage or their retirement, or both. So when Freedman died in 1915, he bequeathed money to build the auspicious Andrew Freedman Home at 1125 Grand Concourse in The Bronx, not too far from where Yankee Stadium would rise.

The home was intended to serve as a final residence for "aged and indigent persons of both sexes," who had once been in good shape financially. Each resident would live at the Andrew Freedman Home rent free. There would, of course, be free servants.

The home functioned for many years until the endowment ran down to nothing. Thereafter, the building took many forms. Today, it is a New York City Designated Landmark. It serves as a day care center and an event space, often with some interesting exhibits by local artists. Things could have turned out worse.

The Giants of The Polo Grounds

Brush financed the purchase of the New York Giants in 1903 by pawning off his bankrupt Cincinnati franchise on the Brothers Fleischmann — Max and Julius — whose family had made a gloriously inflated fortune in yeast. The brothers hoped that an influx of cash would — if you'll pardon the expression — cause the affairs of the club to rise in much the same manner.

Of even greater significance, however, was the arrival in New York over the winter of 1902–3 of the American League. In the first season of competition between the American and National Leagues, the Senior Circuit had outdrawn its upstart little brother by about 600,000 paying customers. But in 1902, basking in bad publicity, the National League had lost 200,000 of its own paying customers and had been outdrawn by 250,000 by Ban Johnson's loop. With both leagues in the mood for peace, an agreement came into effect in January of 1903. By its terms, a New York franchise would be established in the American League and Pittsburgh would stay in the National League with no competing club. Some blood was pumped into the motionless corpse of the Baltimore Orioles — and the club was transferred to New York.

There they were known politely as the Highlanders, primarily because one of the seven stockholders, and the club's first president, was Joseph W. Gordon. The Gordon Highlanders were the best-known regiment in the British Army. The motif was further enhanced by the team's eventual playing grounds, a ramshackle, hastily constructed park in the "highlands" section of Manhattan at 168th Street and Broadway. The park was known as Hilltop Park and occupied the site upon which the Columbia-Presbyterian Medical Center today stands.

Joseph W. Gordon, not entirely by coincidence, was the brother-in-law of John Day, the Giants' founder. If you're wondering the obvious, why Tammany Hall finally stopped shooting public

boulevards through any potential American League playing field,

The Giants of The Polo Grounds

the answer is equally obvious. Tammany's power was diminished, but not entirely deflated. The American League finally moved into Manhattan by cutting the proper deal. All seven Highlander stockholders had impeccable Tammany credentials.

Gordon, for example, was the New York City Inspector of Buildings, a position profitable far beyond the measure of its official salary. Another was Thomas F. McAvoy, a former police inspector who was now a private building contractor. McAvoy was also the Tammany Democratic leader for the Twenty-Third District, in which-by startling coincidence, the new team would play its home games.

Even more fragrant, however, were Frank Farrell, the vice president of the team, and William (Big Bill) Devery, a minority stockholder. Farrell was, to be blunt, the biggest legal and illegal bookmaker in the city of New York. He was the head of a syndicate that ran two thirds of the hundreds of gloriously sordid pool rooms and gambling halls that pockmarked the city.

While a kid, Farrell, seen here in mid-snarl, had become a bartender at a saloon near the headquarters of Tammany Hall. As he poured the watered-down drinks, Farrell shot the breeze and struck friendships with Boss Croker's warriors and foot soldiers who patronized the establishment. The Tammany brigade liked young Frank and dispensed street wisdom to him.

Eventually, Farrell opened up his own joint at Sixth Avenue and 30th Street, near the heart of the city's notorious Tenderloin district. Not too far away was a breath-takingly corrupt police precinct run by Big Bill Devery Farrell's future co-owner of the New York Americans and possibly the most corrupt man to ever carry a badge in New York City.

William Devery was a tireless collector of the "honest graft" that bloated the bank accounts of Tammany chief "Boss" Richard Croker. Every saloon, betting parlor, brothel, gambling den, dance hall, and other abode of iniquity in the Tenderloin provided Devery and his emissaries in blue with generous protection stipends. Devery then

The Giants of The Polo Grounds

kicked a healthy percentage of the take up to a man called "Big Tim" Sullivan, alternatively called "Dry Dollar" and "The Big Feller." Sullivan was Devery's political benefactor and a Tammany powerhouse second only to Boss Croker himself.

Just how did Big Tim fit in?

Timothy Daniel Sullivan – seen here looking at you suspiciously across a century - controlled Manhattan's Bowery and Lower East Side districts as a prominent leader within Tammany Hall. He amassed a large fortune as a businessman running vaudeville and legitimate theaters, as well as nickelodeons, race tracks, and athletic clubs. Imposing of stature, gruff but charming, he was a man who could hold a drink, or several of them, and, though married, romance many of the female stars of his theatrical productions.

In 1911, Sullivan pushed through the legislature the Sullivan Act, an early gun control measure. He was also a strong supporter of organized labor and women's suffrage. In retrospect, he was a bad guy who embraced what history has judged to be good causes.

Sullivan was born in the notoriously violent slum of Five Points in lower Manhattan to immigrants from County Kerry, Ireland. His father, a Union veteran of the American Civil War, died of Typhus in October 1867 at age thirty-six.

Five Points was a 19th-century neighborhood in Lower Manhattan, New York City. The neighborhood was generally defined as being bound by Centre Street to the west, the Bowery to the east, Canal Street to the north, and Park Row to the south. Through the Twentieth Century, the former Five Points area was gradually redeveloped, with streets changed or closed. The area today is occupied by the Civic Center to the west and south.

At age eight, Sullivan began shining shoes and selling newspapers in lower Manhattan. By his mid-twenties, he was the part or full owner of six saloons, which was the career of choice for aspiring politicians. From behind the bar, he gradually built one of New York's most powerful political machines. Sullivan, while still a young man, would control virtually all jobs and vice below 14th Street in Manhattan. His base was his headquarters at 207 Bowery. No one messed with him. Eventually, he was elected to the New York State Assembly and the U.S. Congress.

It did not take long for Farrell and Devery to find each other in the final years of the Nineteenth Century. They became business partners and personal friends, a relationship that thrust Farrell into Big Tim's orbit. By means now impossible to confirm but easy to surmise, Farrell parlayed his association with Sullivan and other Tammany bigwigs into a quick fortune. By the turn of the century, Farrell was New York City's "Pool Room King," with dozens of off-track betting spots under his control. He also became a principal of the protection syndicate that was said to scam two to three million dollars a year.

To no one's surprise, Devery was one of Farrell's dearest friends. They went back many years together, to the time when Farrell was an aspiring saloon keeper in a popular dive bar at Sixth Avenue and 30th Street. Devery was the lumbering uniformed captain of a police precinct that shared the same block. That Farrell's den of vice was never closed down by the gendarmes is a foregone conclusion. The two men rose through the city's nether region almost as a tandem.

Let us consider Devery for a moment.

Big Bill was a major figure in Turn of the Century New York. As a flamboyant and notoriously corrupt police official, a Tammany Hall bagman and district organizer, Devery was a frequent target of reform politicos and their allies in the press. He was more than casually corpulent: he stood six feet tall and weighed, when he could find a scale to accommodate him, 260 pounds. His face was florid. He sported a luxuriant mustache. He was a chain smoker of stinky cigars. His passions for food, liquor, late hours and loose women were local legends.

Devery was a product of Manhattan's Lower East Side, the pugnacious son of Irish Catholic immigrants. His adult working life began as a bartender in seedy various Bowery establishments. He also made money on the side as a local club boxer. Eventually, in 1878 at the age of 24, he found a place where his predilections for brawling and corruption would be a perfect fit: in the notoriously corrupt police force of New York City of the day.

The Giants of The Polo Grounds

By May 1884, he was promoted to a sergeant. In 1897, thanks to some meddlesome reformers, he was arrested and charged with bribery and extortion. After conviction, he was dismissed from the force. He appealed. A friendly judge connected to Tammany Hall ruled that Bill wasn't such a bad fellow. The judge overturned the conviction. Bill went back on his beat to serve the public.

On December 30, 1891, after 13 years on the force, Big Bill rose to the rank of captain. As a police captain he made a memorable speech to his men in which he said, "They tell me there's a lot of grafting going on in this precinct. They tell me that you fellows are the fiercest ever on graft. Now that's going to stop! If there's any grafting to be done, I'll do it. Leave it to me."

The speech was followed by gales of laughter by the men, the deep rich thigh-slapping variety of laughter. It meant that Devery would be the conduit for the distribution of bribes.

The upward trajectory continued. Devery was promoted to inspector on January 7, 1898, and Deputy Chief on February 14, 1898. Devery, corrupt beyond description, was then appointed Chief of Police on June 30, 1898.

Lincoln Steffens was a popular journalist of the day. In 1904, he published a reformist polemic fittingly titled, *The Shame of the Cities*. The book was an anthology of right-thinking articles which Steffens had penned for *McClure's Magazine*. It called out the corrupt political machines in several major U.S. cities. To no one's surprise, New York did not escape mention. Not fondly, Stephens wrote of Devery, "As a Chief of Police, he is a disgrace, but as a character, he is a work of art."

In 1902, *Harper's Weekly* had a political cartoonist named William Allen Rogers. Rogers had succeeded Thomas Nast but could skewer a corrupt individual just as skillfully as his predecessor. Rogers zipped off one titled *The Big Chief's Fairy Godmother*. It showed a sleeping man in a police uniform, unmistakably New York City Police Chief William Stephen Devery, seated on a fire hydrant. A fairy, the old-fashioned kind, with wings decorated with playing card suits held a wand over him to

The Giants of The Polo Grounds

shower him with coins, suggesting that the Commissioner's accounting of his wealth was a fairy tale. Devery was not a fan of the cartoon.

Nonetheless, when Farrell, the bookmaker, and Devery, the crook-of-all-trades, took over their new team in town, The Highlanders needed bodies to form a ball club. The ex-Baltimore franchise didn't have much. Indeed, the league had repossessed it following the Brush-McGraw raid of the previous July and had subsequently turned it over to Joseph Gordon for $18,000. Just before the peace between the two leagues, however, the franchise staged a raid of its own, coming away with at least one man who could pitch, Happy Jack Chesbro of Pittsburgh, one who could hit, Wee Willie Keeler of Brooklyn, and one who could manage, Clark Griffith. Griffith was on loan from Charlie Comiskey of the White Sox, who, like the rest of the owners of the new American League, was anxious for the New York franchise to succeed.

As for Hilltop Park, not a shovel of dirt was overturned until February of 1903, two months before the baseball season would start. Then, in the dead of winter, Frank Farrell suddenly produced a crew of five hundred workmen who were in the employ of McAvoy's construction company. They went to work clearing an area that consisted of rocks, trees, and even a bit of swamp. When shovels were too slow, workers dynamited and blew out approximately thirty thousand square feet of rock and wood. This was hauled away. No sooner was it gone than other workmen reappeared with some nice soft soil that had been pulled out of an excavation site for a downtown subway tunnel, another project underway by McAvoy, the favored Tammany brave. In April, the construction guys poured a cement foundation. On April 18, five days before the season's road opener, a gigantic pile of lumber became a grandstand.

Would miracles never cease? No, they wouldn't. The New York Highlanders opened in Washington, won 3–1 behind spitballer Jack Chesbro, and then continued their road trip until late in May, when they again beat the Washington Senators at their home opener. The score was 6–2. By this time the team was also being called the Hilltoppers, the Porch Climbers, and even the Burglars, the latter a sly reference to the club's ownership. The team would play respectably and finish fourth that year. The name the team would eventually be known as — the New York Yankees — was nowhere in sight. But the American League had

The Giants of The Polo Grounds

arrived in New York with all the subtlety of a mid-afternoon armed robbery.

The year 1903 saw a dramatic shift of fortunes for the Giants, too. The team trained in Savannah, Georgia, that spring. The ballpark was a long hike from the hotel. McGraw permitted his players bicycles, both for training and for transportation. Boys, however, would be boys, even in 1903. When the training exercises turned into frantic races that resembled the Tour de France, McGraw took back the bikes.

Christy Mathewson married a pretty young woman named Jane Stoughton that spring. He had known her from his days at Bucknell, her family being from Lewisburg. McGraw, thirty years old, and Mathewson, twenty-two, knew each other well by this time and proved to the world the attraction of opposites. McGraw, at five-foot-seven, the fiery foul-mouthed little Irishman, and Mathewson, the handsome, rugged, blond, six-foot-two-inch paragon of white Protestant middle-class values, got along perfectly - *so* perfectly that the McGraws and the Mathewsons, a happy foursome, took up residence together when the Giants returned to New York.

The two couples rented a ground floor, seven-room apartment at Columbus Avenue and 85th Street. It was furnished and, by all accounts of the day, was a charming spread. Fifty bucks a month were turned over to the tyrannical landlord. The Mathewsons paid for the food and the McGraws settled the rent and gas bill. The elevated railroad that ran uptown to the Polo Grounds was only a block away. So was Central Park. Best of all, Jane Mathewson and Blanche McGraw were fast friends. The living arrangement allowed McGraw to pour baseball into his prize pupil night and day throughout the season. And, conveniently, neither wife would be left alone during the long summer road trips.

This was the summer when the modern Giants began to move. McGraw had fashioned them into an exciting team by the end of the 1902 season, largely through the force of his own personality. Now they opened to a Brooklyn crowd of sixteen thousand on April 19, a game which New York won, 4–2. A few days later the Giants opened at home to eighteen thousand fans, who watched Joe McGinnity dispatch the Phillies, 6–2. McGraw took aim on Pittsburgh owner Barney Dreyfuss and his champion Pirates, kept a running feud going both on the field and in the sports pages, and drew two whopping crowds, one in May and one in June, of 31,500 and 32,000 to the Polo Grounds for Pittsburgh visits, featuring Jack

The Giants of The Polo Grounds

Chesbro (the future Highlander) and Honus Wagner.

John T. Brush, seeing his investment paying dividends, gleefully hired carpenters to expand the grandstand. But the team drew well on the road, too. It was now John McGraw and the New York Giants. The team was a drawing card.

Heywood Broun, the great sportswriter who covered the Giants for the New York *World* later in the century, once wrote: "I suppose it is an important part of McGraw's great capacity for leadership that he would take kids out of the coal mines and out of the wheat fields and make them walk and talk and chatter and play ball with the look of eagles."

Never was this more dramatic than 1903.

The team surged up to second place, failing to overtake Pittsburgh, but winning more than 60 percent of its games. From the dismal previous season, the team batting average leaped from .238 to .272. Runs scored rose from 401 to 729. Stolen bases, that trademark of scrappy, Baltimore Oriole-style "inside baseball," rose from 187 to 264. Even several players from whom little had been expected were taking on "the look of eagles."

Frank Bowerman, a catcher who had been with Baltimore in the 1890s, was playing a particularly scrappy defense. Roger Bresnahan, who had come to New York in the previous summer's raid, played six different positions and hit .350, the best average of his life and good for fourth in the league. Sam Mertes, a holdover from the Freedman regime who had never distinguished himself before, suddenly led the league in RBIs with 104. And George Browne, a young outfielder whom McGraw had bought from Philadelphia (where he had never hit above .260) in 1902, had blossomed into a star, hitting .313 and scoring 105 runs.

Either McGinnity or Mathewson pitched almost every day. On three occasions, McGinnity pitched and won both ends of doubleheaders, enhancing the Iron Man motif. Sometimes both appeared. They each had two "saves," though that statistic was created decades later. The two hurlers appeared in 100 of the club's 139 games. Between them, they won 61 games, 13 more than the entire Giants' staff had won in 1902.

Mathewson personally beat Pittsburgh eight times in eight games. The constant one-two punch of Mathewson and McGinnity, thrown relentlessly at opponents, paid double dividends. First, paying customers were almost always assured of seeing a Giant ace. And second, Mathewson refined his own art by watching the Iron Man.

From McGinnity, he picked up the idea of the change of pace, putting it in his repertoire along with the big curve, the explosive fastball, and the quixotic fadeaway. Watching the tireless McGinnity, he also learned the science of pacing himself, always leaving something in reserve for that moment when a pitcher *had* to get a man out. "Pitching in a pinch," Mathewson would call it. It was about this time that Sam Crane, the baseball writer and former player whom Freedman had banned from the Polo Grounds, hung a title upon Mathewson, one which would always remain with him.

Big Six was the nickname of New York's most dependable Sixth Fire Brigade. "Mathewson," Crane wrote, "is the Big Six of pitchers."

Muggsy. The Iron Man. Big Six. Some of the pieces were already in place. But McGraw could never be satisfied with a second-place finish. As an improvement it was fine. As a habit, never.

Even before 1903 was out, McGraw was putting the rest of the puzzle together. With access to Brush's checkbook, McGraw made the deals he wanted. He purchased Harry (Moose) McCormick, the leading hitter in the Eastern League, from Jersey City. Then he picked up Art Devlin, a slim, rangy six-footer of a third baseman, from Newark. Devlin would be a fixture at that position, McGraw's old position, for eight years. Like Mathewson, Devlin was a college man, having attended Georgetown University in his native Washington, D.C.

Then, over the winter, McGraw pulled off a coup with his old corporate cousins across the estuary in Brooklyn. McGraw packaged two of his expendable regulars, shortstop Charlie Babb and pitcher Jack Cronin, to Brooklyn for a player cast in McGraw's own image: Bill Dahlen.

Dahlen was known around the league as "Bad Bill," an understated tribute to the pugnacious style with which he played his position. "Now. I have the man I've wanted ever since I've had charge of this team," McGraw crowed when he made the deal. Dahlen, a slick fielder and a skilled batsman, was three years older than McGraw and would be the field leader that McGraw would have been had his leg not been injured. Dahlen, sometime after his arrival at the Polo Grounds, also helped fan the fires of the interborough rivalry.

"It has always been my ambition to play in New York City," announced Dahlen, who had been a regular with the Brooklyn team for the previous five seasons. "Brooklyn is all right, but if you're not with the Giants, you might as well be in Albany." Dahlen's remarks also received considerable attention in Chicago, where the infielder had played for eight years before arriving in Brooklyn.

Then, finally, in a deal that almost seemed like a throwaway at the time, McGraw signed a twenty-four-year-old left-handed pitcher named George (Hooks) Wiltse to a Giants' contract. Wiltse had no major league experience. He would, however play in 339 games for New York over the next eleven years. With that move, McGraw was ready for 1904, and set to take the Giants up one more notch to the top of the standings.

An Artist's Reminiscence – Douglas Cooper

My memories of the Polo Grounds are like those of most who once shared a father's passion for baseball and grew up near New York during the 1950s: a foul ball that I almost caught; a center field with Willie Mays and a depth that made a fastball down the middle a wise defensive pitch; and the huge Knickerbocker above the center field scoreboard—smiling down

The Giants of The Polo Grounds

from under a powdered wig and a colonial hat and holding out a beer-filled glass. But these were not the reasons I drew it when I completed a series of artworks for a show on New York's bridges several years ago.

   I drew it for its location along the Harlem River where the bridge-types all change. It was just below that point where the Harlem River emerges from the Manhattan Schist (the same rock we find in lower Manhattan). The location has prominence. Upriver the bridges are all high arches spanning hilltop to hilltop, with buttressing anchorages in the schist walls below. One is still named "High Bridge" and carried the original aqueduct that brought water to Manhattan from Westchester's reservoirs and made the city possible. Downriver where the Harlem crossed the broader sandy plain of the Bronx and lower Harlem, the bridges shifted to *turn bridges* whose clearance was sufficient for barge traffic and needed turning only for the occasional boat with a high mast.

Douglas Cooper
June 2018

{Editor's Note:} Douglas Cooper is a distinguished American artist who has created many large panoramic murals of cities in the USA and abroad. He is best known for his 120-foot long mural which is now a permanent installation at the Senator John Heinz Regional History Center in Pittsburgh. The work gained acclaim throughout the city and was featured in a documentary on WQED TV. Cooper is a professor of Architecture at Carnegie Mellon University, and has authored two books on drawing: *Steel Shadows* (University of Pittsburgh) and *Drawing and Perceiving* (Wiley).

Print *Coogan's Bluff* © Doug Cooper 2014.

Chapter 18 The First New York Giants Pennant

"There has been only one manager and his name is John McGraw."

Connie Mack

The Twentieth Century, in the form of the internal combustion engine, reared its ugly head on Opening Day, 1904.

Charlie Ebbets, president of the Brooklyn club, hired two large gasoline-powered automobiles to drive through the streets of Manhattan to Madison Square, where they picked up John McGraw and several other executives of the New York Giants. Then the cars crept through the excited crowds that lined Fifth Avenue. The cars continued toward Washington Square, where they turned east, traveled to and across the Brooklyn Bridge, and finally found their way to Brooklyn's Washington Park at 3rd Street and Fourth Avenue.

The day was a Friday, April 15. An early snowstorm in the morning hours nearly thwarted this departure from the old-fashioned horse-and-carriage pregame parade. But by noon the sun was shining, and the snow had melted, perhaps partly due to several hours' worth of hot air released by city officials at pregame ceremonies at Washington Park.

The crowd was estimated at more than sixteen thousand, a record for a baseball game in Brooklyn. The start of the game was delayed until four o'clock in the afternoon by all the hoopla before the first pitch could be thrown. But already there was an edge to a Brooklyn-New York game. The Giants, after all, had surged past Brooklyn the previous season. There were scores to settle.

Brooklyn would be settling none of them this day, however. The sun went under a blanket of clouds right when the game began. A harsh wind whipped up, and baseball was played in near-freezing weather, an April tradition that lasts to this day.

Early in the contest, however, McGraw's men built a pair of runs, Baltimore style.

George Browne singled. Art Devlin, the Georgetown kid, moved Browne to second on a sacrifice. Dan McGann, the big first baseman, singled, scoring Browne. McGann, with McGraw waving wildly from his coaching box at third base, took second on the throw to the plate. Sam Mertes singled two pitches later, scoring McGann. By the bottom of the first, Christy Mathewson had a two-run lead. Though he later batted in a run himself, Mathewson needed no more. The Giants took a 3–1 victory and established the style that would be a hallmark of the 1904 season.

McGraw's legion played before large enthusiastic crowds both home and away. They served notice quickly that they were — despite the presence of strong Chicago, Pittsburgh, and Cincinnati clubs — the team to beat in the National League. The Giants had the best infield: McGann at first, Devlin at third, nasty Bill Dahlen at short, and fleet-footed Billy Gilbert at second. McGraw was all but finished as a player by now, inserting himself into the lineup in only five games all year, mostly a result of juggling or injuries.

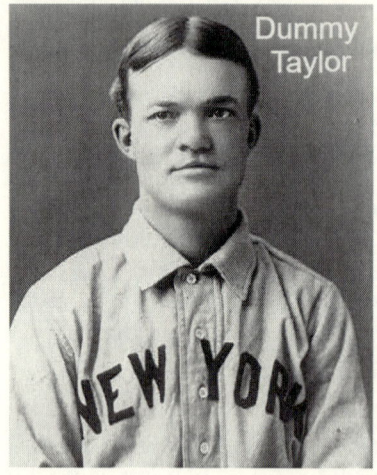

The Giants also had a player who would become the league's best catcher. Roger Bresnahan, known to all as "The Duke of Tralee," began to come into his own. The regular center fielder in 1904, he took over at catcher in 1905. Roger spoke with one of the most charming Irish brogues in the league. Hence his nickname. Never mind that he hailed from Toledo, Ohio. Bresnahan was as Celtic as a shamrock.

Pitching? Of course. McGraw used Mathewson and McGinnity relentlessly again. Mathewson would be 33–12, 2.03, and not even be the number one starter. McGinnity was magnificent, leading the league in wins (35), innings pitched (408), shutouts (9), ERA (1.61), winning percentage (.814), and saves (5), although the latter statistic was not officially kept till decades later.

Yet now McGraw could pick his spots closely with his two aces. Dummy Taylor (who accidentally broke McGraw's nose with a thrown baseball during infield practice earlier in the year) responded to Mac's guidance and amassed 21 wins. Hooks Wiltse, whom no one had been watching, was 13–3. The Giants now had a pitching

The Giants of The Polo Grounds

staff, not just a one-two punch. The achievement of the affable Iron Man was particularly noteworthy. Over the winter he had complained to McGraw that he didn't "feel good." Then he had pitched more than 400 innings for the second year in a row. At one point in 1904, he also put together a streak of 14 straight wins.

McGraw, of course, was always tinkering. Despite the fact that the team was edging out in front of the league, McGraw sensed the need for an extra ingredient: an outfielder who could hit hard, run hard, and shake up a team on the field.

There was one such player in the league who soon became available. His name was Mike Donlin. He played for Cincinnati and was hitting so well that he and Honus Wagner were battling for the batting championship. Donlin was a scrappy, wild-eyed player who was a fan favorite. His problem, such that it was, was that he was one of the great lounge lizards of the era, the undisputed nightlife champ of either league. "Turkey Mike," as he was called for the way he strutted onto a ball field, didn't much care for such trifling matters as training rules and curfews. He also didn't care too much for law enforcement, having spent one six month stretch in the clink for his part in a drunken barroom brawl.

Donlin had driven August (Garry) Herrmann, the president of the Cincinnati team, to utter distraction. Herrmann was so peeved at Donlin that, despite Turkey Mike's rip-roaring batting average of .356, Donlin's name was placed on the waiver list. Herrmann had a deal worked out that would send Donlin to the St. Louis Browns, who were currently wallowing in the second division of the American League. To dispatch Donlin, however, necessitated his clearing waivers. Six National League managers nary raised an eyebrow, such was Mike's reputation for nocturnal exploits. McGraw, however, would rather have his teeth pulled than let an opportunity like this escape.

McGraw did the unthinkable, claiming the feisty Donlin and bringing the league's nightlife champ to New York City. Donlin responded with exactly the type of hard hitting and key base running that McGraw sought. He personally became a factor in keeping the Giants in the lead in the four-way pennant race. As early as July, New York would open a margin of seven full games.

At the end of the previous season, Boston had defeated Pittsburgh in the first modern World Series. The peace agreement between the two leagues stipulated that such a series would continue. New York fans began to speculate on the prospects of Muggsy McGraw taking on his old enemies in the Junior Circuit. A delicious matchup was shaping.

In the American League, much to the consternation of Brush and McGraw, the New York Highlanders were off to a rousing start and engaged the Boston Pilgrims (later known as the Red Sox) in trench warfare for the pennant. But Brush and McGraw still bore some grudges.

On July 27, McGraw himself broke the bubble for a postseason series.

"The Giants," he announced, "will not play a postseason series with the American League champions. Ban Johnson has not been on the level with me personally, and the American League management has been crooked more than once." With monumental contempt, McGraw then dismissed the rival circuit as a "minor league."

"My team will have nothing to do with the American League," McGraw sniffed in conclusion, "and nothing will make me change my mind."

Nothing did.

Lee Allen, the historian at the Baseball Hall of Fame for many years, once wrote that McGraw was a "psychologist without a degree." Definitely. For all the ugly brawls and for all the profanity exchanged with opponents and league moguls, McGraw invariably knew just what to say to one of his own players to elicit the player's best performance. He also knew how much and when.

Two incidents from the 1904 season still stand as shining examples. In an early-season game, Christy Mathewson served up a fastball to Cub center fielder Jimmy Slagle. Slagle rarely hit with power but did hit fastballs well. This one he drove out of the park for one of his two career home runs.

McGraw was livid but said nothing until he was alone with Mathewson the next day. "Don't you know that Slagle murders fastballs?" asked McGraw, barely controlling himself.

"No, I didn't know," Mathewson answered. "Bowerman called for the pitch and I gave it my best."

"Don't ever throw him one again," McGraw said.

Matty never did, and McGraw never brought the point up again.

The other incident also involved Bowerman, who split the catching duties with John Warner that year. Bowerman had encountered a dry spell at the plate as, for that matter, had the entire team. Muggsy was looking for a way to perk his team out of the doldrums. Bowerman, who was normally sullen, was in good spirits in the clubhouse before a game.

"Why the smile?" asked McGraw.

"As I came in today, I saw a team of white horses pulling a brewery wagon past the Polo Grounds," said Bowerman.

"So?" asked McGraw.

"That's a good sign," said the catcher. "Watch me kill the ball today."

Kill it he did, and the Giants won. Bowerman spread the tidings about the white horses around the clubhouse. The next day another player saw them and, superstitious as Bowerman, started whacking the ball, too. Then the next day a third player saw them and so on, until the Giants were devastating any pitching they saw.

"Funny," shortstop Bill Dahlen finally remarked, "how that same team of horses goes past the Polo Grounds just when we're reporting for the game. It sure is lucky."

McGraw agreed but remained silent. He had, of course, tracked down the driver of the brewery wagon and the team of horses the day after Bowerman had first seen them. McGraw now paid the man to bring the team of white horses past the park at the same hour every day. By the time anyone suspected anything, however, the Giants were on a roll that carried them through the summer and into the final weeks of the season.

Late in August the Giants went on a western road trip that included games in Pittsburgh, Chicago, and St. Louis. The Giants under McGraw had blossomed into the most hated team in the league by now, characterized in the Pittsburgh newspapers as "rowdy" and "stuck-up." It was a role, that of the arch-villain, that McGraw was careful to cultivate.

"It is the prospect of a hot feud that brings out the crowd," he liked to tell people. McGraw brought out plenty of crowds on the trip. Meanwhile, the team won 12 of the 14 games in the West and returned to the Polo Grounds with the pennant all but mathematically settled.

That final bit of business took place at the Polo Grounds on September 22, 1904, before a beaming John T. Brush and a crowd of twenty-two thousand. The Giants were scheduled to play two games with St. Louis that day. Despite the presence on the roster of four players who could catch — Bresnahan, Bowerman, John Warner, and Bill Marshall — McGraw reached back into the John

The Giants of The Polo Grounds

Day era of the club's history.

Word had reached him that Orator Jim O'Rourke, by this time a successful attorney and minor league baseball executive in Connecticut, longed to take a final spin with his old club. This was exactly the type of misty-eyed romanticism for which the cantankerous, rough-and-tumble John McGraw had a soft spot. So McGraw invited him to sign with the team and catch the first game. Not by coincidence, a win in that contest would clinch a pennant for New York.

O'Rourke, fifty-two years old, received a rousing ovation from his old fans, as well as a three-foot floral horseshoe presented to him before the game. O'Rourke caught all nine innings, rapped out a single in four plate appearances, and scored a run. The Giants won, 4–3. Simultaneously, the Cubs lost to the Phillies in William Penn's sleepy city. Orator Jim had caught the pennant-clinching game, and the New York Giants finished first in the National League for the first time since 1889.

A few blocks away, the Highlanders greeted the final morning of the baseball season trailing Boston by a game and a half, but with a doubleheader scheduled against Boston at home. Had New York won both games, Clark Griffith's team would have a championship in their second year in the league. It was not to be, however.

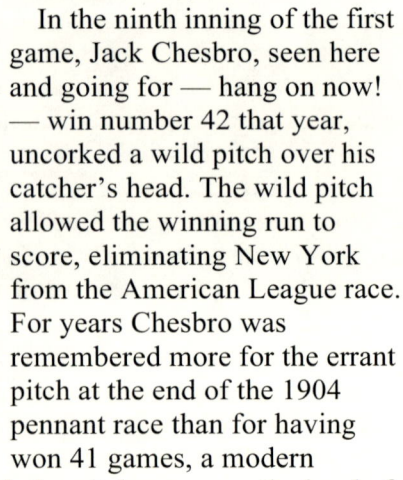

In the ninth inning of the first game, Jack Chesbro, seen here and going for — hang on now! — win number 42 that year, uncorked a wild pitch over his catcher's head. The wild pitch allowed the winning run to score, eliminating New York from the American League race. For years Chesbro was remembered more for the errant pitch at the end of the 1904 pennant race than for having won 41 games, a modern baseball record. Indeed, although the pitch was over the head of Highlander catcher Jack Kleinow, Chesbro's widow, following his death in 1931, conducted a long, unsuccessful campaign to

The Giants of The Polo Grounds

have the official scoring of the play changed to a passed ball.

There was, by the way, an ominous note for Giant management amid the Highlanders' loss that afternoon: Playing in a ramshackle, makeshift park in an inaccessible stretch of Manhattan, New York's American League squad drew nearly thirty thousand people to their park. The crowd overflowed the ballpark and at one point stood fifteen deep behind ropes at the edge of the outfield. Notice was given that New York could be a two team town.

Nonetheless it was the Giants who concluded the year with a championship and a sprawling civic celebration. At Broadway and 45th Street, a special benefit was held at Klaw and Erlanger's Theatre to commemorate the first baseball championship of the Twentieth Century in New York.

Tod Sloan, an elfin little man who was the Eddie Arcaro of his day, was the master of ceremonies. Sloan was one of the greatest thoroughbred jockeys of the day, both in England and the United States. Sloan's success on the racetrack, where he revolutionized the crouching position high up on a mount, combined with a flamboyant lifestyle filled with beautiful women who were a head taller than he, made him a major international celebrity. Sloan palled around with McGraw and Diamond Jim Brady. His reputation, in the United States and England was such that he was the inspiration for *Yankee Doodle* in the George M. Cohan Broadway musical *Little Johnny Jones*, immortalized forever by Jimmy Cagney on screen. Sloan was also the basis for the character of Butler in Ernest Hemingway's short story, *My Old Man*.

Louis Mann, another celebrity McGraw pal and one of the great stage actors of the era, presented McGraw with a pair of diamond-studded cuff links, a symbol of appreciation from the city of New York. Joe Humphries, a young Madison Square Garden sports announcer said to have a "silver voice," presented a large

Jockeys Skeets Martin (left) and Tod Sloan in 1899

The Giants of The Polo Grounds

loving cup to the entire Giants team. Other actors, including Digby Bell, Dan McAvoy, and Gus Edwards, presented skits with star actresses Grace Cameron and Helen Bryon. John T. Brush bought the first and largest subscription box to watch the event, paying $5,000 for the privilege of honoring his own employees.

Though sadly forgotten today, Mann was a major figure of the New York stage at the turn of the Twentieth Century. He played everything from comedy to melodrama to Shakespeare. In 1903, he produced his own starring vehicle, *The Consul*. Shortly after, appearing with a smart, lovely lady named Clara Lipman, he fell in love with his co-star.

Lipman, also sadly forgotten today, was a gifted actress and writer. Mann would collaborate with her for the rest of her career. Lipman wrote twenty-two plays and was frequently on Broadway. Mann and Lipman were best known by audiences of their time their memorable performances in *The Laughing Girl, The Strange Adventures of Mrs. Brown, The Girl from Paris, The Telephone Girl,* and *All on Account of Eliza*, major hits. *The Telephone Girl* was a farce, translated from the original French version. The play made its New York debut at the Casino Theatre on December 27, 1897. Clara starred as a zany chick named "Estelle Cookoo." Mann portrayed a dude called "Hans Nix." It was a sexy farce. The critics slammed it, but what did they know? Audiences loved it. Mann and Lipman later went on the road with it during an extensive tour of North America. As a husband-wife team, they were also active in the women's suffrage movement.

At the special benefit at Klaw and Erlanger's Theatre, the public bought another $20,000 worth of tickets. The receipts were divided evenly among the among the New York players.

(Photo. Louis Mann and Clara Lipman.)

There had been talk, once Brush and McGraw had dismissed

the idea of playing the American League champions at the end of the season, of reviving the Temple Cup format, with the Giants playing a series against second-place Pittsburgh. The idea never took off, however.

There were also some mutterings among Giant players that a series would be played with Boston anyway. It would be organized by the players, the story went. One Giant was quoted both prominently and anonymously in several sporting pages. "Our manager is not afraid of playing anybody. He's being held back by the powers that be."

That meant Brush. It's possible that his hefty and well-publicized donation to the October 2 benefit was an attempt to sooth whatever feathers were ruffled among his champions.

But the 1904 World Series never took place. The players would have to wait for another year to meet the American League. McGraw had built a winner, and — if anything — the 1904 edition of the team had prepared the way for the great squad of 1905.

Chapter 19   A Second Pennant

"I have seen McGraw go onto ball fields
where he is as welcome as a man with the black smallpox . . .
I have seen him take all sorts of personal chances.
He doesn't know what fear is."

—Christy Mathewson

Buoyed by their pennant winning season of 1904, the young 1905 Giants, McGraw's first great team, were basking in the inevitable glory of their league championship. As the season progressed, McGraw made calculated, carefully orchestrated efforts to bring out large hostile crowds wherever the Giants traveled. The key adjective here was "large."

On Pittsburgh's first visit to New York, McGraw heckled a young Pirate pitcher named Mike Lynch, a Brown University product, until Pirate manager Fred Clarke threatened McGraw in retaliation. The umpires eventually banished McGraw, who refused to leave the premises but, rather, sat inside a closet near the Giants' bench. The eighteen thousand fans at the Polo Grounds went wild when Pittsburgh demanded McGraw's physical removal from the closet.

The next day the New York baseball writers castigated the umpires for picking on McGraw while the newspapers in Pittsburgh bemoaned the unruly crowds in New York. No sooner had this dust settled than McGraw appeared in Cincinnati, goaded the populace over the declining competence of their ball club, and offered to fight everyone in the grandstand. Fortunately, everyone did not accept.

Shortly thereafter, the world of bats and balls was treated to the celebrated "Hey, Barney!" case, again involving Pittsburgh.

Pirates owner Barney Dreyfuss had decided to complicate his life by attending a Pirates-Giants game at the Polo Grounds. Shortly before the official festivities were to begin, McGraw, still in the clubhouse, spotted Dreyfuss talking to friends near the ballpark's entrance.

McGraw appeared on the clubhouse balcony and yelled, "Hey, Barney!" until he not only had Dreyfuss' attention, but that of several hundred bemused fans as well. McGraw then berated

Dreyfuss with: (a) a series of scatological references; (b) the accusation that Dreyfuss controlled certain umpires; (c) the allegation that Dreyfuss had become a deadbeat on thousands of dollars of gambling debts; and (d) a bellicose challenge to wager $10,000 on the outcome of the day's game. Not by coincidence, Mathewson, at the peak of his form, was scheduled to pitch that day.

Dreyfuss attempted to slink away from McGraw, but later formally complained to Henry Pulliam, the president of the National League. "Steps should be taken," Dreyfuss suggested, "to protect visitors to the Polo Grounds from the insults of the said John J. McGraw."

"The said John J. McGraw" naturally took up the cudgels in the newspapers, noting that Pulliam had been Dreyfuss' team secretary in Louisville and Pittsburgh. "We might as well be in Russia," scoffed McGraw. It was an interesting allusion, as McGraw often liked to boast, "With my team, I am the absolute Czar."

Pulliam called a league meeting for June 1 to pass judgment on Dreyfuss' charges. The New York newspapers thundered their support of McGraw. Muggsy himself sensed Pulliam's uneasiness and continued on the attack. He telephoned the league president and bawled him out. Pulliam responded by fining McGraw $150 and suspending him for fifteen days. Once again McGraw had succeeded in creating the Alamo psychology (Us versus The Hostile World) for his fans and players. The New York *Evening Journal* then took up McGraw's cause and collected twelve thousand signatures from New York baseball fans calling on the National League directors to dismiss the charges against McGraw. Meanwhile, McGraw tossed names and insults in every direction, as did John T. Brush.

By this time Dreyfuss was unable to produce any witnesses to the incident that had started all the trouble, and the league directors exonerated McGraw. Then, thoroughly intimidated, they reprimanded Dreyfuss for engaging in a public spat with a manager and further commended Pulliam for his sagacious handling of the matter.

But McGraw wasn't finished. "What about the $150 fine?" he asked.

The fine stood, said Pulliam. And so did the suspension. Like hell it did, answered McGraw.

The Giants were in Boston at the time. Lawyers for the club went into Boston Superior Court and received a restraining

The Giants of The Polo Grounds

order that they slapped on the president of their own league. Mortified, Pulliam sat by as McGraw, strutting around like the cock of the roost, appeared in uniform that very afternoon to command his troops against the Boston team.

In time, the real loser was Dreyfuss. Ever after, in any enemy park in which he appeared, the crowd would merrily chant, "Hey, Barney!" and remind him of the day he tangled with John McGraw.

This, of course, was just a small sample of what went on during the 1905 season. In Brooklyn McGraw tossed a few insults at Charlie Ebbets, who was sitting in a front row box. Ebbets, quite shocked, didn't hear McGraw's exact words. So he stood and asked heatedly, "Did you call me a bastard?"

"No," McGraw answered, loud enough to be heard throughout the field boxes, "I called you a son of a bitch!"

And then, to keep the beat going, McGraw fashioned yet another incident against the Pirates. This one was in Pittsburgh and featured McGraw hurling a baseball at umpire Bob Emslie. Emslie, of all the umpires in the league, was McGraw's least favorite. McGraw always called him, "Blind Bob."

Lest you draw the wrong conclusion, there were some pleasant notes for 1905, plus some first-class baseball on the field. McGraw's friend Hughie Jennings, the old Oriole who later would find fame as Ty Cobb's manager at Detroit, had kept busy in the off-season and had earned a law degree from Cornell University. Eddie Brannick, who would serve the Giants in various capacities for half a century, began work as an office boy for Brush and McGraw. And Muggsy himself would welcome into the league a young umpire named Bill Klem, with whom McGraw would maintain public feuds and a private friendship for the rest of his life.

As for the team itself, it rolled through the league, winning 105 games and losing 48. Matty won 31 of 39 decisions (including his second career no-hitter) and also led the league with an ERA of 1.27. McGinnity and Red Ames won 21 and 22 games, respectively, while Dummy Taylor and Hooks Wiltse each captured 15.

"Turkey Mike" Donlin was the driving force behind the Giants' championship season. He smacked 216 hits, good for that .356 average, a career year. He led all Major Leaguers by scoring 124 runs. McGraw loved Donlin's aggressive manner of playing the game.

The Giants of The Polo Grounds

It was a year of dead baseballs but lively feet as the Giants led the league in home runs, a mere 39, and stolen bases, an astounding 291. Pittsburgh, who eventually finished second, nine games back, were knocked out of the race in late September. The Giants went into St. Louis on October 1 and methodically blew out the Cardinals, 9–2, with most of the runs coming in the first two innings.

The win clinched the pennant. This year, however, there would be a World Series.

Waiting for the Giants at the end of a long, contentious season were the Philadelphia Athletics, co-owned and managed by the saintly, unflappable, genteel Connie Mack, the perfect foil for the rambunctious John McGraw.

On Connie Mack's squad was a big ingratiating free spirit of a pitcher named George Edward (Rube) Waddell. Rube was the name hung on him by the sportswriters. His friends called him Eddie. Connie Mack called him the best pitcher he managed in his sixty-four years in baseball, as well as his biggest headache.

Waddell was the Athletics' best pitcher that year. A strapping left-hander from the coal region near Punxsutawney, Pennsylvania, home of the famous ground hog. Waddell distinguished himself with 26 wins and 4 saves and led the league with 287 strikeouts and an ERA of 1.48. He also drew attention to himself with off-the-field behavior that angered his teammates and convinced many rational observers that he was crazy. Still other observers knew what Mr. Mack and his teammates knew but didn't talk about: Rube liked to take a drink now and then.

In 1903, for example, Waddell took time off from a 22-win season to jump the team and go fishing. He had a passion for fire engines and was known to leave the ballpark to chase one. On another occasion, when Connie Mack ordered him into a game as a relief pitcher, Waddell was found under the grandstand playing marbles with a group of boys. All of this, however, pales with the time that Connie Mack, trying to get an angle on how to handle him, promised him three days off to go fishing if Waddell pitched a doubleheader.

Waddell did, but with his own flourish. He pitched seventeen innings against the Chicago White Sox, won his own game with a triple, did handsprings from the mound to the bench after the

The Giants of The Polo Grounds

last out, then returned to throw a 1–0 shutout in the nightcap.

Tall, acetic, dour Connie Mack put up with many things over the course of his long career, but Waddell was *sui generis*, Normally, Mack tried to grin and bear it, figuring that it was God's chosen order that a manager would have to endure a little hardship for such a talented pitcher. Mr. Mack was *not* amused, however, by an incident involving the irrepressible Waddell on the eve of the 1905 World Series.

Waddell had "declared war" on the fashionable straw boaters worn by many men. Rube liked to grab 'em and smash 'em, this being Waddell's idea of a good joke. One that he tried to smash was on the head of one Andy Coakley, a Holy Cross University graduate who had found post academic employment as a member of Connie Mack's pitching rotation. Coakley was an intelligent young man who had just won 20 games — a third of his career victories — and who would later become Lou Gehrig's baseball coach at Columbia University. On the day that Rube Waddell spotted the boater on his head, he was standing on a train platform in Providence, Rhode Island.

All things being equal, Coakley did not want his boater smashed. When he resisted Waddell, some horseplay ensued. Waddell fell backward over a suitcase and smashed his left shoulder against the door of a train. He pitched in pain for the last month of the baseball season. When his performance "slipped," Mack accused him of malingering. As the shoulder became worse, however, the team sawbones convinced Mack that Waddell's injury was serious. The docs also said that Mack could kiss Waddell good-bye for the 1905 World Series.

One story surfaced to the effect that New York gamblers had bribed Waddell to stay out of the Series. Rube was hot when he heard that one. Waddell was a flake, yes, but a crook, no. He indignantly answered that he would "serve the gamblers' interests better and quicker by playing" than by remaining on the sidelines.

Such logic prevailed. The rumors disappeared.

The Athletics won a coin toss held in New York and would be allowed to open the Series in Philadelphia. New York and Philadelphia were the two largest cities in the United States and the matchup captivated the public from coast to coast. The city of Philadelphia was even roused from its normal slumber by the invasion of John McGraw's ruffians. To keep public spirit directed in the right way, and to sell newspapers, the Philadelphia *North*

The Giants of The Polo Grounds

American hung a huge "victory gong" west of City Hall at 15th and Market streets. The gong would peal once for an Athletics' double, twice for a triple, and three times for a home run. McGraw didn't shy away from puffing up his own guys with psychological games, either.

"In my opinion," Muggsy announced before the Series even began, "the Giants of 1905 can do anything the champion Orioles of 1894, 1895, and 1896 did, and have a shade on them besides."

Then, playing the role of the villain, McGraw outfitted his brigade in striking new uniforms: an imposing pitch-black with white trim, white caps suggestive of the bad-assed 1880s, and huge block letters NY across the fronts of the jerseys.

"I will never forget the thrill I got," McGraw confessed years later, "when the Giants trotted out from their dugout clad in uniforms of black flannel. Hundreds of Giant fans had escorted us to Philadelphia. Giant rooters were all over the place."

McGraw, getting a little pudgier in his nonplaying role, looked like an early-day Darth Vader in his black uniform. But he was already one up on the opposition. Compared with the Giants, the Athletics, wearing the dirty, tattered uniforms that had seen them through the American League season, looked like losers.

There was a unique footnote to the splendid 1905 season, both sporting and literary.

McGraw had a young outfielder on the team in June. His name was Archie Graham. He was the son of parents who were both college graduates and was well educated, himself. He had played baseball at the University of North Carolina at Chapel Hill, then in the minor leagues at Charlotte, North Carolina, Nashua, New Hampshire, Lowell, Massachusetts and Manchester, New

The Giants of The Polo Grounds

Hampshire. He had started the 1905 season with the Binghamton Bingoes in the Class B New York State League, but the New York Giants, had purchased his contract. He reported to the team in May but was stuck on the bench.

On June 29, the Giants were pounding the Brooklyn Superbas 10–0 at Washington Park in Brooklyn. McGraw started to empty his bench in the fifth inning. At the end of the top of the eighth inning, Graham replaced George Browne in right field. In the top of the ninth inning, Graham was on deck when Claude Elliott flied out to end the inning. Graham went back to the outfield to finish the game in right field. No ball was hit anywhere near him.

Shortly thereafter, Archie was shipped back to the New York State league as the Giants, with a tight eighteen-man roster, went on to win the pennant and the World Series. He continued with his medical studies away from the ball park. Graham completed his medical degree from the University of Maryland in 1905. While there, he had also played on the university's 1904 and 1905 baseball teams.

Doc Graham never played in the majors again. He did practice medicine, however. His first residency was at the Chicago Ear and Throat Hospital. Not long afterwards, he went to a medical conference in Rochester, Minnesota. There he heard about the wonderful fresh air of the Iron Range Mountains. Impetuously, he resigned from his post in Chicago and took a train into Minnesota, going as far as the last station on the rail line. As if driven by fate, or destiny, Graham stepped down onto a platform at Chisholm, Minnesota.

Doc Graham discovered that several weeks earlier most of Chisholm had been destroyed by a raging fire. Eventually, he found the local hospital. The hospital had no doctor. Graham then announced that they had one now. Graham became the trusted physician to the immigrant miners and their families who had come to America from Eastern European countries like Croatia and Serbia. Graham had found his calling in life. He wasn't moving.

He married a local woman and started a family. In August and September of 1910, a typhoid epidemic spread through the Chisholm area. Thanks in part to Graham's numerous precautionary measures, the town had a lower death rate than most others in the area. The same happened during a polio epidemic in later years. Dr. Graham also was the doctor for the town schools. For years he made and fitted eyeglasses at no charge to local students.

Graham stayed in Chisholm as a physician for fifty-four years, until his death in 1965.

The end of the story for Archibald Wright Graham, M.D.?

No way.

As an underused scrub on McGraw's 1905 Giants, Graham had two nicknames on the team. One was "Doc," for obvious reasons. The other came from a note in The New York Evening *World* a few weeks after his acquisition by the Giants. The paper wrote, "Dr. Archie Graham, who is to join the Giants as soon as he completes his examinations at the Baltimore Medical College, is known as 'Moonlight' because he is supposed to be as fast as a flash."

In the 1970's, an aspiring Canadian English professor and aspiring writer named William Patrick Kinsella, later known as W. P. Kinsella, was passing time in the Devil's Workshop by browsing through *The Baseball Encyclopedia*. He came upon the bizarre entry for "Moonlight Graham" who played in one game but had no statistics and never played again.

Kinsella noted Moonlight Graham's nova of a career, contacted some people who remembered the real-life doctor and recreated a fictionalized Graham as a character in his 1982 novel, *Shoeless Joe*, the late Mr. Kinsella's first novel and finest work.

Enter, Hollywood, with lawyers, typewriters and money.

Shoeless Joe became the movie *Field of Dreams*. Kevin Costner became a star, playing Ray Kinsella, the author's alter-ego. Burt Lancaster, not long before his own death, played the aging Moonlight Graham.

In the film, the Kevin Costner character speaks to Moonlight Graham in dialogue written by writer-director Phil Alden Robinson.

"Fifty years ago, for five minutes you came this close… It would kill some men to get so close to their dream and not touch it. God, they'd consider it a tragedy."

Moonlight replies, "Son, if I'd only gotten to be a doctor for five minutes … now *that* would have been a tragedy."

Chapter 20 The First World Championship

"Mathewson was the greatest pitcher who ever lived. He ad perfect control and form. It was wonderful to watch him pitch when he wasn't pitching against you."

Connie Mack

Before Game One of the 1905 World Series, McGraw and Lave Cross, the captain of the Philadelphia Athletics, met at home plate with the two umpires assigned to the series, Jack Sheridan and Hank O'Day, the old Giants' pitcher from the 1890s. (O'Day, with his back to you here and with McGraw in his black uniform to O'Day's right, by this time had picked up the nickname of "Tank" O'Day, a not-so-subtle allusion to his beer guzzling.) When a discussion of ground rules was complete, Cross reached into his pocket and pulled out a miniature white elephant. He handed it to McGraw. The game would take place at The Columbia Avenue Grounds, which occupied the block bordered by 29th Street, Oxford Street, 30th Street, and Columbia Avenue (a thoroughfare in North Philly since renamed Cecil B. Moore Avenue, in honor of the local civil rights leader).

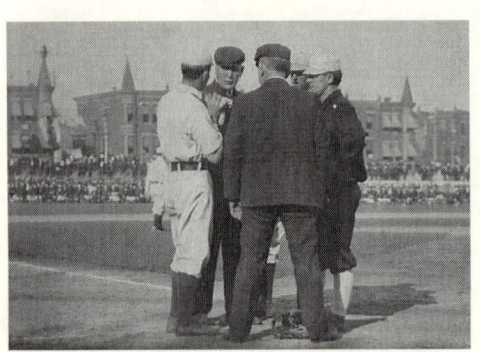

Three years earlier, when asked about the future of an American League team in the Quaker City, McGraw had answered with his usual sweeping contempt. "Connie Mack will have a white elephant on his hands," Muggsy had said. The Athletics had taken on the white elephant as a team symbol and on this day had even put one into McGraw's palm. McGraw accepted it graciously. With equal grace over the ensuing century, the elephant has adorned the A's uniform and logo, following the franchise to Kansas City and Oakland.

The Giants of The Polo Grounds

Then, looking spiffier than ever in his new black uniform, Christy Mathewson took the mound in Game One. He was opposed by Eddie Plank, an old college rival from Gettysburg University. Plank was currently a consistent 20-game winner for Mr. Mack.

The New York Giants had arrived in Philadelphia earlier that same morning, traveling in a special car hooked onto a regularly scheduled train. In their party traveled a number of New York celebrities from the sports and theater worlds. Among them were two of McGraw's fast friends, Gentleman Jim Corbett, the boxer and brother of the ex-Oriole pitcher, and Louis Mann, the vaudevillian.

But back to baseball. . . .

Game One of the 1905 World Series, played on October 9, took place before an unprecedented Philadelphia crowd of 17,955 at Columbia Park, a ball field located at 29th Street and Columbia Avenue in North Philadelphia. The area was known as Brewerytown for exactly the reasons one might expect. The abstemious Mr. Mack managed from the dugout in street clothes with the smell of hops, fermented barley, and fresh beer everywhere around him, including the breaths of fans and players.

Game One proceeded scoreless into the fifth inning. Thereupon Mathewson started a rally with a single. Roger Bresnahan forced him at second base, but then stole the base and came home when Turkey Mike Donlin, always a dangerous clutch hitter, lined a single to center. Donlin went to second on a throw to the plate, then scored when Sam Mertes doubled. The Giants added a run in the ninth, but Mathewson already had what he needed. He shut out the Athletics on four hits, three of them doubles, a small concession to the noisy early version of *The Gong Show* going down on Market Street.

The show shifted back to the Polo Grounds the next afternoon. A crowd of 24,992 enthusiastic souls packed John Brush's ballpark, seen here during the 1905 Series, looking for more of the same.

They got it, with Iron Man McGinnity opposing Connie Mack's greatest "money pitcher," Charles Albert (Chief) Bender. Bender

The Giants of The Polo Grounds

was a full-blooded Ojibwa Native American who always seemed to win when it counted. "If everything depended on one game, I just used Albert, the greatest money pitcher of all time," Mack once said of Bender. "I'd tell Albert when I planned to use him in a crucial series. Then I relaxed. He never let me down."

This day proved Mr. Mack's point. Bender, who pitched for Mack for the Philadelphia Athletics from 1903–14, then later again after a defection to the Federal League, threw a gem. The Philadelphians reversed the outcome of Game One, winning 3–0. To McGraw's horror, sloppy fielding contributed to the scoring.

A day off followed. Then Mathewson opposed Andy Coakley in Game Three in William Penn's snoozing town. This one was no

match. Mathewson had mastered the fadeaway by this time, giving it a great deal of spin with tight finger pressure, then releasing it.

The ball would appear to be traveling much faster than it really was, then break the wrong way. The Athletics had never seen the pitch before. They weren't seeing much of it on this day, either. Seven unearned runs on four errors sabotaged Coakley. Mathewson spread four singles over nine innings. The Athletics never scored. The Giants coasted, 9–0.

Just as the momentum of the Series had shifted back to New York, so did the Series itself and the army of fans who followed it back and forth. Baseball excitement gripped Manhattan for Game Four on October 13. Newspapers were filled with accounts of packed hotels and restaurants. McGinnity pitched again, this time against Eddie Plank.

Plank deserved a better fate. Neither pitcher gave up an earned

The Giants of The Polo Grounds

run. In inning four, Sam Mertes, the Giants' left fielder, bounced a tricky roller to Lave Cross, the Athletics' field captain and third baseman. Cross fumbled the ball. Mertes advanced to second on an out, then scored on a single. McGinnity's big sweeping curveball mystified the Athletics all day. The Giants won, 1–0. Before one of the games in New York, a team picture was taken: missing was Christy Mathewson who no doubt was warming up.

(Public domain Photo Courtesy of Wikipedia; 1905 NY Giants, left to right: Left to right: Sam Mertes, William "Boileryard" Clarke, George Browne, George "Hooks" Wiltse, Art Devlin, Claude Elliott, Dan McGann, Mike Donlin, Billy Gilbert, Luther "Dummy" Taylor, Bill Dahlen, Sammy Strang, Joe McGinnity, the team mascot, Roger Bresnahan, "Red" Ames, John McGraw.)

McGraw came back with his ace, Mathewson, the next afternoon in New York. Before 24,817 howling, ecstatic customers at the Polo Grounds, the great Matty pitched his third shutout in six days. New York scored a run without a hit in the fifth inning and Mathewson scored a run himself in the eighth. Mathewson went to the ninth inning firmly in control of a 2–0 lead. He had pitched twenty-six innings in six days and he was still tinkering with the champions of the other league: Bris Lord of the A's bounced a ball back to Mathewson. So did Harry Davis. Lave Cross grounded weakly to shortstop. Then it was over. The final game had taken a little more than ninety minutes and the Giants had won their first World Series, four games to one. Donlin had been the star of the show after Mathewson. In the first game, he drove in the Giants' first run, all that Christy Mathewson needed to win Game One, and scored three times in the Game Three rout as the Giants took the title in five games.

Pandemonium reigned at the Polo Grounds. Fans charged onto the field and attempted to carry the players to the clubhouse in right center field. A band struck up a victory march and hundreds of fans danced around the infield. Seat cushions flew from the upper grandstand down onto spectators in field boxes who

The Giants of The Polo Grounds

joyously flung them back. Some of the Giants eventually appeared on the second floor porch of the clubhouse, the same porch from which McGraw had berated Barney Dreyfuss earlier in the season. They tossed caps and gloves to the fans who refused to leave the park. Predictably, a wild scramble for souvenirs followed. That evening the spirit of celebration spilled over into the restaurants and saloons of the city, lasting until the following dawn.

Much has been written over the last eighty years on the subject of Mathewson's pitching in the 1905 World Series. But his line in the composite box score probably is the most eloquent statement to have appeared: 27 IP, 0.00 ERA.

He also hit .250 in eight trips to the plate. The Athletics' team batting average for the Series was .161. Years later, toward the end of his long managerial career, McGraw also uttered a definitive word on Big Six. "There was never another pitcher like Mathewson," McGraw said. "And I doubt that there ever will be."

For the time being, the New York Giants were the undisputed champions of the world, a mere three years after John J. McGraw had defected from the Orioles and arrived to find them mired in Freedmanism and eighth place.

The hitting stars of the Series had been Donlin (.316), Bresnahan (.313), McGann (4 RBIs), and Mertes (3 RBIs). Each Giant, however, came away with a winner's share of the Series money: $1,142 in cash. There was much that a man could do to entertain himself with $1,142 in the days when good cigar cost two cents.

The victory was also a boost for the National League, which had suffered public humiliation by losing to Boston in 1903 and had been a laughingstock by refusing to play a World Series in 1904.

The Giants of The Polo Grounds

The general mood of the times, however, particularly in New York, could be found on the sporting pages of the New York *American* following the Giants' win. Writer W. E. Kirk penned a parody of Scottish poet Thomas Gray's *Elegy Written in a Country Churchyard*, written in 1750, to see the baseball nuts through the winter.

> *Far from the madding crowd's ferocious yells,*
> *The Polo Grounds will miss the Giants' tricks.*
> *Until a crowd of thirty thousand tells*
> *That we have started season Nineteen-six.*

Chapter 21   Bright Lights, Big City

"**Mabel Hite is one of the cleverest comediennes in the land. Mike Donlin, her husband, has become under Mabel Hite's tuition an interesting stage figure. They will appear in a musical sketch entitled 'Stealing Home.'**"

Variety

As the 1906 baseball season was set to open, the armada of writers who covered the Giants asked McGraw the obvious question: Would the New York Giants repeat as champions?

"Yes," McGraw said.

No qualifications. No conditions. The Giants would repeat and that was all there was to it. McGraw was, to be sure, strutting his stuff by the spring of 1906. He had taken a moribund franchise and recreated it as a smooth, efficient winner at the Polo Grounds so easily that his feat almost looked magical.

Mathewson, rescued from the misguided clutches of Horace Solomon Fogel, he of the questionable wisdom, had thrived under McGraw. So had Bresnahan, McGann, Devlin, McGinnity, and all of McGraw's other shining Celtic knights. With John T. Brush in the background, this was McGraw's team. He deserved much credit for it, took even more credit for it, and, as long as he had it, he flaunted it.

What could go wrong? Two possibilities: anything and everything.

The first sign of trouble? That came in February, when Mike Donlin, that career recidivist, was arrested for leading a band of drunks in some mayhem on a train to Albany that included waving a pistol in a porter's face. Mike avoided jail time when Giants management intervened and made nice with the railroad.

The team trained in Memphis that spring, then the club traveled north to open the season. On the day before the season began, Mike Donlin turned his boozy life around when he married Broadway musical comedy star Mabel Hite. Hite, a Christian Scientist, helped Donlin stop drinking, at least for a while.

McGraw had new uniforms once again. These were cut from the same villainous pitch-black broadcloth that the Giants had worn the previous October. But instead of the bold N.Y. emblazoned across the chest, McGraw's 1906 players wore black uniforms bearing the inscription: WORLD'S CHAMPIONS. This was in a day when the Giants dressed at their hotel and then rode to the game in open horse-drawn carriages. The horses that drew the carriages got in on the fun also, bedecked with woolly yellow blankets bearing the same inscription.

This was showmanship, pure and simple. The Giants were the best draw in baseball, but as usual McGraw never missed an opportunity to enrage the locals in whatever city he visited. In many cases, the Giants' carriages were followed through alien streets by large angry crowds, some of which threw rocks and garbage at the procession. Those same large angry crowds, however, paid their way into the park. This, combined with the healthy gates in New York, enriched the Giants to the point where they could bid competitively for any player they wanted, an advantage they would maintain for the next several decades.

For a while, it appeared as if McGraw's prediction about the 1906 season would be justified. The birth of John Christopher Mathewson, the first child of Christy and Jane Mathewson, augured well for the campaign. But after a quick start in the first four weeks, things suddenly fell apart. Mathewson himself contracted diphtheria and had to be separated from his new family as well as the team. He would eventually pitch nearly a hundred innings less than usual in 1906. Roger Bresnahan was beaned by a pitch, never fully recovered, and batted twenty points lower than 1905. Then Turkey Mike Donlin compounded everything by breaking a leg on a hard slide into third base against Cincinnati. Donlin, who had led the team in batting and had tied for the team lead with 7

The Giants of The Polo Grounds

home runs the previous season, played in only 31 games all season, excluding six pinch-hitting appearances, and hit only one home run.

It got worse fast.

Bad Bill Dahlen, McGraw's feisty shortstop began to slow down at age thirty-six. It should be noted, however, that "slowing down" on the 1906 Giants meant, in Dahlen's case, meant stealing "only" 16 bases, the lowest total of any regular on the team. The 1906 squad was a band of thieves, playing old-style Baltimore Oriole "inside baseball" and compiling an astronomical 288 stolen sacks, though it will be recalled that the Giants stole 291 the previous season.

It is possible that all this made no difference. Nineteen Six was the first great year for the Tinker to Evers to Chance Chicago Cubs who won an astounding 116 of 152 games played before being upset by the crosstown White Sox in the World Series. The Cubs were paced by in addition to the much-celebrated double-play combination, third baseman Harry Steinfeldt (a more effective hitter than his infield partners), right fielder Frank (Wildfire) Schulte, and pitchers Mordechai (Three Finger) Brown (upon whom more later), Jack Pfiester, and Reulbach. The Cubs were a powerhouse and would win pennants four of the next five years.

For the Giants, 1906 was an unusually frustrating year. Mike Donlin took his absence from the lineup as an opportunity to further familiarize himself with the New York night scene. Donlin made noises about taking up an acting career and joining his wife in show biz. Henry Mathewson, Christy's brother (younger by six years), took a turn on the mound for the Giants, losing the only game he started. But as the season drew to a close, McGraw must have sensed the task before him. Already, he would have to rebuild. The Giants won 63 percent of their games, but still finished 20 games behind Chicago.

McGraw was bellicose as ever as he set to this task. In the middle of the 1906 season, he denied admission to the Polo Grounds to Jimmy Johnstone, an umpire for whom he had a heated dislike. In July he unloaded Edward (Doc) Marshall and Sam Mertes to the St. Louis Cardinals for William (Spike) Shannon, a switch-hitting outfielder.

During the off-season he proved correct his critics who claimed Muggsy would fight with anyone or anything: On the evening of January 10, 1907, out for a quiet evening on the town, McGraw rode

The Giants of The Polo Grounds

in a horse drawn carriage with his wife and one other female companion. A trolley and the driver struck his carriage and he was thrown to the sidewalk. The team of horses bolted. McGraw leaped from the carriage, Roy Rogers-style, and was dragged through the mud for two city blocks before wrestling the horses to a halt.

The 1907 season began on much the same note. The Giants trained in Los Angeles, then, before the season started, traveled to New Orleans where a "rematch" of the 1905 World Series was staged with the Philadelphia Athletics.

In the first game, Iron Man McGinnity defeated Jack Coombs. The next day, the series fell apart when Roger Bresnahan, batting against Eddie Plank, claimed that Plank had committed a balk. McGraw supported Bresnahan in a violent argument with umpire Charlie Zimmer. Zimmer ended the argument by ordering the New Orleans police to escort Bresnahan and McGraw off the field and out of the park. McGraw went, but he took his entire team with him, ending the day's festivities with a forfeit.

On the following morning, McGraw announced that the Giants wouldn't play that day either unless Zimmer was replaced. That game, too, turned into a forfeit. Then an "unofficial match" was arranged with a local umpire. The Giants played in that contest, but not very hard. Philadelphia won, 7–0, at which point McGraw forfeited the remaining games.

Later in the same day, McGraw encountered John Shibe, who owned the Athletics, in a hotel lobby and went out of his way to engage Shibe in a noisy name-calling contest. Thereupon, the local newspapers branded the Giants "New York brawlers" and "hoodlums," echoing an opinion in favor around the National League.

The season itself didn't turn out much better. After a contract dispute with McGraw, Mike Donlin went on a vaudeville tour and announced he would sit out the entire campaign.

"He was born on Memorial Day and has been parading around ever since," an angry McGraw said of Donlin.

Then Bresnahan raised eyebrows on Opening Day by introducing shin guards to the National League. When a sharp foul tip rapped off one of the guards in the fifth inning, sparing the Duke of Tralee from injury, the guards had officially arrived. The game, against the Phillies, also came to a bizarre conclusion: When New York fans refused to stop pelting umpire Bill Klem

The Giants of The Polo Grounds

with snowballs, Klem forfeited the game to the Phils.

The Giants would drop to fourth by the end of the year, the lowest finish by a McGraw squad since the dark days of Andrew Freedman. But while the team played over .500 and while Christy Mathewson effortlessly racked up a league-leading 24 wins, McGraw was drawing plans for the future. In July there arrived at the Polo Grounds a dark-haired, handsome kid of twenty years named Larry Doyle.

Doyle was a second baseman whom "Sinister Dick" Kinsella, McGraw's former Cedar Rapids teammate and now his top minor league scout, found playing with Springfield of the Three-I League. In his first game as a Giant, Doyle had made four errors in the field. But McGraw, thinking back to his own rough initiation as a Baltimore Oriole in 1891, sympathized. He also knew Doyle could swing a bat. So McGraw kept him in the lineup.

One cannot let a name like "Sinister Dick" pass without explanation.

Kinsella owned the Springfield team in the Three-I League from 1904 till 1911. At this time, he began his long scouting career by serving as McGraw's one-man scouting staff.

Kinsella "was called Sinister Dick," wrote Tom Meany, who covered baseball at various times, for the New York *Journal*, the New York *Star*, the Brooklyn *the Daily Times*, the New York *World-Telegram* and *the Morning Telegraph*, "because his eyebrows looked like fright wigs."

According to a New Jersey newspaper of the day, Kinsella was a "fastidious dresser, square-topped derby, square-toed shoes, long sack coat, high stiff collar, a heavy gold watch chain across his middle." He was a light-complexioned man with jet black hair and bushy eyebrows. While he was working for McGraw a newspaper wrote of his "gruff ways and beetling brows."

Sinister? It was the eyebrows that did it. If he had been staring at you in a restaurant, you might have chosen to get up and leave.

Which brings us to Larry Doyle, sent to McGraw by his ominous bushy-browed scout.

The word "sinister" was never used for Larry Doyle. But "guileless" was. Frequently.

Doyle was a big, trusting, open-faced kid who earned the name "Laughing Larry" within his first few weeks in New York.

The reputation of his trusting nature circulated quickly around the league, however.

Frank Graham, the veteran cigar-chomping, snap-brim-fedora-clad newspaperman who covered McGraw and the New York Giants for *The New York Journal American* for decades, recalled the first time Doyle came to bat against Brooklyn in July of 1907.

A sly thirty-four-year-old veteran named Bill Bergen was catching.

"You look like a nice young fellow. What's your name?" Bergen asked.

"Doyle, sir."

"Doyle, eh? Do you like it up here in the big leagues?"

"Yes, sir."

"And what do you like to hit?"

"A fastball. On the inside."

"High?"

"No, sir. Not too high."

Bergen squatted behind the plate, flashed signals to his pitcher, and Doyle spent the day flailing at curveballs high and away.

Later that same year, Sinister Dick sent another young man to the Polo Grounds. His name was Fred Merkle, he was eighteen years old, and he too came to New York billed as a second baseman. McGraw tried him out at second, then turned him over to Dan McGann, the veteran who held down first. McGann would be in

The Giants of The Polo Grounds

charge of tutoring his own eventual replacement.

But McGraw wasn't finished. He drafted another infielder named Charles (Buck) Herzog out of the Pennsylvania League. And, for reasons that appeared to be no more than sentimental, McGraw drafted a catcher named Otis Crandall from Cedar Rapids.

McGraw spent the first month and a half of the season battling Chicago for first place. But in June, the Cubs again took over, shutting down the Honus Wagner Pirates and the No-Name Phillies in the process. On a final trip to the western cities, the Giants lost 9 of 13 games.

His team had settled into mediocrity. McGraw seethed.

Then the season ended.

The following spring, McGraw pulled off the first blockbuster trade of his managerial career. One day before the Detroit Tigers of old friend Hughie Jennings were to open the 1907 World Series against the Cubs, McGraw shipped Dahlen, McGann, Bowerman, George Browne, and a seldom-used pitcher named George Ferguson to Boston. In return, McGraw received Boston's manager-first baseman Fred Tenney, a young shortstop named Al Bridwell, and a utility catcher named Tom "Deerfoot" Needham.

The trade was roundly criticized in other National League cities as the type of five-for-three swap that robs the poorer clubs, in this case seventh-place Boston, of their stars. That case could be made. But the fact was that Tenney was thirty-five and slowing down.

Bridwell had only hit .218 and Needham had slugged a whopping .196 with one home run. What was really at work here was McGraw's instinct. Tenney was the field captain he wanted with the demise of Dahlen.

Bridwell, he sensed, was a future star. Needham came along to carry the luggage and replace Bowerman, the extra catcher. Like many roundly criticized trades, this one stuck. And it also prepared the New York Giants for the memorable events of the following year.

Chapter 22   Touching Second...or Not.

**"I wish I'd never gotten that hit that set off the Merkle incident.
I wish I'd struck out. . . . It would have been better all around."**

—Al Bridwell in 1966

i

Unhappy with the Los Angeles training site of the previous spring, John McGraw moved the Giants' 1908 camp to the town of Marlin, Texas. Marlin was a whistle stop that featured hot springs and warm weather. It was — and still is — in the north central part of Texas, not far from Dallas, Fort Worth, and Houston, where large crowds could be counted upon for weekend exhibition tilts.

McGraw lodged his players at the Arlington Hotel, which was Spartan but adequate. The ballpark, located a half-mile's hike down a stretch of train tracks from the hotel, was conducive to serious training. Equally important, the natives were friendly: Texas was one section of the United States where John McGraw and the New York Giants were not viewed as ogres. So the Marlin camp worked out well in 1908. The venue would remain part of the Giants' spring regimen for the next ten years. McGraw had the team cranked up again. Fresh from the personnel moves that had changed the face of the squad, the team got off to an inauspicious start by dumping three out of four games to the increasingly inept Brooklyn team at the Polo Grounds. From that point on, they chased Frank Chance's Cubs through the National League season, playing tag with Pittsburgh at the same time.

Mike Donlin was back. Turkey Mike's initial flirtation with the stage was sated (there would be others later, however) and the outfielder had an excellent season, hitting .334 — second in the league to Wagner again — stealing 30 bases, and leading the club in home runs (6) and RBIs (106). The man had a potential Hall of Fame career, not that there was a Hall of Fame yet, if he could just focus on baseball. Fred Tenney, experienced and smart (he was an alumnus of Brown University where he had also been a left-handed catcher on the college baseball squad), had a steady year at first base. Cy Seymour, the 1905 batting champ who was acquired from Cincinnati in mid-1906, was equally competent in the outfield, as was Art Devlin at third and Roger Bresnahan behind the plate. Then there was the Kiddie Corps: Doyle, Merkle, Crandall, Bridwell, and Herzog. All played like the "eagles" noted by Heywood Broun.

Then there was Mathewson. Perhaps no National League pitcher has ever had a better year. Mathewson was fully healthy again and pitched more than ever before, 390.2 innings. He won 37 games and lost only 12. He allowed only 42 walks the entire season (against 285 strikeouts) and had a supernal ERA of 1.43.

There were also the memorable events, which would build in magnitude over the course of the year. The funny stuff started during an April series in Boston, where there was no love lost between McGraw and Dan McGann, whom McGraw had peddled as part of his housekeeping efforts.

McGraw encountered McGann in the lobby of the Copley Plaza Hotel. McGraw, always pleased to ignite something in a hostile city, called McGann an "ice wagon" — or perhaps something a stronger — for hitting into a double play. McGraw got his hat crushed and his shoulder bruised in the discussion that followed. This, however, was only a warmup for an event that would transpire in Boston in July.

McGraw was sitting in the stands, watching the Giants play. He was under suspension for having called Jimmy Johnstone, one of his favorite targets, "a piece of cheese," or so the newspapers chose to temper the exact words. The Giants had built up a comfortable lead by the third inning. Then it started to rain. The game, the first of two scheduled that day, was called.

McGraw might have ambled back to his hotel without incident, but on his way out, his attention settled upon a fan who was engaged in a dispute with the management of the ballpark. The fan was waving around a rain check, demanding a check that was good for a doubleheader.

The fan was a small fellow. McGraw must have empathized when the Boston club set two large Pinkerton guards upon him. The guards started to rough up the little guy. Out of nowhere appeared Iron Man McGinnity to protect the noisy fan. When McGinnity got into it with the guards, McGraw leaped in. Next, a group of fans entered the fracas on the side of McGraw and McGinnity, and within seconds a full-scale riot was under way. City police were called in. McGraw and McGinnity were arrested and escorted out of the ballpark and out of town. The next day the Boston newspapers tarred-and-feathered the two Giants for starting the riot. It was that type of year.

The Giants drew astride Chicago in the standings in late August and passed them in early September. Then there occurred, on September 4, a game between Pittsburgh and Chicago that proved to be an eerie harbinger of things to come.

Manager-left fielder Fred Clarke of Pittsburgh was on third base and a utility player named Warren Gill was on first in the home half of the tenth inning. The game remained a scoreless tie, with Honus Wagner batting and Three Finger Brown pitching. There were two outs. Brown threw the ball and Wagner launched one of his 3,430 career hits to center field.

The ball landed on the outfield grass, Clarke waltzed across the plate, and Wagner ran to first base. Okay so far. But Gill stopped several feet short of second base and turned toward the clubhouse, assuming the game was automatically over.

Cub center fielder Artie Hofman, seeing this, picked up the ball and threw it in to Johnny Evers, who caught it and stepped on second base, claiming a force-out.

Umpire Hank O'Day, the old Giants pitcher from the 1890s, refused to call the out, claiming that he hadn't seen the play. Evers exploded.

Today the play would be clear-cut, and Gill, forced at second, would have been called out. In 1908, however, despite the fact that Rule 59 of the prevailing rulebook dictated an out call, some umpires ruled that a hit to the outfield was "automatic." The force rule was applied lazily and inconsistently. And on this day in Pittsburgh, Hank O'Day refused to apply it.

The Cubs, badly needing the win to stay in front of both New York and Pittsburgh, argued long and loud, stressing that in a game this important there was no reason to be lax about the rules. O'Day would not be swayed. He left the park without changing his mind.

The Cubs traveled back to their hotel but were still fuming. Team owner Charles Webb Murphy wired an official protest to National League president Henry Pulliam. Murphy demanded that Gill be called out and the game be declared a tie. Pulliam refused. The Pirate victory of 1–0 stood and the Cubs dropped all the way to third place.

The instant replay occurred nineteen days later at the Polo Grounds. Again the Cubs were the visiting club and again Hank O'Day was the umpire stationed at the base paths.

When the sun rose that morning, the Cubs and the Giants were tied for first. The Pirates were a game and a half behind.

There was but a week to go in the season. The Cubs had put themselves back into contention by winning a doubleheader against the Giants the previous afternoon, September 22. Now, on the afternoon of September 23, things were hanging tough.

A huge crowd had filled the Polo Grounds to watch Mathewson oppose Jack Pfiester. So far, the fans were getting their money's worth. Mathewson had held the Cubs to five hits over nine innings and had struck out nine. The only Cub run had scored in the fifth inning when Joe Tinker had homered.

New York, however, was having its problems solving Pfiester. In the sixth, Buck Herzog had singled to third and had taken second when Harry Steinfeldt had thrown wildly to first. Bresnahan bunted Herzog to third. Our pal Mike Donlin then singled Herzog home, tying the game. That's how it remained going into the last of the ninth inning.

The skies were darkening, but there probably would have been time for two or three more innings. Cy Seymour opened the Giants' half of the ninth by grounding out, Evers to Chance. Then Art Devlin singled, putting the winning run on first. The Polo Grounds, silent a few seconds earlier, came alive with rhythmic clapping. The huge crowd sensed a Giant victory and wanted it now.

Moose McCormick followed with another ground ball to Evers. Evers tossed the ball to Tinker, forcing Devlin at second. Up came nineteen-year-old Fred Merkle.

Merkle was in his first major league game as a starting player. He would never have been in the lineup at all had Fred Tenney, the regular first baseman, not awakened that morning with an acute backache. But Merkle surprised and delighted the crowd when he ripped a long single down the right field line. The ball was fair by only a few feet and would normally have been a double. But the Giants were taking no chances. McCormick went to third easily and Merkle stayed at first.

That brought up Al Bridwell, the New York shortstop, with a chance to end the game. Bridwell stepped into the batter's box. He noticed a long lead Merkle was taking at first and stepped out again, sending Merkle back to first. Then Pfiester threw a waist-high fastball and Bridwell connected with it.

The drive was a solid one that sent Bob Emslie, the umpire behind second base, diving to get out of the way. Bridwell sprinted to first and McCormick crossed the plate with what should have been the winning run. Merkle went halfway to second, saw the huge crowd already leaping out of the grandstands and flooding onto the field, and turned toward the clubhouse. In what was to become baseball's most famous lapse, Merkle never touched second base.

Oops. Want to get away?

For the past hundred and ten years, there have been various versions of what followed. Here's the one given greatest credibility.

Cub second baseman Evers, immediately thinking back to the Pittsburgh game of September 4, raced to the outfield and signaled frantically for the ball. Center fielder Hofman chased it down and threw it back, but the ball overshot Evers and bounded toward first base. Enter the Iron Man, Joe McGinnity, coaching at third that day, who saw what Evers was up to. As the ball bounded loose, and as the infield area was overrun by jubilant New York fans, the six-foot Iron Man outwrestled five-foot-nine-inch Joe Tinker for the ball. McGinnity, with Tinker hanging on his back, threw the ball toward the left field grandstand, hopefully into oblivion.

About the same time, *a* ball — but not necessarily *the same* ball — landed near the shortstop position in the infield. Floyd (Rube) Kroh, a second-line Cub pitcher, saw a fan pick it up. Kroh, up until this point, hadn't even been in the game, but rushed after the ball and demanded it from the New York fan. When the fan gave the Cub pitcher a typical New York response, Kroh punched him and repossessed the baseball.

Kroh later claimed that he gave the ball directly to Evers.

McGinnity claimed that he, McGinnity, took the ball back from Kroh and heaved it into the grandstand. McGraw not only claimed that he had witnessed McGinnity's version of events, but also added with justification that since Kroh had never been announced into the game, *any* ball Kroh touched was a dead ball. Nonetheless, as the Giants piled into the clubhouse and celebrated their victory, little Johnny Evers appeared on second base with *a* ball and, just as he had in Pittsburgh, demanded a force-out from Bob Emslie, the umpire on the base paths. Emslie, however, claimed he hadn't seen the play at second. He had been too busy picking himself up and making sure that Bridwell touched first.

But when Emslie asked Hank O'Day, the plate umpire, whether Merkle had touched second, O'Day confirmed that he had not. Then Emslie called Merkle out. And O'Day, making the rulebook call on a force play, disallowed the run. That meant, of course, that the game was still in progress.

Or was it?

O'Day surveyed the field, saw it filled with spectators and called the game on account of darkness. Then he got out of there. Fast.

Over the next few hours, accounts of the Giants' 2–1 victory shot across the nation's telegraph lines. Many of the New York Giants left the Polo Grounds believing the Giants had won the game. Many accounts, in fact, had it that Evers left the Polo Grounds still arguing with O'Day. What is beyond question, however, is that after the game, as the accounts of the bizarre finish circulated, Henry Pulliam, the National League president, summoned O'Day to the New York Athletic Club, then at Sixth Avenue and 59th Street, where Pulliam maintained his residence. O'Day conferred with Pulliam over the events of that afternoon, then returned to his own hotel room to write out his official version of things.

The Chicago and New York clubs, meanwhile, realized that the result of the game was actually in doubt. At ten o'clock that evening O'Day "officially" called Merkle out.

"If Merkle was out," McGraw roared when he learned this, "the game was a tie and O'Day should have cleared the field and resumed play. If not, we won the game."

Well, they had, but they hadn't.

During the next day, Pulliam took the worst possible course of action. He did nothing. The Giants and the Cubs played another scheduled game (which Mathewson won easily) and Chicago was allowed to leave town without a replay of the September 23 contest. Still, even many Chicago supporters couldn't believe that the victory would be taken from the Giants. Merkle's play had actually been in keeping with the method of play of the day. And further, if Gill wasn't out on September 4, how could Merkle be out on the same play nineteen days later?

There the matter simmered for several days, with most newspapers assigning a Giant victory in their standings. The Giants built a small lead, then began to lose again. Next it appeared that Chicago, New York, and Pittsburgh might be headed for a three-way tie on the last day of the year. That's when Henry Pulliam reversed himself and said that a replay of the Merkle game would be necessary. The game of September 23 was officially a 1–1 tie.

New York filed a protest with the league's board of governors, maintaining that they had won 2–1. Chicago filed a counter protest, claiming they should be awarded the victory by way of forfeit for two reasons: (1) because of McGinnity's interference (Chicago made no mention of Kroh's being on the field), and (2) because New York had let it be known that they *refused* to replay the game as part of a September 24 doubleheader.

Both protests were turned down. The executive board of the league, headed by Pulliam, ruled that a replay of the game would be necessary if the game were to have a bearing on the pennant race. Naturally, Chicago and New York finished the season with identical 98–55 records. The Giants won a coin flip and the replay was scheduled for the Polo Grounds on October 8.

ii

John McGraw probably wanted to win this game more than any other game he ever managed. Waiting for the National League to decide their pennant winner were the Detroit Tigers, led by the great snarling Ty Cobb and managed by Hughie Jennings. McGraw could think of no greater joy than opposing his old friend in the World Series. It was not, however, meant to be.

An angry boisterous crowd turned out at the Polo Grounds for the replay. They numbered in excess of thirty thousand and quickly overflowed the ballpark. Even the seats normally assigned to sportswriters were filled with "belligerent early arrivals," a turn of events that helped found the Base Ball Writers of America in time for the following season. Then, before the game even began, the crowd knocked down part of the fence in right field and threatened to overrun the ball park before police with fire hoses convinced them to retreat. Chicago players were pelted with bottles, cushions, and anything else that could be launched through the air.

The game was a surprisingly calm affair, considering that there was much bitterness between the two clubs and that the players shared the fever pitch with the fans. Mathewson went to the mound for New York. Jack Pfiester pitched for Chicago. Through much of his brilliant career, luck would always desert Matty at key moments. And through much of *his* eight-year, 70-victory career, Pfiester was known as "Jack, the Giant Killer." Today form held, but only somewhat.

Pfiester was wild, and the Polo Grounds erupted with glee when the Giants picked up a run on the Cubs in the first inning. But Chicago manager Frank Chance was taking no unnecessary risks. He pulled Pfiester immediately and replaced him with Chicago's usual answer to Mathewson: Three Finger Brown. Brown would eventually reel off nine consecutive victories in games where he was matched against Mathewson. This was one of them. As Brown shut down the New Yorkers, the Cubbies went to work on Big Six.

The bad inning was the third. Joe Tinker, a perennial nuisance for Mathewson, started the inning with a triple. Wildfire Schulte and Frank Chance followed with doubles. By the time the inning was settled, the Cubs led, 4–1. The Giants put together a run in the seventh, but Brown slammed the door thereafter. The Cubs left New York with the National League pennant. Six days later, they completed a five-game rout of the Detroit Tigers to win the World Series. They would not win another for one hundred and ten years, but what the heck, anyone can have a bad century.

As for John J. McGraw, for the rest of his life he insisted that the Giants had been "robbed" of the 1908 pennant. They had been robbed not by Merkle's play, as much of the press mercilessly claimed, but by the vacillating, ambiguous rulings of Henry Pulliam, McGraw's old adversary from 1906.

Merkle, whom McGraw developed into a fine first baseman for the Giants in subsequent years, was the target of vicious riding for the rest of his baseball career. The press and fans saddled him with the nickname "Bonehead." In addition, the verb "to Merkle" entered the American lexicon for many years, meaning "to not arrive." None of the criticism, however, ever came from McGraw, who raised the young man's salary $500 for the following season and spent many years rebuilding his confidence.

"It is criminal," McGraw frequently said, "to say that Merkle is stupid and to blame the loss of the pennant upon him. In the first place, he is one of the smartest and the best players on this ball club. In the second place, he *didn't* cost us the pennant. We lost a dozen games we should have won."

Nonetheless, whenever Merkle would hit safely, fans would taunt, "Don't forget to touch second." *The Sporting Life*, in late 1908, noted that their Cincinnati correspondent frequently delivered a lecture titled "Running Life's Bases," and suggested that "Fred

Merkle might profit by hearing it." And when Johnny Evers published a quasi-autobiographical book on baseball in 1912, the title was predictably enough, *Touching Second*.

Strangely enough, Merkle was a victim of an incredible conspiracy of circumstances more than anything else. Johnny Evers had screamed so long and so loud at Hank O'Day after the September 4 incident that O'Day, in sober afterthought, had realized that Evers was right, according to a strict observance of the rules. O'Day had thus decided that he would call the play Evers' way if it ever came up again. What were the odds that O'Day would be the umpire in New York when the same play occurred, and that Evers would be the second baseman? What if Merkle, who had slashed the ball down the right field line, had gone for a double instead of "playing it safe?" What if Bridwell, as he often later wished, had struck out instead? What if the National League president had been someone other than Henry Pulliam, the Dreyfuss protégé, and a longtime McGraw enemy?

iii

The latter situation gave rise to its own strange series of events, which resulted in two more tragedies, one involving Dr. Joseph M. Creamer, the Giants' team physician, and the other involving Pulliam himself.

While the Cubs were busy defeating the Tigers in the World Series, a rumor surfaced in several major league cities that someone had tried to bribe Bill Klem, the umpire chosen along with McGraw's old nemesis, Jimmy Johnstone, to work the playoff game with the Cubs. The rumors persisted through the autumn, even surfacing in the newspapers. No names were ever mentioned only "someone connected with the Giants."

McGraw was indignant. He denied the stories and labeled them "absurd."

Pulliam, however, launched his own investigation in December. Soon the accused man, Dr. Creamer, was named.

Klem (in photo) maintained that Creamer had approached him shortly before the start of the playoff game. Creamer had shown Klem a wad of money. "Here's $2,500," Klem recalled Creamer saying. "It's yours if you give all the close decisions to the Giants and see that they win. You'll know who is behind me and you needn't be afraid of anything. You will have a good job for the rest of your life."

Klem further alleged that Creamer had said that the money came from three unnamed members of the Giants' squad who wanted to make sure they played in the World Series.

In his own defense, Creamer maintained that he had never spoken to Klem in his life. "It's a job to ruin me," he testified tearfully. "I have been interested in sports for nearly twenty years, and nobody has ever accused me of any wrongdoing. I cannot understand why the umpires have mixed me up in this unless it's a conspiracy of some kind."

Creamer was, in fact, a well-known and highly respected Manhattan physician. He was in his forties and had practiced sports medicine for many years in the best of amateur and professional circles. It seemed inconceivable that he would appear under a grandstand behaving like a racetrack tout.

Yet it seemed equally incredible that Bill Klem would be wrong or would be lying. And there was one damaging bit of evidence heard. John T. Brush, the Giants' owner, hadn't even known that Dr. Creamer had been on the team payroll. It was only after his bill for salary had come in at the end of the year for $2,840 that Brush had learned who he was and paid him. That tidbit tipped the scales in a choice of whom to believe. Pulliam and his board of directors believed their umpire and ruled again against an employee of the Giants. Dr. Creamer was barred from every major league ballpark for the rest of his life. Immediately, he disappeared from baseball.

Pulliam, too, would disappear, but under even worse

circumstances.

The pressures of the job, evolving from the Merkle and Creamer affairs, weighed heavily upon him. At the league meeting in December he had been reelected National League president by seven of the eight members. Only the Giants withheld their approval. Yet stress, fostered by behind the back criticism by some who had voted for him, convinced him that all of the owners were his enemies. In February 1909 in Chicago, Pulliam spoke at a meeting of major league baseball executives and surprised the gathering by announcing his resignation at the end of the calendar year. The executives responded with applause.

On the next morning, a leave of absence was arranged for Pulliam. His assistant, John A. Heydler, a former umpire and sports editor, took over his job. Meanwhile, Pulliam disappeared from Chicago, literally leaving his hat and coat behind, and popped up in St. Louis a few days later, where he announced his engagement to a young woman whom he appeared to have just met.

Harry Herrmann, owner of the Cincinnati club, was a longtime Pulliam friend. He sensed his friend had slowly slipped away from his rational processes. Herrmann took Pulliam under his wing and three months later Pulliam appeared to be back in control of things. He moved back into his room at the New York Athletic Club and reassumed the presidency of the league.

For a while, everything appeared to be all right. The truth of the matter was that Pulliam was an incurable idealist and romantic, a man who deeply disliked the disputes and petty bitterness of baseball. Seen in its proper light, Pulliam's indecisiveness of September 1908 was the action of a man unable to penalize either side in the dispute, a man who wished baseball would solve its own problems, rather than relying on him.

Pulliam was a Kentuckian. Lee Allen once reported that Pulliam, as a young baseball man, had received a florid invitation to return to his home state to attend a local celebration. It read, "Come back to the land of Bluegrass and Pennyrile, where the crystal waters make music where they ripple through the meadow, where the birds sing sweetest, where the horses are the fleetest, and girls are the prettiest."

Not to be outdone, young Pulliam took out a pen and paper and wrote back to confirm his attendance. "That day will find me," he wrote, "seated beneath the shady branches of an old oak tree with plenty of fried chicken and cream gravy and mint juleps in front of me and flanked on either side by a pretty young Kentucky girl in white."

Pulliam never married. But he did find a way to return to Kentucky. With the pressures of his office mounting, Pulliam took his dinner as usual at the New York Athletic Club on the evening of July 29, 1909. Then he went to his room.

Two hours later, the switchboard operator noticed a signal flash from the telephone in Pulliam's room. Unable to summon a response from his telephone, she sent a club employee named Thomas Brady to see what Pulliam wanted.

Brady opened Pulliam's door to find him lying on a divan, clad only in his underwear, with a severe gunshot wound in the head. By his side, not far from his hand, lay a five-shot revolver with only one chamber discharged. A self-inflicted bullet to the right temple had traveled through Pulliam's brain. Both of his eyes had been blown out of his head.

Incredibly, he was still breathing and semiconscious. There were no notes, no final explanations. He died the next morning at age forty. He was laid to rest in Cave Hill Cemetery in Louisville five days later. Most of baseball's notables went to his funeral. John McGraw and John T. Brush were unable to attend.

Chapter 23   Give My Regards to Broadway

"I don't care if I never get back…."

Jack Norworth

Lest the season of 1908 close on too somber a note, consider a few show business updates.

Mike Donlin had sat out the 1907 season in a salary quarrel with John T. Brush. Now he had bounced back nicely in 1908 with what would turn out to be his last great season, batting .334, stealing 30 bases, and driving in 106 runs as the Giants fell just short of another pennant. Before October was over, he and his drop-dead-gorgeous wife Mabel Hite opened at New York's Hammerstein Theater in *Stealing Home*, a production whose success was more due to Hite's talent and beauty than Mike's oily charm. The show then went on the road and played out in the boondocks, as the New Yorkers might have said at the time. The accompanying advertisement is from the Grand Theater in Indianapolis.

And who cares if you can sell tickets? For more than two years, they toured the country with the show, providing Mike with a larger income than he could hope to pry out of Brush. Playing ball was no longer a priority for him, and the decision to become an actor essentially ended his baseball career at age 30.

Thereafter Mike and Mabel were likely to pop up almost anywhere, on the stage, on the screen or at a ball game: even in ads for the snazzy new Made in the USA Everitt motor car ($1350 in 1910). If the ad could be believed, Mike even let his wife drive. What was the world coming to? What the heck? With this fun couple anything was possible. In any case, life was treating them well for a while.

Consider also the work of Jack Norworth and Albert Von Tilzer. Neither can be found as players in *The Baseball Encyclopedia*, but they made a monumental contribution to the game.

Norworth was a composer and Von Tilzer a lyricist. They wrote tunes for vaudeville and turned out songs with considerable success. Some were lasting: *I'll Be with You in Apple Blossom Time*, for example. Some were not: *Oh! How She Could Yacki, Racki, Wicki, Wacki, Woo*, which you probably haven't heard anyone humming recently.

Norworth was married to an actress named Nora Bayes in 1908. They were a vaudeville act and performed together with great success for several years. (They subsequently divorced in 1913. Bayes would go on to even greater fame by being the first to perform George M. Cohan's patriotic anthem *Over There!* As America entered World War One.)

According to a story that Norworth told in subsequent years, the composer used to commute to work by train into Manhattan. Each morning he would pass the Polo Grounds. Norworth had never been to a ball game. He had never gone by himself and no one had ever taken him. But one morning his eyes settled upon a sign:

BASEBALL TODAY POLO GROUNDS

Norworth started playing with words and thoughts. He wished someone would take *him* out to see the Giants. By the time he arrived at work, he had a new set of lyrics, which he promptly turned over to Von Tilzer. A short time later, they had a popular song. Thus was conceived and written baseball's longtime anthem, *Take Me Out to the Ball Game*. So perhaps 1908 wasn't such a disaster after all.

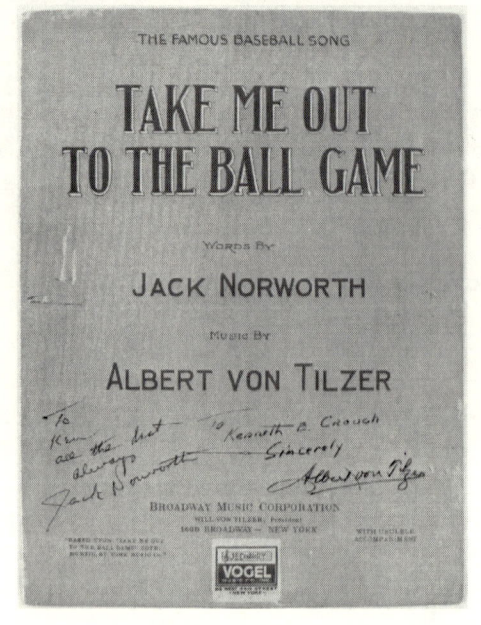

Chapter 24 Karma in the Age of Cobb

"Goddamn! It's great to be young and a New York Giant."

Larry Doyle, when he was both

At the league hearings in 1908 that resulted in the lifetime ban for the unfortunate Dr. Creamer, McGraw learned that the St. Louis Cardinals were seeking a new manager. The St. Louis club was almost bankrupt and field leadership was nonexistent. The glimmer of hope within the organization could be found in the strong young arms of the pitching staff. The talent would never mature in that setting, however, which is what set McGraw to thinking.

McGraw cornered Cardinal co-owner Stanley Robison in the bar of the Waldorf Hotel in New York. "I'll give you a manager for your ball club," McGraw said, "if you help me swing a deal that involves a couple of your players."

"Who's my future manager?" Robison asked.

"Roger Bresnahan," said McGraw.

Robison was dumbfounded. Bresnahan, who played every position in baseball over his career, still reigned as one of the outstanding field leaders in baseball and was, along with Johnny Kling of the Cubs, one of the league's top two catchers. He was not yet thirty years old and was coming off a respectable season. The Duke of Tralee had always nurtured the idea of managing. The prospect of having him as a catcher and manager combining two salaries on the payroll was enough to have Robison salivating.

"What do you want for him?" Robison asked.

"I want Jack Murray and Bugs Raymond from you," McGraw answered. "And I want you to get George Schlei from Cincinnati to take Bresnahan's place."

The terms were reasonable. John (Red) Murray was a good outfielder, but the Cardinals could spare him. Arthur (Bugs) Raymond was in a category by himself.

Raymond was a fireballing pitcher who, at age twenty-six, could throw with the best of his era. The fact that he had just completed a season in which he owned an ERA of 2.03 with 25 losses suggests the problem he was having with the low scoring St. Louis team. Or, rather, it suggests one of the problems. Raymond, one of the greatest spitball pitchers ever when he was on his game, was an incurable drinker. He would quaff virtually anything alcoholic, from Scotch to hair tonic. Robison, anxious to unload an undisciplined problem child, agreed to the deal. He quickly dispatched two young pitchers Ed Karger and Art Fromme to Cincinnati for Schlei. Then he packaged Murray, Schlei, and Raymond to the Giants for Bresnahan.

McGraw also signed John (Chief) Meyers, a Cahuilla Indian from California who had spent a year at Dartmouth College before playing with Butte and St. Paul in the minor leagues. McGraw had acquired Meyers' contract in 1908 against the day when Bresnahan would leave. Now Schlei was McGraw's insurance policy in case Meyers didn't mature quickly enough for 1909.

Schlei and Meyers would work out fine that year, and so would Red Murray, who played an excellent right field and led both the team and the league in home runs with 7. Bugs Raymond, however, was something else.

McGraw was a drinking man himself and sought to address the problem. At training camp in Marlin that spring, McGraw sat down with Raymond and had a long chat. McGraw gave Bugs the best contract of his life, a far more generous one than Raymond deserved. He glowingly promised bonuses and incentives if Bugs could just lay off the booze for the baseball season. McGraw then hedged his bets by sternly warning all the bartenders in Marlin not to give Bugs a drink, not even a tiny one to wet his whistle, under any circumstances. With that done, McGraw arranged to pay Bugs' salary directly to Mrs. Raymond, a sweet long-suffering lady who deserved better than an alcoholic husband.

"If she gets paid, let her pitch," Bugs replied. But once the laugh was over, the choice to Bugs was clear. Sobriety and salvation on one hand. Drunkenness and damnation on the other. McGraw made it abundantly clear that if Raymond didn't toe the line, he would dump him on baseball's scrap heap.

In theory, it seemed like just the sort of kick in the pants that Raymond needed.

But in practice?

Everything went well in Marlin, where the bartenders lived in mortal terror of McGraw's legendary wrath. Dallas, however, was a bigger town. Bugs survived Saturday night when the Giants traveled there to play a weekend exhibition series, but Sunday was too much.

On that evening, the Oriental Hotel served a six-course meal for $1, with a Manhattan or Martini tossed in. Naturally, the occasion was popular among the ballplayers. Bugs found himself waiting for dinner one Sunday night when he noticed a side door to the dining room where the waiters were darting in and out. Raymond wandered through the door and found himself confronted with a long table lined with dozens of the Martinis and Manhattans. The drinks had been premixed for the convenience of the waiters. It was, to be sure, an unfair turn of fate. Despite his best protestations to McGraw, Raymond lunged. He had downed six cocktails and was well on his way to being seriously drunk before a pair of waiters pried him away from the table.

McGraw was livid. But on this issue, as well as all others, McGraw was a fighter. Well, here was a tough case. He stuck with Raymond again in Beaumont when Bugs got himself in a brawl in another barroom, this time for seizing drinks placed in front of other patrons and downing them in a single gulp. It would come as no surprise to learn that the "Bugs" nickname had nothing to do with insects. It was from the term, "Bughouse," a not so nice pejorative for an insane asylum. Warner Brothers used the term later on for their well-known wacky gway wabbit, the one with the Brooklyn accent.

There seemed, that spring, no end to Bugs Raymond's ingenuity when faced with no cash in his pocket and a craving for alcohol. Raymond would prevail upon some of the famous Giants, such as Mathewson, to sign a baseball or two "for some friends," then turn up in a saloon to barter the signed balls for some booze. At least once he victimized McGraw with the "shirt trick," which worked as follows.

Raymond complained to McGraw that he had no more presentable shirts. "Mac," asked Raymond, "advance me some money so I can go get some new ones."

McGraw smelled a con job but wasn't sure what it was. "Go to the store and pick out six shirts," McGraw said. "I'll send another player over with the money."

Off went Bugs. He returned shortly. He had, he explained, picked out six lovely shirts for $2 each. McGraw pulled $12 out of his pocket, gave it to another member of the team, and sent the other player and Raymond back to the store. Then the $12, never passing through Raymond's fingers, were handed directly to the store clerk. A few hours later, Bugs was drunk again, having worked out a kickback scheme with the store clerk. The shirts had cost $1 each, not $2, and the clerk had pocketed part of the extra $6 while returning the rest to Bugs. Raymond pulled the scam with suits also, returning the more expensive one, buying a cheaper set of threads and drinking the difference.

On the mound and while sober Raymond had good stuff, however. "Bugs drank a lot, you know, and sometimes it seemed the more he drank the better he pitched," remarked Rube Marquard many years later. "They used to say he didn't spit on the ball. He blew his breath on it and the ball came up drunk."

So McGraw stuck with him through several benders over the course of the season. Complicating the situation was the fact that New York offered more alcoholic diversions than any other city around the league. That, and the fact that Polo Grounds fans took a liking to Bugs and were amused by the press reports of his slipping his leash to drink behind McGraw's back.

During the season, McGraw even went so far as to assign a "keeper" to Raymond, a private detective named Dick Fuller, a salty former New York cop. Fuller shadowed him, or tried to, and kept him out of as many bars as possible. Under these circumstances, Raymond was 18-12 and became the number two man in the pitching rotation behind Mathewson. The press, not caring to see the darker side of Raymond's situation, loved him. The writers followed him around, even if they couldn't print many of their best Bugs Raymond stories. In the winter following the 1910 season, Raymond made headlines by signing on to wrestle professionally in Chicago.

Once, for example, when Bugs had eluded Fuller, a barman in a Manhattan watering hole asked Bugs how he threw his spitter. Eager to oblige, Raymond stood up and gripped a glass tumbler. "I wet these two fingers like so," he explained. Then he threw the tumbled through the window, shattering the glass.

"Notice the break," he said as he sat down. Six weeks before the season ended, Raymond made his way back into Chateau Bow Wow with McGraw by quitting the Giants to tend bar on Upper Eighth Avenue. He hung his uniform in the window to advertise his presence. He frittered away his chance to become a 20-game winner, but still won 18 and finished with a 2.47 ERA.

Richard (Rube) Marquard, of whom much was expected that year, was a dreadful disappointment at 6-13. The press quickly became critical of him and began terming him the "$11,000 lemon." McGraw also introduced to the Polo Grounds a young shortstop from Texas named Art Fletcher, a brash kid whom McGraw had noticed during the 1908 season, and Fred Snodgrass, who had spent most of the 1908 season as a third string catcher behind Bresnahan and Tom Needham.

But the future plans were nothing more than that in 1909. The Cubs were finally vulnerable. But it was Pittsburgh who raced past the Giants to overtake them, pushing New York back to third. At the end of the season, McGraw shipped Buck Herzog, with whom he had a blossoming love-hate relationship, to Boston.

The 1910 season wasn't much better. The Cubs lashed back at Pittsburgh and had another fine year, winning the pennant going away. Pittsburgh dropped to third. To some extent, the Giants were ignored, which was a mistake. McGraw finally had the proper pieces together again.

With the exception of Mathewson and Art Devlin, the third baseman, there was little left that resembled the championship squad from 1905. Merkle had matured and replaced Tenney at first. Laughing Larry Doyle was the regular at second and Bridwell was at shortstop. Chief Meyers was the regular catcher, just as McGraw had known he would be. Very quietly, Red Murray had become one of the steadiest of Giants in right field and Josh Devore joined the outfield on a regular basis, after spending parts of the preceding two seasons on the Giants' bench. Center field? Snodgrass.

As Snodgrass later recounted it himself, McGraw came to him one day and asked how he would enjoy playing center.

"With what club?" he asked.

"Why, *this* club, of course," McGraw huffed. There Snodgrass remained for the next five years.

Bugs Raymond, you ask? Problems as usual.

Raymond plunged into a professional tailspin in 1910.

As the team barnstormed north from Texas, Raymond wrote out free passes to Giants exhibition games and traded them to bartenders in exchange for drinks. Later, McGraw had to ban Bugs from having unopened packs of cigarettes because his boozy pitcher was re-selling them to buy liquor. Even Dick Fuller, the ex-cop, hit his limit with Raymond. Their relationship, such that it was, began well but ended in a public fist fight on a torrid August day in St. Louis. Fuller, who knew how to throw punches, gave Bugs a black eye. Raymond, who would finish the season with a 4-9 record, complained to McGraw, who promptly punched him in the other eye. Fuller quit in disgust.

Despite all this, it was a time when things were coming together again, even if the W-L record wasn't where McGraw wanted it. It was a time when famous names combined with new names and old names.

Each day the choice boxes at the Polo Grounds were filled with McGraw's usual assortment of celebrity friends: Mabel Hite, Louis Mann, DeWolfe Hopper, an actor, devout Giants fan and theatrical producer best known for performing the popular baseball poem *Casey at the Bat*. John McCormick, the famed Irish tenor was a regular. Stars from the world of horse racing would appear on off days: Davey Johnson, John E. Madden, and Tod Sloan, now a partner with McGraw in a Times Square billiards parlor.

Gentleman Jim Corbett, the retired heavyweight champion, was constantly in attendance as well. In uniform was Arlie Latham, whom McGraw hired as a coach and court jester of sorts, though McGraw actually put him into four games in 1909 when Latham was fifty. In 1910 he also hired his old pal Wilbert Robinson to come to New York as a coach.

The old names? Mickey Welch became a gatekeeper and Bill Dahlen was given a job in maintenance. Henry Fabian, who had seen McGraw from Cedar Rapids to Baltimore almost two decades earlier, was hired to head the grounds crew. Dan Brouthers, an old teammate on the Orioles, became a watchman; Silver King became a sweeper of the infield; and Amos Rusie, the Hoosier Thunderbolt himself, watched the main turnstiles.

Greatness again beckoned for the Giants. Yet there was a final rear-guard action to be fought, thanks to another of the periodic resurgences of the Giants' crosstown adversaries.

The Highlanders had enjoyed a successful season, finishing second. Joseph W. Gordon, the titular owner, was gone by now and Frank Farrell and Big Bill Devery, the retired saloon keeper and the obese scandal-plagued graft-fueled former police captain, revealed themselves as owners. The leaders of their team were an enormously talented and equally corrupt first baseman named Hal Chase and a talented spitball and scuffball pitcher named Russell Ford, a Canadian from Brandon, Manitoba.

One thing led to another. Political forces in the city prodded Brush and McGraw into accepting a challenge to play a city series after the regular season. As the potential receipts for such a series promised to be healthy, management and players on both sides were willing to play. To make matters complete, Hughie Jennings had been hired to cover the series for the New York *World.* Considered an expert on the American League and an expert on John J. McGraw, Jennings was available for postseason employment for the first time in three years. Connie Mack's Athletics had finally wrestled the Junior Circuit title away from the Tigers.

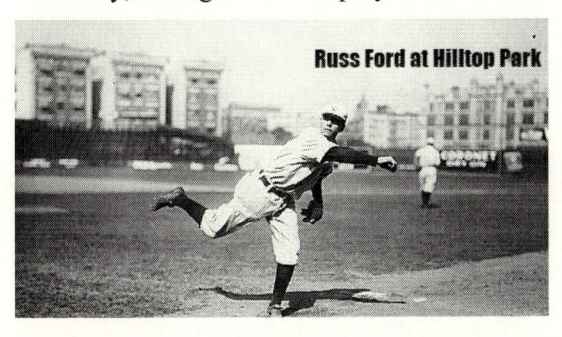

Russ Ford at Hilltop Park

Often such city series go the way of All Star games: interesting contests, but ones in which the athletes go through the motion. This series, scheduled for the best of seven games, was something more. It was, in fact, a harbinger of other autumns later in the century when New York teams squared off against one another.

On October 13, 1910, twenty-five thousand fans packed the Polo Grounds. They roared when McGraw and Chase posed for photographers at home plate. They roared again when Mathewson walked to the mound and proceeded to retire the first three Highlanders with little effort. Then the other half of the crowd roared as the stocky Canadian-born Russ Ford set down the first three Giants. Ford had a curveball, plus a wet one that could break either way. (Ford would be inducted into the Canadian Baseball Hall of Fame in 1989, many years after his death.) He and Matty matched each other pitch for pitch. By the eighth inning, the game was a 1-1 tie.

Then, in the bottom of the inning, Mathewson singled to right. Devore bunted for a single. Doyle then bunted toward first, attempting to sacrifice. Chase, a brilliant fielding first baseman, snatched the ball and fired to Jimmy Austin at third. But Austin bobbled the throw. Bases loaded. But Ford could bear down in the clutch the same way Mathewson could. Ford fanned Fred Snodgrass and Red Murray.

Two outs, bases loaded, bottom of the eighth. Ford threw an

221

inside pitch to Al Bridwell, who pulled what the next day's newspapers gleefully referred to as "an old Oriole trick," allowing the ball to hit him on the ankle, forcing in a run. The play shattered Ford's concentration. Devlin, Merkle, and Meyers followed with singles. It was 5-1, and had there been television sets in 1910, folks could have turned them off right there. Mathewson fanned 14.

The next day at Hilltop Park the shoe was, so to speak, on the other foot. Jack Warhop bested Hooks Wiltse when Wiltse walked in the winning run with the bases loaded in the ninth.

Back to the Polo Grounds the next day. The Giants built up a 5-1 lead after six innings. Then the Highlanders started pecking away at it as darkness and fog rolled down from Coogan's Bluff into the Hollow. In the seventh, Mathewson appeared in relief and saved the game, 6-4. On Monday, October 17, darkness halted a 5-5 tie. Tuesday was Mathewson's day again, which is another way of saying that the Giants won. The score was 5-1 and the only Highlander run was unearned. But back at Hilltop Park on Tuesday, the Highlanders bounced back, winning a 10-2 slugfest in which both sides accounted for two dozen base hits.

It rained on Wednesday. On Thursday John McGraw started Mathewson again, anxious to get the series finished. The Highlanders scored once in the third and, behind Jack Warhop, flirted briefly with the idea of evening the series. They might have known better. In the bottom of the third inning at the Polo Grounds, Larry Doyle came to the plate with two runners on base. Warhop delivered one of those spitballs that might break either way. This one didn't break at all. Doyle, who was sitting on it, lined it like a frozen rope into the upper grandstand in right field. Staked to a lead, Mathewson never looked back, winning 6-3.

The series was over, too, a 4-2 triumph and the reassertion of the Giants as the dominant team in New York. It was also a personal triumph for Christy Mathewson, who had won three of the games and saved the fourth.

The series had been a success, however, for *all* the participants. Paid admissions had been in excess of 100,000 for the six games. Each Giant took home a player's share of $1,110.62. One Giant, Art Fletcher, warmed the heart of the big cold city by using his cut of the fall follies to marry his childhood sweetheart, a young lady with the virginal sounding name of Blanche Dieu. No kidding.

Even more significant was a statistic buried in the box scores of the New York, New York series. Over the course of seven games, including the tie, the Giants stole 19 bases, led by Josh Devore, who swiped 6. McGraw had plans for the following season, and the city series of 1910 had afforded him a dress rehearsal.

Chapter 25 Ragtime Renaissance

> "The Giants were dressed in their baggy white uniforms with black pinstripes. McGraw wore a heavy black cardigan over his barrel trunk with the letters NY emblazoned on the left sleeve. He was short and pugnacious. Like his team he wore socks with thick horizontal stripes and the small cap with a peak and a button on the crown... [He] stood at third base unleashing the most constant and creative string of vile epithets of anyone. His strident caw could be heard throughout the park."
>
> E. L. Doctorow, *Ragtime*

Just after midnight on April 14, 1911, a night watchman on the elevated train tracks adjacent to the Polo Grounds saw flames in the vicinity of the ballpark. Looking more closely, the watchman realized that the flames were *in* the park and shooting up from the stands. The Polo Grounds was on fire.

The blaze had started in the right center field bleachers, probably as a result of a discarded cigarette. Once it got going, however, it developed into one of the most spectacular blazes in New York City history. Before the horse-drawn fire apparatus had a chance to arrive, the blaze had spread into the horseshoe shaped stands that surrounded the infield. Nothing could be saved except a section of outfield bleachers. So here were the Giants, poised on the brink of a return to championship form. But now, over the course of three days, they'd lost their first two home games of the season, plus their playing field as well.

The logical question was where the Giants would play their 1911 schedule. The illogical answer came from Frank Farrell, owner of the Highlanders. After years of feuding with McGraw and Brush, Farrell invited the Giants to move temporarily into Hilltop Park. Brush accepted immediately.

Brush himself was not much healthier than his devastated ballpark. A victim of locomotor ataxia, Brush was frail and practically an invalid. Nonetheless, the day after the massive fire, he appeared at the charred Polo Grounds to assess the damage. He was unable to walk. He conducted the visit in a wheelchair. A picture appeared in the New York press of players and writers inspecting the damage.

With Brush was his wife, Elsie. A less stubborn man might have taken the insurance settlement, sold the team, and spent his remaining days in peace.

Not Brush.

In Philadelphia, the Shibe family had brought baseball out of the wooden grandstand era by constructing a marvelous new concrete-and-steel structure that was named, not surprisingly, Shibe Park. Barney Dreyfuss had built Forbes Field, named for American Revolutionary War General John Forbes, in Pittsburgh and had opened it in the same year era. (The choice of names for the new park presented a strange irony to Dreyfuss, who had fled Germany at age seventeen to avoid conscription into the Kaiser's army.) And similar plans were afoot by the Boston team in the American League. Now here was Brush, confined to a wheelchair and thinking well into the future.

"Elsie," he said, "I want to build a concrete stand. The finest that can be constructed. It will mean economy for a time. Are you willing to stand by me?"

What could Elsie say, particularly with the press hanging around? The team moved temporarily up to 168th Street. Brush's architects started drawing up the blueprints the next day. By May the team was ready to call a press conference at the fashionable

Claremont Inn, located across the street from Grant's Tomb, to unveil the plans for what was, in the hyperbole of the day, said to be the Eighth Wonder of the World, a new concrete-and-steel structure for baseball, containing forty to forty-five thousand seats, built where the ruins of the old park now stood. The initial plans were to call it Brush Stadium. But by the time it opened for business in August, with work continuing on some of the farther reaches, the name of Polo Grounds was still in common use. So it would remain.

In whatever park they played in, however, the Giants of 1911 were as noble a band of thieves as ever played ball. The team stole 347 bases, a figure never equaled and approached only once in modern times by the 1976 Oakland A's. Every time opponents looked up, the Giants were on the run. Josh Devore stole successfully 61 times and Fred Snodgrass, 51. Merkle and Red Murray had 49 and 48, respectively. Three part-time players - Art Fletcher, Beals Becker, and Buck Herzog (back again, McGraw had received him in midseason from Boston in a trade for Al Bridwell) - had more than 60 among them. The players did so much sliding in the form of stealing and trying for extra bases that the uniforms the Giants wore actually began to come apart.

"On one trip west we arrived in Chicago," McGraw once recalled of his 1911 squad, "with a club in rags and tatters. Every player on the club had slid out of the seat of his pants. We had to telegraph [back to New York] for new uniforms. On the day we sent the wire, Josh Devore slid into second base and couldn't get up. His pants had actually come apart. Players had to surround him and walk him off the field. There was nothing left to pin."

"The 1911 team," John McGraw once said, "stole the pennant."

And they did. This crew was so larcenous that the slowpoke of the five base-stealing regulars was Larry Doyle with 38. Unquestionably, Doyle damaged his own totals by leading the league in triples (25) and the team in home runs (13).

By this time Doyle had matured into a leader, both with his bat and with his glove. McGraw had appointed him captain of the team. Meanwhile, as Christy Mathewson reeled off a typical total of victories (26), McGraw's pitching staff responded to the coaching of Wilbert Robinson, the old Oriole catcher. The prize pupil was a surprise: Rube Marquard, who had gone from a lemon to, in the words of Mrs. McGraw, "a peach."

The turning point for Marquard had come in May in a game that

Mathewson had started. The victims were the St. Louis Cardinals of Roger Bresnahan. The Redbirds were better off these days and had moved up a few notches in the standings. This day, however, was not one of glory. After Mathewson had retired the Cardinals in the first inning at the Polo Grounds, the Giants slugged out thirteen runs in the bottom of the inning. This was not a day upon which McGraw was planning to waste Mathewson.

"You can take the rest of the day off," McGraw said to Matty. "I'm putting in Marquard."

Now, cynics might have suggested that Marquard had pitched so poorly over the previous two seasons that McGraw was being a sport and trying to make a game of it. The truth is more prosaic. McGraw felt Marquard needed to throw without pressure and find a groove. He was right. Marquard allowed five runs, but his fastball started popping. He struck out fourteen batters in the last eight innings, making many of them look amateurish as they flailed at his deliveries. It was a turning point in Rube's career. He won 24 games over the course of the 1911 season, was defeated only 7 times, and led the league in strikeouts with 237. His contribution on the pitching staff tipped the balance of the National League. The Giants broke away from the pack in August, moved into their new park and won the pennant by seven and a half games over Chicago.

This was also the year of Charles "Victory" Faust.

Center fielder Fred Snodgrass, in Lawrence Ritter's stellar collection of baseball interviews, *The Glory of Their Times,* recalled the arrival of Faust. Snodgrass didn't get all of his facts straight in his conversations with Ritter. Memory can be a tricky thing. But the essence of what he recalled was true. It formed the centerpiece of one of baseball's strangest tales.

"Early in the season we were in St. Louis . . . having batting practice," Snodgrass recalled, "when out of the grandstand walked a tall, lanky individual in a dark suit, wearing a dark derby hat. He…said he wanted to talk to Mr. McGraw. So some of us pointed McGraw out, and he went over to him,

"'Mr. McGraw,' he said, 'My name is Charles "Victory" Faust. I live over in Kansas, and a few weeks ago I went to a fortuneteller who told me that if I would join the New York Giants and pitch for them that they would win the pennant.'"

But there was more. The fortuneteller also told Faust that after leading the Giants to a pennant he would meet a beautiful girl named Lulu and become the sire of a long line of baseball heroes.

McGraw had heard many things in his life. This was probably no stranger than many others. He listened with great equanimity, then addressed the only point Faust had mentioned that interested him. "You're a pitcher?" McGraw asked. "All right. Let's see what you got." McGraw picked up a catcher's mitt and Faust went to the pitcher's rubber. Faust, wearing his suit, wound up in a funny, windmill style.

After half a dozen pitches, McGraw knew he had nothing resembling even a minor league prospect. But other Giants stopped what they were doing to watch.

"Can you hit?" McGraw finally asked the Kansan.

"Of course," Faust answered.

With a couple of players hanging around the infield, McGraw lobbed a ball to the plate and Faust managed a little roller. No one cleanly fielded the ball. Faust ran the bases, sliding into all four with exaggerated gestures. McGraw congratulated Faust and dismissed him from the field. The players had a good laugh, if a slightly cruel one, and never expected to see the Faust again.

That evening the Giants took a train to Boston. One by one, the Giants were astonished to meet the new member of their team. "Boys," said McGraw, "we're taking Charlie along to help us win the pennant."

And sure enough, there was Charles Victor Faust, now known as Victory Faust, traveling with the big club.

McGraw was a superstitious man, just as many ballplayers of the day were. But he also believed in keeping his squad loose, going along with a good joke, and playing all angles of the psychology of victory. So, why *shouldn't* Victory Faust have joined the team?

Conveniently, the Giants quickly went on a winning streak and Faust developed a reputation as a good luck charm. As the season continued, McGraw kept him around, paid him out of his own pocket, and warmed him up to pitch in almost every game. He never pitched, of course, but was always ready. On occasion, he spooked the players from other teams. Meanwhile, Faust kept up the banter on the bench and in the clubhouse. Somehow, he also developed the ability to accurately predict the results of games and series, doing this successfully just frequently enough to enhance his mystical reputation.

In September the Giants put together a modest winning streak that finally left Pittsburgh and Chicago in the dust. On October 4, in a season that would run to Columbus Day, the Giants clinched the pennant when Mathewson defeated Brooklyn, 2-0, at Washington Park.

Then, on the last day of the season, with the final standings already decided, McGraw gave the players and Charlie Faust what they had been waiting for. In the second game of a doubleheader at the Polo Grounds, McGraw inserted Victory Faust as a pitcher in the top of the ninth inning.

The score was already 5-2, Brooklyn.

Faust went out to the mound in his crisp Giants' uniform, took the familiar windmill windup, and heaved his weak delivery toward the plate. Brooklyn went along with the gag. The Superbas were soon retired without scoring.

Then, in the bottom half of the ninth, Faust came to the plate. The Brooklyn pitcher, Eddie Dent, must have been in a pretty good mood that day because he went right along with the joke, grazing Faust with a slow curve that put Victory on base. Then Brooklyn allowed Faust to swipe second, third, and home. The reporter from the New York *Times* sniffed that the episode was "pure burlesque."

Maybe, but it was good burlesque and a fine lead in for the Giants to prepare the Giants for the World Series. And as for Charlie Faust, he had realized the dream of millions of American boys: if for no more than an instant, he was a big-league ballplayer. Better still, he had played for McGraw's New York Giants. And as for his that funny windmill still of pitching, years later that would be recreated by comedian Joe E. Brown in the 1935 feature film *Alibi Ike*.

Chapter 26   Ticket Back to Philly

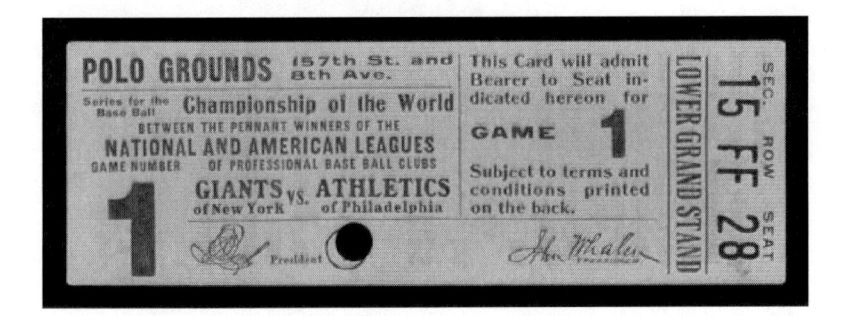

The 1911 World Series opened with much fanfare. It was billed across the country as a rematch of 1905, the World Series that so far had best captured the imagination of the public.

To make things look as much like 1905 as possible, and perhaps to provoke the same result, John McGraw again decked out his players in those imposing pitch-black uniforms. And again, Mathewson and Chief Bender were tabbed to pitch against each other in Game One at the Polo Grounds.

What would a World Series in New York be without media overkill? It will perhaps be reassuring to a modern audience to know that 1911 was little different than, say, 2018. The sporting press packed the Polo Grounds. The "4M" punch of the Giants - McGraw, Chief Meyers, Mathewson, and Marquard - struck deals with various New York newspapers to "write" daily reports on the Series. Not to be outdone, the Philadelphia papers hired their own heroes: Mack, Eddie Collins, and their own Native American, Chief Bender, the Athletics' great hurler, to reveal their own accounts. Naturally, ghostwriters assigned by the papers fashioned articles out of postgame interviews. But it was an age of innocence. The public ate up such "firsthand" articles.

The newspapers gushed over the fact that the Series was to be played in the two newest and most magnificent ballparks in America, brick turreted Shibe Park in Philadelphia and the new digs in New York. Upward of fifty thousand fans would watch some of the games in New York, the press continued. The only act of moderation anywhere was on behalf of the Philadelphia *North American,* which this time didn't bother with the "victory gong" at 15th and Market Streets. The memory of only sounding the damned thing five times in five games was too fresh.

Mathewson was still working on his string of World Series shutout innings, but the Athletics put an end to that in the second inning of Game One. Harry Davis, the Athletics' first baseman, singled Frank Baker home from third. But the Giants tied the game in the fourth when Fred Snodgrass, who had walked, scored on an error. The Giants won the game in the seventh when Chief Meyers doubled and Josh Devore singled. The Giants were again off and running.

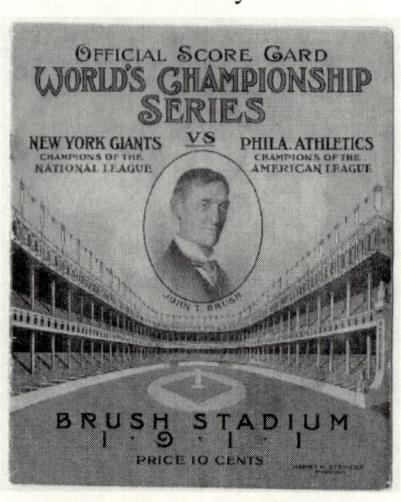

There was no game on Sunday. Monday found the teams at Shibe Park, where the game was knotted, 1-1, in the sixth inning. Eddie Collins, an alumnus of Columbia University, doubled. *(Roar Lion! Yes, he really graduated, unlike non-grads Lou Gehrig, Alexander Hamilton and Jack Kerouac.)* Up came Frank Baker, a fastball hitter. Rube Marquard, after sneaking two curves past Baker, decided to go with some heat. It was a mistake. Baker plastered the ball and drove it over the twelve-foot-high fence in right field, giving the Athletics a 3-1 lead that held up for the final score. In the next day's paper, unbeknownst ahead of time to Christy Mathewson, Mathewson's ghostwriter, Jack Wheeler of the New York *American,* roundly criticized Marquard for serving up a plump fastball for Baker.

Marquard sizzled when he read the criticism in print. The Athletics had a good laugh. They enjoyed an even better laugh the next day when Baker hit a home run off Mathewson - earning his

230

nickname of "Home Run" Baker - that was instrumental in a 3-2, eleven-inning Philadelphia victory. Then the Athletics sat back and read Marquard's ghostwriter return the criticism of Mathewson in the next morning's paper.

Next came the October rains, six days' worth. The Series resumed October 24. Immediately, McGraw went with Mathewson. But the Athletics were waiting for him this time and roughed up Christy for ten hits and four earned runs in seven innings. Philadelphia won, 4-2, and now led, three games to one.

The Giants won a reprieve in Game Five when they rallied for two runs in the ninth to tie the game, 3-3, to keep their Series hopes alive. Larry Doyle opened the tenth with a double to right, then advanced to third when Fred Snodgrass was safe on a fielder's choice. Red Murray popped out. But then Fred Merkle hit a sacrifice fly on which Doyle attempted to score.

Doyle and the ball arrived at almost the same time at home plate, Doyle going in first with an elaborate hook slide. Jack Lapp, the Athletics' catcher, never bothered to put the tag on Doyle, which was a shame from the Philadelphia standpoint: Doyle had slid past the plate, not across it. Umpire Bill Klem watched in amazement as both teams left the field, figuring the game was over. Klem never made a call of safe but declared the game over after the teams were gone. The Giants had "won," since the Athletics had never completed the play. But if anyone had tagged Doyle, he would have been out.

On the next day, however, the Series did reach its conclusion. The Athletics built a lead against Marquard, then put the game away with seven runs on seven hits in the seventh inning. Superstitious members of both teams must have spent the winter throwing salt over their shoulders. But the Athletics were the champions of the world, walking away with a 13-2 rout in Game Six.

McGraw was bitterly disappointed, but this time managed to be magnanimous in defeat. He told Connie Mack after the Series that the Athletics were one of the greatest teams he had ever seen.

"They must be, Connie," he concluded. "I have a great team, too. But you beat us."

McGraw was less civil, however, when he heard that his old friend George M. Cohan was throwing around afresh wad of banknotes at The Lambs Club. Cohan had scored a betting coup in the Series, picking Philadelphia to beat his old friend's Giants, then taking all wagers available from the pro-Giant members of The

Lambs. Cohan came into a fair amount of wealth from the wagers but spent a chilly winter at The Lambs where McGraw's circle refused to speak to him.

After the season, McGraw took the Giants to Cuba for a brief exhibition tour. It was McGraw's first trip to the island since 1890, yet he was astounded to discover that the baseball mad *Cubanos* still remembered him as *"El Mono Amarillo."* McGraw traveled with his wife and punctuated an otherwise pleasant trip with a Thanksgiving evening brawl in a Havana cafe. Still, McGraw took to the city and included a trip to Havana in his winter plans for most of the remaining years of his life. One other matter was resolved in 1911: the career of Bugs Raymond. McGraw's patience with his alcohol-prone pitcher was saintly. But it had limits. The limits were reached during a game against Pittsburgh at the Polo Grounds while the 1911 pennant was still up for grabs.

Marquard was having problems that day. In the fifth inning, McGraw handed Raymond a ball in the dugout and sent him down to the bullpen to warm up. But Marquard got out of his jam and McGraw left him in the game. In the seventh inning problems began again for Marquard. With two out and runners on first and third, Honus Wagner was the batter. McGraw walked to the mound, pulled Marquard, and signaled Bugs into the game.

Raymond warmed up and all seemed under control. Then his first pitch landed at the backstop, one runner scoring and the other going all the way to third. McGraw stared at what had happened but chalked it up as one of those painful things. Still, his worst suspicions were realized on the next pitch.

Wagner hit an easy hopper back to the mound. Raymond caught it and had a routine play at first. Instead, however, he threw toward the plate. Toward, not *to.* The ball sailed high over Chief Meyers' glove, scoring the runner from third and sending the amused Wagner all the way to second.

McGraw started out to the mound. Raymond started toward the dugout. That's when McGraw noticed that his pitcher was staggering.

Later McGraw learned what had happened. When he had sent Raymond down to the bullpen in the fifth inning, Bugs had kept going straight out onto Eighth Avenue and into one of the many seedy gin mills that lined the thoroughfare. There he had traded the baseball for three quick jolts of third rail whiskey. Still, he might have been okay if he had come directly into the game. The problem was, by the seventh inning, the booze had settled in and Bugs had a buzz.

It was a situation that, sadly, McGraw could no longer tolerate. He told Raymond to go to the clubhouse, take off his uniform, leave it for the equipment manager, and get out. He was off the team. And just as McGraw had warned him three seasons earlier, this had been his last shot in the big leagues.

Bugs never caught on with another major league club and, for that matter, never sorted out his life. He fell on hard times, could not hold a job, and separated from his wife. Over the following summer, misfortune struck from another angle. An influenza epidemic took the lives of his two small daughters.

In September, Bugs holed up in a Chicago hotel room. He was recovering from a recent brawl, or several of them, during which he may have suffered brain damage. There he drowned his sorrows in some cheap, strong stuff. Eventually, he overdid it. He felt a pain creeping up his arm, then a strangling shortness of breath, combined with what felt like pressure in the center of his chest.

Alone in the cheap hotel room, he collapsed. A few minutes later, at the age of thirty, Bugs Raymond was dead.

McGraw later sadly commented that Bugs Raymond had probably taken 7 years off McGraw's life. Bugs probably took 40 off his own.

Chapter 27   1912: Two Flags in a Row

"As far as teams were concerned, I was always
a New York Giants' man . . .
The Giants represented the New York of the brass cuspidor,
that old
New York which was still a man's world...
the days of swinging doors, of sawdust
on the barroom floor, and of rushing the growler."

Harry Golden, *For 2¢ Plain*

i

    The Giants had won the pennant in 1911 with a late season surge that carried them past the Cubs. In 1912 the surge came early, right at the start of the season. Instrumental was Rube Marquard, now an established star, who shut up his critics forever by winning 19 straight games to match the number set by Tim Keefe twenty-four years earlier. Marquard beat George (Nap) Rucker of Brooklyn by a comfy 18-3 score on April 11 to start the streak, then beat the same Rucker and the same Dodgers on July 3 by a more modest 2-1 score to notch number 19. The streak ended five days later when Jimmy Lavender of the Cubs defeated New York, 7-2. In between, the Giants, who held first place from May 15 until the end of the year, had virtually run away with the pennant.

    "Actually," Marquard told Lawrence Ritter half a century later, "I won 20 straight, not 19, but because of the way they scored then, I didn't get credit for one of them. I relieved Jeff Tesreau in the eighth inning of a game one day with the Giants behind, 3-2. In the ninth inning, Heinie Groh singled and Art Wilson homered. We won, 4-3. But they gave Tesreau credit for the victory instead of me."

    Tesreau? Well, yes. "Jeff" Tesreau was actually born with the name of Charles Monroe Tesreau in that bustling metropolis of Middle America: Ironton, Missouri. Tesreau, as a prelude to coming to the New York Giants, grew up big and strong, about six feet two, 220 pounds' worth. Something of a hunk, in modern parlance. He also bore a remarkable resemblance to Jim Jeffries, the fighter who was known as, "The Great White Hope" of the day. The Great White Hope was also known as "Big Jeff," and thus so was Tesreau, despite the fact that the White Hope had been battered to a pulp by the audacious black champ, Jack Johnson, in Reno, Nevada, on July 4, 1910.

In any case, Big Jeff Tesreau joined the Giants in the spring of 1912. He was a sly spitballer, crafty and strong. He was 16-7 with an ERA of 1.96, lowest in the league. "Tesreau has curves which bend like barrel hoops and speed like lightning. He's just the kind of a strong man McGraw has been looking for," said the New York Times that year. As if on cue, Tesreau pitched a no hitter in September.

As Marquard went on to lead the league in wins with 26 and Mathewson chipped in with 23, the Giants coasted to a 103-48 record to finish 10 games ahead of Pittsburgh. The margin would have been even greater had New York not slumped in July and August. But this was still the era of "Dead Ball and Lively Feet" at the new Polo Grounds. The 1912 Giants racked up another astonishing total of stolen bases: 319. Snodgrass led the club with 43. Even substitutes Josh Devore (27) and Arthur (Tillie) Shafer (22) were well into double figures.

There was another significant new arrival at the Polo Grounds that year. His name was George Burns, a young outfielder whom McGraw had acquired from Utica in the New York State League in 1911.

When McGraw's gaze settled upon a prospect destined for stardom, he no longer trusted the lad to minor league managers, even his own. So it was with Burns, who had played in 6 games for the Giants in 1911.

"You won't play much this year," McGraw told the twenty-two-year-old at the spring camp in Marlin. "You'll sit next to me on the bench and you'll learn how we play ball up here. I'll get you into the lineup only now and then."

Burns chose to be patient, spending most of the 1912 season sitting by McGraw's side in the dugout as "The Little Round Man," as the players now called him behind his back, set his defenses, gave signs to his batters, and called pitches for every one of his hurlers except Mathewson. Burns kept quiet, munched peanuts by the handful, and, to use Yogi Berra's terminology from many years later, observed a lot just by watching. Burns found his way into only 29 games that year. But the apprenticeship would be rewarded in 1913, when McGraw dropped Beals Becker from the everyday lineup and inserted Burns as a regular. Burns would remain with the Giants until 1921.

John T. Brush, the owner of the club, broke his hip during the summer of 1912. His health failed rapidly thereafter. But he did witness another World Series at the Polo Grounds.

The Boston Red Sox, whom McGraw had avoided when they were called the Pilgrims in 1904, had put together an awesome array of talent that won 105 out of 152 games, finished first by 14 games and made a joke of the American League pennant race.

Gone were the stars of 1904: Jimmy Collins, Bill Dinneen, and Cy Young. In their place were Joseph (Smoky Joe) Wood, who had won 34 of 39 decisions that year, Hugh Bedient, who won 18, and the greatest outfield to ever play together as a unit: George (Duffy) Lewis, Tris Speaker, and Harry Hooper. Together, they brought a flag to Boston's new temple of baseball, an impressive then-modern edifice called Fenway Park, so named by Red Sox president John I. Taylor since it was located naturally enough in the Fens, a marshy area of Beantown. No point wasting good Back Bay real estate on a ballpark, after all.

As is the case whenever Boston plays New York in anything, this turned into an extravaganza.

McGraw got things rolling, so to speak, by announcing before the Series began that he wasn't afraid of Smoky Joe Wood's fastball and that Tris Speaker was probably the only player of major league caliber on the Red Sox. With the gauntlet down, the two teams converged on New York for Game One.

Invading the city also, transported by four special trains, were over a thousand Red Sox boosters who had formed a fan club called the Royal Rooters. They were led in their travels to the Big Apple by Boston Mayor John (Honey Fitz) Fitzgerald and by one William Pink, a man who was, not surprisingly, a liquor merchant in Boston.

Braced with an ample amount of Pink's merchandise, the Rooters arrived in Grand Central Station on the eve of the Series. Then they swarmed across the city and, right under John McGraw's nose, swept through town with tens of thousands of dollars that they attempted to wager upon the Red Sox. Many expressed their dissatisfaction with the absence of takers along the Great White Way.

But the Royal Rooters were a spectacle unto themselves. Author Joseph Durso described it magnificently in *The Days of Mr. McGraw:*

"That night the sky over Manhattan was lit with a torchlight parade down Broadway in which they demonstrated their loud solidarity behind the Red Sox, to say nothing of their loud harmony behind Honey Fitz.

"Marching diagonally across the busy island, the Royal Rooters and their allies touched off a rollicking celebration in anticipation of a victory in McGraw's own backyard. They serenaded the enemy along the sidewalks with numbers like *Tessie* and *When I Get You*

Alone Tonight and every couple of blocks the procession would stop while Honey Fitz himself lifted his Irish tenor in solo salutes to the finest baseball club in the world, the Red Sox."

As all of this transpired, and as the Royal Rooters encountered small surly bands of Giant fans who didn't take kindly to their pro-Boston enthusiasm, a line formed at the Polo Grounds at 9 PM that evening for the few remaining tickets for Game One. Meanwhile, the two teams readied themselves for battle.

McGraw opened with more gamesmanship. Under normal circumstances, a manager leads off a World Series with his best pitcher. But McGraw, always thinking, reasoned that Mathewson would be better equipped emotionally to pitch in hostile Fenway Park in Game Two than rookie Jeff Tesreau. And since few batters in the National League had been able to make much sense out of Tesreau's wet pitches over the season, why not start off with him?

Herein lay the danger of too much thinking. Manager-first baseman Jake Stahl of the Red Sox, who had been a reserve catcher on the 1903 Boston champs, went with Smoky Joe's smoke. "There's no man alive who can throw harder than Smoky Joe Wood," Walter Johnson had commented earlier that year.

{Author's note: Tesreau and Wood would remain friendly adversaries for much of their lives. After retirement, Tesreau accepted the position as baseball coach for Dartmouth College, a position he held until his death at age 58 in 1946. He often coached against Joe Wood, who had become the head baseball coach at Yale University.}

Game One was played before a crowd of 35,730 that packed the Polo Grounds. Managers McGraw and Stahl shook hands for the press before the game. The Giants scratched out two runs in the third on a walk, a pair of singles, and some tentative Boston fielding. Then the Giants chipped in with some nonsense of their own. Speaker hit a long line drive to deep center in the top of the sixth. Josh Devore went for the ball and had it lined up. At the last moment, however, Fred Snodgrass cut in front of him, trying for the catch. The ball flew by safely. Speaker had a triple and at last Boston, when Duffy Lewis grounded out a few seconds later, was on the board. With the ice broken, the Red Sox added three runs in the seventh and came away with a 4-2 win. Joe Wood, in a harbinger of the bad news that would await the Giants, grew stronger as the afternoon progressed, striking out eleven and walking only two.

On the following afternoon, Fenway Park was done up with bunting and flags for the arrival of the Series. Boston's fanatical brigade of followers arrived en masse and were again led in song before the game by the Red Sox' self-proclaimed number one fan, Mayor Honey Fitz, who would find his greater historical footnote five years later when a grandson named John F. Kennedy would be born. On this day, however, he had to content himself with presenting Jake Stahl with a gleaming new automobile and smiling beatifically, as other fans presented Red Sox shortstop Charles (Heinie) Wagner with a silver bat, apparently in appreciation of his .274 batting average.

Somehow, it all disconcerted the Giants. As McGraw fumed, and as Big Six pitched well before more than 30,000 noisy Bostonians, the Giants made five errors, accounting for four unearned Boston runs. The Giants did some hitting, however, and the game continued through eleven innings, tied 6-6. Home plate umpire Silk O'Laughlin ("The Pope for religion. O'Laughlin for baseball. Both are infallible," O'Laughlin liked to tell anyone who would listen listen.) then called the game on account of darkness.

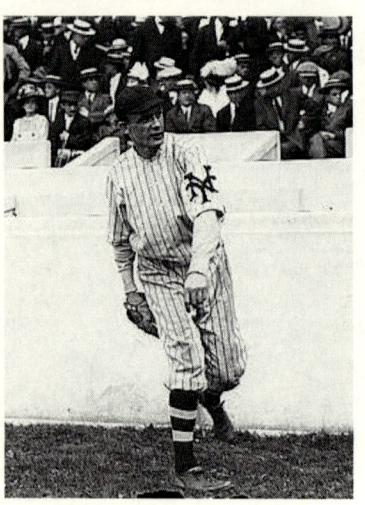

Darkness became a factor in Game Three, also, as Rube Marquard (above) pitched one of the finest games of his life.

Going into the last of the ninth, lefty Marquard, who can be seen here warming up, had allowed the Red Sox five hits and no runs all afternoon. Then, after Speaker popped up, Duffy Lewis singled. Larry Gardner doubled, scoring Lewis. Jake Stahl bounced back to Marquard, who made an excellent stop of a ball that might have gone through the middle. Marquard threw to third, surprising Gardner and gaining the second out of the inning.

The Boston fans were on their feet now, demanding a victory. At the same time, a lazy autumn mist enshrouded Fenway. It grew darker by the moment as Marquard looked for a way to find the final out.

Jake Stahl called for a pinch runner for himself, a speedy young outfielder named Olaf Henriksen. Henriksen's nickname was "Swede," perhaps because he was born in Denmark. Perhaps not. In any case, he was the runner on first when the next batter, Heinie Wagner, grounded to Art Fletcher. Fletcher fielded the ball to Buck Herzog at third, who threw to Merkle. Merkle, rapidly becoming the Marv Throneberry of his day, dropped the ball. Henriksen went all the way to third. Seconds later, Wagner stole second without a throw.

Now Rube had himself in a jam. The tying run was on third, the winning run was on second, the darkness was setting in, and the Giants should have been in the clubhouse.

With nothing else to do, Marquard threw the ball to the next batter, Boston catcher Forrest (Hick) Cady, who clouted it far out into the mist in deep right field. Most people in the park saw only two things: Josh Devore racing after the ball, appearing to have little chance of catching it, and Henriksen and Wagner darting for home. Suddenly, the ball was nowhere to be seen. Devore cut his momentum slightly and continued toward the clubhouse, then located in center field. The fans cheered, wildly for what looked like a Boston victory.

Only it wasn't!

Devore had caught the ball on the short, stumpy fingers of his glove and then had pulled the ball close to his body. Umpire Silk O'Laughlin, infallible again, had run out to see the play. He called it correctly, despite the fact that thousands of fans left the park thinking they had seen a 3-2 Boston victory. Only when they opened their newspapers the next day did many of them learn that the Giants had won, 2-1.

Smoky Joe Wood outpitched Big Jeff Tesreau for the second time at the Polo Grounds on October 11. Hugh Bedient squeaked past Mathewson the following day in Boston, 2-1, an error again undoing Matty and accounting for the winning run. Jake Stahl reasoned he could go with Wood again to clinch the Series in Game Six. He ran into a contrary front office, however. Jimmy McAleer, the new president of the Boston club, ordered his manager to start Thomas (Buck) O'Brien, who had pitched effectively in Game Three, instead. Stahl was furious but did keep in mind whose signature was on his paycheck. He started O'Brien, then watched helplessly as the Giants batted around for five runs in the first inning. Ray Collins relieved O'Brien, but the damage was done, as Marquard coasted.

Then, when Wood started Game Seven, he was ineffective. The Giants scored six runs in the first in Fenway and were officially back from the dead as Jeff Tesreau's spitter finally baffled the Sox. It had been a bad day all around for the Red Sox and their supporters. Tickets to an entire section of Fenway Park had been sold twice, leaving the organized cheering section, the Royal Rooters, with no seats. The Rooters thereupon behaved like a swarm of bees dislodged from its hive, marching around the field with its noisy brass band playing, delaying the start of the game. Eventually, mounted police took the field and drove the Rooters behind some makeshift rails at the edge of the playing field.

Not by coincidence, it was during this long delay that Joe Wood, already warmed up, felt his arm tighten as he waited to pitch. What followed was his worst outing of the year. The only bright spots of the day for Red Sox fans were William (Larry) Gardner's home run (Captain Larry Doyle's homer for New York in that game was the only other homer of the Series) and an unassisted double play by, of all people, center fielder Tris Speaker. Speaker played a notorious short center field. In the ninth inning, he picked off a line drive from the bat of Art Fletcher, then continued in on the full run to double Giant catcher Art Wilson off the base. The other bright spot, of course, was that everyone left the park knowing who had won.

But the Series was tied, 3-3. A final game in Boston would decide. The Giants went with their best, Mathewson, and the Red Sox called upon Hugh Bedient, the winner of Game Five. It was a cold, bleak day. Only 17,034 fans showed up, including a noisy contingent of 2,000 who had taken the train from New York.

The Giants scratched out a run in the third when Josh Devore walked, then scored on Red Murray's double. The Red Sox escaped further damage in the fifth inning when Larry Doyle followed Devore's single with a drive to right that cleared the outfield fence. What prevented a pair of Giant runs was the fact that outfielder Harry Hooper cleared the fence at the same time, catching the ball in midflight. He emerged from the stands holding the ball and the umpires called Doyle out.

The Red Sox scratched for a run of their own in the seventh when Jake Stahl singled. A double by pinch hitter Henriksen brought him home. Thereupon, Joe Wood, shelled in the first inning of Game Seven (this was an eight game series due to the Game Two tie, remember) twenty-four hours earlier, came into the game to match arms with Mathewson.

The game proceeded through nine innings, tied 1-1. Then in the tenth the Giants found the break they needed. Red Murray doubled, his fourth two bagger of the Series. Then Fred Merkle, atoning for a few of his past sins, drove the ball past second. When Speaker juggled the ball in an attempt to make a quick pickup, Murray scored. Mathewson, working the bottom of the inning, needed only three outs to secure the Giants' first World Championship since 1905. Yet what followed was a half-inning that haunted Big Six for the rest of his life.

Clyde Engle, batting for Wood, lofted a lazy fly to center.

A real cupcake.

Fred Snodgrass floated in for the ball and: "Well," Snodgrass said later, "I dropped the darned thing. It was so high that Engle was sitting on second base before I could get it back to the infield."

Hooper was up next. He blasted a ball that should have tied the game.

But Snodgrass, a fine outfielder, made some amends for the previous play. Hooper recalled the play many years later to author Lawrence Ritter. "Ninety-nine times out of a hundred no outfielder could possibly come close to that ball. But . . . Snodgrass ran like the wind and dang if he didn't catch it. I think he *outran* the ball. Robbed me of a sure triple."

He also turned and threw, nearly doubling Engle off second. Think it was a strange inning so far? The strangest was yet to come.

Mathewson lost his control and walked Steve Yerkes, the Bosox second baseman. Then Speaker, on the first pitch, popped a ball up between first base and home plate in foul territory. Three Giants converged on the ball: Mathewson, Meyers, and Merkle. Meyers, the catcher, was the farthest from it, lumbering up the base line on his battered, slow legs. Inexplicably, Mathewson called the play. "Chief! Chief! Chief!" he yelled. Merkle, who had an easy catch, backed off. Mathewson stood by. Meyers lunged, and the ball rolled off his glove.

Speaker taunted Mathewson as the pitcher walked back to the

mound. "Well, that's gonna cost you the ball g a m e !"

It did.

Speaker lashed the next pitch to center, scoring Engle and moving Yerkes to third. Moments later, Larry Gardner hit a long fly to right field. Devore caught it, but his desperation throw to the plate wasn't even close. Yerkes was in with the run that ended the World Series and brought Boston a championship.

Someone in the press box figured that the difference between the winning team's share of the World Series money and the loser's share was $30,000. So out went the headlines: SNODGRASS' $30,000 MUFF COSTS GIANTS VICTORY! McGraw was as angry over that angle on the story as he was over the loss itself. When he also saw stories that he had berated Snodgrass in the clubhouse after the game and threatened the young player with a release, he was even angrier.

"Snodgrass!" McGraw roared for days after to any reporter in earshot. "Snodgrass didn't lose that game. The game was lost when Speaker's foul wasn't caught. I'll tell you what I think of Snodgrass: I think he's the best outfielder I have and one of the best in baseball. I'm going to give him a better contract next year than he's ever had!"

True to his word, McGraw did just that.

Chapter 28   No Business Like Show Business

"The main idea is to win."

John McGraw

Late in November of 1912, the New York Giants suffered an even greater loss than that of the Word Series. John T. Brush started for California in his private railroad car. A few miles west of St. Louis, he died.

In death, Brush was mourned by Giant fans as the man who had salvaged the franchise from the avaricious clutches of Andrew Freedman. "What a wonderful, what a beautiful character was John Brush," said a profoundly saddened McGraw on his boss' passing.

McGraw also might have had an eye upon the future. Ownership of the Giants was now in the hands of Mrs. Brush and her daughters. Over the next few weeks, stock transactions were made, and the estate was settled. When the dust had cleared, Harry N. Hempstead, a son-in-law of Mrs. Brush by an earlier marriage, was the new president of the Giants.

Ascendant in power was John B. Foster, the club's secretary. Also in the picture was Charles Stoneham, a businessman and professional gambler, whose holdings included the Oriental Park Racetrack, and Havana Casino in Havana, Cuba. He eventually sold these operations in 1923, as part of an anti-corruption campaign forced upon baseball by Commissioner Landis. However, he continued his horse racing operations in New York for several more years. According to a story Stoneham himself later told, he finally gained control of the New York Giants Baseball Club in a game of poker against then-owner Harry Hempstead.

"The whole nation had become Giant conscious," Mrs. Blanche McGraw later wrote of this era, "and fans couldn't get enough news of them."

Correct. Larry Doyle's exclamation of it being great to be young and a Giant was never truer than in the years before World War One. Not only was it great to be young and a Giant, it was also profitable.

McGraw went on a vaudeville tour after the 1912 World Series. The tour lasted fifteen weeks and McGraw did well. He told baseball stories, woven around anecdotes written by his close friend Bozeman Bulger, the baseball reporter for the New York *Evening World.*

Friends at The Lambs Club coached McGraw on his delivery and helped him rehearse his performance. Frequently, McGraw's act followed that of a pretty, nubile young woman called Odiva, "The Goldfish Lady." Exactly what thespian talents Odiva possessed are unrecorded, but she was able to build a career around immersing herself in a glass tank filled with water and staying under for a full two and a half minutes. Odiva wore a billowy but diaphanous gold gown, so presumably the males in attendance were holding their breath along with Odiva. It was, to stretch a point, sort of the soaking wet T-shirt exhibition of the day. How McGraw felt about following an act like that is unclear, but McGraw followed the Goldfish Lady more than once. Presumably, baseball yarns were a good means of cooling off the hot-blooded males in the audience after they'd been craning their necks at Odiva.

The tour before the footlights swelled John McGraw's income to between fifty and sixty thousand dollars for the year, an impressive sum in the days before the avaricious Internal Revenue Service. Eventually, McGraw would yield to temptation even further and star in a silent film called *The Detective*. McGraw filled the title role, that of an Irish gumshoe.

At the same time, Christy Mathewson expanded his activities with Jack Wheeler, the cigar chomping newspaperman from the New York *Herald* who had ghosted his column during the 1911 World Series. Mathewson and Wheeler now published a book titled *Pitching in a Pinch*. The book incorporated Mathewson's philosophy of pitching, with a sprinkling of observations designed to titillate readers young and old.

For example, "Many fans look upon an umpire as a sort of necessary evil to the luxury of baseball, like the odor that follows an automobile."

Want another? Try this:

"A young ballplayer looks upon his first spring training trip as a stage-struck young woman regards the theatre. She can only think of the lobster suppers and the applause and the colored lights."

244

As Mathewson's book sold briskly, two other Giants were doing well in the "applause and colored lights" department. Rube Marquard was keeping the gossip columns of the day busy with a much publicized, rip snorting, white hot affair with Blossom Seeley, one of the reigning queens of the vaudeville stage. We see her here on a publicity shot from 1912. Blossom took Rube into her act, both on the stage and off, which would have been fine, except a gentleman named Joe Kane, who happened to be Seeley's husband, took exception. He filed an alienation of affection suit against Marquard, claiming that the pitcher had broken up his happy home life. Once, in the midst of a performance in Atlantic City, Rube and Blossom fled the stage when process servers arrived from New York. They later fled their hotel room via the fire escape when the servers knocked at their door. Blossom's husband was a genuine nuisance, as husbands can frequently be. Eventually, Blossom dumped the bum, the legal shenanigans stopped, Marquard settled the suit in cash, and she and Rube married. They went on offseason vaudeville tours together for the next three years.

All in all, 1912 had been a good year for Marquard: He was 26-11, won 2 games in the World Series, put his name in the record books with the 19-game winning streak, and went to Hollywood to make a film titled *Nineteen Straight* with silent film stars Alice Joyce and Maurice Costello. In his free time, the Devil's workshop, so to speak, he had swiped another man's wife.

The other Mathewson teammate doing well in show biz was Turkey Mike Donlin, who by this time was an ex-teammate. Mike had driven McGraw crazy with salary disputes and holdouts, the latter of which were so extreme that Donlin had taken a hike for the entire 1907, 1909, and 1910 seasons to pursue a budding acting career in Hollywood. He also continued to team with Mabel Hite, his wife. Hey, were the Giants winners in this era, or what? Little Mabel had fallen for Turkey Mike the same way Blossom tumbled for Richard William Marquard. Donlin would be in and out of movies for the rest of his life, frequently playing villains, often cadging roles through his new best buddy, John Barrymore. If you ever have the occasion to see the Buster Keaton classic *The General,* made in 1922, watch closely when three Union Army generals come on the screen. The one in the middle is Turkey Mike Donlin, who didn't look bad in the Civil War regalia.

How did Mike get into a Buster Keaton film? Keaton loved baseball. When stuck for an idea, he would often shut down a production and play baseball with other studio members until he came up with the idea he wanted. There was a joke that the job application for the Keaton Studio had two questions: Do you know how to make movies? Can you play baseball? Passing grade was 50%.

It was a time, with no exaggeration, that the entire world cried out for a view of McGraw's fabulous New York Giants, from delivery boys in New York to kings in foreign lands. Albert Spalding, who had taken a contingent of ballplayers on his world tour of 1888, now in the final years of his life, met with McGraw and Charlie Comiskey to plan a similar tour for the winter of 1913-14.

At the same time, McGraw signed the man who, during the 1912 Olympics in Stockholm, had stood before King Gustav of Sweden and had been pronounced "the greatest athlete in the world." He was, of course, Jim Thorpe, and even if he couldn't play baseball as well as he could compete in the pentathlon and decathlon, he could still run. More importantly, he would bring crowds out to the Polo Grounds, even when he took batting practice.

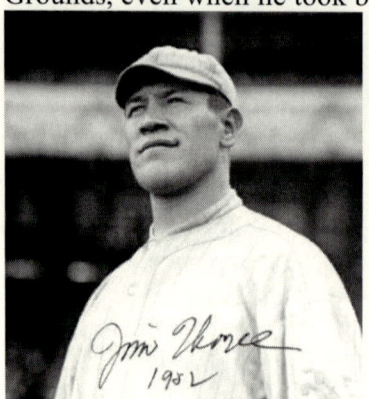

"By thunder, there was a man who could outrun a deer," Edd Roush said of Thorpe. Chief Meyers, Thorpe's roommate and the other Native American on the club, recalled Thorpe with equal admiration.

"Gee, he was an Adonis!" said Meyers. "Built like a Greek god. The greatest athlete who ever lived!"

For the kid on the streets of New York in the second decade of the Twentieth Century, there were no greater heroes than the New York Giants, either. Author Harry Golden – Ukrainian born, but a popular Jewish-American writer in the mid-Twentieth Century - once recalled the era and the feeling with predictable brilliance:

On warm spring days we walked from the East Side to the New York World building on Park Row to watch the baseball game on the electrically operated board. I also saw many a game on summer vacations . . . On the Bowery at Houston Street was a large bakery which sold pretzels to the Polo Grounds concessionaire, Mr. Harry M. Stevens. We kids in the neighborhood alternated the delivering of those pretzels and I got the job as often as any of them. The pay was twenty-five cents for the errand and ten cents carfare, plus the privilege of seeing the game . . . I got to know the players and made myself useful around the clubhouse . . . I became friends with the Giants' Captain, Larry Doyle, and players George Wiltse, Al Demaree, Leon Ames, Otis Crandall, George Burns, Buck Herzog, and Jeff Tesreau, and received many a smile from the aloof but kindly Christy Mathewson himself.

There was a billboard behind the center field bleachers advertising flypaper:

"Last year George Burns caught 198 flies, but Ajax Flypaper caught 19 billion, 865 million flies" ... I also recall a lady with a very large black picture hat sitting in the front row of the center field bleachers . . . and just as the Giants took the field you could hear her battle cry in every corner of the Polo Grounds" Come on, Artie!" and the shortstop Arthur Fletcher would wave his glove at her, everybody would applaud, and then the first visiting batter would step up to the plate."

Shameless Self Promotion - Noel Hynd

When I was writing the original edition of *The Giants of The Polo Grounds*, the story about Rube Marquard and Blossom Seeley in Vaudeville (and their then-scandalous romance) before World War One fascinated me. There was very little known about their act and their relationship at the time. Both were deceased, as were most of their friends and relatives who knew them personally, though I did find Rube and Blossom's son and I did speak to him. By that time, if I recall, he was in his eighties. A very nice man, he lived in Michigan. We spoke on the phone a few times. As a little boy, he hung out in the Giants' dugout from time to time during the McGaw era.

I set out to learn more.

I struck gold in the Theater Library at Lincoln Center New York, more formally known as New York Public Library for the Performing Arts, at Dorothy and Lewis B. Cullman Center, 40 Lincoln Center Plaza. That's at 65th St and Columbus Avenue in Manhattan. The library had in its possession a clipping file on the third floor on both Marquard and Seeley. The clippings - literally little pieces of paper clipped from newspapers - were from original dailies of their day, papers which were never microfilmed and no longer were in business. The paper was disintegrating week to week. The file had been created, I was told, by a woman who was obsessed with vaudeville and Broadway in the early part of the 20th Century. She kept daily clippings on people she liked. When she died, the collection was donated to the library

I managed to photocopy everything I could over the course of many weeks. I gradually put together a story that no one knew, a tale of baseball and illicit romance in the Ragtime era. Major publishers wanted no part of it: it was too remote and too far in the past. But I had a friend and editor who loved baseball, Wally Exman, who later landed at a small publisher in Massachusetts. I did a book for almost no money. I just loved the story. I went back to look at the same files a few years later and the entire file had turned to dust within its folder. It was heartbreaking

The book had solid reviews. "Hynd (*The Giants of the Polo Grounds*) has captured the spirit of the times in this quaint and entertaining sidelight to sports and show-biz history," said *Publishers' Weekly*. Well, thanks.

The book is still available on Amazon Kindle. A newly revised version is currently up and running. A new print copy will be available the first week of October through Amazon.

You might enjoy it.

Noel Hynd
Los Angeles
September 2018

Link: **http://a.co/9Z4nksO**

Chapter 29   Sunday Baseball & Hizzoner the Mayor

"I will say to the people that try to erase the Sabbath
from our statute books, we will swim our horses in blood
to their bridles before you will ever
get us away from it."

Billy Sunday

i

One of the biggest stories of the Twentieth Century also touched the Giants' 1912 season. On April 15 of that year in the early morning in the North Atlantic Ocean, the RMS *Titanic* sank after hitting an iceberg three hours earlier. In keeping with the practices of the era, *Titanic*'s lifeboat system was intended to ferry passengers to rescue vessels, not to hold everyone on board at one time. The ship was unsinkable, correct? As a result, when *Titanic* went under, more than a thousand passengers and crew were still on the ship. The maritime catastrophe resulted in the deaths of more than 1,500 people. There were about a thousand survivors. Some of them were wealthy. A larger number were now destitute.

Less than a week after the *Titanic* sank, a small ad appeared in the sports page of the April 20, 1912 issue of The New York Times. It read, "Ball Game for Titanic Survivors."

President John Brush of the Giants and President Frank Farrell of the Yankees had given approval their clubs for playing an exhibition game at the Polo Grounds. The game was to take place the next day, Sunday, April 21, 1912, for the financial benefit of the survivors of the disaster at sea. The contest game would be the first sanctioned Sunday game ever played at the Polo Grounds and sanctioned only because it was a charity event. It drew more than 14,000 spectators, a solid number on such short notice.

In uniform for the Giants that day was Phifer Fullenwider, a pitcher from North Carolina who had been to spring training with the Giants that year. Fullenwider never pitched the majors, but they had "lent" him to Buffalo in the American Association for the season. The Giants called him up to bolster the squad that day, however. Fullenwider. The name just jumps off one's lips. In a 2009 blog, sportscaster Keith Olbermann referred to Fullenwider as "the greatest *name* in baseball history." Also there, setting the tone, was McGraw's old good luck charm, Charles "Victory" Faust, the early Twentieth Century version of Forrest Gump.

On game day, a pasted-together Giants squad battered a depleted Yankees team, 11-2. More importantly, the game's gate raised nearly $10,000 for *Titanic* survivors.

But that was only part of the story.

A few days before the game, Broadway showman George M. Cohan contacted newspaper titan William Randolph Hearst with a concept. If Hearst would publish a special Sunday edition of his New York *American*, Cohan would fork out $5,000 for the first copy, the dough to go to the charity. Additionally, Cohan would personally shuffle around Manhattan hawking copies of the *American* to benefit the *Titanic* survivors. It was a nice stunt for a good cause.

Hearst agreed. Cohan started to shuffle.

According to the rival New York *Tribune*, Cohan "covered the city from the Battery to The Bronx and netted a sum that will amount to nearly $20,000." In the afternoon of his Sunday paper route, Cohan stopped by the Polo Grounds for the special

Yankees-Giants ballgame. A photographer captured him in the pair of photos, including the one seen here.

Etched onto the eventual newspaper versions of the two photographs was the name "Geo. Cohan" and the event, "'Titanic' Benefit Game." There was also a young man seen trailing behind Cohan, also carrying a stack of newspapers. The same *Tribune* article identified the young man as Jack Sullivan, "founder of the Newsboys' Home." The article stated that Sullivan assisted Cohan selling papers.

Fine and good so far.

Over the years, however, experts on crime in New York City have identified "Sullivan" as Jacob A. Reich (or Rich), who was at the time better known as "Jack Sullivan." Sullivan may have been doing nothing other than basking in the wake of Cohan's fame. But three months after the *Titanic* disaster, the man who was called "King of the Newsboys" was in the public eye again under his various names, figuring prominently in the murder of a midlevel gangster and gambler named Herman Rosenthal.

On July 16, Rosenthal walked out of the Hotel Metropole at 147 West 43rd Street, just off Times Square at 6 a.m. He was shot to death by a squad of gangsters from the Lower East Side. The case was one of the headline stories in New York that summer. Four men would be executed for the slaying, five if you include Charles Becker, a New York police lieutenant who was later executed in an ensuing case.

The incident got a prominent mention in F. Scott Fitzgerald's *The Great Gatsby*, in which Meyer Wolfsheim was based on Arnold Rothstein, the alleged fixer of the 1919 World Series:

"The old Metropole," brooded Mr. Wolfshiem gloomily. "Filled with faces dead and gone... I can't forget so long as I live the night they shot Rosy Rosenthal there. It was six of us at the table and Rosy had eat and drunk a lot all evening. When it was almost morning the waiter came up to him with a funny look and says somebody wants to speak to him outside...

"Then he went out on the sidewalk and they shot him three times in his full belly and drove away."

It will be noted that the Titanic benefit game was played on a Sunday. That, too, was an event unto itself, as professional baseball was prohibited in New York on Sundays due to blue laws.

The fight over blue laws and professional baseball in the late 19th and early 20th centuries provides a lens not only into legislation and church-state relations in the U.S., but also into the shifting cultural mores of the United States. A cursory glimpse through this lens reveals with startling clarity how much the legislative, political, and theological approaches to American life changed during the 20th century.

Throughout the 18th and 19th centuries, first in New England, and then across the south and mid-west, blue laws were written and passed: laws limited what activities could occur on Sundays. Often targeting Jews, Seventh-Day Adventists, saloon owners, and non-religious persons, the laws carried stiff penalties for engaging in non-Christian activities on Sunday. In many cities, one could be arrested for playing cards, dancing, buying and selling, fixing wagon wheels, and – horror of horrors! - playing baseball. But as the country's demographics shifted, a number of cities began to strike down aspects of their no-fun-on-Sundays legislation. Chicago, St. Louis and Cincinnati struck down legal prohibitions on baseball in 1902.

Yet, during this time a number of teams, and prominent baseball figures didn't like what was happening. Notably, Methodists Branch Rickey and Christy Mathewson refused to play on Sundays. And then there was center fielder turned professional Bible-thumper Billy Sunday.

Sunday games were frequently played in Brooklyn's Washington Park despite the law, as some tried to find loopholes in it. At some events, promoters stopped selling tickets and put out a contribution box. Sunday games were also going to be attempted at the Polo Grounds in 1904, according to the New York *Times*. But a posse of blue-nosers called the New York Sabbath Committee caused trouble. They said they would "have arrested Sunday baseball players and take the case to the highest court in the State if necessary."

This battle went on for years. When a Sunday game was attempted at the Polo Grounds in 1917 between the NY Giants and the Cincinnati Reds both team managers, John McGraw and Christy Mathewson (of all people!), were arrested afterwards.

The most drawn out controversy over the Sunday baseball laws predictably took place in Philadelphia. As early as 1911,

Connie Mack had urged support for Sunday baseball in the sleepy Quaker City. The A's teetered on the brink of financial ruin for decades, as did their local rivals, the flea-bitten Phillies. The prospect of Sunday games was a prospect for financial survival, if not stability. John B. Shibe, the vice-president of the Athletics, estimated an average flow of $20,000 to the team for each Sunday baseball game it could play in Philadelphia. But no one was listening. Support to maintain the supposed tranquility of the Sabbath across the state was unwavering.

All this led to yet another built-in disadvantage for the Phillies, Athletics and Pirates. The three clubs had been juggling their schedules for years because of Sunday prohibition, making Pennsylvania teams travel out of state on Sundays. A baseball writer named Charlie Bevis once describe the futility of all this, even after Sunday baseball became legal in New York.

"The Athletics often made the train trip to Washington to play the Senators on Sunday, with occasional one-day forays to New York to play the Yankees. The Phillies played many weekends in New York, playing the Giants at the Polo Grounds on one day and the Dodgers at Ebbets Field on the other day. The Pirates ventured from Pittsburgh frequently on one-day Sunday excursions to Cincinnati and Chicago."

In New York, however, the solution moved into place in the person of one James John Walker. Walker was the son of an Irish-born a carpenter and lumberyard owner who was at various times a Democratic assemblyman and alderman from Greenwich Village. Walker was a so-so student, but prodded by the old man, eventually graduated from New York Law School in 1904. Walker at first decided that he would rather write songs in Tin Pan Alley and make a living on Broadway or in the music industry. And so he did. In 1905, a romantic at heart, he penned Tin Pan Alley hits such as *There's Music In The Rustle Of A Skirt* and *Will You Love Me in December As You Do in May?*, the latter with its bittersweet refrain:

Will you love me in December as you do in May,

254

Will you love in the good old fashioned way?
When my hair has all turned gray,
Will you kiss me then, and say,
That you love me in December as you do in May?

Nonetheless, the young songwriter eventually entered politics in 1909. Now known as Jimmy Walker, seen here on the phone, he was a member of the New York State Assembly and later the State Senate. Charming, charismatic, he tied his fate to the powerful Tammany Hall Machine. As he gained power in the state senate, Walker sponsored causes that were close to him.

He condemned the Ku Klux Klan, who were powerful in the national Democratic Party at the time and backed a steady progression of social welfare legislation. He was also the key sponsor of the "Walker Law," which legalized professional boxing in New York. He was honored a number of times over the years by the boxing community. To this day, Walker is a member of the International Boxing Hall of Fame and was given the Edward J. Neil Trophy in 1945 for his service to the sport.

The other bit of crucial work Walker accomplished as a State Senator was "The Sunday Baseball Law," which legalized the professional game on Sundays and enabled all three New York teams to draw huge crowds of working men on the Sabbath. For years, games didn't start till two p.m. so that fans could go to church first, in theory at least. It also allowed them to tank up at a local saloon if they were so inclined. The bill was signed by Governor Al Smith on April 19th, 1919. It would come as no surprise to learn that Walker was a diehard Giants fan.

On May 4th, the NY Giants played their first legal Sunday home game to 35,000 fans at the Polo Grounds. They lost to Philly, 3-1. It was also a big day in Brooklyn, where 25,000 turned out for the first legal Sunday game at Ebbets Field. Brooklyn won.

Walker's reputation as a flamboyant man-about-town made him a hero to many working-class voters. He was often seen at busy speakeasies and Broadway shows. He was dapper and a clothes horse. A shrewd and charming campaigner, he was elected Mayor of New York City in 1926.

Walker and Babe Ruth were probably the two most iconic symbols of New York City during the back end of the 1920s. (Chicago had Capone and the lingering stench of the Black Sox scandal.) Yet much as he was the hero of the Catholic working man, the guy who allowed booze and games on Sundays, his reputation for tolerating corruption made him suspect to middle-class and moralistic voters.

In the initial years of Jimmy Walker as mayor, the city prospered. Many public works projects gained traction. However, Walker's tenure was also known for the proliferation of speakeasies during Prohibition. Walker led his administration in challenging the Eighteenth Amendment by replacing the police commissioner with an inexperienced former state banking commissioner. The new police commissioner immediately dissolved the Special Service Squad, the guys who would go around raiding warehouse, smashing barrels of booze and closing your favorite speakeasy. Since Walker did not feel that drinking was a crime, he "discouraged" the police from enforcing Prohibition law or taking an active role unless it was to curb excessive violations or would prove to be newsworthy.

Then there was Jimmy's private life, which was not so private. His affairs with "chorus girls" were widely known. He left his wife, Janet, for a bodacious showgirl named Betty Compton, seen here looking gorgeous in a publicity photo from the era. Walker and Compton would frequently show up at the Polo Grounds and hobnob with players and management.

Reformers challenged Walker in 1929. Voters decided that nothing needed reforming, or at least the people counting the votes made that decision for them. But Walker's fortunes began to slide after the stock-market crash of 1929. Patrick Joseph Hayes, the Cardinal Archbishop of New York, publicly suggested that the immorality of the mayor, both personal and political, in tolerating "girlie magazines" and casinos was a cause of the economic downturn. Heaven forbid! But eventually

Tammany Hall yanked away its support for Walker.

Scandal followed scandal until it became wearisome. Walker was not above leaving the country to avoid process servers. Money that had been paid to him as overt bribes he termed, "beneficences." Eventually the new governor of New York State, Franklin Roosevelt, talked Walker into resigning. FDR was gearing up for a run for President in 1932 and didn't want to be associated with a corrupt Democratic machine in New York City.

Walker resigned as mayor in September of 1932 and quickly took off for Europe until the legal heat on him subsided.

Nonetheless, from the time Sunday baseball became legal in New York, Walker in his lifetime (he died in 1946) was a regular at Giants games at the Polo Grounds, frequently throwing out the ceremonial first ball of the season in April.

Even in the final team yearbook in 1957, the team carried his picture, double-breasted overcoat, snazzy fedora, tightly knotted tie and flashing an all-Erin grin. The Giants organization never forgot him. The team's official history referred to him as "hizzoner," New York's "first citizen" and the "father of Sunday baseball."

The gratitude was that great and Sunday baseball was that important, as were the huge boxing crowds that would eventually see great matches at the Polo Grounds in the next decades.

ii

Although Sunday professional baseball wasn't played in New York legally until 1919, that doesn't mean the Polo Grounds was empty on Sundays. Various entrepreneurs would frequently stage events.

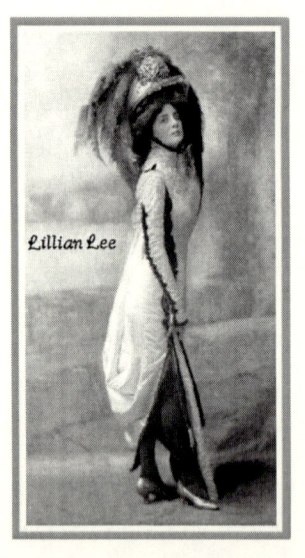

Among them, the actors and actresses of the Broadway and vaudeville stages would often present benefits on Sundays. One of the most successful was in 1908, which included a benefit "baseball game" for a fund for crippled children. Prominent was an actress named Lillian Lee, who was one of the original Ziegfeld Girls in the first Follies in 1907, seen here in Follies garb and also kicking back at the Polo Grounds where she played first base.

Three years later in 1910, there was an extravaganza again produced by the Actor's League. "It's more fun than a barrel of monkeys," remarked *Moving Picture World,* at the time. "Regular village cut-ups are those actor chaps and actresses. They don't keep still a minute when they get loose on the village green at the Polo Grounds. The band begins to play and the procession starts from Madison Square in "buzz wagons" and keeps moving until they get to the grounds where every actress and actor in town passes in review before the grandstand of political and social celebrities there assembled. Here they come now: Eddie Foy, Bert Williams, Marie Dressler, Lew Fields, Marshall P. Wilder. George M. Cohan, Victor Moore. Jim Corbett, Tim Sullivan, Joe Humphreys, Emma Carus, Louis Mann, Terry McGovern, Annie Oakley, Irene Franklin and, well, just watch them as they pass by and you can pick them all out. This show takes in every show in Manhattan and the suburbs. There goes the wild men of Borneo in a Salome war dance.... Burt Williams and Billy Reeves in a sparring exhibition would make an owl laugh, and the 'greased pig chase just before the pie-eating contest." A short film, which still exists, was made of the event and put into newsreel release across the country.

A group of chorus girls staged a baseball game, "in pretty blue bloomers," said the New York *Times*. And the great Annie Oakley, fifty years old and with some white hair, put on a shooting exhibition. Presumably one needed to be careful where one sat for that.

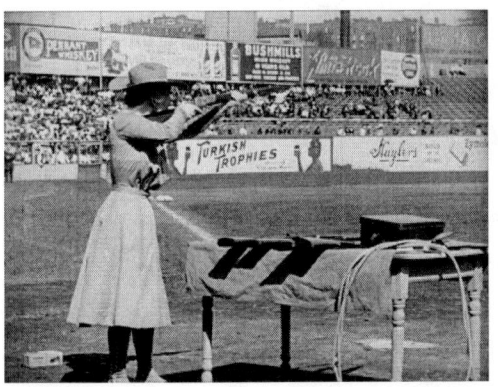

On June 4, 1916, while the Giants paused in a series against Cincinnati, a group that called itself the National Open Air Festival Society presented a performance of Verdi's *Requiem*, (at one time called the *Manzoni Requiem*.) The work was Verdi's musical interpretation of the Roman Catholic funeral mass. It was composed in memory of Alessandro Manzoni, an Italian poet and novelist whom Verdi admired. Manzoni was a giant of world literature in the Nineteenth Century but is pretty thoroughly forgotten today. The first performance, at the San Marco church in Milan on 22 May 1874, marked the first anniversary of Manzoni's death.

The Polo Grounds performance was presented by the National Open Air Festival Society. There was a chorus of 1,200 singers, chosen from the leading choral societies of New York. An augmented New York Philharmonic Orchestra of 120 players played the music. The soloists were Lucile Lawrence, Maria Gay, Giovanni Zenatello and Leon Rothier, pictured here with the Polo Grounds bleachers and scoreboard in the background. The performance was conducted by Louis Koemmenich, one of the great conductors of his day. Sadly, he would die by suicide from cooking gas on August 14, 1922 in his apartment at 347 West 91st Street.

Chapter 30   Three In A Row!

"You are born with two strikes against you. So don't take a third one on your own."

Connie Mack

The Giants of 1913 won their third straight pennant in workmanlike fashion. At the outset of the season, they jockeyed for the league lead with the Cubs and the Pirates, then put together a June winning streak that pushed both competitors back into the pack. Rising quickly in pursuit, however, were the (gasp!) Philadelphia Phillies, paced by the hitting of right fielder Clifford (Gavvy) Cravath and the pitching of Tom Seaton and Grover Cleveland Alexander, who together won 49 games.

There were, inevitably, additions and subtractions over the course of the season. Needing a fifth starter as insurance against injuries to his pitchers, McGraw picked up veteran righthander Art Fromme from Cincinnati. The price was high. McGraw gave up Josh Devore, Leon (Red) Ames, and infielder Henry (Heinie) Groh, plus twenty thousand of Harry Hempstead's dollars.

A month later, this time for cash alone, McGraw added Edward (Harvard Eddie) Grant, an outstanding dugout leader and reserve infielder, to his roster. You do not need to be told from which eastern university Eddie Grant had earned two academic degrees: one undergraduate and one from the law school. Famously, maybe because of his Harvard background, Grant refused to ever call for a fly ball by yelling, "I got it!" Instead, he would only shout the grammatically correct, "I have it!"

Harvard Eddie once set off a near riot during a spring training game in Texas. Needled by a bunch of rednecks along third base, Grant finally turned to them and announced that his grandfather, the Civil War general, President, and legendary drinker of the same surname, had taught the South a thing or two about humility and he, Eddie, would be happy to, also. Harvard Eddie was no more of a relation to Ulysses S. Grant than he was to the Eddy Grant of *Electric Avenue* fame. But the remark had the predictable effect upon the fans.

No less an event in 1913 was the opening of Ebbets Field in Brooklyn. Charlie Ebbets, the Dodgers' owner, had spent the years 1908 through 1911 acquiring parcels of land in the unfashionable Pigtown area of Brooklyn, a section known for its malodorous shanties. By March of 1912, however, the first spade of dirt had been turned over in the construction of a new ballpark. By April of the following year, the new ballpark was ready.

The tone of the entire operation was soon established. The Dodgers hosted the crosstown New York Yankees, as they were now called. Casey Stengel, a starting outfielder for Brooklyn, opened the scoring in the new place by lining a long drive to center field. Yankee outfielder Harry Wolter retreated for the ball.

He retreated and retreated...

Then the ball landed a few feet in front of him. It bounced sharply, hit Wolter in the foot, and careened to the center field wall. Brooklyn fans, who knew a good show when they saw one, hooted wildly as Casey circled the bases with an inside the park home run. There were 25,000 fans there that day. Most of them left happy after the Dodgers blew a 2-2 lead, then scored in the bottom of the ninth to salvage a victory. Also noteworthy was Yankee pitcher Ray Caldwell, a so-so righthander but the owner of a legendary appetite for Jewish food. Ray used to spend his off-hours prowling the city in search of the perfect bagel or knish or gefilte fish.

A few days later, Ebbets Field opened for real, and the goofy mythology of the park began to take shape. On the official Opening

Day, it was discovered that, even though local newspaper editors had approved the stadium's design, there was no press box, a detail that might have pleased many future Dodger managers. This was "temporarily" rectified by removing two rows of seats from the park's upper deck and designating the area as the press section. (A real press box would not be added until 1929.) But even this discovery was pale in comparison to the actions of the opening date gatekeeper, assigned to open the park, who forgot to bring the keys. Eventually, the gates were opened, the crowd poured in, the knights of the local keyboards were seated, and the players, the Dodger brass, and a big noisy band marched to center field for a flag raising ceremony.

Problem. No flag. The Dodgers had forgotten to order one. Once all this got settled, the Dodgers then played a three game series with the Phillies and lost all three by scores of 1-0.

The year 1913, however, was not one of brotherly love between the Philadelphia and New York clubs. The two cities looked upon each other with, say, the same mutual feelings as the residents of Paris and London in the 1780s. (And Paris and London didn't field ball clubs against each other.)

McGraw, unpopular as ever in the other cities of the league, was particularly unappreciated in Philadelphia, where memories of the 1905 and 1911 World Series still lingered. It will be recalled that McGraw would fight with everyone or anyone and, like a belligerent drunk in a saloon, occasionally liked to challenge the whole house. On June 30 in Philly, he got his opportunity to do all three. Following an eleven inning, 11-10 Giant triumph, McGraw became embroiled with Phillies pitcher Addison (Ad) Brennan in a spirited shoving match. The grandstands were emptying at the time and Brennan had the good fortune to be joined by several thousand loyal Phillies fans, all anxious to get their licks in against their tormentor, McGraw. Brennan eventually was fined a hundred bucks for the incident, but McGraw, who had instigated it as much as anyone, received no fine. It was felt by the league honchos that the Quaker City fans had already meted out sufficient punishment.

Those were about the only lumps McGraw took during the 1913 season. His team played quiet, diligent baseball. The only standout at the plate was Chief Meyers, who hit .312. The *team* batted a collective .273, tops in the league. But it was the pitching that carried the day. Mathewson, Marquard, and Tesreau won 70 games among them. In the process, Christy Mathewson established a National League pitching mark by hurling 68 consecutive innings without a walk. In all, it was enough to enable the Giants to coast to their third pennant in a row and their fifth in ten years, finishing a comfy 12.5 games ahead of the ornery Philadelphia Phillies.

When the World Series arrived, however, the Giants discovered that they weren't finished spending long afternoons in Philadelphia. Connie Mack's Athletics were waiting for them yet again. This time Mr. Mack arrived equipped with his "$100,000 Infield" of Home Run Baker, Jack Barry, Eddie Collins, and John (Stuffy) McInnis. He also brought some pitchers named Plank, Bender, and Bush.

The Series opened at the Polo Grounds on a gloomy, overcast October day. The weather actually lifted the confidence of Bender and Plank who, for reasons best known to themselves, enjoyed pitching in the gloom. The Giants also had other cause for alarm, with both Fred Snodgrass and Fred Merkle ailing from leg injuries.

If John McGraw tormented other players and fans around baseball, at least the gods brought some measure of fairness to the world by sending McGraw a few tormentors of his own. One of them, as will be recalled from 1911, was Home Run Baker.

McGraw started Rube Marquard against Chief Bender in Game One. The contest was relatively even until inning five when Baker parked yet another World Series home run into the right field grandstand. The blow put the A's up, 5-1. Bender got roughed up a little by the McGraw men later in the day, but Philadelphia hung on to win, 6-4.

Game Two promised to be a disaster. McGraw's catcher, Chief Meyers, split a finger in pregame practice and had to be scratched from the lineup. Merkle was too lame to even take the field and Snodgrass was hobbling.

McGraw improvised. Second-string catcher Larry McLean went behind the plate, Tillie Shafer went to center field, and Snodgrass went to first base. But more significantly, Christy Mathewson went to the mound and proceeded to throw goose eggs at the Athletics. The scoreless game took a stranger turn in the third inning when Snodgrass went from first to third on a single by Mathewson but aggravated his leg so badly that he had to leave the game. McGraw gambled, sending pitcher Hooks Wiltse in to run for him, then left Wiltse in the game at first base. The move seemed set to explode on McGraw in the bottom of the ninth inning when the A's, with the game still scoreless, put runners on second and third with none out.

If ever there were a goal line stand in a baseball game, this was it. Mathewson, of course, was never better than in such situations. This was what pitching in a pinch was all about.

As Amos Strunk and Jack Barry led off third and second, respectively, Jack Lapp, Mr. Mack's catcher, smacked the ball sharply. Naturally, it went straight at Wiltse, the pitcher playing first. Wiltse fired to the plate, where Larry McLean tagged Strunk sliding in. This was a great game for fans who liked to see potential winning runs thrown out at the plate. The Wiltse to McLean play promptly repeated itself as Eddie Plank also hit a ball sharply right at Wiltse. This time Wiltse threw out Jack Barry trying to score. Philadelphia fans moaned. Their agony was complete when right fielder Eddie Murphy bounced back to Matty to end the inning. Buoyed, the Giants then racked up three runs in the top of the tenth. Mathewson continued to mesmerize the Athletics, and the Giants evened the Series, 1-1, with the 3-0, ten inning victory.

McGraw promptly announced that momentum had shifted back to New York. Perhaps it had, but it was gone again by the time the teams returned to the Polo Grounds. It was, in fact, gone for the year.

Joseph (Bullet Joe) Bush, Philadelphia's hotshot rookie, started Game Three. Bullet Joe was not to be dodged, limiting the Giants to one run as the A's raked Jeff Tesreau and Doc Crandall for eight runs. Chief Bender came back to hurl Game Four for Connie Mack, found himself staked to a 6-0 lead after five innings, then hung on to win, 8-5. In desperation, McGraw went with Mathewson in Game Five at the Polo Grounds, just three days after Matty had pitched his ten-inning shutout. This was not, however, to be the great Matty's day. The Athletics collected three runs in the first three innings before Mathewson had found his range. Only two of the runs were earned, but Eddie Plank, anxious to get things finished, allowed the Giants only two singles all day. New York eked out a run in the fifth, aided by a walk and an error. But the Giants had come up short again, losing the game, 3-1, and the Series, 4-1. For the third consecutive year, McGraw had led his troops all the way to the Fall

Classic, only to run into hot representatives of what he had once called a minor league.

There was some melodrama at the end of Game Five.

After Larry Doyle had popped up to end Game Five, Mathewson walked slowly across the playing field to the clubhouse beyond the outfield. The friendly crowd at the Polo Grounds converged on Matty. Those closest to him attempted to console him in defeat. Art Fromme, who hadn't played in the Series, joined Mathewson on the long walk. The crowd opened gently before them.

Nearing the clubhouse, Fromme placed a mackinaw across Mathewson's sturdy shoulders. But as Mathewson climbed the steps to the clubhouse, the coat came loose, slid from him, and lay on the ground. Matty entered the clubhouse and closed the door behind him.

It was a strange vision, and one that stayed with many who saw it. It gathered a certain eeriness through the years, carrying as it did a sense of finality and, beneath the leaden fall skies, gloom.

What witnesses had seen, as it turned out, was Christy Mathewson's final appearance in a World Series though no one could possibly have imagined it at the time. Big Six had started eleven World Series games and completed ten, still a record. He had thrown shutouts in four of them, another record, and compiled an ERA of 1.15 with only ten walks in more than 100 innings. Yet his won-loss record was 5-5. On four different occasions, unearned runs had cost him potential victories.

McGraw was unpredictable as ever in the bitterness of his third consecutive Series loss. He congratulated Connie Mack lavishly. "You've got the greatest infield I've ever seen," McGraw told the A's mentor. "You deserved to win." Then he turned his wrath upon his old friend Wilbert Robinson, his first base coach and friend, dating back two decades earlier to the Diamond Cafe in Baltimore. In the three years since he had joined the Giants, the affable Robinson had done a magnificent job bringing along such pitchers as Marquard and Tesreau. But after the 1913 Series, McGraw accused his first base coach of missing a sign that resulted in the slow-footed Fred Snodgrass being tossed out on the bases.

The two old friends argued viciously, with the dispute culminating in Robinson's firing. Not long afterward, Uncle Robbie found his place in the sun as manager of the Brooklyn

Dodgers. And, as Lee Allen once wrote, "for eighteen more years, they would glare at each other from opposing dugouts."

Another personality left the Giants at the end of the 1913 season. Charlie Faust, the occasional team mascot who had first appeared before McGraw in 1911 at the behest of a fortuneteller. Faust had parlayed his notoriety of 1911 into a series of vaudeville appearances of his own. Once when the Giants were on the skids in 1912, however, McGraw had sent for his court jester and the team, its spirits lifted, responded with a winning streak.

In 1913, there was a similar turn of events. Faust visited the team for a few days and the team won. He then resumed his vaudeville tour and the Giants lost four games in a row. McGraw invited him back and the team went on a winning streak again.

There was, of course, nothing magical about Charlie Faust. Nor had he any baseball talents or insights. But having him around, letting him be the brunt of many of the Giants' benign jokes, seemed to keep up club morale. The Giants usually won when Faust was around.

Toward the end of the 1913 season, however, it all took on an unhealthy glow for McGraw and he made plans to quietly get rid of Faust for the 1914 season. But before he could, Faust vanished of his own accord. He wasn't heard from again until the following spring, a few weeks after Comiskey and McGraw had completed their world tour. At that time, Faust (suffering from what now would be diagnosed as dementia) was a resident in an insane asylum in Portland, Oregon. Eventually, he was transferred to another institution. He died in the state of Washington in June of 1915.

The world was on the brink of change in 1913. So was baseball and so were the Giants. Faust and Robinson were gone, and so would be many of the great names of the 1911-13 champions - Mathewson, Marquard, Meyers, Merkle, Snodgrass, Doyle, and Fletcher - before another pennant would fly at the Polo Grounds. Yet perhaps the spirit of the times and the attitude of the players was summed up most concisely half a century later. Lawrence Ritter interviewed Fred Snodgrass, just short of the latter's eightieth birthday. Snodgrass put everything in perspective in *The Glory of Their Times:*

"Well, life has been good to me since I left baseball. My lovely wife, Josephine, and I have enjoyed success and things have gone well, very well, through these many years. In contrast, my years in baseball had their ups and downs, their strife and their torment. But the years I look back on most fondly, and those I'd like to live over, are the years when I was playing center field for the New York Giants."

Chapter 31   Ida Schnall, Female Giant

> "A kiss on the hand maybe quite continental
> But diamonds are a girl's best friend...."
>
> From *Gentlemen Prefer Blondes* (1949)
> written by Jule Styne and Leo Robin,
> based on a novel by Anita Loos.

The 1912 Olympics in Stockholm, at which Jim Thorpe won Olympic gold medals in the pentathlon and decathlon, were noteworthy in Giants history on account of another extraordinary athlete, this one a woman named Ida Schnall.

The hosts of the Stockholm Olympic Games opened the competition that year to competitive events in swimming and diving. The secretary of the United States Olympic Committee, James E. Sullivan, however, viewed himself as a defender of modesty. The European female athletes had opted for comfortable bathing suits for pool events. Australian swimmer Mina Wylie, who won the 1912 silver medal in the 100 meter freestyle, can be seen here in one of the scandalously comfortable swimsuits that Sullivan objected to. Sullivan, a founder of the A.A.U., banned the American women from competing, citing modesty and decency.

Twenty-four year old Ida Schnall was one of the American athletes prevented from competing. She never forgot the slight, nor did she ever give up the challenge of female athletes finding a fair and level playing field. The next year, still simmering over her treatment in Stockholm, she penned a letter to the NY *Times*. The *Times* published it.

"I read in the newspapers wherein James E. Sullivan is again objecting to girls competing with the boys in a swimming contest. He is always objecting, and never doing anything to help the cause along for a girls' A.A. U. He has objected to my competing in diving at the Olympic games in Sweden, because I am a girl," Schnall wrote. "He objects to girls wearing a comfortable bathing suit. He objects to so many things that it gives me cause to think that he must be very narrow minded and that we are in the last century. It's the athletic girl that takes the front seat today, and no one can deny it. I only wish that some of our rich sisters would consider the good they can do with only a small part of their wealth and start something like an A.A.U. for girls…"

{Author's note: Bravo!}

Over the course of the next few years Ida Schnall won the women's bicycle race from New York to Philadelphia and starred on Broadway in Al Jolson's revue, *The Passing Show of 1912*, where her fancy diving in the harem scene won her plaudits. She won the grand prize at the San Francisco Exhibition of 1915 for being "the most beautifully formed woman in America." Then in 1916 she went to Hollywood and starred in *Undine*, an American silent fantasy drama film which featured the athletic actress Ida Schnall in a water-themed story based upon the French fairy tale *Undine* by Friedrich de la Motte Fouque, first published in 1811.

Never mind the plot. As seen here, Schnall played the Princess and leader of a team of comfortably attired (James Sullivan would have been horrified!) enchanted water nymphs. In the film, Schnall dived off a 135-foot cliff in the Channel Islands off California. No stunt double necessary. Then she led her team of aqua-maidens around an enchanted island in a gauzy fantasy. No stunt doubles for this, either.

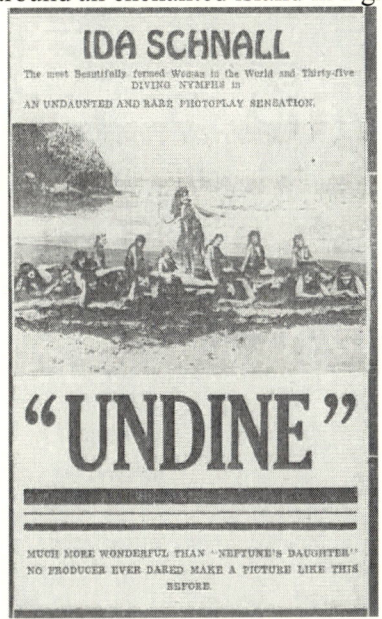

The film sparked an obscenity trial in Kentucky, which the would-be censors deservedly lost. According to baseball historian John Thorn in his splendid 2012 book, *Baseball in the Garden of Eden: The Secret History of the Early Game,* one critic stated, "No one really cared much about the plot of *Undine*: It was enough that sylphlike Ida Schnall showed up from time to time in various stages of near nudity." Another critic suggested that a better title would have been *Undressed* due to Schnall's wardrobe, or paucity thereof, in the film. Needless to say, the film was a financial success. Sadly, no prints of the entire film are known to remain.

But in 1913, even before going to Hollywood, Schnall and about two dozen other female athletes found that "game of ball." They formed an all-female baseball team named The New York Female Giants and proceeded to play a very brief schedule, including appearances at The Polo Grounds.

The Female Giants comprised 32 players. The women split into two teams, Reds and Blues, and played games against each other. It is likely that the Female Giants were created at least in part by John McGraw. The athletes were mostly high school students.

They were a perhaps a curiosity and seen by many as a mere stunt. But the games were played in earnest and the athleticism legitimate. Ida Schnall, twenty-five years old at the time, was the captain and star player. She also usually pitched. Once at the Polo Grounds, she posed for pictures with Giants' star lefty Rube Marquard. In regular street clothes, right Schnall hummed a few fastballs for him.

The Female Giants' first game was played on the grounds of the Westchester Golf links on April 27, 1913. More than a thousand fans attended. A game subsequently played on Sunday, May 25, 1913, ended with what can only be described as a police raid. Not only were the ladies violating blue laws, but one of them attempted sell scorecards. The press just happened to be there.

"The batter hitched up her skirt. The pitcher nervously adjusted a side comb," wrote a scribbler for the New York *Tribune*. "Girls will be boys, and the Reds and the Blues of the New York Female Giants were playing an exhibition game at Lenox Oval, 145th Street and Lenox Avenue."

Was this something new? Not exactly.

Female athletes had been playing baseball, sort of, at the 'Seven Sisters' colleges of the Northeast since the 1860s. Annie Glidden, a student at Vassar College, was an early player of note. She once wrote a letter home mentioning, "They are getting up various clubs now for out-of-door exercise....They have

270

a floral society, boat clubs and base-ball clubs. I belong to one of the latter, and enjoy it highly, I can assure you."

Here we see Schnall on the mound, pitching.

Good looking, athletic women were no strangers to the Polo Grounds even in the 1890s. Broadway star Helen Dauvray was a fixture at the ancient oval. Recall that she even married a Giant, shortstop John Montgomery Ward. In 1887 La Dauvray funded the first World Series trophy, the "Dauvray Cup," won by the champion Detroit Wolverines.

The first woman to play in Organized Baseball was Lizzie Stride (or Stroud) who on July 5, 1898, with the blessings of the president of the Atlantic League, Ed Barrow, later famous as the general manager of the NY Yankees tossed an inning for the Reading Coal Heavers against the Allentown Peanuts. (Two hits no runs.) She later pitched for many years on barnstorming tours. Women also played with professional traveling teams like the "Boston" Bloomer Girls, which was actually based in Kansas City. (Go figure.)

There is no record of the New York Female Giants operating past the 1913 season. They apparently played several games that year and drew more than passing interest from the public. The gates to American female athletes competing in Olympic swimming and diving events opened after 1914 when James Sullivan died.

As years passed, Ida Schnall joined the women's wrestling tour, was a fitness trainer and played tennis on a nearly professional level. Gussy Moran, an American tennis star of the 40s and 50s who played twice in Grand Slam finals, said in 1950 that Ida was, even in her fifties, the greatest woman tennis player who ever lived. "Maybe she hasn't got the snazziest backhand in the world," Moran noted, "but she tries real hard and cheats like mad. She's great because it's fun to watch her play."

In later years, Schnall moved to Los Angeles, married and stayed there, other than when business or sports put her on the road. She had a love for baseball. She kept forming ball clubs. She reorganized the New York Female Giants in Hollywood in 1928 as well as at least one local team. She died in Los Angeles 1973 at age 85. She is largely forgotten today – except for here where she rates her own chapter – at least partially because female athletes of the early Twentieth Century received such meager press in their day. Those who knew her, however, always said that the episode in her life of which she was most proud – echoing the sentiments of Fred Snodgrass - was when she twenty-five years old and pitched for The New York Female Giants.

Ida Schnall, Captain of the Feminine Baseball Club at Los Angeles.

Chapter 32   The Feds and Big Tim

> "In playing or managing, the game of ball is only fun for me when I'm out in front and winning. I don't give a hill of beans for the rest of the game."
>
> **John J. McGraw**

Into the confusion of professional baseball in 1914 came the Federal League. The league was an insurgent outfit attempting to set itself up as an equal partner to the two existing leagues. The Feds would survive for two years, long enough to cause trouble. They took on the majors in Chicago, St. Louis and Pittsburgh and tried to elevate such minor league metropolises as Indianapolis, Baltimore, and Kansas City to major league status.

They were well-financed. Harry Sinclair was one backer. Sinclair's fortune was estimated as high as $60 million, mostly from oil leases. Sinclair was an avid owner of sports properties, and a force in American thoroughbred racing. Horses from his stable won the Kentucky Derby and three Belmont Stakes. His name was later to become a household word, though a tarnished one, in the Teapot Dome scandal of the Harding administration. The founder of Sinclair Oil, Sinclair would later serve six months in prison for jury tampering. Afterwards he returned to his former life and enjoyed its endless prosperity until his death.

Chicago lunch counter tycoon Charles Weeghman was another. Weeghman had made a fortune serving only cold sandwiches. His diners would eat in one-armed school chairs so Weeghman could fit more chairs into his restaurant. At one point, Weeghman owned fifteen of these downscale diners, with the one located at Madison and Dearborn serving cheap eats to more than thirty-five thousand hungry Chicagoans each day.

Phil Ball, the ice baron of St. Louis, was a third. Then there was Robert B. Ward and his brothers, who owned the family bakery that produced Tip Top bread in Brooklyn. Ward had built modern bakeries in which the bakers' hands never touched the bread, something he advertised heavily. There was a notion, probably more than a little correct, that bakers had dirty hands and spread disease. Some other bakeries were notorious for grit, insects and things like fingernails in the bread, which for some reason some customers found unappetizing.

To distance themselves, the Wards built gleaming white clean baking factories, highly mechanized, and made a fortune. Now they also owned the Brooklyn club in the new league. The team played in a refurbished Washington Park, and added just the right classy touch to the operation by naming their club after the bread. The Brooklyn Tip Tops. Remember basketball's New York Tuck Tapers? Well, there was the prototype. These days, we have the New Jersey Red Bulls.

The owners of Federal League ball clubs threw money in every imaginable direction, a happy occurrence for all who surrounded them. One direction was the construction of new ballparks. Today's Wrigley Field in Chicago, one of the remaining jewels of baseball, was originally Weeghman Field, home of the Chicago Whales of the Federal League. Another direction was the players. Eventually, Joe Tinker, Hal Chase, and Three Finger Brown defected to the Feds. Others, such as Walter Johnson and Tris Speaker, drew salaries as high as double what they had been receiving to ward off the overtures from the new league. One name which the Feds badly wished to have in the fold was that of John J. McGraw.

Rumors of the day, which Mrs. Blanche McGraw later confirmed, had it that $100,000 was offered to him to join and manage a franchise in the new league. "You cannot realize what such a sum meant in those days," she later wrote. With the domestic acumen expected of a wife in the first fifth of the Twentieth Century, she further made her case. "Flour cost four dollars a barrel. Coffee was eleven cents a pound. The best steer beef was eight cents a pound. The offer was an opportunity to be a man of wealth and independence whether the new league succeeded or failed."

True enough. Another rumor had it that McGraw was offered a five-year pact at $50,000 per year. But in the end, he turned down the upstarts and then gave all his own players generous raises to ward off defections.

Still, his own team came apart at the seams in 1914. There had been some unpleasantness over the winter when Harry Hempstead, co-owner, had traded Buck Herzog to Cincinnati for outfielder Bob Bescher.

"Who's managing this ball club?" McGraw raged to the new owners.

"Why, you are, John," they purred.

But McGraw wasn't convinced. In the past, McGraw had made his own deals, frequently telling John Brush about them days after they'd been made. Now things were different.

Mac was seeing different results on the field as well. By the first of June, McGraw's squad was in first place. They were there still on July 4.

If McGraw was looking over his shoulder, surely his eyes were not upon the eighth place Boston Braves. But almost invisibly, the Braves began to move. Granted, the teams were tightly bunched for most of the midsummer, but the Braves had crept to seventh place by July 15. On August 1, they were fourth. But by then they were behaving like monsters and, by the fifteenth of that same month, they were breathing down McGraw's neck.

Then the Giants faltered as the Braves smashed their opponents. The Boston pitchers Bill James, Dick Rudolph, and George (Lefty) Tyler pitched the Miracle Braves past the Giants on Labor Day. Then the lead changed hands from day to day before the Hub club of manager George Stallings, a onetime medical student, continued on their closing rampage of 34 wins in 44 games. Boston won the National League pennant by 10.5 games over the Giants, then zapped the unsuspecting World Champion A's four straight in the Series. It was a hell of a roll for Boston Braves fans and they did well to savor it; the team wouldn't win another pennant for thirty-four years.

McGraw, as the roof caved in, grew surly and bitter, berating his own players for their overconfidence, though he had obviously shared it earlier in the season. In turn, the Polo Grounds crowds turned nasty to match, heckling McGraw savagely when he made appearances on the field. The fans drew from McGraw in return, according to Frank Graham of the New York *Sun,* "language that would curl their ears." Use your imagination.

There was a postseason series with the Yankees, but McGraw didn't stay around for it. Instead, he went to the World Series in Boston and Philadelphia. More important, however, were the events of that winter.

Please recall that noble son of Erin, Timothy Daniel "Big Tim"

Sullivan, the New York Congressman and political fixer and who helped make the city work and, more importantly in the world of baseball, was a mentor to Frank Farrell and Bill Devery, the Yankees' owners.

Recent years had not treated Sullivan with kindness. Always a debonair man about town and a favorite of many ladies, Sullivan was now suffering from tertiary syphilis, a cruel turn of events in the era before penicillin. His health deteriorated in the first decade of the new century. A court judged him mentally incompetent and finally committed him to a sanitarium in mid-1912.

According to the incompetency hearings, Sullivan elicited paranoid delusions. He believed spies were watching him and that his food was being poisoned. On January 12, 1913, the New York *Sun*, which kept its readers in the know about such things, reported in a prominent page two article that he was mourned after being committed, "beyond cure."

The newspaper did not mention the ailment. Wink, wink. Everyone on the street knew.

After about a year, in early 1914, Sullivan escaped from the sanitarium. According to some accounts, he had slipped away from orderlies after an all-night poker game at a private residence. Within a few hours, a train hit him on the tracks in the Eastchester area of the Bronx, New York. He was pronounced dead at the scene.

Sullivan's body was brought, and held, at the local Fordham morgue for ten days. No one identified him. Or no one chose to identify him. Sullivan was classified as a vagrant and scheduled for burial in Potter's Field, this despite his expensive clothing and "TDS" diamond monogrammed cufflinks, which miraculously had not (yet) been stolen.

Just before removal of his remains for burial, a police officer named Peter Purfield, assigned to the ever-pleasant morgue detail, was peeking under various sheets at the "odd cold ones" that came in. Purfield's eyes went wide.

"That's 'Big Tim' Sullivan," Purfield said.

Sullivan's family was notified. The death hit the newspapers. Things started to happen.

The engineer of the train that struck Sullivan stated that he thought the body was already deceased. The New York *Times*, ever anxious to cause trouble, speculated that Sullivan might have been killed and placed on the tracks. And, adding to the speculation of foul play, Thomas Reigelmann, the Bronx coroner and Tammany political appointee who signed the death certificate, failed to recognize the body of his longtime friend despite the lack of trauma to the decedent's face.

Hmmmmm...

In any event, the one thing everyone agreed on was that Big Tim Sullivan was dead.

More than 25,000 people turned out for his funeral at St. Patrick's Old Cathedral on Mott Street in Manhattan. The funeral was at Calvary Cemetery, Queens, New York, where Big Tim remains to this day. But how did this affect New York City baseball, you ask?

Monumentally.

The death of Big Tim Sullivan in 1912 had closed off the access of Frank Farrell and Big Bill Devery, the Yankee owners, to Tammany-related revenue. Simultaneously, Farrell and Devery had grown tired owning the second rate American League franchise in New York. They wanted out. Worse, Farrell had frittered away a fortune on a new stadium project and his thoroughbred racing ventures were dripping in red ink.

Devery, who never had a Farrell-sized bankroll to begin with, was in no better shape. The two men, longtime friends and business partners, had also begun to bicker, not just between each other but with their manager, Frank Chance, the former famed Cubbie first baseman, who was now leading the Yankees to another less-than-impressive seventh-place finish. There were issues of player discipline, or the non-existence of it.

Things hit the bottom after an ugly loss to Connie Mack's A's. A clubhouse encounter between Chance and his bosses turned physical. Writers, players and sportswriters pulled the husky manager and the even larger, but much older and more lethal, Bill Devery away from each other.

It was time, to understate things, for Farrell and Devery to scram from the baseball business. Part of being a successful crook, after all, is knowing when to fold up shop.

Farrell discounted rumors that he had been in sale negotiation with the Ward brothers, the wealthy bakers and owners of the Brooklyn Tip Tops in the new Federal League. "The report is without a grain of truth," asserted Farrell. "My club is not on the market at any price."

Sure thing. Like most statements from Farrell, this one was at variance with the truth. Giants manager John McGraw, a Farrell friend, knew who might be able to buy what.

Soon after, Colonel Jacob Ruppert, a former United States Congressman (with the support of Boss Croker at Tammany Hall), and head of a thriving New York City brewery, expressed interest in purchasing the Giants.

"My team isn't for sale," McGraw answered. "But the other New York team might be."

Colonel Jacob Rupert was more than just a millionaire beer baron. Ruppert also had stellar New York political connections. Ruppert had been elected to the United States House of Representatives in 1898 as a member of the Democratic Party to the United States Congress, defeating incumbent Philip B. Low of the Republican Party in New York's 15th Congressional District. Ruppert and the effulgently named Lieutenant Colonel Tillinghast L'Hommedieu Huston, a retired army engineer who had made a fortune in construction in Cuba, approached Ban Johnson and attempted to buy the floundering New York Americans.

McGraw steered the pair to Frank Farrell. Eventually, in return for $460,000, which Farrell and Devery reportedly split down the middle, control of the New York Yankees passed into the hands of Colonel Ruppert and Captain Huston. With league president Johnson serving as broker, the transfer officially happened in late January 1915.

Not everyone celebrated the departure of the Yankees founders, particularly Farrell.

"I exceedingly regret that Farrell is out of the American League," Johnson informed the press. "Mr. Farrell is a perfect baseball man, one who is popular with every club owner in the league and I know that his associates ... as well as myself regret his passing from our organization."

Farrell make have been a bit of a racketeer and crook, but he was seen as an honorable racketeer and crook, as much as such a thing existed. He was also good on his word and personally likeable.

The two new Yankee partners made an odd couple: As opposed to Ruppert, the soft-spoken, well dressed patrician who spoke with a distinctively Teutonic accent, the physically larger Huston was a self-made man known for his craving for challenge and adventure and disheveled dress.

Nonetheless, the new owners were intent on turning around the fortunes of the New York Americans. This they did, pumping the team with new blood, new money and renewed political clout in the process. The team was known as the Yankees now and things would be different. Then McGraw compounded everything for the future by allowing them to play in the Polo Grounds and pay rent as tenants.

Meanwhile, the battle over the estate of Big Tim Sullivan plodded along: for the next seven or eight years, the same amount of time that Ruppert and Huston would be co-owners of the Yankees. There was a protracted battle over Sullivan's estate, which, by some estimates, ranged as high as $2.5 to $3 million.

Creditors took their bite first, then the bulk of the assets went to Sullivan's full siblings, Patrick H., Mary Anne, and half-brother, Lawrence Mulligan. Sullivan had one child with his wife Helen, a daughter who died in infancy. He did, however, get around town a bit: he fathered at least six illegitimate children, many with actresses affiliated with his theatrical ventures.

Two of the actresses who bore Sullivan's children were Christie MacDonald and Elsie Janis. They have long been forgotten today but they led interesting and accomplished lives.

MacDonald was a Canadian-born American opera singer and musical comedy actress. Her child with Timothy Sullivan was placed in the New York Foundling Hospital in 1904. She returned to the stage that same year and remained active until 1920, performing almost non-stop and recording several early gramophone recordings. The hit 1913 musical *Sweethearts* was specifically written for MacDonald by composer Victor Herbert. She retired from the stage after appearing in a successful 1920 revival of the musical comedy *Florodora*.

Elsie Janis, another of the ladies who brightened Big Tim's life, was an American singer, songwriter, actress, and screenwriter. She was a headliner on Broadway and London. On Broadway, she starred in a number of successful shows, including *The Vanderbilt Cup*, during which she shocked audiences by driving an automobile on stage. She entertained the American troops stationed in Europe during World War One and became known as "the sweetheart of the American Expeditionary Force."

Janis also enjoyed a career as a Hollywood screenwriter, actor, and composer. She was credited with the original story for *Close Harmony* (1929) and as composer and production manager for *Paramount on Parade* (1930). She and director Edmund Goulding wrote the song, *Love, Your Magic Spell Is Everywhere* for Gloria Swanson in her talkie debut film *The Trespasser* (1929). Janis' song, *Oh, Give Me Time for Tenderness* was featured in the Bette Davis three-hankie-classic, *Dark Victory* in 1939, also directed by Goulding. In 1934, she became the first female announcer on the NBC radio network.

Like Christie MacDonald, Elsie lived a long productive life into the 1960s, outlasting even the Giants in the Metropolitan area.

Chapter 33   The Lawful Skies

> "There is a world-old controversy that crops up whenever women attempt to enter a new field. Is a woman fit for that work?
> It would seem that a woman's success in any particular field would prove her fitness for that work, without regard to theories to the contrary."
>
> **Ruth Bancroft Law**

The year 1915 opened on just the right note in Daytona Beach, Florida, where the Brooklyn team trained. Giving exhibition flights in a small airplane was a young pilot named Ruth Law, also known by her married name, Ruth Law Oliver. A photogenic lady of twenty-eight, Law was one of America's great early aviatrixes. Harry Atwood and Arch Freeman at Atwood Park in had Massachusetts taught her to fly. Keep in mind, this was just a dozen years after the Wright Brothers' first successful flight at Kitty Hawk. To see a controlled aircraft in the sky remained a stunning sight for many people. Even more stunning was flying one of those machines, and more incredible than that was a female pilot. But Ruth Law received her pilot's license in November 1912 and was damned well going to use it.

Not surprisingly, her brother, Rodman Law, was an aviator and stunt man in silent movies. From time to time, he was known as "The Human Fly."

The first licensed woman pilot in the United States was Harriet Quimby in 1911. Katherine Wright, sister of the Orville and Wilbur, had as much to do with the first flight at Kitty Hawk as did her brothers. Women flew airplanes before they could vote. So in some ways it wasn't surprising to find Ruth Law at Daytona Beach in 1915 giving a demonstration of aerobatics before a large astonished crowd. She announced ahead of time that she was going to perform a loop for the first time, and proceeded to do so, not once but twice, to the heart-stopping amazement of her husband, Charles Oliver.

Wilbert Robinson, 1916

Among those who knew of Ruth Law was Wilbert Robinson, formerly McGraw's number one coach, now the manager of the Brooklyn team. Robbie also knew that a few years earlier Gabby Street, the former catcher of Walter Johnson in Washington, more recently with the crosstown Highlanders, had generated a bucket of publicity for himself by catching a baseball tossed out of the observation window of Washington Monument, some 550 feet toward the sky. Street had muffed the first dozen baseballs that were dropped but snagged the lucky thirteenth.

Someone on the Brooklyn team egged Robinson on, which was never difficult. How would Robbie, the pleasantly profane old catcher, feel about catching a ball tossed by Ruth Law out of her Wright Model B airplane at some 525 feet above the ground? Robinson, who always bumbled into borderline-crazy events like this, said he would have a go at it.

The day arrived. So did the intrepid Ruth Law in her biplane.

Out of the plane at the appointed hour came a small round object that at first was at first a dark spec in the sky. Then as it fell it grew both brighter and larger until, with the porky Uncle Robbie (seen here in 1916) circling under it, it came closer and closer and...

Splat!

"It caromed off the edge of his mitt and hit him right in the chest," Casey Stengel, the Brooklyn right fielder, a witness, later recalled. "It spun him around. Then he fell over, like in a Western picture where you see an Indian that's out on the hill, and they shoot him, and he goes around in a circle and falls dead."

Concerned, the Brooklyn players and some Giant friends raced to Robinson's side, where they found him covered with a sticky reddish-yellowish gooey mess, the remains of a pink grapefruit that had been substituted for a baseball. Robinson at first thought he had been mortally wounded, seeing the reddish remains of the fruit. Then he took it in stride.

Ruth Law explained later that part of her flight that morning was dropping golf balls onto a local golf course. When she arrived over the baseball field, she couldn't find the baseball. So she substituted the fruit. That was her story and she stuck to it.

It was the last thing McGraw had to laugh at all season.

After all, 1915 was the year of the Great Collapse for baseball's two greatest managers, Connie Mack and John McGraw. Mack refused to pay the salaries required to compete with the Federal League. He released Bender, Plank, and Coombs less than two years after they had won a World Series in 1913. Then, in various deals that strengthened every team except his own, the Philadelphia genius peddled away Eddie Collins, Jack Lapp, Herb Pennock, Jack Barry, and Bob Shawkey.

"Philadelphia fans," mused Mack, "are bored with perfection."

So Connie gave them imperfection, and plenty of it, instead. The team fell from first to eighth, winning 56 fewer games in 1915 than 1914. And the fans were even more bored.

Mack, however, had an opportunity to salvage his franchise and change forever the nature of Philadelphia baseball in 1915. His friend Jack Dunn, who owned the International League's Baltimore Orioles, was getting squeezed by the Baltimore Terrapins, the Federal League entry. The Feds had given Baltimore the illusion of big league ball and the city had responded by ignoring the Orioles, despite the latter's famous roots. Dunn wanted to sell off two of his young players, both pitchers, one of whom could hit pretty well, to turn a few bucks. "No, Jack," was Mack's famous response. "You keep those fellows and sell them to someone who can give you real money for them."

Dunn did. He passed them along to the Red Sox, who in turn, with the same shrewd financial savvy, passed along the two pitchers, Ernie Shore and Babe Ruth, to the Yankees.

The collapse of the Giants was more complicated. It was part age and part desire. Rube Marquard had been 12-22 in 1914. McGraw believed him to be finished. Riding him, challenging Marquard to turn things around, McGraw eventually threatened in the clubhouse one day to unload Marquard for $7,500 if only he could find a taker.

"Okay," Marquard answered. "Can I use your phone?"

"Sure," said McGraw.

Marquard telephoned Wilbert Robinson and traded himself to Brooklyn, against whom he had tossed a no-hitter earlier in the season. He would pitch for the "Robins," as the Dodgers were now called under Robinson's tutelage, and propel them into the World Series in 1916 and 1920. That same month, August of 1915, Fred Snodgrass was unceremoniously jettisoned to Boston, also for cash.

Toward the end of the season the Giants plopped into last place. There they stayed, the great Mack and the great McGraw occupying the basement at the same time. The Phillies won the National League pennant and the Boston Red Sox won the World Championship. How's that for an upside-down year? The Phillies and the Red Sox. Think about that.

Larry Doyle won the batting championship and Fred Merkle, who played the outfield sensationally as an emergency replacement late in the season, hit .299. But the saddest aspect was the decline of Mathewson. After throwing more than 4,600 innings since 1900, his wing was gone. He won only 8 games all year. He had, in fact, only 4 more wins left in his great right arm.

Back to Ruth Law for a moment, who was having a better mid-decade.

In the spring of 1916, she took part in an altitude competition, twice narrowly coming in second to male fliers. She was furious, determined to set a record that would stand against men as well as women. Eventually, she set a new cross-country distance record by flying from Chicago, Illinois, to Hornell, New York, in a Curtiss Pusher biplane similar to the one seen below.

After the United States entered World War One in April 1917, she campaigned unsuccessfully for women to be allowed to fly military aircraft. Stung by her rejection, she wrote a feisty article entitled *Let Women Fly!* in a new magazine, *Air Travel*. She argued that success in aviation should prove a woman's fitness for work in that field. Ruth Law then proved her point by earing as much as $9,000 a week for exhibition flights in 1917.

Many patriotic American women volunteered to fly and fight for their country in World War One, including Ruth Law. None was accepted by the military. Princess Eugenie Shakhovskaya and Princess Sophie Alexandrovna Dolgorunaya flew in combat for Czarist Russia in Europe. Still, American women pilots volunteered, none were taken seriously.

After the great war, Law continued to set records and participate in aircraft exhibitions.

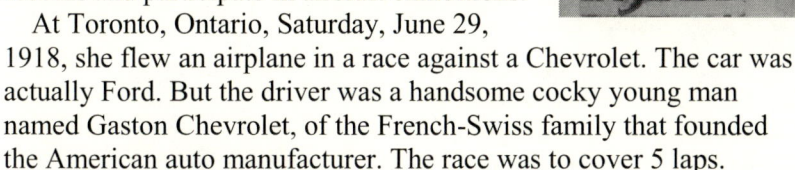

At Toronto, Ontario, Saturday, June 29, 1918, she flew an airplane in a race against a Chevrolet. The car was actually Ford. But the driver was a handsome cocky young man named Gaston Chevrolet, of the French-Swiss family that founded the American auto manufacturer. The race was to cover 5 laps.

Chevrolet was given a one-lap head start and won the race by half a lap with Ruth noisily gaining on him overhead. Smoke billowed from both vehicles and they hit the finish line seconds apart.

After Raymonde de Laroche of France set a women's altitude record of nearly 13,000 feet on June 7, 1919, Law set a new French woman's record on June 10, flying to 14,700 feet. Laroche in turn, however, broke Oliver's record on 12 June, flying to a height of 15,748 feet.

During World War Two, however, Ruth Law's ideas finally found receptive ears. Women were admitted to an auxiliary corps. Among them was Women Airforce Service Pilots (WASP) which trained and ferried military planes from base to base within the United States. Between September 1942 and December 1944, the WASPs delivered 12,650 aircraft of 78 different types. Each woman who flew freed a male pilot for combat missions, a dubious honor.

Thirty-eight WASP fliers lost their lives in accidents while serving. Eleven died during training. Twenty-seven perished on active duty. Because they were not officially part of the military, under the existing guidelines, a fallen WASP was sent home at

285

family expense. Traditional military honors or notes of heroism, such as medals, permission to allow the U.S. flag to be placed on the coffin or displaying a service flag in a window, were not allowed.

Nonetheless, Ruth Law saw many of her early ideas become reality. She died in San Francisco in December of 1970, sixty-five years after the day she dropped a grapefruit on the unsuspecting Uncle Robbie.

There was a footnote on Gabby Street, the old catcher and later manager whose attempts to catch the ball off Washington Monument led to Uncle Robbie being splattered by the foxy aviatrix's grapefruit.

Almost three decades later, Street returned to St. Louis where he had been a player and manager. He was now a broadcaster. As a color commentator on the St. Louis Browns radio broadcasts after World War Two, he worked with a younger microphone partner who had been born in St. Louis with the name of Harry Christopher Carabina.

As a younger man serving time in Joliet, Illinois, the town not the prison, Carabina had been advised by WCLS station manager Bob Holt to change his name to something less awkward on the air. Thus – Holy cow! - Harry Carabina became Harry Caray, seen here with a microphone, and began a Hall of Fame career up and down the American Midwest as one of the most popular baseball broadcasters of all time.

All in all, he did far better than Gaston Chevrolet who had beaten Ruth Law around that oval in Ontario. After his May 31, 1920 victory at the Indianapolis 500, Chevrolet moved on to California to the compete in the Beverly Hills Speedway, a 1.25-mile wooden board track. That track was built for early auto racing on a parcel of land today includes The Beverly Wilshire Hotel. Chevrolet (seen here to the left) died when his Frontenac crashed on lap 146 of the 200-lap race. He was 28 years old.

286

Chapter 34   Mordechai and Matty

"You can learn little from victory.
You can learn everything from defeat."

Christy Mathewson

McGraw was not a man to sit still with a losing hand.

When the Federal League went belly-up during the winter of 1915-16, McGraw attempted to pick up the best pieces. He purchased the contracts of pitcher Fred Anderson and catcher Bill Rariden, as well as two outfielders, Benny Kauff, the Federal League's best hitter, Edd Roush, and infielder Bill McKechnie.

With those signings accomplished, McGraw packed off Chief Meyers to Brooklyn, where he was reunited with his one-time coach, Robinson, and his favorite pitcher, Marquard. Then the Giants opened the season by losing eight in a row. McGraw planned to tear apart the whole franchise and build again from the ground up, but his plans were tempered by a torrid winning streak of seventeen in a row, all on the road. Another slump followed.

Eventually, McGraw did the inevitable. He moved Mathewson off the ball club. "Trade" is perhaps too strong a word, though that is what happened. Mathewson had entertained the idea of managing for many years, and McGraw was not inclined to surrender his own job. The solution arose with the Cincinnati club, which needed both a persona and a leader. Mathewson figured to be both. After over six hundred games in a Giant uniform and a career total of wins that has yet to be surpassed in the National League, Mathewson was shipped to Cincinnati with Roush and McKechnie, two of the ex-Federals, for Buck Herzog and an outfielder named Wade (Red) Killefer.

Upon Mathewson's departure, McGraw was genuinely moved.

"He's not only was the greatest pitcher I ever saw," McGraw said, "but he is my friend. He could stay with the Giants as long as he wanted to. However, I'm convinced his pitching days are over.

He is ambitious to become a manager and I have helped him to gratify that ambition." McGraw helped in a second manner, also. Upon Mathewson's departure, he suggested that if Roush were played in center field every day, he would rise to greatness.

Mathewson took McGraw's suggestion and started Roush on a career that landed him in Cooperstown, New York.

Mathewson's Cincinnati club would finish the season tied for seventh, while the Giants, finishing fourth, would climb back to the first division, mostly due to a late season winning streak of 26 games. It would be, however, a year of further emotion and adjustment. Among the older players who also moved along that season was Larry Doyle, who went to the Cubs on August 28 in a five-player deal that brought Bronx-born, broad shouldered third baseman Henry (Heinie) Zimmerman to the Polo Grounds.

"The Great Zim," as he called himself.

Doyle took the trade hard, sitting tearfully in the clubhouse after learning that he was gone. Doyle had given rise to the well-publicized saying, "It's great to be young and a New York Giant." Now he coined another one. "Batting champion one year, traded the next."

It was on September 4 in Chicago that year, however, that an era of baseball came to an end. Since the early 1900s, the Chicago Cubs and the New York Giants had dominated the National League. During the ten years from 1904 through 1913, the Giants had won five pennants and the Cubs four. Five times the teams had finished one-two. Inevitably, as showdown games between the two clubs had come around, Mathewson had opposed Three Finger Brown. Matty's no-hitter against the Cubs in 1905, for example, had come at the expense of Brown, who allowed only one run and one hit until the ninth. Yet Brown had won 9 matchups in a row, from July 12, 1905, until October 4, 1908, the playoff for the pennant following the Merkle incident. Now, in 1916, they would oppose each other a final time in the second half of a doubleheader between the Reds and the Cubs.

Mordecai Peter Centennial Brown was a sturdy, affable Hoosier who was known as "Miner" to his friends and teammates. A miner was what he had been back in Indiana before baseball had come to his rescue. His patriotic parents hung the Centennial on him to celebrate his date of birth: 1876. But he was best known by the nickname the sportswriters gave him, "Three Finger" Brown. Actually, he had a Fellini-esque eight and a half fingers. Five on one hand and the remainder on the "paw," as he called it, that threw a baseball for a living.

In 1908, Brown's greatest season, he won 29 and lost 9, plus two World Series victories (and an ERA of 0.00) over Ty Cobb's Tigers. That year in 312 innings he walked 49 batters, threw 9 shutouts, and won 11 starts in a row. He also made his contribution to the science of pitching. It was Three Finger Brown's innovative theory that you got a hitter out by working against his batting stance.

"If a batter had a straight up stance, close to the plate," he once explained, "I'd pitch inside to him. If he crouched, I'd try to keep the pitch a little high, and a fellow who stood away from the plate was fed outside pitches. The main objective is to take the power away from the hitter keep him from putting much wood against the ball."

Now, about that hand. You've heard of Brown and you know his nickname. But you've never seen the hand, right?

You're going to. Now.

When Brown was seven years old, his older brother was operating a feed-cutting machine that ground up hay or alfalfa with grain on the family farm. Young Mordecai rammed his right hand into the shaft where the blades revolved. His forefinger was cut off below the second joint. The second finger

was also mangled and broken. A few weeks later, while the hand was still in splints, Brown was chasing a hog across a field. He fell, broke the third and fourth fingers on the same hand, and pushed the reset tip of the second finger far back into his hand. This time there was no doctor around. When the splints finally came off, the hand was grotesque, with not one finger normal.

But there was no pain. So, in accordance with medical procedure of 1883, nothing was done. All that was left at the end of Mordecai Brown's right arm were two swollen, twisted fingers, one misshapen finger, an amputated finger, a thumb, and 239 career wins.

But Brown claimed the accident was a stroke of luck, as it gave him a far greater "dip" on his curveballs. It also made him a perfect foil for Mathewson: the gnarled workingman's hero as opposed to the vision of middle class perfection. And it made him famous. Everyone wanted to *see* that hand, even John McGraw, who was notorious for not fraternizing with opposing players.

Once in 1906 after Brown had shut out the Giants, McGraw strolled close enough to Brown to get a good look at the famous paw. McGraw winced. "As Mac walked away," Brown recalled years later, "he said, 'I'm going to have the first finger on the hand of each of my pitchers cut off tomorrow.'"

Brown slipped suddenly to 5-6 in 1912. The Cubs released him. After an 11-12 season with Cincinnati, he drifted over to the new Federal League, where competition was less keen, for a couple of seasons. He became the manager of the St. Louis team for a while, then moved on to Brooklyn. Meanwhile, Mathewson's arm expired with similar abruptness. In 1915 he was 8-14. The "fadeaway" was gone and so was the supernatural talent of always retiring the key hitter. The end for both men was in sight.

Brown, at age thirty-nine, drifted back to the Cubs in 1916. He pitched only sparingly. At the same time, McGraw was deeply depressed over the fate of Mathewson, thirty-six, whom he had come to regard as a surrogate son.

"He can't pitch anymore," McGraw confided to many intimates between the 1915 and 1916 seasons. That's when McGraw first entertained the notion of sending Mathewson west to manage Cincinnati.

Mathewson approached his new challenge with the same grace and dedication with which he had pitched. The Reds improved under his command, but the season was already a loss. August passed. The team was due in Chicago for a Labor Day series with the Cubs. And Mordecai Brown announced that he would, in the second game of the September 4 doubleheader, pitch his final game as a Cub.

Mathewson had been looking for a spot to test his own arm, to see if it was as dead as he believed it was. What better place than the same game? So Christy Mathewson would oppose Three Finger Brown for the final time over twelve years of competition.

As the date approached, public interest in the game built and the doubleheader was soon a sellout. The Cubs won the first game, 3-0. The great ovations began when Brown and Mathewson took the field to warm up for Game Two. There was a short ceremony to mark Brown's retirement. Then a bulky display of long-stemmed American Beauty roses was presented to each pitcher. And the game began.

Mathewson had announced in the days before the game that he would pitch as long into the game as Brown did. Brown responded that Matty better be in good shape, because he intended to pitch all nine innings. But in the first inning, the Cubs touched Mathewson for two easy runs. It looked like Matty would be gone quickly, despite his promise.

Brown gave up a run in the second inning to make the game close. Matty started to settle down. But by the end of three innings, the score was 3-3.

Brown allowed three runs over the next two innings. Matty hung a particularly poor pitch to Cub first baseman Vic Saier, who pounded it for a two-run homer. At the end of five, it was 6-5, Reds. Under other circumstances the great Mathewson and the great Three Finger Brown would have been gone.

But not today.

Grimly and resolutely, the two pitchers continued, neither willing to leave before his rival.

Brown singled twice off Mathewson. Mathewson doubled and singled twice off Brown. Hits flew in every direction. In the top of the sixth, Cincinnati added two more runs for an 8-5 lead. Neither pitcher had much left. Both survived on guts, guile, and endurance. The crowd was silent. Mathewson gave up hits, but each time escaped. And now Brown was being pounded. The Reds added runs in the eighth and ninth for a 10-5 lead. But Brown retired a final Giant in the top of that inning to mark the complete game. The crowd rose and gave him a tremendous ovation as he walked off the field. He tipped his cap with his famous disfigured paw.

Then Mathewson ran out of gas. The Cubs hit him virtually at will in the bottom of the ninth. But there was no manager to pull him because he *was* the manager. Gritty, tough, stubborn, he refused to pitch any less baseball than Brown. The crowd savored what might be the final irony: Mathewson might win, but Brown might pitch the complete game. Two runs scored before a long fly was the first out. A line drive became the second out, but a single brought in a third run. It was 10-8. Mathewson had nothing left except willpower. The tying run came to the plate. *Pitching in a pinch.* Mathewson reached for the old reserve a final time and somehow found it. Pinch hitter Fritz Mollwitz who had been a ten-year-old boy in Germany when Mathewson first pitched for the Giants popped up a final fadeaway. Third baseman Heinie Groh caught the ball. It was over.

Cincinnati won it, 10-8. Mathewson had given up fifteen hits, Brown nineteen. It was Matty's ninth career win against Brown, versus Brown's thirteen career decisions against Mathewson. The two hurlers shook hands at the pitcher's mound after the game and a standing ovation sent them to their respective dugouts.

"Never again," Matty told reporters as he trudged to the locker room, "will I go into a ball game." He didn't. And neither did Brown in the major leagues. Three Finger couldn't resist temptation, however, and kicked around the American Association and the Three I League until 1920.

There was, of course, a great deal of sadness in that confrontation between the old pitching aces that afternoon. An era ended, certainly, and if anything was demonstrated it was that greatness had departed from the arms of both men. But there was also a suggestion of the tragic in that final matchup, setting a tone that was to bedevil Mathewson for the next decade.

That Mathewson won the final encounter only underscored the fact that when it had counted, Brown had always won. Similarly, it was Brown, the maimed old workingman, who had come home to bask in the adulation of his adoring fans. Mathewson was in the enemy city in an alien uniform. Like Babe Ruth as a Boston Brave or Duke Snider taking his final cuts as a San Francisco Giant many years later, Mathewson looked like the victim of some terrible prank. All this while giving up eight runs and fifteen hits. Matty that afternoon looked like a Greek god who had fallen from grace. And though he never pitched again, tragedy followed him.

The following summer, Christy's younger brother Henry died suddenly of influenza at the age of thirty-one. Christy, wishing to get away from baseball at last, quit as Cincinnati manager at the end of the 1918 season and enlisted in the United States Army. He was sent to France, arriving shortly after the end of World War One. Yet somehow, he was exposed to poison gas, which injured and weakened his lungs.

He returned to the United States the following year, but he had contracted tuberculosis, one of the deadliest diseases of the day. (It had also claimed the life of Ruth Law's brother, the stunt man, while he was in the Army Air Corps in 1919.)

For the next few years Matty lived in a sanatorium at Saranac Lake, New York, receiving and answering letters from friends and fans.

In many ways, Three Finger Brown had bested the unfortunate Matty once again. When Brown finally retired from baseball, he went quietly home to Indiana and for much of the rest of his life owned and operated a service station at 7th and Cherry streets in Terre Haute. A simple sign hung outside above the gasoline pumps.

It said: MORDECAI BROWN.

Brown lived out his life comfortably, a lean, quick man who was usually seen in rimless glasses and a tweed suit, chewing on an unlit cigar and talking baseball with anyone who brought up the subject. Friends there called him "Brownie." Never "Three Finger."

Brown died in 1948, having outlived Christy Mathewson by twenty-seven years. Yet it was only fitting that a year after his death Brown, too, was elected to the Baseball Hall of Fame. For a final time the two ancient rivals had been reunited.

Chapter 35   Ty Cobb and The Winds of War

"If you were a younger man, I'd kill you."

**Ty Cobb, who
meant it, to John McGraw in the
in the lobby of the Oriental Hotel,
Dallas, Texas, 1917**

By the spring of 1917, John McGraw had managed the New York Giants for almost fifteen years. He had elevated the franchise up from the National League's basement, brought it to the heights of one World Championship and five pennants, had managed great pitchers and great hitters, had spawned younger managers in his own image, had traveled the world and met kings, and had played baseball on four of the world's five continents. He had become wealthy and famous. He was the manager for whom young players aspired to play. He was also forty-four years old and embarking upon the most turbulent eight years of his life.

At spring training in Marlin that year, there was a kid of nineteen whom McGraw liked instantly. The name the boy had been born with was Royce Middlebrook Youngs. Somewhere along the line, the Royce had been changed to Ross. Thus Royce Middlebrook Youngs had become Ross Youngs by the time he arrived in Marlin in 1917.

Today an athlete Youngs' size would be considered a tall dwarf. He was only five feet eight, 150 pounds, but he was solidly built, fast, and aggressive very much the way McGraw himself had been at a similar point in his career. Youngs was a Texan from the town of Shiner and as a teenager had attended West Texas Military Academy, an institution that could never be confused with a party school. There Youngs had distinguished himself as a track star and as a halfback on the school's football team.

But all Youngs lived for was baseball. At the age of sixteen, he went directly from the military academy to the Texas League. The jump proved too precipitous, however, and Youngs drifted to lower leagues for the next three seasons. In 1916, however, he hit a robust .362 in the Western Association. As usual, McGraw's spies were everywhere. The Giants acquired him.

In camp in 1917, Youngs impressed his manager. But McGraw, realizing that the kid wasn't quite ready for the big time, turned Youngs over to Mickey Doolan, the manager of Rochester in the International League. At the time, the Giants had a working agreement with Rochester.

"I'm going to give you a kid who is going to be a great ballplayer someday," McGraw said to Doolan. "Take good care of him, because if anything happens to him, I'll hold you responsible."

So Doolan took Youngs to Rochester. McGraw would open the season with an outfield of Benny Kauff, Dave Robertson, and veteran George Burns. He could wait for Ross Youngs.

In early April, the Giants began a trip north with the Detroit Tigers, still managed by Hughie Jennings. McGraw may have been at the height of his career as a manager that year, but Ty Cobb was at the height of his career as a player. Cobb was a crowd favorite but had few friends among other ballplayers. The Giants were ready for him.

In Dallas on a Saturday afternoon, Cobb swaggered onto the field moments before game time. "Who do you think you are, you bum?" Giant shortstop Art Fletcher called to Cobb. "Why didn't you stay back at your hotel? We could have gotten along without you."

"Why, Mr. Fletcher," sportswriter Frank Graham recalled second baseman Buck Herzog adding, "don't you know better than that? Don't you know all these people are out here today just to see the great Ty Cobb? Like the star of any show, he has to come on late to take his bows."

For bench jockeying of the time, it was pretty tame stuff. Cobb didn't react. But by the time he batted for the first time and got hit by an inside pitch by Jeff Tesreau, he was pretty mad. Arriving at first base, Cobb jawed at Tesreau. The entire Giant bench started riding Cobb. Herzog then made the moment complete by glaring at Cobb from second and daring him to steal the base.

Furious, Cobb attempted to steal on the second pitch. Anticipating him, Jeff Tesreau pitched out and catcher George (Lew) McCarty fired the ball to the bag. It arrived with Cobb several feet away from the base.

But it was not second base that Cobb was after. It was the second baseman.

Cobb came into the base with his sharpened spikes high in the air, taking aim and hitting squarely Herzog's legs. Cobb's cleats ripped into Herzog's uniform and flesh, sending Herzog sprawling. Herzog counterattacked. Art Fletcher, sharing the same opinion of Cobb as most of the Giants, attempted to kick him in the head. Hey, this was an *exhibition* tour. Can you imagine what a World Series would have become?

Umpires, teammates, and the Dallas police managed at length to pull the two players apart. As soon as they were upright and released, they attempted to get at each other again. In the stands, clusters of Giant fans went at it with Tiger fans. Eventually, the umpire tossed Cobb and Herzog out of the game.

Herzog went quietly. Cobb, who was a sorehead even when he was in a good mood, never went quietly. He complained angrily to Hughie Jennings that if he was out of the game he would quit the entire series with the Giants. As Cobb presented main gate attraction and as there were several games left to play on the joyously friendly springtime journey north, this was a serious problem.

Jennings bitched to the umpire, who was unmoved. "Get him out of here," he said. "He started it. Get him off the field."

Now, were both teams staying in the same hotel? Of course they were. There the festivities continued.

In the lobby of the hotel that evening, who should cross paths but Cobb and McGraw? It was not the type of encounter McGraw would shy away from, despite the fact that Cobb was bigger, stronger, and a dozen years younger. McGraw hurled every expletive he could think of at Cobb.

"If you were a younger man, I'd kill you!" snarled Cobb.

"I'm young enough. Start killing," McGraw raged.

A crowd of hotel guests ringed the potential combatants. Cobb kept his temper in check and walked away from McGraw. The Giant manager shouted after him. A few minutes later, Herzog found Cobb in the hotel dining room. Still wanting a piece of him, Herzog approached Cobb's table.

"What's your room number?" he asked. Cobb gave it.

"I'll be there at ten o'clock," Herzog said. "I'll bring one player with me and you can have one of your players there. You can have (Detroit Tiger trainer) Harry Tuttle there, too, as referee."

Cobb never broke pace with those twin demons, the knife and fork.

At ten PM, when saner men were easing into sleep for the night, Herzog and Heinie Zimmerman appeared in Cobb's room. Cobb was there. So was Tuttle. And so were eight other Detroit Tigers.

The two men stripped to their waists. Herzog threw the first punch, which decked Cobb. But Cobb came back up swinging, got to his feet, and administered a merciless pounding to Herzog until Tuttle stepped in. As might be expected, accounts varied as to the severity of the fight and the prowess of the combatants.

"They fought like a couple of washerwomen," Tuttle said later.

Others had other opinions. Baseball writer Joe Williams, who wrote New York baseball for 34 years for the New York *World Telegram and Sun* and

Heinie_Zimmerman 1917

its predecessors, dubbed it, "the Louis-Schmeling fight of baseball."

But one of the Tigers, noting that Herzog was bloody and reeling when he left Cobb's room, maintained that the fight had only been broken up when Cobb had Herzog bent backward over the front of a bed. Kindly old Tyrus was jumping on him, trying to break his back.

Incredibly enough, Cobb and Herzog hadn't had enough of each other by the end of this day. They intensified the insults they threw at each other during games, then staged a rematch of the Texas fisticuffs in a hotel room in Wichita Falls. Eventually, both men were satisfied. Herzog had knocked Cobb down in front of his teammates, while Cobb felt he had given Herzog the worst of the pounding, which in fact he had.

Herzog never missed a game on the tour. Cobb jumped the Tigers eventually and joined the Cincinnati club for the rest of spring training, having made the necessary arrangements with manager Mathewson. This amused the Giants greatly. When the Giants and Tigers parted company in early April, having partaken in a few lesser brawls to round out the spring, the New York Giants sent Mr. Cobb a postcard from Manhattan, Kansas.

"It's safe to rejoin your club. We've left," the card said. It bore the signature of all the players on the New York club.

The card, however droll it may have been, got lost in the newspaper headlines of the day. It was April 6, 1917. On that day, the United States Congress declared war on Germany. The United States was now an active participant in the World War One.

Chapter 36   1917: The First Wartime World Series

"Every day above earth is a good day."

Ernest Hemingway in *The Old Man and the Sea*

On June eighth of the same year, McGraw embarked on one of the most chronicled of his disputes with umpires. Leaving Redland Field in Cincinnati, catcher Tom Clark of the Reds was still jawing at umpire Bill (Lord) Byron. Byron was a colorful fixture around the National League. He was known as "The Singing Umpire" for his sometimes-irritating habit of humming segments of popular tunes between pitches. Some batters and catchers claimed the musical interludes drove them to distraction. On this particular afternoon, however, it was Lord Byron's calls around home plate that had driven both sides to a frenzy.

Hearing the Reds catcher berate Byron, McGraw, happening by, couldn't resist poking in his two cents' worth.

"I don't know what you just said, Tom," McGraw said, "but it goes double for me."

Byron turned toward McGraw. "I wouldn't say that if I were you," the umpire warned.

"I'll say anything I please!" McGraw answered.

"You talk big. I guess you didn't used to be so tough," Byron continued. "They say you were run out of Baltimore."

Now McGraw was warming up. "'They say'?" McGraw screamed. "Would you say it?"

Byron thought for a moment, then gave the wrong answer.

"Yes. I'd say it," he said.

McGraw punched Byron in the face with a short righthanded jab, bloodying the ump's upper lip. As Byron staggered toward the runway to escape, McGraw kept after him, taking a few more swings. First to the umpire's rescue was Matty Schwab, the Reds' excellent groundkeeper. Bill Rariden took care of Schwab with a clout to the side of the head. Then players from both teams joined the mayhem and piled in, as did fans and police. Byron was escorted to the umpires' dressing room, while cops pulled McGraw to the Giants' locker room.

Reporters, who had been at the scene, filed their headlines right away: McGraw had struck an umpire. There would be hell to pay. Everyone knew it.

While Byron remained silent, McGraw spoke freely about what had happened. This was not, he stressed, an incident between a manager and an umpire, even though he knew it would be interpreted as such. This was man-to-man. Byron had told "an infamous lie" about him, McGraw claimed. He had never been "run out of Baltimore." McGraw said he would have popped *anyone* who said such a thing to his face. And he probably would have.

Five days later, John K. Tener, a former pitcher, a former governor of Pennsylvania, and currently president of the National League, suspended McGraw for sixteen days and fined him $500.

The Giants were in Pittsburgh that day. The news of the fine and suspension first arrived via a telegram that was opened by Sid Mercer, covering the Giants for the New York *Globe*. Mercer wrote on baseball and boxing and had once been the road secretary for the usually inept St. Louis Browns. Mercer took the telegram to McGraw, who was at his hotel.

"Do you have anything to say?" Mercer asked, getting out his pencil and his notepad.

"Yes. I have plenty to say," responded a furious John J. McGraw. The "Little Napoleon" then launched into a detailed tirade that focused on the incompetence of National League umpires in general and the dishonesty of Tener in particular. The latter, stretching things considerably, was said to be a tool of the Phillies and had been put into his position by the Philadelphia owners.

"Do you want to be quoted on this?" Mercer asked.

"On every word of it!" McGraw howled. The story was passed around the press corps. McGraw reconfirmed his statements and even stood by his opinion the next day when confronted by Pittsburgh writers.

"I have nothing more to say," McGraw said in conclusion. "It's all in that story."

"That story" would haunt McGraw for the rest of his days.

After a series in Chicago, McGraw traveled back to New York by train, summoned by Harry Hempstead and Cornelius J. Sullivan, the Giants' general counsel. When he rejoined the team at Braves Field in Boston, he had issued a signed statement repudiating the interview with Mercer.

"Don't take it so seriously," he told the enraged sportswriters. "I had to sign that statement to quiet Harry Hempstead and Cornelius Sullivan. It will all be forgotten in a few days."

"Not by me it won't," answered Sid Mercer.

The writers felt that the wording of the repudiation had challenged their integrity. McGraw pronounced the incident as "closed," but the New York Chapter of the Baseball Writers' Association demanded a hearing from the National League to vindicate Mercer and three other writers who filed the story. The writers from other cities lined up behind their New York colleagues. The incident escalated. Faced with adverse publicity for the league, John Tener scheduled a hearing at league headquarters, then at 8 West 40th Street in New York. John Conway Toole, counsel for the league, was appointed to take testimony and issue a finding.

Sid Mercer, as a result of the flap with McGraw, now covered the

Yankees. As the incident had given greater visibility to Mercer and aroused a certain amount of sympathy on his behalf, his dispatches had an increased audience, which in turn gave the Yankees greater visibility in New York.

Mercer was the star witness at the hearing, though he was ready to drop the whole matter. What was the point of an investigation, he asked. "McGraw called me a liar and I called him one right back. I don't think anyone has any doubt who is telling the truth."

The Baseball Writers' Association did press the hearing, however.

Questioned by the distinguished trial lawyer Martin W. Littleton, the counsel for the Baseball Writers' Association, Mercer concisely restated his story and how he came to file it. Littleton was as high profile a mouthpiece as existed in that year. He had defended Harry Kendall Thaw in 1908 at his trial for the murder of architect Stanford White. He had also defended Harry Ford Sinclair, the head of Sinclair Oil, from criminal charges resulting from the Teapot Dome scandal. Littleton had served one term as United States Representative from New York from 1911 to 1913, representing a district in Brooklyn.

But Mercer was unshaken by the interrogation by McGraw's lawyer, John Montgomery Ward, the former player who had picked off a law degree from Columbia after hanging up the spikes. McGraw then made a lousy witness in his own behalf, confirming part of Mercer's story in a roundabout way, then denying other parts of it.

Two days later, Tener accepted Toole's finding.

McGraw, the hearing ruled, had not been misquoted. Mac was thus fined another $1,000. It had cost McGraw $500 for popping the Singing Umpire in the lip, then twice that for talking about it.

Mercer wired Tener and asked the league president to rescind the fine. But it stood. McGraw paid it, though McGraw remained unfriendly with both Mercer and Tener for the rest of his life. Mercer refused to ever again cover the Giants.

While all of this was going on, the New York Giants were

playing great baseball. When the team demolished the Phillies in a September series at the Polo Grounds defeating their old adversary Chief Bender, who was doing a final cameo appearance with the other Quaker City club, second place Philadelphia dropped out of contention to stay. Though most of the country was spending more time reading war news, the Giants streaked to a pennant, winning by 10 games. For the second time, McGraw had moved a tail-end team to the pennant within two seasons.

This year McGraw's troops had backed balanced pitching with two of the league's six .300 hitters, the majors' home run champion (Dave Robertson tied Gavvy Cravath of Philadelphia with 12), and the National League leader in RBIs (Heinie Zimmerman with 102). An August road trip upon which the Giants won 12 of 17 games had put the team in first place to stay. Pitcher Harry (Slim) Sallee had defeated St. Louis, 3-1, on September 24 for McGraw's sixth National League pennant.

The 1917 World Series against the Chicago White Sox opened amid a backdrop of patriotic fervor. The United States was now at war. The stands at Comiskey Park in Chicago were almost invisible under two tons of red, white, and blue bunting. The White Sox themselves nearly disappeared under the same colors. Gone was their normal black broadcloth uniform. Gone also were even their white socks. For the occasion, the Sox wore new bridal white uniforms with a huge red and blue *S* upon their hearts. Their leggings were red, white, and blue, like Uncle Sam's spats.

In the first game, Eddie Cicotte of the White Sox opposed the Giants' Slim Sallee. Cicotte (28-12; 1.53), featuring a "shine ball" that was midway between a slider and a spitter, was termed "unbeatable" by the press. That day he was. The White Sox won when Chisox center fielder Oscar (Hap) Felsch lofted a lazy, drifting fly ball to left center field in the fourth inning. Burns and Kauff ran for the ball and camped under it. As Burns pounded his glove to make the catch, a sudden gust of wind carried the ball into the bleachers. Chicago won, 2-1.

The second game was played on Sunday, October 7, the first Series game ever played on the Sabbath. In a pregame ceremony, a $50 Liberty Bond was presented to Hap Felsch, the hero of the previous day, by McGraw's pal Al Jolson. Jolson had jumped his touring show *Robinson Crusoe, Jr.*, in which he performed in blackface, just to attend the game.

{Author's note: This show was not the high point of Jolson's career; skipping out to the World Series was a great idea. Sample lyrics from the show:

"Over a thousand years, or maybe more
Out on an island on a lonely shore
Robinson Crusoe landed one fine day
No rent to pay
No wife to obey..."}

McGraw started his ace, Ferdie Schupp, in an attempt to even the Series. Schupp was pounded. The White Sox won, 7-2, and took a two-game lead on the road to New York.

Game Three provided a New York version of the same wartime pageantry. The city proclaimed the day as Liberty Loan Day and if Comiskey Park in Chicago was festooned with two tons of streamers, the massive, sprawling Polo Grounds was burdened with four tons. Banners in every section of the Polo Grounds announced the million-dollar loan drive to support the war in France. Three marching bands clomped noisily through the stadium, playing even as the game progressed and crossing the field between innings. The bands were followed by a legion of patriotically attired young men and women with red, white, and blue collection plates in order to, in the words of Giants president Harry Hempstead, "disgorge bank notes from the forty-five thousand fans at the game." Most fans were called upon to "disgorge" once every three innings. And all that was preceded by some other giving.

A group from Connecticut presented Benny Kauff with a walking stick with an ivory horse's head as a handle. A group from Manhattan presented a gold Swiss watch to Hank Gowdy, the first National League player to enlist in the Army. And a group from Chicago, who traveled all night by train to see the game, presented a box of raspberries to their least favorite Giant, Heinie Zimmerman.

The box was delivered directly from their box seats, hurled with a high majestic arc midway through the third inning. Zimmerman was apprised of the gift when it hit him between the shoulder blades as he attempted to bat.

Zimmerman, as a Giant, always seemed like a lightning rod for strange events. Once he tired of a fan who had heckled him all season. Zimmerman climbed into the stands and, in the best Bronx fashion, decked the loudmouth. Recalling the incident in the 1950s, the wonderful writer and humorist Harry Golden moaned, "That personal touch in baseball is gone. It is more of a business today."

With the game scoreless in the fourth, the Giants' Dave Robertson defied gravity and climbed the Polo Grounds' eleven-foot fence in deep right field to rob Charles (Chick) Gandil of a potential triple or inside-the-park home run. Robertson's catch ended the inning, stranding two White Sox runners.

Inevitably, Robertson led off the home half of the inning. He was still receiving a standing ovation for his catch when he smacked a standup triple. He scored one play later. The Giants had all they needed as John (Rube) Benton shut out the Sox, 2-0. Cicotte, winner of Game One, was the loser.

Ferdie Schupp returned in Game Four and pitched a gem. The Giants won, 4-0, to tie the Series. Benny Kauff pounded two homers off Red Faber. One was inside the park, lost for several minutes in the rosebushes in front of the center field clubhouse. That set the stage for the return to Chicago. The White Sox had not scored a run in twenty-two innings and the momentum was clearly with the Giants.

Game Five began like a continuation of the last two. While the White Sox hung zeroes on the scoreboard in their halves of the innings, the Giants quickly dispatched Ewell (Red) Russell, the Chicago starter. At the end of five innings, it was 4-1, New York.

Enter the wind again, and the Giants began to unravel.

In the seventh a windblown popup landed between three Giants with two outs and the bases loaded. When Dave Robertson relayed the ball to second baseman Buck Herzog, Herzog too became afflicted with the dropsies. The runner from first crossed the plate and tied the score as Herzog grappled with the ball, unable to even pick it up. In the next inning, Heinie Zimmerman, launched a throw to second base that landed at the right fielder's feet. A run scored. Then four singles followed. The final score was 8-5, but not before Urban (Red) Faber, scheduled to start Game Six for Chicago, had to be summoned to get the final two outs when New York brought the tying run to the plate.

Faber might as well have slept on the mound overnight. He started the next day as planned. Woeful hitting sabotaged him. Chicago tallied no earned runs that day, just enough to win. Inexplicably, the normally smooth Giants were still afflicted with iron gloves.

The first run of the game was one of the most famous in World Series history. Former Philadelphia Athletic Eddie Collins opened the inning by grounding to third baseman Zimmerman. Zimmerman's throw landed in the seats behind first, allowing Collins a free trip to second. Shoeless Joe Jackson lofted a cupcake fly ball to Robertson in right. Robertson dropped it. Collins went to third, Jackson stayed on first. Rube Benton then concentrated upon the ever-dangerous Hap Felsch and induced him to bounce the ball back to the mound. Benton charged off the mound with the ball and ran to the third base line. Collins, who had been trying to score, ran back toward third. Bill Rariden, the Giants' catcher, moved up the line to help his pitcher in an anticipated rundown, leaving the plate unguarded.

Benton threw the ball to Zimmerman. Collins turned away from third. In a moment that must have remained with him forever, he saw a completely open baseline in front of him with an unguarded plate at the far end. Collins, who was fleet enough to steal 743 bases in his career, took off. Zimmerman, finding no one to throw the ball to, took off after him, comically holding the ball with the elongated fingers of his outstretched arm.

McGraw stood in the dugout screaming, red in the face with rage, as his third baseman chased Collins ninety feet down the baseline and across home plate, never catching him. The Giants never caught the White Sox, either.

Chicago scored another unearned run in the fourth and two more in the ninth when Benny Kauff dropped a fly ball with two out. Chicago won the game and the Series, 4-2. The incensed McGraw left the clubhouse fifteen minutes after the game's conclusion, returning home to sulk. Zimmerman was roasted by the Giant fans and in the press, particularly in New York, where one reporter wrote a long-paraphrased takeoff on Kipling's *Gunga Din*, refraining it with, "I'm a faster man than you are, Heinie Zim."

Zimmerman, in his defense, spent the rest of his life insisting that the plate was unguarded. "Who should I have thrown to?" he demanded the day after. "Klem?"

"I was afraid he would," answered umpire Bill Klem, who had worked the plate that day.

But the Giants of 1917 were defeated, and John J. McGraw had lost his fourth consecutive World Series, this time to a franchise that would not win another one for eighty-eight years.

McGraw never blamed Zimmerman for the bizarre twist that had ended the Series. Just as in 1908 when a weird play had cost the Giants the pennant, and in 1912 when a team miscue had cost the Giants the Series, McGraw refused to single out the player to whom others wanted to donate the goat horns.

"It wasn't Zimmerman's fault," McGraw reflected in the clubhouse after the game and for years ever after whenever the subject of 1917 came up. The man to blame, he said, if anyone, was first baseman, Walt Holke, who stood at first base watching the play instead of covering the plate.

Not so fortunate, however, were those who tried to extend sympathy. At the end of the Series, Chicago White Sox manager Clarence (Pants) Rowland ran to meet McGraw as the two teams started off the field. Rowland, magnanimous in victory, extended his hand to McGraw. "Mr. McGraw," he said. "I'm glad we won. But I'm sorry you had to be the one to lose."

The answer was vintage McGraw: "Get away from me, you god damned busher," he said.

A Fan's Reminiscence – David Lippman

My grandfather became a Giants fan in 1908 as a little kid, when his older brother introduced him to the game. My great-uncle worked for John J. McGraw in the poolhall he co-owned with Arnold Rothstein. He became a bagman and enforcer for the "Big Bankroll," helping to fix the 1919 World Series. Grandpa became an honest pharmacist but got good seats for a lot of Giants game. The great-uncle, Sam "Izzy" Lippman, skimmed the take from Rothstein, who found out. Izzy is forever a cornerstone in the infrastructure of New York. He's holding up the Hellgate Bridge.

(Photo: Arnold Rothstein in 1926. NY Daily News)

David H. Lippman
New York, 2018

Chapter 37 War and Remembrance

"There is no charity in baseball.
I want to win the pennant every year."

Colonel Jacob Ruppert, Owner, New York Yankees

McGraw, never averse to surprising people, surprised everyone in January of 1918, possibly even himself. He traded Buck Herzog for Larry Doyle. Also tossed into the bargain was a young righthander named Jesse Barnes, who was a few years away from proving he was a major league pitcher.

The trade was one of the few times in McGraw's career where he might correctly have been accused of giving in to sentiment. He loved Doyle in much the way he had loved Mathewson. He had always disliked Herzog. By this time, he despised him and was pleased to pack him off once again, the third and final time, this time to the Cubs where he would end his career amidst controversy and accusations, never substantiated, that he had conspired to fix a game versus the Phillies. In 1924 Herzog managed briefly at Newark in the International League, and he managed Easton in 1925 and 1926. He then signed on as baseball coach at the U.S. Naval Academy.

"The old man and I had our arguments," Herzog would recall many years later of Mr. McGraw and his time as a Giant. "I guess because we both liked to win so well. But, when he got into a pinch and needed someone to put fire into his team, I am glad to remember he always was calling back Buck Herzog."

Doyle, it turned out in 1918, could still hit and field adequately and formed a competitive infield with Walt Holke, Art Fletcher, and Heinie Zimmerman. In the outfield, Ross Youngs came up from Rochester and was more than ready. He hit .302 and stole 49 bases to lead the league. He fit into right field well, with Benny Kauff in center and George Burns in left. Slim Sallee (left, looking ebullient) and Jeff Tesreau (right, looking bored out of his mind), seen here at the Polo Grounds on Opening Day 1918, were part of the pitching staff.

Yet the pitching was no more than ordinary and the war in Europe took its toll. Pitcher Jesse Barnes was the first Giant to don a doughboy uniform. Relief pitcher John (Spitball) Anderson was next, followed later in the season by Kauff. Walt Holke also left the team to serve in a defense plant. McGraw was a patriotic soul, and never complained. But when the Cubs rushed past the Giants in early June, it was clear that New York would never catch them. The Giants gave a reasonable chase, but Chicago won the pennant by ten and a half games, even though the regular season halted abruptly on September 2 in support of the war effort. The Red Sox were back in the World Series, defeating the Cubs, 4-2.

A brash young pitcher for the Red Sox named Babe Ruth won two games, including a shutout. Combined with the win and games Ruth had pitched in 1916, Ruth had pitched 29 consecutive scoreless innings, a World Series record that would stand for 42 years. His World Series record was 3-0 with a 0.87 ERA. There it would remain. He would never pitch in a World Series again, but he sure would hit.

The Giants drew less than a quarter of a million fans to the Polo Grounds that year of 1918: the lowest figure in the Twentieth Century and a direct result of the war. There was another bitter wartime note, too. It came after the season ended.

On October 5 in the Argonne Forest in France, three weeks before the Armistice, Major Eddie Grant, McGraw's Harvard-educated third baseman of a few seasons earlier, was part of an infantry detail that attempted to rescue the "Lost Battalion" of Major Charles White Whittlesey. Grant, who was now in private law practice in Boston, he was a Harvard guy, after all, had been one of the first men to enlist when the United States entered World War One in April 1917. He served as a captain in the 77th Infantry Division.

During the battle of the Meuse-Argonne Offensive, all of Grant's superior officers were killed or wounded. He took command of his troops on a four-day search for the "Lost Battalion." During the search, an exploding shell killed Grant on October 5, 1918. He was the first active or former Major League Baseball player killed in action in World War One. He was buried at the Meuse-Argonne American Cemetery in Lorraine, France, where he remains to this day.

Over the winter, with the war at an end, Harry Hempstead began making noises about selling his ball club. McGraw was only too pleased to help him along. Looking for new ownership that would allow him a free hand to run the club, McGraw turned to Joe Vila, the longtime New York sportswriter, for advice. Vila suggested George Loft, the founder of a New York based candy company that bore his name.

A deal with Loft was nearly worked out. But on the morning of January 14, 1919, the New York press was notified that the New York Giants would make an important announcement at their headquarters, then situated at Fifth Avenue and 23rd Street. Loft was nowhere present at the press convocation.

Instead, reporters were presented to one Charles A. Stoneham. "The costliest franchise in baseball has changed hands," said a press release. So had $1 million Stoneham's money, which went to the Brush Estate. Stoneham now owned 1,300 shares of Giants stock, while Francis X. McQuade, a city magistrate, took 70 shares to become the organization's treasurer. McGraw, the new vice president of the club paid $50,000 for 70 shares also, realizing a longtime dream to own at least part of the New York Giants.

The sale to Stoneham came as a surprise, if not a shock, to newsmen, most of whom had never heard of him. The betting had been that if Loft failed to purchase the club, George M. Cohan or Harry Sinclair were waiting in the wings. So where had this guy Stoneham come from?

The answer was not so readily apparent. Initial press reports identified Stoneham as "a Wall Street broker." Charley Stoneham modestly termed himself, "a Giant fan all my life."

But so were a lot of people.

The truth was that Stoneham was indeed active on Wall Street, but not as one might have suspected. Stoneham was the owner of a "bucket shop," a stock establishment that took orders to buy and sell stock, but never executed the orders. They were thoroughly legal up until the time of the Great 1929 Crash, a form of gambling establishment that sought to make good on their clients' bad purchases by replacing stock after it had gone down in value.

It was a dubious business, made even more so by some of the characters Stoneham associated with. One of his partners was Arnold Rothstein. Rothstein was a multi-millionaire gambler who would finance young bootleggers Jack (Legs) Diamond, Waxey Gordon, and Dutch Schultz. He was also believed to be, at the time, the key financier of the international heroin trade.

Arnold "The Brain" Rothstein may have done more to corrupt American sports than any other person in the 20th century, a high distinction since many others had their greedy fingers in the pot. Rothstein always denied it, but he was the man suspected by many of engineering the Chicago "Black Sox" baseball scandal, when players threw the 1919 World Series. He became a central figure in the Black Sox scandal of 1919-20.

Rothstein had a passion for gambling: sporting events, casinos, cards and horses. He used an extensive network of "advisers" to take the chance out of certain games of chance and had other people in his employ to perhaps influence the outcome of some events. He was accused of engineering the outcomes of many horse races, for example. He reportedly operated an illegal casino in Manhattan. If you thought the roulette wheel in *Casablanca* that spun for Humphrey Bogart was rigged, you should have seen some of Rothstein's.

Rothstein was the inspiration for Meyer Wolfsheim in *The Great Gatsby*. He would achieve even greater notoriety when he was shot to death during a high-stakes poker game at the Park Central Hotel in 1928.

Rothstein was also, "The Brain" in several of Damon Runyon's short stories about New York in the 1920's. As a newspaper writer reporter, Runyon knew Rothstein personally. He later was assigned to the trial of Rothstein's alleged killer. This being New York in the 1920's, the accused killer was acquitted.

At the time of the sale, Rothstein had also bribed Judge McQuade in a case involving a fatal shooting at one of his illegal casinos, a joint known as The Partridge Club. What was clear by that time was the missing link that had brought Stoneham to the Giants. His ties to Tammany Hall, including then-Mayor Alfred E. Smith, were impeccable. No one had ever owned a major ball club in New York City without the blessing of the Tammany Tiger.

With all of these unsavory associations linked to the Giants, McGraw then went out and added yet another. He traded hardworking Bill Rariden, his catcher, and Walt Holke to Cincinnati for Hal Chase.

Christy Mathewson had accused Chase of giving something less than his best efforts for the Reds in 1918. What Mathewson was really saying was that Chase had "tanked" games in order to win payoffs from gamblers.

Mathewson had made a formal complaint, which was heard by the league during the winter of 1918-19. By this time, however, Mathewson was in Europe, serving as a captain in the U.S. Army and somehow never responded to the cabled inquiries for a disposition in the Chase case. More than likely, Matty never received the requests. But without Mathewson's testimony, Chase was exonerated. Chase had, however, worn out his welcome in Cincinnati and had been blacklisted by the entire American League on suspicion of dumping ball games. He had nowhere to go and appeared to be finished. Then McGraw traded two good players for him.

To make the absurdity complete, when Mathewson returned from France and World War One, he resigned as the manager of the Reds, only to be hired a few days later as a coach for John McGraw. So there they sat together on the Giants' bench: Chase, the accused; Mathewson, the accuser; and McGraw, who had given jobs to both.

It was cozy. With Chase and Mathewson gone, the Reds won the pennant, then surged past the corrupt White Sox to win the World Series. The Giants, with Hal Chase as a regular, finished second.

By that year, however, the New York Yankees were making waves. In late July, Jacob Ruppert signed Carl Mays to a pitching contract. Mays, the Red Sox ace, had jumped the club on July 12 after losing 11 of 16 decisions. Now he revivified the Yankees, pushing the team into the American League pennant race for the first time in public memory.

The Yankees fell short by seven and a half games, finishing third behind Chicago and Cleveland. In a funny portent of things to come, New York led the American League in home runs with 45.

There was another vision of the future that season. As McGraw's team was chasing Cincinnati to no avail, the world of bats and balls was agog over one George Herman Ruth, who pitched for the Red Sox but more often than not played the outfield.

On September 20, on Babe Ruth Day at Fenway Park in Boston, Ruth had banged home run number 28 of the year over the far reaches of the right center field fence.

The home run had broken a major league home run record that had been so remote up until this season that Gavvy Cravath, who had hit 24 home runs for the Phillies in 1915, had been widely believed to be the holder of the single season record. As Ruth's totals mounted in 1919, however, baseball historians dug out the fact that Edward (Ned) Williamson, a Chicago White Stockings third baseman in 1884, had hit 27. Most of them had been hit over the inviting left field wall, which was just over two hundred feet from the plate at Chicago's miniscule Lakefront Park. But the number *had* been 27, and that was the record until Babe Ruth Day in Boston in 1919. One of the witnesses to the new record was Lieutenant Colonel Tillinghast L'Hommedieu Huston of the Yankees, Harry Frazee's old pal.

Four days later, Ruth brought his act to New York for a two-game series at the Polo Grounds, where the Yankees were currently playing their home games. In the second of the two games, Bob Shawkey of the Yankees, Ruth's friend and future teammate, hung the Babe an off-speed curveball about shoulder high.

Ruth waited. Then he uncoiled.

The ball rocketed toward right field, rose, rose . . . and continued to soar. Most observers claimed that the ball was still rising when it cleared the double deck grandstand in right field. What was unarguable was that the ball *did* clear the grandstand completely and eventually crashed down among the bottles, rocks, winos and tall grass of a nearby field.

Up until that moment, the hardest ball ever hit in the Polo Grounds had been believed to be one hit by Joe Jackson, then playing for Cleveland, which had cleared that same grandstand in 1913. Ruth's blast had dwarfed Jackson's. It had also tied the game, 1-1, in the ninth inning, a contest that the Yankees would eventually win in thirteen, 2-1.

But that was lost in the shuffle. Colonel Huston witnessed the clout of September 24, saw the crowd's reaction to it, and made up his mind about the future of Babe Ruth.

On January 5, 1920, the two colonels heralded in the new decade and the Jazz Age itself by completing the purchase of Ruth from the Red Sox. The price was $125,000 cash, plus a $300,000 loan from Ruppert to Red Sox owner Harry Frazee so that Harry, who also produced Broadway shows, could get his theatrical projects on the boards. The collateral on the loan, by the way, was Fenway Park.

Frazee would eventually make a fortune producing *No, No, Nanette!* on Broadway with Ruby Keeler, but someone should have said, "No, no!" to Harry before he sold the Babe to New York. Ruth had set a new home run record, led the league in RBIs and runs scored, hit .322, and had a 9-5 record as a pitcher in his spare time. Despite the fact that in preceding and subsequent years, Frazee would dispatch such quality players as Tris Speaker, Harry Hooper, Duffy Lewis, Ernie Shore, Carl Mays, Waite Hoyt, and Joe Dugan from Boston, Ruth was "The Franchise," the soul of the club. Now he was gone. Boston fans screamed in indignation, not for the last time.

Ruth screamed, too. The Babe was reluctant to come to the big town.

Frazee, who sometimes just couldn't shut up, changed that, too, by publicly claiming that he was forced to unload the troublesome Ruth. The latter's well-known boozing and lechery were all but destroying the moral character of his ball club.

Oh?

When Ruth read about this in the Boston papers, he was happy to take a few shots himself, recalling how Frazee was such a "cheapskate" that at the previous season's Babe Ruth Day, which had packed Fenway, Ruth had to pay for his wife's ticket. Then, at the end of the afternoon, according to Ruth, Frazee had given him a "cheap cigar" as a reward for his cooperation.

"That's a fair example of his liberality," Ruth said. And with that sour taste in his mouth, Ruth was happy to get out of town and head toward the bright lights of Broadway

In a funny kind of way, the Yankees and Giants intersected at time. Despite the fact that the Giants were vastly the more successful franchise, both were building for the coming decade. Both were pretenders to the thrones of their respective leagues. And both, gradually were getting tired of each other.

McGraw, taking a cue from the way the Yankees were plucking players from the Boston Red Sox, put together a deal in August 1919 in which the Boston Braves' best southpaw, Art Nehf, came to the Giants for three expendable pitchers: Joe Oeschger, Cecil (Red) Causey, and Johnny Jones, a minor league catcher named Mickey O'Neil and $55,000.

The following June, McGraw unloaded Art Fletcher, who had been his regular shortstop for nine years, to the Phillies for Dave (Beauty) Bancroft, who would fill that same position for the next four seasons. (Fletcher would eventually have the dubious honor of managing the horrible Phillies in 1923.) These were good trades that began to put the pieces together for the next generation of great New York Giant teams.

A Fan's Reminiscence – Bart Bramley

When I moved to Dallas in 2003, a mutual friend introduced me to a man named Jack McCormack, who had grown up in New York. McCormack was an early Texas Instruments executive who had a lifelong passion for baseball.

I didn't meet Jack until he was almost ninety. He was born eight days before JFK in 1917, but our shared love of baseball made us instant friends. Jack and I would see each other at local bridge tournaments several times a year and we also had a few dinners and other non-bridge meetings over the years. Jack had his (still mostly) red hair and beard all of his life, along with a gentle soft-spoken voice and a constant twinkly grin. I was fascinated to meet someone who was not only incredibly knowledgeable about the game, but who had actually witnessed some legendary events.

Jack's father was both a baseball fan and a theatre lover. On weekends they were often at Yankee Stadium or the Polo Grounds. Jack was 25 months old in 1919 when his father, a New York Giants fan, took him to see the New York debut of future Hall of Fame player Frankie Frisch.

Jack's baseball memories went back into the '20s and players like Cobb and Ruth. Carl Hubbell was his pick as the greatest pitcher ever. Jack was a little young to have seen Walter Johnson or Christy Mathewson, but he saw every great one since then. He once recounted that the best game he ever attended was Carl Hubbell's 18-inning shutout at the Polo Grounds on July 2nd, 1933, part of a pair of 1-0 wins. The nightcap took only nine innings.

Those were also the years of musicals by George Gershwin, Cole Porter and Rodgers and Hart. Jack saw Fred and Adele Astaire, Ethel Merman, Bob Hope, and George M. Cohan. He also saw Abbott and Costello when they first appeared on Broadway and did their *Who's on First?* skit.

When studying at Columbia University in 1940, Jack obtained a commission as a reserve Ensign in the U.S. Navy Supply Corps. After graduation, in November 1941, he was assigned to the Naval Air Station at Pearl Harbor. When the Japanese attacked on December 7, battleship row was not far from his quarters. His introduction to World War Two was the sight of the Rising Sun on the wings of a plane overhead.

I made sure to "consult" with Jack on baseball matters at critical junctures, like when the Giants and Rangers met in the 2010 World Series. I had assumed that he was still a Giants fan, but I discovered that after living in Dallas for more than fifty years his allegiance had switched to the locals. (I could never imagine not rooting for my beloved Yankees in similar circumstances.)

I talked to him just a couple of weeks before he died, in October of 2012, at the age of ninety-five. The Giants were again on a deep post-season run, and he sounded as sharp as always.

Bart Bramley
Dallas, April 2018

{Author's note: What a remarkable life! Was there anyone else in the 20th Century who personally witnessed the attack on Pearl Harbor, Fred and Adele Astaire dancing and Carl Hubbell's 18 inning 1-0 victory? I doubt it.}

Chapter 38 The Violence of the Lambs

**"I don't want to belong to any club
that will accept me as a member."**

Groucho Marx

The 1920 season began on a strange note.

One of McGraw's many friends had returned from a hunting trip in Mexico, where he had captured three wildcat cubs. The Giants had moved their spring training site to San Antonio to open the new decade. There McGraw's friend presented the New York skipper with one of the cubs as a pet.

Not Surprisingly, McGraw took a shine to the animal and named it "Bill Pennant." According to witnesses, it was a handsome creature, no bigger than a house cat, but had spots like a leopard and large padded feline feet. "He'll bring you luck, John," the hunter had promised. Again, not surprisingly, the cat took a liking to McGraw, perhaps sensing a kindred spirit

There was no mistaking what this animal was. Larry Doyle and a number of other Giants wouldn't go near it. McGraw took great delight at brandishing the wildcat at key moments. Once that spring in Asheville, North Carolina, Bill Pennant was unleashed to roam the grounds of a hotel. As McGraw sat in the hotel's writing room, the cat hopped up on the windowsill, walked into the room, and slowly meandered among pens and paper.

A few minutes later, a soldier entered the room and didn't see the cat until he was about to sit down to write a letter. At that moment, he quickly recoiled and stared at McGraw. "Does that belong to you?" he asked.

"Yes," McGraw answered. "It's a wildcat."

The soldier thought for a moment. "Are you an animal trainer?" he asked.

"Yes," said McGraw. "My name is Hagenbeck. Did you ever hear of me?" McGraw was referencing a man named Carl Hagenbeck, a German exotic animal merchant well known in the era. Hagenbeck had died in 1913, but apparently the news had not yet reached the American hinterlands.

"Yes, Mr. Hagenback. Sure, I heard of you. Everyone has heard of you." The soldier moved to the door. "Jesus! A wildcat for a pet!" he said.

Then he fled.

Less amusing, however, was the trip north. McGraw had arranged at the end of the previous season to tour northward with the Boston Red Sox. McGraw had hoped to capitalize on Babe Ruth's increasing box office power. But by this time, Ruth was gone.

The Giants arrived in New York but got off to a slow start. One problem was at first base, where George Kelly, after riding the bench for most of five seasons, had finally replaced Hal Chase, who took his odor of corruption with him when he left after one season.

George Kelly was a gangly, strapping young man of six feet four inches and 190 pounds. The New York sportswriters, in the un-subtle way they had with words, had hung the nickname "Hickpockets" upon him.

Kelly was clumsy at first base, particularly in contrast to the charmingly corrupt Chase. He had not yet learned to use his height and reach to his advantage. When fans got on him, he sulked. His batting average fell at the same time. After one particularly galling afternoon, McGraw called Kelly into the manager's office.

"I wanted to remind you," McGraw told him. "I'm the only one you have to care about around here. I'm running this ball club. Not the fans behind first base, the gamblers behind third, or the writers in the press box."

It was the same avuncular conversation that in previous years McGraw had laid upon Rube Marquard, Fred Merkle, and Fred Snodgrass. Again, it worked. Kelly began to hit and field.

The team, however, faltered. As soon as the Kelly crisis was solved, Frankie Frisch was sidelined by an appendectomy. A sub named Fred Lear filled in at third. This Fred bore the regal nickname of "King," but there was nothing royal about his batting average of .253 or his stolen base total of zero. It was closer to tragic. Like his namesake, Lear was a **man more sinned against** than sinning. And with Frisch out and Chase gone, the Giant attack, with speed as its premise, was at a halt. Doyle at second was slowing and Fletcher at short was, also. Hence the deal for Bancroft in June.

By the middle of July, Frisch returned. Immediately he proved his value to the team. The Giants, with Frisch and Bancroft now in the infield each day, rose from the cellar to third place in three weeks. They would make a distant run at the pennant before finishing second, seven games behind the Brooklyn team of Wilbert Robinson. But *that* was not the biggest storm cloud of 1920.

The problem was Babe Ruth.

The American League, sensing the ticket-selling power of Ruth, had slipped a new cork-centered baseball into play for the 1920 season. No one loved it more than the Bambino and, in a preview of coming distractions, no one launched the new balls more often, either. Batting against Bill Burwell of the St. Louis Browns, a reliever who had a great career in the minor leagues, Ruth launched one of the new cork-centered jobs out of the Polo Grounds on July 15. It tied Ruth's previous season home run record of 29.

Four days later, a White Sox pitcher named Dickie Kerr watched a couple of his best deliveries exit the Polo Grounds via the air corridor above the right field grandstand. Now Ruth had 31 home runs at the midway point in the season. This was, to say the least, just about incomprehensible.

In his outstanding biography, *Babe,* Robert W. Creamer compared the 1919 Yankees to John the Baptist, preparing the way for the Lord. Now, in 1920, the Lord was working his miracles. Often several each week. Ruth would hit the stratospheric total of 54 home runs that year. The next best slugger in the American League would have 19. No other team in the American League hit more than 50 home runs and the Giants, en masse hit only 46.

Meanwhile, Ruth's nocturnal prowling around New York only hyped the gate at the ballpark. No one printed the stories about The Babe (now 24 years old and with an apparently raging libido) drinking and womanizing, but the stories got around. It was difficult to find a New Yorker who *hadn't* heard any.

McGraw seethed.

He hated this new style of baseball. He had a growing personal dislike for the man who personified it. Worse still, the public flocked to the Polo Grounds to see the resurgent Yankees while the Giants vainly chased the Robins. The old single season attendance record of 910,000, set by McGraw's 1908 Giants, was surpassed by a whopping 400,000 by the Yankees.

So. The Robins were beating the Giants on the field, the Yankees were clobbering them in attendance in their own ballpark. People wanted to see Ruth knock the tar out of the baseball and they wanted to read about it. Ruth was pushing everyone else out of the lead position on the sports pages.

At the same time, McGraw came to the sad conclusion that Benny Kauff would never be the player for the Giants that he had been in the Federal League. McGraw released him to Toronto. And finally, Christy Mathewson's health was failing again. Big Six had left baseball indefinitely and had gone off to Saranac Lake, New York, for a rest. Can there be, then, any question as to the frame of mind McGraw must have been in on Friday night August 8, 1920, an evening which will live in legend forever in the world of New York nightlife?

McGraw had repaired to The Lambs Club for the evening, as was his habit. There he held court among his Broadway friends, discussing the day's events on the stage or at the Polo Grounds. Although Prohibition was the law of the land, this was a gentlemen's club, and was not unknown as a place of an occasional shot of bootleg booze.

McGraw arrived at The Lambs and wandered into the club's grill room. There he spotted, among the other members in the crowded room, a pair of cardplayers in one corner. One of them was John C. Slavin, a vaudevillian, comedian and a McGraw pal. The other cardplayer was William Boyd, a Broadway actor of the day, but not to be confused with the "other" William Boyd who later found fame as "Hopalong Cassidy."

McGraw apparently had a load on by the time he arrived at The Lambs for he mistook Boyd, his friend, for another actor, Walter Knight, whom he detested. McGraw strode over toward Boyd, an Englishman, and began cursing him loudly.

Boyd, stunned by the verbal assault from a man he had presumed to be his friend, stood and asked McGraw to shut up. Boyd told McGraw, "As a man I like you, as a baseball manager I like you, but I don't like your language." This exchange evolved into an argument over the superiority of American or English stage actors, and whether John Emerson should have defeated Wilton Lackaye for Presidency of the Actors' Equity. According to witnesses, Boyd asked McGraw to temper his language in the presence of several cleaning ladies, who were already at work at this late hour.

Temper his language? McGraw? Not very likely.

Moments later, punches were flying in every direction. One of the two combatants, witnesses differed as to who, grabbed a water carafe. Boyd and McGraw apparently took turns trying to crown each other. Like most fights in exclusive gentlemen's clubs on Saturday nights, this one was quickly broken up by cooler heads, but not before Muggsy, for all his pugilistic experience, had gotten the shorter end of the deal. Well, McGraw was on the floor and Boyd was still standing, so draw your own conclusion.

Slavin, who moments earlier had been peacefully playing cards, then helped pick McGraw up. Slavin and a resident of the club, a man named Winfield Liggett, a blustery retired U.S. Navy commander who was living at the club, decided it might be a good idea to escort McGraw home in a taxi.

As the three men stepped out of a cab about a half an hour later in front of McGraw's home at Broadway and 109th Street, another argument erupted. According to what the cabbie later recalled, McGraw shoved Liggett back into the cab and lurched through the doorway of his own apartment building. But when Liggett emerged from the cab a few moments later, he found Slavin unconscious on the sidewalk. When Slavin would not come out of it, the low comedy turned serious. An hour later, Slavin was admitted to St. Luke's Hospital in critical condition.

Enter the gendarmes, who were alerted by St. Luke's when the medical staff there determined that Slavin, who would remain unconscious for several days, had a fractured skull, a cut lip, two front teeth missing, and a badly bitten tongue. The police, hearing an account of things from Liggett and the cab driver, called on McGraw in the middle of the night, awakening him. McGraw was sporting a black eye and badly bruised forehead. He told police that he and Slaven had parted "on the best of terms." The unfortunate actor, suggested McGraw, "must have fallen."

Now here's the best part of the story: the police seemed perfectly content with this account of things. Boys will be boys on Saturday nights, they reasoned, so no charges were filed at the time.

The story did not sit well, however, with one James S. Shevlin, the chief Prohibition enforcement agent in New York. Shevlin someway somehow just kind of had this sneaking suspicion that some alcoholic refreshments may have had something to do with the events of August 8, 1920.

Shevlin and his professional blue-noses raided the famous club and arrested an employee who was caught trying to dump some expensive imported stuff down a sink. Then Shevlin got an indictment against McGraw for possessing a bottle of liquor, an act he admitted in a statement he gave to the police. The directors of The Lambs Club, of course, expressed shock - shock! - that any alcohol had been consumed on their premises.

By now Manhattan District Attorney Harold Swann was feeling left out. But not for long. He started making public noise about indicting McGraw for something. But he didn't know what, since Slavin at first remained unconscious, then refused to make any formal complaint against McGraw. Slavin instead sued McGraw after leaving the hospital. The number tossed around in the civil action was $25,000.

Not that the eye of this storm needed one more celebrity participant, but one entered anyway. This was William J. Fallon, one of the great criminal lawyers of the Twentieth or any other century. Fallon was known in the New York tabloid press as "the Great Mouthpiece." And he was exactly that, smooth and polished – when he needed to be.

Fallon was a prominent defense attorney during the Jazz Age who defended the gangster Arnold Rothstein and his accomplice Nicky Arnstein during the trial in which they were accused of fixing the World Series. He later inspired the Warner Brothers films *The Mouthpiece* (1932), *The Man Who Talked Too Much* (1940) and *Illegal* (1955). It was said that he also served as inspiration for the celebrity lawyer Billy Flynn in the musical *Chicago*. Fallon was a notorious drinking man himself who used to go on long sodden binges between high profile trials. He would later die at age 41 of what might have been termed acute life-style poisoning.

McGraw, during his heyday with the Giants, knew everyone in New York worth knowing. So it was no surprise that Fallon had been a friend of McGraw for many years. The attorney now rose up in righteous eloquent indignation when McGraw was being branded as the instigator of all this trouble.

The charges against McGraw proceeded with all the speed that one would expect from a New York court calendar. First McGraw was cleared of any problems with the local D.A. when Slavin settled out of court and never told his account of things. Then there was the federal problem involving possession of alcohol. That was handled admirably by Fallon, who delayed the case until the following spring.

Fallon, when sober, was brilliant. He had graduated Valedictorian of the Fordham class of 1906, and then continued to graduate from Fordham Law School in 1909. From the Jesuit education, he learned eloquence and oratory, skills he wielded like sabers. He was also known to grease a few juries in his day.

When John McGraw's day in court arrived, McGraw entered on crutches, the result of a "spring training injury." Under the guidance of The Great Mouthpiece, he told his version of things to Judge Learned Hand and a jury that Fallon had made certain contained a heavy sprinkling of Giant fans.

By that time, the federal case had been tossed into the lap of a young assistant prosecutor. Fallon made mincemeat out of him. The jury deliberated less than five minutes, returning with a verdict of not guilty.

By this time, however, the legal travails of John J. McGraw were small potatoes compared with the larger baseball issues before the courts. At the close of the preceding season, the entire scandal of the fixing of the 1919 World Series by the Chicago White Sox had broken onto the front pages of the newspapers. In comparison to eight White Sox tanking the series, McGraw's pugnacious evening didn't seem like much to get worked up about.

There were, however, some footnotes to the end of the 1920 season. Immediately after Tris Speaker's Cleveland Indians had beaten the overachieving Brooklyn Robins, 4-3, in the World Series, McGraw announced that his old friend Hughie Jennings, who now had a law degree from Cornell University, would be joining the Giants as a coach. Everyone wondered how, as Johnny Evers and Patrick (Cozy) Dolan currently held those jobs with the Giants. The answer soon came from Chicago, where the Cubs announced that Evers would succeed Fred Mitchell as manager. Benny Kauff, McGraw's disappointment in the outfield, was banned from baseball for life for his participation in a stolen car ring. Heinie Zimmerman and Hal Chase were also banned for acting as go-between for professional gamblers.

Then, finally, there was the matter of The Lambs Club.

The club bounced John McGraw as a member following the unsavory publicity generated by the events of August 8. The suspension would last for three years. Muggsy didn't take this lying down. He promptly had certain members' passes to the Polo

Grounds confiscated the next time they were presented.

The members came out on the short end of that exchange, also, for soon the year was 1921. Quietly and brilliantly, almost as if no one had noticed what he was doing, in the midst of all the other drinking, brawling and madness, McGraw had put together his greatest squad since 1905 and probably the greatest assemblage of talent in the history of the franchise.

Those poor little Lambs Club members who had lost their way couldn't possibly have picked a worse moment to forfeit their passes to the Polo Grounds.

Chapter 39   Another Pennant.

Anything goes!

Cole Porter

John McGraw was forty-eight years old by the time the 1921 season began.

No longer was McGraw be confused the wiry thin young third baseman of the Baltimore Orioles that he once had been. The years had taken their toll. Mac had a paunch, his face was reddish, and his hair had long since begun to gray. With the passing of years, he had also become more contemptuous than ever of defeat, aware that the years ahead were limited in their number. The players on his team had taken to calling him, "The Old Man." There was no mistaking what they meant by that.

The New York Giants had long been the dominant force in professional baseball. They were the most famous team in America, the most loved, the most hated, the most feared, and the most imitated. John J. McGraw's vision of the game, "inside baseball" or "scientific baseball," still remained. Now he had rebuilt his club from the pennant winners of 1917 and had a squad that could elevate his vision into a high art. It was only fitting that his tormentors would continue to be the upstart New York Yankees, his noisy tenants, who played no strategy at all other than to stand on the bases and wait for the Bambino to hit one over the roof of the upper deck. So, by the end of 1920, McGraw had had enough. He handed the Yankees an eviction notice. Nothing personal, just go away. Play your games anywhere you see fit: Central Park, the waterfront, or the floor of the Stock Exchange. Just take leave of the Polo Grounds, the most famous ballpark in the United States. The Yankees agreed to start looking for a new home.

McGraw entered the 1921 season feeling that, position by position, he had assembled the best team in baseball. But by the middle of the season, the Philadelphia Phillies, who were in the business not of competing with the stronger teams in the league but rather of selling off their stars at a profit, sent Dave (Beauty) Bancroft, Johnny Rawlings, Irish Meusel (whose brother Bob played for the Yankees) and Casey Stengel to the Giants. The acquisition of Rawlings for second base allowed McGraw to shift sparkplug Frankie Frisch to third. The advent of Stengel and Meusel allowed McGraw to "platoon" his outfielders.

Stengel was so pleased to return to New York, where he had played on the other side of the Brooklyn Bridge, that he left Philadelphia immediately upon learning of the trade.

"I wanted to get there before Mr. McGraw changed his mind," Casey would say years later.

But by late August, the Pittsburgh Pirates were seven and a half games in front of the Giants. They swaggered into the Polo Grounds for five games and announced that they only had to win two of them to settle the pennant race.

McGraw called a clubhouse meeting the night before the Pittsburg series was to start. What followed, in the words of Tom Meany, who obtained his account directly from Stengel and several other players, "may have been ranked with the invectives of Cato or the deliberately cajoling logic of Clarence Darrow." The gist was a tirade that was brutal even by McGravian standards.

McGraw started by telling his players that they could have been part of one of the greatest squads of all time, but they were now on the verge of being one of his worst. He reminded everyone how he had predicted the rise of the New York Yankees a few years earlier and had calculated the money to be made from a Giants-Yankees World Series. Babe Ruth (on his way to amassing an incomprehensible total of 59 home runs, many hit at the Polo Grounds) squaring off against the Giants, McGraw raged, would be one of the great showdowns of the century. But, he said, his bums had blown it.

"Now it's gone!" he screamed. "Gone because you're all a bunch of knuckleheaded fools! Pittsburgh is going to come in here tomorrow laughing at us. Pittsburgh is going to take it all! Pittsburgh! A bunch of banjo-playing, wisecracking humpty-dumpties! You've thrown it all away! You haven't got a chance! And you've only got yourselves to blame!"

With those words, McGraw departed, leaving his legion to think things over. He reappeared for the first game of a doubleheader the next day. He stood in a corner of the dugout, icy and silent, arms folded across his chest on a torpid Wednesday afternoon.

Sullen and downcast, his players sat along the dugout bench, watching the Pirates. On the field, the Pirates, chipper and confident, laughed their way through batting and fielding practice. In the Pirate dugout, Charlie Grimm strummed his ukulele. Pittsburgh looked like a team of joyous college kids at their end-of-term softball outing. Then they all assembled, right there at the Polo Grounds, and had their team picture taken for the upcoming World Series program.

McGraw just stared.

It is possible that Pittsburgh never knew what hit them that afternoon. The Giants blasted them, 10-2, behind Art Nehf in the first game of the doubleheader. Then Shuffiin' Phil Douglas, an erratic right-hander whose career revolved around spitballs and highballs, shut out the Pirates, 7-0, in the nightcap.

The jubilant Giants stormed into their locker room after the second game, delirious over the two wins. The Pirate lead was down to five and a half games. "I guess we really showed the Old Man up," said one young Giant.

"Wonder what he'll say now," said another.

The team whooped it up for several minutes. Then McGraw appeared.

Uncharacteristically, he was in street clothes, having changed in private.

As the room fell silent, he walked to a wash basin and briskly scrubbed his hands. For several seconds, there was not a word.

"I told you fellows last night that you didn't have a chance," said McGraw without looking up. "Well, I was wrong. You have a chance. A bare chance. If my brains hold out."

Then he strode from the room.

"It's a good thing he got out then," George Kelly recalled later, "or he might have been skulled by a shower of bats."

The next afternoon the Giants demolished the big sweeping

curveball of "Jughandle Johnny" Morrison for five runs in the second inning. Giant pitcher Fred Toney contributed to the barrage with a home run, then held Pittsburgh to two runs the rest of the way. The Giants won the third game and the Pirates were shaken.

Phil Douglas, who had pitched the second game on Wednesday afternoon, came back to pitch the fourth on Friday, winning 2-1. The key play was a spectacular catch made by Dave Bancroft behind second base on a line drive by Charlie Grimm. The shot should have scored the game's tying run and could have opened up a big inning. Instead, Bancroft turned it into a double play.

Another facet of John McGraw was on view during the Pittsburgh series, but his players and the public never knew about it. By 1921, Christy Mathewson had entered the sanitarium at Saranac Lake. After each game with Pittsburgh, McGraw would telephone Mathewson and boost the ailing Matty's spirits with an account of what had happened. Years later, Blanche McGraw recalled her husband's side of the conversations:

"You never saw such hitting, Christy... Yesterday [Earl] Smith caught and murdered the ball ... Today I put [Frank] Snyder in against [Wilbur] Cooper and he hit ... Kelly will hit over .300 this year. Remember how he was laughed out of the park five years ago?

"...Imagine that, Christy... We can take this Pittsburgh crowd now, for sure... They don't have much left. Call you tomorrow night... Take it easy... Tell Jane hello... And young Christy..."

By Saturday, the Pirates just wanted to get out of New York alive.

McGraw's old adversary, Barney Dreyfuss, had already constructed extra grandstands and bleachers back at Forbes Field in anticipation of his first World Series since 1909. Now Barney (to the chorus of "Hey, Barney!" of course) was squirming. He got to squirm some more on Saturday afternoon. Pennant fever had gripped Manhattan. Thirty-eight thousand fans packed the Polo Grounds and howled with delight. Art Nehf pitched again. Aided by a home run by Frankie Frisch, Nehf shut down the Pirates, 3-1.

"Not bad," growled McGraw after sweeping five games. "But Pittsburgh is still in first place."

Not for long. The Pirates won two out of three from Brooklyn at Ebbets Field, but the stuffing had been knocked out of them. The Giants visited Forbes Field in September and continued where they had left off at the Polo Grounds, sweeping three more from the stunned Pirates. From there on, there was no race at all.

The Giants finished four games in front, having made up 11 games over the course of the season's final five weeks. Crucial had been the season series with Pittsburgh, which the Giants had won, 16-6.

Chapter 40   1921: World Champions Again

**"Why shouldn't we pitch to Babe Ruth?
We pitch to better hitters in the National League."**

John J. McGraw on the eve of the 1921 World Series.

As McGraw had predicted, the World Series of 1921 was to be played against the Yankees. It was the first Series to be played all in one ballpark and the last to use the cumbersome five out of nine format. It also presented McGraw with the greatest challenge of his career.

Not only had McGraw failed in his last four attempts to win a World Championship, but he now found himself face to face with his irritating tenants. Not only did McGraw hate Yankee-style baseball, but he also disliked the Yankees personally. Worse, McGraw felt the Yankees had humiliated him by outdrawing the Giants in the Polo Grounds. This was, to be sure, the adversary he wanted. But he wanted equally to pin back their ears.

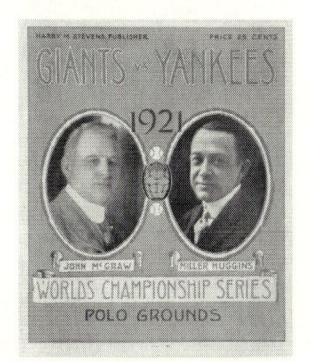

There was another touch that McGraw found mortifying. McGraw had signed a Brooklyn schoolboy a few years earlier by the name of Waite Hoyt. He had pitched in one game for the Giants, then McGraw had tried to pack him off to the minor leagues for seasoning. Hoyt had balked, then argued with McGraw. This was not the type of personnel move that McGraw intended to debate with an eighteen-year-old kid from Flatbush, so McGraw had cut him. Sometime later, the Red Sox signed Hoyt and, as was their habit, packed him off to the Yankees as soon as he began to show some potential. In 1921 he was the number two pitcher on the upstart Yankee staff, winning 19 games behind Carl Mays' 27.

The Series opened on October 5 with the grandstand less than packed. Rumors had swept the city that the game was sold out and tickets were impossible to obtain, so many fans never bothered to go to the park. Down in the choice seats, however, old-timers Ned Hanlon and Monte Ward turned out for the event, sitting a few boxes away from Irving Berlin, Florenz Ziegfeld, George M. Cohan, and Governor Nathan Lewis Miller of New York. Just before the game started, McGraw glowered across the field at Ruth and gave his pitching staff their most important instructions.

"Just remember," McGraw said, "don't give that big baboon anything but low curves."

Carl Mays won the first game for the Yankees, 3-0, a game best remembered by the steal of home (seen here) in the fifth inning by Yankees' Mike McNally, a utility infielder.

Waite Hoyt came back the next day to win by the same score. The game had been particularly uncomfortable for the Giants, as they had worn their gray road uniforms in their own park. So into the clubhouse the Giants went for another tirade, this one topping the one in August which preceded the series with Pittsburgh.

Player by player, McGraw berated his troops for failing him at the final moment. With just a few victories between them and the World Championship, he raged, the Giants were about to disgrace themselves again. One particular player whom McGraw had been on all year was George (Highpockets) Kelly, his first baseman. McGraw kept challenging Kelly to, "do something brilliant." It was an odd challenge: Kelly had led the National League in home runs that year with 23. But McGraw stayed on Kelly relentlessly, wanting not just excellence but brilliance.

So did the Yankees get bombed the next day?
Was McGraw Irish?

The Yankees roughed up Giant starter Fred Toney for four runs in the second inning of Game Three, but the Giants fought back savagely, winning 13-5. Frankie Frisch, the brunt of some of the worst of McGraw's upbraiding, played like a man possessed, raising his Series batting average to .700.

In Game Four, Phil Douglas, the spitballer, kept the Yankees guessing, winning 4-2. In this game Babe Ruth hit a solo home run, his only one of the Series.

Game Five saw Hoyt beat the Giants again. It also saw Ruth take a strategic potshot at McGraw by laying down a perfect bunt in the fourth inning, astounding everyone in the park. Art Nehf, the Giants' pitcher, was so shaken by the play that he then grooved a ball to Bob Meusel, who hit a long Polo Grounds double that scored Ruth from first. But it was Ruth's last involvement in the Series. When he arrived in the dugout, he collapsed, suffering from an inflamed elbow and an. aching knee. Or something less family-friendly. The Yankees' team doctor removed him from starting subsequent games.

The next day Fred Toney and Jesse Barnes combined to defeat the Yankees, 8-5. The Series was even, 3-3. But the momentum was back with the Giants.

Phil Douglas shuffled back to the pitching mound to defeat Carl Mays in Game Seven. The contest was tied, 1-1, in the seventh when Yankee second baseman Aaron Ward allowed Johnny Rawlings to reach base on an error. Frank Snyder, the Giants' catcher, then doubled Rawlings home. McGraw was just one win away from his first World Championship since 1905.

In Game Eight of the Series, Waite Hoyt of the Yankees faced Art Nehf of the Giants for the third time. The Yankees were the "home" team for the fourth time. A surprisingly small crowd of 25,410 witnessed one of the strangest World Series games of all time.

Hoyt started the game by getting George Burns to ground to third. Bancroft walked. Frisch fouled to Wally Pipp at first base. Then Ross Youngs, who by now had acquired the nickname of "Pep," walked. There were runners on first and second with two out. George Kelly hit an easy ground ball to Roger Peckinpaugh, the Yankee shortstop. How easy? So easy that Peckinpaugh took his eyes off it, allowing it to hop untouched between his legs out into left field.

Bancroft, running like the wind, scored.

From that unearned run onward, both pitchers slammed the door to opposition batters. Johnny Rawlings doubled to start the second inning, advanced to third on a sacrifice, but was thrown out at the plate. Rawlings again doubled to lead off the fourth, but again failed to score. In the bottom of the same inning, the Yankees left the bases loaded without denting the plate.

Pitch for pitch, inning by inning, Hoyt and Nehf were superb. Hoyt fanned seven and Nehf struck out four. When the Yankees came to bat in the last of the ninth, trailing by the single unearned run that had scored in the first inning, they had amassed a paltry three singles for the day. The Giants had six hits, including three by Rawlings.

Desperate to get something started, Yankee manager Miller Huggins sent Ruth up to bat for Wally Pipp. Seeing nothing but low, slow breaking stuff, Ruth grounded to Kelly at first. Giant fans howled with delight. Ruth trotted back to the dugout, apparently finished for the year. Then the crowd quieted when Aaron Ward walked.

McGraw left Nehf on the mound. The batter was none other than Frank (Home Run) Baker, the old Giants nemesis from the 1911 World Series. Baker, thirty-five years old, was winding down a distinguished career with spot duty for the Yankees. He was, as always, dangerous particularly in a park like the Polo Grounds with a friendly 257-foot right field foul line.

Years later, Johnny Rawlings, playing the game of his life that day, recalled succinctly what happened when Baker hit the hardest shot of the afternoon.

"Baker was a tough left-handed pull hitter and I would have been playing him over toward first anyway," Rawlings remembered. "But with a man on first, I figured he had to be trying to hit behind him and I edged over even more. It was a good thing I did, because Frank hit right through the hole. I was lucky to get my glove on the ball. I fielded it cleanly but fell down and threw to Kelly at first base on my knees to get Baker."

Rawlings was modest in relating the play. The line drive was like a frozen rope. Knocking the ball down and throwing out Baker was one of the great clutch plays in World Series history. But there was more, as Rawlings remembered.

"It was the hit-and-run, of course, and (Aaron Ward) Wardie was off at the crack of the bat. He saw where the ball was hit and never hesitated at second, but kept right on for third, figuring it for a single. Kelly was on his toes, too, and Long George [Kelly], with that great arm of his, whipped the ball across the diamond to Frisch at third. Frankie put the ball on Ward as he slid in, and we were the champions of the world!"

Bang, bang, bang.

Just your normal second to first to third double play to end an eight game World Series. The Giants, finally, were back where McGraw wanted them. They were the World Champions of baseball.

For every player on the 1921 squad, this was the first time that the Little Napoleon had guided them to the top of the mountain. The date of the last New York Giant championship, 1905, was a boyhood memory, if even that, to most of the players. A few, Burns, Slim Sallee, and George Kelly, had been on the 1917 team that had lost to Chicago in the World Series. To almost the entire squad, then, winning was something new.

They also knew that McGraw, who had berated, cajoled, and prodded them along, had elicited a championship from a team that otherwise wouldn't have won one. Overnight, to the seven players who would be key to McGraw's success over the first part of the decade - Frisch, Youngs, Kelly, Snyder, Meusel, Nehf, and Wilfred (Rosy) Ryan - McGraw had proven himself to be the belligerent genius they had always heard him to be. Now they had experienced it.

Mac was, of course, quick to take credit. There was a rousing victory party at the Waldorf, a bash that predictably carried into the morning hours of the following day. At the party and afterward, McGraw took particular relish in his personal victory over Babe Ruth.

"I signaled every pitch to Ruth," McGraw told anyone who would listen. "It was no secret. You could see [catchers] Snyder or Smith turn and look at the bench before signaling the pitcher. We pitched only nine curves and three fastballs to Ruth during the entire Series. All the rest were slowballs, and of the twelve of those, eleven set him on his ear."

McGraw's comments, widely reported around New York, made their way back to Ruth. The Ruthian response was nothing that could be quoted in the daily papers of that or this day.

Most baseball historians maintain that McGraw's strategies for handling Babe Ruth dated back to an incident in spring training in 1918, when the Giants were playing the Ruthian Red Sox.

In the second inning of an exhibition game, the Giant pitcher, a lanky right-hander from Byram, Connecticut, named Columbia

George Smith (Smith had attended Columbia University) decided to see if he could pop one of his fastballs past Ruth. Smarter ideas have come from other Columbia alumni.

Ruth connected squarely with Smith's pitch and launched something that had never been seen before in the era of "dead ball" baseball. The ball rocketed out toward right center field and soared. Ross Youngs, playing right, looked like David chasing Goliath's blast.

The game was being played at a racetrack that had been hastily converted to a baseball park for this occasion. The ball hopped a low fence at the far end of the park and continued to roll, with Youngs in hot pursuit as Ruth trotted around the bases.

Later, sportswriters approached Youngs and asked him to take them to the spot in a neighboring lot where he had retrieved the ball. They paced the distance back to the plate, then checked it against a tape measure. According to Ed Barrow, the Red Sox general manager, and a witness to the event, the ball traveled 579 feet. From this day on, John McGraw determined that no pitcher of his would ever again treat Ruth to a fastball in the strike zone.

Just as McGraw had promised his players, the first Subway Series had drawn a whopping gate: $900,233 in cash receipts. This was translated to the players' benefit in the happiest of fashions. Winners' share of the World Series loot was $5,265. The losers' shares totaled $3,510. These were, needless to say, hefty paychecks in those days. The Twentie$ were $tarting roar. And with the go-go stock market of the postwar economy, several players parlayed them into tidy sums of money that would see them through later years.

It seemed now that McGraw could do no wrong. His legal troubles solved, he had ordered the Yankees from the Polo Grounds, then dispatched them and Ruth in a spectacular World Series. He had told his players that they would rise to greatness and get rich if only they had the brains to listen to him. He had been right.

Even when McGraw had gone against prevailing wisdom, he had been proven correct. The Yankees had lumbered into the Series with a team batting average of .300 and an unprecedented total of 134 home runs. Against the Yankees, McGraw had thrown three pitchers: Art Nehf, Phil Douglas, and Jesse Barnes for 68.1 of the Series' 71 innings. They had responded with ERAs of 1.38, 2.08, and 1.65 respectively, in a ballpark that featured foul lines of 279 in left and 257 feet in right.

It was as if a mystic quality had come over McGraw's leadership.

Over the winter, and in years afterward, many of those who had been Giants in 1921 thought all the way back to a key play in the first game of that important Pittsburgh series in August. With the game still close, Highpockets Kelly faced Babe Adams, an excellent curveball pitcher with razor-sharp control. (Adams was 14-5 that year and walked only 18 in 160 innings.) Adams had three balls and no strikes on Kelly with one man on base.

Kelly looked to McGraw in the dugout, expecting the take sign. McGraw instead let him hit, a heretical baseball move for the National League in that era. On the bench was Casey Stengel, recently arrived from Philadelphia, who was studying McGraw and was absolutely shocked at the sign.

Adams threw a fastball down the middle of the plate, Kelly swung on it and lofted a fly ball that cleared the left field stands and landed in the railroad yard across the street. It was one of those plays upon which a season can turn. The home run put the game out of reach. The game set the tone for the series. And the Pittsburgh collapse against New York cost them the pennant.

Several years later Casey was on a world tour with McGraw. The play still bothered him. On a boat crossing the English Channel, Stengel asked McGraw about the play. Naturally, Mac remembered it perfectly.

"If Kelly took the 3-0 pitch, which would be right down the middle," McGraw explained, "Adams would get a piece of the plate with his curve for strike two. And then the load would be on Kelly. How many times that year did you see Long George march back to the dugout with the bat over his shoulder after a pitcher got him 3 and 2, especially a cagey pitcher like Adams?

"I figured," McGraw concluded, "that the 3-0 pitch would be the last fastball Kelly would get from Adams on that particular afternoon. Why not let him have a full cut at it?"

Why, not, indeed?

It was from such lessons that Stengel would later say, "What I learned from McGraw I used with all of them. They're still playing with a round ball, a round bat, and nine guys on a side."

Frankie Frisch and Dave Bancroft also learned the lessons. Both would go on to become McGraw-style managers.

It's equally noteworthy of the 1921 squad that whatever grumbling they did among themselves or to reporters, they had genuine affection for McGraw. After they had won the World Series, the players chipped in and commissioned a silver trophy to be created.

On it, a batsman stood astride a baseball on top of a loving cup. The inscription dedicated the cup to McGraw, "in appreciation of his qualities of leadership."

The cup remained one of McGraw's most cherished possessions for the rest of his life.

Chapter 41 Another Pennant, Another Scandal

"Born? Hell, Babe Ruth wasn't born. He fell from a tree."

Joe Dugan, Yankee teammate

The glitter was still fresh upon John McGraw's second World Championship when he went to work to secure a third. At the National League's winter meetings that December, McGraw executed two player transactions. In the first, the Giants sent George Burns and bullpen catcher Mike Gonzalez to Cincinnati for Heinie Groh, whom McGraw had shipped to the Reds in 1913, along with Red Ames, Josh Devore, and $20,000, for Art Fromme and Eddie Grant. Now Groh had developed into one of the premier third basemen in the league. McGraw wanted him back.

Groh was a small but powerful man, one of the greatest bat doctors of all time. He used a 46-ounce bat with a handle that had been shaved down until the whole bat looked like an elongated Bordeaux bottle. But more importantly, the acquisition of Groh enabled Frankie Frisch to move from third base to second, his natural position and a spot where his abilities as a field leader could flourish.

Then McGraw talked owner Charles Stoneham into writing a check for $75,000 to purchase a first baseman named Jimmy O'Connell. The price was a record for a minor league ballplayer. But O'Connell, twenty-one and a graduate of Santa Clara University, had hit .337 in a challenging league in his second season in organized baseball. McGraw was convinced that O'Connell was a star of the future, and left instructions that O'Connell remain with San Francisco but be retrained as an outfielder.

Mr. and Mrs. McGraw vacationed briefly in Havana and rang in the new year of 1922. Then McGraw turned his attention to two of his scouts.

One, Norman (Kid) Elberfeld, a former infielder who had bounced around the majors with six clubs over the first fourteen years of the century, was currently the manager of Little Rock in the Southern Association. Elberfeld touted a young shortstop named Travis Jackson. McGraw signed Jackson immediately. Then another old McGraw crony, Tom Watkins, owner of the Memphis club in the same league, steered McGraw to his own young star, one Bill Terry.

Terry could pitch, hit, or play first, all with varying degrees of success, ranging from brilliant to adequate. But he carried with him a unique problem as a recruit for the McGraw organization. He had a potentially more lucrative career outside of baseball.

Terry had pitched first in the Georgia-Alabama League and then with Shreveport of the Texas League from 1917 through 1919. He had pitched well, but no major league scouts had beckoned. He was, in 1919, an intelligent young man with a wife and baby and knew better than to wait for offers that might never come. Thus he took a job with Standard Oil, did well, and found himself promoted quickly in John D. Rockefeller's sprawling organization. He played semi-pro ball for the hell of it for the next three seasons. By the time McGraw found him in early 1922, he was singularly unimpressed by the prospects of playing baseball.

Watkins arranged a meeting between the two men at the Peabody Hotel in Memphis. McGraw, dancing around the issue a little, asked, "How'd you like to come to New York with me?"

"What for?" asked Terry.

"Well, to play for the Giants, maybe."

"For how much?"

It is possible that McGraw had never been asked such an impertinent question. He gagged for a moment, then answered. "Do you understand what I'm offering you? I'm offering you a chance to play for the New York Giants. If you're good enough."

"Excuse me if I don't fall all over myself," Terry answered. "But the Giants don't mean anything to me unless you make it worth my while. I've got a nice home [in Memphis] and I'm in no hurry to leave. If you care to make me an offer, you can reach me care of the Standard Oil Company."

"They tell me you're a great hitter," McGraw eventually tried.

"Did they also tell you I'm a great pitcher?"

And so it went. Miraculously, McGraw eventually talked young Terry into accepting a Giant contract and reporting to Toledo in the

335

American Association. There owner-manager Roger Bresnahan took charge of McGraw's new recruit. On the same team was a sixteen-year-old infielder named Freddie Lindstrom who had quit high school in Chicago to play ball for Bresnahan. Terry would play first base for most of 1922 in Toledo, and Lindstrom would play third.

Meanwhile, back in New York, the Giants started the 1922 season in defense of their championship. They found themselves in first place in late April and hit stride in June following a beanball incident involving the Phillies that resulted in a brawl that was only broken up by New York City police.

Then the pitching staff - led by Art Nehf, Jesse Barnes, Rosy Ryan, and Shuffiin' Phil Douglas - faltered in July. McGraw knew that additions would have to be made. Pittsburgh, Cincinnati, and St. Louis were still giving chase.

One addition was easy. The always-strapped Boston Braves were easily seduced into peddling pitcher Hugh McQuillan to McGraw for one hundred thousand of Charley Stoneham's dollars.

The second addition was less predictable, though it was equally a typical McGraw stunt. The story has fairy-tale proportions, all of which are apparently true.

There had been, the previous few years in the league, a big, slow-moving, slow-thinking North Carolinian named Jack Scott. Scott was a farm boy by birth and a pitcher by vocation. He had had a fair record on a bad club, the Braves, and had been traded to the Reds in February of 1922 for, of all people, thirty-two-year-old Rube Marquard.

Scott had been assailed by more misfortune than playing with Boston and Cincinnati. He was a farmer in the off-season. During the most recent winter, the barns in which he had stored his crops burned to the ground. They were uninsured. Somewhere along the way, he also injured his arm. Early in the 1922 season, the Reds released him after one game.

Jack Scott in 1922

He went home to North Carolina in May and tried to put his farm and his life back together. But tobacco prices had crashed, his entire county was broke, and within two months he realized that the farm, without working capital, was going to be a lost cause, too.

You might not think so, but the gods were actually smiling upon Jack Scott. He was too naive a man to give up hope. It occurred to him that after two months of not throwing a baseball his injured arm might not be so bad anymore. If only someone would give him a chance.

Here's where Scott's innocence comes in. Normally a player released by a second division team would be unlikely to catch on at all, much less with the league leader. But Jack Scott never thought of that.

"McGraw was the one man I thought of, right from the beginning," Scott recalled much later. "I knew that of all the managers, he was the one who would give me a chance."

With the last money he had in the world, Scott traveled from Ridgeway, North Carolina, to New York. He walked into McGraw's office in the Polo Grounds unannounced. "I believe I can still pitch, Mr. McGraw," he said. "I ain't asking much. I'd just like to stay around here and work out for a while.

McGraw gave him money from his own pocket and allowed him to work out at the Polo Grounds on the understanding that he wouldn't sign with the Yankees while the Giants were on the road. Scott, grateful for the chance, promised, worked himself into shape, and signed with the Giants when McGraw returned from a western swing. The Yankees, in fact, saw Scott working out on the fringes of the Polo Grounds and ignored him completely. To them, as they were busily winning their second pennant in a row, Scott was just another sore-armed pitcher engaged in a hopeless quest for rehabilitation. Many of the Yankees felt sorry for him.

McQuillan won 6 games for the Giants in 1922 and Scott won 8. Scott's total was particularly intriguing, as the Giants finished 7 games in front of second-place Cincinnati, the team that had released him. The Boston Braves, with their usual savvy management of players - having unloaded both McQuillan and Scott - finished last.

It might have been a smooth trip to the World Series for McGraw, but it wasn't. First, the entire city clamored for a rematch of the previous season's finalists. So pressure existed on both the Yankees and the Giants to win their flags. Second, the Yankees had acquired a ten-acre tract of land from William Waldorf Astor, who was now a British subject. The land was across the Harlem River from the Polo Grounds. The Yankees bought it for $600,000.

There in the south Bronx, a little too close for comfort, they were building their own palace. Then there was Earl Smith, McGraw's big, strapping catcher who irritated McGraw so persistently that Mac eventually dubbed him "an anarchist" and began making plans to unload him. And finally, McQuillan teamed with Jesse Barnes not just to win games but to play practical jokes in the clubhouse and to crawl through nocturnal New York with an enthusiasm unseen since the days of Mike Donlin some fifteen years earlier. McGraw dubbed McQuillan and Barnes, "Gallagher and Shean," after a pair of popular stand-up comedians on the vaudeville stage. The two pitchers took it as a compliment, though it hadn't been meant as such.

Then came the Phil Douglas incident.

Shufflin' Phil was off to his finest season (he would eventually be 11-4) but, like Bugs Raymond before him, couldn't control his predilection for booze. Again, like Bugs Raymond before him, Douglas received a "keeper" from his manager.

The "keeper" was a private detective named O'Brien. He was assigned to watch Douglas and keep him sober and out of trouble. Douglas rebelled at first, then decided that he liked O'Brien. Since he liked O'Brien, he went on his best behavior so that the poor man wouldn't lose his job. Now, O'Brien was appreciative of all this, and since, as a detective, he knew all the best speakeasies in New York, he began taking Douglas to one of the snootier ones for a few harmless beers after home games. Douglas was pleased with this arrangement. He had his keeper but had his beer, too. Happy and reasonably sober, he pitched well.

Enter McGraw again. Sensing the close bond that had developed between detective and pitcher, McGraw figured that O'Brien was being too lenient. Hence, he sacked him and replaced him with Jess Burkett, another of the many McGraw friends and one of the only three men (along with Ty Cobb and Rogers Hornsby) to hit over .400 three times in the majors.

Douglas didn't like Burkett. He resented McGraw's firing of O'Brien. So Douglas slipped his leash one night and went on a four-day drunk. When he returned to the clubhouse, disheveled and possessed by a dreadful hangover, McGraw physically hauled him into the manager's office and gave him one of the great tongue-lashings of McGraw's career.

Off went Douglas to sober up. He returned to the team the next day and all seemed right again for a while. Then the roof caved in.

On August 16, newsmen were summoned to McGraw's suite at

the Schenley Hotel in Pittsburgh. They were surprised to find a sullen John McGraw staring out the window at Forbes Field. At the desk of the suite, they were even more astonished to see Judge Kennesaw Mountain Landis, the commissioner himself.

"Gentlemen," Landis intoned solemnly, "I have just placed the name of Phil Douglas on the permanently ineligible list."

The writers gasped, then unleashed a torrent of questions. McGraw refused to answer them and deferred to Landis.

Soon the story was told. There before the newsmen and the commissioner was a ragged letter that Douglas had written on New York Giants stationery. The letter had been sent to Leslie Mann, a utility outfielder for the St. Louis Cardinals. In it, Douglas suggested that if the Cardinals made it worth his while, Douglas would sit out the rest of the season, helping clear St. Louis' road to the pennant.

Mann, with the memory of the Chicago Black Sox scandal of 1919 fresh in his mind, wanted no part of such a thing and turned the letter over to his manager, Branch Rickey. Rickey gave it to Landis. And Landis, who had been hired by baseball to root out just such knavery, was unable to distinguish between outright crooks, such as Hal Chase, and a man like Douglas who was an alcoholic and mentally ill. Thus Phil Douglas, one of the heroes of the 1921 World Series, not only sat out the rest of the 1922 season as offered, but sat out the rest of his life, as well.

Chapter 42   "He Hit .118"

"You little bastard!"

Babe Ruth to the Giants' Johnny Rawlings, 1922 World Series

The Giants clinched the National League flag on September 25, assuring the city of the matchup it wanted. So what that the rest of the country was out in the cold? The city wasn't called New York, New York, for nothing.

Radio made its first appearance on the premises for a World Series. In 1921 a reporter at the Polo Grounds had had an open telephone line to relay play-by-play information back to radio station WJZ in Newark, New Jersey. This year WJZ had put a microphone right into the Polo Grounds and placed before it a young sports commentator named Grantland Rice. An astonished nation crowded around radio sets and loudspeakers to hear Rice's voice and the actual roar of the crowd, crack of the bat, and yell of the peanut vendors in faraway Manhattan. The country, as the Series began, heard the future and the future worked. The second Subway Series thus began. Miller Huggins of the Yankees sent that year's ace, Bullet Joe Bush (26-7), to the mound in Game One.

McGraw started Art Nehf. He also imparted some strategy to his players before the game began.

"Wait out Bush," McGraw said. "He'll tire."

By waiting him out, McGraw meant to take a pitch or two. Bush, however, was a clever soul and quickly noticed what was going on. He retaliated by firing fastball strikes against most of the Giants who faced him. Ahead of each hitter, he coasted through seven scoreless innings. The Yankees, meanwhile, had a pair of runs. In the sixth, Ruth singled Joe Dugan home and in the seventh Aaron Ward sent Bob Meusel home on a sacrifice fly.

McGraw changed his instructions as Dave Bancroft prepared to lead off the bottom of the eighth for the Giants. "Start swinging at the first pitch," Mac said.

Bancroft singled. Groh singled. So did Frisch, and suddenly "The McGrawmen," as the tabloids called them, had the bases loaded with none out.

Up came Irish Meusel, who was swinging at the first pitch also. He lined it just past Bush's outstretched glove into center field, scoring Bancroft and Groh and tying the game. Now the Polo Grounds fans were revved up and screaming.

Huggins settled them down by calling in Waite Hoyt to relieve Bush. Ross Youngs was the next batter. Youngs got hold of a Hoyt fastball and took it deep to left field. Center fielder Whitey Witt ran it down. But Frisch scored easily after the catch. Then Hoyt struck out George Kelly and Casey Stengel. But the damage was done. The Giants won, 3-2.

The second game was one of the most unusual World Series contests ever played. In the first inning, Groh and Frisch singled and Irish Meusel followed with a home run into the left field grandstand. But the Yankees chipped away with runs in the first, fourth, and eighth to tie the game. There it remained through ten innings, knotted 3-3.

At four forty-five in the afternoon, the sky was still blue. The sun was shining. That's why everyone in the park was surprised-and suspicious-when umpire George Hildebrand held his mask aloft at the end of the tenth inning, circled his arm as if calling a home run, and bellowed, "Game called on account of darkness!"

Darkness?

You could have suffered a sunburn from this darkness. It was also suddenly very hot. Not the weather, but the reaction from fans. At the top of the inning, umpire Hildebrand had walked over to Commissioner Landis, sitting behind the Giants' dugout, and exchanged a few words with him. When Hildebrand then called the game for darkness, the 37,020 fans who had packed the Polo Grounds assumed incorrectly that Hildebrand had been acting on Landis' orders. Many of them - some estimates said several thousand - stood and jeered Landis when the teams abruptly started off the field. The terms "crook" and "robber" were bandied readily about, the suggestion being that baseball wanted an extra day of receipts and thus encouraged the inconclusive game.

A phalanx of city police finally made its way to Landis and escorted the stern-faced, white-maned old jurist out of harm's way. To settle down the mob, upon his departure, Landis also announced that the game's receipts would be given to various war charities, a gesture that was not cheerfully received by the ownership of the Giants and the Yankees. With that, Landis made his way into his car and fled northern Manhattan.

The actual villain of the piece had probably been Bill Klem, who had been umpiring at second base. Klem had gently reminded Hildebrand a few innings earlier that the pace of this game had been slow. Two years earlier, a Brooklyn-Cleveland World Series game had ended in the dusk, much to the dissatisfaction of everyone. Hildebrand hadn't wanted to preside over a replay of that situation. Thus he had called this game too soon rather than too late.

The 3-3 tie put McGraw in the mood to play a hunch. "My pitcher for Game Three," he announced, "is Jack Scott."

Scott?

The castoff from the Braves and the Reds? Scott, the sore-armed chucker whom the Yankees ignored as he did wind sprints on the far reaches of the Polo Grounds outfield the previous summer.

Scott, indeed.

He took the mound in the first inning and threw nothing but high smoke all day, even to Ruth. The Yankee sluggers, accustomed now to seeing slow breaking stuff from McGraw's staff, were thoroughly off-balance all afternoon. Ruth went hitless. Wally Schang had a double. There were three other Yankee singles all afternoon. The Giants pecked away at Waite Hoyt, scored two unearned runs and one legitimate one, and Jack Scott came away with a 3-0 victory. McGraw had picked a pitcher off the scrapheap, had given him a second chance, and had been rewarded with a complete game shutout over the most fearsome lineup in baseball.

There was also a slightly less seemly aspect to what was going on down on the field.

For a few years it had been known that the only real way to shackle Ruth was to distract him verbally. That usually meant jockeying him fiercely enough so that he forgot about the ball game.

Ty Cobb, who personally disliked Ruth and his style of play, was a master of this and did it on and off the field. With Cobb, the jockeying centered around Ruth's personal cleanliness and habits of hygiene. During a winter barnstorming tour, Cobb had once discovered that Ruth rarely changed his underwear and even more rarely bathed. Thus, whenever Ruth came near, Cobb would make a habit of sniffing loudly, as if he hadn't seen Ruth coming but had noted a strange smell. Then Cobb would hold his nose and walk away.

The Babe didn't think this was particularly funny. Nor was he amused when several of the Giants suggested that Ruth's inordinate physical prowess - athletic and sexual - stemmed from a Negro ancestry.

Ruth's chief tormentor during the 1922 World Series was Johnny Rawlings. Rawlings had been the Giants' regular second baseman in 1921 but had been benched in favor of Frisch. He was still very much in the game, however.

Fed lines by McGraw, Rawlings (seen in the photo here looking innocent) stayed on Ruth incessantly through the first three games of the Series, the racial epithets becoming fouler and more graphic as the games wore on. By the end of Game Three, at which time Ruth was 2 for 11, the Babe had heard more than enough. So had Yankee teammate Bob Meusel.

As Robert Creamer described it in *Babe*, the masterful biography of George Herman Ruth, Ruth and Meusel appeared suddenly in the Giants' clubhouse after Game Three.

"Where's Rawlings?" Ruth demanded.

"Right here," said Rawlings, who was six inches shorter and sixty pounds lighter.

"You little bastard!" Ruth said. "If you ever call me that again, I'll choke you to death."

Rawlings, still sitting by his locker, grinned at him. "Can't you take it?"

"I can take plenty, but I can't take that."

Jesse Barnes, a Giant pitcher, said, "You got a hell of a lot of nerve complaining after some of the things you called me yesterday."

"I didn't call you anything."

"You're a goddamned liar!"

Ruth went for Barnes, but other players got between the two. Earl Smith, one of the Giants' catchers, who was called Oil and was said to be the toughest man in baseball, had been in the bullpen during the game and had missed the bench jockeying. Mildly, he asked, "What did he call you, Babe?"

"He called me a nigger."

"That's nothing," Smith said. He turned away.

Ruth was calming down rapidly. When one of McGraw's coaches told him he had better leave, he said, "All right. I know I shouldn't have come in here, but I wanted to get things straight. Listen, I'm sorry, fellows. Tomorrow let's cut out the rough stuff and just play baseball."

Heinie Groh, the Giants' third baseman, hooted. The day before Ruth had slid into Groh like a fullback hitting the line. "Baseball?" said Groh. "Look who's talking. Yesterday I thought we were playing football."

Everybody laughed. Ruth and Meusel started to go, but at the door Babe turned back for a moment. "Don't get me wrong, fellows," he said seriously. "I don't mind being called a prick or a cocksucker or things like that. I expect that. But lay off the personal stuff."

Then he left.

The Yankees were still angry the next afternoon when they jumped on Hugh McQuillan in the first inning of Game Four. Singles by Witt and Dugan opened the game. That brought up Ruth, who blasted one. But McQuillan already knew what generations of Polo Grounds pitchers would later come to learn. Get the other team's power hitter to take the ball to straightaway center and you can throw just about anything.

Ruth's shot was one of those tremendous blasts that brings a crowd collectively to its feet. It would have left most parks, possibly including Yellowstone. But here at the Polo Grounds it went far back in center field and remained in play. Bill Cunningham, Stengel's platoon partner in center field that year, was already playing deep. He went back, back, back, and finally pulled in the ball, not too far from where another New York center fielder would pull in a Vic Wertz blast thirty-two years later.

Witt went to third and later scored. Dugan later came around too. But the Yankees had been deprived of their big inning. The Giants rallied for four in the fifth, then held on when Aaron Ward homered to left in the seventh to make the score 4-3. That was all McQuillan was giving up that day, however, and the Giants led the World Series three zip.

Clearly, God was wearing a New York Giants cap in the autumn of 1922. McGraw tossed his ace, Art Nehf, at the Yankees in Game Five. There were 38,551 fans at the Polo Grounds, the largest World Series crowd to date - another sign that baseball had come of age in the Roaring Twenties. The Yankees got a run in the first, which was set up when Ruth bunted to sacrifice Joe Dugan from first to second. The Babe and the Yankees were that much off their game. The Giants retaliated with two in the second, the key hit being a two-run single by Cunningham. The Yankees then scratched single runs in the fifth and the seventh and maintained the lead in the bottom of the eighth when the Giants came to bat.

Bancroft grounded out. Then Groh singled and Frisch doubled. The Giant fans who packed the park howled with delight as they sensed the kill. But the Yankees drew the infield in. Irish Meusel hit the ball sharply to Everett Scott at shortstop, who fired the ball to Wally Schang, the Yankee catcher, nailing Groh after a short rundown. Frisch was safe on third and Meusel went all the way to second on the play.

Now Miller Huggins ordered Joe Bush, the Yankee starter, to walk Ross Youngs. Bush obeyed but was insulted. As he threw four wide ones, he punctuated each with insults hurled at the Yankee manager. Then, still rattled, Bush faced George Kelly, who was sitting on the first pitch. Kelly swung and lined the ball into center. Frisch darted home from third and Irish Meusel roared all the way to the plate from second. The Giants were up, 4-3, and the crowd was delirious.

Kelly remained at first, with Youngs on third. Up stepped a journeyman outfielder named Lee King, making the only plate appearance of his life in a World Series. King had gone into the game at the top of that inning as a replacement for Cunningham, for whom Earl Smith had hit in the seventh. King singled to left, a little pop fly over short that fell at Bob Meusel's toes. With his one swing in the Series, King had iced the Yankees, driving in the insurance - and final - run of the day.

In the top of the ninth, Bob Meusel, Wally Schang, and Aaron Ward all hit harmless fly balls, setting off a wild celebration in the Polo Grounds and across the city. Again, the Giants were the champions of the world. The old guard had again prevailed over the young pretenders, and the Yankees, McGraw was quick to point out, were leaving the Polo Grounds with their tails between their legs. McGraw, on the other hand, was mobbed with adoring fans after the final out and took a long time before he was able to push his way to the center field clubhouse. Later that evening at the Waldorf, the team threw a victory bash that became legendary even by McGravian standards. Describing the party many years later, the ever-sour columnist Westbrook Pegler recalled the celebrants leaving the classy Waldorf long after dawn the following morning: "hurtling, bruised and disheveled, like bums out of a barrel house."

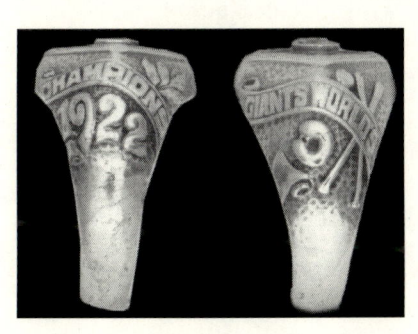

Such behavior, of course, was routine in the days of Prohibition.

The 1922 edition of the Giants, who were rewarded with World Series rings by the ownership, was probably the greatest squad in the history of the franchise, with apologies to the stalwarts of 1905 and 1954. No fewer than five players - Kelly, Frisch, Bancroft,

Youngs, and Stengel - were future Hall of Famers, as was coach Jennings and manager McGraw.

They had won more than 60 percent of their games in a difficult league, had hit .305 as a team, and had demolished the Yankees without losing a game. Particularly demolished was the Bambino himself, who had one single and one double in seventeen official at-bats. Ruth's power failure prompted *Baseball* Magazine to print the following ditty, much to the delight of Giant fans:

HE HIT .118
Lives of great guys Oft remind us
That they sometimes Fail Their Trust.
Ruth for Instance In the Series.
Holy Moses! What a bust!

After the game, the great sportswriter Fredrick G. Lieb, who covered the Yankees that year, rode down to the Commodore Hotel with Colonel Huston, co-owner of the Yankees. Huston was furious at the world in general, but his anger had settled upon his manager. Particularly repugnant, with the benefit of hindsight, was the intentional walk to Youngs that had made an autumn hero out of the frequently maligned George Kelly.

Braced with a shot of some bootleg spirits, Huston angrily cleared the bar in the hotel by sweeping away every glass in sight with his right arm. Simultaneously, he let out a scream of pain and proclaimed, "Miller Huggins has managed his last game as a Yankee!"

Well, not quite. Later that evening, Huston came across Jacob Ruppert, who made the point that Huggins had just guided the Yankees to two pennants, which was two more than the team had ever won without him. It might be, Ruppert continued, seen as an ungracious gesture to sack a manager with such a successful track record.

Huston was unmoved. The dispute expanded to several other points and, within a matter of months, Ruppert had bought out Huston's interest in the team. One of the beer baron's first act as sole owner was to extend Huggins' contract and impress upon some of the more wayward players that Huggins was in charge of the team.

Thus McGraw's handling of Ruth and defeat by the Giants didn't get a manager fired, but rather dispatched an owner. Lest you weep for the memory of Lt. Colonel Tillinghast L'Hommedieu Huston, however, it might be further noted that the half of the New York Yankees that he sold drew him a check for $1,500,000, six times what he had paid in 1915. There were many pleasant things that a healthy man could do in New York City - in the years before capital gains taxes - with a check for $1,500,000.

(Above: The remains of the 1922 Pennant that once flew over the Polo Grounds. It was recovered from the rubble by the wrecking company that tore down the ball park in 1964.)

An Editor's Reminiscence – Wally Exman

One sunny afternoon in the summer of 1963, former major league pitcher Waite Hoyt escorted me to the radio announcers' booth high up behind home plate in the Polo Grounds. Hoyt had broken in with the Giants in 1918 as a high school student. Later he had become a star with the Yankees and Red Sox, returned briefly to the Giants, and pitched in the big leagues for more than twenty years en route to a place in The Baseball Hall of Fame.

When I first met him, he had been broadcasting the Cincinnati Reds baseball games for years and had built a substantial fan base due largely to the yarns he spun about his days playing with the 1920s Yankees. Whenever it rained in Cincinnati in the summer, folks tuned their radios to the Reds' station just to listen to Hoyt's stories about the on-field and off-field shenanigans of Ruth, Gehrig, et al. An LP record, ***The Best of Waite Hoyt in the Rain*** had persuaded me to contract with him for a book about his life in baseball.

Waite Hoyt, NY Giants, 1918

The Reds-Mets game Hoyt had invited me to watch with him in the radio booth that afternoon went badly for the Reds. I recall that the Reds manager, Fred Hutchinson, who was famous for his low boiling point, sat alone and by himself in the Reds dugout long after his players had departed for the clubhouse. But for Hoyt there was always an upside. This was Pete Rose's rookie year, and Hoyt praised his hustle and scrappy attitude. "Just like the players in my day," he said proudly.

I was an editor with the World Publishing Company at the time and had arranged for Waite to have a coauthor. Hoyt eventually looked at the first draft and scrapped the project. He didn't feel the writer had captured his persona as he, Hoyt, perceived it.

Hoyt was touchy about his standing among his baseball peers. He felt a need to separate himself from the many players who were "just off the farm." Hoyt grew up in Brooklyn and had graduated from Erasmus Hall High School, of which he was a proud alumnus. I don't want to make him out to be a holier-than-thou prude, for he wasn't that at all. He was a warm and generous person. When he later went back to Yankee Stadium for an Old Timers game, he invited me to tag along. I never saw so many half-naked, overweight and out-of-shape middle-aged men in one place at one time as I did that afternoon in the Yankee clubhouse.

I regret his book never saw the light of day. The spring after our meeting at the Polo Grounds, the Mets moved across the Harlem River to their new home in Queens, New York. Shea Stadium. That same spring, a wrecking crew wearing Giants jerseys began dismantling the Polo Grounds. It took a crew of 60 workers more than four months to level the structure.

Wallace Exman,
Osterville, MA
April 2018

(Editor's note: Over a distinguished thirty-plus year career in book publishing, Wally Exman edited many sports books, including two *New York Times* best sellers: *Out of Bounds* by Jim Brown with Steve Delsohn, and *The Duke of Flatbush* by Duke Snider with Bill Gilbert. Mr. Exman also edited several other books well known to baseball fans: *Real Grass, Real Heroes: Baseball's Historic 1941 Season* by Dom DiMaggio with Bill Gilbert, *"AARON, r.f." The Story of My Life, the Good Times and the Bad, from Mobile to Milwaukee to Atlanta* by Henry Aaron as told to Furman Bisher, *The Giants Win the Pennant! The Giants Win the Pennant!: The Amazing 1951 National League Season and the Home Run that Won It* by Bobby Thomson with Lee Heiman and Bill Gutman, *Bill Mazer's Amazin' Baseball Book: 150 Years of Baseball Tales and Trivia* by Bill Mazer with Stan and Shirley Fischler, *Don't Knock the Rock: The Rocky Colavito Story* by Gordon Cobbledick and *Marquard and Seeley* by Noel Hynd.)

Chapter 43   Twenty-three Skidoo!

"Ruth crushed to earth shall rise again."

Heywood Brown

Construction on the new Yankee Stadium, which many fans thought should be called, "Ruth Field," began in early 1922. The whacking of hammer and nails and the roar of construction equipment could be easily heard at the northern end of the Polo Grounds. And by the spring of 1923, at the tidy cost of $2,500,000, the new shrine of lively ball baseball was set to open.

Not only did it open, but it opened with a flourish.

President Warren Harding of Ohio loved any and all Opening Days. So he turned up on April 18, 1923 at the new Yankee Stadium to throw out the first pitch in New York, in the ball park "Root" – as Colonel Ruppert invariably called him with his beer and bratwurst accent - had built for the Giants' evicted tenants.

The game progressed before an announced crowd of 74,217, Babe Ruth – who else? - launched the first home run in the new place and the Yankees defeated the Boston Red Sox, 4-1. The first hit in the new park, by the way, came off the bat of a George Burns, no relation to McGraw's onetime center fielder or Gracie Allen's show biz partner.

Warren Harding might be ranked low in the presidential success chart, but he did know his baseball. As a youth, he had been a teammate in Marion, Ohio, with a boy named Bob Allen, who grew up to be a shortstop for the Philadelphia Phillies, the Boston Beaneaters and the Cincinnati Reds, as well as a temporary manager for both the Phillies and Reds. Harding scored games like an expert and at one time owned a minor league team in his hometown, Marion, Ohio.

He loved the game.

Two days after the opener at Yankee Stadium, President Harding would throw out the first pitch of the season's home opener for the Washington Senators at Griffith Stadium.

With that, the 1923 season was underway.

The Yankees streaked to a pennant and coasted, Yankee-style, to the World Series by sixteen games.

McGraw's Giants won the pennant also, though not as easily. McGraw waived Johnny Rawlings to the Phillies in midseason. Travis Jackson took his place on the team. McGraw traded Jesse Barnes to the Braves. Jimmy O'Connell became a regular in center field and a new pitcher named Jack Bentley claimed a spot in the rotation.

Bentley, whom McGraw had purchased from Jack Dunn of the International League Baltimore Orioles in early 1923 for $65,000, knew how to hit as well as throw. He was 13-8 as a pitcher, and .427 as a hitter, including a torrid 10 for 20 as a pinch hitter. Yet, with all this additional talent, Cincinnati still chased the Giants all the way to the wire. The New Yorkers won the flag by four and a half games and went into the 1923 World Series ready to settle the Yankee challenge for once and for all.

Along the way, however, there had been some national distraction.

On the evening of August 2, 1923, the nation's number one baseball fan, President Harding died in a San Francisco hotel room. The poor man's body was barely cold when the rumors of scandal or even worse started to circulate, promulgated by the conspiracy theories of the day. Oddly, the tin foil hat folks existed even before there was tin foil.

Today, most historians accept that Harding, 57, had keeled over from a heart attack brought on by being overweight and an overindulgent lifestyle. There was also ample evidence of cardiac problems. But that wasn't the original cause of death cited in 1923.

So rumors kindled quickly.

There was no autopsy done on the body of the president, at his widow's request. Dr. Ray Lyman Wilbur, a Harding friend who was also the president of Stanford University, was at the hotel when Harding was stricken. In his memoirs, he recalled the events that followed. "We shall never know exactly the immediate cause of President Harding's death, since every effort that was made to secure an autopsy met with complete and final refusal," he said.

That meant you, Mrs. Harding.

An outraged public, upset with the sudden death of a popular but incompetent president, took out its anger on the widow and the doctors. Harding had more than half a dozen personal physicians. One by one the nuts of the era targeted them. There was even a well-known medical gadfly of the day named Dr. Albert Abrams who was famous during his lifetime for inventing machines which he claimed could diagnose and cure almost any disease. They were a big business, with about three thousand practitioners employing them in the United States. A legion of Dr. Abrams' followers took aim on the late President's doctors and kept the controversy rumbling.

Dr. Abrams' machine was called "The Dynomizer." He claimed it could analyze a patient's illness and cure it. It looked something midway between a table radio and an automobile battery. These pieces of apparent quackery were a hefty business, among those willing to believe in them. They were leased to practitioners for about $200 with a monthly $5 charge thereafter. The practitioner also had to pay for a course in how to operate the contraption. Then the lessor had to sign a binding contract stating the device would never be opened and examined. Try not to laugh. Abrams explained that this would disrupt their "delicate adjustment." Giggle, giggle.

Abrams, who was terrific at promoting himself and his machines, used his Dynomizer to perform diagnoses on dried blood samples sent to him on pieces of paper in envelopes through the mail.

The business fell apart in 1923 when an elderly man who was diagnosed in the Mayo Clinic with inoperable stomach cancer went to a Dynomyzer practitioner, who declared him "completely cured" after treatments. The man died a month later.

In a separate case, a respected physician mailed a blood sample to an Abrams practitioner, and got back a diagnosis that the patient was an adult human male and had malaria, diabetes, cancer and syphilis. Oops. The blood sample was in fact from a rooster.

Nonetheless, the Abrams contingent was convinced that Mrs. Harding had murdered her husband. Abrams piled on to Harding's death as several dozen others did. It kept him on the front pages in the popular press, along with lurid tales of the late president's sex life and many alleged mistresses. The President's doctors were accused of starving the President to death or overfeeding him to death or assisting in slowly poisoning him.

The Harding scandals, or alleged scandals, occupied much of the news of the day. Harding was popular while in office.

He was elected in 1920 primarily by rural Americans. He stood for high tariffs, against immigration, against booze, against corruption in Washington and for reduced regulations on business. The economy boomed under Harding, largely because he inherited a strong economy from his predecessor, Woodrow Wilson. Wilson was a strong internationalist, and the country was in the mood to reject internationalism.

However, Harding's reputation was badly tarnished following his death when Americans learned of corruption within his administration. In one infamous incident, known as the Teapot Dome Scandal, Secretary of the Interior Albert Fall rented public lands to oil companies in exchange for gifts and personal loans. Fall was later convicted of accepting bribes and spent nine unpleasant months in prison.

(Fall's background and degrees of separation from weirdness get even stranger if you follow it. In addition to being the first American cabinet member to go to the slammer, as a young attorney in 1908 Fall successfully defended Jesse Wayne Brazel, the accused killer of former Sheriff Pat Garrett, famous for killing outlaw Billy the Kid in 1881. A little over thirty years later, in early July 1947, Fall's nephew William "Mac" Brazel gained fame in the so-called Roswell UFO incident when he found "strange debris" on his ranch some 70 miles northwest of Roswell, sparking the claim that a flying saucer crashed on the ranch where Brazel was foreman and that the government subsequently instituted a cover-up.)

Other government officials took payoffs and embezzled funds. Harding had extramarital affairs and (gasp!) drank alcohol in the White House, a violation of the 18th Amendment which he was on record as favoring. He had a daughter out of wedlock with a woman named Nan Britton, but the White House covered this one up, too, and Harding's party attacked Britton viciously when she came forward and published her book, *The President's Daughter*, in 1927. (DNA proved the daughter was his many decades later.) None of this was any surprise to the people who knew him. But it was a complete shock to many of the yokels who had voted for him, who tended to categorize any negatives stories about him as "made up."

The immigration policies failed and so did the tariffs. But the stories and the scandals did get traction in the press and the final answer on the overheated economy wasn't apparent till the Wall Street crash of 1929.

The dirty laundry in 1923 tended to push the pennant race off the newspapers. Nonetheless, the Giants took the lead in their pennant race and the Yankees bolted to the front in the American league.

On the 17th of September, Hickpockets George Kelly, posing for you right here, put on a display from the batter's box when he homered in the 3rd, 4th and 5th innings against the Chicago's Vic Aldridge. The Giants cruised to a 13 - 6 win in Chicago.

Kelly was the first player ever to homer in three consecutive innings. An odd footnote: Kelly had six dingers off cousin Aldridge in 1923, a record off one victimized pitcher that would be tied by Ted Williams in 1941 off Johnny Rigney of the White Sox and Ted Kluszewski in 1954 off Pittsburgh's Max Surkont. And so the 1923 World Series beckoned as a possible New York-New York extravaganza once again, a mere six weeks after the death of the President. It would take some doing to grab back the national headlines, but the two New York teams were doing their best.

Chapter 44   This Time, He Hit .358

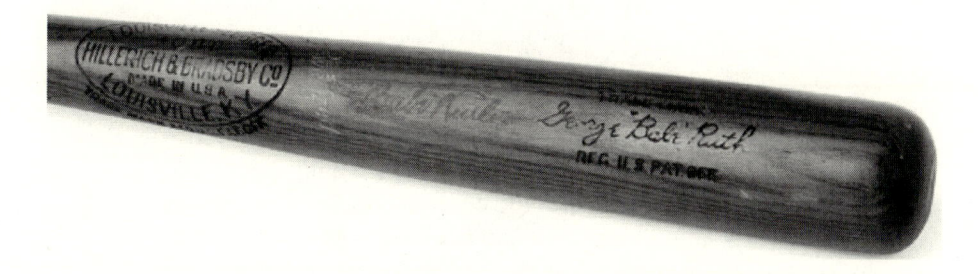

McGraw went into the 1923 World Series on the threshold of his most cherished goal: three consecutive World Championships. All his Giants needed to do was dispatch a team they had already handled twice.

But first, there had to be some final hostilities between the two clubs.

This time the center of the storm was twenty-year-old Lou Gehrig. McGraw's scouts had spotted Gehrig in 1921 at Columbia University, where Gehrig had a football scholarship. Through some quick talking, they had signed him to a professional baseball contract, then hidden him at Hartford of the Eastern League under the name Henry Lewis. It was not an uncommon practice of the day, but who should happen to attend a Hartford game, but a former A's and Highlanders hurler Andy Coakley, former owner of the straw boater that had kept Rube Waddell out of the 1905 World Series. Coakley also happened to be the Columbia baseball coach.

"What," Coakley demanded of Gehrig, "are you doing in that uniform?"

Lou tried to explain. Coakley dragged Gehrig back to New York, saved his scholarship, and extricated him from the Hartford contract. Gehrig continued to play football and baseball for Columbia, then the Yankees signed him in the spring of 1923. Where did they send him? Hartford, of course. He tore up the league. The Yankees brought him up at the end of the year and he hit even harder: .420 in thirteen games. The Yankees, it appeared, had another treasure.

But Gehrig had come to the big club after September first. Coincidentally, first baseman Wally Pipp had suffered a painful rib injury. The Yankees requested that Gehrig take Pipp's place on the World Series roster. Commissioner Landis responded that Gehrig could play, but only if the opposing manager consented.

McGraw, keeping the events of 1921 in mind, was quite happy to withhold consent. First Hoyt had gotten away to the Yankees. Next Ruth. Now Gehrig. It was too much for McGraw. "The hazards of the game," he said. "The rules are clear." Lou couldn't play. Pipp was trussed up like a mummy and the World Series of 1923 began.

So disdainful was John McGraw of everything connected with the Yankees that he refused to even use the new Yankee Stadium dressing rooms. His players could change sweatshirts in the stadium's clubhouse. Nothing more. For Yankee home games, McGraw's team used its home locker room at the Polo Grounds, then took the bridge across the Harlem River to the enemy territory.

In the ninth inning of the opening game, Casey Stengel, with the score tied at 4-4, lashed what might have been a single to left center. Left fielder Bob Meusel had been guarding the line. Whitey Witt in center had shifted toward right. Before anyone could quite figure how it had happened, the ball was between them, hopping toward the 450-foot sign. Casey was running as if his life depended on it. And, since anything involving Stengel had to have a comic touch, he was cheering himself on at the same time, much the same way as a jockey would a horse, yelling, "Go on, Casey, go on!"

Yankee third baseman Joe Dugan had an excellent view of it. "It was the damnedest sight," he said.

It was. Rounding second, Casey felt a sponge break free from the inside of his left shoe. Rounding third, he wobbled like a cripple. Sliding home, as you can see here, Casey signaled himself safe. Fortunately, umpire Billy Evans agreed.

Damon Runyon truly had a ball with this one. Here's the account that appeared on October 11, 1923, in the New York *American*:

This is the way old Casey Stengel ran, running his home run home to a Giant victory by a score of 5-4 in the first game of the World Series of 1923.

This is the way old Casey Stengel ran, running his home run when two were out in the ninth inning and the score was tied and

the ball was bounding inside the Yankee yard.
This is the way-
His mouth wide open.
His warped old legs bending beneath him at every stride.
His arms flying back and forth like those of a man swimming with a crawl stroke.
His flanks heaving, his breath whistling, his head far back...
The warped old legs, twisted and bent,
by many a year of baseball campaigning, just barely held out under
Casey Stengel until he reached
the plate running his home run home.
Then he collapsed.

Casey, while he cherished the publicity, wasn't wild about Runyon's poetic account. At the age of thirty-three, he had just married his beloved Edna. He had not yet met his in-laws, however, and feared that they, in reading the account, might conclude that their daughter had fallen in love with a doddering old man.

{An old news clip, by the way, has been remounted to the MLB site under the title of *Stengel runs the Bases* at MLB.com. The video doesn't support the accounts of the day, but actual time is difficult to judge.}

But, ah.... Only Casey Stengel.

Not only had McGraw's player-coach stolen the show, but he had also deprived Ruth of hitting the first World Series home run at Yankee Stadium. And the Giants had the run that would win Game One. The 1923 Series already looked like a replay of the previous two years.

But, as Heywood Broun wrote the next day, "The Ruth is mighty and shall prevail." True enough. The Babe walked in the first. Then, in the fourth, Ruth caught a Hugh McQuillan curveball and launched it three hundred feet. That was the altitude, again according to the hyperbolic Broun. The distance was never measured, as the ball disappeared in a high arc over the right field grandstand. The Yankees kept the rally going, bringing Ruth back up in the fifth with the bases empty.

Walk him? McGraw had answered that question before the game. "Why shouldn't we pitch to him?" said the Little Napoleon. "We pitch to better hitters in the National League."

Oh? The new Giants' pitcher, Jack Bentley, showed the Babe a slow curve. Ruth showed Bentley a fierce line drive into the lower deck. The Yankees had a 4-1 lead and the game. And almost inexpressibly, the tide seemed to be turning. The Babe was starting to catch up to Giants' pitching.

The unexpected hero in the third game was again Stengel. In a scoreless contest, Casey- who hit with moderate power during his career, amassing a career total of 60 home runs - lined a ball into the right field seats at Yankee Stadium. It would prove to be the only run of the game, but not the only fun. The target of relentless heckling from the Yankee dugout, Stengel turned toward the Yankee bench and appeared to be flicking a fly off his nose with the tip of his thumb. Only 62,430 people saw Casey's clear gesture of ill will. Jacob Ruppert demanded that Stengel be punished. But Commissioner Landis refused.

"Casey Stengel," Landis said with unusual understatement, "can't help being Casey Stengel." Even the Bambino, one of the targets of Stengel's nose thumbing, was amused.

"I didn't mind," Ruth said. "Casey is a lot of fun."

The Giants had a 2-1 lead in the Series. Game Four was played on October 13, 1923, a turning point for professional baseball.

In the second inning of the fourth game, the Yankees finally went to work on McGraw's pitchers. The Yankees scored quickly and often. Six runs blew the game out of reach early. It was 8-0 going to the bottom of the ninth when the Giants, with a late rally, fell four runs short.

"It was a bad game for a good team to lose," McGraw remarked when it was over. But maybe he sensed something, too, for Game Five, played at Yankee Stadium, was also a rout: 8-1, Yankees. But it wasn't as close as the score suggested. The Yanks had scored three runs in the first and four in the second to turn it into a no-contest early in the afternoon. The turnaround was absolutely stunning. Forty-eight hours earlier, riding the heroics of Stengel's second home run, McGraw and his players seemed on the brink of their elusive third straight Series title. Now their backs were against the wall.

Game Six was played at the Polo Grounds and it turned into a classic, final struggle between old baseball and new.

Ruth set the tone early with a home run. Then the Giants, playing their traditional game, chipped away for single runs in four different innings. There it stood until the eighth. Then came the big inning.

Art Nehf, the Giants' pitcher, had been coasting. He had pitched a shutout three day earlier, but now Wally Schang and Everett Scott singled. Then Nehf walked two pinch hitters on eight pitches, forcing in a run and losing his stuff so quickly that McGraw didn't have time to warm up Rosy Ryan, his best reliever.

But Ryan had to come in anyway. Ryan walked Joe Dugan and the Yankees had another run. The score was 4-3 and, naturally, Ruth was up next.

From somewhere, Ryan pulled himself together. In a final gasp of old time "inside baseball," Ryan fanned Ruth. Perhaps he then thought the worst was over and the Giants could hold on. If so, he thought wrong. There was no Gehrig to follow Ruth yet. McGraw had seen to that. But there was Bob Meusel, who lined a ball right back to Ryan - and past him. When Bill Cunningham kicked the ball around in center field, the bases emptied. The Yankees had five runs in the inning, plus the lead. About twenty-five minutes later, they returned to Yankee Stadium with their first World Championship.

McGraw was strangely gracious and philosophical when the 1923 World Series was over. "The best team won," he allowed. "The old guard changes, but never surrenders."

He must have been thinking of himself, and he must have had an inkling of time passing him by. At age fifty, his face was lined, his hair was white, and his stomach was thick. Worse, he must have known the way the public would interpret the 1923 World Series: The mighty Giants had been dethroned by the sluggers from the Bronx, Within another season, all the young players would be holding big bats by the end and swinging from the heels.

That is, of course, exactly what happened.

The stars that evolved over the next few years were all sluggers: Ruth, Gehrig, and Hornsby; Jimmie Foxx, Hack Wilson, and Chuck Klein. "Inside baseball" was discredited. The home run and the so-called 'big inning' were now what fans would pay to see.

As for the Yankees, the nucleus was in place for the great explosive teams that would dominate baseball for the next half century. Playing exactly the type of ball that McGraw so loathed, the Yankees would bring forty pennants and twenty-seven World Series titles to their park in the Bronx as of 2018. It may have been "The House That Ruth Built," but John J. McGraw, the perfect foil, had certainly helped.

"New York," proclaimed Yankee manager Miller Huggins when Ruth had joined the Yankees, "is a home run town."

By now it surely was.

McGraw, falling two games short of a third consecutive World Championship, knew it was again time to rebuild. He had a kid named Travis Jackson, who was ready to take over at shortstop. He had a powerfully built young slugger named Hack Wilson, who had led his minor leagues in home runs and batting average for the last two seasons. And McGraw also had the diligent young Bill Terry, who at the age of twenty-four had managed and slugged Toledo to the American Association championship in 1923.

Room had to be made.

The key man to go, ironically enough, was Stengel. Casey had sat at McGraw's side on the bench for the past two seasons, evolving strategies, analyzing games, and serving as a coach without portfolio. As a platoon player over the previous two seasons, Casey had rewarded McGraw with batting averages of .368 and .339. At the time of Stengel's heroics in the 1923 World Series, McGraw had commented, "There isn't anyone I'd rather have seen make that homer than Casey."

Nonetheless, Stengel was history with the Giants twenty-eight days after Jack Bentley, batting for Rosy Ryan, had grounded out, Ward to Pipp, to end the 1923 Series. Stengel went to the dismal Boston Braves with Bill Cunningham and Dave Bancroft for Joe Oeschger (who had previously pitched a complete game, twenty-six-inning 1-1 tie with Brooklyn) and Billy Southworth.

The trade seemed lopsided, to say the least. Oeschger was thirty-two years old and had just lost 15 of 20 decisions. Southworth was a good everyday outfielder, but with no power and no great defensive skills. In return, Bancroft was a leader who would manage the Braves as well as play shortstop. Stengel and Cunningham were equally competent players who would be in the lineup more often than not.

The real motivation behind the trade, as well as opening up space on the Giants' roster, was to aide McGraw's old friend Christy Mathewson, who had been named president of the Boston Braves earlier that year by Judge Emil Fuchs, the Boston owner.

Mathewson's title was largely that of a figurehead, but Big Six was feeling well enough to leave the sanatorium at Saranac Lake and return to the real world. McGraw was happy to send Matty some warm bodies, particularly if it helped the Giants in the process.

Stengel, on his part, was miffed by the deal that ended his time with the New York Giants, though eventually he would end up managing the Braves and owning part of franchise. But for the moment, he was despondent over leaving his mentor, McGraw, and New York, where he had been a media star. Never at a loss for words, Casey reportedly got off a zinger as he left the Big Apple.

"The paths of glory," he muttered corrosively, "lead but to the Braves."

Chapter 45   The Giants of the Ring

> **"He [Firpo] had been well named. He was really like a sullen human bull.**
> **Dempsey could not be still. As he got his last instructions, he fidgeted nervously and kept his head down, a little to one side, not meeting Firpo's sullen and stolid look."**
>
> **Thomas Wolfe – *The Web and The Rock*, 1939**

When the Yankees built Yankee Stadium in the early 1920s, they didn't just have baseball in mind. They were also thinking about boxing. The two emerging American sports stars of the decade were Babe Ruth and Jack Dempsey. The powers that ran the Yankees wanted a venue that could showcase both.

The perfect spot to construct a ring, it was theorized, was directly above the spot where second base would be located. Accordingly, a fifteen-foot vault was installed directly under the ground beneath second base. It was wired so members of press row could telegraph stories to their editors. (It seems primitive today, but it was high tech for the era.) During the next four decades, The Stadium hosted thirty championship fights, the first of which was the 1923 lightweight bout between the great Jewish-American champion Benny Leonard and challenger Lew Tendler, a great boxer from Philadelphia who somehow never won a world title. Leonard won a unanimous decision in fifteen rounds. (Leonard is seen here 'taking a punch' in a publicity shot with Australian swimmer Annette Kellerman, another formidable Jewish athlete of the era. Kellerman, who would go on to be a successful actress, writer and swimwear designer, also later found fame as the first star performer, male or female, to perform nude in a Hollywood film, *A Daughter of The Gods*.)

In its time, the Polo Grounds was equally popular as Yankee Stadium for boxing. It was the site of two of history's most memorable heavyweight scuffles. Writer Red Smith, who spent more than a few days and nights at the Giants' park referred to it as "the sweltering funnel," a crucible for those who practice the art of pugilism. And as the years evolved, Yankee Stadium may have had more fights. But the Polo Grounds always seemed to host the great ones.

Few battles could equal the Monday, September 24, 1923 Polo Grounds brawl between Jack Dempsey and the Argentine heavyweight Luis Firpo, the Wild Bull of the Pampas, while the New York Giants were on their final significant road trip of the season.

Not only was the Dempsey-Firpo match one of the great fights of the Twentieth Century, but it also transformed the public image of Jack Dempsey, aka The Manassa Mauler. Dempsey was an unpopular figure for the majority of his championship reign, rarely more so than when he stepped into the ring against Firpo.

Born into a poor family in Manassa, Colorado, Dempsey had

362

begun fighting under the name of Kid Blackie in rough towns in Utah, Colorado and Nevada. He once knocked out a professional fighter in Salt Lake City in fifteen seconds, then knocked out the man's brother in twenty seconds a few minutes later. He would fight anyone. Victory after victory mounted. He lived in logging camps, flop houses, hobo villages and, when lucky enough, whore houses.

When he was twenty, he married a thirty-five year old woman whom he described as "the sexiest woman I'd ever met." Her name was Maxine Cates. She played the piano in a saloon and was an occasional prostitute. There were rumors over the years that he pimped for Maxine. No proof was ever offered and Dempsey always denied it.

After winning the world title in 1919, Maxine sued for divorce. The accounts of the trial became a full-blown scandal. It brought before straight-laced Puritanical America Dempsey's checkered background. Maxine's testimony also suggested that the Mauler had perhaps not fully deserved his deferment to avoid the military draft during World War I. The term "slacker" (meaning draft dodger) hung painfully upon him.

Thus Dempsey became the 'villain' in most of his matches. His promoter, Tex Rickard took full advantage, most notably in Jack's bout with French war hero Georges Carpentier, a valiant World War one aviator known for his speed, his excellent boxing skills and his extremely hard punch. That clash between good and evil was on July 2, 1921, in Jersey City, New Jersey, at a site known as Boyle's Thirty Acres. Dempsey, a brutal and stunningly hard puncher, attacked the Frenchman from the opening bell. Carpentier suffered a knockout in the second minute of the fourth round. The fight created the first million dollar gate but did nothing to rehabilitate the heavyweight champion's dark surly image. For three solid years Jack Dempsey had to endure the disapproval of the general public, not to mention taunts of "Slacker!" everywhere he went, all this while Babe Ruth – a legendary carouser who also missed World War One - was adored by the public.

By 1923, Luis Firpo was the legitimate challenger to Dempsey, though few gave him a chance to win. Big and tough at 6-2 ½ and two hundred twenty pounds, the Argentinian had defeated the gigantic - 6-6, 240 pounds - Jess Willard and Gunboat Smith to establish himself as the top contender. Eighty thousand fans thus packed the Polo Grounds to witness Dempsey's fifth title defense.

Immediately after the referee had delivered his instructions, the fighters tossed away their towels and robes. The crowd let out a collective gasp over the difference in size between the two men. Firpo outweighed the champion by 25 pounds and had a far bigger upper body. Some began to wonder if Dempsey might finally be in trouble.

But at the bell, Dempsey attacked, as was his no-nonsense style. He missed a wild left and Firpo, retreating in the face of Dempsey's assault, countered with a right and dropped Dempsey to one knee. The crowd roared, rising as one to its feet. No one would sit down again until the ferocious battle had ended.

Dempsey rose. The fighters came together again in the center of the Polo Grounds, muscling each other in close before finding punching room and letting loose huge haymakers, both men connecting. At the twenty second mark, Dempsey landed his left, knocking Firpo down. Firpo lurched to his feet. The fighters resumed grappling and pounding, every blow thrown with intent to render the other man unconscious, the massive Polo Grounds crowd howling as the fighters punched and slammed each other.

Dempsey continually whirled and spun, turning Firpo in the clinches and then hitting while the Argentinian was still off stride. Firpo, while bigger and stronger, lacked Dempsey's footwork and balance. Dempsey scored two knockdowns via hard shots to Firpo's midsection.

Incredibly, Firpo hit the canvas seven times in the first round. More than once it appeared that he wouldn't get up. But he did. Dempsey was allowed to hover over his foe at each knockdown and pound Firpo the second his gloves left the canvas.

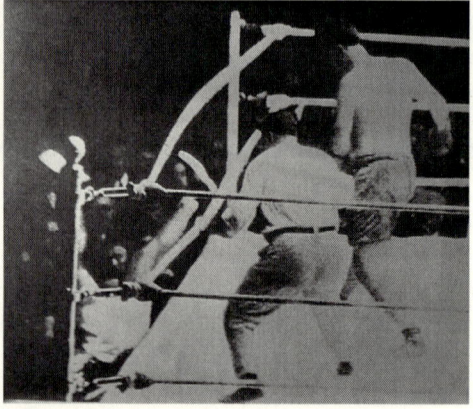

Amazingly, after the seventh knockdown, and with less than a minute left in the round, Firpo unleashed a brutal counterattack that almost ended the fight. Firpo put Dempsey on the defensive with a volley of rights, driving the champion to the ropes. Firpo's explosive right hand then detonated on Dempsey's jaw and propelled him through the ropes and out of the ring.

Few could believe what they were seeing. Dempsey, his feet high in the air, fell directly onto the table of the ringside press. At this time there were no aprons on boxing rings. Several writers pushed him back through the ropes, frantically working to get him off their typewriters so they could continue recording what was taking place.

For a moment, it looked as if Firpo would become world Heavyweight champion. But Dempsey was helped into the ring at the count of nine (Despite having been seventeen seconds outside the ring, fighters are given a twenty-second count when they are knocked through the ropes.) "A champion is someone who gets up when he can't," Dempsey often said. It was never truer.

In the ring again after the famous long count, and back on his feet, Dempsey, stunned, backpedaled as Firpo resumed his attack. The challenger desperately hammered away with his right but the champion weathered the storm and came back with two hard rights of his own just before the bell finally rang.

In their corners between rounds, both battlers were suffering the effects of the wildest round in ring history. Some witnesses said that Dempsey, sitting on his stool, was unconscious until Jack Kearns, his wily manager, found the smelling salts and put them under the champion's nose. Dempsey blinked and looked at his handlers who were slapping him and dousing him with water and asked, "What round was I knocked out in?"

The second round began. But Firpo's punches lacked snap. He was wobbly. Dempsey had Firpo on the defensive. Dempsey was back from the dead. The champ launched a series of left hooks that put the challenger down for the eighth time.

Firpo climbed to his feet yet again. He took one last right hand swing before Dempsey struck with a sharp one-two, the final punch a right to the jaw as Firpo was already going down. The challenger rolled over onto his back. The fight, perhaps the most savage two rounds in boxing history, was over after barely four minutes. Then, in a moment almost as stunning as the fight, as soon as Firpo was counted out, Dempsey the assassin of just seconds before turned into a comforter. Dazed himself, he left his own corner to stoop down to help up his bloody, beaten foe. The more than 80,000 in attendance at the Polo Grounds roared their approval.

Magnanimous in victory. A giant of a man. The American spirit.

The brief but electrifying brawl at the Polo Grounds had provided more thrills than all of Dempsey's previous title defenses put together. Newsreels caught the whole fight. The impact of seeing the American heavyweight champion of the world pounded through the ropes by the Argentinian challenger won new respect for Jack Dempsey.

Suddenly, he was an early "Rocky," an indomitable American working guy who didn't give up and climbed back into the ring to eventually floor his most formidable opponent. The late great American boxing historian Bert Randolph Sugar called Dempsey-Firpo, "the greatest fight in the history of the sport." Few would argue.

For years The Mauler had been the invincible champion no one could relate to or care about, especially after the scandals of his divorce and the accusations of his being a draft dodger. But seeing him come so close to defeat changed his public image and made him human again, at least in the United States. So for the next three years Dempsey burnished that more appealing image as he stayed out of the prize ring and instead became a full-time celebrity, appearing in various exhibitions, stage plays and movies, and then marrying gorgeous film star Estelle Taylor, seen above being hoisted trophy-style by Dempsey in 1925. Thus, Dempsey was more popular than ever by the time he finally fought again against Gene Tunney in 1926.

Despite "losing" in the ring, Firpo garnered immense fame and respect all over Latin America. The feat of dropping Dempsey, much less putting him through the ropes, was superhuman: punched or shoved, it didn't matter. The fight was so inspirational that a Salvadorian football club, C.D. Luis Ángel Firpo, was named after Firpo in 1930. The club exists and competes to this day. The team colors are red and blue: the colors worn by the football club that Firpo supported in Buenos Aires, the Club Atlético San Lorenzo de Almagro. Various schools, streets and avenues across Latin America have also been named after him.

The fight had an immeasurable impact on American culture. This

366

is the fight at which Clark Gable and William Powell's character meet in the 1934 movie *Manhattan Melodrama,* a fine George Cukor film, but best remembered as the movie that gangster John ("I rob banks for a living, what do you do?") Dillinger attended on the night he was shot to death by FBI agents.

Author Thomas Wolfe referenced the fight in Chapter 15 of his 1939 novel, *The Web and the Rock*, published posthumously, a year before his masterwork, *You Can't Go Home Again*. In the book, the main character, George Webber, has a friend, Jim, who is a young reporter. Jim makes a visit to Luis Firpo's training camp. He is also at the Polo Grounds on the night of the fight. With him is another friend named, Monk. They watch the fight and go downtown to a bar where they start a fight. Wolfe's descriptions of the evening are detailed and vivid, as was his style. Since nearly everything Wolfe wrote in his four major novels was autobiographical, one assumes that Wolfe, too, was at the fight.

Later in the century the fight was mentioned in Steve McQueen's *The Sand Pebbles* (1966) during the fight between Po-han and Ski. It was also referenced in the 1976 film *Rocky* by character Mickey Goldmill, portrayed by Burgess Meredith, who says he fought an opponent on the same date.

The fight was on the radio. But there were no televisions, and at the time it wasn't possible even to see fight films in theaters. That would come in the 1930s. There were newsreels in movie theatres, but the product was occasional and inconsistent. The ways in which the glories of Jack Dempsey were visually conveyed to the public were the words of the men who saw him fight and a handful of grainy photographs in newspapers. So how did the fight embed so deeply in the American psyche?

A newspaper, the New York *Evening Journal*, commissioned an artist named George Wesley Bellows to make sketches of the fight. Bellows was well known in his time. He was an American realist painter, known mostly for his bold depictions of urban life in New York City. Bellows was frequently called "the most acclaimed American artist of his generation."

He was from what art critics might call the second generation of the 'Ashcan School,' the group of realistic artists, many of whom had started as newspaper illustrators in New York and Philadelphia, who first exhibited in New York as a movement in 1908.

The 'Ashcan' guys were known for their gritty urban subject matter, dark palette, and gestural brushwork. Their spiritual genius was the American painter Robert Henri. They believed in the worthiness of immigrant and working-class life as artistic subject matter and in an art that depicted the way people really lived, rather than an elitist ideal. Bellows, who had been an outstanding semi-pro baseball player before coming to New York to be an illustrator, was influenced by the 'Ashcan' style, but was less concerned with realism, as we will see.

Bellows sat ringside sketching. In the first round Dempsey kept Bellows working furiously as Dempsey knocked Firpo to the canvas seven times. But then all of a sudden, not far above Bellows, Firpo landed the perfect punch to Dempsey's chin and knocked him, or shoved him, through the ropes and out of the ring, falling onto the table of sportswriters sitting ringside.

That was the moment that Bellows painted.

As the referee began counting to ten, the sportswriters helped push the dazed Dempsey up and back into the ring. Among them was the legendary Paul Gallico, who later insisted it was his typewriter that Dempsey landed on, causing a noticeable gash in the champ's head. It was an odd coincidence: Gallico's career had been launched by an interview with Dempsey a few years earlier in which Gallico asked Dempsey to spar with him and not hold anything back. Gallico thus described how it felt to be knocked out by the heavyweight champion.

The fight continued. Later, inspired by what he had seen, Bellows decided to turn one of the sketches into a painting. Or, more accurately, he turned one of his sketches into a masterpiece of Americana. Bellows produced a worked called *Dempsey and Firpo* in 1924, depicting the champ's exit from the Polo Grounds ring. It's a large oil painting, about 5 feet long and 4 feet high.

It hangs today in the Whitney Museum of American Art in Manhattan, way downtown at 99 Gansevoort Street, only a few mile from where Jacket Dempsey landed on a sea of typewriters.

Bellows strived to capture the essence of the fight and he nailed it. Take a close look.

You see the fight as if you're sitting on one side of the ring, perhaps in the first row, your line of vision about the height of the ring floor. (Assume you're a mob-connected guy or a gangster's doll and that's how you got such a great ticket. Further assume you were there with your moll.) You look up through the ring ropes to see the boxers. The ropes are very light gray, almost white. A strip of the ring's white canvas floor covering runs horizontally, all along the edge of the ring. These white lines stand out against the darkness of the arena in the background. You can make out the heads of the crowd on the far side of the ring, but not much else.

In front of you are eight men, sportswriters presumably, all along the length of the ringside. You see them from their backs, from the waist up, as they twist away from or reach out to cushion the fall of Jack Dempsey. The champ is captured in mid-fall, his arms and legs flailing. He crashes backwards through the ropes and down onto the writers. The men in the picture are boxy and geometric in shape. They are portrayed with coarse brushstrokes that feel energetic, rippling with movement and emotion.

In contrast to the falling Dempsey, above him in the ring the sturdy relentless Firpo stands like a giant, concluding the great swing of his powerful left arm and fist. Also in the ring, on the right, the referee, Johnny Gallagher, stands pointing his finger at Dempsey, counting him out. The painting, not surprisingly, is often referred to as, *Dempsey Through the Ropes*.

A strange quirk: In the artwork, the right-handed Firpo knocks Dempsey out of the ring with his left hand. Why the left? Look at the lines. Most likely Bellows thought it better drew the viewer's eye to the moment of impact.

"George Bellows did for visual art what Ring Lardner did for journalism," wrote sports journalist Allen Barra in *The Atlantic* in 2012. "You got all the details and a vivid account of the action that was at the center of the narrative. You could smell the sweat and cigar smoke and feel the heat coming off the crowd."

Stunning. And here's a footnote. At the left edge of the painting, sitting ringside there is a bald man. That was the artist, George Wesley Bellows.

Gradually, the painting by Bellows made its way around the nation, in newspapers, by original lithographs and by magazines. The visual image took root in American minds. There were giants in those days, or rather that's the way working men wanted their heroes to seem. But the only medium of the time that could really suggest monumental nature of what happened on that night in upper Manhattan was George Bellows' moody violent magnificent canvas.

The fight was not without controversy. Film that exists to this day shows the referee, Johnny Gallagher, reaching the count of four by the time Dempsey was finally back in the ring. Ringside observers with stop watches at the time said the time was fourteen seconds. A speedier count, it has been conjectured, would have made Firpo the victor. But a speedier count didn't happen.

Bellows began his painting just weeks after the fight. He died of a ruptured appendix in 1925, a little more than a year after he finished *Dempsey and Firpo*. Seven years later Firpo and Jack Dempsey agreed to jointly manage an Argentine heavyweight named Abel Evaristo Cestac. Cestac was an amateur boxer when Firpo discovered him. According to Firpo, he came across Cestac fighting a steer because the latter could not find any men his equal in strength.

Firpo lived to age 66 and died in 1960. Dempsey died at age 87 in 1983. Both Firpo and Dempsey were wealthy men after the showdown in New York.

    After the great fight of September 24, the New York Giants returned home that Friday. They quickly clinched the pennant against Boston and Brooklyn. Once again, baseball was back at 155th Street and Eighth Avenue. And the crosstown Yankees would be waiting in the World Series, for which the Fight of the Century had been a preliminary at the Polo Grounds

***

{Author's note. Much of the Dempsey Firpo fight can still be found on You Tube. Like many Polo Grounds events, it was extraordinary… For those interested, some wonderful photos and film clips of the talented Annette Kellerman exist on-line and on You Tube, also. I recommend both.}

Chapter 46   Springtime in Sarasota

> **"I like Florida. Everything is in the 80's. The temperatures, the ages and the IQ's."**
>
> **George Carlin**

    John Ringling, the circus impresario, was one of McGraw's many influential friends during the Twenties. Sometime after the Yankees had defeated the Giants in the 1923 World Series, Ringling talked McGraw into trying Sarasota, Florida, as a spring training site. Ringling, as it turned out, knew as much about baseball as McGraw knew about, say, sword-swallowing.

    Ringling didn't exactly own Sarasota, but he owned more of it than anyone else. He housed his circus there when it wasn't on the road, he owned one of the finest winter mansions in the city, and he tied up his luxury yacht conspicuously at the town's best pier. The owner of a lavish art collection, Ringling made way for some new canvases in his own digs by weeding out several dozen old ones and presenting the town with a public art gallery. He also dabbled in local real estate, which was equivalent to saying that Rockefeller dabbled in oil.

Normally McGraw was familiar with a town he had selected as a spring training site, but Sarasota was an exception. Thus things began to go wrong when McGraw, in February of that year, arrived with a caravan of five dozen ballplayers, a couple of dozen wives, and an array of newspapermen who changed by the hour. The Giants' contingent was too large for the hotel into which Ringling had booked them.

McGraw complained to his friend, who quickly became exasperated.

"What kind of baseball team did you expect me to bring?" Mac raged. "Nine men?"

Well, yes. That was what Ringling had expected. So McGraw broke his delegation in half, lodging his veterans, the writers, and wives into the snazzy Mira Mar Hotel, an expensive joint overlooking the bay. Rookies and other newcomers were bivouacked at the more austere Watrous Hotel, a wood-framed structure down the street. The Watrous overlooked nothing more breathtaking than its own shadow.

Since the sportswriters were present, spending the money of their tyrannical bosses back up north, stories had to be filed. As nothing of particular interest had happened, several writers filed cute stories on the confusion upon the team's arrival. When this well ran dry, the scribes filed accounts of sunless gray skies and near-freezing weather. This did nothing to endear the Giants to the locals. Soon clippings of offending newspaper stories were posted in the town square, annotated with such handwritten comments as, "If you don't like our weather, keep your damned mouths shut!"

As Jack Benny might have said, "Well. . . !"

Certain writers who followed the Giants - Bozeman Bulger, Bugs Baer, W. O. McGeehan, and George Herbert Daley, in particular - were filing some truly sour dispatches from Florida, most of them at the expense of the natives. A contingent of the citizenry approached McGraw and asked him to muzzle the writers. McGraw only shrugged. "I can't tell them what to write," he answered, suddenly an expert on the rights of a free press.

No, he couldn't.

But certain members of the Sarasota population decided that they would give it a shot. One night soon thereafter, all the lights suddenly failed on the main street, where the Mira Mar and the Watrous stood. A strange bugle call was heard in the distance. And then, upon cue, a long white row of hooded, torchlit Ku Klux Klansmen trudged into town.

We are speaking here not of a modern Twenty-first Century

American South, but a backward South of cross burnings, lily-white segregation, Bible Belt temperance, *The Birth of a Nation* by Kentuckian D. W. Griffith, and Governor Huey Long of Louisiana. It was a time, in other words, when Klansmen held a terrible influence that they've long since relinquished among decent people. Still, the troublemakers from up north were hardly intimidated. The newspapermen and the ballplayers piled out of the two hotels to catch the ugly spectacle.

For several moments there was an uneasy silence. Then the first words were spoken by Cozy Dolan, an ex-player and now a coach for McGraw.

"Just give me a fungo," Dolan griped, "and I'll lick all of these bums myself."

First the ballplayers began to laugh, then the newsmen. The rest of the crowd started to giggle. Suddenly, the so called White Knights of the Invisible Empire were nothing more than what they really were: a silly group of ignorant men parading around in cheap sheets. Off they slinked into the darkness. The incident was reported in the northern newspapers, then forgotten. Soon even the weather improved, and the spring training trip began to resemble many others.

There was one casualty, however.

McGraw spent many evening hours prowling the doorways and lobbies of the Mira Mar and the Watrous, looking for players breaking training. One rookie who always seemed to be caught in McGraw's net was a pitcher named Pat Malone. Eventually, McGraw released the young man to Toledo after the Giants had broken camp and arrived in New York. McGraw didn't make too many mistakes in player personnel, but this was one. Malone was picked up by the Chicago Cubs, for whom he would have seven distinguished seasons, winning 20 or more games twice to lead the league in victories. In 1929 and 1932, he would help pitch the Cubbies to a pennant. He would later turn up with the Yankees and won 134 games over the course of his career.

Even with the loss of Malone, however, the Giants had a surplus of talent as they pursued an unprecedented fourth straight pennant. Hack Wilson was ready to take over an outfield position and young Travis (Stonewall) Jackson, the slick, graceful young man from Arkansas, had made himself a fixture at shortstop. Billy Southworth, whom McGraw had obtained in the Stengel trade, was a good hitter and a smart, seasoned outfielder. Heinie Groh was possibly winding down at third base, but McGraw had an eighteen-year-old phenom named Freddie Lindstrom ready to take over.

First base was also an embarrassment of riches. Highpockets Kelly was coming off a .307 season with 16 home runs. Yet young Bill Terry, who had destroyed American Association pitching in 1923, was understandably restless. "Why don't you try me in the outfield?" Terry suggested one day.

"Think I want you to get hit on the head and be killed?" McGraw growled.

"I played the outfield in Shreveport," Terry countered.

"This isn't Shreveport," McGraw shot back with just the right tone of condescension. "Take it easy. Learn to play first base. Forget about the outfield." Thus Bill Terry prepared to take a seat on the bench for much of the season.

McGraw's pitching was also set. Nehf, McQuillan, Bentley, and Virgil Barnes, Jesse's brother, would form the starting foursome, with Rosy Ryan and a rookie named Wayland Dean working in and out of the rotation. McGraw was confident enough of his club's chances to answer the biggest question of all at a press conference before the season started.

"Mac," asked a New York sportswriter, "who's going to pitch the opening game of the World Series?"

"Nehf, I suppose," McGraw replied. "He always does."

Chapter 47   1924 and Another Scandal

"Fans like home runs. And we have assembled a pitching staff to please our fans."

Clark Griffith, Owner, Washington Senators

Early in the 1924 season, someone hit upon the curious notion that the Brooklyn club was always dangerous in the year of a presidential election. The genesis of this bizarre belief was, of course, the fact that the Flatbush squad had won pennants in 1916 and 1920. As you may recall, the team was widely referred to as the Robins, a salute to their affable leader Wilbert Robinson. (In the shorthand of the sports pages, the Robins - to continue feathery metaphor - was further contracted to "the Flock," a term that could still be seen in the New York tabloid sports pages well into the 1950s.)

The idea that the Robins would magically rise on leap years made dandy press. No one had the heart to suggest that the years 1904, 1908, and 1912, when the Brooklyn team finished sixth, seventh, and seventh, respectively, might disprove the theory. The fact was, the Brooklyn players had read so much along these lines in early 1924 that they began to believe it themselves. Never mind that they'd finished sixth, 19.5 games behind the Giants, in 1923. In 1924 they were off and running.

The Giants, on the other hand, bloated with overconfidence, were off and stumbling. As the season progressed, Pittsburgh, Cincinnati, and Chicago fell back into the pack. The Giants maintained a lead, but Brooklyn came on with a terrifying rush. Every time the Giants won, Brooklyn - paced by Dazzy Vance and Burleigh Grimes, who would combine for 50 victories - would win, also. McGraw was jolted out of his good humor and his rages were frequent and violent. He juggled his lineup when Groh struggled, establishing Lindstrom at third base. He forced Terry into the batting order by putting him at first, shuffling Kelly off to center field and platooning his regular outfielders: Southworth, Youngs, Meusel, and Wilson.

Still, the Robins stayed close and stalked the Giants, frequently from a second-place position only a game or two off the pace. By mid-August, McGraw was so much fun to be with that an observer of the New York Giants' dugout would frequently see him by himself at one end of the bench with the entire team huddled at the other end, with every player carefully avoiding Mac's gaze.

Meanwhile, the fair-haired boys from Gowanus kept coming.

First baseman Jack Fournier, a discard from St. Louis, would hit .334 with a league-leading 27 home runs. Zack Wheat would hit .375, his finest of many fine seasons. But who were the rest of these guys?

Johnny Mitchell? Milt Stock?
Andy High?
Eddie Brown?
Art Decatur? Bill Doak?
Who?

Over the last weekend in August, this gang of nobodies ambushed the Giants and took three games in a row from them. On September

6, Uncle Robbie's club plowed into first place. McGraw was fit to be tied. By winning the second half of a doubleheader against the Phillies, the Giants edged back into first place that same afternoon.

The next day a single game was scheduled at Ebbets Field. It was tied, 3-3, after seven innings, only to have the Giants score five times in the top of the eighth. Before a riotous crowd, however, the Robins charged back with a run in the eighth and three in the ninth before Hugh McQuillan, in relief of Jack Bentley, put out the fire.

Not all the excitement was on the field. The city's riot squad had to be called out to deal with several hundred fans of conflicting loyalties who hadn't been able to buy tickets to the game. Many of them did get into the park by breaking down a left field gate and invading the grandstand. But by the time the sun set, the Giants were clinging to a slim game and a half lead.

Still, the Robins stayed with the Giants. On the morning of September 20, McGraw made a strange and sudden announcement. Heinie Groh and Frankie Frisch would be out for the rest of the season due to "injuries." There was rejoicing in Brooklyn.

On September 22, the Robins were only half a game back with a week left in the season. The Giants went to Pittsburgh for a series against the tough third-place Pirates. McGraw slapped his players together, gave them a rousing lecture in the clubhouse, and somehow cajoled them into sweeping the Pittsburgh club.

Now, despite being pursued all year, the Giants' magic number was two. New York had three games remaining with seventh-place Philadelphia, while the Robins had the same number with cellar-dwelling Boston. It was a strange set of circumstances, with McGraw and Robinson trying to steer their clubs to a pennant against each other, and against teams managed by former New York infielders: Art Fletcher of the Phillies and Dave Bancroft of the Braves. But the pennant race ended suddenly. New York beat Philadelphia and Brooklyn lost their first game to Boston. The Giants would go to the World Series for the fourth consecutive year.

Or would they? After the season ended, and before the World Series began, something happened that would mar McGraw's fourth straight pennant and which, for a time, threatened to again rip baseball apart.

According to John (Heinie) Sand, the shortstop for the Phillies, he, Sand, had been approached at the Polo Grounds by Giants outfielder Jimmy O'Connell just before the pennant-clinching game. O'Connell, according to the story, offered Sand $500 if he "wouldn't bear down too hard" that day against New York.

Sand walked away from the offer and might have said nothing about it. But in Sand's mind, there remained the image of Chicago White Sox third baseman George (Buck) Weaver.

Weaver had been an honest member of the 1919 Black Sox, had played his hardest in the fixed World Series, but had been banned from baseball for life - much to the chagrin of John McGraw, who wanted to acquire him for the Giants. Weaver's sin had been knowing that the fix was in, but not reporting it. Heinie Sand did not want to be the Buck Weaver of the mid-1920s. Accordingly, he reported the bribe attempt to his manager, Art Fletcher. Fletcher reported it to John Heydler, the National League president. Heydler passed it along to Judge Landis, baseball's warrior against both types of corruption: real and imagined.

Landis interviewed O'Connell in New York in September after the season ended. Guileless, he freely admitted that he had attempted to bribe Sand. "Who put you up to it?" Landis asked.

"Why, Cozy Dolan," O'Connell answered. He also named Frankie Frisch, Ross Youngs, and George Kelly as other players who were in on the scheme.

Landis summoned the three players named, plus Dolan. The players categorically denied O'Connell's story. Dolan made a poor witness. Grilled by the commissioner, all Dolan could say was, "I don't remember."

Over and over, Dolan would answer question after question with, "I don't remember." Landis pointed out to Dolan that it was not terribly believable that a man wouldn't recall whether he had had a conversation on such a significant subject. But nothing jostled Dolan's memory. Landis was left in a position of taking everyone's story at face value. Frisch, Youngs, and Kelly were cleared of any involvement. Landis used O'Connell's admission to ban him from baseball. The same fate befell Dolan, whose clumsy amnesia convinced no one of his innocence. Sand, by the way, was commended by the commissioner for bringing the story to light.

For their part, McGraw and owner Charles Stoneham initially reacted with bewilderment to L'Affaire Sand-O'Connell. "I can't understand what these men [O'Connell and Dolan] did," McGraw told reporters. "The chances were 100-1 that New York would win the pennant anyway."

McGraw, who was also angry that the matter had gone through John Heydler to Landis before he knew about it, attempted to haul out his favorite legal eagle, William J. Fallon, to defend his old friend Dolan. Dolan, however, bypassed Fallon, feeling that Landis would eventually reinstate him. Landis never did.

Amid this stench, the World Series prepared to open. Much to the delight of the rest of the country, a team from somewhere other than New York would participate for the first time since 1920. Incredibly - and that is the only word that fits the occasion - the Washington Senators had outlasted the New York Yankees in a torrid American League race. Babe Ruth, to no one's astonishment, had battered his circuit's pitchers to the tune of .378 and 46 home runs, leading the league also in hits, runs, walks, slugging percentage, and total bases. Paced by this and the other artillery that Colonel Ruppert had sprinkled through his lineup, the Yankees won 18 of 20 games during one particular rampage in September. Still, Washington, led by aging Walter Johnson and manager-second baseman Stanley (Bucky) Harris, reached the finish line two games ahead of the dreaded Yankees.

Washington was on its ear with excitement. And the rest of the country was similarly thrilled. Not only were Johnson and twenty-seven-year-old Bucky Harris two of the most popular players in baseball, but there was a notion out in Middle America that the World Series ought not to be a private arrangement between the boroughs of New York City. Add to that the odor still in the air from the O'Connell-Dolan mess and it is easy to understand how much of the country would be rooting for the Senators. The steely-eyed oddsmakers, however, favored the New York Giants.

After the King Kong vs. Godzilla flavor of the previous Giants-Yankees Series, it was difficult to imagine the Senators even taking the field against McGraw's crew. As a team, they had 22 home runs, 12 of which had been hit by Leon (Goose) Goslin, their third baseman. All they had was pitching, defense, a lineup packed with contact hitters, and an uncanny way of eventually finding ways to win, as the Series would illustrate.

Chapter 48   One for "The Old Man"

> "He's got a gun concealed about his person.
> You can't tell me he throws them balls with his arm."
>
> **Ring Lardner, writing of Walter Johnson**

The new American President, Calvin Coolidge found much of life a damned bore, and baseball was therein included. But he showed up at Game One of the 1924 World Series at Griffith Stadium in Washington and grimaced for the photographers. Senators Manager Bucky Harris presented the Commander-in-Chief with a baseball to throw as a ceremonial first pitch.

Coolidge warmed up and threw it.

It landed nowhere near any of the players.

Trying a second time, "Silent Cal" did much better. He then settled in to watch Art Nehf, just as McGraw had predicted in the spring, oppose Walter Johnson, though it is doubtful that Coolidge had any idea who was pitching. The First Lady, a dignified but vocal gray-haired woman named Grace Coolidge, sat by her husband's side, kept a scorecard with no help from anyone, and passionately exhorted the Senators to victory.

Alas, the baseball gods were not smiling on Walter Johnson on October 4, 1924. Johnson pitched masterful baseball. "The Old Man," as he was called, scattered base hits all over the place, but through eleven innings only Highpockets Kelly, with a home run in the second, and Bill Terry, with a home run in the fourth, had actually burned him. But Art Nehf matched him nobly, en route to his fourth career World Series win. Both pitchers hurled complete games, but Johnson's worst enemies - the rest of his own Washington squad - caught up to him at last in the twelfth inning.

Two Senator errors allowed the Giants to pull the game out, 4-3. As a footnote, Giants pitcher Art Nehf much later proclaimed that his proudest feat in baseball was not outpitching Johnson that day, but rather collecting three singles off him in five at-bats. A news photo of the day caught Goose Goslin being tossed out at first base on an outstanding play by shortstop Travis Jackson to first baseman Bill Terry. All three players would later join the Baseball Hall of Fame.

The next day the Senators bounced back, winning by the same 4-3 score with a run in the last of the ninth. Jack Bentley pitched admirably for the New Yorkers, but Goose Goslin and Bucky Harris stung him for home runs, keeping the Washington club in the game until the ninth inning rally won it.

Then the two clubs took turns throttling each other. The middle three games of the Series were played at the Polo Grounds, each before crowds just shy of fifty thousand. The Giants and the Senators both used four pitchers in Game Three and reliever Rosy Ryan, who hit his first and only World Series home run, was credited with the 6-4 win. The next afternoon, however, Goose Goslin was again a problem for McGraw's pitchers. Goslin's four-for-four day included another home run as George Mogridge defeated the Giants' Virgil Barnes, 7-4.

It will be recalled that in 1923 McGraw had obtained a hard-hitting pitcher named Jack Bentley from Baltimore in the International League. Casey Stengel once called Bentley one of the best "natural" hitters he had ever seen. Indeed, Bentley had hit .350 with 22 home runs in 1922, his final International League year, playing first base when he wasn't pitching. But Bentley had also had a previous life with the Senators from 1913 through 1916. There he had amassed - if that's the word for it - a 6-9 won-lost record in 39 games. But now, eight years later, he was back in the majors, squaring off in Game Five of the 1924 World Series against Walter Johnson.

Bentley did not waste the opportunity, getting a single and a two-run home run in three at-bats as he earned the victory. Two of the new kids did well against "The Big Train": Lindstrom, with a four-for-four afternoon, and Bill Terry, with a rousing triple. Back to the District went the Series. Washington garnered only four singles in seven innings against Art Nehf, and none off Rosy Ryan in relief. But one of those singles, struck by Bucky Harris, drove in two runs. Behind a masterful pitching effort by Tom Zachary (who would become a baseball footnote himself three years later by serving up the pitch that Babe Ruth converted into home run number 60) Washington won, 2-1.

That brought the Giants into Game Seven of the World Series, winner take all, for the championship of professional baseball. The Senators had the home park, but they also had a problem: Bill Terry was hitting a flat .500 over the first six games of the Series and showed no sign of letting up. If only, Bucky Harris mused, that meddlesome Terry could be removed from the New York lineup.

Terry was, of course, a left-handed hitter. The other Giant first baseman, George Kelly, hit right-handed. Normally, McGraw started Terry at first only against right-handers and either benched Kelly or put him in the outfield, depending on how he was hitting. Here the wheels began to spin.

When the New York Giants arrived at Griffith Stadium on October 10, they were stunned to see Harris warming up a right-hander named Warren (Curly) Ogden. Ogden had been acquired from the A's during the season and had won 9 games for the Senators. But he was also a journeyman starter, probably the sixth-best pitcher on the staff, the owner of a career record under .500, and possessor of a lifetime ERA of more than 5.00 runs per game. Ogden made no sense as a starter. But there he was.

McGraw sensed what Harris was up to, but he wasn't about to fall for it. Not yet, anyway. Ogden struck out Freddie Lindstrom to start the game, then walked Frisch. Out to the mound came Harris, who yanked Ogden - in accordance with his prearranged plan - and brought in lefty George Mogridge. Harris was challenging McGraw to either leave Terry in against a southpaw pitcher or remove his best hitter in favor of a right-handed batter.

McGraw left "Memphis Bill" in the game.

Mogridge induced Terry to ground out to second in the second inning. He struck Terry out in the fourth. Harris homered in the fourth.

Bucky Harris scoring his home run in the 4th inning in the 7th game of the World Series. 10/10/24

The Senators led, 1-0 going to the sixth and the trap was ready to spring shut on the Giants.

Ross Youngs started the inning by walking. Highpockets Kelly singled him to third. Now Terry was up, and New York needed runs. Terry was hitless in two at-bats against Mogridge. The last thing McGraw needed was a strikeout or a ground ball. McGraw knew that if he pinch-hit for Terry, Harris would make a move of his own. But McGraw's hand was forced. He couldn't allow Terry to make an easy out.

McGraw inserted Irish Meusel to hit for Terry. Harris responded by taking Mogridge out of the game and replacing him with Fred (Firpo) Marberry, his ace reliever. Still, for a while it looked as if McGraw would duck the bullet. Meusel hit a sacrifice fly that scored Youngs. Hack Wilson followed with a single, then Travis Jackson and catcher Hank Gowdy reached base safely on Washington errors. When the dust had settled, the Giants came out of the inning leading, 3-1.

There it remained until the bottom of the eighth inning. The Giants needed only six more outs to win the Series. They got the six outs, but not before a bad hop single off the bat of Bucky Harris careened over Freddie Lindstrom's head in the bottom of the eighth inning, scoring two runs. Art Nehf relieved Virgil Barnes, the starter, and retired the side.

But the game was tied. Harris then pulled shut the trap door on McGraw. With the dangerous Terry gone, Harris trudged into the game an unexpected visitor, Walter Johnson, the greatest right-hander in American League history, making his third appearance in the Series. This was serious heat coming in out of the bullpen.

It was as if the die was now cast. McQuillan relieved Nehf and Bentley relieved McQuillan, as McGraw scrambled to stay in the game. Fate played out its hand in the twelfth inning, just as it had in Game One.

In the bottom of that inning, Washington catcher Herold (Muddy) Ruel, hitting an awesome .050 for the Series, lifted a pop foul behind the batter's box to start the disaster. Hank Gowdy, Ruel's New York counterpart, tossed away his face mask and circled under the ball. But as he circled, Gowdy trapped his own foot in the discarded mask. He hobbled like an animal caught in a snare, lost track of the foul pop, and allowed it to drop.

Blessed with a second life, Ruel slapped a clean double past third, raising his Series average from 50¢ to 95¢.

Walter Johnson was up next. He hit the ball hard at Travis Jackson and, predictably enough, the sure-handed Jackson fumbled the ball. Johnson was safe as Ruel held second. The Washington crowd, watching the unbelievable, roared with approval.

It ended moments later. Previously hitless in five at-bats that day, Earl McNeely, the Washington center fielder, hit a grounder directly at Freddie Lindstrom at third.

Lindstrom had two alternatives. He could take the force at third and hope for a double play at first. Or he could go around the horn immediately for the double play. He had these alternatives, that is, if he caught the ball. He probably had one of these plans in mind when the ball - just as it had in the eighth inning - hit something in front of him and took a wild hop over his head.

The Giants stood by and watched, helpless and disbelieving, as Ruel dashed from second to home plate. There was no throw. The Washington Senators had the only World Championship they would ever claim. Even President Coolidge, who managed to sit through the three-hour game, cracked a huge smile at the Washington victory and applauded.

"The ball hit a pebble," Heinie Groh explained after the game. "It wasn't Freddie's fault. It was bad luck."

Clark Griffith, according to Goose Goslin, always maintained that God had been on the Senators' side in the seventh game. How else, Griffith would ask, could those pebbles (which were never found) have positioned themselves in the way of a batted ball twice?

Jack Bentley, the losing pitcher in the fluky seventh game, had a similar explanation. After the disconsolate Giants had trundled aboard a train for New York, the entire team sat in a long sullen silence until Bentley finally spoke.

"Cheer up, boys," he said. "It just looks as though the Good Lord couldn't stand seeing Walter Johnson get beat again."

A "victory" party had been scheduled that same evening at the Commodore Hotel on 42nd Street. Despite the loss of the World Series and despite McGraw's bitterness at having dropped a pair of World Series in a row, Mac bade the party go on.

The bash at the Commodore lasted until five in the morning, but it had a decidedly subdued air. Instead of the rousing, raucous affairs that had marked Giant triumphs in the past, this one resembled the piano room on the Titanic's final voyage. Art Nehf played *On the Banks of the Wabash Far Away* on the piano as his wife and father led with the singing. An Irish tenor named Jimmy Flynn lifted his smooth vocal cords in a rendition of Dear *Old Pal of Mine*. And naturally, in these dark days of Prohibition, the booze flowed freely.

Meanwhile, three hundred miles to the south, the capital was agog with excitement over the Senators' very own World Championship. President Coolidge issued an official proclamation congratulating the new champs. Then Calvin celebrated a second time less than a month later by easily defeating John W. Davis and Robert M. LaFollette for the presidency.

Chapter 49   A Winter of Discontent

Do you know what the cardinal sin was on that ball club? To begin a sentence to McGraw with the words, "I thought."
"You thought?" he would yell. "With what?"

Freddie Lindstrom, years after his retirement

The tour of Europe that McGraw and Comiskey had planned the previous year finally took place that fall. Everyone had a good time. Several players who were on neither the Giants nor the White Sox came along to round out the rosters. Notable among the extras were Muddy Ruel, who had batted the ball that had hopped over Freddie Lindstrom's head, and Casey Stengel, seen here, who had gotten over his bitterness about being shipped to the Braves. Casey was back by McGraw's side on the bench.

The trip was a financial disaster, however. Typical autumnal weather on the Continent - rainy and cold - followed the two squads across England, France, and Ireland. Fortunately, both McGraw and Comiskey were wealthy men by this time. They were able to underwrite expenses out of their own pockets. They forged along with the trip without a complaint. Along the way, the Giants were presented to King George V of England. A photo appeared worldwide of coach Hughie Jennings walking behind the monarch as King George shook the hand of Art Devlin.

McGraw personally met another good Irishman named George Bernard Shaw. The latter pronounced McGraw "the most authentic and real Most Remarkable Man in America" and seemed surprised that McGraw was polished, cordial, and in good spirits. Then, toward the end of the tour when the Giants played ball at Stamford Bridge, Arthur Conan Doyle, writing in the Times of London, predicted that baseball would "sweep England" as it had America. With such foresight did the empire begin to crumble.

Home from Europe, John and Blanche McGraw repaired to Havana in midwinter. McGraw was fifty-one years old by this time. He had been either playing or managing baseball for the better part of the last four decades. Many stories filled the New York newspapers that winter. Some said that McGraw was contemplating retirement, which he wasn't. No story, however, had any real sense of perspective because it was impossible to really know what the big story was. Namely, by the first day of January 1925, John McGraw had completed his finest times as manager of the New York Giants.

The years remaining to him would not be without excitement, intrigue, or merit. But they would, in the end, be marked by a slow and inexorable fall from grace.

For the previous four years, the Giants had accomplished the unprecedented feat of winning four consecutive league championships. Their domination of the National League was all the more impressive as they had had, during this time, no batting champions and no dominating slugger who could approach the likes of Ruth or even Hornsby in the National League. The championships had been carefully created in the image McGraw wanted, that of a team effort, executing properly and preventing opponents from scoring. So in 1925 there was no reason to suspect that the New York Giants would not steadily proceed to their fifth straight pennant.

A series of injuries - notably to Lindstrom, Groh, and Frisch (seen here) - hobbled the team in April and allowed the Pittsburgh Pirates, not the New York Giants, to jump in front of the National League. On top of this, McGraw developed abdominal problems and left the club for a week early in the year.

Hughie Jennings ran the Giants in McGraw's absence. At about the same time, Sam Crane, the sportswriter of the New York *Evening Journal* and longtime McGraw bridge partner and crony, fell ill during a road trip. He was escorted home by his fellow New Yorker Frankie Frisch and never again saw the Giants play. Crane died at age seventy-one on June 25. Crane's death not only saddened McGraw, but shocked and depressed him. The two men had known each other since McGraw's days as an Oriole. Worse, rumor reached New York that Christy Mathewson had returned to Saranac Lake for further treatment for his tuberculosis.

The portents for 1925 were wretched.

Chapter 50   Greb vs. Walker; Guttman vs. Benfica

**"Prizefighting ain't the noblest of arts
and I ain't the noblest artist."**

**Harry Greb
American light heavyweight champion (1922-3)
and world middleweight champion (1923-6)
W 261 L 17 D 19 KO's 48**

Less than two years after the monumental Dempsey-Firpo boxing match at the Polo Grounds, one of the other great fights of the Twentieth Century took place in the same ring. As the Giants were away on a brief road trip to Philadelphia and Boston, Mickey Walker, the world welterweight champion, better known as "The Toy Bulldog," went up in division to challenge World Middleweight Champion Harry Greb. Fifteen rounds were scheduled. Fifty-five thousand people attended and, like Dempsey-Firpo, the brawl at the ballpark was memorable.

{Mickey Walker (left) against Harry Greb (right) at The Polo Grounds in 1925.}

Harry Greb fought professionally more than three hundred times from 1913 to 1926. He had floored opponents who outweighed him by more than thirty pounds. At various points in his career he owned the world middleweight and light heavyweight titles. Dubbed "the Pittsburgh Windmill" because of his brawling freewheeling style, Greb also crossed racial lines, taking on all challengers regardless of race. He was a fighter's fighter. Like Walker, he was ranked by the late American boxing historian Burt Randolph Sugar as one of the greatest pound for pound of all time.

Mickey Walker, former champion of the world, is on anyone's list as one of the greatest fighters in boxing history. Born just after the start of the century, he was in the ring when boxing was the most popular major American sport after baseball. There were only eight championships, and Walker held two of them - welterweight (1922-1926) and middleweight (1926-1931) - over a nine-year period. He fought at a time when powerful fighters packed each weight division. Walker fought them all from welterweight up to heavyweight. Walker was also a great personality who loved life and lived it to the fullest.

Of his opponent this night in the Polo Grounds, Walker always spoke with admiration and respect. "Harry Greb could hit from impossible angles," Walker recalled years later in 1954 to writer Stanley Weston in *Boxing and Wrestling Magazine*. "Once, after Harry missed a right to my face, he spun all the way around so that his back faced me. I relaxed my guard and waited for him to turn around. But before I knew what was happening, his left was stuck in my mouth. I still don't know how he did it, but he hit me while his hands faced in the opposite direction."

But on July 2, 1925 at the Polo Grounds, The Toy Bulldog gave The Pittsburgh Windmill as much as he could handle. Plus a little more later in the evening, according to legend.

Here's how it went down.

On the night of the fight, many observers feared that Greb would have trouble making the 160 pound weight limit. But Greb weighed in at 157 1/2 pounds and became the 9–5 favorite at match time - not that there was any wagering going on or anything.

During the opening rounds, Walker came out with body punches to Greb as the defending champion tried to stave off cramps in both his legs. In the fifth round Walker suddenly shifted his attack to Greb's head. A solid left smash by Walker caused Greb to spit out parts of several teeth. Greb hesitated momentarily, but quickly caught himself. Starting with the next round he cut loose and began to whittle away Mickey's early lead. Soon, Walker's face was badly puffed and he was bleeding from his mouth, nose and right eye.

"The two men stood toe-to-toe in round after round, hitting out for all they were worth," wrote *Boxing News* in a contemporary account of the fight in 1925. "Each man (was) badly shaken but carried on, with Walker getting somewhat dazed in the fourteenth round, but managing to hold on until his brain cleared, and then putting up as hot a fight in the final stanza as in any of the previous ones."

The endgame rounds belonged to Greb. Here's how Damon Runyon saw it from his usual perch at ringside:

"One tremendous splurge of wild fighting in the 14th round, during which (Greb) had Mickey Walker tipsy and teetering from his smashing punches, probably saved the title of middleweight champion for Harry Greb, the "Pittsburgh Windmill," here tonight. Walker made a determined attack on the Greb's body, round after round, and frequently hurt him with left hooks to the stomach and under the heart. Greb took a lead in the early rounds, loafed a bit and had been lagging along a bit behind up to the 14th when he suddenly clipped Walker on the chin with a swinging right that dazed the fighting Irishman from New Jersey. Walker backed into his own corner as Greb emptied every punch in his locker on him. Walker outfought Greb in the 15th and last round but Greb had offset anything Walker might now do."

The judges awarded Greb a unanimous decision. He retained the championship. But the guys weren't finished, according to legend.

Out on the town after the fight, Walker happened upon Greb after midnight at a mobbed-up speakeasy called The Silver Slipper at Forty-eighth and Broadway, both in the company of "ladies." The Silver Slipper was quite a joint. Located in a hotel, it was supplied with top-shelf, uncut booze by "the Broadway mob" - Meyer Lansky, Lucky Luciano, Bugsy Segal and Frank Costello. Luciano was the front guy for the liquor business and ran things from his offices at the now demolished Hotel Claridge, located at 1500 Broadway, just a few minutes' walk south at 44th Street.

According to the stories that circulated, the two fighters sat discussing their match over a drink when Walker made a comment stating that had it not been for Greb thumbing him in the eye, he would have won the fight.

Greb took great umbrage and jumped to his feet to fight. As Greb ripped off his jacket, Walker landed an uppercut that put him down for the proverbial count.

Or at least that's how Walker recounted it.

The story that circulated through Manhattan eventually had it a little different: Greb and Walker took it outside, the tale went, and started to hammer away at each other in a free-wheeling a violent street brawl for the second time in the same evening, with Greb coming out on top the second time, also. The doubleheader joined boxing's mythology and persisted among ring fans for years, adding to the urban mystique of big fights at the Polo Grounds.

Walker elaborated in 1970 to author Peter Heller. According to Walker, Greb and he enjoyed some drinks and left together, sans female companionship. Once outside, Walker teased Greb about his less-than-sportsmanlike style. Greb offered to pick up Round 16 right there in the street.

"So he started to take his coat off, and when he had his coat down around both his elbows so he couldn't move his arms, I wound up with my best punch and hit him on the chin," said Walker. Just then, a cop happened to walk by and separate them. "And nobody was around," Walker said. "Only Pat Casey (the cop), to see that I won the second fight. I licked Greb the second time."

The account given by Walker put a positive spin on Walker's loss. But Damon Runyon, who knew a bit about spinning a sports yarn, once said, "Ninety-five percent of sports tradition is fiction. Lies, if you like. But harmless. Who the hell cares if the facts get twisted?"

So the second fight, the one outside the Silver Slipper? It was bursting with jazz age 1920's style, world class pugilists, a speakeasy, easy women, gangsters, a big night at the Polo Grounds and mayhem far into the morning. Even an understanding Irish cop. It persisted for years. But, "The better a story is, the more likely it's a lie," Bert Randolph Sugar told ESPN.com a few years ago. "But what a wonderful story."

Take a second look at it. Walker and Greb left together but without their female companions? And the street was deserted outside a high profile speakeasy? Greb, who could tangle with heavyweights, got tangled up in his coat?

When writer and columnist Arthur "Bugs" Baer had heard the story too many times he tried to kill it. "Walker may have scuffled with him, and Greb may have cuffed his ears, but there was no second fight," Baer wrote in 1937.

A 1946 biography of Greb titled *Give Him To The Angels* by James Fair dissed the story. Fake news. Few of Greb's friends gave the story any credence, often citing the fact that Greb was a pro fighter and wouldn't be dumb enough to risk injury without a payday.

Columnist John Lardner, Ring's son, resuscitated the tale in 1947. In this version, Greb won. Eight years later, Lardner recanted, largely because a friend of Greb's, Eddy Deasy, had offered $1,000 to charity if any reliable witnesses came forward. There were no takers. No friendly officer Casey.

During the 1950s, the staunchest supporter of the myth was Mickey Walker himself. By that time Walker was enjoying a new career as an artist, his primitive water colors gaining good notices and selling in European galleries. Naturally, the story of the Silver Slipper resurfaced. By this time Greb had died. Walker owned the story. And ironically, despite all his triumphs in the ring, the alleged brawl outside the Silver Slipper was what people wanted to hear about, even decades later.

So in one of the more inventive accounts of the story as told by Walker, Greb landed on top of a parked taxi, leaving a large dent in the fender. Then, after the pugs left in separate cabs, Walker began to worry about his girlfriend. From his hotel, Walker called several nightclubs looking for her, only to learn that his girl was now shacked up with Greb.

Uh huh.

Walker was at it again in 1961 when his autobiography was published. "I lost the first fight to Greb, but I always thought I won the second one," he wrote.

In 1971, Walker told the story to the Syracuse *Post Standard*. This time, Walker spiced it with a new character, a former fighter named "Sailor Grande" (whom no one else had ever heard of) who was the Silver Slipper's doorman. Mr. Grande patiently held the door while Greb and Walker fought.

Sailor Grande at the door of the Silver Slipper.

Yeah. Right.

"Great stories have legs," said Burt Randolph Sugar. "Stories are what made the Roaring Twenties roar."

In a 1921 fight, Harry Greb had taken a thumb to the eye from a tough light heavyweight known as Kid Norfolk. He apparently suffered a retinal tear, which would eventually lead to permanent blindness. Incredibly, he kept the injury a secret from all but his wife and closest friends. He memorized the standard eyecharts and tricked physicians during pre-fight physicals for the latter half of his career. He fought half-blind for the final years of his life, including the fight against Walker in 1925. He retired in 1926.

Shortly afterwards, he had his right eye removed and replaced with a glass prosthesis.

Jack Dempsey, preparing for a fight against Gene Tunney, offered Greb a job as a sparring partner. Greb had defeated Tunney in a light heavyweight match in 1924. Greb declined the job. Greb eventually presented himself to an Atlantic City clinic for surgery to repair damage to his nose and respiratory tract, injuries caused by his ring career.

However, complications occurred and he died of heart failure on the afternoon of October 22, 1926. He never woke up from the anesthetic. He was thirty-two years old. At his funeral, Gene Tunney was one of the pallbearers. The 1924 loss to Greb would be the only loss in Tunney's long distinguished career, out of 86 decisions. A subsequent biography of Greb was titled, *Live Fast, Die Young*, which pretty much got it right.

Mickey Walker lived much longer, enjoying life as a raconteur, celebrity and artist. But he spent the final part of his life in a Freehold, New Jersey rest home. When Burt Sugar visited one afternoon shortly before Walker's death in 1981 at age 79, Sugar asked about the Silver Slipper incident of more than a half a century earlier.

"Nah, never happened," Walker scoffed.

"Mickey said they were just nightclub-hopping, trying to get lucky," Sugar said. "It seemed to me he didn't want to talk about it."

By that time, maybe not. But the place of Harry Greb and Mickey Walker in boxing folklore was established, much thanks to the wild night at Eighth Avenue and 155th Street in front of tens of thousands of fans in 1925 and the second fight that either did or didn't spill out onto Broadway.

***

In addition to boxing, the Polo Grounds hosted countless international soccer matches over the course of seven decades. The first soccer at the Polo Grounds was in 1894 when the management of the various baseball teams thought it would produce revenue in the off season. They were quite mistaken. Six famous baseball franchises formed Association Football sections. The New York Giants soccer team took the field in all-white uniforms with black socks and played six games, often playing their matches in midweek in front of a few hundred sleepy folks who had paid 25 cents or less to be there.

More positively in 1926, Hakoah, an all-Jewish side from Vienna, Austria, drew the largest crowds ever to watch soccer in the United States up to that time. Three successive games at the Polo Grounds drew close to 100,000 fans. The highlight was a May 1, 1926 exhibition game between Hakoah and an "All-New York" team (which won 3-0) which drew 46,000 fans.

Playing for Hakoah at the Polo Grounds was the famous Béla Guttmann, a Hungarian footballer and later coach. After the exhibition in 1926, however, with an eye on the hideous tide of anti-Semitism rising in Central Europe, Guttmann and several teammates remained in the US. After first playing for Brooklyn Wanderers, Guttman (pictured here with

Hakoah) signed for the New York Giants of the American Soccer League, playing 83 games and scoring two goals over two seasons. When he finally did return to Europe, he was captured by the Nazis and deported to a Nazi slave labor camp. He somehow survived and later played as a midfielder for MTK Hungária FC, SC Hakoah Wien, Hungary and a handful of clubs in the United States.

Much later he left a more lasting mark on his sport, however, as a coach and manager of A.C. Milan, São Paulo FC, FC Porto, Benfica and C.A. Peñarol. His greatest success came with Benfica, the great Portuguese side. Guttmann guided them to two successive European Cup wins in 1961 and in 1962.

After defeating Real Madrid in the 1962 European Cup Final, Guttmann asked for a pay raise from the Benfica board of directors. The board decided they had other things to do with their money. On leaving Benfica in a huff, Guttmann cursed the club, declaring, "Not in a hundred years from now will Benfica ever be European champions."

They shoulda paid the man, already!

Benfica have gone on to lose all eight of their subsequent European finals, including five European Cup finals in 1963, 1965, 1968, 1988, and 1990.

Guttmann died in 1981. The 1990 final was played in Vienna, the city where Guttmann is buried. The great Portuguese striker Eusébio {Eusébio da Silva Ferreira}, one of the greatest footballers of all time, prayed at Guttmann's grave and asked for the "curse" to be lifted.

It wasn't. Subsequently, Portugal has lost three UEFA Cup/UEFA Europa League finals in 1983, 2013 and 2014, the same years as Eusébio's death. Eusébio's remains are in Portugal's National Pantheon in Lisbon. Guttman rests in Vienna. The curse apparently has a few more decades to go.

Chapter 51   Good Night, Sweet Prince

> "Christy Mathewson brought something to baseball no one else had ever given the game... a certain touch of class, an indefinable lift in culture, brains, and personality."
>
> — Grantland Rice

As the second half of the 1925 baseball season resumed at the Polo Grounds, the Giants spent the remainder of July in second place, then edged in front of the startled Pirates in early August. The late rush for the pennant was enough to nudge aside two other major news stories: the Scopes "Monkey" trial in Tennessee, later to be dramatized and immortalized in the Spencer Tracey film, *Inherit The Wind*, and Babe Ruth's mysterious collapse (labeled "a bad dose of clap" by one of his teammates) on a railroad depot in North Carolina, later to be kept completely out of any news fit for public consumption.

McGraw shuffled his roster.

He farmed out Hack Wilson to the appropriately named Toledo Mud Hens of the American Association. (McGraw's younger brother Jimmy, not coincidentally, was the secretary of the club.) Then he added an unorthodox broad-shouldered young pitcher, Freddie Fitzsimmons, to the Giants.

McGraw had seen Fitzsimmons at Indianapolis the previous spring. One of the Giants, in watching Fitzsimmons' strange delivery, remarked that the young pitcher "looked like a guy swinging Indian clubs." Indeed, he did. ("Indian clubs" were a popular form of resistance exercise in the Victorian era, big clunky bowling pin style pieces, which were Persian in origin, rather than Indian.)

Fitzsimmons had an odd windmill-style delivery that was strangely reminiscent of Charles (Victory) Faust, McGraw's resident mascot of the previous decade. Fitzsimmons not only would whirl his arms going into his windup, but also would turn his back on the batter at the last second. Then he'd unleash a pitch with surprising speed and a knuckleball-style flutter.

Four days after McGraw sent Hack Wilson to Toledo, Fitzsimmons joined the Giants. In his first appearance, he worked the final four innings in a 5-3 loss to Pittsburgh. Fitzsimmons pitched scoreless ball in a game spiced by a healthy fistfight between the normally mild-mannered George Kelly and the Pirates' gentlemanly Pie Traynor. Pennant races could bring the animal, it seemed, out of anyone.

Pittsburgh, however, led by Traynor, Max Carey, and Kiki Cuyler, had leapfrogged over the Giants again by this time. A crucial series loomed at the Polo Grounds late that same month. On August 22, fifty-five thousand fans packed the place - much to the delight of owner Charles Stoneham - and set a new club home attendance record for a single date.

Thirty thousand more fans were turned away. The Pirates should have been turned away, too, however, as they swept the Giants, pushing New York five games back. The next day, before fifty-eight thousand fans, New York and Pittsburgh split two more games. The Pirates left town with a lead they would never relinquish. The Giants finished out of first place for the first time since 1920.

There would be deeper sadness that year, too.

Early in the season, on April 18, Charlie Ebbets of the Brooklyn club succumbed to the heart condition that had plagued him for years. He went in style, at least, his heart finally giving out in a suite he maintained at the Waldorf. His funeral cortege passed both Washington Park and Ebbets Field on its way to Green-Wood Cemetery, where you can still visit him to this day. Green-Wood, which has its main gate at 500 25th Street in Brooklyn, is now a National Historic Landmark. It is also the resting place of Leonard Bernstein, Boss Tweed, Charles Jean-Michel Basquiat, Louis Comfort Tiffany, Horace Greeley, and scores of other early baseball pioneers.

Ed McKeever, Ebbets' former partner, was named the new president of the club. At Ebbets' funeral, however, McKeever caught a chill that rapidly developed into something more serious. Eleven days after Ebbets, McKeever too passed away. The ownership of the ball club was then split, fifty-fifty, between the Ebbets heirs and the McKeever heirs, two factions that agreed that Wilbert Robinson should become the club president. But in the ensuing years, they would agree on little else.

Then, during the Pittsburgh-Washington World Series that year,

John McGraw received the jolting news that Christy Mathewson had died. A long moment of silence preceded Game Two of the World Series. Both clubs wore black armbands in memory of one of the National League's finest gentlemen and greatest pitchers.

John and Blanche McGraw departed from the World Series immediately and traveled to Mathewson's last home at Saranac Lake. From there they accompanied Jane Mathewson, Christy's widow and Mathewson's body along the arduous trip to Lewisburg, Pennsylvania. There, a few dozen yards from the campus of Bucknell University, with McGraw and Larry Doyle acting as pallbearers, Christy Mathewson was laid to rest.

Christy Mathewson's grave stone in Lewisburg, PA

Chapter 52　First and Long

> "Just tell me one thing. Now that I
> have a franchise, what do I do with it?"
>
> Tim Mara, having newly acquired the New York
> Football Giants as an NFL franchise in 1925.

Nineteen twenty-five also was the first season that the Polo Grounds had a new tenant, The New York Football Giants, one of five teams that joined the early National Football League that year and the only one that survives to this day. The Football Giants began their season just one day after the baseball Giants concluded theirs, though McGraw's team played their final fourteen games on the road. Baseball concluded at the ancient oval on September 12.

The founding genius, or investor, or both, was a man named Tim Mara, a businessman and bookmaker. (It was legal then.) Mara's bankroll was five hundred dollars. Mara ponied up the money in a moment of inspiration, figuring that "an exclusive franchise for anything in New York is worth $500," according to David Neft, Richard Cohen, and Rick Korch in *The Complete History of Professional Football from 1892 to the Present*. The Franchise, such that it was, had previously been in a shaky association known as the APFA, the American Professional Football Association, which can today be viewed as the wobbly ancestor of the National Football League.

Mara purchased the franchise despite having never having watched a single pro game. Well, one thing he needed to do was find a place to play his home games. Thinking big, he rented the Polo Grounds for several Sundays. Then he hired Jim Thorpe, the former baseball Giant, to carry the ball for him, even though Thorpe was 37 years old and hardly his Olympian self from 1912. But Thorpe had name recognition and that's what Mara needed: stuff that attracted attention.

Thorpe also had some quirky footnotes to his football career: When Thorpe was playing for the Carlisle Indian Industrial School in 1912, Carlisle recorded a 27–6 victory over Army (or West Point). Thorpe had a 92-yard touchdown run that was nullified by a teammate's penalty. No problem: on the next play Thorpe rushed for a 97-yard touchdown.

Playing against him was a twenty-two year old blond-haired blue-eyed linebacker who just didn't seem to have much liking for native Americans. According to West Point lore, it was believed that a cadet would become famous if he knocked "the Indian" out of the game. The linebacker, Dwight David Eisenhower, the future soldier and President, did his best, but was eventually tossed from the game when the refs thought his hits carried an intent to injure.

Professional football was the Rodney Dangerfield of sports in the mid-1920's. No respect at all. The college game had the school spirit and the youthful charm and the lively drinking songs that inspired young men to reach into their racoon coats for the thoroughly illegal hip flasks. The top college players of the day were expected to go into respectable business after graduation so that they could help overheat the economy and contribute to the Wall Street crash of 1929. Be that as it may, college football at the various locations known as the Polo Grounds went all the way back to 1880 when Harvard defeated Columbia. The most curious score on record at the old Polo Grounds, however, was from November 3, 1885 when Princeton beat the Columbia Law School, 72- 0, at the old venue in the northeast corner of Central Park between 110th and 112th streets. The only surprise was that Princeton didn't get sued.

But in the 1920's, the pro game was something else. The public viewed it as not much more than a gang rumble for guys who couldn't even get a good factory job. There were few organizational rules and forget about player rights or loyalty. The pro game was such a professional crap shoot that Red Grange, the greatest player of his era, had to argue with his father in order to obtain his family's blessing to join the Chicago Bears.

And speaking of the Bears, no respect for them, either. The team made a stop in Washington, D.C. for an exhibition game in the mid-1920's. The players were introduced to President Calvin Coolidge as being "members of the Chicago Bears."

"Glad to meet you fellows," said the President. "I always did like animal acts."

The New York Football Giants, as they were called by almost everyone to distinguish them from McGaw's gang, played their first contest as an away game against All New Britain in New Britain, Connecticut, on October 4, 1925. Shock of shocks, they won it 26–0 before an announced crowd of ten thousand people, which was not to be confused with ten thousand paying customers.

Jim Thorpe played, sustained an injury, and his Football Giants career ended. His absence left the team without a star or an identity for the new season. The team lost three first three games, including the home opener on October 18 at the Polo Grounds against the Frankford Yellow Jackets, the antecedents of the Philadelphia Eagles. The score was 14-0 and 27,000 people attended, again not all of them paid. Let's just say, no one was yet going to Disney World.

Over the course of the season, Tim Mara pumped $25,000 of his own cash into the franchise just to keep the gates open at the Polo Grounds. Players received less than a hundred bucks per game. A lot less. To break even, Mara needed $4,000 a game to cover his own outlays and $2,000 to $6,000, depending on the opponent, to pay the visitors and break even. He slashed ticket prices and gave out over 5,000 free tickets a week to fill seats that would have been vacant. He gave out the tickets, that is, if he could find people to take them. Sometimes he couldn't.

Mara pulled some high visibility promotional gimmicks - several players from the visiting Kansas City Cowboys tarted themselves up in Old West cowboy outfits and galloped terrified horses around New York City to promote that week's game, scattering pedestrians. But Mara's ship came in on the eleventh game of the season when Red Grange and the Chicago Bears came to town. Seventy-three thousand fans showed up on December 6th, 1925 to see the 'Galloping Ghost' of Illini fame. Twenty thousand fans were turned away at the gates, which must have broken Mara's hart. Grange gave the people what they wanted to see and scored the game's final touchdown on a thirty-five yard interception return. The Bears won 19-7. The influx of revenue saved the franchise. The Giants are seen here in the darker uniforms in that game, doing something that became all too common in certain seasons to come: punting.

The next week, the team ended their inaugural season in Chicago at what was then known as Cubs Park, a joint that was rechristened Wrigley Field the next year and which has also survived. The Giants won, 9-0.

Despite having lost their first three games and having lived hand to mouth financially all season, the Giants finished with a surprising 8–4 record, including the 9-0 victory against the Bears on the final day. (They also played five 'non-league' games that did not count in the standings. They were 11-6 overall.) Having made it through the initial season, they would then remain tenants of the Polo Grounds for another thirty years before moving to Yankee Stadium in 1956.

Despite some gloomy interludes along the way (the Yale Bowl era, anyone? The G-Men won one game in Connecticut in two seasons. Ouch!) the Football Giants have 19 overall championship appearances, more than any other NFL team. They are in third place among all NFL franchises with eight NFL championship titles, four in the pre–Super Bowl era (1927, 1934, 1938, 1956) and another four since the advent of the Super Bowl, Super Bowls XXI (1986), XXV (1990), XLII (2007), and XLVI (2011) . Their championship total is bettered only by their old pals the Green Bay Packers (13) and the Chicago Bears (9).

If you have a jersey, you may wear it with pride.

Chapter 53 Pennant Park & The Rajah

"You've followed me in baseball, now follow me in real estate!"

John McGraw in NY *Times* advertisement

The world of John McGraw - and hence that of the New York Giants - was shaken a second time the ensuing winter. In mid-January 1926, much to the surprise of the New York sporting public, there appeared in the New York *Times* a full-page advertisement centered around the glowing countenance of John McGraw.

The text, designed to appeal to baseball fans, extolled the virtues of a new real estate development in Sarasota, Florida, site of the Giants' miserable spring training camp of two years earlier.

In part, the ad read:

"I am building another winner in which you may share . . . Today I am building something to last long after my ball teams are forgotten. It is my hope that people in years to come will thank me for giving them the chance to find health, happiness and opportunity on the shores of matchless Sarasota Bay..."

Uh-oh.

McGraw, with every good intention, was fronting for a pair of out-of-state real estate hustlers.... uh.... "developers" named Louis Polokow and Israel Perlman, although the ad, needless to say, didn't exactly reveal that. Polokow and Perlman had options on some oceanfront property and this was the peak of the Florida real estate boom. They also had a grandiose scheme called Pennant Park, which is where McGraw came into the picture.

The real estate development, the ad went on to say, would be a fancy, pleasurable community with the New York Giants as its theme. Mathewson Boulevard, for example, was to roll right smack-dab down the middle of the community. And hey, what right-thinking New York baseball fan wouldn't feel his spirits soar each time he gave his address as Frisch Street? That was just a pop fly away from Bresnahan Street and a line drive short of Nehf Square.

All of this led up to the "bargain" price for homesites - $3,500 to $5,000 - and the lucky reader could get in on the ground floor, so to speak, just by sending in the coupon on the lower left-hand corner of the page. The coupon, naturally, began with the ominous phrase, "Herewith my check."

Yes, it all might have seemed like a slick swindle had the announcement carried the crafty visages of Messieurs Polokow and Perlman. But instead, there was McGraw with his beatific smile of success. One could have been every bit as confidant buying real estate from Mother Teresa.

Exactly why McGraw got himself involved in such a project defies ready explanation, although the phrase "sheer stupidity" does come to mind. Polokow and Perlman bought a tract of land exactly where Pennant Park was planned. The project was to be located on Sarasota Bay, adjacent to Whitfield Estates, where another sports star, golfer Bobby Jones, was selling property. A Florida bank issued a mortgage. Polokow and Perlman didn't hang around to see the project collapse. Nor were they around when it was apparent that few, if any, homes would ever be built. And they sure weren't anywhere in sight a year later when disgruntled investors - and there were scores of them - called on McGraw to make good on their losses. The ad, it was recalled frequently, had said in so many words said that John McGraw personally guaranteed the success of Pennant Park.

Over the years that followed, John McGraw did the honorable thing.

Though he had been gulled into fronting for the scheme by one of the two principals, who had promised him a piece of the profits. McGraw began shelling out thousands of dollars from his own pocket to repay investors who had bought homesites. Some twenty years after McGraw's death, Blanche McGraw recalled the evening in the late 1920s when John took a late evening telephone call, spoke at some length, then crawled into bed.

"Well, the last one is paid," he said. "Thank God that's over."

Pennant Park had cost McGraw about $100,000 to salvage his good name.

Unfortunately, by the summer of 1926, baseball offered McGraw no respite from his troubles. Where once he had to worry about gopher balls being served up to Mr. Home Run Baker and Mr. Babe Ruth, McGraw was now bedeviled by the likes of Rogers Hornsby in his own league and folks like Frankie Frisch and Freddie Lindstrom on his own team.

Mel Ott arrived that year from Gretna, Louisiana, seventeen years old and carrying a straw suitcase. The owner of a unique batting stance, Ott would raise his right foot and bend his knee - something like a hunting dog - before lashing out at a pitch. But McGraw brought Ott along with kid gloves, not allowing him to fraternize with the "adult" players and not allowing any minor league manager to tamper with him. Casey Stengel, now the skipper at Toledo, pleaded for Ott, but McGraw refused to option him, even to Casey.

When the team hit the second division, however, other drastic measures were in order. McGraw verbally flailed his entire team from day to day, with captain Frankie Frisch - whom he not-so-affectionately referred to as, "Krauthead" - bearing the worst parts of the abuse. Such tongue-lashings had worked in the past, and McGraw probably didn't understand why the new generation of players didn't respond to them. Instead, players such as Frisch and Lindstrom sulked at first, then conspired behind McGraw's back. Meanwhile, the St. Louis Cardinals in general and their player-manager Rogers Hornsby in particular were tearing up the league.

McGraw tried to clean house and shake up his roster.

He released Heinie Groh and Art Nehf.

Groh caught on with Toledo, then made it back to the majors for a few games with the Pirates in 1927. Nehf was picked up on waivers by Cincinnati, but the Reds claimed that Nehf's arm was shot. McGraw maintained that everyone in the league knew the condition of Nehf's arm and insisted that the transaction stand. The president of the National League, John Heydler, eventually upheld McGraw.

In August, however, with the Giants destined for their first second division finish since 1915, the tensions on the club reached the breaking point. Frankie Frisch, who had once appeared to be McGraw's heir apparent as manager of the Giants, bolted the club in St. Louis and returned to New York. McGraw didn't know of Frisch's departure until game time the next day at Sportsman's Park. It was not the type of surprise McGraw needed.

Frisch and McGraw talked over their differences upon the team's return to New York. All that was ironed out, however, was that Frisch would soon be an ex-Giant. No one walked out on John McGraw.

The other shoe dropped in December, just about the time that the city of St. Louis was recovering from its first World

Championship. The shoe was in the form of a blockbuster trade.

Not only had Rogers Hornsby guided the Cardinals to a memorable seven-game victory over the mighty Yankees in the World Series, but he had also worn out his welcome with the club owner, Sam Breadon, whom he rarely addressed without profanity. If you consider that Hornsby had hit over .400 three times in the previous five years and had led the league in home runs twice, you get the idea of what an insufferable, crusty, cold-blooded character Hornsby was. Sort of a National League version of Ty Cobb.

"He had been born in the Texas town of Winters," Lee Allen once wrote of Hornsby in a moment of understatement, "and there were some who found him chilly."

Breadon offered Hornsby a one-year contract of $50,000, not a bad piece of change in 1927. Hornsby said the money was right, but he wanted a three-year contract. Breadon refused. Old animosities surfaced between the two men. Then Breadon heard that Frankie Frisch, whom he greatly admired, was available. As if by the grace of God, both men were second basemen.

Breadon telephoned McGraw, who fell all over himself at the prospects of both ridding himself of Frisch - thus reasserting his tyrannical rule on the Giants - and bringing Hornsby to New York. A deal was quickly worked out. To Breadon's great pleasure, McGraw also threw in Jimmy Ring, a journeyman pitcher, and some cash. The latter two elements, Ring and the money, were a spiteful touch by McGraw, who didn't want Frisch to get the idea that he was Hornsby's equal.

In St. Louis, Sam Breadon was initially worried about negative reaction to the trading of Hornsby. His worst fears were not realized. They were exceeded.

Breadon was assailed daily by furious fans and lambasted in the newspapers. The Chamber of Commerce issued a resolution condemning him and a number of organizations that bought blocks of Cardinal tickets threatened to boycott the ballpark. The entire city, in short, would have been quite pleased to put Breadon together with a noose and a sturdy tree limb. One Cardinal fan went so far as to sneak onto the roof of Breadon's house one night and decorate the front porch with black crepe.

Back in New York, Hornsby proved that even though a man couldn't be in two places at once, he could easily cause trouble in both. Partially, this was the fault of McGraw, who appointed Hornsby captain of the New York Giants upon the latter's arrival in

Sarasota.

McGraw already had enough troubles in Florida, both on and off the diamond. His pitching was undependable, and the staff had no big winner. An attempt to acquire Adolfo (The Pride of Havana) Luque from Cincinnati failed.

Rube Marquard, released by the Dodgers, showed up in camp looking for a job. But after 536 major league games and 201 wins, Rube's arm was shot. The experiment ended in Florida.

The outfield had potential for disaster, also. Ross Youngs hadn't felt well during the off-season and didn't seem to be himself. Edd Roush, recently returned from the Reds, had rejected McGraw's latest contract terms and was threatening to sit out the season. Then there was, as noted, Captain Hornsby.

Before even reporting, Hornsby caused a commotion. In January, some three weeks after McGraw had signed Hornsby to a $40,000-a-year contract for two years, Hornsby was hit with a $70,000 lawsuit by a Kentucky gambling commissioner named Frank Moore.

Moore claimed Hornsby owed the money in bad wagering debts on horses. Hornsby, whose contract made him the second-highest paid player to Babe Ruth, eventually won the suit, despite provoking the ire of Judge Landis, who had seen enough of gamblers hanging around ballplayers. Then there was another nasty complication that McGraw had overlooked in his haste to swap Frisch to the Redbirds. The largest holder of St. Louis stock, aside from Sam Breadon, was Hornsby.

Here was a detail that everyone thought could be easily ironed out after the trade. Anyone who knew Hornsby should have known better. National League president John Heydler and Commissioner Landis, on hand to root out any possible conflict of interest, ordered Hornsby to sell his Cardinals stock before playing for the Giants.

Hornsby said fine and offered the stock to Sam Breadon at $116 per share. Breadon, owner of two of the game's tightest fists, howled that Hornsby had only paid $45 per share a few years earlier.

"That," the Rajah replied to Breadon with his usual humility, "was before I won the pennant for you."

Hornsby and Breadon stood firm on their prices, and the league stood firm on not letting Hornsby play. McGraw, already short of good players, threatened to sue baseball, a move that struck terror into the hearts of the seven other National League owners, as any lawsuit could eventually disrupt baseball's delicate labor structure.

Everyone was at an impasse.

Finally, the six other National League owners - believe it or not - took up a collection and paid Hornsby's price.

Hornsby reported to training camp with the Giants, but black clouds continued to follow him. Appointed to the captaincy, Hornsby took the assignment literally, pulling rank on players who had been with the team for years. McGraw, unhappily, was absent from the camp for business and health reasons from time to time. At these occasions, Hornsby attempted to retrain players to do things his way, not McGraw's.

One day third baseman Freddie Lindstrom challenged Hornsby's instruction following a play at third. "That's the way the Old Man wants us to make the play," Lindstrom said.

"Then when he's here, make it that way," Hornsby shot back. "When I'm here, make it the way I tell you."

The rest of the players gathered around. "Who the hell do you think you are?" Lindstrom finally challenged. "When you put the bat down, you're no bargain,"

"You do as I tell you and keep your mouth shut," Hornsby snarled. He looked around him, saw the unfriendly faces of the rest of his teammates, and retreated not an inch. "That goes for the rest of you, too," he said.

He returned to his position at second base. For the rest of the camp, his only companions were a handful of reporters - Bozeman Bulger, George Phair, and Kenneth Smith - and occasionally his wife and son. The gloom in the camp was only heightened when Ross Youngs' physician diagnosed him as having Bright's disease, a chronic and serious kidney ailment for which no cure existed. Youngs was not just out for the season, he was battling for his life.

Burleigh Grimes, the stubble-bearded old spitballer, came to the Giants from Brooklyn and would win 19 games. In later years, Grimes would insist that McGraw, in five minutes, had retaught him the science of curveball pitching. ("McGraw showed me that right-handed hitters had to pull a curve to the left side of the diamond, because their bats were all the way around when they made contact with the ball. Fifteen years of experience had not taught me a simple, obvious piece of strategy, but McGraw laid it on the line for me cold.") Meanwhile, Freddie Fitzsimmons matured quickly and chipped into the cause with 17 victories of his own.

Six Giants regulars hit over .300 in 1927: Hornsby, Jackson, Lindstrom, Terry, George Harper, and Roush, who finally did come to terms. McGraw's squad was a good one, but it was burdened by a slow start: They got hot late in the season and came close to league-leading Pittsburgh.

On September 25, however, Clarence (Dazzy) Vance of the Robins led his club to a 10-5 victory over New York at Ebbets Field. The loss eliminated the Giants from the National League race. They finished two games behind Pittsburgh and, ironically enough, half a game behind St. Louis, now led by Frankie Frisch.

In 1927, a year that presaged the future, Lindbergh flew across the Atlantic and Al Jolson's film debut in *The Jazz Singer* spelled doom with a capital D for the silent movies. But for McGraw, there were portents of more frightening things to come.

The Yankees now dominated baseball. Ruth hit his monumental 60 home runs, followed by Gehrig, whom McGraw had once wanted to sign, with 47.

(It is interesting to note that the Yankees had moved past their initial disappointment that Lou Gehrig was not Jewish. A Jewish star, a slugger at that, would have been a gold mine in New York City. When Lou had politely replied to a question by Miller Huggins that he was a Lutheran, and then began to hit, the Yankees decided that the nice Gentile boy would work out anyway. Who knew? It is equally intriguing to note that at much the same time Bronx-born Hank Greenberg was clamoring for a tryout with the Yankees or Giants. Neither team, however, would look at him.)

The Yankees won a staggering 110 ball games out of 154 played, then crushed a strong Pirate team in the Series that McGraw himself had been unable to catch.

Over the course of the season, McGraw had marked his silver anniversary with the Giants, twenty-five years which included ten pennants. There was a ceremony commemorating McGraw's arrival at the Polo Grounds. Friends from Broadway gathered. Joe Humphries, the silky-voiced announcer who normally introduced the boxing matches at the ball parks and Madison Square Garden, acted as M.C. He held McGraw's arm aloft like he would a fighter's, pronouncing McGraw a "champion of champions."

It was supposed to be a happy occasion. But in many ways, it wasn't. To McGraw, it suggested again that time was passing and while the Giants were struggling, the mighty Yankees were trashing their entire league.

Then there was the matter of Ross Youngs, whose strength was failing day by day. By the end of October, at the age of thirty,

Youngs would be dead. For the second time in three years, McGraw would be a pallbearer to a fine athlete and a surrogate son, dead before his rightful time.

Chapter 54   Cohen & Hogan, Hartnett & Capone

"I'm a kind person, I'm kind to everyone, but if you are unkind to me, then kindness is not what you'll remember me for."

Al Capone

It could be argued that the year 1928 marked the final stage of the era of John McGraw. Hornsby, cantankerous and obnoxious as he was, had become something of an antihero around the Polo Grounds. There were fans in those days - just as there are today - who get their jollies from athletes who like to tell the boss to go to hell. Hornsby specialized at this, just as Billy Martin would a generation later. Management did not particularly savor this, particularly Charles Stoneham, who was merely the owner of the club and whom Hornsby insulted whenever he saw fit.

Accordingly, it angered but hardly surprised fans to learn on January 11, 1928, that Hornsby had been traded to the Boston Braves for a pair of journeymen, catcher Frank (Shanty) Hogan and outfielder Jimmy Welch. But there was an extra significance to the deal. McGraw had been in Havana when it was made. Stoneham had completed it on his own.

In a cynical effort to appease the New York fans, who complained about Hornsby's departure almost as noisily as they'd wailed about Frisch's, the Giants elevated an engaging young Jewish player named Andy Cohen from the minor leagues to take over Hornsby's position.

Cohen, smart, personable and talented, was immediately popular.

Author Peter Levine, a professor of history at Michigan State, in his 1992 book *Ellis Island to Ebbets Field: Sport and the American Jewish Experience*, suggested that Eastern European Jews traditionally honored scholarship and learning over athletic prowess, a notion that doesn't seem too farfetched. In Dr. Levine's words, the

Jewish immigrants were "people of the book rather than people of the hook, right cross, or home run."

Nonetheless, the New York teams were always looking for possible Jewish stars to boost the ticket sales. A good-looking kid like young Andy Cohen had great potential. Jewish immigrants found their kids engrossed by American sports, to the shock of most and the horror of some. By the 1920s, city-dwelling Jewish athletes moved admirably into the urban gym-rat game of basketball, even if they were still being victimized by questionable stereotypical reporting in the sports pages.

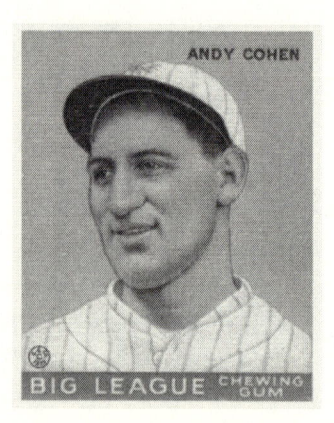

"Basketball," wrote Paul Gallico, the sports editor of the NY *Daily News* in the 1930s, "…places a premium on an alert, scheming mind, flashy trickiness, artful dodging and general smart aleckness." Even better, he argued, Jews were rather short and so had "God-given better balance and speed."

You read that right: being short was an advantage in basketball.

Jews had made their mark in the nose-crunching world of boxing with two-time lightweight champion, Benny Leonard, a product of Manhattan's Lower East Side, who is still seen a century later as one of the greatest lightweights of all time. But big-time stardom in baseball, in the person of Hank Greenberg, was still a few years away.

Often forgotten was the great 1906 season of "Silent George" Stone. Playing for the second division (as usual) St. Louis Browns, Stone led the American League in batting average, hits, total bases, and slugging percentage while finishing second in triples, third in RBI, and seventh in home runs. Personally Stone was a quiet man, not given to self-promotion and thus acquired the nickname "Silent George." Most fans had no idea he was Jewish.

Cohen was raised in an observant Jewish home. At the University of Alabama, he was the captain of his college baseball team, and pledged a Jewish fraternity. He declined to change his last name when entering professional baseball, unlike a previous generation where many Jewish players changed their names if they were "too ethnic" to avoid the wrath of some of the drunken bigots in the grandstands who had better vocal chords than brains.

So fans at the Polo Grounds were ready for Andy.

How ready? Very ready.

Cohen whacked three hits in the Giants' 1928 season home opener, led the team to victory, and was carried around the Polo Grounds after the game on the shoulders of fans. In New York, he was hailed as the long-awaited Jewish baseball hero, the Benny Leonard of the ball game, the first prominent Jewish major leaguer. *Time* Magazine, made him the cover boy and noted his popularity. They reported on a letter from an adoring fan. It read, "I understand you are Jewish and single... if you would care to meet a brunette... Anyway drop me a little note."

This was one of several hundred such letters Cohen said he received that year. Similarly, the Giants successfully cashed in on his success on the field. Refreshment vendors sold "Ice Cream Cohens" at the concession booths at the Polo Grounds.

So it was only natural that when Rogers Hornsby got off to a slow start at the plate in 1928, the New York *World* started printing a little box in the sports pages carrying Cohen's batting average next to that of Hornsby, the sour-natured Protestant from Texas.

"That's a lousy trick to play on the kid," said Hornsby, full of himself as usual, on his first trip to New York with the Braves. "I ain't hittin' now, but when I start, I'll lose him."

Hornsby, who had been a negative for McGraw in New York, then turned into a positive for the Braves. He would eventually lead the league in hitting with a .387 average and also hit 21 home runs. Cohen dropped to .274 and 9 HRs, and the *World* discontinued its box in midseason. And another trade backfired, also. At Stoneham's urging, the Giants sent Burleigh Grimes to Pittsburgh for a right-handed pitcher named Vic Aldridge. The latter would win 4 games for the Giants. Grimes would enjoy his finest season, winning 25 games for the Pirates.

Despite all of this, McGraw kept his team close. On the bench, the tempers of the New York players were usually worn raw from McGraw's berating, a method of inspiration that failed to work with the new generation. Now they were completely frayed. Yet in mid-September the Giants clawed their way into first place. There they seesawed back and forth with St. Louis.

Scout Dick Kinsella, the sinister one, still worked diligently for John McGaw. He had always been involved with the Illinois Democratic Party. In 1903 he lost the election as the Democratic candidate for sheriff of Sangamon County. He was the sergeant-at-arms at the Democratic National convention in 1912, and head doorkeeper at the St. Louis convention in 1916, both of which nominated Woodrow Wilson.

As a delegate to the 1928 Democratic National Convention in Houston, Kinsella snuck out to see a baseball game and scouted a southpaw screwball pitcher whom the Detroit Tigers had rejected and who was now pitching for Beaumont of the Texas League. The pitcher's name was Carl Hubbell.

Kinsella liked what he saw. He convinced McGaw to spend $30,000 to buy Hubbell's contract. Hubbell arrived in New York at midseason.

On September 27, New York engaged the Chicago Cubs in a doubleheader. The Cubs, led by Joe McCarthy, were no day at the beach in this era. St. Louis led the Giants by half a game, but New York, behind rookie Carl Hubbell, led Chicago, 3-2, in the sixth inning. Art Nehf, the old Giant whose arm troubles seemed to have disappeared, was pitching for Chicago.

With Andy Reese running at third for the Giants and Leslie Mann at second, Shanty Hogan drove a ball back to Nehf with one out. Nehf trapped Reese off third. But when Reese ran toward the plate, Cub catcher Charles (Gabby) Hartnett collided with him, then wrapped his arms around him. "To keep from falling," Hartnett later explained. But he kept his arms around Reese just long enough to impede him from scoring. Meanwhile, Cub third baseman Charlie Beck raced down the third base line and tagged Reese.

McGraw, charging onto the field with the rest of his team, howled in protest to Bill Klem, who had called Reese out. McGraw claimed interference. Newspaper photographs the next morning showed that McGraw was right. But the Cubs escaped the inning without the Giants scoring. Eventually, Chicago won both that game and the nightcap. It was a painful climax to the season for McGraw, as the Cardinals, led by Frisch and slugging first baseman Jim Bottomley, won the pennant by two games.

Critics were quick to point out that, had the Giants kept Hornsby, Grimes, and Nehf (who won 13 games for the Cubs), they would have won the pennant going away. It made little difference that in the annual dance with the Devil at Yankee Stadium, the National League's entry in the World Series again got blown away in four games.

Not blown away, however, were the new teammates Andy Cohen and Shanty Hogan.

In the off-season, the two Giants channeled some Rube Marquard and Mike Donlin and teamed up in a successful vaudeville act, performing on the Loew Circuit. Their first appearance on stage was at the Loew's Commodore Theatre in the Manhattan on October 15, 1928. The theater was at 102 Second Avenue at Sixth Street. Forty years late it became the Fillmore East and booked rock concerts including the performance debut of *Tommy* by The Who in 1969. That's right: Roger Daltrey and Keith Moon were on the boards that Hogan and Cohen once trod.

In New York, they billed themselves as Cohen and Hogan. Then they went on tour and called themselves Hogan and Cohen in Boston in deference to Boston's large ticket-buying Irish population. The formula of the Irish and Jewish comedian working together was as old as vaudeville itself and would last even longer. Think of Burns and Allen. Far into the future, consider Stiller and Meara, Ben's parents. (One could argue Abbott and Costello as such a tandem and one would be half-correct. Lou's given name was Louis Francis Cristillo. His father was from Calabria, Italy and his mother was an American of Italian, French, and Irish ancestry. Lou changed his name to Costello - a commonly recognizable Irish surname originating in County Mayo - in the early 1930s.)

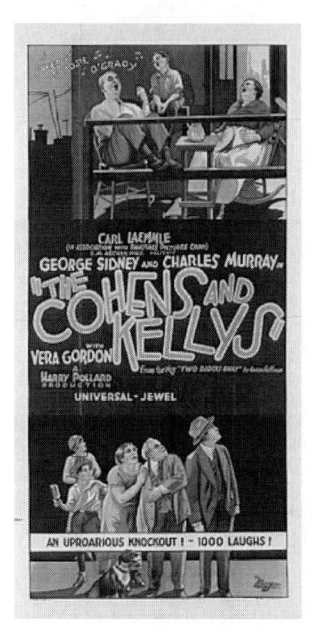

Once again, the critics were lukewarm, at best. The public loved them.

The Cohen and Hogan names together on a marque also evoked another popular entertainment of the era. A film titled *The Cohens and Kellys* was a classic 1926 silent comedy film directed by Harry A. Pollard and starring Charles Murray, George Sidney, Kate Price and Jason Robards Sr.

The film was the first of the popular "Cohens and Kellys" film serials, followed by followed by *The Cohens and the Kellys in Paris* in 1928 and five others. In the film series The Cohens and the Kellys portray an Irish family and a Jewish family living as close neighbors in a Manhattan slum. They don't like each other. Even the family dogs are antagonistic. The Cohens have a daughter, the Kellys have a son. The Jewish father is in the garment business. Wouldn't you know it, Mr. Kelly is a cop. The children are in love, secretly marry and the fun, such as it is, begins.

So the public appetite for Irish-Jewish entertainment was in vogue that winter. Somehow there was something inherently funny about the Irish-Jewish set-up. Hogan and Cohen, or Cohen and Hogan if you prefer, told stories and sang parodies, receiving a whopping paycheck of $1,800 per week. Cohen even inspired poetry. One poem was called, *Cohen at the Bat*, a satire of the Ernest Lawrence Thayer classic. In Providence, Rhode Island, the hulking Hogan reduced Cohen to uncontrollable laughter by introducing a mild but loud obscenity into a purported McGraw telegram Cohen was supposed to read as part of the act, ordering the men off-stage and back to baseball.

A real telegram was not needed. Both the corpulent Hogan and the charismatic Cohen reported to the Giants spring training in 1929, richer in both dollars, sports and show biz experience. Years later, after vaudeville disappeared, Cohen would recall the vaudeville experience with whimsy and affection.

"We didn't kill vaudeville," he frequently quipped, "but we sure helped."

Speaking of killing people, everyone likes a ball game and everyone likes a dad who takes his son to the game, right?

In September of 1931, more than a few eyebrows shot sky-high when the star Chicago Cubs catcher Gabby Hartnett wandered over to the expensive seats at Comiskey Park to sign a baseball for a fan and his son. The fan was Al Capone and the boy was twelve-year-old Alphonse Jr., whom Dad called, Sonny. On the other side of Sonny, watching carefully, was Roland V. Libonati, a lawyer and then an Illinois state legislator, later elected to the US Congress from Illinois. The occasion was a charity game, Cubbies against Pale Hose, to raise money for the unemployed. Big Al had already financed several soup kitchens around Chicago, nurturing his Robin Hood image. Al had recently served a short jail sentence for carrying a concealed weapon. A few months later he would begin an eleven year prison sentence for tax evasion. He would serve eight years.

Check out the gentlemen in fedoras behind Scarface. Those are the boss's bodyguards and were not to be messed with. Look at the guy right behind Capone, identified by reports that day as "Machine

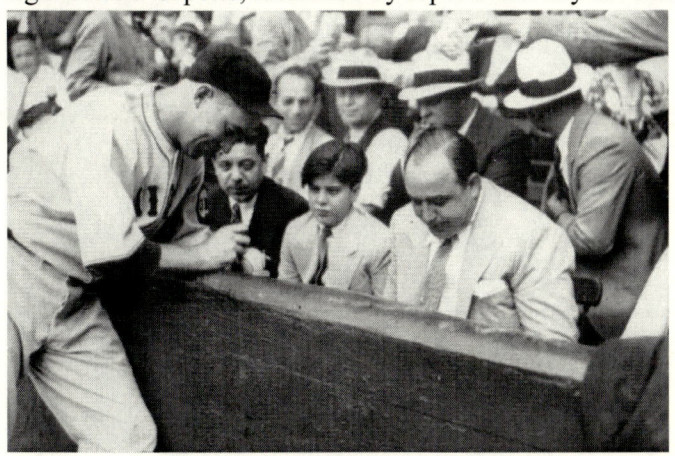

Gun" Jack McGurn, who had been born in Sicily as Vincenzo Antonio Gibaldi. McGurn was a small time boxer, a night club owner and a Capone bodyguard. A vendor looks to have accidentally rubbed his shoulder and "Machine Gun" is either reaching for his wallet or is on alert to protect his boss. McGurn, alleged to be one of the planners of the infamous St. Valentine's Day Massacre was shot to death five years later at the second-floor Avenue Recreation Bowling Alley, at 805 N. Milwaukee Avenue in Chicago.

After prison, Capone spent time trying to recover his health. He moved to Miami. Sonny, who was a quiet kid with chronic health problems, eventually went to St. Patrick High School in Miami with Desi Arnaz and graduated in 1937. He then attended the University of Miami. Dad died in 1947. Sonny later changed his name and lived out of public view as much as possible. He died in Florida in 2004, 85 years old. Three of his four daughters are alive today.

But on this afternoon in 1931 it was all father-and-son (plus the mouthpiece and three gunmen) and the enjoyment of a good baseball game. Harnett graciously signed a ball for Sonny.

Commissioner Landis got after Gabby Hartnett after this photo and several others went public. The commish sent a message to the Cubbie catcher telling him to stop signing autographs for gangsters.

Hartnett, who would end his career at the Polo Grounds with the New York Giants in 1941, replied and told the commission the *he, the commissioner*, should tell the mob guys to stop asking if he felt strongly about it. This was Chicago after all.

Chapter 55   Mr. McGraw Goes Home

"I'm quitting."

John McGraw

By 1929, as the specter of a sixtieth birthday loomed before McGraw, the nucleus of a fine ball club was again forming.

Carl Hubbell, for example, was showing flashes of the form that would take him to Cooperstown. Giants catcher Shanty Hogan loved Hubbell's screwball and advised Hubbell to keep throwing it. It would become Hubbell's money pitch for the next 15 seasons.

On May 8 Hubbell threw an 11-0 no-hitter against Pittsburgh, one of 18 wins that year and the last no-hitter ever to be thrown by a New York Giant. Ott, at the ripe old age of twenty, hit .328 with 42 home runs, attaining full-fledged stardom. Bill Terry hit .372, but so antagonized McGraw with his annual holdouts that he and his manager barely spoke. Yet with all this, the Giants finished third, far behind the Cubs who, not by coincidence, now had a .380 hitter named Rogers Hornsby. Hornsby, whose ornery nature antagonized almost everyone, eventually wore out his welcome with every club he played for, managed or worked for. But for the while, he was still a Cubbie.

By 1930 McGraw's own nerves were shot and his health was beginning to falter. The Giants' stars - Terry, Hubbell, Lindstrom, Fitzsimmons, and Ott - performed well, particularly Terry, who hit .401 to lead the majors, the last National League to hit .400 to this date. But the club was beset with bickering, both between the younger and older players and in the front office as well.

Francis McQuade, McGraw's longtime friend and confidant, had been sacked as club treasurer by the board of directors. Leo

Bondy had been voted in. McQuade sued Stoneham, and while he eventually lost, the Giants' internal problems were thus hung out for all to hear in New York State Supreme Court. The Giants finished third, five games back.

Things could have improved in 1931 but didn't. The Depression had a firm grip on the land. Attendance sagged badly. The Empire State Building opened in Manhattan and Pearl Buck published *The Good Earth*. But the lively Twenties, which had begun with three years of Ruth-McGraw showdowns at the Polo Grounds, were nothing more than a lovely memory.

Even the Yankees fell on leaner times now, with Ruth starting to slip and Connie Mack ascending to the top of the American League with his last great A's teams. But by 1932, the Yankees were on top again with young players named Charles (Red) Ruffing, Vernon (Lefty) Gomez, and Bill Dickey in supporting roles for Ruth and Gehrig. Eventually, Mr. Mack threw in the towel and, faced with slumping attendance, sold off his champion players.

In June of 1932, McGraw found himself in a strange position. His players were in active rebellion against him, resenting his old-fashioned Napoleonic methods and the "company spies" he hired as coaches. His pitchers, even the great Hubbell, resented his insistence at calling every pitch from the bench. The team was in and out of last place and the fits of rage and frustration increased in intensity.

One day, Dave Bancroft, who had returned to the club as a coach, found McGraw seated in his hotel room at midday, the shades drawn and the lights off. A few days later, Mrs. McGraw, at the urging of friends, forced her husband to see a doctor.

McGraw had suffered most of his adult life from sinus trouble – the result, no doubt, from having taken too many fists and baseballs to the face during his brawling days - and ptomaine poisoning within the last year.

But now there were kidney problems that were accelerating, plus a general wearing down of energy and health. Just as there were a finite number of wins in a pitcher's arm, there were probably a finite number of victories in a manager's soul. On June 3, 1932, Lou Gehrig punctuated a pleasant afternoon in Philadelphia by hammering 4 home runs over the short right field wall at Shibe Park. To show it was no accident, the "Iron Horse" just missed a fifth.

Normally, Gehrig's feat would have had the sports headlines to itself. But it was always Gehrig's fate to display his finest performances in the shadow of someone else. So it was this day, too.

It was raining in New York, but the Giants were at the Polo Grounds in case their game could be played. As it turned out, the game was postponed. Bill Terry, however, was called to McGraw's office early in the afternoon.

Terry was surprised at being summoned, as he and McGraw hadn't spoken for several weeks. There'd been a mean-spirited holdout that spring, after which Terry had had to suffer a pay cut of $5,000 from his 1931 salary of $23,000. The cut, presumably, came from the .052 drop in his batting average, all the way down to .349.

Terry arrived at the manager's office, knocked, and walked in. "Sit with your back to the door," McGraw instructed routinely. The door remained open. There was a long pause. Most likely, Terry figured he had been traded.

Then McGraw asked, "How would you like to be manager of this ball club?"

Terry, years later, would recall being unable to speak. He listened, barely able to believe what he heard as McGraw continued.

"I'm quitting," said McGraw. "I want you to think it over for a few days before answering."

Terry didn't need the few days, just as McGraw hadn't needed a few days when Andrew Freedman offered him the position thirty years earlier.

"I'll take it right now," Terry answered.

There was a meeting a short time later between Terry, McGraw, and Charles Stoneham. But as easily and shockingly as that, the Giants' torch had passed. Ironically, the team was in eighth place, exactly where McGraw had found it. Most likely, that small detail had told him that it was time for his departure.

Later that day, the newspapers trumpeted the news that McGraw of the Giants had quit. Before the news reached the public, however, McGraw returned home to Pelham to inform Blanche that he had resigned. In later years, Mrs. McGraw recalled that John had seemed pleased that evening. He behaved, she said, like a man who had had a great burden eased from his back.

In fact, one had been. But now it belonged to Bill Terry: an intelligent man, a great athlete, and an individual untried as a major league manager.

Lest the John McGraw era close on too somber a note, consider the career of Shanty Hogan, the backup catcher obtained from the Boston Braves in the Rogers Hornsby trade.

Shanty had broken into the major leagues with the Braves in 1925 and 1926. He had played a few games in the outfield, then settled in as a reserve catcher. He was a huge, grinning, strapping kid with clear brown eyes and thick wavy hair. He was a local on the Boston squad, having been born in nearby Somerville in 1906. He was also blessed with a resonant baritone voice. He liked to serenade other players with Irish favorites. Hometown fans loved him.

Now, he did have a chest on him that compared favorably with Beacon Hill. His actual weight, spread around a six-foot-one frame, was something of a mystery but was easily 260 pounds when he hit the big leagues. Nonetheless, he called a smart ball game and knew which end of the bat to hold. When he hit .288 in seventy-one games for the Braves in 1927, he caught the attention of another prominent Hibernian around the National League: John McGraw.

McGraw, in his twenty-fourth year as manager of the New York Giants, sensed greatness in Hogan. As it turned out, the greatness was to be of an unexpected sort. But when McGraw put together the deal with the Braves that brought Hogan to New York, Shanty at first responded. He hit .333 in 1928, his first full season with the Giants, the one he followed with a spin around the vaudeville circuits with his pal, Andy Cohen. He followed with a .300 year and then battered the ball at a hefty .339 in 1930. His defensive skills were fine, too. But it was not behind that plate that Shanty Hogan attained stardom. You see, for the thirteen years he played major league ball, Shanty Hogan was American sports' number one gourmand, trencherman, and behemoth. Not since William Howard Taft, America's only 300-pound President, took the first seventh-inning stretch had the public seen anything quite like this.

While in spring training with the Giants, Hogan brought his mother to camp to cook for him. She was a delightful little gray-haired Irish woman who spoke in the lilting brogue of Boston and the Old Sod. "My boy Francis," she used to tell anyone who would listen, "hasn't he a grand appetite?"

Well, yes, he did.

Elephantine would have been an appropriate adjective. A family of wolves couldn't put away a meal faster than J. Francis Hogan. Naturally, this took its toll. He gradually moved up in uniform size.

Hogan was "growing in too many directions," commented John Kieran, the fine New York *Times* sportswriter of the day. Shanty was becoming, well, kind of obese. Polo Grounds crowds still loved him, and Boston fans remembered him kindly. But some taunts did begin in some enemy parks, notably Ebbets Field. "Who's that crowd behind the plate?" was a common barb. No one ever determined whether the remark was conceived at a ballpark or in a restaurant.

As Hogan blimped up past the 250-pound mark, John McGraw began a long futile war against Shanty's midriff. Muggsy began to monitor Hogan's meal vouchers in the hotel restaurants where the Giants stayed on the road. But Hogan's intake was surprising. To all

Rabbit Maranville and Shanty Hogan chow down in Boston.

appearances, he was a vegetarian. The meal receipts showed order after order of carrots spinach, and black-eyed peas. Yet Shanty continued to gain.

This in itself perplexed McGraw. But eventually the Giants' manager came upon the truth. Hogan had turned his Celtic charm upon the waitresses. That, or he had bribed them. In any case, the meal vouchers were coded. Spinach was roast beef. Peas were pork chops. The carrots were baked potatoes. And McGraw was furious. Yet in this particular holy war, McGraw's martyrdom was endless. While many players were into the innocent habit of stashing crackers in their hotel rooms to munch as a midnight snack, Hogan was not above sneaking down to the hotel dining room to prepare himself a steak. When McGraw cruelly put a stop to this, Hogan stashed crocks of beef stew under his pillow to ward off the demons of late-night hunger. Then there was a memorable incident in Havana.

The Giants were spending spring in Cuba. During siesta hour one afternoon, McGraw noticed that all his ballplayers were calmly enjoying their daily sandwich and milk. But something seemed wrong. McGraw counted heads. One missing. Hogan. Instinctively, McGraw circled back to the hotel dining room. There he found his catcher finishing one steak and beginning another.

McGraw confronted Hogan. Hogan's response became an immediate part of team folklore. "Aw, come on, John," Shanty demurred from behind the plate. "The first steak was just a little one. If it had been a fish, I'd have tossed it back."

Here the story turns sad. Hogan's production at the other plate fell off in 1932: 8 home runs and a .287 average. Worse, he was so saddled with fat around the shoulders, neck, and arms that throws to second base had to be made sidearm. Larcenous runners were having their way against Hogan. And the Giants, from whom John McGraw retired in midseason for medical reasons, plopped into the second division for the first time since 1915. The new manager, Bill Terry, made changes in the off-season. One of them was to send the popular Hogan back to Boston for $25,000.

There Shanty's fortunes tumbled further. The only one of his statistics that rose was the one on the scale in the trainer's office. By 1935, weighing in excess of 270, he was back in the minor leagues. His best fans in mudville were the team cooks. It looked as if Shanty Hogan had dug his own grave with his teeth.

But not quite.

As Shanty later explained it, he was riding the team bus one night when the vehicle hit a terrific bump. Hogan shot upward in his seat and hit his head on the roof. "I'd been sound asleep. I woke up. I started thinking," Hogan told writer Jack Miley of the New York *Daily News*. The grand epiphany continued. Shanty would soon be out of baseball at age twenty-nine if he didn't do something drastic. So he did. He began to flirt with a diet.

The Washington Senators brought Hogan up for a cup of coffee - black, no sugar - at the end of the 1936 season. He excelled. And the fans, always a consideration in Washington, loved him anew.

"Shanty gets more applause when he strikes out than most of our boys do when they hit a two-bagger," commented Senator manager Bucky Harris. Hogan's batting average stayed in the .320s and he pegged little bullets to second base. Everything seemed set for a last hurrah. Then steely-eyed owner Clark Griffith took Shanty aside at the end of the season and pushed him onto a scale. It read: 278 pounds.

Griffith's instructions were clear. "Lose fifty pounds," he said, "by Opening Day."

Over the winter, Hogan, with the appetite of a lion, held to the diet of a sparrow. He starved himself. He exercised. He starved himself some more. At training camp the following spring, he worked out in heavy underwear, three woolen shirts, and a rubber jacket. He sucked chunks of pineapple for nourishment and wouldn't even drink water until his thirst was unbearable.

"I'm suffering," Shanty Hogan told writers, "the tortures of the damned. I'd give ten points off my average for an ice-cold bottle of beer."

But Hogan didn't have the beer and didn't give away the ten points. Instead, he played again like an ambitious rookie. Fans cheered him, and friendly baseball scribes termed his new frame, "cadaverous." Opening Day neared. Shanty stepped on the scale again for Griffith: 228 pounds. The 50 pounds were gone. Right on the nose. Rumors swept Florida and Arizona that the lowly Senators might have the best catcher in baseball that season.

Had it only ended that way. Washington got off to a particularly painful start that season and soon had plopped into last place in the American League. And as the Senators went down, Shanty Hogan went down with them.

Hogan without his girth was like Sampson without his hair. Gone was more than 50 pounds. Gone was the bat, the power, the glove, and the stamina. After twenty-one games, Hogan had four doubles, six singles, and a listless .152 batting average. May it be a lesson to anyone who goes on a successful diet. Hogan never recovered. With almost a thousand major league games to his credit and a career .295 average, Shanty was finished in the major leagues, though he did briefly surface in sunny San Diego in the Pacific Coast League a short time later.

His legacy, however, remained. Many years later, New York Yankee star Reggie Jackson had a candy bar named after him. Well, so what? In his own day, McGraw's leviathan catcher had a whole meal named for him.

There was, you see, for many years near the Polo Grounds a German restaurant popular among players and fans. It served great steaks of four different sizes. The small one was one pound.

The medium one was two pounds and the large one was three.

Then came the real extravaganza, a five-pound special that could probably have sustained a construction worker for a week.

Its size designation? It was called simply, "The Shanty Hogan."

PART THREE:

THE BILL TERRY YEARS

Chapter 56   The Reign of King Carl

"Such control in a left-hander is incredible. There must be a skeleton in Hubbell's closet somewhere, perhaps a right-handed maternal grandmother."

Heywood Broun

Not long before opening day of 1933, manager Bill Terry was asked was asked by sportswriters how his Giants would fare that year.

"I think we'll do third or better," answered Terry, who could always be counted on for an honest answer. The writers started to chuckle. So much for overconfidence in a manager starting his first full year. But Terry continued.

"I'm telling you guys," Memphis Bill insisted, "we're a cinch for the first division if Parmelee and Schumacher come through. Of course, I'm taking Fitz and Hubbell for granted. If any of you think I'm kidding, put your money where your mouth is."

Several dollars were placed accordingly, Depression or no Depression. Terry's confidence in his team was fine, but the Giants had no earthly reason to be near the top of the first division. They had two certifiable hitters: Ott and Terry himself. They had two reliable pitchers: Fitzsimmons and "King Carl." And beyond that, they had nothing but new faces and question marks. The moral of the story, then, is never make a bet with a man who has hit .401.

There were, of course, some predictable components to the team. Hughie Critz, the Mississippian, was a solid second baseman. Johnny Vergez was equally adept at third but was coming off of injuries. Jo-Jo Moore was a dependable outfielder, as was George (Kiddo) Davis, though the latter didn't hit much. Gus Mancuso, obtained from St. Louis in the off-season, was an adequate catcher, but he wasn't going to make anyone forget about Mickey Cochrane or Buck Ewing. As for the pitchers, LeRoy Parmelee's nickname was "Tarzan," a comment not so much for his ability to swing from vines and amity with apes, but rather his control challenges.

Parmelee threw sidearm. The result was a prodigious sailing fastball that veered as sharply a slider or cutter. He was also a handsome dude. He was built like a pitcher: 6-feet-1, 200 pounds, with hunky shoulders and thick forearms. When the nickname of Tarzan first appeared in the New York *Daily News* via writer Jimmy Powers, Parmelee took it as a compliment to his muscular build. Powers soon set him straight. It was because of his wildness.

"Every time you pitch you seem to be out on a limb," Powers explained.

Hal Schumacher had a career record of 6-6. Adolfo Luque, the Cuban relief pitcher the Giants had finally been able to obtain, was a museum piece: forty-two years old, and nearing the end of a career that stretched back to the Boston Braves of 1914.

The rays of hope were few. Travis Jackson was still suffering knee problems, but a young graduate of Holy Cross, John (Blondy) Ryan, was a possibility in the infield. Hank Leiber, an outfielder from Arizona, had originally been sent to John McGraw by Art Nehf, who had retired after 1929. There was also a young catcher named Paul Richards, who would much later manage the Baltimore Orioles in the 1950s.

This was a squad that appeared to have some talent, but which would need considerable shaking up if it were to move as high in the standings as Terry predicted. Some of the shaking began on March 11 in Los Angeles while the Giants played at exhibition game at Wrigley Field against the Cubs. An earthquake struck, rumbling the ground while the grandstands swayed. Horrified players grouped at second base, expecting catastrophe. Then the quake subsided. Aftershocks continued for the next few days, but the Giants stoutly remained in La-La Land until the exhibition schedule brought them east to open the season.

There were two casualties en route. Travis Jackson's knees were still ailing, so Blondy Ryan assumed the shortstop position. Then coach Billy Southworth went home, said to be also suffering from a knee injury. Southworth had wrenched his joint during a game in El Paso. But the rumor had it that he and Terry had had a dispute of some sort, despite the fact that both men denied it. There would have been nothing to the rumor at all, except that Terry was mysteriously sporting a shiner, and dependable old Frank Snyder, McGraw's hulking catcher from the 1920s, took over for Southworth "indefinitely."

Terry suffered another injury - a fractured wrist - soon after the season started. At that point, the sportswriters figured their wagers with Memphis Bill were practically bankable. But no one panicked.

The pitching came around. The Giants, in traditional Giants fashion, made a habit of winning low-scoring games. Ryan and Critz began to work smoothly in the middle infield and the Giants were in third place by Memorial Day, two and a half games behind the Pirates.

Terry's wrist healed. That's when he dealt his extra first baseman, Sam Leslie, to the Dodgers for Francis (Lefty) O'Doul. O'Doul was thirty-five years old, but his bat didn't know it. Able to pinch-hit or play the outfield, O'Doul had led the league in hitting in 1932. Giants fans liked the trade. The Giants went into first place and began jockeying for the league lead with St. Louis, a team still rebuilding from their 1926 World Championship.

Much of the attention in baseball that year centered upon what was being billed as "The Game of the Century." The contest in question was baseball's first All-Star Game, a much-touted promotion that was to be held at the Chicago World's Fair on July 6. The hype for the game was so intense that the sporting public took little note of a key series to be played in New York the weekend preceding the Chicago contest. The St. Louis Cardinals, playing better ball each week, were to invade the Polo Grounds. If they swept the Giants, they could go into first place.

The Cardinals already had the nucleus of the club that would form the famed "Gashouse Gang" of 1934. In Frankie Frisch and Johnny (Pepper) Martin they had two of the scrappiest players in the game. In Jay Hanna (Dizzy) Dean they had a topflight pitcher. Even in weak hitting shortstop Leo Durocher, dubbed "The All-American Out" by Babe Ruth, they had the era's best defensive shortstop. And after the first two games of the series at the Polo Grounds, they also had the Giants on the run. New York was beginning to stumble, and St. Louis had now won seven straight.

The Giants stopped the Cardinals in the third game on Saturday, July first. That set the stage for the final two games of the series, which were to be played as a Sunday doubleheader. St. Louis manager Charles (Gabby) Street had James (Tex) Carleton, ready to pitch the opening game. Bill Terry relied on the man who had already astonished the baseball public with a streak of twenty-six consecutive scoreless innings earlier that year: Carl Hubbell.

Hubbell, at the age of thirty, was still nothing more than a reliable pitcher with flashes of brilliance. On a good day his "scroogie" was almost impossible to hit, and, true, he had tossed a no-hitter against Pittsburgh in 1929. But he had never won 20 games and he had never led the league in any important statistic. The Hall of Fame credentials were not yet there. On the other hand, they were not too far off in the distance, either.

At a few minutes after two o'clock, Hubbell trudged to the mound. He had lost his last start against Pittsburgh and a good effort today was crucial to keep the surging Cardinals at bay. Hubbell stood in the bright New York sunlight, rearranged the clay of the pitcher's mound with his spikes, hitched up his perpetually sagging trousers, and retired Pepper Martin to start the game. Then he retired Frankie Frisch. Then down went Ernie Orsatti, a durable center fielder who had once been Buster Keaton's stunt double in a Hollywood movie titled *Our Hospitality* in 1923.

In their half of the first, the Giants were up and down almost as quickly. Tex Carleton, the Cardinal right-hander, was Gabby Street's number two pitcher behind Dizzy Dean. He had beaten the Giants in the first game of the series on Thursday and, knowing how crucial the doubleheader was, requested to work again. From the first inning, it was clear that Carleton was as sharp as Hubbell.

Both pitchers worked routinely through the opposing lineup. Then they worked through it again. The game speeded along, but only toward the seventh inning did any tension begin to build. Neither team was able to construct anything resembling a scoring threat, though it might be argued that with the left field foul pole only 279 feet from home plate and the right field pole 257 feet, anyone standing at the plate with a bat was a scoring threat.

Similarly, there were hitters on both teams who were no strangers to home runs: Mel Ott, Bill Terry, and Johnny Vergez of the Giants. James (Rip) Collins and Joe (Ducky) Medwick of the Cardinals. Yet nine innings passed with astonishing suddenness. The Cardinals had three hits and the Giants four. There was no score. Hubbell hadn't walked a batter and the Giants hadn't committed an error. So St. Louis had had but three base runners.

Only now, after approximately two hours of play, did the near capacity crowd sense what they were watching. In the eleventh the Cardinals sent up Rogers Hornsby - who was primarily a pinch hitter in his second tour with the club - to hit for Durocher. He grounded weakly back to Hubbell. Then, in the bottom of the inning, the Giants started something.

Lefty O'Doul walked to open the inning. Bill Terry replaced him with a pinch runner, Bernie James, then successfully sacrificed him to second. That brought up Mel Ott, who was walked intentionally.

The Cardinals walked the next batter, Johnny Vergez. The Giants had the bases full with one out. Tex Carleton, on the mound, was staring at an eleven-inning 1-0 loss.

Jo-Jo Moore grounded to Frisch, who brought the crowd to their feet by throwing home. James was forced. Gus Mancuso popped out to end the inning.

In the twelfth, Rip Collins got as good a hold on a Hubbell pitch as anyone had all day. He drove it deep to center - inside-the-park home run territory - but Jo-Jo Moore pulled it in with a sliding acrobatic catch. Then in the bottom of the thirteenth, Johnny Vergez tagged one of Carleton's pitches and sent it streaking down the left field line. The Polo Grounds erupted with a tremendous roar as the ball landed in the lower grandstand. But the roar turned to groans a moment later when the third base umpire signaled that the ball had gone foul. Vergez's shot had missed the pole by less than a foot.

Into the fourteenth, the two pitchers matched each other, conjuring up images of turn-of-the-century scoreless baseball. But games like this one, as sportswriter Jimmy Powers of the New York *Daily News* reported, had gone out with moustache cups and the turkey trot.

Into the fifteenth Carl Hubbell continued his mastery of the Cardinals, the wicked screwball seeming to jump through enemy bats. Then, in the bottom of the fifteenth, the Giants again had their chance. With two out, the ballpark thundered as Bill Terry drove a tremendous shot to left center. Terry raced around the bases as the Cardinals frantically relayed the ball back in. Terry stopped at third. Now Carleton faced Mel Ott. Again Carleton intentionally walked Ott. That brought up Johnny Vergez, who had just missed the foul pole on his previous at-bat. With the crowd on their feet, Vergez popped up. So Hubbell returned to the mound in the sixteenth and routinely continued to set the Cardinals aside.

Terry's triple, however, must have conveyed a message to Cardinal manager Gabby Street. Having given up eight hits, seven walks, and no runs in sixteen innings, Tex Carleton left for a pinch hitter. Jesse Haines, a sly thirty-nine-year-old veteran, relieved. He retired the side in the seventeenth. Hubbell retired the side in the eighteenth and was scheduled to hit in the bottom of the inning.

But for Jesse Haines, the bottom of the Giants order proved elusive. Jo-Jo Moore walked. Gus Mancuso sacrificed him to second. Then ailing Travis Jackson batted for Blondy Ryan, the shortstop. Jackson walked intentionally, forcing manager Bill Terry to send Hubbell to the plate or remove him from the game.

Terry gave the crowd what they pleaded for: Hubbell at bat.

It might have been poetic justice if he had won his own game. Instead, he forced Jackson at second, putting himself at first base and Moore at third. The crowd was again on its feet waiting for Hughie Critz, the second baseman (two-for-nine in the game), to do something.

It had now been four hours since the game began. A sunny warm day was now overcast. A cool wind was whipping in off the Harlem River. Critz, as was his habit, stuffed some tobacco in his mouth, took a few practice swings, and stepped into the batter's box. Haines worked the count to two and one before Critz slapped the ball past Haines' ear out into center field.

For a moment the park was stunned. Then a roar went up that probably could have been heard at Yankee Stadium across the river. Moore came home. Hubbell stood on second as his Giants teammates mobbed him. Straw boaters, torn programs, and shredded Sunday papers rained onto the field. It was finally over, and Carl Hubbell had pitched a game that has never been seen before or since. The ovation continued as Hubbell walked all the way to the clubhouse in center field. It didn't abate until King Carl disappeared.

The magnitude of Hubbell's performance remains to this day.

Facing a pennant contender, Hubbell had allowed six base runners in eighteen innings. Twelve of the innings were perfect. He had struck out twelve and walked no one all day. Pepper Martin and Frankie Frisch, a pair of .300 hitters, had no hits in a total of fourteen at-bats. Four of the six St. Louis hits were scratch. Only one runner reached third base. And the game had lasted four hours and three minutes.

Now, recall: This was the first game of a doubleheader.

Between games, Gabby Street was so incensed by the loss that he threw Dizzy Dean at the Giants for the second game. Rain was beginning, and the day had turned dark. What better way to get even - and remain three and a half games behind - than to use Dean?

Ole Diz had already beaten the Giants on Friday. But he wasn't complaining about the one day of rest. Instead, he came out and threw. Roy Parmelee pitched for the Giants.

Again the zeroes mounted. After the monumental battle in the first game, with all the elements of sudden death for the last nine innings, game two seemed like an anticlimax. In the fourth inning, Johnny Vergez, who had almost been the hero in game one, lined a Dean pitch into the left field grandstand: 1-0, Giants. And that's how that game ended, too, in the darkness and the rain at a few minutes after eight o'clock. Two runs had scored in twenty-seven innings, the equivalent of a tripleheader, and the Giants had swept two games.

Breathtaking. The day's performance by the Giants and Cardinals had run longer that a Metropolitan Opera production of *Die Gotterdammerung* – without being anywhere nearly as funny.

For the Cardinals, the two losses by 1-0, combined with the 11-1 loss of the previous day, started the team on a slide: 19 losses in 26 games. It cost them the 1933 pennant and it cost Gabby Street his job later on in July. But Branch Rickey, who headed the Cardinals at the time, made a shrewd change, elevating Frankie Frisch to the position of player-manager. The move was too late to change the season but paid its dividend the following year. Making Frisch the manager was the final element that made winners of the Cardinals. The season that followed, 1934, was the year of the Gas House Gang and a World Championship in St. Louis. As for the Giants, shortstop Blondy Ryan was spiked on a play at second base in the second game of the St. Louis series. He left the game and required thirteen stitches. When the Giants went on their next road trip, Ryan was still unable to play. He remained sidelined until the team was in St. Louis.

It was at that time that the weak-hitting and somewhat porous fielding Ryan sent a telegram to his teammates. Advised by his doctor that he could play again, he dispatched the message: AM ON MY WAY! THEY CAN'T BEAT US!

Although Ryan never intended it, the two sentences were interpreted as cause and effect: THEY CAN'T BEAT US! as voiced by the popular Ryan, became the team's rallying cry that year. And no one did beat them.

Hubbell turned in his first great season: 23-12, a 1.66 ERA, and 10 shutouts, all of which led the NL. Along the way, he also had 5 saves. Hal Schumacher was now "Prince Hal," with 19 wins. Parmelee had controlled himself and his right arm enough to notch 13 wins. Fitzsimmons had 16.

Hitting? Of course. Terry was fourth in the league in average (.322) and Ott was third in both home runs (23) and RBIs (103).

Johnny Vergez hit 15 other home runs besides the one that beat Ole Diz on July 2, and Lefty O'Doul hit .306 for the Giants in a reserve role.

Vergez was lost with appendicitis late in the season, but by that time Travis Jackson was ready to play again. Ryan stayed at second. Jackson took third. The team went on a road trip in mid-September, split with the Pirates in Forbes Field, then knocked the Cubs out of the race by taking four of six in the Windy City.

Thus the Giants clinched their first pennant in nine years, their first ever without John McGraw, in St. Louis on September 19. On that day second-place Pittsburgh lost to the Phillies. As that announcement was made in Sportsman's Park, Mel Ott blasted his final home run of the season over the famous pavilion in right field.

The Giants took a train back to New York and were greeted by a delirious throng of ten thousand fans and two brass bands all packed into a raucous Grand Central Station. This was the middle of the Depression, after all. Franklin D. Roosevelt had been President for only a few months and New York, as much as any city, craved heroes. Given the boisterousness of the occasion, it was difficult to believe that this was New York City's twelfth pennant in the last thirteen years.

The official celebration of the pennant took place the next morning on the steps of City Hall. Mayor James O'Brien congratulated the team on behalf of the city. (Mayor O'Brien was serving out the final term of Jimmy Walker, the champion of Sunday baseball, who had fled to Europe until the danger of indictment subsided. O'Brien was a Tammany guy, too. When asked at his post inauguration news conference, who the new police commissioner would be, O'Brien responded honestly with, "I don't know. They haven't told me yet.")

Brief speeches followed by National League president John Heydler and, appropriately, John McGraw, looking old and ailing. He also looked awkward as he stepped to the background and watched the gathered throng of fans cheer for Bill Terry and a new generation of Giants.

Later in the day came the news that the city had expected. The Washington Senators, led by Joe Cronin, Henry (Heinie) Manush, Goose Goslin, Earl Whitehill, and Alvin (General) Crowder, had dethroned the Yankees for the American League pennant.

Crowder was a dour guy. He had put in almost three years in the

United States Army during World War I, including assignments in the Philippines and nearly a year with the American Expeditionary Force in Siberia. However, he never reached the rank of "General." His nickname, "General" Crowder, came from General Enoch Crowder, who had presided over America's World War I draft lottery. As a private in the U.S. Army, he had learned to play baseball.

More importantly, Washington would oppose the New York Giants in the World Series. Again.

Chapter 57 World Champions Again

> "The screwball's an unnatural pitch.
> Nature never intended a man to turn his
> hand like that throwing rocks at a bear."
>
> **Carl Hubbell**

This time there were no rocks. Or pebbles.

The World Series opened at the Polo Grounds on October 3, 1933. There were approximately eight thousand empty seats in the grandstand at a reasonable buck ten, a testament to the sour economic conditions in the United States. Around the country, however, millions of Americans clustered around console radios.

There was little question who would pitch for New York.

Carl Hubbell had become the most devastating pitcher in baseball in 1933. Joe Cronin, however, decided upon a strategy, starting his number three hurler, Walter (Lefty) Stewart, instead of Crowder or Whitehill. Ott greeted Stewart accordingly, lining a typical Ott home run - a sharp line drive - into the lower right field stands in the bottom of the first inning. Jo-Jo Moore was on base. On his next at-bat, Ott singled in Hughie Critz, Ott's second of four hits and third RBI for the afternoon. Already the Giants had more than enough. Hubbell would be touched for two unearned runs late in the day, but Game One was no contest. New York won, 4-2.

On the next afternoon, Hal Schumacher and General Crowder were warming up for Game Two when photographers posed them together. One cameraman asked Crowder to smile.

"Why?" he asked. Time in Siberia makes for a subdued personality.

Good question. Crowder had even less to smile about two hours later when New York erupted for six runs in the sixth inning before 35,461 happy Giants fans and approximately 20,000 empty seats. The big blow was a single by Lefty O'Doul, batting for George Davis, that knocked in two runs. It also knocked Crowder out of the game. Goose Goslin hit an early home run for the Senators, but the Giants won easily, 6-1.

Game Three was in Washington, after the teams had hustled aboard a train from New York. The Senators would win, 4-0, behind Earl Whitehill, but the star of the day was a New Yorker: President Franklin D. Roosevelt, whose New Deal legislation had passed Congress that same summer.

A steady drizzle threatened the game all morning and held attendance down to 27,727, about 2,000 under the capacity of Griffith Stadium. But toward game time, the skies cleared. Roosevelt, blessed with his inordinate good fortune, chose that moment to arrive at the game by car. The auto pulled down a Griffith Stadium runway as both teams and United States Army band stood at attention. Incredibly, the sun chose that very moment to emerge from the clouds. Surely, if FDR could have that impact on climactic conditions, happy days were here again.

Clark Griffith, the Senators' owner, greeted the President, who was rolled to his seat in a wheelchair. No photos permitted. He would rise from it to stand and throw out the ceremonial first ball. Photos encouraged. "We're glad you're here, Mr. President," Griffith said. "And we hope to win this one for you."

Roosevelt, flashing the world's most famous smile, was quick to answer, and even quicker to remember which

434

state had the greatest number of Electoral College votes.

(Photo: FDR with Joe Cronin and Bill Terry: Library of Congress, Prints & Photographs Division, photograph by Harris & Ewing)

"Wait a minute, Clark," Roosevelt answered. "I'm neutral. Don't forget, I may be living in Washington now, but I'm from New York." Ah, politicians. Earl Whitehill then tossed an artistic five-hitter, sending most of the non-neutral Washingtonians home happy.

The loss never daunted the Giants. Terry knew he was coming right back with Hubbell, and he knew Hubbell was practically unhittable. Game Four turned into one of the finest World Series games ever.

The contest was scoreless until the top of the fourth inning, when Bill Terry drove a long home run into a distant section of the right center field bleachers.

Washington scored in the seventh when Hubbell fumbled Joe Kuhel's bunt, allowed Ossie Bluege to sacrifice Kuhel to second, then yielded a two-out single to James (Luke) Sewell. There the game remained through nine innings, tied at 1-1, with a stalwart Monte Weaver, the Washington right-hander, matching Hubbell pitch for pitch.

Then came the eleventh. Travis Jackson surprised the entire stadium by laying a perfect bunt single down the third base line. Gus Mancuso bunted Jackson to second, bringing up the light-hitting Blondy Ryan, as in, THEY CAN'T BEAT US!

With first base open, the situation presented both managers with strategic decisions. Should Ryan be walked to force Hubbell to either bunt or hit a possible double-play ball? Or, for Terry, should he waste a pinch hitter for Ryan, knowing that Lefty O'Doul, the most logical pinch hitter, would probably be passed intentionally?

Terry let Ryan swing, despite a .238 average for 1933. Weaver came in with a fastball and Ryan straightened it out, singling to right, sending Jackson, gimpy knees and all, racing home with the tie-breaking run.

Hubbell singled on the next pitch, moving Jackson to second. Cronin pulled Weaver. Reliever Jack Russell retired Jo-Jo Moore and Hughie Critz to thwart any further Giants rally.

The damage was already done for Washington. But the Senators weren't finished. Joe Schulte singled. Joe Kuhel bunted toward first, attempting to sacrifice. But Bill Terry let the ball roll. It never crossed the foul line. Terry snatched the ball in disgust and returned it to Hubbell. Then Ossie Bluege successfully bunted Schulte to third and Kuhel - the potential winning run - to second. Luke Sewell was intentionally walked to load the bases.

Then Cronin pulled what might have been an excellent bit of strategy. He sent a young catcher named Cliff Bolton up to hit. Bolton had spent most of the year with Chattanooga of the Southern Association before coming to Washington and batting a lofty .410 in a part-time role.

There was no "book" yet on Bolton in the major leagues and most National Leaguers had never seen him. In this key situation, after which the Giants would either have a commanding 3-1 lead in the Series or be tied, 2-2, no one knew how to pitch to Bolton. Further, Terry had a choice in strategies again. He could play in for a play at the plate - the conventional move that would also increase Bolton's chances of rapping a game-winning hit through the drawn-in infield - or he could play deep for a double play.

On the Giants' bench, however, was Chuck "Cholly" Dressen, a veteran reserve third baseman who would never play in the 1933 Series. He did, however, make a crucial contribution. Cronin had forgotten that Dressen had been Bolton's manager at Chattanooga in 1932. Dressen wasted no time in speaking to Terry. Bolton, according to "Cholly," ran like a Galapagos tortoise.

"Make him hit the ball on the ground," said Dressen, "and you'll have a cinch double play."

Blondy Ryan and Hughie Critz also wanted to play deep, so Terry went with the unconventional strategy. Hubbell spun a low screwball to Bolton. Bolton hit it sharply to Ryan. Ryan flipped the ball to Critz, who zipped it to Terry at first before Bolton was anywhere close to the bag. It was the easiest double play of the Series and gave the Giants a 3-1 advantage in the series.

The final game was also in Washington. It, too, was a nail biter. This time Schumacher faced Crowder. The Giants built a 3-0 lead after five and a half innings, but Washington came roaring back in their half of the sixth. With two out, trouble began when Manush and Cronin each singled. Then Fred Schulte launched a three-run homer into the left field seats, tying the game. Kuhel followed with a single off Hughie Critz's leg. Ossie Bluege smashed a ball off Travis Jackson's glove at third. Bluege's hit sent Kuhel to third and Schumacher to the showers.

In trudged "The Pride of Havana," Adolfo Luque, who had last pitched in a World Series against the Chicago Black Sox in 1919.

Luque induced Luke Sewell to ground out to Critz. Then Luque and Jack Russell, who relieved Crowder in the top of the same inning, exchanged zeroes through nine innings.

Here were the New York Giants and Washington Senators heading into extra innings yet again, just as they had on the previous afternoon, and just as they had in Games One and Seven nine years earlier. The resolution of this one was to be every bit as spectacular.

Hughie Critz opened the top of the tenth with a fly to Heinie Manush in left. Terry hit a harmless grounder to Charles (Buddy) Myer at second. Ott, zero-for-four, was up next.

Jack Russell worked the count to two and two, then came in with a fastball. Mistake. Ott cocked his right leg and lifted a long fly toward the right center field bleachers. Fred Schulte went waaaaaay back, back, back for it and arrived just as the ball did in front of a three-foot-high fence that enclosed some temporary bleachers.

Schulte reached up, grabbed for the ball, hit the wall, and felt Ott's hit go off his fingertips over the fence. Schulte, a victim of his own momentum, toppled over the fence after the ball.

Second base umpire Cy Pfirman called it a ground rule double. Terry protested and found sympathy among umpires David Moran and John Moriarty. The latter two overruled Pfirman and awarded Ott a home run, despite a vehement protest from Washington. As Ott crossed the plate with the run that would bring the Giants their first World Championship since the great McGraw squad of 1922, all that was needed was some good relief work from Luque.

{By curious coincidence, Pfirman was no stranger to the Giants or Hubbell. Pfirman, who at one point he umpired 1,710 consecutive National League games, would be the plate umpire in the 1934 All-Star Game when Carl Hubbell struck out Babe Ruth, Lou Gehrig, Jimmie Foxx, Al Simmons and Joe Cronin in order.}

Among those on their feet to cheer the Giants on in the enemy ballpark was John McGraw. He and Blanche had attended every game, though he kept very much in the background. Now, as the ageless Luque faced Goose Goslin, the Little Napoleon leaned forward intently.

Goslin grounded to Terry, who flipped to Luque covering first. One out. Heinie Manush lined the ball to Critz at second, who caught the ball cleanly. Two outs.

Then, keeping the Senators' hopes alive, Joe Cronin singled, the second hit off Luque since the sixth inning. Then Schulte walked on four pitches.

Terry came to the mound, aware that Luque was showing his age. Joe Kuhel was the next hitter. Kuhel was not an easy out. He had had his difficulties with the Giants in the Series, but he had hit .322 for the season with more than a hundred extra-base hits. He was overdue. And an extra-base hit here would send the World Series back to the Polo Grounds.

Only one team, however, was destined to return to New York. Luque, with a flourish, drew a deep breath and hitched up his belt. He looked at catcher Gus Mancuso, then started his windup.

Luque struck out Kuhel on three pitches and the Giants were champions of the world.

Chapter 58   The Old Guard Fades Away

"May Flights of Angels Lead You On Your Way"

paraphrase of the ancient
Latin funeral hymn, *In Paradisum*

The Giants returned to New York for the party that ex-manager John McGraw threw at the New Yorker Hotel.

For a while it was like the old days, with booze and good cheer flowing into the morning hours. Hubbell (no earned runs in twenty innings) and Ott (2 HRs, .389) were seen as stars of the Series. Hubbell eventually went on a vaudeville tour and Terry received a new five-year contract as player-manager at a whopping $40,000. It may have been the Depression, but Charles Stoneham was both grateful and generous, at least for now. Ott returned to his home in Louisiana to receive a more unusual award: his high school diploma, given to him at age twenty-four, seven years after he had dropped out of school to join McGraw's Giants.

As for McGraw, Terry's victory in 1933 had given the Old Man his last great thrill in baseball. He had celebrated his sixtieth birthday before the season had started, but his health was spiraling downward now.

He was afflicted first with uremia, then prostatic and intestinal cancer. He was wise enough a man to know that his time was limited. He had promised Terry, upon the latter's appointment, that he would never enter the Giants' manager's office again. He didn't. But during a Giants road trip a friend had come in and removed two photographs: one of Mathewson and one of Ross Youngs. The pictures were moved to McGraw's desk in his home at 620 Ely Avenue in Pelham. Just as death had closed in on the two players he most loved, he now must have known it was closing in on him.

Tim Keefe had died earlier that year and Old Dan Brouthers, who had worked for McGraw from 1907 until 1927 as a night watchman and press box guard at the Polo Grounds, had passed away in 1932.

Billy Gleason, who had sent McGraw to Baltimore from Cedar Rapids those many years ago, had also passed away, as had William (Kid) Gleason (no relation). But most jarring of all was the death of McGraw's personal physician, Dr. William Walsh. Walsh was shot to death by a former convict in his office at 656 Riverside Dr. William Walsh. The murderer, who committed suicide that same day, had an old festering grudge against one William Walsh, M.D. Unfortunately, a case of mistaken identity had been involved and the convict had murdered the wrong man.

McGraw attended the annual dinner of the New York Baseball Writers Association on February 4, 1934, then dropped by a New York Giants "victory dinner" afterward at a different location. He only stayed for an hour.

Less than two weeks later, considerably weakened, he checked into New Rochelle Hospital. Nine days after that, he died "from an internal hemorrhage brought on by uremia."

So said the hospital.

The New York *Times*, which didn't waste much front-page ink on sports figures, had some space on Page One for McGraw the next day. The headline read:

**JOHN J. MCGRAW IS DEAD AT 60.
CALLED BASEBALL's GREATEST FIGURE.**

At the time of his death, he certainly was. Shortly after McGraw's death, his widow Blanche, found among his private papers a list of all the black players he wanted to sign over the years.

In the New York *Herald Tribune* on February. 26, 1934, an observer wrote, "Baseball to John J. McGraw was a feud, not a game....He brought to the Polo Grounds dozens of players whose deeds made separate chapters in baseball's history, and through his knowledge of baseball, knowledge that made popular the phrase 'master minding' and made McGraw 'The Little Napoleon,' he trained many players who learned their lessons so well that they afterward became rivals of their old master."

Babe Ruth said, "What, John McGraw dead! He was one of the three greatest baseball generals. I rank him with my late friend, Miller Huggins, and Connie Mack."

And Bill Terry, his successor, added, "The man who made the Giants stand for what they do is gone, but his code lives on. It was under McGraw that I learned what I know about baseball and I will try to carry on and teach the same things to those who never had the chance to benefit directly from the greatest manager baseball has ever known."

Following a funeral tribute in New York, McGraw was buried at New Cathedral Cemetery in Baltimore.

Bozeman Bulger had died the previous year, leaving Joe Vila as the only reporter in New York who had been on the job when McGraw had stolen away from the failing Baltimore Orioles to rebuild the Giants three decades earlier.

Vila had revolutionized sportswriter in New York, one of the most influential scribblers during the first third of the Twentieth Century. He was a graduate of Harvard College and attended Harvard Law, but never graduated. He didn't literally scribble, either.

In 1889 Vila arrived in New York City, where he wrote for decades for The New York Evening *Sun*, one of the city's prestige dailies. He covered baseball and boxing. He was the first sportswriter to use a typewriter at ringside, clackity clack, while dictating to a typist round by round the fight between James J. Corbett and Tom Sharkey and sending the resulting copy to a Western Union operator. As a result, other reporters who customarily wrote in longhand stopped scribbling and switched to typewriters.

Now Vila mourned McGraw in the pages of the *Sun*. Included

was a sorrowful quote from Wilbert Robinson, who had buried the hatchet with his old Baltimore Oriole pal a few years earlier. Even with his success and fame as a player, McGraw would best be remembered for his managing, especially since he had guided the most popular team of its era.

McGraw's 2,763 victories ranked second overall behind only Connie Mack, records that endure into the second decade of the Twenty-first Century. Mack didn't pass McGraw until a few months after the latter's death. McGraw also still holds the National League record with 2,669 career wins. Only Tony La Russa with 2728 wins in the two major leagues has crept anywhere close.

McGraw was probably the best player to become a great manager in the history of baseball. For generations he also held the dubious Major League Baseball record for most ejections by a manager, 132, until Bobby Cox, also an ex-infielder, broke the record in 2007.

What was it that McGraw had said after the 1923 World Series?

"The old guard changes but it never surrenders."

Mac had been right about that, too, in an eerie way.

Joseph Vila collapsed at his desk a few weeks later while covering the opening of the horse race spring meeting at Jamaica Race Course. He was hospitalized, then driven to his home in Brooklyn. He died later of a heart failure at the age of 67, April 8, 1934.

Wilbert Robinson had become the president of the Atlanta Crackers minor league team after his retirement from managing Brooklyn. He died in Atlanta at 71 years of age following a brain hemorrhage. His body was returned to Baltimore and was buried in the New Cathedral Cemetery, August 8, 1934, not far from his old friend and partner.

The old guard was indeed passing from the scene, opening the way for a new generation of stars at the Polo Grounds, and writers and opponents to bedevil them.

Yours truly,
John J. McGraw.
1911.

Chapter 59 The Borough of Churches and Bad Ball Clubs

"I wish you were in Dixie!"

**Placard to Bill Terry
from a Dodger fan at the Polo Grounds**

In January of 1934, Bill Terry was in New York to attend the annual business meetings of the American and National leagues. Several sportswriters converged on Terry at the Hotel Roosevelt across from Grand Central Station.

Terry held court on the Giants' chances for 1934, which were widely viewed as excellent. Terry named Pittsburgh, Chicago, St. Louis, and Boston as other threats to dethrone the champion Giants.

"What about Brooklyn, Bill?" asked Roscoe McGowen, who covered the Dodgers for the New York *Times*.

"Brooklyn?" asked Terry, gently teasing McGowen. "I haven't heard anything from them lately. Are they still in the league?"

The writers laughed. The writers reported the remark. But in print the next day the question didn't have the playful tone in which it had been spoken. Nor was it well received on the other side of the Brooklyn Bridge. Come to think of it, out of context it does sound pretty nasty.

Bob Quinn, the new head of the Dodger front office, was used to suffering. But Terry's remark not only irked him, because it diminished the character of Brooklyn baseball, but he also thought it might diminish the box office in Brooklyn. How wrong he was about that.

Quinn leaped on Terry's remarks and launched several well-crafted insults of his own, most of which found their way into print. Meanwhile, Quinn was also irked that Max Carey, the Brooklyn manager, had made no public response to Terry's jibe.

As the situation heated up, Quinn grew angry with Carey, fired him, and on February 23 replaced him with Casey Stengel. This was Casey's first managerial position in the majors. His old mentor, John McGraw, would have been pleased for him. McGraw, however, was in New Rochelle Hospital with forty-eight hours of life left in him. He probably never knew of Stengel's appointment.

"The first thing I want to say," said Casey, who always had an assortment of things to say, "is that the Dodgers *are* still in the league."

So there it was, February 23, 1934. Already the gauntlet was down for the season.

In fairness, it is easy to understand Terry's remark, both in its intent and tone. Brooklyn had, for many years, been the closest thing baseball had to offer to a Mack Sennett comedy.

Under Wilbert Robinson, despite pennants in 1916 and 1920, the team had become known as "The Daffiness Boys." Anything capable of happening *did* happen at Ebbets Field. There was the much-chronicled incident in which Floyd (Babe) Herman doubled into a double play, an exercise in baseball futility which had three runners, including Herman and Dazzy Vance, diving into third base from different directions all at the same time. There was also the day Casey Stengel, as a young Brooklyn outfielder, tipped his cap and a bird flew out. There was another time when Robinson was in the dugout watching a game when an opposing batter slashed the ball down the left field line. Robinson sprang to his feet trying to see the play but couldn't. He asked Herman, who was seated nearby, whether the ball had been fair or foul.

"I don't know, Robbie," came the answer. "I was reading the newspaper."

Under such leadership, the Dodgers quickly became a playground for uninspired ball players, a franchise that in no way suggested the hard-nosed competitive spirit that prevailed on the team in the 1940s and '50s. Losing was both accepted and expected, prompting one sportswriter in the early 1930s, not long before Quinn took over, to remark that "overconfidence could eventually cost Brooklyn sixth place."

Ironically, Stengel would do nothing to improve the situation. Later in his life he would refer to Brooklyn as "that borough of churches and bad ball clubs, many of which I managed." He would preside over the incident in which Frenchy Bordagaray would be tagged out while standing on second base. When Casey came out to argue, Bordagaray confessed that he had been tapping his foot and he guessed he had been tagged between taps.

Whenever Nick Tremark, a five-foot five outfielder got on base, which was not very often, Stengel held his hands to his eyes as if he were looking through binoculars, trying to find Tremark on the great big ball field. Then there was the incident with Hack Wilson and Dodger pitcher Walter (Boom-Boom) Beck at the Baker Bowl in

Philadelphia.

The Phillies had been trashing Beck's pitches all afternoon. Wilson, playing right field in front of the tin fence that occasionally kept balls in the park, had been chasing down the results of many of Beck's pitches. Casey came out to remove Beck. Beck didn't want to go. Wilson, who had a reputation for indulging in alcohol close to game time, or during, as well as after, was studying his shoes during the discussion on the mound.

Relieved of duty, Beck refused to hand the ball over to Casey. Rather, with what must have been his best throw of the day, he turned and heaved it toward right field. It carried over Wilson's head and boomed against the fence. Startled, Wilson heard the ball hit the fence, figured it was another Philadelphia double, retrieved it as fast as possible, and played it into second base. Not long after, Wilson was traded to Philadelphia, where he could play in front of that fence every day.

There was no end to such anecdotes. Bill Terry had witnessed enough by himself to be prompted to make his remark. But that didn't make it any better received in Kings County. Nor was Terry received well there either.

The Giants got off to a good start in 1934, but on the first trip to Brooklyn, Terry had to have an inkling of what he was in for. The fans hurled verbal abuse at him that was rough even by Flatbush standards. When Casey Stengel tried to pose with Terry for some photographs, fans chucked firecrackers at both of them. Eventually, Stengel retreated to a safer spot, which was anywhere Terry wasn't.

There were some changes in the lineup from the pennant-winning combination of 1933. Paul Richards filled in frequently for Gus Mancuso, who had suffered from typhoid in late winter. Travis Jackson, his knees finally coming around, moved to shortstop and made a utility player out of Blondy Ryan, the previous year's inspiration.

George Watkins came from the Cardinals in a trade for the lighter-hitting George Davis. But the pitching staff remained intact. Even Adolfo Luque was back for another turn around the league. Somewhere there had to have been a portrait of the man that was aging in his place.

On Memorial Day, the Giants visited Ebbets Field a second time, sold the place out, and took two games from the Dodgers. The abuse heaped upon Terry hadn't abated. It had increased and now spilled over onto other Giants, such as Travis Jackson and Mel Ott, who had always been popular in Brooklyn. Terry barely cared, happy to leave with the two victories. The Giants were tied with the Cubs for second place, a game and a half behind St. Louis.

In June and July, the Giants stayed as hot as the midsummer weather, maintaining leads over St. Louis and Chicago that hovered consistently around three to five games. There was a break in July for the All-Star Game, held that year at the Polo Grounds. Terry, as the manager of the reigning champions, skippered the National League squad. He started his own best pitcher, Carl Hubbell.

Hubbell worked carefully to Charlie Gehringer, who led off the game. Gehringer singled. Then Hubbell walked Heinie Manush, his adversary from the previous autumn. At that time, Hubbell's catcher for the event, Gabby Hartnett of the Cubs, visited the mound.

"Come on, Hub," said Hartnett, "throw that *thing.*" He meant the screwball. "Hell, I can't hit it and they can't either."

One of baseball's most memorable feats followed, as Ruth, Gehrig, and Jimmie Foxx swung wildly at a pitch they had never before seen. Foxx at least managed a foul tip. In the next inning Hubbell fanned Al Simmons and Joe Cronin with "the thing" before Bill Dickey broke the spell with a single. Hubbell then struck out pitcher Lefty Gomez of the Yankees to end the inning. Gomez, whose eventual career batting average proved to be .147, would in later years use the incident to equate himself with Ruth, Gehrig, and company as a hitter.

Through the rest of July and August, New York continued to play great baseball. Ott was having an outstanding year: He would share the home run lead with Rip Collins of St. Louis with 35 and win the RBI title outright with 135. Terry would hit .354, second in the league to Paul Waner's .362.

Hubbell was stellar as usual, winning 21 times and coming on in relief so often that he also led the league in saves with 8. So why then, given that the Giants had a six-game lead in early September, did they finish s e c o n d ?

The answer is that they slumped badly in mid-September, and St. Louis got hotter than a cheap pistol. This was 1934, the year of the "gashouse gang," a rough and tumble team that featured several former or future Giants. An opposing player one day alleged that the Cardinals players usually went into the field in stinky sweaty uniforms. Reputedly, shortstop Leo Durocher referred to his team as "a bunch of "gashousers." The phrase "gashouse" referred to factories of the era that turned coal into gas for a town's lighting and cooking. They stank like hell.

So as fatigue, both mental and physical, mounted on the Giants, the smelly Cardinals closed the gap. The Dodgers, meanwhile, had settled into their habitual spot of sixth place. But Bob Quinn, Casey Stengel, the players, and hundreds of thousands of leather-lunged fans had not forgotten Terry's remarks of the previous January.

On Sunday morning, September 21, the Giants led the Cardinals by three and a half games. Freddie Fitzsimmons beat the Phillies at the Polo Grounds that afternoon while a larger story was unfolding in Brooklyn, where Dizzy Dean beat Brooklyn on a three-hit shutout in the first game of a doubleheader. Then Paul Dean tossed a no-hitter in the second game.

Afterward Dizzy was credited with a quote almost as famous as Hubbell's five strikeouts in the All-Star Game: "If I'da knowed Paul was gonna throw a no-hitter," Dean said, "I'da throwed one too." But the Giants lead had now been whittled to three games. That too evaporated over the next week. With two games left on the final Saturday and Sunday of the season, St. Louis and New York were dead even. St. Louis went to Cincinnati to visit the cellar-dwelling Reds. The Giants were home at the Polo Grounds. Brooklyn was visiting: not just the team, but every Dodger fan in the borough.

The Dodgers' faithful had been salivating in anticipation of this moment all season. For that matter so had the players. This Brooklyn team was not to be confused with the docile bunch of patsies who poked out three hits against the Dean brothers in eighteen innings the previous Sunday. These guys were brutal.

So were the fans. They clanked cow bells, blew whistles, and howled at Bill Terry every time he poked his head out of the dugout or took his position on the field. They carried signs. BILL WHO? and YES, WE'RE STILL IN THE LEAGUE. Meanwhile, the Dodgers battered Tarzan Parmelee for five runs while Van Lingle Mungo held the Giants to one. Out in the Rhineland, Paul Dean handled the Reds easily, winning, 6-1. The Giants went home that day a game behind, after leading the league for most of the season.

Sunday was every bit as disastrous. The New Yorkers hopped on Brooklyn's starter, Ray Benge, for four runs in the first inning, routing him. But on the Polo Grounds scoreboard, the news was not good. St. Louis had scored two quick runs against Cincinnati. Paul Dean's older brother was pitching, looking for win number 30. There was no way Dizzy was going to mess that up. The

Giants lost their concentration, their lead, and eventually the game and the pennant. Even Carl Hubbell was unable to staunch a Dodger rally. Brooklyn won, 8-5, and Dean shut out the Reds. The Giants finished two games back.

Apparently, yes. Brooklyn was still in the league.

Though dispirited and exhausted, Bill Terry was a gentleman in defeat. "I'm not blaming anyone, and I have no alibis," he said at season's conclusion. "St. Louis made a great finish. I rank them above the Tigers in the World Series." Unlike his pronouncement of earlier in the year, this one looked good almost immediately.

In the off-season, Terry made an initial attempt at rebuilding, sending Watkins, Vergez, Ryan, minor league left-hander John (Pretzels) Pezzulo, and $75,000 in cash to the Phillies for Dick Bartell, a shortstop. Bartell was better known around the league as "Rowdy Richard." He was an infielder in the old-school style of John McGraw, meaning he approached baseball the way a modern hockey player might. He was well known for two spiking incidents, both involving the Dodgers. Nowhere in baseball was he more hated than at Ebbets Field. He was, then, a natural for stardom at the Polo Grounds.

When the next season, 1935, started in Boston, Babe Ruth was with the Braves. He had spent the winter thinking about Carl Hubbell's screwball, the one he had been unable to touch at the All-Star Game. He straightened one of them out for a towering 430-foot home run up into the "Jury Box" at Braves Field, then winked to Hubbell as he jogged between first and second to indicate he had figured out the pitch. Hubbell smiled back. The Braves even won the game, 4-2, deceiving their fans into believing that they were not one of the most godawful squads ever assembled. They were, winning only 38 games all year. They finished 61.5 games out of first place, and 37 games out of seventh.

The Giants led the league for a while and looked to be in position to rebound for a pennant. But late in the season the Chicago Cubs won twenty straight games and drew away from everyone. On one horrifying afternoon in St. Louis, however, Hal Schumacher collapsed on the mound during a blistering hot midwestern afternoon. The Cardinals' team sawbones, Dr. Robert Hyland, packed Schumacher in ice, sent him off to the hospital and, in the words of Blondy Ryan, by then traded by the Phillies to the Yankees, "brought him back from the dead."

The team had been predicted to finish second that year. Instead, the Giants finished third. So in the off-season of 1935-36, Terry continued to deal. He reacquired Sam Leslie from Brooklyn, then traded Tarzan Parmelee to St. Louis for Burgess Whitehead. Whitehead was tabbed to take the place of Hughie Critz, who had retired. With Bartell, Whitehead - a Phi Beta Kappa graduate of the University of North Carolina - would provide some needed youth for the middle of the infield.

Youth also took over elsewhere in the Giants' organization that winter.

On January 6, 1936, Charles Stoneham died in Hots Springs, Arkansas, a city famous for gambling and bootlegging, after spending several days in a coma. The Giants' owner was the last living member of the trio that had purchased the team in 1919, McGraw and McQuade having preceded Stoneham in death.

Stoneham, by anyone's measurement, had been a good owner of the team, standing quietly in the wings while experienced baseball men - McGraw and Terry - had run his operations. His name popped up in corruption scandals in New York from time to time, but not in connection with the Giants.

Following his funeral, the front office of the National Exhibition Company, the Giants' corporate name dating all the way back to the Jim Mutrie years, was realigned. Leo Bondy was elevated to vice president, in addition to his duties as treasurer. Eddie Brannick, thirty years after coming to the team as McGraw's clubhouse boy, was the team secretary. And replacing Charles Stoneham was son Horace, thirty-two years old, the Giants' fourth owner since the redoubtable Andrew Freedman.

Stoneham the Younger would preside over the club's fortunes for the rest of their tenure east of the Hudson River.

Chapter 60 "The Yankees have a guy named DiMaggio...

> "…..Sometimes a fellow gets a little tired
> gets a little of writing about DiMaggio. A fellow thinks,
> 'There must be some other ballplayer in the world worth
> mentioning.' But there isn't really, not worth mentioning in the
> same breath as DiMaggio."
>
> **Red Smith**

One of those grand seasons when American professional baseball thrived, 1936, was a brief unhurried breath of time between the Great Depression and a second world war. The established stars - Lou Gehrig, Mel Ott, Jimmie Foxx, Dizzy Dean - are now part of baseball's firmament. Joe DiMaggio was a flashy rookie. So was Bob Feller at age seventeen. Ten cities had at least one major league team. Franklin D. Roosevelt was looking forward to winning a second term, and the Chicago Cubs were the defending National League champions.

New York City was gradually crawling out from the effects of the Depression. *Gone With the Wind* was in all the bookstores and, with the return of legal liquor, the lights were brighter than ever along Times Square, a region described by showman Billy Rose as "a triangle full of squares running around in circles."

There were changes in the National League, too. Less than a year after being dismissed by the Dodgers, Bob Quinn had come to Boston to operate the Braves. In a move that attempted to distract the public from the team's recent, incompetent past, Quinn made an asinine move every bit as awful as some of the stuff transpiring on the field.

The Braves were renamed the Bees, as in *buzz. buzz.* Cuter still was Quinn's attempt to get everyone to call Braves Field, "The Beehive." Can you picture all the good Irishmen from Southie tumbling out of those taverns and announcing they were on their way to see the Bees? Can you envision a Harvard classics professor or a Beacon Hill Brahman stepping into a cab, requesting, "The Bee hive, puh-leeze?" No one else could picture it either. The experiment died of natural causes after a few short years.

The Giants opened the season with three contentious games against the Dodgers at the Polo Grounds. The Giants would win all three, but the center of the storm arrived in the second game. Giants' shortstop Dick Bartell kept alive his long-running feud with anyone in Dodger blue. Bartell hit an easy ground ball to Dodger first baseman Buddy Hassett who trotted to first to stamp on the bag long before Bartell could arrive. Pitcher Van Lingle Mungo came over toward first, however, and according to witnesses gave Bartell a little shot with his hip. Bartell, three inches shorter and at least thirty pounds lighter than six-two, 195-pound Mungo, went sprawling.

Bartell tumbled for several yards, landed hard on his back, and came to his feet with fire in his eyes. Then they went for each other's throats.

The dugouts emptied, as they frequently did during Giant-Dodger get-togethers. Beans Readon, who happened to be the third base umpire, waded through sprawling bodies and pulled Mungo and Bartell apart. Then he heaved them out of the game.

The next day, in a strange twist, the new National League president, Ford Frick, fined Mungo and Bartell a crummy $25 for the fight, while apologizing for the low amount of the penalty.

"These fines are the smallest for a fistfight in a good many years," Frick said. "I made them," he continued philosophically, "because there are degrees of fights. This one was not premeditated. No one got hurt and no one even got a black eye." What Frick was saying, in other words, was that it was a puny fight, which was to be punished with a puny fine.

Mungo, quite by coincidence, was hit with something more painful that same day. Pitching in relief at the Polo Grounds, he nursed a 6-5 lead into the top of the ninth. He retired the first two Giants. Then Whitehead walked and Ott singled. Next Hank Leiber popped up a ball that should have ended the game.

Freddie Lindstrom, our old friend from the final John McGraw years, was playing left field for the Flock. He moved in for the routine catch and in the process bowled over Brooklyn infielder Jimmy Jordan, who was moving out for the same catch. The ball popped out of Jordan's glove as the two fielders, having cracked their heads together, fell away in opposite directions. Whitehead and Ott circled the bases to win the game.

"I've been in the league twelve years," Lindstrom moaned after the game, his head pounding, "but that never happened to me until I was a Dodger."

Lindstrom then thought better of spending an entire season caught up with the Daffy Dodgers. He retired several games later. Several weeks afterward, Mungo walked out on the same club, demanding to be traded from this "bunch of inefficient semi pros." He didn't get his wish and went on to be tagged with 19 losses for the s e a s o n .

Terry juggled his lineup to keep the Giants near the top of the league through May. He alternated himself at first base with Sam Leslie, and let young Eddie Mayo, called up from Baltimore, share third base with Travis Jackson. Hank Leiber, coming out of an excellent 1935 season (.331, 22 HRs, 107 RBIs) started terribly and was platooned in center field with young Jimmy Ripple. Gradually, though, by the end of June the Giants were starting to slip down the 1936 tubes.

In early July, about the time of the All-Star break, New York was in fifth place and looking downward. "I guess," said Horace Stoneham, "the best thing that could happen would be if the team were torn to pieces and rebuilt from the ground up." And writer Ed Hughes, in the Brooklyn *Eagle,* chortled in print that the Giants were playing "the forlorn punch-drunk type of game supposedly the sole possession of our diabolically inventive Dodgers."

The Cubs, meanwhile, were on a tear. They put together a fifteen game winning streak in June that took them to the top of the league. Although they battled to create daylight between themselves and the Pirates and Cardinals, they won games even when they shouldn't. On July 13, for example, they got all of two hits at Wrigley Field against Carl Hubbell and the Giants. Still they combined the two hits with an error and a walk, manufactured a run, and beat the Giants, 1-0. Never mind that the Cubs hit only four balls out of the infield all day. The loss dropped Hubbell's record to 10-6.

The loss also came at about the time the Giants hit bottom for the year. From Chicago the team went to Pittsburgh, where they dumped a doubleheader, fell eleven games behind, and found themselves closer to the cellar than the top. That's when the season turned around.

Ott homered in the eighth inning the next day to seal a come from behind victory. Then in the final of four games against the Pirates, Carl Hubbell chucked a 6-zip shutout, assisted by four Giants triples. What followed was a hot streak by the team that is the equal of any in the history of the National League, and a pitching performance by Carl Hubbell which, in its sustained brilliance, remains incomparable to anything before or after.

Two days after the whitewashing of Pittsburgh, Hubbell picked up a relief win against the Reds. Without missing a turn, he pitched a ten inning 2-1 win over St. Louis. More followed. By August 2, King Carl had suddenly won 5 in a row while the Giants were on a roll during which they clicked off 17 wins in 18 games. The torrid pace continued through August, highlighted by a doubleheader sweep at Wrigley Field which included Hubbell's win number 20. At that point King Carl had 10 in a row, a cornerstone of the 38-9 pace that the Giants had set since mid-July. No longer was the team in fifth place. They were in first, 4 games in front of the Cardinals.

St. Louis came into the Polo Grounds and the Giants took 2 of 3 from them. In the rubber game of the series, with Bill Terry engaging in a battle of wits with Frankie Frisch, his old teammate and currently the St. Louis manager, Hubbell opposed Dizzy Dean *in relief.* Hubbell won, 7-5, victory number 24 of the year. It was also his fourteenth in a row. From there on, the Giants mopped up with the also-rans. Hubbell added two more triumphs to his long skein and the Giants won the pennant by 5 games over Chicago.

As was often the case with Giants pennants of that era, the story was Hubbell on the mound and Mel Ott at the plate. Hubbell, who would eventually be elected the Most Valuable Player for that year, led the league with 26 wins, a winning percentage of .813, and an ERA of 2.31. He also had sixteen straight victories by season's end, the first time since Rube Marquard's streak of nineteen in 1912 that anyone had won sixteen or more in a row. Ott, meanwhile, had hit .328, led the league in home runs with 33, and finished three off the league lead in RBIs with 135.

Ott, it might be noted, led the Giants in home runs every year from 1928 through 1945.

Things had been lively that year on the northern banks of the Harlem River also. Two years earlier the New York Yankees had purchased Joe DiMaggio from the Pacific Coast League's San Francisco Seals for $25,000 and four players. The price would have been higher - at age eighteen Joe had hit in sixty-one (gasp!) straight games for the Seals in 1933 - had DiMaggio not injured his left knee in a freak taxi-cab accident in California. The Yankees left him in the Bay City for 1935, at which time he destroyed PCL pitchers at a .398 clip. In 1936, according to Jacob Ruppert and Ed Barrow, the Yankees' new chief operational officer, DiMaggio was ready for the big time.

The Yankees scored an astronomical 1,065 runs that year, more than three hundred more than the Giants. Yankee pitcher Red Ruffing hit .291 with 5 home runs. There wasn't a soft touch anywhere in the lineup. Often the pitcher's spot was dangerous, even beyond Ruffing. Watching the Yankees in operation, one gained the impression that even the groundskeeper could come off the bench, take a couple of pitches, then line a double to right. As a team they hit .300.

All of this figured prominently in the destiny of the New York Giants. The Yankees shocked no one by winning their pennant by 19.5 games, setting up a new Battle of Broadway. It was the first subway series - the fare was still a nickel, by the way - since 1923, and the town was agog over the upcoming spectacle.

There were two groups who were less than elated, however. First there were the Broadway bookies, who installed the Yankees as prohibitive favorites in the series. To place a wager on the Giants, you had to bet with your heart, never a good idea. Second were the Giants' pitchers, notably Hubbell, Schumacher, and Fitzsimmons, who would be in charge of cooling down the Yankee lumber.

Game One was played in a steady downpour at the Polo Grounds on September 30. Carl Hubbell opposed Red Ruffing. Selkirk of the Yankees and Rowdy Richard Bartell of the Giants traded solo home runs through the first five and a half innings. Then Gus Mancuso singled Ott home in the bottom of the sixth, giving the Giants a 2-1 lead.

Trouble came when the Yankees batted in the eighth. Crosetti doubled. Rolfe bunted safely when Hubbell, fielding the bunt, slipped on the wet infield turf. Hubbell then faced none other than the Yankee Clipper.

Hubbell worked on DiMaggio with low screwballs. DiMaggio found one he liked and smashed it. Burgess Whitehead, now a steady second baseman for the Giants, speared the ball, robbing DiMaggio. With a quick flip to Terry, he doubled Rolfe at first. Buoyed by the clutch fielding, Hubbell then induced Bill Dickey to ground to Terry, ending the inning. In the bottom of the same frame, the Giants, working with singles, walks, and an error, scratched out four runs. In an upset, the Giants led the Yankees, 1-0, in the Series.

The next day the spell was broken. The Yankees showed up at the Polo Grounds looking for blood. They found it in the third inning, chasing Freddie Fitzsimmons with seven runs, before a crowd of 43,543. Included among the spectators was President Roosevelt, whose campaign for a second term had brought him to Manhattan.

In an 18-4 Yankee triumph, Lazzeri had the big hit, a third-inning grand slam, and DiMaggio had the most sensational play. With two outs in the ninth, Hank Leiber hit a monstrous long line drive to the deepest part of center field. DiMaggio ran back, back, back, turned one way, then the other, then nailed the ball beyond the front screens of the bleachers and just in front of the steps to the clubhouse. The ball was 480 feet from home plate, but just as easily the Yankees had turned it into an out. Blithely, DiMaggio continued directly into the clubhouse, stopping only at the top of the steps in honor of the President, who was leaving via car across the outfield.

The President gave DiMaggio a salute. DiMaggio acknowledged.

At Yankee Stadium on October 3, 64,842 watched Game Three. This time Yankee pitching carried the day, 2-1, as Crosetti lined a ball off Fitzsimmons' glove in the eighth inning to score the winning run. The next day, 66,669 watched the Yankees win again. (The attendance set a World Series record for the second day in a row.) Hubbell was back and so was his screwball. But this time the Yankees solved it - if three runs in seven innings can be considered a solution. The Yanks won, 5-2.

Game Five was the best game of the Series, both from the Giants' view and from the view of the game itself.

Prince Hal Schumacher opposed Red Ruffing on a warm autumn day at Yankee Stadium. The Yankees went for the kill, but the Giants began the game with three runs in the first inning. Then the game seesawed until the top of the tenth. It remained tied, 4-4.

Then Jo-Jo Moore opened the tenth with a double. Bartell bunted him to third. Terry lifted a high fly to DiMaggio and Moore scored. When Schumacher held the Yankees in the bottom of the inning, the Series was a game closer at 3-2.

The Series returned to the Polo Grounds for Game Six. Those with their hearts in the Giants' camp mumbled hopefully about a stunning comeback. But these were, unfortunately, another magnificent assemblage of Yankees, certainly the equal of the powerhouses of the mid-1920s and early 1960s. No team had ever won four World Series in a row - none of Mack's great squads, none of McGraw's. But the New York Yankees were on their way toward doing it.

Freddie Fitzsimmons got the call again, with Lefty Gomez working for the Yankees. Ott doubled in two Giants runs in the first, but the Bronx Bombers chased Fitzsimmons with 5 runs in 3 2/3 innings. The Giants struggled back and had the tying runs on base in the seventh inning. But Yankee skipper Joe McCarthy pulled ace Johnny Murphy (who would later be the general manager of another

455

New York team called the Mets) out of the bullpen. Murphy retired the side. The Yankees then iced the Series in Yankee fashion. As diehard Giants fans streamed from the Polo Grounds, the sluggers from the Bronx battered Giants pitchers Dick Coffman (who didn't get anyone out) and Harry (Gunboat) Gumbert for seven runs in the ninth. The final score was 13-5. The Yankees won the World Series, four games to two.

"That club," said Bill Terry, shaking his head in the locker room after Game Six, "has everything. They're the toughest club I've ever faced." Just as McGraw had been magnanimous in defeat fourteen years earlier, Joe McCarthy was gracious in victory. "The Giants," McCarthy said of his underdog opponent, "are a much better team than people give them credit for. They gave us a whale of a battle."

Indeed, they had. Many experts saw a moral victory - if there are such things - in the two games the Giants had won from the Yankees. There was another ironic touch also. Just as McGraw had uttered about the old guard changing in 1923, so it was again. Travis Jackson's legs were gone. So were Terry's. Both would retire as players during that winter. (Both would also be elected to the Baseball Hall of Fame after too long a wait.) Though no one knew it at the time, Gehrig had hit his last World Series home run. Conversely the new guard, in the person of Joe DiMaggio, had arrived.

Then there was the final touch. The biggest Yankee bat of all had been carried by Jake Powell, the left fielder who had arrived from Washington in midseason for the aging Ben Chapman. Powell led all hitters with a .455 Series clip. Again no one knew it, but the Yankees had begun one of their lesser traditions: getting a key season or half season out of unexpected players. It was a mold into which such names as Enos (Country) Slaughter, George McQuinn, Nick Etten, Johnny Sain, Luis Arroyo, Bob Turley, and even Bobby Shantz would fit neatly in the future.

Chapter 61   24-0: 7-17-36 -> 5/17/37

"If I'm playing cards for pennies, I want to win."

Carl Hubbell

There were no significant personnel changes on the Giants over the winter of 1936-37. The only significant change in New York baseball came from the Brooklyn team. John Gorman, the Dodgers' general manager, had fired Casey Stengel as manager and hired Burleigh Grimes, the old spitballer. But that didn't keep the team off the sports pages.

Attention began to focus on Carl Hubbell's winning streak. Twenty-five years earlier, Rube Marquard had reeled off nineteen straight wins, all during the 1912 season. If Hubbell surpassed that total in early 1937, would the new streak supplant Marquard's in the record books?

Carl Hubbell himself was asked. "How the hell would I know?" he answered.

Demand grew for a ruling, particularly the following spring when Hubbell blanked the Braves 3-0 in his first start. Ford Frick, the president of the National League, was the man on the spot. Somehow Frick didn't like excitement to grow. He ruled that Marquard's record would stand no matter what Hubbell did. Consecutive wins, he reasoned, had to be all in one season. Promptly, much of the press lost interest in Hubbell's string of wins. Years later as commissioner, Frick would toss Roger Maris an asterisk under similar circumstances.

The Giants trained in Havana, a convenient circumstance for Adolfo Luque, a native of that city. Inconvenient was the presence of one Bob Feller with the Cleveland Indians, the club with which the Giants barnstormed north as a prelude to opening the season.

Previously the Giants had only heard about Feller. They hadn't seen him. When he was pitching against them, they had trouble seeing the ball also. Rapid Robert's delivery was *that* fast. Toward the end of the 1936 season, Feller had made headlines by striking out seventeen of Connie Mack's A's in an American League game. Seventeen was also Feller's age.

Two Giants who quickly became authorities on Feller were Dick Bartell and Hank Leiber. Bartell, after seeing the kid for the first time, made the mistake of commenting that several pitchers in the National League were "definitely faster." Feller proceeded to strike out Bartell thirteen of the eighteen times they faced each other. Leiber found out about the Feller speed a more difficult way. He was hit on the head with a Feller fastball in New Orleans. Leiber was lucky he wasn't killed, but recurring headaches stifled his effectiveness all season. There were no batting helmets in 1937.

The season began at Ebbets Field with Bartell being hit in the back with a tomato lobbed from the lower box seats. The Flatbush faithful cheered loudly as Rowdy Richard toweled off. Bartell made a mental note and dished out the receipt a few days later when the Dodger second baseman received a tag across the teeth while sliding into a base guarded by Bartell. The umpires stepped between them before the benches could clear.

The real fun started in St. Louis, however, under circumstances that boggle the imagination. Bartell was involved in this one, too. Burgess Whitehead was on second while Bartell batted. Dizzy Dean was pitching. Dean looked to second and threw to the plate. Bartell lifted a harmless fly to the outfield and was retired.

Or was he?

Umpire George Barr called a balk on the pitch, giving Bartell a second life. Angrily, Dean quick pitched Bartell as the at-bat continued. Bartell was ready and lined the ball to right fielder Pepper Martin. Martin was *not* ready and missed the ball, opening the door to a three-run rally.

Dean was furious. He exercised his temper by throwing at New York Giants baseball caps while the Giants hitters still had their heads in them. After several Giants had dropped like flies in the batter's box, and after the home plate umpire took a boys-will-be-boys attitude toward the events, crusty Giants' center fielder Johnny Ripple took matters into his own hands.

After being dropped, but not hit, by a pitch himself, he looked into the New York dugout as if to give his team a cue. "All right, you hillbilly bastard!" he shouted at Dean. "The next one is going down the first base line. Let's see if you have the guts to c o v e r."

The next pitch was bunted down the first base line. Dean

covered. But the ball was bunted too hard and went out toward second base, where Cardinal shortstop Jimmy Brown fielded it. Dean, who no longer belonged in the play, kept coming toward first, dead set on not being intimidated by Ripple. As if to see how much fun he could have with the play, Brown held the ball for an extra second, allowing Dean, the ball, first baseman Johnny Mize, and Ripple to all arrive at the same moment.

Crash.

Dean and Ripple, forgetting all about the play, plowed into each other simultaneously. Fists were flying before the players hit the ground. The Giants bench emptied, as did the Cardinal bench. As a side event, catchers Gus Mancuso and Mickey Owen squared off in their own private heavyweight match.

Eventually, umpires called in the St. Louis police to separate the players. Incredibly, Dean and Ripple were allowed to stay in the game, but Mancuso and Owen were booted. The next day Mancuso and Owen were fined by league president Frick, who, moving in his usual mysterious ways, declined to fine Dean and Ripple for instigating the brawl. And the only physical casualty was suffered by Don Gutteridge, the Cardinals' rookie third baseman, whose eye was blackened by contact with the fist of Dolf Luque, who may have been a coach but craved a good rumble.

Through all this, even when baseball fans were paying more attention to the fight results than the pitching performances, Carl Hubbell kept his winning streak intact. There was a 3-0 whitewashing of the Bees on April 23, and an 11-2 laugher against the Dodgers a week later.

Then, surprisingly enough, there was trouble against tail-end Cincinnati on May 4. Hubbell was coasting through the middle innings with a 7-0 lead when the magic failed. The screwball refused to jump, and the supernal control was gone. The win would have been his nineteenth straight, but it was slipping away. Hubbell allowed six runs and departed in the seventh with men on base. Disaster loomed. Then a relief specialist named Dick Coffman slammed the door on the Reds. It had seemed to be one of those games a man is destined to lose, but Hubbell emerged with the win.

Another three wins followed, all complete games. Then Dick Coffman appeared again to stifle a Pittsburgh insurrection with two out in the ninth. Hubbell's streak was at 23. Next there was a relief win against Cincinnati. By then it was clear: Hubbell might never lose another game in his life.

On a sweltering Memorial Day in 1937, the Giants had scheduled another episode in their annual gang war with the crosstown Dodgers. This time it took the form of a holiday doubleheader. It was an event. *By* twelve-thirty that day, the fire department of New York City had already closed the gates to the Polo Grounds. The police were busy turning back an estimated 25,000 ticketless fans; 61,756 would eventually jam the ballpark. By the time Carl Hubbell emerged from the Giants dugout to warm up - as if it were necessary on such a day - the standing-room crowd was bulging at all the barriers along the outfield grandstand. Some fans were actually nestled into the rafters of the upper deck. Every one of them seemed to scream at once when Hub threw his first pitch: a bad ball, far off the plate. Ominous. Then he threw three more.

An infield hit followed, then a sacrifice. Next, Dodger first baseman Buddy Hassett drove in a run on a ground ball. Well, so what? The Giants were good for a run. It was only when Long Tom Winsett, Brooklyn left fielder, boomed a triple off the left center field fence that thousands of Giants fans began to think the unthinkable: Hubbell didn't have it that day.

Yet Cookie Lavagetto fanned to end the inning. Hubbell blanked the Dodgers in the second. So it was only 2-0. If King Carl settled down, a comeback was well within reach. But then came the third inning.

It was a completely uncharacteristic performance. With one out and a man on, Hubbell hit one batter, then walked the next, loading the bases. Lavagetto cooperated again by popping out. Then to bat came a player named Paul Chervinko - not one of the big names around the league. He was a frightened, pudgy country kid from Trauger, Pennsylvania. He was catching his first major league game and seeing New York and the Polo Grounds for the first time as well. Chervinko would last exactly 42 games in the major leagues over two seasons. He would have 11 career hits and 5 career RBIs. He was exactly the type of inexperienced hitter that Hubbell normally ate alive. Chervinko smacked a line-drive single to right, scoring two runs and nudging the game out of the Giants' reach. When the bombardment continued in the fifth inning, Bill Terry mercifully pulled his ace pitcher. Enter Dick Coffman again. But by this time things were out of control. Giants fans gave Carl Hubbell a long, thundering roar of tribute and appreciation as he trudged to the clubhouse in center field. But the streak was over at 24.

The game ended, 10-3.

Before the second game, Hubbell graciously appeared again. He smiled and waved to the crowd during a prearranged presentation of his 1936 MVP award. Babe Ruth, who had retired as a player after the 1935 season, looking very benign and portly in a tan suit, handed the award to Hubbell. It made little difference that the Giants would win the nightcap, 5-4. What mattered was that the cops and firemen had barred the wrong people from the Polo Grounds that afternoon. It was the Brooklyn Dodgers who should have been locked out.

The Giants stayed close to the league lead into June, without actually taking it. Just before the trading deadline of June 15, they tried to acquire help. In a shocker that turned out poorly for New York, Freddie Fitzsimmons was sent across the bridge to Brooklyn. Literally. Fitzsimmons, downcast to the point of tears, took a taxi to the "other" ballpark the next day, He was, however, to have the last laugh. Freddie would win 47 games for the Dodgers and become a fan favorite in Flatbush, particularly in 1940 when he was 16-2. In return, all the Giants received was Tom (Rattlesnake) Baker. Baker, a Texan, would eventually win only 2 big league games for New York prior to his release in 1938. More than one wag suggested that Terry, on this deal at least, was "snake bit."

New York also acquired right-handed slugger Wally Berger from Boston, an attempt to compensate for the disability of Hank Leiber, who was still recovering from Feller's errant fast one. In another move they picked up, if that's the right term for it, Walter (Jumbo) Brown from Cincinnati. Brown was a relief pitcher whose nickname derived from the famous circus elephant of the same name. At six feet four and believed by some to be in excess of 300 pounds, Brown and the elephant, to the casual observer, appeared to be approximately the same size. Fortunately, on most occasions Brown pitched better than his namesake, though the elephant would have drawn more fans to the Polo Grounds.

Thereafter, Bartell and Mancuso both suffered injuries. Hubbell went into a mild slump following his long victory streak. Though the team had spent several days in first place, the Chicago Cubs nudged them aside and eventually moved seven games in front.

Thereupon Bill Terry silenced many of his critics. For years the press, even some of the New York press, had been sniping at Terry. While no one ever questioned his credentials as a player, as a manager he was called "too aloof" by one writer and "the most unpopular manager ever to win a pennant" by another. At some points the New York locker room had been closed to reporters as Terry warred with those who abused him in print. This, naturally, only worsened the situation and led to some inspired second-guessing of managerial decisions.

Now, however, Terry managed to pull the 1937 season out of the hat.

To beef up the hitting in the Giants' lineup, Terry moved Mel Ott to third base. Jimmy Ripple stayed in as a regular and Hank Leiber went back to center, headaches and all. The Cubs then helped, as Cub teams frequently do, by slipping into a long, lovely slump through the dog days of August. By September first, the New York Giants had slipped back into first place.

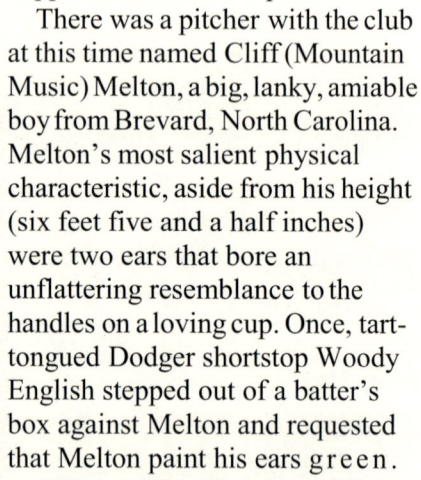

There was a pitcher with the club at this time named Cliff (Mountain Music) Melton, a big, lanky, amiable boy from Brevard, North Carolina. Melton's most salient physical characteristic, aside from his height (six feet five and a half inches) were two ears that bore an unflattering resemblance to the handles on a loving cup. Once, tart-tongued Dodger shortstop Woody English stepped out of a batter's box against Melton and requested that Melton paint his ears green.

"What for?" asked the guileless Melton, taking the set-up line.

"To give us a good batting background," said English. Melton, however, grinned good-naturedly and won the game.

He also won 19 other games that season and led the league with 7 saves, which is the point of the anecdote. It was Melton's best year as a big leaguer. Hubbell managed 22 wins, an ordinary year for him, but tops in the league. Harry Gumbert chipped in with 10 and Prince Hal contributed 13. Dick Coffman won 8 in relief and saved 3 more. Ott, as he did on five other occasions, led the league in home runs. In total, it was enough to win the flag by three games over the Cubs, whose August walkabout cost them the chance to get beaten up by the Yankees in the World Series.

Beaten up is exactly what happened.

Chapter 62   New York, New York

As Fall Classics go, this one was as unmemorable as any ever played. Most casual observers reasoned that it would matter very little what opponent was tossed into the ring with the Bronx Buzzsaw. The results would be the same.

Hubbell faced Lefty Gomez in Game One on October 6. The Yankees won it, Yankee-style, with seven runs in the sixth at Yankee Stadium. That inning even set the tone for the Giants' miseries in the matchup.

When Hubbell had already been pasted for six runs, Terry walked to the mound and pulled him from the game. He signaled to the bullpen in deep right field for Dick Coffman. Coffman, carrying his jacket over his shoulder, began the long hike to the mound.

As Coffman approached the infield, the public-address announcer boomed out the pitching change. But the pitcher announced as coming into the game was Harry Gumbert.

This astonished many people in particular. But among the most astonished, aside from Bill Terry, was Harry Gumbert, who had been relaxing in the Giants' dugout when he heard his name. He sprung to attention. He *was* in the game, though he hadn't warmed up for several days.

The source of the confusion was catcher Gus Mancuso.

Mancuso had mistakenly informed home plate umpire Red Ormsby that Terry was bringing Gumbert into the game. Terry actually wanted Coffman. But Mancuso's notification to Ormsby was official, even though it had been in error. Gumbert was thus surprised to find himself in the game.

Straight from the bench to the mound he went. He took his warm-up throws, then heaved a few balls to first base. Then he induced Tony Lazzeri, always a tough out, to ground the ball to Burgess

Whitehead at second. Whitehead kept the Yankee rally going by allowing the ball to scoot through his legs. Then Coffman came in and allowed the final Yankee to run of the day.

Against this fine edition of the New York Yankees, it didn't matter who was pitching. The next day, again at the Stadium, the Yankees leaped upon Melton, Gumbert, and Coffman for eight runs, to win, 8-1, behind Red Ruffing. Game Three was at the Polo Grounds, and the Giants were never in this one either, losing, 5-1.

Ruth was gone, sure. But Murderers' Row was alive and well. Joe DiMaggio had come of age that year, with a .346 average and a league leading 46 home runs. Gehrig, his health still intact, hit .351 with 37 home runs. In comparison, Bill Dickey was a sure out at .322 and 29 home runs.

Hubbell stopped the juggernaut in Game Four, making his last World Series appearance but riding a six-run Giants second to a 7-3 win. The next day, in Game Five, the Giants' hopes flickered for a few moments when Ott hit a two-run home run to overcome an early Yankee lead. But the Yankees came back with two runs in the fifth against Cliff Melton, ears and all. It was over. And the next year the National League (represented by the Cubs) would win *no* games over the Yankees. The whole thing was probably summed up most accurately by sportswriter Joe Williams in the New York *World-Telegraph.* Williams wrote after the Series: "The turning point came when the Yankees suited up for the first game."

Actually, there was a turning point in New York baseball during the Series, but it had nothing to do with the Yankees and the Giants. The Dodgers traded four healthy players - Jim Bucher, Johnny Cooney, Roy Henshaw, and Joe Stripp - to the St. Louis Cardinals for a fading, thirty-four-year-old shortstop named Leo Durocher.

The trade was all the more an oddity since Babe Ruth was currently employed as a coach for the Dodgers. Ruth and Durocher still hated each other. Somehow, the Babe's watch had never turned up.

Durocher would bat .219 as the Dodger shortstop in 1938, but he was obviously being groomed for other things, much to the mutual dismay of Burleigh Grimes, who already managed Brooklyn, and of Ruth, who wanted to.

The same year saw the beginning of a long slide at the Polo

Grounds. Yes, the Giants were coming off two pennants, but the Yankees swaggered astride New York baseball. Soon, as the Yankees again crashed through the American League, the Giants were struggling to keep their own heads above water.

Hal Schumacher's rickety pitching motion eventually took its toll on his fine arm. There were fragments of bone in his elbow. Melton's arm cooled down. He won only 14 and lost as many. Stoically, quiet and dependable Harry Gumbert won 15, but the great Hubbell had an ailing wing also. Ty Cobb's prophecy about the screwball was coming true after all those years. The left arm hurt. There was a bone chip in the joint. Hub won only 13. The team finished third, five games back, and watched from a safe distance as Joe McCarthy's Bombers smashed the Chicago Cubs. Later that same month Orson Welles shocked part of the country with his Mercury Theatre broadcast adaptation of H. G. Wells' *The War of the Worlds*. "Shocked" is a polite way of saying that some segments of the listening audience were dumb enough to think the Martian invasion was actual news coverage.

The winter of 1938-39 was the end of that peculiar era between the two world wars. It was a time of change and tumult, even in baseball. Burleigh Grimes was at last fired in Brooklyn, and when the smoke cleared Leo the Lip was the new manager of the Dodgers.

Not only was Europe on the brink of war, but so were the three New York ball clubs, a situation made worse by shifting balances of leadership. As long ago as 1935, radio broadcasts in other cities had fed fan interest and increased the turn of the turnstile. The three New York clubs had opposed radio, but now Larry MacPhail of the Dodgers was giving it another thought. By mutual consent, the three clubs had stayed off the radio for the five years from 1935 to 1940. But MacPhail announced that he would no longer honor that pledge. The Dodgers, who had brought night baseball to New York in 1938, would put their games on the air in 1939.

Eddie Brannick, the Giants' secretary, was furious. He countered that if the Dodgers followed through on their threat, he would put the Giants' games on the most powerful transmitter he could find and, in his words, "blast the Brooklyns into oblivion."

Brannick's mistake here was making the threat instead of just doing as promised. MacPhail quickly enlisted General Mills to sponsor Dodger games on WOR radio. Then he hired the best play-by-play man in the game, Red Barber, who had been doing games for the

Cincinnati Reds since 1934 and the World Series since 1935. Now MacPhail had the best transmitter, an excellent sponsor, and the premier broadcaster, though some of Barber's Southern inflections were received in Brooklyn as a foreign language might be. Now MacPhail was ready to blast the other two clubs into oblivion.

But the Yankees and Giants quickly took a "me too" position on the radio. Mel Allen and Arch MacDonald were hired to cover all home games except those on Sundays. Radio station WABC was to be the means of conveyance.

But even by then, MacPhail had greater things in mind. On August 26 he added to a growing list of Dodger firsts by installing a single television camera on the third base side of the second deck in Ebbets Field. NBC carried the game, and Red Barber moved over from the radio booth to do some commentary. Ivory Soap, Mobilgas, and Wheaties chipped in with commercials. The visiting Cincinnati club chipped in with a 5-2 win.

Never mind that out there in "television land," as 1950's TV host Jack Paar would eventually call it, there were no more than a few hundred sets. The game was piped to the press box where a receiver was set up and where the press corps could ogle the future. Another set was placed at the RCA exhibition a few miles away at the New York World's Fair. There the telecast was such a hit that the exhibition had to close its doors to keep the crowd away.

August of 1939 was, of course, the month when the war in Europe broke out for real. But to make matters worse for Giants fans, their team was going in the same direction as the rest of the planet: the wrong direction. For a while the Dodgers, riding the crest of MacPhail's gift for promotion and Durocher's talent for kicking his players along, were as high as second place. The Giants at the time were in seventh.

"I'm sure," grumbled Bill Terry, "that Mr. Durocher feels as out of place as I do."

But Mr. Durocher didn't. The Dodgers fell back a bit but finished third, a successful season. It was all the more successful (and enjoyable) because the Giants, their tormentors for all these years, had become mired in the second division. New York finished fifth, and no one was giggling at the Dodgers any longer.

Within another year, as the collapse became all the more apparent. Horace Stoneham quickly shelled out $125,000 to equip the Polo Grounds for night baseball. But the ball that was played there would have been better left in the darkness. Even shrewd Bill

Terry couldn't reverse the slide.

The events of August 7, 1940, at the Polo Grounds served as an unintentional metaphor for the times. This was Mel Ott Night, an evening of appreciation for the little slugger, now in his fifteenth year with the Giants.

On a table inlaid with the number 4, Mel's uniform number on the Giants, several gifts were assembled. The focal point was a sterling silver tea service of two hundred and some pieces, as well as a set of golf clubs, which was probably much more useful. It was almost as if they were retiring Mel, which they weren't, though it had uncharitably been suggested many times in the press that Master Melvin was slipping

It was also something of a nostalgia night. Carl Hubbell, aging and on the way to another 11-win season, pitched. Freddie Fitzsimmons, undergoing a joyous new life with the Dodgers, hurled for the Brooklyn opposition. Gus Mancuso, the ex-Giant, caught. Nostalgia all around. But the Dodgers also won the regularly scheduled game, 8-4. The Bums from Flatbush even shelled poor Carl Hubbell, part of the new order of things.

Through it all, Ott looked uneasy. Maybe he had his suspicions about the decade that was to follow. Then again, if he had known for sure what was in store for the New York Giants, he might have fled completely.

Seventh Inning Stretch – Rolfe Humphries

Chances are, you're never heard of Rolfe Humphries.

George Rolfe Humphries was an American poet, translator and teacher. He graduated cum laude from Amherst College in 1915. He served as a First Lieutenant who commanded a machine gun unit in France in World War One. Later, he was a teacher of Latin in secondary schools in San Francisco, New York City, and Long Island through 1957. Thereafter, he taught at Amherst College and at many poetry and creative writing workshops.

Humphries is probably not on your baseball shelf, but he may be somewhere else in your library. In the seven and a half decades that comprised his life, he published seven books of original poetry and eight volumes of translations.

Remote stuff? Not entirely.

Humphries' translation of Virgil's *Aeneid* has sold more than a quarter of a million copies since 1951 when Scribner's first published it. It was deemed, "a formidable work" by W. H. Auden. His 1960 translation of Ovid's *Metamorphosis* from Latin to English is still considered the definitive translation nearly sixty years later. Ezra Pound reportedly ranked Humphries' Ovid translations as "essential to the pursuit of a liberal education."

But Humphries was also a diehard baseball fan. One of his poems ruminated upon a game between the Giants and the Dodgers at the Polo Grounds. The poem first appeared in *The New Yorker* of August 22, 1942.

The work includes many players on the 1942 Giants, several of the Dodgers and many of the great Giants stars from previous eras.

Give it a look.

Polo Grounds

Time is of the essence. This is a highly skilled
And beautiful mystery. Three or four seconds only
From the time that Riggs connects till he reaches first,
And in those seconds Jurges goes to his right,
Comes up with the ball, tosses to Witek at second,
For the force on Reese, Witek to Mize at first,
In time for the out—a double play.
(Red Barber crescendo. Crowd noises, obbligato;
Scattered staccatos from the peanut boys,
Loud in the lull, as the teams are changing sides) . . .
Hubbell takes the sign, nods, pumps, delivers—
A foul into the stands. Dunn takes a new ball out,
Hands it to Danning, who throws it down to Werber;
Werber takes off his glove, rubs the ball briefly,
Tosses it over to Hub, who goes to the rosin bag,
Takes the sign from Danning, pumps, delivers—
Low, outside, ball three. Danning goes to the mound,
Says something to Hub, Dunn brushes off the plate,
Adams starts throwing in the Giant bullpen,
Hub takes the sign from Danning, pumps, delivers,
Camilli gets hold of it, a long fly to the outfield,
Ott goes back, back, back, against the wall, gets under it,
Pounds his glove, and takes it for the out.
That's all for the Dodgers. . . .
Time is of the essence. The rhythms break,
More varied and subtle than any kind of dance;
Movement speeds up or lags. The ball goes out
In sharp and angular drives, or long slow arcs,
Comes in again controlled and under aim;
The players wheel or spurt, race, stoop, slide, halt,
Shift imperceptibly to new positions,
Watching the signs according to the batter,
The score, the inning. Time is of the essence.
Time is of the essence. Remember Terry?
Remember Stonewall Jackson, Lindstrom, Frisch,
When they were good? Remember Long George Kelly?
Remember John McGraw and Benny Kauff?

> Remember Bridwell, Tenney, Merkle, Youngs,
> Chief Meyers, Big Jeff Tesreau, Shufflin' Phil?
> Remember Mathewson, Ames, and Donlin,
> Buck Ewing, Rusie, Smiling Mickey Welch?
> Remember a left-handed catcher named Jack Humphries,
> Who sometimes played the outfield, in '83?
> Time is of the essence. The shadow moves
> From the plate to the box, from the box to second base,
> From second to the outfield, to the bleachers.
> Time is of the essence. The crowd and players
> Are the same age always, but the man in the crowd
> Is older every season. Come on, play ball!

Humphries addresses the distinct noises, patterns, and influence of the crowd throughout the game of baseball. He mentions that time is important. He must feel that way because he tells us six times. He also sees the game as something of a concert; he employs musical terms such as "obbligato", "crescendo", and "staccatos" to describe the sound levels and patterns of the crowd during different parts of the game.

He presents us with a double play, always a good thing when the Giants were on defense, Jurges to Witek to Mize. He reminds us that it only took "three or four seconds."

Nonetheless, time is passing. Names come and go. The sport doesn't grow old and our memories stay with us. "Remember John McGraw and Benny Kauff? Remember Bridwell, Tenney, Merkle, Youngs, Chief Meyers, Big Jeff Tesreau, Shufflin' Phil? Remember Mathewson…Smiling Mickey Welch? Remember a left-handed catcher named Jack Humphries…?"

John "Jack" Humphries (seen here) was the poet's father, who played 49 games for the Giants in 1883 and 1884 and who died in 1933. Notice the shadow moving across the field at the end of the poem. From "the plate to the box". The "box" representing a coffin, perhaps, the shadow representing an eventual death? A double play in baseball takes but a few seconds. The game is languid. Players come and go and time passes for all of us. So as we age, let us not waste time.

"Come on. Play ball!" he exhorts us.

Rolfe Humphries, this guy who was a teacher of creative writing at Amherst, Smith and Dartmouth, was a complicated man. He was one of the preeminent Latin scholars of his time, but he had a personal lexicon that could make a sailor blush. And his fascination with football gridirons, baseball diamonds and horse racing tracks constantly pulled him away from academia. *Time* Magazine commissioned him to write a full-page poem on the reopening of Belmont Park race track in 1968. "Riders up! the bugle sounds First Call ...," Humphries wrote with enthusiasm. Makes you want to rush to the $50 win window and play a 12-1 long shot, doesn't it?

He also helped lead a major literary effort on behalf of the anti-Franco Loyalists in the Spanish Civil War. He was the main organizer of a fund-raising volume, *...And Spain Sings. Fifty Loyalist Ballads* (1937). He translated two volumes of poetry of Federico García Lorca, the brilliant Spanish poet and playwright murdered at the beginning of that war and a symbol of the intellectual life that Spain lost.

Humphries may be best remembered for a notorious literary prank.

Somewhere along the years, Humphries locked horns with a man named Nicholas Murray Butler. Butler was an American philosopher, diplomat and educator. He was President of Columbia University from 1902 to 1943. He was also a recipient of the Nobel Peace Prize. He was so well known that the New York *Times* printed his Christmas greeting to American people every year and he was so full of himself that he actually wrote such a thing. The Butler Library at Columbia is named after him.

He was also viewed as an autocrat at Columbia and was widely disliked by many faculty members. To be blunt, they considered him an obnoxious stuffed shirt.

In 1939 *Poetry* Magazine asked Rolfe Humphries, no fan of Butler, to contribute a piece of new poetry to their magazine. Humphries complied. He wrote 39 lines which the magazine published. The work contained an acrostic: The first letters of each line spelled out Humphries feelings toward Butler. "Nicholas Murray Butler is a horse's ass," it read. The editor later printed an apology and Humphries was banned from the publication until 1941.

But back to baseball, not a moment too soon.

To an aspiring young poet concerned about the monotony of his text, Humphries once wrote, "In prosodic terms… in a dominantly iambic pentameter poem, you would once in a while break the cadence with a trochaic trimester or put in a good long rest instead of a foot, or do as Shakespeare did in that opening speech of *Twelfth Night*…."

But Humphries also described the solution this way in the same correspondence:

"Don't fire every ball over the plate with the same speed, at the same height, over the same corner; take a little off the pitch, move the ball around, change up on 'em every once in a while."

Rolfe Humphries, a baseball guy from his youth to his final days, died of emphysema on April 22, 1969 in Redwood City, California. His private papers remain archived at Amherst College.

PART FOUR:

THE GRIM WORLD WAR

TWO YEARS

Chapter 63   Another World War

> "Hermie had done all that could humanly be done with the small bedroom in the bungalow that had been allotted to him. One wall, the one with the window, he decorated with autographed pictures of Mel Ott, Johnny Rucker, and Hank Danning because he was a Giant fan. All the autographs were forged because the Giants were in New York and Hermie lived in Brooklyn, and to wait till the Giants came to Brooklyn and then to have the audacity to be seen asking the Giants for autographs - it was much too risky."
>
> -Herman Raucher,
> *Summer of '42*

In October of 1940, fourteen months after the war had begun in Europe and fourteen months before the attack on Pearl Harbor, the United States began forming its Army for World War Two. On October 16, every American male between the ages of twenty-one and thirty-six was required to register for the Selective Service. Included were several thousand men under contract to major and minor league baseball clubs. But since President Roosevelt had vowed to do everything possible to keep the United States out of a European war, many looked on registration as a formality: patriotic duty, perhaps, but a formality nonetheless.

Selection to the Armed Forces was done by lottery, with a man's likelihood of being drafted increasing with the ranking of his lottery number.

Two men who registered on October 16 realized on November 18, the day the lottery numbers were drawn and assigned by birthdate, that registration would soon turn into more than a formality. They were Hugh Mulcahy, the Phillies' beleaguered pitcher, and Hank Greenberg, the Detroit slugger. Greenberg had blasted 58 home runs in 1938, just two seasons previously, and at age twenty-nine he was one of the prevailing stars of the game.

Mulcahy was a good pitcher, though his entry in *The Baseball Encyclopedia* doesn't indicate this. A tall, strong right-hander from

Brighton, Massachusetts (who much later in life became a fine instructor of minor league pitchers in the Chicago White Sox organization), Mulcahy had the misfortune of being called up to the Phillies in 1935.

Over the years that followed, he became the workhorse of a poor pitching staff on an equally poor baseball club. It was still the policy of Phils' owner Gerry Nugent to finance his club's operations by peddling his best players elsewhere, such as to the Dodgers and the Giants. Under such astute management, the Phillies finished no higher than seventh from 1933 through 1945. One of the victims of this policy was Mulcahy.

Over the course of four seasons, from 1937 through 1940, Mulcahy pitched in 176 games for the Phils. Blessed with their usual support, he was awarded the loss in 76 of them. Don't get the idea that he won the other 100. Mulcahy came away from this stint in sports purgatory with 40 wins, an achievement in itself. The suffering inflicted on the valiant Mulcahy was so thorough that "Losing Pitcher" was repeated by sports commentators and stadium announcers so often with his name tacked onto it - as in "Losing Pitcher, Mulcahy"- that it became *part* of his name.

Losing Pitcher Mulcahy - just like Babe Ruth or Catfish Hunter or Stan the Man Musial.

Thus it was not without irony that the twenty-seven year old Mulcahy, on March 8, 1941, became the first major league ball player drafted into the United States Army. Mulcahy was set to leave his Massachusetts home to report to spring training with the Phillies at Miami Beach, Florida, when the induction notice arrived.

Mulcahy went willingly to the Army, announcing, "I will do my best." What could basic training or the war in Europe hold in store that could have been any worse than pitching for the Phillies? With another touch of irony that was probably unintentional, the Phillies eventually decorated the cover of their 1941 scorecard with a picture of Mulcahy holding two bats arranged in-of all things-a *V* (for-victory) symbol.

Mulcahy ended up taking a four-year detour away from the major leagues that pretty much put an end to his professional baseball career. Mulcahy was assigned to Camp Edwards, near Cape Cod, Massachusetts, for infantry training. His time there ended on December 5, 1941. Two days later Japan attacked Pearl Harbor and Mulcahy was back in the Army. Eventually, he was assigned to New Guinea and the Philippines. He rose to the rank of Master

Sergeant.

He never saw combat, but dysentery struck him in 1945 in the Philippines. He lost 30 pounds. He was discharged in July with a Bronze Star. While he eventually made it back to the major leagues, he was never an effective pitcher again. Some observers called him the most talented but unluckiest pitcher ever to play.

Mulcahy, spoke to a writer named John Perrotto before his death in 2001 at age 87. Mulcahy didn't see himself as having been unlucky. "I don't look back on it with any anger or bitterness," said Mulcahy.

After retirement as a player, he spent three decades in baseball as a scout and minor league manager and coach. He also had a one-year stint as the pitching coach for the Chicago White Sox in 1970.

"Our country was at war," he recalled, "and that was more important than baseball… You didn't think twice about it, though, because you are doing your duty by serving your country. A lot of guys went to the war and didn't come back. I came back and had a long career in baseball. I feel I was fortunate, not cheated."

On May 8, 1942, however, events took a more serious turn when Greenberg became the second major league player inducted.

The loss of Greenberg, the 1940 American League MVP, dropped Detroit from first place to fifth in 1941, while the Phils, without Mulcahy, finished last. The only other losses to the military were three part-time players, outfielder Joe Gallagher of Brooklyn, and pitchers Oad Swigart and Johnny Rigney, of Pittsburgh and the Chicago White Sox, respectively. Outfielder Morrie Arnovich of the Giants tried to get into the action by volunteering but was rejected because he was missing a pair of occluding molars, a physical attribute he demonstrated to reporters by pulling out his false teeth shortly after his rejection. When the United States finally entered the war, recruiters were not so choosy. Arnovich didn't need molars to pull a trigger, and he eventually served for three years. He would return to the Giants for one game in 1946.

In the end, the 1941 Giants baseball season proved to be a repeat of the mediocre 1940 season, as well as a harbinger of the lean war years to follow. The Giants were eight and a half games behind by Memorial Day, nine games back by the Fourth of July, and sixteen games behind by mid-August. There was a good pennant race going on between the Dodgers and the Cardinals, but the Giants only read about it in the newspapers.

There were, however, more serious world events upon the

horizon, and they seemed to intersect with the downward turn in the New York Giants' fortunes, a turn that would run through the decade.

On May 27 President Roosevelt addressed the nation in one of his fireside chats. This one discussed a national "emergency" and proclaimed the American intention to stand up to further Nazi efforts to interfere with American shipping to Europe. At the Polo Grounds, umpire Jocko Conlon stopped a game with the Braves and the entire stadium sat for three quarters of an hour as Roosevelt's patrician radio voice boomed from the speakers atop the center field clubhouse. Players sat in the dugouts and on the steps to the clubhouse and listened.

Several weeks later, a bit more arbitrarily, a game against the Pirates at Forbes Field was stopped in the fourth inning so that Iron City fans could listen to fight news of a different sort. Pittsburgh's Billy Conn was spending that evening trading punches with Joe Louis in front of 54,800 people at, of all places, the Polo Grounds. Pirate management had promised to broadcast the boxing in the ballpark. Conn, the Irish light heavyweight champ went into the fight at 174 against the baddest heavyweight on the planet, Joe Louis, who weighed 199.5.

Many fans wondered if Louis still had the clout which made him one of the most feared heavyweight champions of all time. In the first two rounds Louis launched a brutal attack on Conn. But Conn stayed on his feet.

As the fight wore on, Conn steadied his own attack. By the middle rounds, Conn was using his superior speed and lightning punches to draw even with Louis. By the end of the 8th round Louis appeared to be tiring.

By Round Ten, Conn was ahead on points. At times Louis appeared to be befuddled by Conn's speed. In the eleventh round the crowd began to sense that Conn may actually be able to pull off what would be one of the hugest upsets in boxing history. The 12th round saw more of the same as Conn began to pile on what appeared to be an insurmountable lead. Toward the end of the 12th round "The Pittsburgh Kid" staggered Louis and had him holding on at the bell. Conn's seconds tried to calm him down between rounds and implored him not to trade punches with Louis in the 13th round.

Conn, however, had visions of knocking out the great

heavyweight champion. That was not to be. The 13th round turned into a brawl. For a while Billy held his own. Then The Brown Bomber caught Conn with a paralyzing right hand to the jaw that appeared to freeze him. Louis followed with a wicked left hook to the body. A series of lefts and rights followed and Conn fell to the canvas where he was counted out.

The Ring Magazine still ranks the 1941 Louis vs. Conn fight as the sixth greatest title fight of all-time. Along with the Dempsey-Firpo bout and the Greb-Walker fight, it was probably the third greatest fight at the Polo Grounds during the Giants' tenure.

But one listener who was not terribly pleased was Bill Terry at Forbes Field, particularly after the ball game went to eleven innings tied at 1-1 after a thirteen round fight. Baseball was stopped by a midnight curfew.

Terry was losing patience with everything, but the Louis-Conn broadcast particularly ticked him off. A presidential address, *yes*. But a prizefight? Come on....

"Next time," he growled, "they might as well hold up the game to listen to Jack Benny or Bob Hope." Fortunately, Los Angeles was not yet in the league.

The team collapsed completely in August, winning two games and losing eleven on a swing through the western cities. With the club in Pittsburgh, Terry hinted to the sportswriters that he was thinking of resigning. He was, but Horace Stoneham talked him out of it. Then the club dropped into the second division to stay.

In the closing days of the season, some names of the future turned up in box scores. Dave Koslo, at age twenty-one, won his first game as a Giant. Sid Gordon singled in his first plate appearance and was promptly picked off first a few minutes later. Gordon had been born in the Brownsville section of Brooklyn in 1917. His father had emigrated from Russia and became a plumber and a coal dealer in the United States. Sid graduated from to Samuel Tilden High School and drove a few of his father's coal trucks before his baseball career took off. In Gordon's first game with the Giants, he was one of four Jewish players in the line-up, the others being Morrie Arnovich in the outfield, Harry Feldman pitching and Harry Danning catching.

A husky young outfielder named Babe Barna came up from Minneapolis billed as Ott's eventual successor. He homered in his first time at bat but hit only .214 in 10 games. There was no one anywhere to get excited about. There was, on the contrary, much to disturb a Giants fan.

Hubbell won only 11 games that season and was nearing the end. Ott hit 27 home runs but also showed signs of fading. Bill McGee, a consistent winner for St. Louis, won only 2 of 11 decisions while the consistent Harry Gumbert had gone 11-5 for the Cardinals.

Manager Bill Terry kept making noises about wanting out. Already out were Jumbo Brown, the 300-pound reliever, and former Cubs catcher and manager Gabby Hartnett, both unceremoniously dumped at the close of the schedule.

Worse, when the campaign was complete, the Giants finished fifth, six and a half games out of the first division. Pittsburgh, managed by the old Fordham Flash himself, Frankie Frisch, finished one notch higher. Even more mortifying was the presence of the Brooklyn Dodgers in the World Series for the first time since the days of Uncle Robbie, he of the dropped grapefruit from Ruth Law, the enchanting aviatrix.

In 1939 the Dodgers had amassed six straight losing seasons. But the new manager, Leo Durocher had reversed things. The Dodgers had also purchased a young shortstop, Pee Wee Reese, from the Boston Red Sox. Reese impressed Durocher so much that he gave up his spot as the regular shortstop so Reese could get a chance to play. In his third season as manager, Leo led the 1941 Dodgers to a 100–54 record and the National League pennant, their first in 21 years. Led by Pete Reiser and Dolf Camilli, Brooklyn battled with St. Louis for the entire season before overtaking Branch Rickey's Cardinals late in September and winning the flag by two and a half games. All this was for the privilege of being trashed by the Yankees in the World Series, 4-1.

A pantheon of stars led the Bronx team: Bill Dickey, Phil Rizzuto, Red Rolfe, Red Ruffing, Tommy Henrich, Charlie Keller, Lefty Gomez, Spud Chandler, and a San Francisco-born outfielder who had hit in 56 straight games that year. Let's face it. The Dodgers - who hit .182 in the Series - would have been blown out even if catcher Mickey Owen hadn't famously been crossed up on the third strike to Henrich.

On the first day of December, owner Horace Stoneham and club treasurer Leo Bondy found themselves in Jacksonville, Florida, attending the minor league meetings. They had major league business on their minds, however.

The New York newspapers were filled with reports that Bill Terry was about to become the only living ex-Giant manager. Either Dick

Bartell or Bill Jurges, the stories went, would succeed Memphis Bill.

The fact was, Stoneham and Bondy had decided to replace Terry but were at a loss for a way to do it graciously. Stoneham was, in the end, a man who treated his employees like family members. No matter what disputes he may have had with Memphis Bill, Stoneham wasn't about to heave him out on his ear.

Terry traveled to Jacksonville and huddled with Stoneham and Bondy. At about the same time, Mel Ott left his home in Metairie, Louisiana, to converge on the same spot.

Ott was disgruntled also. He felt he was facing a pay cut off his previous season's performance. He also felt that management was rushing the Barna kid along, acting too anxious to find a new right fielder. Eventually Ott walked into Stoneham's hotel suite in Jacksonville to hash out these issues. He found Stoneham, Bondy, and Terry waiting for him.

The discussion Ott had envisioned never took place. "I have a new job for you, at more money," Stoneham said as Ott arrived. Then Stoneham grinned at Terry and informed Ott what the job was: manager of the New York Giants.

Just as Terry had stood in disbelief before John J. McGraw a decade earlier, Ott now stood incredulously before Stoneham. When Stoneham finished, Ott looked to Terry, then back to Stoneham. "You aren't kidding, are you?" he asked.

Terry eased the situation along. "Go on, son, take it," he said. "I want you to take it."

"I guess a fellow couldn't refuse a chance like this, could he?" Ott finally said. He agreed, then sank back into a chair.

The news was released to the press on December 2. Ott was only the third Giant manager since 1902. Terry finally moved into the front office, now in charge of the Giants' minor league and scouting operations. Of course, five days later, the whole matter got shoved to remote sections of the newspapers as the Japanese dropped some bombshells of their own on Pearl Harbor.

Thus, almost simultaneously, the world was again at war and the Giants had new leadership. Everyone knew baseball would be greatly affected by the war and that almost all able-bodied players would be going into the service. Nonetheless, four days later, Ott pulled off the first major trade of his regime, sending catcher Ken O'Dea, first baseman Johnny McCarthy, pitcher Bill Lohrman, and a check for $50,000 to St. Louis for Johnny Mize, "The Big Cat," the soft-spoken Georgian with the sweet, powerful swing. Ott, who held the National League record for career home runs at the time with 511, insisted that the Giants make a deal for the 28-year-old slugger.

Mize had one season in a Giants uniform (.305 average, 26 homers, and a league-leading 110 RBIs) before going into the United States Navy. He served for three prime years, and as has been suggested about many baseball stars of that era, there's no telling how stellar his Hall of Fame numbers might have been had his career not been interrupted.

"I know what kind of baseball New Yorkers want and I promise to give it to them," Ott said not long after the Mize trade. What he meant was winning baseball. What he also meant was baseball in his own mold: slugging. The trade for Mize was interpreted in New York as a signal that Horace Stoneham would not take kindly to being the one New York team out of three to be excluded from the World Series. It was known that Brooklyn was trying to land Mize also. Giant fans were elated to have acquired the Big Cat right under the nose of Dodger president Larry MacPhail.

One deal that the Giants didn't manage to complete would have changed baseball history. The St. Louis Cardinals had a twenty-year-old kid at Springfield, Missouri with a kinky left-handed batting stance that they thought could be effective at the Polo Grounds. They offered $40,000. Branch Rickey, who was running the Cardinals, was close to taking the deal. But Sam Breadon, the owner, had reservations. Breadon had become a self-made millionaire as the owner of Pierce-Arrow auto dealerships in the first decades of the Twentieth Century. He hadn't become rich by making poor decisions. He made another good one here and nixed the Giants' offer. Thus Stan Musial would remain a Cardinal and would do twenty years of damage at the Polo Grounds and Ebbets Field as a highly respected visitor.

On December 5, 1941, as Master Melvin was still getting over the shock of being appointed to Jim Mutrie's old job, Hank Greenberg was discharged from the Armed Forces. Greenberg was the beneficiary of a revised Selective Service regulation which permitted draftees twenty-eight years of age or older to cut short their time of service. Greenberg at the time was a month shy of his thirty-first birthday. Two days later Pearl Harbor was bombed. Greenberg promptly reenlisted, trading his $50,000-a-year job as Detroit first baseman for that of a sergeant in the U. S. Army, at sixty bucks a month, plus all the bullets he could duck.

Making a similar gesture at exactly the same time was twenty-three-year-old Bob Feller. It is difficult today to understand how Feller had captivated the American public, coming out of the heartland of America in the years following the Depression with a fastball reminiscent of Walter Johnson's. In an age when $10,000 was a laudable salary, Feller too drew $50,000 a year to play baseball. Though perceived as barely more than an adolescent at the time of Pearl Harbor, Feller already had won 107 American League games, lost 54, and had whiffed 1,233 batters. His graduation from high school in 1937 - a year after he had first pitched for the Cleveland Indians - had been broadcast live on radio. He was, without question, one of the most recognizable athletes in America. Thus, when Bob Feller enlisted in the Navy on December 9, this too was broadcast live to the nation, as well as shown on movie newsreels across the country.

The enlistments of Greenberg and Feller set the moral tone of the day, as concerned organized baseball's attitude toward the war. There were no publicized gaffes such as the one that had occurred during the war preparedness days of 1918 when Cub pitcher Harry Weaver, as reported then by *The Sporting News,* asked for a deferment from his Warren, Pennsylvania, draft board on the grounds that the Cubs had "a chance to win the pennant."

Indeed, by early 1942 the only real question facing the American and National leagues was whether they would be allowed to play at all. Seeking guidance, Judge Landis scribbled a handwritten note to President Roosevelt on January 15. In part, it said:

"Baseball is about to adopt schedules, sign players, make vast commitments, go to training camps. What do you want it to do? If you believe we ought to close down for the duration of the war, we are ready to do so immediately. We await your order."

FDR's orders came back a day or two later. The first line of the response was all that really mattered. The President wrote, "I honestly feel that it would be best for the country to keep baseball going."

So the game, with conspicuous absences, continued.

Chapter 64   Ninety-Six and A Final Curtain

> **"You know how I really feel? I feel like a baseball team going into the ninth inning with only eight men left to play."**
>
> **Franklin D Roosevelt in 1944**

Two men doomed to suffer aftershocks from the attack on Pearl Harbor were Donald Barnes, president of the St. Louis Browns, and his general manager, Bill DeWitt. The Browns had, by this point in their history, become the prototype for a bad, failing franchise. Sharing Sportsman's Park with the more successful Cardinals, the Browns had the worst facilities in major league baseball. The lockers were not air-conditioned, showers resembled standpipes, and the infield was habitually reduced to a dust bowl by July. They also had the smallest fan base.

For a game at the end of the 1933 season, the paid attendance was 34, meaning there were more players in the park than spectators. For the 1935 season, the Browns drew less than 85,000 fans. And by 1939, the home attendance had climbed no higher than 109,000, an average of approximately 1,400 hardy souls per home game. No wonder that the grounds crew, according to legend, occasionally didn't cover the field when midsummer rainstorms began. They just let the rain fall. That way everyone could go home.

Remember the old jingle that Senator fans used to recite about their team?

Washington: "First in war, first in peace, and last in the American League"? Browns fans, presumably all 34 of them, had their own version, playing on their city's fame for manufacturing quality footwear and good beer. "First in shoes," it went, "first in booze, and last in the American League." And while it was evident that St. Louis and Washington couldn't occupy last place at the same time, particularly with Connie Mack's miserable bargain-basement A's in the same league, those three teams annually maneuvered in a somber holding pattern of incompetence around the league's low rent district, maintaining a stranglehold on the league's bottom three places for a frightening number of years.

Sitting astride such a franchise, Barnes and DeWitt hatched out a solution that was years ahead of its time. They would move the club to Los Angeles for the 1942 season. Southern California had been clamoring for major league baseball for some time and had well received McGraw's teams when the Giants had trained there among the palm trees, starlets and earth tremors.

Southern Californians hadn't indicated that they would embrace the country's worst team with open arms, but major league ball was major league ball. Barnes and DeWitt saw dollar signs beckoning from the cheap land, surf and palm trees. They received approval from enough other American League owners to move the Browns. They planned to have the move formally ratified at league meetings in Chicago in December of 1941. Then came Pearl Harbor, and the prospect of inevitable wartime travel restrictions. The Browns' shift to Los Angeles was, if you'll pardon the expression, dead in the water by December 8.

At the Polo Grounds, the Giants inaugurated the 1942 season with a series against - who else? - the defending National League champion Brooklyn Dodgers. On Opening Day, managers Ott and Durocher - a contrast in personalities if ever there was one - met at home plate and shook hands for photographers. Also in the picture was Mayor Fiorello LaGuardia, who presented the two skippers with war bonds in the amount of 10 percent of their first salary checks of the year. Then the Dodgers christened the new campaign by scoring four runs in the first inning off Ott's old roommate, Carl Hubbell. Ducky Medwick had the big hit, a bases-loaded double. When Pee Wee Reese homered in the fourth inning, the Dodgers had a 6-0 lead, and the Giants were on their way to the first loss of the Ott administration.

On the next afternoon, rookie Willard Marshall, playing left field, cracked a grand slam to beat the Dodgers behind Cliff Melton. But Dave Koslo lost to pitcher Ed Head (Yes, that was his real name) in the third game of the series. Already Ott was down a series to the Bums.

Edward Marvin Head, the Dodger pitcher, was memorable in many ways aside from his unusual name. A natural left-hander, at the age of 15 he was involved in a car accident that killed his girlfriend and nearly resulted in the amputation of his left arm. Surgery saved the arm, but Head could no longer use it to pitch. So he switched hands and became a righty.

Ott had another "first" the day after the Dodger series. The Giants were in Beantown when umpire Ziggy Sears tossed him from the game along with Hal Schumacher and Billy Jurges. It promised to be another long season, ending in the second division. But then, as if by magic, the middle part of the lineup started hitting: Ott, Mize, Marshall, Leiber, and Harry Danning, who hit in the third through seventh positions. Simultaneously the team began to win.

Ott found the duties of a player-manager to be a burden. He was the first since Ty Cobb and Tris Speaker to attempt those concurrent duties from an outfield position. The role took its mental and physical toll. This was, remember, in the days before a manager was limited to two trips to the mound per pitcher. Often Ott had to call time to trot to the mound several times per inning from deep right field on those squat, aging legs.

Once he reported "being startled" while concentrating on game strategy in right field and looking up to see a hard-hit fly ball coming his way.

On another occasion, he was at bat when he accidentally put on the squeeze play by tapping the plate with his bat, a mannerism he had always had. Seconds later, Bill Lohrman, the runner at third, was charging the plate when Brooklyn pitcher Johnny Podgajny delivered. The misplay had a happy resolution. Ott got his bat on the ball at the last split-second. Lohrman scored, winning the game.

The pressures upon Ott manifested themselves in other ways, too.

For many years Ott had had the nervous habit of tapping his foot on the ground while he played his outfield position. Now he wore a bare spot in the outfield grass. Then there was his base running. In a bases-loaded situation against Brooklyn, with Ott on first, Johnny Mize hit a hard smash to first baseman Dolf Camilli. Camilli was thinking double play. So was Pee Wee Reese. So was Ott, who arrived at second as Reese crossed the bag. The normally mild Ott leveled Reese, stunning the whole stadium. Reese's return throw to first went wild, allowing two more Giant runs to score.

The Dodgers retaliated with aggressive base running of their own. And twice, shortly after Ott had leveled Reese, Ott found it necessary to duck pitches aimed at his ear, one from Hugh Casey, the other from Larry French. Such were *de rigueur* from the Dodgers under Leo Durocher. One Dodger pitcher under Durocher once hit every batter in the opposing line-up, a perfect game of sorts.

In 1942 the war first began to significantly affect baseball. Willard Marshall left for the Marine Corps in September and Babe Young went into the Coast Guard. The Giants were entrenched in third place by this time, far out of the Dodger-Cardinal pennant race but comfortably in front of fourth-place Cincinnati. Already, however, the war had affected play at the Polo Grounds.

Civil defense officials early in the season prohibited East Coast teams from playing with their lights on an hour after sunset. This, in effect, blocked night games for the duration of the war. The result was a mongrel known as the twilight game, which began at seven and ended, well, ended arbitrarily.

Two such games with the Dodgers ended in complete chaos. In one, Brooklyn took a 7-4 lead into the bottom of the ninth inning at the Polo Grounds. Bill Werber, the New York third baseman, singled to start the inning. Then Ott walked. Then umpire George Magerkurth started waving his hands in the air, stopping the game. It was 9:10 P.M., precisely one hour after sunset. The umpires awarded the Dodgers a victory, basing the score on the result of the first eight full innings.

Naturally, the umpires had picked this warm evening of August 3, when 57,305 fans were in attendance for the benefit of the Army Emergency Relief Fund, to get picky about the rules. The Giants players were furious, and the fans were nearly riotous.

Enter the Fred Waring Orchestra, accompanied by a 150-member choral group who trudged out to second base, as prearranged, to conclude the evening with their rendition of "The Star-Spangled Banner." The 57,000 assembled baseball fans did not want to hear the "SSB" or any other music and accordingly drowned out the musicians with boos. Order was restored, and a riot was avoided only by shining a spotlight on the American flag atop the roof of the clubhouse in center field.

Not savoring the prospect of his ballpark being torn apart, Horace Stoneham wisely announced that all twilight games remaining on the Giants' schedule would be changed to afternoon times, all of them, that is, except the one the next evening.

Dodger fans, who had been chortling over the Giants' loss on August 3 and who had chided the Polo Grounds faithful for their inhospitality to Fred Waring, did a little moaning the next night.

The game went to the tenth inning. Pee Wee Reese hit an inside-the-park grand slam against Fiddler Bill McGee, breaking a 1-1 tie. Now the Giants were in no hurry to finish the inning and, sure enough, moments later, dim-out time arrived again. The game was ruled a 1-1 tie. Dodger fans howled, but at least they could howl patriotically. There was no orchestra scheduled that night.

Things could, however, have been worse.

The distinguished New York *Times* sports columnist John Kieran reported a few days later in *Sports of the Times* that an even more bizarre incident had occurred in a minor league game at Jacksonville, Florida. The lighting man, Kieran reported, threw the switch at the pre-arranged hour, but without warning anyone ahead of time. As it happened, the lights went out just as a pitch was thrown.

Kieran wrote: "The catcher later claimed it was a perfect strike whereas the batter said it was a foot outside. The umpire said nothing. He went home to bed."

Amid all this Ott had the personal satisfaction of collecting his 2,500th career hit and tying Rogers Hornsby's league record for career RBIs with 1,584.

Late in the year a tall, young right-handed pitcher named Bill Voiselle made his debut as a Giant. Voiselle was from the town of Ninety-Six, South Carolina, and eventually wore that number on the back of his jersey.

The number was not badly suited to Voiselle's six-foot-four frame. Born in Greenwood, South Carolina, Voiselle grew up in the nearby Ninety Six. He received special permission from the National League to wear the number 96 to honor his hometown. In an era long before Twenty-first Century Yankee slugger Aaron Judge, 96 was the highest number ever worn in major league baseball.

The town of Ninety Six had an interesting history. Located in what is now western South Carolina, Ninety Six was founded on the American frontier in the early 1700s. Some prominent English Sephardic Jewish families named Salvador and DaCosta purchased 200,000 acres intending to help poor Sephardic families relocate from London to the New World. The settlement became the capital burg of the "Ninety-Six District" when it was established in July 1769.

Meanwhile, however, the Giants finished where they had spent most of the season: third place. As soon as the position was clinched, the club allowed Polo Grounds favorite outfielder Hank Leiber to take a turn on the mound. In his only major league pitching appearance, Leiber hurled a complete-game 9-1 loss to the cellar-dwelling Phillies. Then at the end of the year, several New York sportswriters lobbied hard for Ott to receive Manager of the Year accolades, as well as Most Valuable Player. The points were not badly taken. Ott had brought the team up to a respectable position in the first division for the first time since 1938. He had played in almost all the Giants' games, other than two in which he had been thrown out. He had led the league in home runs with 30, had hit .295, and had knocked in 109 runs.

The scribes from the other National League cities, in their infinite wisdom, took this into consideration and chose manager Billy Southworth and pitcher Mort Cooper, respectively, for the two awards. Perhaps the writers were trying to tell Mel that he would be better off staying home for the following season. It might have been a good idea.

The Giants lost one of their most impassioned fans on November 5, 1942, when George M. Cohan died at his Manhattan apartment on Fifth Avenue. He was 64 and succumbed to cancer. His funeral took place at St. Patrick's Cathedral at Fifth Avenue and 50th Street. Thousands attended, including five governors of New York, two mayors of New York City and from the baseball community Connie Mack and Joseph McCarthy of the A's and Yankees respectively. With his passing, the last major player from McGaw's "old gang at 42nd Street" had departed.

Chapter 65   April, The Cruelest Month

A MAJOR LEAGUE MIRACLE!

Spalding produces its famous CUSHION CORK CENTER without critical war materials

1943?

Let's get the bad part out of the way first. The 1943 season was one of the worst in the history of the New York Giants. Bill Terry resigned from the organization in December of 1942, twenty-two years after John McGraw had convinced him to go to Toledo. All twenty-two years had been distinguished. But the farm system had shrunk to two teams due to wartime shortages of manpower. Memphis Bill was too straight an individual to accept money for doing nothing.

Shortly after Terry departed, the Armed Forces gained Mize, Danning, Koslo, and Schumacher, leaving the Giants with no one at first, no one to catch, and not much of a pitching staff. Across town, the Dodgers would lose Reese, Casey, Lavagetto, and Reiser to Uncle Sam and the Yankees would surrender Rizzuto, DiMaggio, Selkirk, Ruffing and Henrich. But the Dodgers and Yankees had depth. The Giants did not. Nor did they have anywhere warm to start the season.

In 1943, Commissioner Landis, at the request of Joseph Eastman, head of the Office of Defense Transportation, asked all major league teams to train in the chilly North. This "Landis-Eastman line" replaced the Mason-Dixon line for baseball geographers, drawn as it was along the Ohio and Potomac rivers. Not since 1919, when the nearly bankrupt St. Louis Cardinals trained in a drafty gym at Washington University, had major leaguers welcomed a new season in so frosty a fashion.

The Landis-Eastman line made for some unusual accommodations. The Dodgers relocated from sunny Havana to frigid Bear Mountain, New York. The Cubs swapped balmy Avalon, California, for icy French Lick, Indiana. The Boston Braves, led by Professor Casey Stengel, the ex-Giant, moved into the Winter Exercise Building at The Choate School in Wallingford, Connecticut, alma mater to such glittery alumni as Adlai Stevenson, Alan J. Lerner, John F. Kennedy, Edward Albee, actor/ producer Michael Douglas, and - to cite a less glittery example - the author of this book. So as not to corrupt the morals of minors, the Braves moved to Choate during the school's spring recess.

The Giants set up a camp that was almost as unique in Lakewood, New Jersey, the same little town where the Giants of – cringe! - Andrew Freedman had trained in 1897 and 1898. The site, which the Giants shared with their Jersey City farm club, was upon a wooded estate owned by the Rockefeller family.

The practice diamonds were gently carved out of a golf course where the ornery old monopolist-philanthropist had once handed out dime tips to caddies who had earned his favor. The players stayed in a mansion which had also once been the residence of John D. the First. It featured private rooms for the players, a jukebox, and, most importantly, heat. When spring training began, the edge of the golf course was blanketed with snow.

As the season began, the Giants wasted a four-for-four performance by Ott and got themselves drubbed again by the Dodgers, a recurring theme of recent years. But the larger story was the baseball itself, now one of the casualties of the war.

Though the average baseball fan had probably never thought much about it, the horsehide that had for years covered major league baseballs had come from Belgium and France where the also-rans of one week's *tierce* might wind up at the *boucherie a cheval* a few days later.

The two major leagues were now cut off from trade with occupied Belgium and France but were able to buy horseflesh from Bolivia. So the problem of the ball's covering was solved. But an even greater difficulty loomed: a shortage of rubber.

Rubber had been an essential ingredient in a baseball's core since the lively ball of 1920 had been introduced. But most rubber came to the United States from Malaya and the Dutch East Indies. The Japanese army had interrupted that. And since approximately one ton of rubber was needed to build an American tank, Uncle Sam banned the use of rubber in all products nonessential to the war effort. Baseballs were one such item.

What to do?

The problem of finding a new formula for big league baseballs was to be the headache of A. G. Spalding & Bros., the longtime official maker of the little spheroids. Spalding did its best and concocted a new item that looked and felt like a real baseball. Only it wasn't. It had a granulated cork center instead of the high-grade cork and rubber mixture. Around this center were two shells made of "balata," a nonstrategic hard, rubbery substance which for many years was used in the manufacture of industrial gaskets and as the outer shell of golf balls. Balata, however, lacked rubber's elasticity, a fact of physics that somehow got lost in the rush to make new baseballs.

Lost, that is, until Opening Day.

The new balata ball, as it was called, had all the happy characteristics of a croquet ball. It wouldn't *go* anywhere. The Cardinals, the most potent offensive team of 1942, opened their season with a 1-0, eleven inning loss to the Reds. The next day they lost again, 1-0 in ten innings. Every series in baseball looked like a replay of the all-shutout 1905 World Series. If the baseball of the pre-Ruth era was "dead," this one was positively embalmed. It should have gone to war as a weapon. Detroit Tiger manager Steve O'Neill, who had played as long ago as 1911 for Cleveland, pronounced the ball deader than the one of the Ty Cobb era. Other managers - Ott, Durocher, Southworth, and Bill McKechnie - concurred.

Warren Giles, then the general manager of Cincinnati, was so angered by the situation that he went up to the roof of Crosley Field to conduct a test. Aided by his head groundskeeper on the sidewalk below, Giles chucked balata balls off the roof, followed by a few good old Spaldings left over from the 1942 campaign. On average, the old ball bounced 13 feet in the air. The balata ball bounced 9.5 feet.

A few days later Hy Turkin, a sportswriter from the New York *Daily News,* escorted some balata balls to New York's Cooper Union. There scientists sliced them, unraveled them, and swatted them with wooden mallets. The verdict: 25.9 percent less resilience, a result not too different from the experiment Giles conducted in Cincinnati. No wonder the monster 400-foot home run of 1942 was now the lazy 300-foot fly ball of 1943.

Faced with these results and fearing that the public wouldn't pay to see 1905-style baseball, the two major leagues prevailed upon Spalding to revise their product. Spalding did. By May 9, hitting was back in those places it had existed previously. One place where it never returned that year, however, was the Polo Grounds, where the Giants plodded through another woeful season with the second-worst team batting average in the league. The Giants also had the league's least effective pitching staff, making for a long season and a memorably ugly eighth-place finish.

Along the way, Ott tried to reverse things, but couldn't. He acquired Ernie Lombardi from the Braves in April to fill the vacancy behind the plate. He ditched outfielder Babe Barna on the unsuspecting Red Sox for pitcher Ken Chase, but Chase, with a 4-16 record that year, failed to help the team. He called up a flashy young Cuban named Nap (short for Napoleon, of course) Reyes from Jersey City, but the kid hit no more than .256 with no power.

In July, getting desperate while in seventh place, the Giants picked up aging and grumpy Joe (Ducky) Medwick from the Dodgers, who felt – correctly, as it turned out - that Medwick didn't have too much mileage left on him. him. Then on July 31 came the ultimate indignity. Ott swung a blockbuster trade with Brooklyn. He sent Bill Sayles, Bill Lohrman, and Joe Orengo to La Belle Borough for pitcher Johnny Allen and Dolf Camilli.

This might have helped, except that Camilli announced his retirement rather than report to the Giants. New York got Allen, who won one game then was suspended following a row with an umpire, and Brooklyn kept their three players. Then, to make the 1943 spring debacle complete, Carl Hubbell won the 253rd and final game of his career, a 3-2 win over Pittsburgh, and Ott hit .234 for the year. "It was just a season," said Mel at the close, "when everything went wrong."

For the Giants, maybe, but not for the Yankees and the Cardinals, who squared off again in the World Series. And not for the Dodgers, either, who had made an astute move in the front office before the season had even begun. They had hired Branch Rickey away from the Cardinals to take the place of Larry MacPhail, who was off to war with the rank of lieutenant-colonel. The Dodgers had lost too many key players to contend with the Cardinals, but Rickey already had his eyes on the future. Out there in the heartland of America, while other club managements worried about teetering through the 1943 season, Rickey's best scouts - Tom Greenwade, Clyde Sukeforth, and George Sisler - were busy looking for teenage talent. Under such circumstances, the names Jackie Robinson, Rex Barney, Ralph Branca, Edwin (Duke) Snider, Gil Hodges, and Clem Labine would become familiar in Dodger uniforms in the years that followed.

Rickey, in a move that would affect the rest of the Giants' tenure in New York, also had a keen eye on the managerial situation in Brooklyn. Newly signed to a five-year pact at $75,000 per year as president of the Dodgers, Rickey had recently uttered many nice things about Burt Shotton, manager of the lamentable Phillies from 1928 to 1933.

Before that, Shotton had had a distinguished playing career: he was a quick-footed outfielder, nicknamed "Barney" after the lead-footed race car driver Barney Oldfield, who batted left and threw right. He compiled a .271 batting average with 1,338 hits in 1,387 games played for the St. Louis Browns, Washington Senators and St. Louis Cardinals from 1909 until 1923. He stole 294 bases during his career, but his greatest contribution was his talent at getting on base. His OBP finished in the top ten in the league four times in his career. In 1913 and 1916 he led AL batters in walks and finished in the top ten six seasons.

Rickey had it in his mind that Shotton was the finest manager in the game, even though in seven years with the Phillies and Reds, he had yet to win anything. Nonetheless, it was widely speculated – meaning the nosy New York press kept writing about it - that Shotton, Rickey's old friend from the St. Louis Cardinal organization, would soon be replacing Durocher at the Brooklyn helm.

Blocking the move was the vehemence of the Brooklyn fans. They loved Leo.

Leo loved them right back.

They were, in truth, made for each other. Take that any way you want. The Durocher spirit - scrappy, pugnacious, irreverent, profane and brawling - fit Brooklyn as it would fit nowhere else in the country.

Ah, but there were problems. Leo was due to be drafted. Leo also was widely held to be the central figure in several high-stakes poker games that always seemed to be floating through the Dodger clubhouse. Some observers claimed that clubhouse distractions of gambling - and gambling debts - had distracted just enough from the attention of certain players to allow St. Louis to win the 1942 pennant by two and a half games. Yet Rickey was astute enough to know that firing Leo wasn't the answer. Antagonizing fans unnecessarily was never part of any Rickey game plan.

So Leo and Branch got together for breakfast one morning in St. Louis. Rickey did most of the talking, after which Leo came up with a promise that the clubhouse card games would stop. Branch smiled and rewarded him with a new contract.

Later that same summer of 1943, while the Giants were plunging again toward the National League cellar, Durocher solved his other problem, flunking his Army induction physical due to a punctured eardrum. (Leo was also 37 years old.) "Leo will do his fighting for the Dodgers!" happily proclaimed one Brooklyn newspaper.

And so he would!

Making the picture complete was the increasing prominence in Dodger business of the club's new attorney, a graduate of Penn and Columbia Law. He was the man who, along with Rickey, would eventually buy out the interests of the McKeever-Ebbets heirs who had owned Dodger stock since 1912.

The man's name – which will live forever in infamy in the Borough of Churches - was Walter Francis O'Malley.

Nineteen Forty-three was also the inaugural year of The All-American Girls Professional Baseball League. The AAGPBA, made famous to new generations by the 1992 film *A League of Their Own*, ran from 1943 to 1954. In the movie, the professional all-female baseball league was founded by a publicity-crazed candy maker named Walter Harvey, played by Garry Marshall. In real life, the AAGPBA was founded by Chicago Cubs owner and chewing-gum manufacturer Philip K. Wrigley, who conceived it as a way to maintain sports entertainment during the war. It also gave some fine female baseball players a proper organization in which to play. It survived the war and drew nearly a million paying customers fans in 1948, its most popular season.

Really, what was not to like?

Chapter 66   Dauntless Dan & The 3-Way Game

"The Giants were our team. We left the tourists to the Yankees."

Jimmy Cannon, columnist, New York *Journal-American*

The New York Giants were a mild surprise in 1944, rising to fifth place in a league increasingly bereft of talent. The Dodgers were an equal surprise, but going in the other direction, plummeting to seventh. War time had left the Dodgers with one quality player, Dixie Walker, who hit .357 against the paltry pitching of the day. The real shocker in 1944, however, would be the St. Louis Browns, who, pasted together with aging veterans and kids too young to know any better, fielded their usually ordinary-to-poor team. Yet they won the pennant by one game in the American League, proving the old bromide that in the Country of the Blind, the One-eyed Man is King. Then, in the first World Series to be played entirely in one ballpark since the 1922 Giants-Yankees extravaganza, the Cardinals dispatched their upstart tenants in six games.

There were a few good moments at the Polo Grounds in 1944, too. Before fifty-eight thousand astonished fans one afternoon, the Giants clobbered the Dodgers by a football score of 26-8.

A handful of the individual statistics were as perverse as the game itself. Phil Weintraub, the Giants' new first baseman, batted in 11 runs, one shy of Jim Bottomley's major league record, with two doubles, a triple, and a home run. Ott scored six runs without hitting safely. Leo's pitching staff walked Ott five times, making Mel a significant beneficiary of the seventeen bases on balls dished out that day.

"I had nothing but humpty-dumpties on my staff that year," Leo later admitted, given to understatement for once. Six of the walks had been consecutive. And plodding Ernie Lombardi knocked in 7 runs, which, it might be said, sealed the victory.

Bill Voiselle, tall number 96, would be pitching for a team in transition.

Only Ott and Johnny Rucker, who combined with Joe Medwick

to form the regular outfield, were holdovers from Opening Day of 1943. George Hausmann, Buddy Kerr, and Hugh (Hal) Luby formed the second, short, and third sections of the infield. Ernie Lombardi was the regular catcher but was helped out from time to time by Gus Mancuso. The year 1944 also marked the arrival of one of the era's more memorable Giants, Danny Gardella.

Gardella was, bless him, a native New Yorker who had worked in a naval yard in 1943, making him exempt from the draft. He was a small (5' 7") colorful player who liked the game of baseball and played hard at it. He was exactly the type of player who gets good press in New York, the little guy who's always mixing things up and creating interesting stories.

One thing Gardella mixed up from time to time was fly balls. An outfielder whom the press soon named, "Dauntless Dan," Gardella could turn a routine chance into something far more memorable. Optimists at the Polo Grounds, seeing a ball go airborne in Danny's direction, felt Dan just might catch it. Pessimists feared that Dan would be injured. One sportswriter wrote about a long fly that Gardella had caught "unassisted." He was the bane of Mel Ott's existence. Manager Mel exiled Dauntless Dan to Jersey City in midseason, only to bring him back as a regular the following season.

But Danny made things jump. Sometimes literally, as can be seen here.

Center fielder Johnny Rucker had shown Gardella how to tap his sunglasses into place just like a major leaguer when chasing a fly ball. Early in 1944 Gardella gave his glasses just such a tap while in hot pursuit of a fly ball off the bat of Chicago pitcher Hank Wyse. The glasses came down over Gardella's eyes, but so did his cap, to which the glasses were attached. The ball landed nearby.

Later that same season, Gardella snuck into a high school prom - short men can get away with such things - in a Pittsburgh hotel, befriended the boys in the band, and warbled a solo rendition of *"Indian Love Call*, the cloying Jeanette MacDonald, Nelson Eddy classic.

"When I'm calling yooooooooou, Oo-Oo-Oo-Oo, Oo-Oo-Oo-Oo," sang Dauntless Dan, "Will you answer toooooooooooo?" before the astonished students. A year later, on the day the war ended in Europe, Gardella terrified the staff in another hotel when he combed his dark hair over one eye, pasted on a fake toothbrush-style mustache, and strutted through the building, noisily proclaiming that Hitler, contrary to widely circulated press reports, was still very much alive.

One teammate who didn't think that Gardella was very funny was Nap Reyes, Gardella's long-suffering roommate. Reyes shared Gardella's most memorable moment as a Giant one morning in the Chase Hotel in St. Louis. Gardella had been setting Reyes up for several days, complaining about depression and discussing suicide. Reyes just listened. Then one morning at the Chase Hotel, Reyes was just coming awake when he heard Gardella, who always rose a little earlier, yell.

"Here I go! Good-bye!" Gardella screamed.

Reyes whirled around in his bed and saw an open window, complete with fluttering curtains. With his heart in his throat, Reyes sprung from his bed and ran to the window. There was Gardella, twenty stories above the city of St. Louis, hanging by his fingertips, grinning at the terrified Reyes. If Gardella had been a sport himself, he would have been the roller derby. If he had been a film, he would have been directed by Fellini, with a script by Tarrantino.

With the war in Europe going in the Allies' favor, night baseball returned to the Polo Grounds in May 1944. Less than a month later, on June 3, nine thousand fans at a Giants-Pittsburgh game heard a somber announcement over the park's loudspeakers. The invasion of Europe had begun, it was said.

There was a moment of cheering approval as the game stopped. The players and crowd all stood for a moment of prayer. Then the game, much subdued, continued. It was only much later that it was learned that no such invasion was in progress at all. A teletype operator in London, getting in a little extra training at her machine, had knocked out a line of wishful thinking: FLASH:

EISENHOWER'S HEADQUARTERS ANNOUNCE ALLIED LANDINGS FRANCE.

Accidentally, the operator's line was live when the message was typed. The Associated Press in New York picked it up and transmitted it across the country within seconds. A few minutes later, AP realized that the flash had not been confirmed and tried to kill it. But already the much-prayed-for news had broken before millions of Americans, including those at the Polo Grounds. The actual Normandy invasion did not begin until three days later on June 6. All major league teams cancelled their games that day.

Twenty days later at the Polo Grounds, on June 26, 1944, there took place a unique baseball contest: a "Tri-Cornered Baseball Game" between the Giants, the Dodgers, and the Yankees. The idea was conceived by a group of New York sportswriters and then became a reality in support of the Allied forces in World War Two.

To attend the game, each fan needed to buy a War Bond as a ticket. Forty thousand unreserved tickets were on sale for "$25" each, which was the bond maturity value. The actual cost was $18.75. There were also just shy of six thousand reserved seats in the lower stands, each costing a $100 bond, and 3700-plus box seats each available for $1,000 bonds. New Yorkers, as they invariably do, rallied to a good cause. In addition to the amount raised by fans, Mayor Fiorello La Guardia announced that the city would purchase $50 million in War Bonds. The Bond Clothing Stores chain purchased a one million dollar bond in exchange for an autographed scorecard of the game.

Before the game, five hundred wounded servicemen arrived to attend the game. There was a fungo-hitting contest, which was won by an eighteen-year-old pitcher for Brooklyn named Cal McLish. He knocked a 416-foot 5-inch, shot. There were three heats in a sprint contest. The Yankees Snuffy Stirnweiss beat the Giants' Johnny Rucker, posting a time of 7.8

seconds. In the other two heats, Dodgers sprinters Eddie Miksis and Luis Olmo bested the Giants' Buddy Kerr and the Yanks' Johnny Lindell, respectively. In a throwing-for-accuracy competition for catchers, the Dodgers' Bobby Bragan came closest to throwing the ball from home plate into a barrel at second base, besting five other backstops.

Before the game, the famous clown prince of baseball, Al Schacht, entertained the crowd. Milton Berle presented an array of musical numbers furnished by the Manhattan Beach-based United States Coast Guard band. Former New York City Mayor James J. Walker introduced a contingent of diamond stars from the New York teams, including Zack Wheat, Nap Rucker, Otto Miller from the Dodgers, Wally Schang and Herb Pennock from the Yankees, and Roger Bresnahan, George "Hooks" Wiltse, and Moose McCormick from the Giants. Babe Ruth had been scheduled to appear, but apparently found something or someone more interesting to do.

Each team played in the field for two consecutive innings, then batted for two innings and then sat for an inning until each had played a total of six innings. That blueprint created a nine-inning game – a strange one, but a nine inning game. A Columbia University math professor, Paul A. Smith, created the mathematical concept and attended. He sat in the press box and helped the flummoxed official scorers.

Major league rosters were obliterated by the war, of course, but organizers rounded up some great names: Paul Waner, Joe Medwick and Ernie Lombardi. Other participants included Ralph Branca, Eddie Stanky, Dixie Walker and Snuffy Stirnweiss. Leo Durocher managed the Dodgers. Joe McCarthy guided the Yankees. Mel Ott managed the Giants. Ott at least had his dugout to himself. Durocher and McCarthy, the visitors, managed the game from opposite wings of the same bench.

Final tally: Dodgers 5, Yankees 1, Giants 0. The Dodgers, in other words, beat the Yankees and the Giants on the same evening. The real winner was the American war effort, however, which gained more than $56,000,000 in bond purchases, $50 million of which came from the City of New York, but six million from fans was a good take, also.

The 1944 Giants might have finished higher in the standings had it not been for a disastrous August road trip in which, with Ott injured and out of the lineup, the Giants lost the first 13 games. The streak was the longest series of losses since before John McGraw had taken over the team. Effectively it killed the season, though Ott finished second in the league with home runs at 26, and big lanky Number Ninety Six did his home town proud: Bill Voiselle became the 1944 Rookie of the Year.

Facebook

If you're enjoying this trip through The Polo Grounds and New York Giants' history, you might consider visiting three sites on *Facebook* which bring together men and women with similar interests. I visit frequently. May I suggest:

New York Giants Preservation Society
Polo Grounds New York 1891-1964
(and)
The Polo Grounds Remembered.(1891-1963)

I also like *Classic Baseball Pics, Baseball Books*
(and) Institute For Baseball Studies

And it's difficult not to like *Brooklyn Dodgers Nostalgia Society.* Admit it: We all have friends who are Dodger fans.

N.H.

In Remembrance...

Three men with minor league baseball experience died during the first hours of the D Day invasion of France in June of 1944.

Joe Pinder, who had minor league experience in the Chicago White Sox organization, was a radio operator who hit Omaha Beach in a landing craft. Twice wounded in the water, Pinder refused medical attention despite having the left side of his face shot off. Hit a third time, he died holding his position. The day was also his thirty-second birthday. He was later awarded the Congressional Medal of Honor.

Elmer Wright also came in on a landing craft at Omaha Beach. Most of the men on his vessel were killed before reaching shore. Wright was hit by machine gun fire when he hit the beach and died there.

A pitcher named Forest "Lefty" Brewer parachuted into Normandy on D Day, landed safely, but was killed by enemy fire later that afternoon in the vicinity of Sainte-Mere-Eglise. Six years earlier to the day, Brewer had pitched a brilliant no hitter in the Florida International League.

(L-R) Lefty Brewer (1918-44), Joe Pinder (1912-44), Elmer Wright (1915-44)

Time passes quickly, memories fade. These young men who sacrificed their lives on June 4, 1944 in Normandy for their country, for you and for me, are remembered and honored here.

According to the UD Department of Veterans Affairs, 16 million Americans served in World War Two. Approximately 500,000 are still alive. If you know one, thank him or her again.

***

{Editor's note: An Englishman named Gary Bedingfield is recognized as a leading expert on baseball during WWII and in particular the casualties of that war. Gary's enthusiasm for baseball began, as it did for many of us, with his father. Gary's father who was born and raised in England but, as a musician, toured the American Air Force bases during the early 1960s. Gary developed an interest in baseball during this time by watching the Air Force teams play and participating in the occasional scratch games. He later played for the Great Britain national and Olympic teams, and coached varsity baseball at the American School in London.

"I am privileged to say," he recalls, "I have played against such talented professionals as George Foster, Tug McGraw, Graig Nettles, Mark Fidrych and Luis Tiant."

Gary coupled his enjoyment of the game with his knowledge of history. His writing has appeared in many prominent places. Today he maintains a website on American baseball in wartime. He can be contacted there:

http://www.baseballinwartime.com

I am indebted to Gary's site for the photographs above.

Chapter 67   A Time of Optimism

**"If you don't know where you are going,
you might wind up someplace else."**

Yogi Berra

    Over the winter of 1944-45, Giants manager Mel Ott toured Europe, visiting U.S. military bases with several other major league players. He returned in time to preside over the club's third and final training at Lakewood, New Jersey.

    The team that took the field on Opening Day, 1945, an 11-6 victory in Boston, was much unchanged from the starting lineup of 1944. President Roosevelt had died a few days earlier. The opening ceremonies followed a memorial service. Then the Giants built upon their victory in Boston by winning 11 of their next 15 games. They were at the top of the National League. Ott professed his belief that they could stay there for the season.

    For a while it did look that way. Ott hit home run number 494 in May, passing Gehrig's career total and moving into third place on the all-time list behind Ruth and Jimmie Foxx. At the time Ott's catcher, Ernie Lombardi, was hitting well also, leading the league in home runs on his way to a season's total of 21.

    Bill Voiselle won 8 straight games before losing a heartbreaking contest interrupted by rain in St. Louis. Harry Feldman, the number two man on the staff, won 7 straight. The rest of the pitchers - which included a rejuvenated Van Lingle Mungo, seen here finally in a Giants uniform - were in and out, but Ace Adams, the relief specialist, helped out consistently. Even Danny Gardella contributed with a solid major league season, hitting .272 with an astonishing 18 home runs. Better yet, Dauntless Dan made only 9 errors in the field all year. Would wonders never cease?

By May the war in Europe was over, but so were the Giants' pennant prospects. A series of losses to Brooklyn and Chicago dropped the club to fourth. The worst loss, however, came in June in New London, Connecticut, where the Giants played an exhibition game at the huge naval base.

There, a former Chicago Cub and Cincinnati Red outfielder named Jimmy Gleeson had morphed over the years into U.S. Navy Lt. Commander James Gleeson. Gleeson spoke to Ott by phone about a player on the service team. The player was a young catcher from St. Louis. He was awkward but could hit. Gleeson convinced Ott to come take a look at the young man.

There was a little bit of a backstory to the kid from earlier in the 1940's.

When the young man had turned 18 in 1943, he had put a promising baseball career on hold and joined the United States Navy. Trained as a gunner's mate, the kid worked on a rocket launching boat and served on D-Day. Of that fateful day, he later said, "Being a young guy, you didn't think nothing of it until you got in it. And so we went 300 yards off beach. We protected the troops." For twelve days his boat was ordered to knock down aircraft. They accidentally shot down an American plane, but the crew managed to save the pilot. The young warrior went on to serve in a second assault on France for which he received a medal from the French government.

Ott turned up with the Giants to play an exhibition against Gleeson's navy team and to get a look at the kid. Ott had a difficult time believing the squat, awkward-looking seaman named Lawrence Peter Berra was a potential ballplayer. Then Berra went 3 for 4 against Giants pitching. Ott was then further shocked to learn that "Yogi," as he eventually would be call, was the property of the New York Yankees and was scheduled to join their minor league system.

Ott promptly misplayed his hand by offering $50,000 cash for the kid. Larry MacPhail, who had returned from the war decorated with medals, was the new president and general manager of the Yankees. He knew that if Ott and owner Horace Stoneham were willing to throw that much money after a minor league prospect, the boy deserved a hard look by the Yankee organization. Thus it was "no sale," and Lawrence Peter (Yogi) Berra would find his way to the Bronx, rather than the Polo Grounds, two years later.

The Giant front office, however, remained at work. As the war in the Pacific came to an end in August, punctuated by the horrific atomic bomb attacks on Hiroshima and Nagasaki, Horace Stoneham's organization began rebuilding its minor league system.

Trenton, the Giants' Class B farm affiliate, was the first significant addition. Then a right-handed pitcher, Salvatore Anthony Maglie from Niagara Falls, New York, arrived at the Polo Grounds in the middle of the same month. Maglie had been a fine athlete in high school. Nearby Niagara University had offered him a basketball scholarship. But Maglie wanted to play baseball. Later he held down a job at a local chemical plant and pitched for the company baseball team. That was when he had attracted major league scouts.

Young Maglie would pitch well in this year of 1945. He would win 5 games. But the team would plop into the second division and stay there.

If the year was not an artistic success, it was a financial and moral success.

With the city swollen with returning servicemen, attendance exceeded one million for the first time, the best numbers since the pennant season of 1937. Better, the war was finally over. Quality players would be returning. New prospects, those who had survived the war at least, could look forward to wearing the crisp white, gold, and black uniforms of the New York Giants instead of Uncle Sam's battle fatigues. There was no reason for fans, and the country, not to be optimistic. In an unusual twist, however, part-time outfielder Steve Filipowicz, defected to the New York Football Giants, where he became a quarterback.

At the close of the 1945 season, National League president Ford Frick honored Mel Ott with a lifetime pass to league parks in recognition of Mel's twenty years in the league. Horace Stoneham joined in the general aura of almost-good feeling by tearing up Mel's old contract, which had one year remaining on it, and issuing a new five-year one with a substantial raise.

Meanwhile the Cubs and Tigers prepared to play the last "wartime" World Series.

"It's the fat men against the tall men at the annual office picnic," wrote Frank Graham, who had moved from the New York *Sun* to the shrill New York *Journal-American*. And Chicago sportswriter Warren Brown of The Chicago *Herald-Examiner*, sitting in the press box at the opening of the Series, summed up much of wartime baseball in general and the 1945 World Series in particular when asked who he thought would win. Brown, whom most historians credit with hanging the nickname, "The Sultan of Swat," on Babe Ruth, eyed the two teams carefully.

"I don't think," Brown said, "either team can win."

Well, one of them had to. And the Cubs were in the middle of their Lost Century.

Not by coincidence, Hank Greenberg had returned from the service early that same season. So the team that failed to not win the Series was Detroit. But it did take seven games.

Chapter 68   Safe at Home

"The foul line was on the other side of my living room wall. Bobby Thomson's home run, the one that won us the pennant in 1951, landed on my roof."

Matty Schwab, Jr., Giants Groundskeeper

By the autumn of 1945, Horace Stoneham, owner of the New York Giants baseball team, knew he had many serious problems, and not all of them had to do with the Giants' finish in the second division for the last three years.

One was the ballpark. The Polo Grounds a comfortable, historic old place. But now after World War Two, the playing area was ragged. Rumor had it that the grounds crews were spending more time on long, liquid lunches than on maintaining the field.

The situation was made more acute by Branch Rickey. Whenever Stoneham and traveling secretary Eddie Brannick ventured to Ebbets Field, Rickey loved to crow about what great shape his own field was in.

After Rickey needled Stoneham one time too many, Horace went looking for help. His attention settled on Matthew Schwab Jr., one of the best groundskeepers in the business, if not the best. Matty's grandfather, John Schwab, had first kept the grounds at Redland Field in Cincinnati in 1883. Matty's father, Matthew Sr., was still with the Cincinnati club in the same capacity. As for Matty, well, he was the head groundskeeper at Ebbets Field. He was just what the Polo Grounds needed. So at the end of 1945, when Stoneham learned that Rickey, a legendarily tightfisted employer, had once again denied Matty a long-deserved, long-deferred raise, the Giants' owner sent Brannick to Schwab's winter home in Florida to ask Matty if he would care to come over to the Polo Grounds.

Schwab said yes. Rickey woke up not too many mornings later to discover that Stoneham had swiped his head groundskeeper and was taking him to Manhattan. In the never-ending war between the Giants and the Dodgers, it was a masterful shot.

One problem developed, however. Schwab lived with his wife, Rose, and four-year-old son, Jerry, in a nice apartment on President Street in Brooklyn. The commute by car to the Polo Grounds at 155th Street and 8th Avenue in Manhattan was a killer. For a short time Schwab and his family moved into the Concourse Plaza Hotel near the ballpark. That didn't work out very well. Too expensive, and anyway, what family wants to live in a hotel? Yet there was no convenient, reasonable housing anywhere near the Polo Grounds.

Schwab noticed some unused space below the left field grandstand at the ballpark.

"I asked Mr. Stoneham whether it would be possible to build a place to live right there," Matty, explained years later. "He said it was unheard of. But Mr. Stoneham always took care of his employees. So he asked Joe Traynor, the park superintendent, to see what could be done."

Soon carpenters were at work under the grandstand, followed by electricians and plumbers. Eventually there emerged a cozy two-bedroom apartment with bath, kitchen and living room, plus a private entrance and free parking. In 1946, unbeknownst to most of the thousands of fans who pushed through the Polo Grounds turnstiles, the Schwab family took up residence at the ballpark, just beyond the outfield fence. Matty can be seen above in a New York *Herald-Tribune* photo, the gate to left field on his left.

There were windows on three sides of the apartment; two faced some subway repair yards across the street from the park and another looked out on an alley. Soon Matty began to dream about a fourth exposure. "I asked," he said with a sly chuckle, "if I could put in another window. You know, in the outfield wall facing the field. But Mr. Stoneham finally said no."

Only Rose had the slightest complaint: The place did get a little noisy from time to time, particularly during boisterous doubleheaders when the Dodgers were visiting. Imagine a party going on in an upstairs apartment with 56,000 people in attendance, half of whom hate the other half, and you get the idea.

Schwab may have been partway to paradise, but his son was already there.

"The biggest backyard in Manhattan," Matty used to call the playing field. On warm summer nights, Jerry, an eight-year-old in 1950, would invite friends over, pitch a tent and camp out beneath the stars. The grassy turf that Mel Ott, Sid Gordon and Bobby Thomson—and later Hall of Famers Monte Irvin and Willie Mays—roamed by daylight was Jerry's private playground for countless nights.

"On some nights when I didn't camp out, I would get up every two hours to help my father move the sprinklers around the field," said Jerry, who later became the branch manager of a post office in Fort Lauderdale. "My father used to send me into the dugouts sometimes to turn hoses on or off. It was pitch black. I never knew what monsters might be waiting in the darkness. But none ever were."

Daylight brought the athletes, arriving for work.

"There were three of us kids who were tolerated by the players," said Jerry, "though I was the only one who actually lived there. Me, Chris [son of Giant skipper Leo] Durocher and Dale [son of star pitcher Larry] Jansen. We wore New York Giants uniforms, just like the batboys. We had the run of the park. If we wanted to go somewhere we'd take one of the many underground tunnels and pop out of a manhole. We'd stand behind the batting cage and watch the pitchers. Then we'd work out with the players and shag flies in the outfield. There was only one place we knew not to go: the clubhouse after Durocher had slammed the door. That meant he was about to yell at his players."

Jerry was particularly close to pitcher Jim Hearn, but it was slugger Johnny Mize who was his boyhood hero. "I wore number 15 on my uniform, same as Mize, before they sold him to the Yankees. After he left, I still kept his number."

Then there were the retired Hall of Famers who used to pass by: Bill Terry, Carl Hubbell. Mays arrived in 1951 as a frightened rookie. Then in 1952 there came a 28-year-old rookie with an unorthodox pitch, Hoyt Wilhelm. He and Jerry took a liking to each other.

"Hoyt made me a whiz on my high school baseball team," Jerry recalled many years later. "He taught me how to throw a knuckleball."

As the condition of the playing field improved under Schwab's scrupulous care, so did the Giants under Durocher. There was the miracle pennant in 1951, then the heady World Championship in 1954. Schwab received a full share of the World Series money that year, plus a Series ring. But by then the team was starting to unravel. Irvin retired. Durocher quit. Thomson, Al Dark and Whitey Lockman were all traded.

At the same time, the neighborhood began to change, and the concrete-and-steel structure of the Polo Grounds, erected in 1911, began to creak. Inevitably, talk centered on sites for a new ballpark in New York. It all must have been terribly unsettling for the Schwab family. It was their home that people wanted to abandon.

The Schwab family remained in their home near the scoreboard for the rest of the time the Giants remained in New York. Eventually, they would move west with the team. Matty would take care of the field at Candlestick and Jerry would help me. The father son team surfaced prominently during the 1962 playoff when they just kinda sorta accidentally overwatered the base paths for Maury Wills, Tommy Davis and Willy Davis. Lake Candlestick.

"I'm sorry I never went back to the Polo Grounds as an adult," Jerry many years later, when interviewed in the mid-1980s. "I would have liked to see it through the eyes of a grownup and compare it to my memories as a boy. But I never got back there. It bothers me."

THE POLO GROUNDS
NEW YORK
NEW YORK
SEASON OF 1887.
HOME GAMES OF THE NEW YORK BALL CLUB FOR THE LEAGUE CHAMPIONSHIP.
April 28, 29, with Philadelphia,
May 5, 6, 7, " Boston,
" 9, 10, 11, " Washington,
" 14, " Philadelphia,
" 16, 17, 18, " Indianapolis,
" 20, 21, 23, 24, " Pittsburg,
" 26, 27, 28, " Detroit,
" 30 A.M. & P.M., 31, " Chicago
June 9, 10, 11, with Washington,
" 13, 14, 15, " Philadelphia,
July 7, 8, 9, " Detroit,
" 11, 12, 13, " Pittsburg,
" 15, 16, 18, " Chicago,
" 19, 20, 21, " Indianapolis,
" 23, 25, 26, " Boston,
Aug. 22, 23, with Pittsburg,
" 25, 26, 27, " Chicago,
" 29, 30, 31, " Indianapolis,
Sept. 1, 2, 3, " Detroit,
" 5, 6, 7, " Washington,
" 26, 27, 28, " Boston,
Oct. 5, 6, 8, " Philadelphia

Chapter 69   Fiesta Mexicana con Pistolas y Dinero

"In all my time in sports, I had never seen a ballplayer so heralded before he had played game one in the major leagues.
Not DiMaggio... not Mantle... not Williams nor A-Rod... This guy, at first look, was Shoeless Joe Jackson, Ruth and Bob Feller all rolled up into one."

Bill Gallo in The New York *Daily News* on Clint Hartung

The New York Giants played one more year of wartime-style baseball, even if the rest of the league did not.

The franchise was filled with good vibes moving into the season of 1946. Over the winter Horace Stoneham had acquired Clint Hartung, widely touted as the top prospect in the country. Hartung was a massive six foot five inch Texan who could pitch as well as hit. Or at least he had always been able to do both against non-major-league competition.

Other young prospects included infielders Bill Rigney, who popularized the basket catch at the Polo Grounds several years before Willie Mays, and Robert (Buddy) Blattner, as well as young pitchers Monte Kennedy,

Clint Hartung in 1947

Marv Grissom, and Mike Budnick. Then there were the proven stars set to return: Willard Marshall, Dave Koslo, Sid Gordon, Babe Young, and Hal Schumacher.

In January, Stoneham paid the St. Louis Cardinals $175,000 for

Walker Cooper, perhaps the finest catcher in baseball, to split duties with Ernie Lombardi. It looked as if old times would return to the Polo Grounds.

Instead disaster struck. This time the disaster took the form of a pair of Mexican brothers, Jorge Pasquel and his brother, Bernardo. Jorge Pasquel, a wealthy industrialist based in Mexico City, had in mind to upgrade the Mexican League to parity with the two major leagues in the United States. To this end, he traipsed around from one major league city to the next, often with tens of thousands of dollars in cash in a suitcase. The money was for big league ballplayers if they would sign a contract and come play with him.

The Pasquel brothers had most of their wealth from the manufacture of cheap cigars. In 1914, when Jorge Pasquel had been a child during the Mexican Revolution, American forces had attacked and occupied his home town of Veracruz in what was called an effort to try to preserve trade in the dispute with President Huerta. Jorge may have been driven by nationalism and by a dislike for American imperialism, possibly spurred by the U.S. invasion of his hometown when he was a child.

Pasquel and his brothers were multi-millionaire owners of the Azules de Veracruz of the Mexican League. They also had interests in various other clubs. Jorge In 1946, Pasquel assumed the Presidency of the Mexican League president in 1946. For several years he had already been importing players to Mexico from the American Negro Leagues. Post-war, Pasquel began to offer high salaries to bring white major league talent to Mexico.

Farfetched as this sounds today, this was poison in 1946. Most professional athletes had suffered some sort of hardship or deprivation during the war. If they hadn't been in the service, their salaries had been kept down and precious playing years had been lost. The Pasquel brothers, who often brandished pistols as they went about doing business, offered to make up for this with a quick fix of cash.

The Giants reported for training camp in March of 1946. Mercifully the team trained in Miami. But a few days after camp was in session, Danny Gardella - who else? - shocked the rest of the squad by revealing that he had signed with the Mexican League.

The Dauntless One explained to sportswriters that the Giants had been unappreciative of his "gifted talents." Danny had hit 18 home runs the previous year, he reminded everyone, and yet the tightwads in the front office were offering him only a $500 raise to $5,000 per year. The Giants, said Dauntless Dan in so many words, could take it and stuff it. And by the way, he concluded, his roommate Nap Reyes and pitcher Adrian Zabala were going with him.

Uh-huh.

Ott was not exactly reduced to tears hearing that Gardella would be gone. In all likelihood, little Danny had been earmarked for Jersey City, an allegation that Gardella also made. The loss of Reyes and Zabala didn't hurt, either. The Giants, it seemed to Ott, had a ton of good players.

A month later, however, things were not so funny. The Pasquels had picked off Vern Stephens of the Browns, the American League's home run champion of 1945, and Max Lanier, who had been the Cardinals' top pitcher in 1944. Mickey Owen and Luis Olmo of the Dodgers had also defected. Serious proposals were made to such stars as Phil Rizzuto, who was unhappy with what the Yankees were paying him, and Stan Musial. Then the Pasquels walked off with Giants Sal Maglie, Roy Zimmerman, and George Hausmann. Suddenly the Giants were minus seven players. Soon, after the season began, it was even worse. Pitcher Harry Feldman defected, and so did the club's only relief specialist, Ace Adams. According to Ott, the two hurlers showed up in the clubhouse one day before the other players had reported, packed their gear, and departed.

"I understand," Ott told the press, "that they were flashing a roll of bills totaling about $15,000. Well, I'm missing nothing."

Ott was whistling in the dark. He was missing a third of a major league team and some of his more effective pitchers. Just as the recently-concluded world war had devastated the Giants roster, now the raids by the Mexican League would raid the postwar roster.

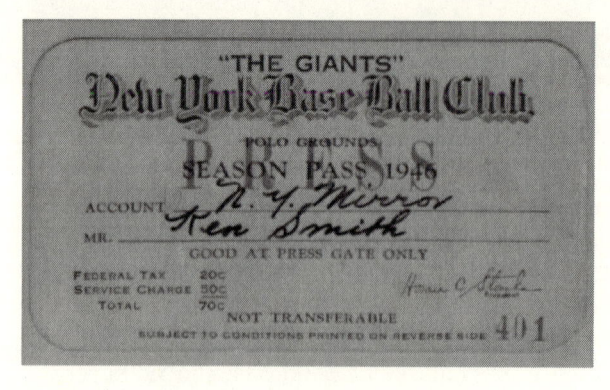

On Opening Day 1946 in Boston, the player pilferages from down south were subject to particular interest. The Dodgers visited the Braves, whose ballpark had been spruced up with fresh green paint. The weather was cold and drizzly, but Boston wanted to give the Brooklyn team, still managed by Leo Durocher, a warm reception. So they hired a mariachi band to play South of The Border in deference to Mickey Owen's defection to the Veracruz Blues. The green paint, however, proved more memorable than the Braves' 5-3 victory.

The paint had not dried properly due to the cold wet weather. What's the polite way to explain what happened? Thousands of fans left the game with green paint on their backsides. The team ran ads offering to compensate any fan for his or her cleaning bills. Claims rolled in from all over North America. The Braves paid all of them. The crosstown Red Sox, however, noted the popularity of the rich green hue and used the same tone to pain their monstrous left field wall by opening day the following year. Thus the Monster became The Green Monster. How far wrong can you go with the color green in Celtic Beantown, after all?

Elsewhere around the league, the weather was even worse.

In St. Louis, ex-Giant and ex-Cardinal Frankie Frisch now managed the visiting Pittsburgh Pirates. Frisch sent some kids out to gather wood before the game and started a fire in a wheelbarrow in the dugout as the game proceeded. The frozen Cardinals lost to the not-as-freezing Pirates, 6-3.

Back in New York, Ott, now in his 20th major league season, would thrill the Opening Day audience at the Polo Grounds by looping a fly ball into the right field stands for his 511th home run. The home run was witnessed by another native Louisiana, actress Dorothy Lamour, well known for the Hope-Crosby-Lamour *Road To* – movies of the 1940s, but even better known as every G.I.'s favorite scantily clad - for the time - pin-up star of the war years. (We see her here in *The Jungle Princess*.) Today, Lamour wore a large sweeping white hat in her seat behind the Giants' dugout, not to draw attention or anything.

A few seats away at the Polo Grounds, sat a man named Tryge Lie.

Who?

Lie was the first United Nations Secretary General, the predecessor of the better-remembered Dag Hammarskjold. Lie, a Norwegian socialist, had once met Vladimir Lenin while on a Labor Party visit to Moscow in the 1920s. Lie later agreed to offer Trotsky asylum in Norway until Joe Stalin allegedly personally contacted him and talked him out of it.

Trotsky subsequently settled in Mexico City where he was assassination by Stalin. (If only he had had the Pasqual Brothers' bodyguards and arsenals, things might have worked out better.) During the war, Lie had been the Foreign Minister of the Norwegian government-in-exile in London.

Post-war, Lie's life would not be without its bizarre moments. Lie was a big heavy man. Uncharitably, he might have been described as porky. Once in Geneva he jammed himself into a small private elevator with Fiorello LaGuardia, by this time former mayor of New York City. The combined weight of the two men approached 500 pounds. When the doors closed on the two gentlemen the elevator, instead of rising, slowly sank out of sight. Multilingual cursing arose from the shaft. A Swiss engineer was summoned, and the elevator was slowly cranked up to its original position to release its angry beefy cargo.

Now, today at the Polo Grounds, because Tryge Lie's life had apparently just not been interesting enough, he was seeing his first American baseball game and meeting Mel Ott and a voluptuous movie star on the same afternoon.

Those who stayed at the Polo Grounds for the full nine innings on this Opening Day 1946 saw the Giants defeat the Phillies, 8-4. Those who stayed did not include Dorothy Lamour, who hustled to the exit after the first inning, perhaps to beat the traffic.

"Against protocol," wrote John Lardner, who at the time was the author of a weekly column for *Newsweek* called "Sport Week." Lardner facetiously suggested that protocol insisted that the Phillies pitcher, that day Oscar Judd, should be allowed to leave first. Judd, an amiable Canadian-born hurler with a predilection for wild pitches, left in the bottom of the second, down six-zip. So far, so good for the New Yorkers, but the season was just hours old.

The next day was catastrophic for the Giants. Mel Ott dived for a ball in the outfield and mangled his knee. He barely played the rest of the year, hitting an anemic .074.

Several players had defected to the Mexican League, as noted, but now for the Giants, the rest of the season went south.

Bill Voiselle, Number 96, the former Rookie of the Year, pitched well but lost 19 games, many of them painful. Hartung remained in the minor leagues. Walker Cooper had an assortment of injuries, as did Johnny Mize. Mize's case was particularly perverse, as he suffered a beaning, a broken hand, then a fractured toe, yet almost led the league in home runs with 22 in 109 games. Ralph Kiner - as in "Going, going, gone! Good-bye!"- led the league with 23.

The team slipped to seventh place in late May. Plop. Every time they seemed to turn a corner, they encountered a manhole. Soon they were playing peek-a-boo with the cellar, just as they had in 1943.

The day to day players, you ask?

Carroll (Whitey) Lockman, who would eventually become one of the most popular Giants of all time, made his debut as a regular outfielder, having been switched from first base. But he also spent much of the year in the army. Johnny Mize replaced him at first base when he was healthy. Buddy Kerr, a native Noo Yawker from Astoria, Queens, developed into a fine shortstop. Outfielder Goody Rosen, a Toronto native born to Russian Jewish immigrants in Toronto, and a former Dodger, acquired from Brooklyn, punctuated the season's series with the Dodgers with a rip-roaring fistfight with Eddie Stanky after the latter had come in hard at second base.

Rosen obviously knew something about throwing his fists. His older brother Jake was a boxer who fought out of New York and Chicago in the 1920s. Bill Rigney became a regular at third.

In 1943, the New York Giants had purchased Rigney's contract from Oakland in exchange for Dolph Camilli, who became the Oaks' player-manager. Rigney was discharged from the U.S. Army in November of 1945 and signed a contract for 1946. When he arrived in New York after spring training, it was the first time he had seen the city. Like many ballplayers of his and prior eras, he played in the first major-league game he saw.

And now the good news!

During all this time, despite the loss of nine players to the Mexican League, despite a record of 61 wins and 93 losses by the end of the season, the turnstiles at the Polo Grounds swirled wildly. A total of 1,234,733 fans paid their way into the park, such was the postwar romance with baseball. It was only fitting then, in an incident that would have ironic overtones for both the New York and Brooklyn clubs, that Mel Ott and Leo Durocher would unwittingly create a bit of Americana late in the year.

The Dodgers played a doubleheader at the Polo Grounds. Mize and Lombardi homered in the first game to win for Dave Koslo. In the second game, the Dodgers gained a split, despite New York home runs by Buddy Blattner, Ernie Lombardi, and Willard Marshall. The next day, Dodger radio broadcaster Red Barber sat near Durocher in the Brooklyn dugout, needling Leo about the events of the previous afternoon.

"Leo," said the soft-spoken redhead, "how about those five home runs yesterday? Your guys were lucky to split."

"Home runs? Home runs?" snapped Durocher, taking the bait. *"Home runs!* Those were line drives and pop-ups that would have been caught in any other park! That's what they were!"

Barber continued, "Why don't you admit they were real home runs? Why don't you be a nice guy for a change?"

The suggestion of being a nice guy ignited Leo. He launched into a soliloquy that probably could have been heard across the Harlem River in Yankee Stadium. Various versions have been recounted over the years, but it went pretty much this way:

"A nice guy?" he roared. "A nice guy! I never saw a nice guy who was any good when you needed him. Go up to one of those nice guys when you need a hundred [dollars] to get you out of a jam, and he'll give you that 'sorry, pal, I'd like to help you, but things aren't going so good back at the ranch.'"

Leo paused and heated up, his voice becoming shrill, according to witnesses. "'I'll take the guys who ain't nice. The guys who would put you in a cement mixer if they felt like it. But you just get in a bind. You don't have to come to them. They'll come looking for you and ask, 'How much do you need?'"

Eventually, Durocher pointed across the field to the Giant bench. "Look over there. Do you know a nicer guy than Mel Ott? Or any of the other Giants? Why, they're the nicest guys in the world. And, where are they? In last place!"

Now Leo was in full gear. He looked at the batting cage where Eddie Stanky was taking his final swings. "Look at that little bastard," Leo said approvingly. "Think he's a nice guy? The hell he is. He'll knock you down and pick you up and say, 'I'm sorry.' That's the kind of guys I want on my ball club. He can't run, he can't hit, he can't do nothing. But what a ballplayer! I wouldn't trade him for any two second basemen in the league!"

Frank Graham, employed by the New York *Journal-American* at the time, was one of those fortunate writers in attendance. The next day Graham printed Durocher's remarks. Somehow the full statement (which was recalled in varying ways by those in attendance) got contracted into the immortal, "Nice guys finish last." With that editing, Leo became one of two ballplayers to earn entry into Bartlett's *Familiar Quotations:* The other is Satchel Paige with, "Don't look back. Something may be gaining on you."

The "nice guys" that Leo designated, Ott and the Giants, *did* finish last that year, eighth in an eight-team league. {The timing of Leo's rant was oddly ironic, as Mel Ott, on a not-so-nice day apparently, had become the first manager to be ejected from both ends of a doubleheader a month earlier against Pittsburgh.} But it might also be noted that Leo's not-so-nice guys, the Dodgers, lost a two-game playoff for the pennant to the St. Louis Cardinals. Bad guys, one might conclude, didn't necessarily finish first, either.

*

Mel Ott would never play again after the 1947 season. He ended his playing career with 511 career home runs, more than 200 more than any other National Leaguer. The total was exceeded only by Babe Ruth (714) and Jimmie Foxx (535). Ott's total of 21 seasons as a player with the New York Giants is the longest of any baseball player to play consecutively with a New York area team, rivaled only by the 21-season tenure of Martin Brodeur, the Hockey Hall of Fame goal tender of the New Jersey Devils.

The New York Giants Preservation Society

No more New York Giants fans? Think again.
The New York Giants Preservation Society exists at an on line site which you are free to visit and join. The group is loosely structured and has occasional meetings in the New York City area. The guiding light is a gentleman named Gary Mintz who inherited NY Giants fandom from his father. You can contact Gary and visit the group page on Facebook or here:

http://newyorkgiantspreservationsociety.com.
There are group meetings in Manhattan at various time of the year and usually at least one trip to Citi Field to see the Giants play the Mets. Here are a pair of pictures from the August 2018 visit.

PART FIVE:

THE FINAL MOMENTS OF GLORY

Chapter 70   Window Breakers

"I come to play. I come to beat you. I come to kill you."

Leo Durocher

When World War Two ended, the America that emerged in the late 1940's was prosperous, impatient, exhilarated, noisy and relieved. Those Americans who had survived could go about their lives again, without the interference of foreign politics. Or so they felt. There was more time for recreation than ever before. This continued to manifest itself in New York City. The turnstiles, in other words, continued to spin like the revolving doors at Grand Central Station at rush hour.

The year 1947 was unlike any before or after in terms of paid attendance. The Brooklyn Dodgers packed 1,807,596 paid admissions - plus all the people who habitually snuck in - into cozy little Ebbets Field, a site that seated no more than 32,500 at any given moment. Frequently, if you left your seat during a game, it was occupied by an imposing stranger in a 'wife-beater' and a Dodger cap by the time you returned.

The Yankees, proving the old adage about the rich getting richer, led the three metropolitan teams with a whopping 2,200,369. The Giants, as was the custom in that decade, brought up the rear, but they did it in healthy fashion. A total of 1,599,784 fans paid their way into the Polo Grounds. John McGraw would have been pleased.

Helping the turnstiles whirl, of course, was the coming of Jackie Robinson. Branch Rickey's well-chronicled move probably would have pleased John McGraw also, as McGraw had many times looked longingly at the talent in the Negro leagues. The addition of Robinson was the precise ingredient missing from the Dodgers in 1946 and was the extra dimension that propelled the Bums into the 1947 World Series, a typical autumnal dogfight with the dreaded Yankees, who, typically again, won in seven games.

When a team finishes eighth one year, with several ballplayers defecting to a foreign country, as was the case for the Giants in

1946, it stands to reason that the next year might be an improvement. And so it was with the 1947 Polo Grounders.

Mel Ott, recovering from the raids from Mexico, had put together a team in his own image. If ever there were a one-dimensional team, this one was it. Ott knew his own bat was gone from the lineup. He wanted to make sure the team had some power.

It did.

The 1947 Giants were a collection of strapping, shuffling sluggers. It was a bitter irony that McGraw's kid, Mel Ott, would resort to this. The Giants played exactly the type of game that McGraw loathed. They played for the home run and the big inning. They never bunted and rarely stole. But unlike 1946, they *did* win some ball games and they *did* make things exciting.

They opened the season in Philadelphia with Bill Voiselle pitching and Walker Cooper catching. Mize, solid as a redwood, was at first. A rookie named Bobby Thomson was, of all places, at second. Sid Gordon was at third, and Bill Rigney, filling in for Davey Kerr, who had been injured in spring training, was at shortstop.

Rookie Al White started in center, flanked by Willard Marshall in right and Clint Hartung in left. If this lineup doesn't sound very familiar, it's because they committed five errors in that first game in Philly, three the next, and three more two days later when the Dodgers opened the Giants' home season at the Polo Grounds. They also hit 6 home runs against the Dodgers, winning for the first time after dumping two games at Philadelphia. The year already promised to be memorable, albeit uneven.

Shortly thereafter, the club fell into a serious slump. Ott rattled the lineup, allowing Kerr to return to shortstop, putting Rigney at third and Buddy Blattner at second. Bobby Thomson moved to center field. Clint Hartung, the most perplexing puzzle on the club, was tried as both a pitcher and an outfielder, and showed alternating flashes of brilliance and incompetence as both. But the team started to win, shocking the entire league by moving into first place by the end of May.

Sid Gordon eventually claimed right field.

Gordon's first full year in the majors had been with the Giants in 1943. He had then spent two years in the U.S. Coast Guard in wartime, not a soft assignment with Nazi submarines lurking off the east coast, Florida and Texas.

Now he turned into a steady player. He also gave fans in New

York a strong solid player to root for. A well-liked, intelligent and highly respected man wherever he traveled, Gordon, Jewish, was nevertheless subjected to ceaseless anti-Semitic taunts by some of the dimmer lights around the National League. In particular, the St. Louis Cardinals rode him mercilessly. Gordon ignored the taunts and took the high road. He used a thirty-one ounce bat, swung it hard, and let the lumber reply to the slurs.

For a while, the Giants were on a merry roll. Three young pitchers whose careers had been delayed by World War Two, began to blossom: Monte Kennedy, Dave Koslo, and Larry Jansen. And the postwar generation of sluggers, the hitters in Ott's own image - Mize, Cooper, Gordon, Marshall, and young Bobby Thomson - started to slug.

The dimensions of the park made slugging easier, of course. By this year, 1947, the Polo Grounds was the way most people would remember it after the team's departure for some place out west. The left field wall – the one on the other side of Matty Schwab's apartment - was 16 feet, 10 inches high, and was 279 feet from home plate. {Author's note: Schwab often insisted he had gone out with a yardstick and measured the distance and found it to be even closer, something many pitchers would have agreed with.} The right field wall was friendlier still: 10 feet 8 inches high, 257 feet from home. In left field, the upper deck overhung the lower deck by about 5 feet.

An outfielder could retreat on a fly ball with the expectation of catching it, only to have it brush the overhang on a downward trajectory and plop at his feet like a dead bird.

Home run.

Similarly, little pop-ups, as Leo Durocher uncharitably suggested when he led the Dodgers, which were harmless flies anywhere else, could tuck themselves around the right field foul pole with disconcerting regularity. More than one checked swing landed in this region. Again, home run.

There was, of course, a quirk.

There was no such thing as a pop fly home run into the lower decks, thanks to those cozy overhanging upper decks. Anything into the lower deck had to be a line drive or, at worst, a humpback liner. Granted, the distance could be short, but the trajectory had to be low and reasonably steady.

The home runs continued to sail out of the park all season, but the pitching faltered in June. Larry Jansen, en route to a 21-5 rookie season, was consistent all year. Koslo and Kennedy were in-and-out, ending the season with 15-10 and 9-12 marks, respectively.

Hartung as a pitcher would be 9-7. As a hitter, in 34 games, he would continue to tantalize with his ability: a .304 average with 4 home runs. The Giants quickly developed a reputation as a high-scoring, highly scored-upon operation.

Trying to shore up some extra pitching, Ott dealt Bill Voiselle to the Braves for Mort Cooper, Walker's brother, reuniting the battery that had won pennants a few years earlier for the Cardinals. Mort Cooper, however, was recovering from an arm operation and was nowhere nearly as effective as he had been in the past.

The team faded back to third place in July but set a National League record by hitting home runs in 16 straight games. "The Window Breakers" was the nickname the press hung on the squad. By August 2, the team had broken the old team home run record of 144 set in 1930. Later that same month, they erased the National League season record for home runs, 171, set by the muscular 1930 Cubs. And in September, the major league record of 182, set by the murderous 1936 Yankees, fell also. But through it all, bad pitching undid games that should have been won. By August the Cardinals and the Dodgers were pulling away, and even the Boston Braves slipped quietly past the Giants.

Still, fourth place was a laudable performance.

It was an improvement from the cellar of the previous year. Horace Stoneham, who watched games through binoculars from his office on the second floor of the center field clubhouse, had to be pleased with attendance. And then there were the individual home run totals. Mize, with 51, tied Ralph Kiner for the league lead and set a Giant club record. Marshall, Cooper, and Thomson had 36, 35, and 29, respectively, to finish third, fourth, and fifth in the league. Bill Rigney had 17. Sid Gordon had 13 and third baseman Jack "Lucky" Lohrke had 12.

Who?

"Lucky" Lohrke came about his nickname the hard way: he earned it several times.

During World War Two as a US soldier, he survived a troop train crash that killed three and injured dozens more. He fought in the D-Day invasion of Normandy and the Battle of the Bulge as a member of the 35th Infantry Division,

On four occasions, solders on both sides of him died in combat, yet Lohrke was untouched. On his way home from the war in 1945, he was bumped from a military transport plane in Ohio to make room "for some big-shot," as he recalled it.

The plane crashed 45 minutes later, killing all on board.

Whatever angel was watching over Jack Lohrke - for whatever reason, he did not like his nickname – it continued to keep an eye on him after the war. He resumed his baseball career in 1946. That season found him playing for the Spokane Indians of the Class B Western International League.

Lohrke was a passenger on the team bus carrying the team as it traveled toward Bremerton, Washington, June 24th to begin a road trip. At the time, Lohrke was hitting .345 in 229 at bats. His performance had earned him a promotion to the Triple-A San Diego Padres in the Pacific Coast League. When he was called up, he was on the team bus in transit between cities.

The Indians' business manager contacted the police along the route and asked that they relay the message to Lohrke, which they did when the Indians stopped for dinner. Lohrke, under orders to report immediately to the Padres, removed his gear from the bus. He said goodbye to his teammates and hitchhiked back to Spokane. That same evening, the team bus broke through a guard rail on a mountain pass, plunged down a hill, and crashed. Nine of fifteen players were killed, including player/manager Mel Cole. The six survivors were badly injured.

Lohrke, seen here, happy to at last be in the majors, reached the Polo Grounds the next year, 1947.

He debuted at third base in the Giants' third game of the campaign. He knocked out his first major league hit, a single, in his first big league at-bat, against the Dodgers' Vic Lombardi. He was immediately caught trying to steal second, proving that no one's luck is perfect. His first major league home run came on June 9 at the Polo Grounds. The lucky pitcher was Pittsburgh's Kirby Higbe. A young third baseman, he also got to meet the man considered at the time to be the greatest third baseman ever, Honus Wagner, when the Giants played against the Pirates at Forbes Field. Lucky again.

In this year of 1947, Jack Lohrke played in 112 games for the Giants, starting 102 at third base. He hit .240 with 11 home runs and

35 runs batted in. One home run had historical significance. It was the Giants' 183rd home run of the season, which broke what was then the major league record for home runs in a season: 182, held by the 1936 Gehrig-Dickie-DiMaggio-Selkirk New York Yankees.

Lohrke shrugged off his contribution to baseball trivia.

"With guys like Johnny Mize, Walker Cooper, and Willard Marshall around, I was pretty much lost in the shuffle," he said many years later.

Nonetheless, the team set a new record with 221 home runs for the year, a mark surpassed many times since by many clubs. The downside, of course, was defense and speed. The Giants had 29 stolen bases for the year, the same number as Rookie of the Year Jackie Robinson. Still, one came away from the 1947 season with the impression that if the Giants had only had a better pitching staff, they could have been in the pennant race, maybe even in the World Series.

Over the winter, the newspapers were filled with the usual scuttlebutt about the Giants. Deals would have to be swung, the sportswriters surmised astutely, to secure more pitching for Ott's team. But none were. Ott maintained that he had some good arms and they would eventually come around.

This manifested itself in the 1948 spring training camp with the presence of forty-one-year-old Thornton (Lefty) Lee, a castoff from the American League, and thirty nine-year-old Bobo Newsom, whose better years with the Browns and Senators were already past. The quirkiest experiment of all was the attempted conversion of Jim Gladd from catcher to pitcher. Well, he had always thrown well but never had hit much.

Perhaps the writing was already on the wall for Mel Ott. Unlike Bill Terry, who had taken over a nucleus of fine ballplayers from the final days of Mr. McGraw, Ott hadn't been left with much to build a future. Then World War Two and the Mexican League had only made a bad situation worse. Now, going into 1948, the Giants hadn't won a pennant in over a decade and hadn't won a World Championship in fifteen years.

The front office, meaning Mr. Stoneham, was getting understandably itchy. And why not? The Yankees had the class and the Dodgers had the flash. The Giants were playing left out.

A Famed Actress Reminisced

I keep a radio going in my dressing room whenever possible so I can hear the Giant games. I have always been a rabid Giant fan. The name Giants is right for my team. Who could stand in awe of a team named the Cubs? Cubs are cute. Or the Dodgers? I never dodged anything in my life. Cincinnati? Too many Republicans. Pittsburgh always depresses me. They beat the Giants too often, and the elevators in the William Penn Hotel are too confusing for words. What I like best about St. Louis is the zoo. And the beer is fine in Milwaukee. But the Giants are a name to look up to. And I simply must know how they are doing every day. Last summer during the Giants' six straight over Brooklyn, I was on stage each day for most of the third act. So one of the cast wrote the inning score on a card and stuck it in his shirt where I could see it when he walked on stage.

Actress Tallulah Bankhead, *Look* Magazine, September 21, 1954

{Tallulah Bankhead (1902 – 1968) was an iconic American film and stage actress, best known for her husky voice, outrageous life style, cigarettes – 150 a day sometimes, the ciggy butts eventually contributed to emphysema and death - unapologetic promiscuity and devastating wit. While her career started in London in 1923, she was one of America's most recognizable actresses well into the 1960s. Her most prominent film role was in Alfred Hitchcock's *Lifeboat*. (Seen here, *Lifeboat* cast, Walter Slezak, John Hodiak, Tallulah Bankhead, Henry Hull, William Bendix, Heather Angel, Mary Anderson, Canada Lee, and Hume Cronyn. Bendix would later play Babe Ruth in *The Babe Ruth Story*.)

Bankhead was well paid, usually $50,000 in the 1950s for a four week or six week shoot. But she disliked Hollywood. At a meeting with producer Irving Thalberg, she once inquired, "How do you get laid in this dreadful place?" Thalberg answered, "I'm sure you'll have no problem. Ask anyone." Well, apparently not just anyone. In 1932 she starred in *Devil and the Deep*. She received top billing over Cary Grant, Charles Laughton, and Gary Cooper. She later said, "Dahling, the main reason I accepted the role was to fuck that divine Gary Cooper." }

Chapter 71   Leo: The News Watch Never Stopped

"Thou shalt not steal. I mean defensively.
On offense, indeed thou shall steal and thou must."

Branch Rickey

i

Another strange series of events which was in motion already, a set of occurrences having nothing to do with the Giants at the outset, yet which determined their destiny for the rest of their stay in New York. The events dated back to November 1946.

At that time Branch Rickey, the president of the Brooklyn Dodgers, sent his top assistant to Cincinnati to urge Commissioner Happy Chandler to contact Leo Durocher. Durocher was the Dodger manager. Rickey was hopeful that Chandler would impress upon Durocher the unsavory quality of what was cryptically described as "Durocher's associations off the field."

Durocher was spending a warm, gentle winter ensconced in the Coldwater Canyon, California home of his good friend actor George Raft. Raft was one of the highest paid movie stars of the postwar years, and his specialty, even then, was an all-too-realistic portrayal of gangsters. Raft's acting ability bothered no one. What bothered Chandler, and Rickey before him, was Raft's well known habits of researching his gangster roles. That and his friendship with Durocher.

Raft had wonderful street credibility. He had been raised in the same rough and tumble stretch of Manhattan's Tenth Avenue as Ruby Keeler and Ray Bolger. He was a childhood friend of gangsters Bugsy Siegel and Owney Madden, a British-born mobster nicknamed "The Killer," who had run The Cotton Club in Harlem and who had become a millionaire during Prohibition.

Raft had run away from home at age thirteen. He tried his hand at being a baseball player, a boxer and an electrician, and finally settled on working as a "paid dancer," a male escort for female patrons, in several clubs including the Roseland Ballroom. His dancing shoes remained there until the time of his death in 1980.

"George did the fastest and most exciting Charleston I ever saw. I thought he was an extraordinary dancer," said another guy who knew how to move his feet, Fred Astaire.

In 1930, Raft was preparing to go on a tour of Florida with the Primo Carnera traveling boxing show, run by Owney Madden, when he auditioned for a role in director Howard Hawks' film *Scarface* (1932), loosely based on Al Capone. Hawks thought that Raft had a "unique look" and signed him to play Guino Rinaldo, "Scarface's" best friend and a role that was based on Capone's real-life bodyguard and enforcer, Frank Rio. In the film, seen here, Raft is the original coin-flipping mobster.

After a few more such juicy roles, Raft was stereotyped as a hoodlum, which, all things considered, was safer than being one. In his personal life, Raft was soft spoken, exquisitely dressed and had excellent manners. He was popular in Hollywood. He was also said to be generous to children and friends in need. He did have his share of bad publicity, however. In 1933, Tallulah Bankhead nearly died following a five hour emergency hysterectomy due to venereal disease. She claimed she had contracted it from George Raft.

And so the public perception was what it was. And no one disputed that Raft was on tight terms with some questionable people.

Chandler tracked Durocher down by telephone. He found him not at Raft's house but at the Hollywood studios of NBC, where Leo was deeply involved in rehearsal for a skit on Jack Benny's weekly radio show. The commissioner requested Durocher to meet him the following week at the Claremont Country Club in Berkeley.

Leo kept the meeting.

Chandler brought with him a list of personalities that he wished Leo to avoid in the future. In addition to Raft, they included such alleged Durocher gangster pals as Benjamin (Bugsy) Siegel (later to be shot to death in his Beverly Hills home) and Joe Adonis (later to die of a heart attack while in the custody of Italian police, following deportation from the United States). In terms of pop culture, Adonis has returned to the world of 2018 as a character in the cable television series, *Boardwalk Empire*.

Another Durocher pal was a man named Connie Immerman, who had formerly managed The Cotton Club for Madden. These days, fortunately perhaps, he was out of town a lot since he ran a casino in Havana, reputedly for Lucky Luciano.

But wait, there was more. There was always more with Leo.

Durocher, who just couldn't stay away from these people, was also buddy-buddy with a Brooklyn gambling czar and racetrack tout named Max "Memphis" Engleberg. Engleberg had full access to the Dodger locker room and ferried bets from players to local racetracks. Engleberg was one of the few Americans to list "handicapper" as his profession while enlisted in the U.S. Army.

"Engelberg was a close friend of Charlie Dressen's and a good friend of mine," Durocher would cheerfully recall years later. "He had been a bookmaker back in the days when bookmaking was legal in New York. At the time I met him he was probably the best horse handicapper I had ever come across. Whenever I went to the track, which wasn't often, I'd have Memphis mark my card. So did all the players."

Red Barber, then an announcer for the Dodgers, once commented that, "Clubhouse doors could be shut at times to newspapermen but never to Memphis or George Raft."

In the course of the Chandler-Durocher meeting, which took place on the Claremont's fairway, the commissioner asked Durocher if he actually knew Bugsy Siegel and Joe Adonis.

"Nodding acquaintances," Durocher answered with a straight face.

"Don't nod to them anymore," Happy Chandler responded. Chandler added that if Leo palled around again with Raft, Siegel, or Adonis (the names of Immerman and Engleberg apparently got lost in the excitement), he would be suspended from baseball.

Leo, holding a new $50,000-a-year contract as Dodger skipper, seemed to understand Chandler's position, though he wasn't happy about it. He moved out of Raft's digs and cut the ties that Chandler found troublesome.

Everything was fine…for about a month.

Even when Leo wasn't overtly palling around with mobsters, he would somehow seem to be involved with them. A renowned playboy, Durocher had a penchant for actresses. In the past he had been romantically linked with Betty Hutton and Linda Darnell.

Most recently, the target of Leo's affections was a blonde named Edna Ryan, seen in a photo here.

Edna was a showgirl who entertained visitors to New York's Copacabana nightclub at 10 East 60th Street in Manhattan. The night club was opened in Manhattan in 1940, financed by the mobster Frank Costello. It was a celebrity hotspot where socialites dined and made small talk with film stars, sporting heroes, politicians, diplomats and diamond-pinkie-ring mob guys. The club, later famous for the 1957 brawl involving Yankees Billy Martin, Mickey Mantle and Hank Bauer, was particularly noted for its chorus girls, who despite the rules against it, would frequently mingle with the male patrons, giving a heavy air of sex and scandal to the place, not that anyone who went there expected otherwise.

No less an authority than Hugh Hefner once offered the opinion that the Copa's chorus line featured the "finest pins on the planet." Edna was the lead dancer, starting in the mid-1940s, and *the* "Copa Girl" of her time. Edna Ryan drew the attention of paparazzi and gentlemen diners and just about anyone else with two eyes and an above average libido. She frequently popped up in gossip columns. She was described by Walter Winchell, the Broadway columnist as a "long-legged blonde stunner out of the front line" and a "one-girl traffic jam."

So naturally, she was dating Leo, giving him more mob links, albeit once removed.

Then in December of that same year, 1946, a man named Ray Hendricks accused Leo of being "a love pirate," not to be confused with being a Pittsburgh Pirate.

Hendricks' wife was actress Laraine Day. Ah, Hollywood. Now the whole affair, so to speak, took on an extra edge. Leo had dumped Edna Ryan and now taken up with Laraine Day, inconveniently another man's wife.

Laraine Day began acting with a small theatrical company in Long Beach, California. She appeared in her first film in 1937 in a bit part in *Stella Dallas*, a ten-hankie tearjerker starring Barbara Stanwyck, the former Ziegfeld girl. The flic was directed by King Vidor and produced by Sam Goldwyn, whose contribution to American culture included dozens of films (including *Pride of The Yankees*) and such quotes as, "The harder I work, the luckier I get," and "A verbal contract isn't worth the paper it's written on," and "I'm willing to admit that I may not always be right, but I am never wrong," and, "In two words, Im Possible."

Day had been born as Laraine Johnson into a family of affluent Mormons in Roosevelt, Utah. Locally, her father had functioned as a Mormon version of Paul Revere, riding around town to warn polygamists that the federal marshals were in town so that they could hide their surplus wives. Her great-grandfather, three of his six wives, and a few dozen of his 52 children had been early settlers in San Bernardino, Calif. So the move to Long Beach for Laraine Johnson with her family when she was nine was not something unusual.

In 1939, she had one line before dying in a plane crash in *"Tarzan Finds a Son"* (1939). She committed suicide in *"I Take This Woman"* (1940) starring Spencer Tracy and Hedy Lamarr.

In 1939, Laraine signed with Metro-Goldwyn-Mayer, and changed her name to Laraine Day. She soon became popular as Nurse Mary Lamont in a string of Dr. Kildare movies beginning with *Calling Dr. Kildare*. Day played the doc's fiancée. Eventually, in the ninth and final Kildare film in 1941, a sob fest wrap-up titled *Doctor Kildare's Wedding Day,* Nurse Lamont is run over by a truck. Kildare rushes to the scene, which, naturally was in New York, where trucks were known to run people over.

"This is going to be much easier for me than it is for you," she says to the man who loves her as she expires in the doctor's arms.

You couldn't make this stuff up.

Thereafter, through the war years, Laraine Day was a quiet dependable working actress, usually a good looking damsel in distress. Privately, she remained faithful to her Mormon upbringing. "It brings me comfort in a confusing world," she told friends. Throughout her life, she never swore, smoked, or drank any kind of alcohol, coffee, or tea. On May 16, 1942, Day married James Ray Hendricks, a charming former dance-band singer who later became an executive of the Santa Monica airport. Together they adopted two girls and one boy.

Through all this time, Day (pictured here in 1943) would have appeared to be living as sane and balanced a life as any woman in the movie industry. True, she wasn't quite "A List," but she was easily on the "B-Plus List." She worked regularly. If there was one complaint in the film business about her it was that she was regarded as a "cold personality without sex appeal." Too nice," was a frequent criticism. "Too conventional" and "too normal." From a studio publicity angle, it was tough to get her into the newspapers. Worse, she seemed to like it that way.

The only missing ingredient, it turned out, was Leo Durocher.

Out of the blue in 1946 James Hendricks alleged that Leo Durocher, while "posing as a family friend," had wooed her and won her. Hence the "love pirate," allegation.

Lest anyone conclude that Hendricks was hallucinating, Mrs. Hendricks and Mr. Durocher announced that they would soon marry.

Judge George Dockweiler, in granting Ms. Day's request for a divorce in California, ruled that she and Leo must live apart for a year, the legal equivalent of an icy shower.

The lovebirds, their hormonal passions raging, had little use for such a decree. Laraine Day flew to Juarez, Mexico and filed for a quickie second divorce. Then Leo joined her in El Paso, just a few quick paces across the bridge from Juarez. There he and Laraine were married - perfectly legally - precipitating a contempt citation from Judge Dockweiler.

Now she had as much publicity as she had never wanted. Now the chilly persona became hot, hot, hot. Her price to do a film doubled. Newspapers and fanzines clamored for tidbits and interviews. She began filming a new pic titled *Tycoon* with John Wayne and Leo hung around the set as much as possible.

She was not the only one to benefit. Her studio released her latest picture, *The Locket*, ahead of its scheduled date to cash in on the publicity. A Brooklyn movie house that did second runs began showing a previous picture, *Mr. Lucky*, and changed its marquee to read, "Starring Mrs. Leo Durocher and Cary Grant." The

Hollywood proverb that "The only bad publicity is no publicity" seemed particularly apt.

Yet while true love had found its way down by the Rio Grande and across American box offices, back up in the National League headquarters in Cincinnati, Happy Chandler was simmering. Then he was burning.

Nor was Chandler the only one upset by Leo's latest behavior. Durocher had been involved in bad publicity before. His case before the public was not helped, for example, when his first wife alleged that Leo tied her up in bed sheets and beat her. In fact, Leo was rarely too far from bad publicity. But now - in the public perception - he had run off with another man's wife. This drew before him yet another formidable adversary: the Roman Catholic Church, for which, to mix the metaphors, this was one toke over the line.

In February of 1947, Reverend Vincent Powell, speaking on behalf of the Brooklyn Catholic Youth Organization, publicly slammed Leo for "undermining the moral training of Brooklyn's Roman Catholic youth by his conduct both on and off the baseball diamond."

This condemnation, while it might draw snickers today, was not something to be taken lightly at the time by Branch Rickey. The Dodger owner always had his eyes on the turnstile. The CYO had no fewer than fifty thousand members in Brooklyn, most of whom attended more than one Dodger game per season. The clear threat, as voiced by Reverend Powell, was that those kids would be packed off to Giant or Yankee home games instead if Leo remained with the Brooklyn club. Leo, always able to come up with a snappy and incendiary response, replied that from what he had seen, the youth of Brooklyn were perfectly capable of corrupting themselves.

ii

Now, as mentioned, Durocher was no stranger to controversy. He had been an infielder with the Ruth-Gehrig Yankees of 1928 and 1929, had spent several years with the Cincinnati Reds. Along with Pepper Martin and Frankie Frisch, he had sparked the St. Louis Cardinals' championship Gashouse Gang in 1934. All that was fine. But Leo's name had surfaced almost as often on pages other than those given to sports.

Durocher, many fans were reminded at the time, had grown up in the industrial slums of West Springfield, Massachusetts, in the early years of the Twentieth Century. As a teenager in Springfield, Leo worked in a factory, then supplemented his income by hustling games at a local pool hall. At this, as in all other respects of hustling, Durocher became quite adept. According to those who knew him in this era, Leo rarely lost.

Durocher signed a professional baseball contract with Hartford in 1925, the same franchise through which the young Henry Louis Gehrig had passed. Shortly after Durocher's arrival, some of the other players began to discover money missing from their wallets. A trap involving a marked five-dollar bill was set. Sure enough, shortly after this bill disappeared from one player's wallet, it was located in Leo's.

The other Hartford players wished to lynch Leo right there, or at least have him suspended from baseball. The Hartford manager, however, was a man named Paddy O'Connor. O'Connor had appeared briefly in the major leagues with four clubs. Perhaps looking out for his own long-term interests as a minor league manager, O'Connor knew he needed a shortstop. He worked out a compromise with his players. He would dispose of Leo at the end of the season, right after the Eastern League pennant race was decided. This O'Connor did by peddling Durocher to the Yankees.

Much like his future pal George Raft, Durocher maintained some lifelong friendships with a jaw-dropping coterie of hoods. "Lifelong" for characters of this sort didn't last that many years, however.

One Durocher crony from Springfield, was a lad named Gerry Chapman, who was also known as "The Count of Gramercy Park" and "Gentleman Gerald." Chapman was the leader of an early Prohibition era gang from 1919 until the mid-1920s. Chapman also had the honor of being the first criminal to be dubbed "Public Enemy Number One" by the press, quite an accomplishment given the amount of competition.

Chapman was in and out of prison most of his adult life. He was serving a 25-year-sentence at the Atlanta Federal Prison when he escaped on December 30, 1923. On October 12, 1924, while on a crime spree in Connecticut, Chapman murdered Officer James Skelly of the New Britain Police Department. Chapman was recaptured on January 18, 1925, in Muncie, Indiana, based on authorities being tipped off by an informant named Ben Hance, who would be murdered not long afterwards.

During his apprehension, Chapman fired at a police officer but missed. President Calvin Coolidge was convinced to reduce the robbery sentence of Chapman in federal prison to time served, but Chapman was then handed over to the Connecticut authorities. Chapman was eventually executed by a macabre device known as an "upright jerker." Rather than dropping down through a trapdoor, the condemned would be violently jerked upright into the air by means of a system of weights and pulleys. This came to pass on April 6, 1926. Meanwhile, Leo, the boyhood pal of The Count of Grammercy Park, was trying to catch on with the New York Yankees as a middle infielder.

In 1928, Durocher made the Yankees.

Dark clouds continued to follow.

Shortly after joining New York in 1928, Durocher was at shortstop against Detroit and the batter was Robert (Fatty) Fothergill. Fothergill was a benign outfielder who stood five feet ten and a half and weighed 230 pounds, though he was a skilled hitter. He was Detroit's answer to Shanty Hogan. With two out in the ninth and runners on base, Durocher called time and trotted to the plate.

"What's going on here?" Durocher complained to the umpire. "You can't have two men batting at once."

At first the umpire didn't know what Leo was talking about. Then he turned and looked at the rotund Fothergill. Leo scampered back to his position as the furious Fothergill cursed the disrespectful rookie. But, his concentration shot, Fothergill fanned to end the game.

Less amusing was another story that rarely found its way into print, but which traveled through baseball clubhouses for years.

Leo, on arriving with the Yankees, also made the mistake of antagonizing Babe Ruth. This wasn't easy since Ruth liked almost everyone. But Ruth, like most of the Yankees, disliked Durocher's brashness. At Durocher's first spring training, Ruth spotted Leo in a tuxedo, getting ready to do the town one evening. "Who's the little gink in the monkey suit?" Ruth asked. Things went downhill from there.

Sometime later, Ruth careened back to the Yankees' hotel one night, drunk out of his mind. He asked for help getting undressed and into bed. This was a duty that other players had learned to avoid. But according to the story that eventually circulated, Leo volunteered. He and the grossly intoxicated Ruth then disappeared down a hallway.

The next morning Ruth decided that his watch had been stolen.

He further decided that Durocher had taken it. The charge was given some credibility by other players due to the $5-bill incident in Hartford. Yet no one had even noticed whether Ruth had been wearing his watch when he had lurched in the previous evening. No one knew which half dozen women he might have been lolling around with, what gutter he could have been rolling through, or in what speakeasy he had tied on his load. There was, in short, not one shred of evidence suggesting that Leo had swiped the Babe's watch.

"Jesus Christ," Durocher once said, "if I was going to steal anything from him, I'd steal his goddamned Packard."

Yet the story followed Leo from club to club. Opponents for years liked to get Durocher's goat by standing on their dugout steps, waving watches at him. Nor was Leo's Yankee career helped in 1929 when he was linked to a series of checks written to merchants around Yankee Stadium. The checks were returned for insufficient funds. Leo, apparently had lived too well on his $5,000-a-year salary. He was waiting for the big World Series check in 1929 to take care of his debts. Unfortunately, the Philadelphia A's became World Champions that year.

Now, Leo loved Brooklyn and generally was well appreciated by the fans there, particularly in 1941 when he guided the Dodgers to their first pennant since the days of Uncle Robbie.

"It was Brooklyn against the world," Leo recalled many years later. "They knew baseball like the fans of no other city. It was exciting to play there. It was a treat. I walked into that crummy, flyblown park as Brooklyn manager for nine years, and every time I entered, my pulse quickened and my spirits soared."

But that in itself did not mean that life always proceeded smoothly for the Lip in the Borough of Churches. In June of 1945 the dark clouds started to surround him again.

One of the habitués of Ebbets Field in those days was a big, noisy 200-pound fan named John Christian, a recently discharged veteran of World War Two. Christian, in the habit of making his views known in no uncertain terms, owned a foghorn voice that could be heard almost to the outfield. Decorum was not an area of Mr. Christian's expertise. According to some of the Dodger players, the term "motherfucker" was tossed in their direction more than once.

One summer evening Mr. Leo Durocher apparently decided that he had heard enough from Mr. John Christian. The vehicle for silencing Christian was a massive, thuggish 270-pound security guard named Joe Moore.

"Among the young rooters who often tried to sneak into the park," wrote Peter Golenbock in his marvelous book *Bums,* "Moore was notorious. He would bellow, 'If I catch you, you're gonna get a kick right in the ass!' Fortunately for the kids, his gross weight slowed him down, and he didn't catch the kids - often."

On June 8, 1945, while a Dodger game was in progress, Moore summoned Christian to a private cubicle not far from the Dodger dugout. Leo was waiting there.

Exactly who struck whom first remains open to question. Whether or not Christian deserved a pop in the mouth depends on one's sense of etiquette. Let's say he did. But the fact was, Christian fled the ballpark moments later, his teeth loosened, his mouth bleeding, his jaw broken, though finally silent.

On the way to the hospital, he stopped off at the Empire Boulevard police precinct and alleged that Moore and Durocher had worked him over with brass knuckles. The next morning Moore and Durocher were arrested for assault.

Moore and Durocher were released on bail. Christian sued everyone and eventually collected $6,750 from the Brooklyn club's insurance company. The criminal case meandered through the courts until Judge Samuel Liebowitz eventually dismissed it.

{This being Brooklyn, Liebowitz was a colorful character in his own right. In his younger days as a trial attorney, he defended mobster Al Capone as well as the Scottsboro Boys, a group of African-American teenagers, ages 13 to 19, falsely accused in Alabama of raping two white women on a train. Later in life, he would hand long prison sentences to the drug smugglers in the "French Connection" case. At the time he dismissed the suit against Leo, Judge Liebowitz was an ardent Dodger fan, not that this could have had any bearing on his decision.}

After the John Christian incident was settled, newspapers started zeroing in on Durocher with other stories. A far-right columnist and professional gasbag named Westbrook Pegler led the charge.

Pegler was a piece of work, also. In a way, Leo and Westbrook deserved each other.

Pegler once lamented the failure of would-be assassin Giuseppe Zangara, who missed FDR and killed the mayor of Chicago instead. Zangaga "hit the wrong man" when gunning for Franklin Roosevelt, said Pegler. Now Pegler took time out from blasting Eleanor Roosevelt and racial equality – he hated both - to draw a bead on Durocher.

In one column, Pegler maintained that actor George Raft had used Durocher's New York apartment to hustle a wealthy sucker out of $12,500 in a crooked dice game. Then other stories began to circulate: Durocher's name had appeared on a series of checks involved in a complicated fraudulent check scheme racket that netted $800,000 for some Hollywood gangsters. And another tale surfaced in which the New York City police had tapped Leo's telephone and knew he had received at least one call from the office of Joe Adonis.

Pegler never pointed out, however, that Raft denied that the dice game ever took place, and no one maintained that Durocher been present. Similarly, Durocher's name was one of a thousand that popped up in the check swindle and Leo had nothing to do with the scam. And the phone call from the Adonis office had been from an underling inquiring about some bats and balls that Leo had agreed to contribute to a church charity.

But, with all of these sordid tales about Leo selling newspapers so briskly, some of the other knights of the newspaper profession dredged up some dirty laundry from the distant past, such as the time in Cincinnati when a local girl claimed Durocher had impregnated her. Durocher had been forced to marry the girl, then she had recanted her story, and the Cincinnati ball club had helped get the marriage annulled.

Or so went the story.

All of this, by the time the CYO was yapping for Durocher's hide in February of 1947, was putting Leo on a very hot seat, indeed.

Then came spring training of 1947.

The Dodgers and Yankees began a series of games in Havana in early March. The Dodgers - for reasons known to no one - selected the Hotel Naçional as their headquarters. The Naçional was a gaudy, neon-bedecked legend owned and operated by one Connie Immerman, an intimate of Lucky Luciano and the other "nodding acquaintance" that Leo had been warned to stay away from. The hotel came equipped with a casino into which – somehow - many players seemed to find their way.

During one Saturday evening game, Immerman and Memphis Engleberg, the other "nodding acquaintance" that Leo had been instructed to avoid, occupied a choice box behind the Yankee dugout. To reporters, they appeared to be in a Yankee box and, therefore, guests of the ball club. Reporters asked Durocher about it after the game, reminding Leo of the warnings he had received over his questionable associations.

"I guess there are two sets of rules," Leo answered, "one for club owners and one for managers."

Larry MacPhail, president of the Yankees, was incensed.

When asked about this by a young reporter named Dick Young, MacPhail shot back that the two mobsters were not in seats in a Yankee box at all. Rather they were in an adjoining box with tickets supplied by the Dodgers. Durocher countered that MacPhail was just trying to make trouble. MacPhail, Durocher maintained, had offered him the job of managing the Yankees in 1947, but Durocher had declined.

MacPhail discounted that completely, then had to add an extra dig. "Leo has always wanted to manage the Yankees," MacPhail clucked. "Fact is, we wouldn't have his type at the Stadium."

Back and forth the charges went. The flames spread when MacPhail hired Chuck Dressen and Red Corriden, Durocher's top two coaches in 1946, to come over to the Yankees. The move seemed to make little sense, except as a provocation.

Durocher took his case to the highly-entertained public.

In a column called *Durocher Says* in the Brooklyn *Eagle,* Leo intensified the invective hurled at the Yankees. MacPhail then filed a formal complaint to the commissioner's office. The complaint gave Chandler just the tool he needed to deal with Leo.

On April 9, just before the opening of the season, the season when Jackie Robinson would break the venal color barrier in baseball and many other African-American stars would follow, Chandler fined Leo's ghostwriter, Harold Parrott, one of the Dodgers' media guys, $500 for the column. Then he suspended Durocher from baseball for one year for "an accumulation of unpleasant incidents...detrimental to baseball."

No specific incident was ever cited. Leo was never convicted of anything in any court. What it really came down to was that Chandler didn't care for Leo's lifestyle.

Burt Shotton succeeded Durocher as manager.

Mel Ott managed the Giants to a third place finish. But the excitement in New York City baseball was elsewhere. The Dodgers and the Yankees, now the two most antagonistic organizations in professional sports, each won their pennant and met in the 1947 World Series.

As usual, the Yankees won.

Funny Cars and Midgets in The Land of Giants

The Polo Grounds saw many strange events over the years, but perhaps the strangest was midget auto racing, which was a surprisingly popular spectator sport in the 1930's, then again with a revival after World War Two. The midgets racing, to be clear, were the cars, not the drivers. "Baby smoke-eaters," they were called, and that pretty much says it all. The cars were stripped down versions of their bigger vehicles: usually four cylinder engines with an impressive power-to-weight ratio. To stretch a point, they were half go-carts and half Messerschmitts.

In June of 1948, a board track was temporarily installed at the Polo Grounds and racing program of midget cars took place. Featured were drivers Bill Schindler, pictured on the program, and Lloyd Ruby, both of whom had extensive successive careers. Ruby raced at places like Daytona, Indianapolis and Le Mans. I suppose there were worse things to do on a warm summer night. Ruby is seen here in his highway version of a Messerschmidt. Schindler, one of the pioneers of midget or "sprint car" racing, lost his left leg from above the knee in a racing accident in 1936 at Mineola, Long Island. He later participated in the Indianapolis 500 with a prosthetic leg.

As for the success of racing at the Polo Ground, not so much:

it was never much more than a curiosity, though a few artifacts remain to this day: a program from 1948 and a photo of the track with some of the tiny putt-putts zipping along. One has to wonder how Matty Schwab, the head groundkeeper felt about what was happening to his beautiful playing field.

Chapter 72   Back From Exile

*"Baseball is like church, many
attend, few understand..."*

Leo Durocher

Considerably humbled, Durocher reported to Vero Beach in 1948 to manage the Dodgers. Shotton gracefully stepped back to the coach's box. Leo remained discreetly quiet in the dugout, rarely arguing with umpires and avoiding both press and controversy. It was almost as if Leo had lost his voice. As the season began, the Dodgers piled loss upon loss, even though they were the defending league champions. Many suggested that Leo's newly found manners ruined him as a manager.

But there were other problems. Eddie Stanky, Leo's favorite infielder had been peddled to the Braves. Jackie Robinson, who had broken in with such a flourish in 1947, had been expected to replace Stanky at second base. Robinson had spent the off-season on the "rubber chicken" banquet circuit and reported to camp a prodigious thirty-seven pounds overweight.

Durocher tried to improvise. He converted a minor league catcher named Gil Hodges to first base. It worked. He brought up Roy Campanella, an untested rookie, from Montreal to catch every day. That worked, too. But nothing else fell into place, By July the Dodgers were languishing in sixth place. Worse, many Brooklyn Dodger fans were spending their evenings watching trotters and pacers at the newly opened Roosevelt Raceway instead going to Ebbets Field to watch Dodgers trot around the bases.

Rickey began to think. At the same time, Horace Stoneham was having his own problems.

The 1948 Giants were off to a terrible start. They remained a team with little pitching, no speed, and porous fielding. Stoneham, like Rickey, was looking to make a move. The first one would be to replace popular Mel Ott as manager. Ott had resigned in private and Stoneham hadn't yet found a successor.

Shortly before noon on July 15, 1948, Stoneham and Rickey met in Manhattan. "Mel Ott resigned," Stoneham said. "I need to replace him."

"Who did you have in mind?" Rickey asked, coy as ever.

Stoneham drew a breath. "I want your permission to talk to Burt Shotton," Stoneham said.

"I have plans for Burt."

"Doing what?"

"Managing the Dodgers."

Stoneham, who could barely believe his ears, waited for several seconds.

"What about Leo?" he exclaimed.

"I'm about to dismiss him," said Rickey. "Why? Do you want to talk to him instead of Shotton?"

Horace Stoneham answered that he would very much like to talk to Leo. And by that evening, the baseball world was stunned with the news. Durocher, the most hated Dodger of all at the Polo Grounds, had changed allegiances in the course of a few hours.

One woman who appeared to change allegiance best was Laraine Day. When reporters found her at home in Manhattan and broke the news to her of the big switch, she thought for only a moment. Then she walked to her console radio upon which the Dodger broadcast was about to begin. "I guess I have the wrong game on," she said, flicking to the Giants' station.

Shotton took the helm of the Dodgers. Ott retired. A reserved, subdued, and pensive Leo Durocher - for a short while, anyway - thus became only the fourth New York Giant manager since McGraw arrived from Baltimore in 1902. It was a strange series of events that brought Leo to the Polo Grounds, all set in motion by the off-the-field shenanigans and sexcapades that had resulted in Durocher's suspension.

After Shotton's return to manage, the Dodgers rallied to take the lead in the National League standings by the end of August. It looked as if they had a good chance to win their first pennant since 1941 although the shocking Boston Braves had other plans.

It wasn't just difficult for Giant fans to accept Durocher. After learning to hate him for the past eight years, it was nearly impossible. *Liking* him was almost out of the question.

Even Leo knew this much.

"Like me or not," he recalled much later, "I was going to give the Giant fans a ball club so exciting that they'd come out in spite of me and in spite of themselves."

Yet to picture Leo walking the turf of Christy Mathewson, standing in the dugout where John McGraw had stood, walking to first where Terry had played was like a bad dream.

Yet Leo was there.

Ott, whose number 4 was retired the day he was relieved, never took another field job in baseball. And the move would change the spirit of Giants baseball once again.

"This ain't my kind of team," Leo observed upon arrival, eyeing the lumbering sluggers on his roster.

No, it wasn't.

Nor could anyone expect the scrappy Durocher, who had hit only 24 home runs in his major league career, to take kindly to the array of big, slow, amiable white guys that the Giants had assembled. It was clear from the beginning that Leo would make changes.

Know what? He was right.

When Durocher took over the Giants, the team was in fourth place. Their record was 27-38 and they were tied in the standings with a mediocre Pittsburgh club managed by Billy Meyer. Under Durocher, the team manufactured a modest winning streak, which included a 13-4 bombing of the Dodgers at Ebbets Field, Leo's first visit in the enemy threads.

The game sold out. Thousands of fans, perhaps curious as to how Leo would look in Giants black and orange, were turned away.

Leo looked mildly uncomfortable with the whole thing, particularly posing at home plate for pictures with Burt Shotton. Shotton, Leo's predecessor and successor, still wore street clothes to each game, managing out of uniform from the dugout, Connie Mack style. Shotton was a strange sight, but stranger sights had been viewed in Flatbush.

The pitching then faltered, as Leo had known it would. Inexorably, while still banging home runs, the Giants began their midseason slide toward the second division. It was a strange kind of baseball year all around, with Billy Southworth's Boston Braves out in front of the league, riding the strong arms of Johnny Sain and Warren Spahn and the legendary prayer for rain on any day that the two aces weren't pitching.

{The rhyme was cute and popular, but the truth was the ex-Giant Bill Voiselle was an effective number three guy in the rotation. He won 13 games.}

Third baseman Bob Elliott paced Boston's unforeseen climb with 23 homers and 100 runs batted in. The middle of the Boston defense was the envy of the league, as Leo noted frequently while visiting Boston. Al Dark, the All-American football player from Louisiana State University, was at short. Eddie Stanky, Leo's old second baseman, was now the Braves' new second baseman.

On August 16, Babe Ruth died. Not since the death of Franklin Roosevelt three years earlier had there been a passing that so moved the public. A short time afterward, the Dodgers under Shotton made a run at the Braves.

Just when Brooklyn moved into first place, the Dodgers found themselves scheduled to play four games at the Polo Grounds. Was Leo up for these? Hell, the whole city was up for these.

The Giants swept a twilight-night doubleheader on September 4, a Friday. They increased the misery upon the Dodgers the next day with a 3-0 shutout behind Sheldon (Available) Jones.

The Dodgers salvaged a morsel of their pennant hopes with a victory on Sunday, but the game took twelve innings. The Dodgers had poured their guts out at the Polo Grounds, which is to say that their pennant hopes had been eviscerated. The next day Boston won two from the Phillies and weren't caught again, winning their first pennant since 1914.

Chapter 73   Leo and KOBS

> "You and Durocher are on a raft. A wave comes and knocks him into the ocean. You dive in and save his life. A shark comes and takes your leg. Next day, you and Leo start out even."
>
> **Dick Young**

The Giants played at a 51-38 clip under Durocher, a radical improvement. Leo also salvaged some respect for the Giants, even though the team finished fifth. Hurting the Dodgers helped. And it did not escape the notice of the Polo Grounds faithful that Leo had won the Dodgers-Giants season series from both sides of the river. As Dodger skipper, he was 8-4 against the Giants. At the Giant helm, he was 7-3 against the Dodgers.

Sic transit Leo.

Shortly after taking over, however, Horace Stoneham asked Leo to write out a lengthy report on the Giants. Who should stay? Who should go? Durocher watched his new charges for the last half of the 1948 season and wrote, as he later recalled it, a four-word report: "Back up a truck."

"In other words," he said, "you need a whole new team, Horace."

It was tough advice for Stoneham. He liked his Irish-American middle infield of Kerr and Rigney. He liked his Window Breakers: Mize, Cooper, Marshall, and Gordon. The Giants had outslugged everyone in baseball again, and wasn't that worth something?

No, Leo said, it wasn't.

What good was Buddy Kerr's fielding record for consecutive games without an error, Durocher argued, if he didn't have the range of a Rizzuto or an Al Dark? What good were all the home runs if a manager could use no strategy, no McGraw-style hit-and-run, bunts, or steals?

What good, indeed? Durocher spent many days and nights

arguing the points with Stoneham, endless hours of much disagreement and alcohol.

"To say that Horace can drink," Durocher once wrote, "is like saying Sinatra can sing."

Eventually, Leo got his way. But it took many months, and he only got his way gradually. In the end he would employ one of his favorite tactics: playing men Stoneham liked until they failed in key situations, forcing Stoneham to come around to Leo's way of thinking.

Leo sacked Ott's old coaches, Travis Jackson and Hank Gowdy. Then he traded Walker Cooper to Cincinnati for catcher Ray Mueller.

"I've always felt Durocher would ruin any good ball club," Cooper remarked upon his departure.

Well, maybe. But not immediately.

A young man named Hank Thompson had joined the St. Louis Browns in the summer of 1947, integrating the Browns' lineup two days before Willard Brown made his debut as the second black player on the team. The next day, Thompson played second base and Brown played center field against the all-white Boston Red Sox, managed by Pinkie Higgins, said to be one of the most virulent racists of the era. The game featuring Brown and Thompson marked the first time that two black players appeared in the same major league lineup. One can only imagine Higgins' thoughts in the Boston dugout.

{Higgins, along with owner Tom Yawkey, are often at the center of any discussion of the Boston club's reputation for resisting racial integration. Higgins was said to be notorious for racial slurs as well as profane insults to sportswriters such as Cliff Keane, who covered baseball for The Boston *Globe* from 1939 until his retirement after the 1975 World Series, and who made favorable comment about minority players. The Red Sox didn't field a black player until 1959, twelve years - !!! – after Jackie Robinson had integrated.

{Al Hirshberg, who wrote for the Boston *Post* and the Boston *Herald*, once quoted Higgins as saying, "There'll be no n*****s on this ball club as long as I have anything to say about it."

{Many of the charges against Higgins did not surface in public in his lifetime, so he was unable to defend himself against them. But under his leadership, there would be no pennants, either.}

Coincidence?

A few weeks later, on August 9, 1948 against the Cleveland

Indians, Thompson and Indians outfielder Larry Doby became the first black players of opposing teams to appear on the field at the same time.

The Giants had acquired Thompson's contract over the winter and conveniently parked him in Jersey City. On July 4, 1949, on Durocher's urging, the New York Giants called Thompson up from Jersey City. Thompson thus established himself in a singular historical niche in major league baseball history. He was the first black baseball player to play in both the National and American leagues. Then on July 8, 1949, Thompson and Monte Irvin became the first black players for the Giants.

Irvin had previously been assigned to Jersey City of the International League. There, Irvin batted .373. He debuted with the Giants on July 8, 1949 as a pinch-hitter.

The Giants lumbered to another mediocre finish, ending up in fifth place. Meanwhile Shotton won his second pennant with Brooklyn, capturing 97 regular-season victories. The Dodgers finished a game ahead of the St. Louis Cardinals. Robinson won the National League's Most Valuable Player award and batting championship. But Brooklyn again bowed to the Yankees in the World Series, this time in only five games.

Not surprisingly, however, despite Burt Shotton's two pennants in three seasons, his feet were always feeling the fire from Durocher loyalists on the Dodgers, players who claimed that Shotton was a poor game strategist and lacked Durocher's competitive intensity. Perhaps it was more a liking for Durocher's fiery spirit than anything against Shotton and his drab boxy suits.

Jackie Robinson remarked, "I sure do like to play for that man" when told Shotton was coming back in 1948. Pee Wee Reese, who had succeeded Durocher as the Dodgers' shortstop, was more circumspect. "I'm a Durocher man, myself… But I'll play my head off for Shotton."

Many fans felt Shotton was dullsville. Because he refused to wear a uniform, Shotton was prohibited by league rules from stepping onto the field of play during games. He remained in the dugout during arguments with umpires and pitching changes. One of his uniformed coaches, Clyde Sukeforth or Ray Blades, assumed those wonderful chores, making it look like there was no one home in the manager's office. This was an example of Burt Shotton's division of labor.

According to Gerald Eskanzazi, the great sportswriter for The

New York *Times*, Shotton's failure to wear a uniform struck Dodgers fans as "odd."

Or maybe even more than odd.

Disinterested, maybe. A little bit stick-up-the-butt, sort of. Sometimes Shotton sat there very properly and formally in a suit in the dugout waving his finger at his coaches, not really planning ahead. The mannerism aggravated such players as Ralph Branca, who were accustomed to Durocher's lively profane bench with plenty of mental hardball.

Shotton had also undone himself with the New York press, never a wise move. According to author Roger Kahn, Shotton attempted to ban Dick Young of the *Daily News* from the Brooklyn clubhouse. Young was quoted as saying Shotton was "aloof," "indifferent to his players' problems" and "a vain, stubborn person."

Young, always brash and with a loyal following of readers, had come to refer to him caustically in print only by the acronym KOBS, which stood for, "Kindly Old Burt Shotton." Shotton further alienated and infuriated the New York *Herald-Tribune's* erudite Harold Rosenthal by repeatedly addressing him as "Rosenberg" and "Rosenbloom."

Frequently, the newspapers were filled with rumors that Durocher was on the way out, particularly after an ugly incident involving a fan named Fred Boysen, who alleged that Durocher had assaulted him after a game. (Witnesses failed to support Boysen's version of things, and Leo's thinning scalp was saved.) But Leo was still in the process of changing Stoneham's mind about things and reorganizing the ball club. Many of his moves had been unpopular, including a big move that Durocher talked Stoneham into making over the winter of 1949-50.

Durocher unloaded two of his allegedly immobile sluggers, Willard Marshall and Sid Gordon, to the Boston Braves, along with Buddy Kerr and pitcher Red Webb. In return, Leo got the middle infield that he craved, along with the feisty field leadership that he needed to win. Shortstop Alvin Dark came to the Giants, accompanied by second baseman Eddie Stanky.

Eddie the Brat and Leo the Lip, the two integral elements of the resurgent Dodger teams of the late forties, were now reunited at the Polo Grounds.

To replace Walker Cooper, Durocher summoned a young Wes Westrum back to the club from Jersey City. Westrum had been with the Giants earlier and had not won a spot. But now in 1950 became a regular. A right handed pull hitter, he was dangerous in the Polo Grounds. He would hit 23 home runs in 1950, second on the team to Bobby Thomson's 25. He would eventually have his personally greatest game against Cincinnati on June 24 in the Polo Grounds: three home runs, a walk and a triple. He also scored five runs in the Giants' 12-2 rout of the Reds.

Leo benched Johnny Mize and Davey Kerr. He moved Rigney to short for a while and gave second base to Hank Thompson, the twenty-three-year-old infielder who had once played for the St. Louis Browns, who rarely won anything.

A Fan's Reminiscence - Seth Jonas

My Grandfather, Al Jonas, was a writer for the NY *Journal American*. Every week he ran a baseball clinic at one of the local ballparks. I think this picture is from 1950. Eddie Stanky and Leo Durocher are with the kids. My father, Eric Jonas, is the boy kneeling on the front left not facing the camera. They never had my dad facing the camera because he was there each week and my grandfather didn't want any readers asking why the same kid was there every time.

My dad also once told me a funny story. He was standing in center field one day with his father at the Polo Grounds The Giants were having a lousy season and he said something derogatory. He turned around and Durocher was standing right behind him. My dad said he almost peed in his pants he was so embarrassed.
Seth Jonas
New York, 2018

Chapter 74 Dauntless Dan, The Barber & Death in the Afternoon

"I'm perfectly happy here. My wife likes Mexico and we moved into this super-modern apartment today and everything is dandy."

Mickey Owen in 1946

By 1948, American ballplayers returned from south of the border like survivors from a sinking ship, which in a sense they were. Everything hadn't been so dandy after all. The league hemorrhaged money from lack of attendance until it was bankrupt.

At the end of the 1949 season, Commissioner Happy Chandler was pleased to throw each of the drowning men an anchor. A five-year ban on each of them was in effect. Organized baseball in the United States didn't just want to punish the deserters, it wanted to humiliate them.

One of the survivors of the Taco Circuit was Danny Gardella. Gardella hired a Wall Street lawyer who thought it might be profitable to sue organized baseball both for anti-trust violations and for unfair labor practices: the reserve rule.

This put a tremor of fear through the owners. The ban was eventually trimmed to three years, equivalent by that time to time served. Gardella eventually won his case. He received a settlement which he claimed to be $60,000. The first chips had been made in baseball's reserve clause. Accordingly, the veterans of the Mexican League were free to return to their National and American League teams by 1950. Out of this, the Giants were now in a position to re-sign an extraordinary pitcher named Salvatore Anthony Maglie.

Sal Maglie had pitched for two seasons with the Puebla Parrots. Dolf Luque was his manager, and the flinty old Cuban molded the mild-mannered Maglie into a pitcher along his own lines. Maglie absorbed Luque's methods. He often pitched under adverse conditions. And so a new Sal Maglie was born: a grim, tough, ruthless competitor unfazed by weather, taunts, or pressure, a pitcher who could bend a curve like a pretzel, something he refined with Luque, or knock a batter to the ground with a fastball that grazed his chin, something he learned well in the south of the border circuit.

After 1947 Maglie was still banned from the American major leagues. He then joined a barnstorming squad organized by fellow jumper Max Lanier, consisting of other Mexican League refugees. The squad traveled the United States by bus, taking on local semi-pro teams. The team failed to bring in enough money to cover expenses and disbanded in August of 1948. Maglie returned home to Niagara Falls, New York. He used money saved from his years in Mexico to purchase a home and a gas station and tried to resign himself to life as a pump jockey.

He was not happy.

Who would be?

Invited to pitch in the Provincial League in Quebec, Maglie put in an outstanding season in Canada in 1949, leading the Drummondville Cubs to a championship. If you have been keeping track, you will have noticed that the New York Giants had finished in the first division two times since 1938. Finally, however, they were ready to move. One of the first orders of business was signing Maglie, pictured here.

So now the 1950 season marked a potential turning point for the New York Giants.

Leo finally had his type of team. With Dark and Stanky, as he would later phrase it, "we had two guys who could do things with the bat, could run the bases, and who came to kill you." Mr. Durocher, it will always be recalled, liked players who came to kill you.

By May he also had a semblance of

a pitching staff. Then in late spring, the St. Louis Cardinals were induced to part with a twenty-nine-year-old right-hander named Jim Hearn, who had been an excellent golfer and basketball player in college.

Hearn was a tall, soft-spoken Southern gentleman from Georgia. He had studied at Georgia Tech and served in the U.S. Army in the Philippines during World War Two. He had begun his professional baseball career as a third baseman but had converted to pitching. He had solid seasons for the St. Louis Cardinals in 1947 and 1948, but the wheels had come off his wagon in 1949 and 1950. The Cardinals gave up on him. New York picked up off the cheapo $10,000 waiver wire on July 10, 1950.

Big Jim, as he was called, joined the team in Pittsburgh. Durocher was skeptical. There was a pernicious rumor that Hearn was more interested in golf than baseball. Leo put it to his new pitcher on arrival.

"Jim, they tell me you want to be a golf pro," said Durocher. "If you are interested more in golf than pitching, let's have it right now so we don't lose any time and effort on you."

Hearn said he would be pleased to pitch, given the opportunity.

So pitch he did, and quite well. The Giants had lost nine of their last ten games when Hearn pitched for the first time on July 17 against Cincinnati at Crosley Field. To everyone's shock, possibly even his own, he tossed a complete-game four-hitter to win, 10-3, backed by home runs by Dark, Westrum and Bobby Thomson.

Hearn was a new man with the Giants, going 11-3 for them (11-4 overall for the year), with a league-leading ERA of 2.49 (1.94 as a Giant). Larry Jansen pitched well, too, as he did for several years in a row. But the decisive addition was a familiar name who hadn't received much time on the mound previously: Sal Maglie.

Maglie, who was polite, gracious and gentlemanly off the field, was an imposing 6-foot-2-inch, 180-pound right-hander. His new glowering game-day face bristled with thick black stubble. His pitching style confirmed the fears his appearance aroused. He was ferocious on the mound.

"He scares you to death," said Cincinnati outfielder Danny Litwhiler. "He's scowling and gnashing his teeth, and if you try to dig in on him, there goes your Adam's apple. He's gonna win if it kills you and him both."

Maglie showed up in the Giants' training camp in Tucson that spring, said little to anyone, and failed to gain much attention. Sal sat quietly and kept ready. He worked in the bullpen early in the season, started a game against Cincinnati in June, and was pounded. Then it was back to the bullpen for another month.

In July, Leo needed an extra starter and tapped Maglie. Maglie responded with an eleven inning 5-4 victory over the Cardinals. Afterward no less an authority on National League pitching than Stan Musial admitted that Maglie's curveball was the best he had seen in the league.

That put Maglie in the starting rotation. And that addition made the Giants a red-hot team through the second half of the year. For the rest of the season Sal pitched brilliantly, finishing with an 18-4 record, at one point hurling four straight shutouts. He also had a big breaking curve that looked like the fastball as it approached. Further, Maglie was now an intimidator. As any good New Yorker knows, they called Maglie, "The Barber." Legend had it that he could shave either a batter's chin or the corner of the plate - sometimes both at once - with that big breaking curveball. Or maybe it would just be the mean fastball, right up there under the chinny chin chin.

Maglie won 11 straight games. So did Hearn.

Maglie also threw 45 consecutive scoreless innings before Gus Bell of the Pirates ended the streak with a pop-fly home run down the right field line in the Polo Grounds. When Bell's "clout" cleared the 257-foot sign, Maglie was only four outs short of Carl Hubbell's record for consecutive scoreless innings, set in 1934. Assuredly, Gus made a mental note to be ready to duck the next few times facing Maglie.

All of this contributed to a blazing streak of 34 wins in 46 games through late July and August. The streak carried the Giants into the periphery of the pennant race. Brooklyn was chasing a young upstart club from Philadelphia who were in no way to be confused with the sappy Phillies clubs of previous years. The names were Richie Ashburn, Del Ennis, Willie Jones, Andy Seminick, Robin Roberts, and Curt Simmons. And in a feat equal to that of the 1969 Mets, they held on to win the pennant over the Dodgers. The Giants finished a very respectable third, five games out of first.

Eventually, the Yankees outclassed the Phillies in a quick four-day four game World Series, the last one, by the way, to ever be played by all white teams. But the upstarts had risen, both in Philadelphia and New York.

Strangely enough, however, few people gave much attention to the team from the Polo Grounds. Their own fans did, of course, as more than a million people paid their way into the Polo Grounds again. But it went almost unnoticed that for the last half of 1950, the Giants were again the best team in baseball. All the attention had gone to the Whiz Kids from Philadelphia, who had brought that long-suffering somnambulant city its first National League pennant since 1915 and the days of Grover Cleveland Alexander.

There had been, however, a horrific incident in the middle of the season, one which portrayed the city of New York at its worst.

On the Fourth of July, Bernard Doyle, a 54-year-old retired freight worker went to mass at his church in New Jersey and took Communion. He then travelled to the Polo Grounds to see the New York Giants play the Brooklyn Dodgers in a much-anticipated double-header. Doyle had once been the manager of Irish-American prizefighter James J. Braddock, better known to the world as the "Cinderella Man." Braddock had been the heavyweight champion from 1935 to 1937 and had fought in New York many times, mostly at Madison Square Garden, never at the Polo Grounds.

Doyle had taken with him Otto Flaig, a freckled, 13-year-old boy who was from a neighbor's family. Doyle's seat was Seat 3, Row C, Section 42 in the upper grandstand between right and center field. In the adjoining neighborhood, a 14-year-old boy named Robert Mario Peebles, stood on the rooftop of his Harlem apartment complex at 515 Edgecombe Avenue overlooking the Polo Grounds.

Six months earlier, Peebles had "found" a .45 caliber pistol containing a single bullet in Central Park. He had hidden the gun in his basement, waiting to fire the lone bullet into the air in celebration of the country's independence. At 12:30 PM, Peebles fired the gun straight up into the air, several hundred yards from the Polo Grounds.

At that moment, the Giants and Dodgers teams were running out on the field in front of a nearly packed house of more than forty-nine thousand fans. Doyle had turned to say something to Flaig when the random bullet, descending from the sky as Isaac Newton would have predicted, crashed into his skull, causing him to slouch over.

"Great fountains of blood exploded from his nose and ears and mouth, and Barney (sic) Doyle was dead before he fell back in his seat," wrote the New York *Daily News* the next day The fans nearby heard a popping sound. One witness compared it to "a paper bag breaking."

Flaig asked the man if anything was wrong and got no response. He assumed Doyle had had a heart attack. Doyle had had heart problems recently which is why he had retired. But then there was all the blood, which suggested otherwise. When Polo Grounds attendants came over and checked on him, they saw the entry wound and realized a bullet had lodged in his brain. Doyle had died instantly.

The game proceeded.

Not only did the game go on as scheduled, as did the second game, but "standees fought over Doyle's empty seat as medics carried the dead man away," reported the New York *Daily News*, a paper that would never neglect such a detail. Even Flaig, Doyle's compatriot, seemed more upset that the incident caused him to miss the game than that his neighbor had been killed as he sat next to him. Young Otto himself complained that the detectives' questions were making him miss the ballfield action, the *Daily News* story hummed along. Said The *News*, "I've been dreaming about this game for a month," he grumbled.

Police, acting on a local tip, found Peebles. Peebles confessed to firing the weapon. He was charged with "juvenile delinquency." He went to the New York State Training School for Boys, stayed for less than two years, and disappeared from the public view.

What did not disappear, however, was the beginnings of an idea that many New Yorkers felt, vis-à-vis The Polo Grounds and Ebbets Field. They were not safe places to be. The surrounding minority neighborhoods were crumbling, same as the ballparks. They could be dangerous. To be blunt, many white fans didn't want to go there.

Easier to stay home and watch on your new television. Or at the bar with friends and liquid refreshment. Or at your little neighborhood restaurant. Much more pleasant too.

It was an idea that lurked and would take a few more years to take hold. But take hold, it did.

Chapter 75 From Another World

"I like New York in June, how about you?"

From, *How About You?* composed by Burton Lane, lyrics by Ralph Freed, introduced in the 1941 film *Babes on Broadway* by Judy Garland and Mickey Rooney

The 1951 season began with buoyant expectations by all three New York clubs. The Yankees, with two consecutive pennants under McGraw's old protege, Casey Stengel, were the masters of their league, and, for that matter, of the National League as well. They began their season looking toward a third successive World Series, with Joe DiMaggio still in center field. Two young outfielders flanked The Clipper on Opening Day, Jackie Jensen in left and Mickey Mantle in right.

The Dodgers had new ownership. Walter O'Malley had bought out Branch Rickey's share of the club. Rickey had paid $350,000 for his piece of the Dodgers in 1945. Now he sold out to O'Malley for a cool million. O'Malley was furious at the price and denounced Rickey for manifesting greed in the ownership of such a beloved local ball club. In celebrating his new control over the Dodgers, O'Malley quickly sacked Kindly Old Burt Shotton and replaced him with Unkindly Younger Chuck Dressen.

At the Polo Grounds, Giant fans were quietly confident. This *could* be their year, they felt. Grudgingly they would admit that Durocher had reshaped the ball club pretty well. Many of them couldn't quite recall why they'd disliked him all that while. He didn't seem such a bad fellow now that he was in a Giants uniform.

"If it's in the column under '**W**' for win," Leo explained, "nobody cares how it got there." It was remarkable how many Giant fans had been converted to Leo's line of thought. But at the outset of 1951 there wasn't much in the column under **"W."** The team dumped 11 games in a row in the month of April and plunked themselves firmly into the cellar by the end of the month.

Dodger fans chortled.

"It's like a snake eating its young," Durocher said of the losing streak. "The streak starts, the guys start to press, the worse it gets."

Despite all the trades, and despite the freight-train-style finish of the previous season, the club seemed listless at the outset of 1951. The defense was suspect. The hitting wasn't there. In spring training, Durocher had announced that the Giants would have the best pitching in the National League, with a top four of Maglie, Jansen, Hearn and Dave Koslo. But it wasn't working out that way. In the early season, the pitching was deplorable.

To make matters worse, the Dodgers under Chuck Dressen were off to an electrifying start. No horsing around with the upstart Phillies this year for Brooklyn. Assembled were the nucleus of the last great Flatbush teams: Robinson, Hodges, Reese, Billy Cox, Carl Furillo, Campanella, Snider, Don Newcombe, Erskine, Preacher Roe, and Ralph Branca. ("Name eight Dodgers without Cox," was a popular Polo Grounds one-liner of the day.)

This year the Dodgers were out to shut down everyone in sight. They won 28 of their first 36 games. Arthur Daley, the savant of the New York *Times,* commented on the situation at the beginning of May, with the Dodgers on top and the Giants on bottom.

"It will take," Daley wrote, "a miracle for the Giants to win the championship now."

Daley, it turned out, was correct. But in the meantime, in the absence of an early season miracle, Horace Stoneham was entertaining the terrifying vision of empty grandstands by the middle of July. Something had to be done right away. Several sportswriters tried to help Horace out by suggesting that canning Durocher might be just the right something. But Stoneham had his thoughts elsewhere - in Sioux City, for example. It was there that a minor league ball player for Minneapolis was playing a road game.

An immensely likeable, thin, timid kid from rural Alabama, Willie Mays was celebrating his twentieth summer by obliterating the pitching of the American Association. Halfway through May, Willie was hitting a blistering .477, or about double the Giants' current team average. The parent club could wait no longer.

Mays, as everyone knows, was a scout's once-in-a-lifetime dream. He could run, throw, field, hit for power and hit for average. And he could do it all with excellence. He had played pro ball at age sixteen for a team named the Chattanooga Choo Choos, who were a farm team for the Birmingham Black Barons.

From Chattanooga, William Howard Mays, named after President William Howard Taft, had moved to the Black Barons in 1948. In

28 games, Mays hit .262 with one home run and one stolen base. But he also hit in the clutch. In the Negro American League playoff series against the Kansas City Monarchs, he gave Birmingham a win with a two-out, bases-loaded single in the bottom of the eleventh inning. A double in the bottom of the ninth in Game Two drove in future Giants teammate Artie Wilson with the tying run that sent the contest into extra innings. The Black Barons won three one-run games in succession before the series moved to Kansas City. Mays tripled and scored in a losing effort in Game Seven - a rain-shortened tie extended the series - and made the final putout in the Game Eight clincher.

After the 1949 season, Roy Campanella, now with Brooklyn, led a barnstorming team through the Old Confederacy. In a game between the barnstormers and the Black Barons, Mays threw out Larry Doby, then with Cleveland, at home plate after nailing a fly ball near the center field fence. The play stunned everyone in the ball park, particularly Doby and Campanella.

Campanella implored the Dodgers to send scouts down to sign Willie. A scout, came, saw, and muffed it. "The kid can't hit the curveball," the scout reported.

Around the same time, Giants scout Eddie Montague was watching the Birmingham first baseman, Alonzo Perry, for the Giants. Mays caught his eye. Montague reported that Mays was "the greatest young player I had ever seen in my life or my scouting career."

According to Durocher, Montague later reported that Birmingham had "a kid playing center field practically barefooted that's the best ballplayer I ever looked at. You better send somebody down there with a barrelful of money and grab this kid."

At length, the New York Giants did just that.

The Giants sent Willie was sent to Trenton of the Class B Interstate League. He might have been sent to Sioux City, Iowa, but there had recently been an ugly racial incident the recent burial of a Native American in a local segregated cemetery. Thus Sioux City wasn't a good fit, to put it mildly.

So Mays played his first game for Trenton in June in Hagerstown, Maryland, one of the league cities below the Mason-Dixon Line. He started in center field and was subjected to some of the uglier racial taunts of the era. Mays chose not to respond to the bigots, other than with his hitting and fielding. He would later also remember staying at a blacks-only hotel across town from the team's hotel, and five of his new white teammates came to his room to check on him.

In 1951 Mays trained with the Giants' top minor league club, the Minneapolis Millers of the American Association. (Photo here courtesy of Courtesy of minnbaseball.org.) The major-league team trained in Lakeland, Florida. Their minor league camp was in nearby Sanford. Leo Durocher wanted to see Mays play in person. A game was arranged between the team's two top farm clubs, Minneapolis and Ottawa. Mays doubled and homered.

Durocher began agitating for Mays to play for the Giants right away. Horace Stoneham resisted, claiming that Mays was about to be drafted into the U.S. Army. Willie began the season with Minneapolis as planned.

The New York Giants started their 2-13 spring calamity and Mays rapped out a dozen hits in his first week with Minneapolis.

Durocher continued to lobby for Mays.

In May, Minneapolis was in Sioux City to play an exhibition against the Giants' farm club there. The Millers had an off day. Mays went to a movie where, during the show, he learned that his manager was looking for him. Mays returned to his hotel.

The Minneapolis manager, Tommy Heath, informed Mays that he had been called up to the Giants. "Tell Leo I'm not coming," Mays answered.

Eventually Durocher phoned. Mays told him that he didn't think that he could hit National League pitching. Durocher asked Mays what he was hitting in the American association.

"Four seventy-seven," Mays answered.

Leo colorfully inquired if Willie thought he could hit two fifty in the National League.

"Sure," Mays answered.

Horace Stoneham bought an ad in the Minneapolis *Tribune* to apologize to Twin City fans for filching their young star. Willie, age 20, was on the next plane to meet the team in Philadelphia.

There was, of course, a subtler and less conspicuous reason for tabbing Mays at that moment. Over in Brooklyn "The O'Malley," as true Dodger fans called Walter, had two of the best young black stars of the day in Jackie Robinson and Roy Campanella.

Stoneham didn't care what color people were as long as they surged through his turnstiles. He wanted a "Negro star," too. More accurately, he had fervently prayed for one. Now he had a star in Monte Irvin. He also had a potential superstar in Mays.

The Giants were 17-19, on May 25, the day Willie joined the team at rickety old Shibe Park. Durocher installed the 20-year-old in center field. The Giants won three out of three games in Philadelphia, though Mays was hitless in his first 12 at-bats with six strikeouts. Only once had he even hit the ball solidly. Although he had dazzled Giants fans in Philly with splendid catches and inspired throws, he was demoralized. He wept in frustration. He begged Durocher to remove him from the lineup.

He pleaded to be sent back to Minneapolis.

But Durocher, as usual, had made up his mind. Just as another Giant manager, John McGraw, had refused to send a frightened, struggling young Mel Ott to the minors, Durocher kept Mays in New York. Leo had no way of knowing it at the time, but he was approaching his finest hour as a manager. He spent morning, afternoon, and evening with Mays. He talked baseball relentlessly to him, taking him literally under his arm many times. Everything - everything! - was designed to build the confidence of the overanxious rookie.

Durocher told Mays, "You're my center fielder from now until the end of the season. Now forget about everything else. Just go out and play baseball."

On May 28, Durocher had the temerity to start Mays against crafty Warren Spahn of the Boston Braves. Spahn - lanky, stylish, and hawk-beaked - was the prevailing southpaw in the league, a 20-game winner in three of the four previous seasons. He reminded older fans of Carl Hubbell, and with justification.

Spahn was difficult. His long crooked fingers could virtually twist the horsehide on a baseball. He possessed a cryptic, indecipherable stance on the mound and went through a windup and delivery which somehow resembled a huge beer pretzel coming unraveled. There followed either a prodigious fastball or a tight, quick curve which approached the plate exactly like the fastball but then exploded downward from a lunging batter, away from right-handers or onto the fists of left-handers. Those in the best position to see Spahn's snappy curveball - catchers and umpires - described it as appearing as if it were rolling off a table. Batters had earthier descriptions of it.

Spahn, the sly, talented veteran, against Mays, the gifted, but demoralized and hitless rookie. It was a sunny, mild, lovely spring Saturday. They faced each other for the first time, Spahn was tall, lean, and angular in his bluish gray road uniform with a red and brown tomahawk across his chest beneath the scripted word BRAVES. Mays' uniform was new, crisp, fresh, and bridal white. Across the front were six bold black-on-orange gothic letters spelling, GIANTS.

Mays watched a sneaky curveball that just missed the outside corner of the plate. Then he swung six inches beneath a fastball. That gave Spahn the notion of trying the curve again. Nick the plate with it for a second strike, he reasoned, then come back for a third strike with a fastball on the fists. Mays was thinking along the same lines.

Willie had the final bend of Spahn's curveball measured perfectly. His bat moved in a blur and connected with the loud, instantly recognizable crack of complete contact. The ball did not jump, fly, waft, or arc. It simply soared.

It soared upward and upward toward the green upper facade of the Polo Grounds grandstand, continued, cleared the left field roof, and presumably traveled until it reached Connecticut. It was an awesome, Ruthian blast, disappearing like a little white aspirin tablet out into the blue sky of upper Manhattan. For half a second, the players and crowd could only moan in admiration. Then the center field bleachers let loose with something that sounded like thunder, and it rolled inward across the grandstands in a matter of a second or two until the entire crowd, even the businessmen in their regular box seats, was roaring in one grand ovation.

On the field, the thin rookie was almost embarrassed by the fervor of the crowd. He circled the bases unsmiling and with his head lowered. Spahn busied himself with his feet, hands on his hips in disgust, and rearranged the dirt behind the pitching rubber until Mays had safely returned to the dugout. Durocher, beaming and grinning like a gargoyle, was the first to greet him.

"He was something like 0-for-21 the first time I saw him," Spahn recalled much later. "I'll never forgive myself. We might have gotten rid of Willie if only I'd struck him out."

A sense of the inevitable went through the Polo Grounds, particularly among the players. With one successful swing of the bat, Mays was now a proven big leaguer, part of the team. He was no longer a Minneapolis Miller but a New York Giant. He could feel at home. He could have fun. With his bat, his glove, his arm, his presence-even with his bare hand he could lead and add a new dimension, the missing dimension, to the 1951 team. The season, which was still quite young, was suddenly no longer a disaster, but rather one that could only get better. {A footnote: Yes, Mays hit his first home run, but it was not a good game for Willie. He took a called third strike with two runners on and popped up with a runner on base to end the game.}

After the homer, Mays went on a 0-for-13 slide, leaving him hitting .038 (1-for-26). At this point, in an often-told story, Willie sat in front of his locker, crying, after taking the collar again. Coaches Freddie Fitzsimmons and Herman Franks sent for Durocher. Mays again said he couldn't hit big-league pitching. Durocher replied, "As long as I'm the manager of the Giants, you are my center fielder. You are the best center fielder I've ever looked at." Then he advised Mays to hitch up his pants to give himself a more favorable strike zone.

Willie then went on a 14-for-33 tear. As if by osmosis, the lineup coalesced.

Along the way in 1951, Durocher unleashed one of his more memorable quotes after a Mays round-tripper.

"I never saw," said Leo, "a fucking ball go out of a fucking ballpark so fucking fast in my fucking life."

The scrappy Eddie Stanky led off and played a rugged second base. Alvin Dark, a great contact hitter, batted second and played shortstop. Don Mueller, the "man with the seeing-eye bat," hit third. More often than not, Monte Irvin, still solid and skillful in his thirties, batted cleanup and played left field.

Bobby Thomson - who had once tried out for the Brooklyn Dodgers but had been dismissed - moved from center field to third base. Whitey Lockman, a fixture since the late forties, returned to first base, and Wes Westrum, now the premier defensive catcher in the league, batted eighth.

Mays roamed both center field and the batting order. Durocher, always playing head games with his opponents, inserted Willie anywhere from the third to sixth position, wherever instinct told him Mays would do the most damage on that particular day. This final quirk of Durocher successfully kept the opposition off-balance for much of the season.

Meanwhile, Giants management kept a careful eye on their franchise player. Monte Irvin, a dozen years older and wiser, was assigned as the rookie's roommate on the road and protector. Irvin looked after him like a benevolent big brother, discarding phone messages from baseball groupies, meeting his dates before they went out and generally keeping trouble from finding him.

The Giants arranged for him to live in a Harlem boarding house. David and Anna Goosby became caretakers *in loco parentis* at St. Nicholas Avenue and 155th Street, a few blocks from the Polo Grounds. Willie ate meals there. Anna did his laundry.

He quickly became a neighborhood celebrity. Neighbors often waited outside for Willie to arrive home. His stickball playing became a legend.

{For the culturally deprived or otherwise uninitiated, stickball is a variant of a street game related to baseball, usually formed as a pick-up game. It was particularly popular among kids in New York City and Philadelphia. A broom handle is used as a bat and a rubber ball, typically a spaldeen, or a tennis ball is the ball. The rules are modified from baseball to adapt to a street situation. A manhole or a fire hydrant or mailbox might be used as a base. Buildings or walls were foul lines. The game dates back to at least the 1700's and was widely popular among kids growing up from the Twentieth Century until the 1980s, when video games start to replace outdoor activity, not necessarily for the better.}

Willie often played an hour of stickball before reporting to the

Polo Grounds. Or another hour after a game. On August 30, 1951, Willie hit two home runs in one game against the Pirates at the Polo Grounds, and then homered again in a stickball game later that day. That might be some sort of record. Mays could hit a stickball homer that measured "six sewers," the stretch of six consecutive New York City manhole covers. That's about 300 feet and it too, might be some sort of record.

"If you were a 14-year-old New York kid in the summer of 1931," wrote columnist David Hinckley in the New York *Daily News*, "you couldn't just round up some of your musical pals, knock on Irving Berlin's window and have Irv come out and write a few songs with you. If you were a 14-year-old aspiring vocalist in the summer of 1941, you couldn't just grab a couple of tenors, knock on Frank Sinatra's window and have Frank come join you for a round of harmony. If you were a 14-year-old kid in the summer of 1951, you couldn't just knock on Willie Mays' window at 9 o'clock in the morning and have Willie come out and play an hour of stickball with you. Well, actually, you could."

One of the lasting contributions to American culture in 1951 was a film called *The Thing*, also billed as *The Thing From Another World*. When John W. Campbell wrote his sci-fi novella Who Goes There? in 1938, he could never have expected his story to inspire multiple movie adaptations. The book focuses on a group of Antarctic researchers who accidentally release a shapeshifting alien from a block of ice. But in addition to the killer creature, the scientist also unleashed three feature length films, *The Thing from Another World* (1951), *The Thing* (1982), and *The Thing* (2011) all drew on Campbell's novella for inspiration.

The 1951 flick, released while the Giants-Dodgers pennant race was heating up, was set in the Arctic. In it, an alien creature (played by James Arness in his pre-*Gunsmoke* days) terrorizes an Arctic research team after they inadvertently thaw it out of some ice. The terror then mounts, as you'd expect it would.

The terror here, however, was nothing compared with what the Brooklyn Dodgers began to sense in June of that year because it was in June the New York Giants began to consistently win.

Victories equaled losses and soon surpassed them. Defeat became an only occasional thing. It was only much, much later, of course, that Mays' home run off Spahn in May could be assessed for what it really was: a turning point. It was the first significant hit in the most dramatic pennant race in the history of American baseball.

Reminiscence   -   Gary Mintz

My dad was Louis Mintz. Family man, librarian at the NY Public Library for over 40 years, father, Giants Fan. He loved my mom, loved his 3 boys, my wife, and worshiped the ground of his 3 granddaughters (his girlies, my daughters) and his grandson.

Then there were the Giants. His love of the NY Giants somehow continued when the orange and black moved to San Francisco. Wanting to be like him, I started following the SF Giants in 1969. Up until 2010, I claimed it was the only wrong thing my father ever did. That all changed when Nelson Cruz swung and missed on a Brian Wilson pitch on November 1, 2010. It was the most compelling moment of my sports life as a fan. Forty-one years I waited. In one night, all the hurt and pain was suddenly gone.

Then viola!! Two World Championships in 3 years!! UNBELIEVABLE!! Then 2014!! Make it 3 WS Championships in 5 years!! My only remorse is that "Sweet Lou" wasn't around to savor it with me as he passed in 2003.

I became associated with the New York/San Francisco Giants because of my love and admiration for this man.

Growing up I would hear him say things that would just pop out of the air for no apparent rhyme or reason. There would be the names that he would spew. Alvin "Blackie" Dark, Monte I"rrrrrrrrr"vin, whom he called at times the "Orange Cutie" (evidently Monte Irvin's nickname, though nobody else seem to know of its origins), Bobby Thomson, "The Flying Scot", Sal "The Barber" Maglie, Bill "The Cricket" Rigney, and just plain "Willie".

Then there were the little sayings, the old "PG's", "The June Swoon", and as Frankie Frisch would say, "Oh those bases on balls". Occasionally he would sing the Giants theme song, "We're calling all fans, all you Giants ball fans, come watch the home-team going places, round those bases." (https://www.youtube.com/watch?v=i0StBIbUtaU)

Then there was his mimicking Mel Ott's leg lift and Hoyt Wilhelm's knuckle ball grip. Dad would often tell me how the fans had to leave the Polo Grounds through the center field gate which meant walking on the field. He told me that he was once spiked by Johnny Bernardino near the second base bag. He would also see doubleheaders by going from the Polo Grounds to Yankee Stadium (or the other way around) via the Macombs Dam Bridge. Sometimes he'd see both the football and baseball Giants on the same Sunday afternoon.

My dad left me and his family way too early. When the Giants finally won in 2010, I planted a little World Series Flag by his grave. It still waves proudly there today along with the 2012 flag and the 2014 flag, a triple play. I needed him to know his impact on me and how "we" finally did it. I'm hoping to add another before too long.

I miss the many times, even as an adult when he would say to me after I was forlorn over a loss, "What are you worried about? Do they worry about you?" Although I am now middle aged, I still hope I can be half the man he was. There were the Giants from the Polo Grounds, the Giants in San Francisco, and all the legendary players that donned the Giants uniform in both places.

For my money though, my dad, Louis Mintz, was the greatest Giant of them all!

Gary Mintz
New York
June 2018

(Photo of Louis Mintz, courtesy of Gary Mintz.)

Chapter 76 Sugar Ray

"To be a champ you have to believe in yourself when nobody else will."

Sugar Ray Robinson

The Polo Grounds on the northern edge of Harlem, just north of Sugar Hill. Following the "Great Migration" of the 1920's, Harlem became the best known center of African-American life in the United States. In the 1950's Willie Mays, who lived not far from the ballpark, was perhaps Harlem's Number Two Celebrity.

Number One, easily, was boxer Sugar Ray Robinson, the great middleweight and welterweight champion in the 1940s and '50s. Robinson was not a native New Yorker, he was from Georgia. But by the Forties and Fifties, he presided over Harlem and its nightlife like a duke.

He was born Walker Smith Jr. in 1921. His father was a farmer. His parents separated and his mother moved the family to Harlem when he was twelve in 1933. When he tried to enter his first boxing tournament, he was told he needed to first obtain an AAU membership card. He slipped past the age requirement (18) by borrowing a birth certificate from a friend named Ray Robinson. He fought 85 times as an amateur and won every match. Told that he was "sweet as sugar" by a lady fan, Walker Smith Jr. began to fight as "Sugar" Ray Robinson.

Robinson made his professional debut on October 4, 1940 at Madison Square Garden, winning in the second round over Joe Echevarria of the Philippines.

Robinson won his first 40 professional fights before losing to Jake LaMotta in 1943. He would eventually fight LaMotta six times. "I fought Sugar Ray so many times it's a wonder I didn't get diabetes," LaMotta would say during a comedy routine he used to do to make a few extra dollars during his days running a strip club. The line was later made famous by Robert De Niro in the *Raging Bull*.

Robinson was a fluid boxer who could throw a quick jab and had knockout power in both hands. He fought 202 bouts over a quarter of a century and defeated Jake LaMotta, Carmen Basilio, Rocky Graziano and Kid Gavilan.

"Robinson could deliver a knockout blow going backwards, wrote Burt Randolph Sugar. "His footwork, hard speed and leverage were unmatchable. Pound for pound, he was probably the best ever."

As years passed, Robinson fought frequently in New York, New Jersey and nearby, sort of, Philadelphia. His first fight at the Polo Grounds was in 1941, when he TKOed an American named Peter Lello. Robinson had a home in Harlem and settled his mother into a nearby apartment on St. Nicholas Avenue. He stayed away from mob contact when possible, not the easiest thing in those decades, and presided over the evening in Harlem at his night club, Sugar Ray's, at Seventh Avenue and 124th Street.

By this time, around 1950, Robinson owned most of the block between 123rd Street and 124th Streets, right before the Hotel Theresa. Next to the night spot was Ray Robinson Enterprises, his real estate business, then his wife's boutique called Edna May's Lingerie Shop. (Edna May Holly, seen here with her husband whom he married in 1943, was a noted dancer. She toured Europe with Duke Ellington and Cab Calloway, in 1940 and had also performed at the Cotton Club at 142nd & Lenox.) There also was a Golden Gloves Barber Shop and a beauty salon.

Nothing remains today. But don't get the idea that Ray was locked up behind a desk. He could often be found tending bar at his own place, mixing drinks for the celebrities, politicos and other guests. One of the "unofficial hosts" at the club was a young man named Charles Rangel who would eventually become the U.S. Congressman from the district. Mr. Rangel was a desk clerk at the Hotel Theresa, near the club. Part of his job was escorting female guests to Sugar Ray's.

Robinson wore suits tailored by Sy Martin, who made suits for Duke Ellington. Robinson took his entourage, a prototype for what is now commonplace among celebrities and athletes, on his travels abroad. It included his trainer, his barber, his golf pro, a nutritionist, a manicurist, driver.

Robinson would cruise Harlem in his famous custom pink Cadillac, a car he loved so much that he once shipped it to France so that he could drive it and his entourage around Paris while training for a fight. The French loved Sugar Ray first because of his style and second because they hated Jake LaMotta. LaMotta had defeated the French champion Marcel Cerdan, and Cerdan had died in a 1949 plane crash in Portugal while training for a rematch.

By 1951, Sugar Ray Robinson was considered the best pound-for-pound fighter in boxing history, an assessment that still stands. (He weighed in usually around 150 pounds). That summer, Robinson went to England for a vacation before his scheduled July 10 bout with Randy Turpin. Robinson was heavily favored. To the shock of his fans, the durable young (23) Turpin won a 15-round decision.

Two months later on September 12, while the Giants were being rained out in St. Louis, Sugar Ray came home to New York for a rematch with Turpin. His fans turned out to a establish a new middleweight fight attendance record: sixty thousand people.

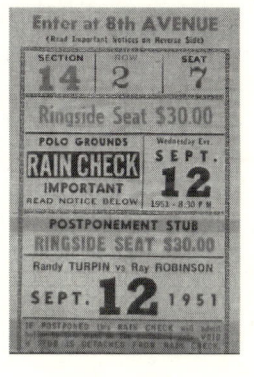

From the first seconds of Round One, Robinson set the pace of the fight. He won each of the first seven rounds decisively. In the eighth round, however, Robinson appeared to tire, and Turpin fought with a new intensity, hitting and hurting Robinson for the first time in the fight. In the ninth round, Turpin delivered numerous right hands to Robinson's head, opening a cut over his left eye. But in the tenth, Sugar Ray knocked Turpin to the canvas with a right to the jaw. When Turpin was ready to continue, Robinson unleashed a barrage of punches to his head and body. Two minutes and 52 seconds into the 10th round, referee Rudy Goldstein stopped the fight. Robinson was the winner on a TKO.

Sugar Ray had gain the world middleweight title, moving up from welterweight. Robinson was showered with adulation from the adoring hometown crowd. Where else could this match have been?

The fight was at the Polo Grounds.

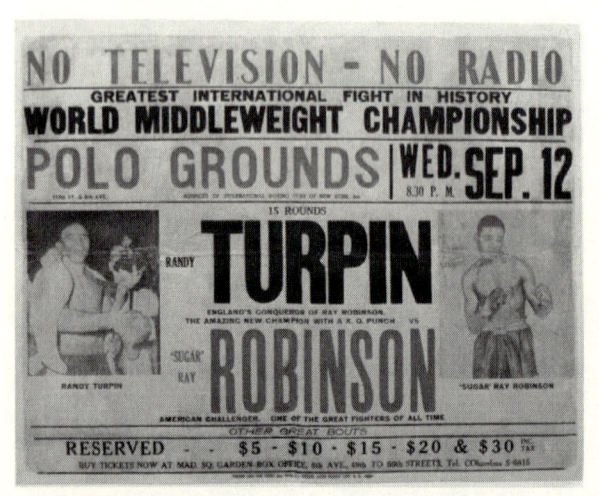

The greatest fight that never happened: World Middleweight Champion Jake LaMotta was scheduled to make his first title defense against the man he won the crown from, the French Champion, Marcel Cerdan, on September 28, 1949, at the Polo Grounds. The match was first postposed, then cancelled a month later when Cerdan died in an airplane crash in the Azores en route to New York. French fight fans would forever vilify LaMotta; had a questionable decision not given LaMotta the win in their first match Cerdan would never have died going to the rematch. For years, unused tickets circulated as macabre souvenirs of the event that never happened.

Chapter 77   "The Giants is Dead"

"All baseball fans believe in miracles. The question is, how many do you believe in?"

John Updike

"The Giants is dead," remarked Chuck Dressen in a genial mood in July of 1951. Actually, the Giants weren't dead. They were just dozing.

But Willie Mays woke them up.

He played with the enthusiasm of a kid, which is what he was. He lifted the spirits of his team through his presence. And when he couldn't remember anyone's name, even after coming up to the Giants, he addressed everyone with, "Say, hey!" So that became his name, too.

"To watch Mays play was to watch Rembrandt paint or Caruso sing," wrote one sportswriter of the era.

"I'm not sure what the hell charisma is, but I get the feeling it's Willie Mays," said Cincinnati Reds slugger Ted Kluszewski.

"As a batter, his only weakness is a wild pitch," said Bill Rigney.

Charlie Grimm, the once and future manager of the Chicago Cubs, said, "Willie Mays can help a club just by riding on the bus with them." Durocher, of course, was the man closest to Willie when he came up. As always, Leo's observation was as astute as it was opinionated.

"If somebody came up and hit .450, stole a hundred bases, and performed a miracle on the field every day, I'd still look you in the eye and say that Willie was better. He could do the five things you have to do to be a superstar: hit, hit with power, run, throw, and field. And he had that other magic ingredient… he lit up the room when he came in. He was a joy to be around."

Well, not if you were pitching to him.

All of this, strangely enough, is a prelude to a memorable event called Wes Westrum Day at the Polo Grounds. The date was August 12, 1951 and the amiable Giant catcher was to be presented with a shiny new Mercury sedan, presumably in appreciation of his high fielding average (.987 at season's end) rather than his batting average (.219 for the year).

A crowd of thirty-some thousand paid their way into the Polo Grounds, perhaps to escape the television, which currently featured Senator Joseph McCarthy's witch hunt. There had to be *some* reason to go to the ballpark because the Giants, although they'd moved laudably up from eighth place to second, were still 13.5 games behind the Dodgers. Only those who believed in sorcery could have been thinking of a pennant. But the Giants knocked off the Dodgers that day. The teams exchanged victories in the days after that. Then on August 15 came a play that set the stage for what was to follow.

The Dodgers were still at the Polo Grounds, losing 3-1 as they batted in the eighth. Billy Cox was on third and Furillo was batting. Furillo hit a ball that sent Willie Mays deep, deep, deep to right center, a certain triple until Mays' glove somehow intersected with the flight of the ball. But Willie wasn't finished.

Mays not only caught the ball but turned in the same motion and rocketed - "threw" is an inaccurate word here - the ball to the plate. There the honoree from four days previously, Mr. Wesley Noreen Westrum of Clearbrook, Minnesota, tagged out an astonished Billy Cox. Cox stared at the ball in Westrum's glove. He understood where Furillo had hit it. What he couldn't understand is how quickly it had returned. Nor could anyone who had looked directly at the play.

The Giants won the game, nipping the incipient Dodger rally. The Giants won again the next day. They did not lose another game until August 28 while the Dodgers played as if they were still in shock over Billy Cox being thrown out at the plate. In this space of time, the New York Giants won 16 in a row and trimmed the Dodger lead down to 5.5 games. A new term, "The Creeping Terror," started to appear in the newspapers. That's what the Giants players were now calling their pennant drive. And yes, it certainly was a pennant drive.

From the standpoint of the Brooklyn Dodgers, it was a living version of those nightmares in which something terrible approaches, but one's feet are rooted to the ground. One goes to scream, but no sound emerges from the throat. In this case the something terrible approaching was the New York Giants.

Oh, what a nightmare.

Campanella, who would be the league's MVP that year, finally left the lineup after a succession of injuries. Snider and Furillo slumped. So did Hodges. Meanwhile, the Giants were on a magnificent roll that would eventually place a phenomenal 37 entries in Leo's "W" column out of 44 attempts.

Four games behind were the Giants.

Then three.

Then two and a half.

On September 25, they beat the Phillies and moved to within one game of Brooklyn. Three days later, the Giants caught the Dodgers and went into a flatfooted tie for first place. Each team had two games left. On the final Saturday of the season, the Giants beat the Braves in Boston. Meanwhile, way down south in Philadelphia, the Dodgers shut out the Phillies at Connie Mack Stadium. So the race was still tied on Sunday morning.

Back to Boston.

Larry Jansen, superb again, defeated Warren Spahn of the Braves, 3-2. The Giants had ended the campaign - or at least the regularly scheduled part of it - with a flourish: seven straight wins. But the Dodgers had a flourish of their own.

The Giants went to board a train back to New York. The train departed at five P.M. from Boston. The last score they'd seen from Philadelphia had the Phillies leading 8-5 in the seventh inning. The Giants rode the New Haven Railroad with champagne cooling in the club car. The Dodgers, however, still had a little magic left in the 1951 season before it all went up in smoke.

En route to New York, the Giants learned that the Dodgers had won. Eventually, they learned how.

Brooklyn had rallied for three runs in the eighth, tying the score. Then Jackie Robinson had saved the game in the twelfth when he stopped a line drive off the bat of Eddie Waitkus that, according to teammates, drove Robinson's elbows into his chest and actually knocked him unconscious for several seconds. Had the ball gone through him, a Philadelphia runner would have scored, ending the season. Instead, the Dodgers stayed alive until the fourteenth inning when - who else? - Robinson knocked a ball far over the rooftops of Philadelphia's North 20th Street.

"That," Rachel Robinson has said many times, "always ranked as one of Jack's biggest thrills in baseball."

The year 1951 was also emblematic of Monte Irvin's greatness as a baseball player. At 32 years of age, the venal segregation of the 30s and 40s, plus the World War, had cost him his prime and exposure in the major leagues. Now, he finished third to Roy Campanella and Stan Musial in the MVP voting with his .312

batting average, 24 home runs, and 121 RBI's. He scored 94 runs, hit 11 triples, and drew 89 walks while only striking out 44 times, and he went 12-for-14 in steals.

He was fifth in batting average, fourth in on-base percentage, seventh in slugging, tied for 10th in runs scored, seventh in hits, ninth in total bases, third in triples, tied for 10th in homers, and led the National League with 121 RBIs, a dozen more than his nearest competitors. Want more? Irvin finished seventh in walks, tied for eighth in steals, fourth in runs created, fifth in times on base, and tied for third in the number of times he was hit by a pitch.

Giant fans, always accused of being laid-back and unenthusiastic compared their noisy Brooklyn counterparts, mobbed the club's train when it arrived at Grand Central Station. The team was astonished. There among them was the boozy restauranteur Toots Shor, one of the most ardent Giant fans on Manhattan Island, leading a contingent of several hundred delirious rooters, many of whom appeared to have spent several hours in Toots' mobbed-up watering hole preparing for the occasion. After all that had happened, after the wretched start by the Giants and the compelling start by the Dodgers, after Dressen's asinine pronouncement, after Mays' taking Spahn over the grandstand, after Maglie's razor-sharp 23-6 season and Preacher Roe's 22-3 campaign, after Monte Irvin's league-leading 121 RBIs and Hodges' 40 four-baggers, the Dodgers and the Giants were even.

They would now play two out of three for the pennant.

Chapter 78   Bottom of the 9th, Brooklyn leads it, 4-2...

"Branca throws... There's a long drive... It's gonna be..."

Russ Hodges on WMCA Radio

The first game of the playoff took place at Ebbets Field on October 1, when 30,707 people paid their way into the ballpark. But millions more listened on the radio. Here one could opt for "Giant Radio" with Russ Hodges and Ernie Harwell on WMCA, "Dodger Radio" with Red Barber and Vin Scully on WOR, or the presumably neutral voices of the Mutual Broadcasting System. There was also television, meaning that the taverns and bars around the five boroughs had busy afternoons.

Whoever one listened to or watched, the scores were pretty much the same. Andy Pafko, a recent Dodger addition from the Cubs, opened the scoring with a second-inning home run off Jim Hearn. But the Giants quickly came back. Bobby Thomson hit a two-run homer off Dodger starter Ralph Branca - yes, that's right - and Monte Irvin, who had played like a man possessed all season, chipped in with a solo homer.

Final score: 3-1, Giants.

The Dodgers, when they ventured to the Polo Grounds for game two, were nearly dead. But they didn't know it yet. Hodges, Robinson, Pafko, and Rube Walker all homered for the Dodgers, battering three Giants pitchers - Sheldon Jones, George Spencer, and Al Corwin - for ten runs. The Giants rapped out five singles, with a double by Bobby Thomson. It added up to a 10-0 Brooklyn victory.

You may have previously heard about game three.

The skies were overcast, rain threatened but never materialized, and 34,320 fans played hooky from school or work to attend the game. All over the city, radios and televisions stayed tuned to the Polo Grounds. One of the early arrivals at the park was Tallulah Bankhead, still a reigning star of Broadway and films, who, along with Toots Shor, was one of the Giants' best-known fans.

Tallulah blithely predicted a win for the home side.

Durocher and Dressen went with their best pitchers - Maglie and Newcombe, respectively. To start, Newcombe was the superior of the two.

In the first inning, Reese walked for Brooklyn. Snider walked. Robinson singled Reese home. Under cloudy skies, Newcombe's fastball was humming. He wasn't striking men out, but he was retiring them steadily on pop-ups and groundouts. "Newcombe," Monte Irvin recalled afterward, "was blinding us."

At a few minutes after 2 P.M., the Polo Grounds lights were turned on by the umpires. Up until the seventh inning, the two teams traded goose eggs.

Then in the Giants' half of the inning, Irvin doubled. Whitey Lockman bunted him to third. Bobby Thomson, who had hit well against the Dodgers all year, cracked a long fly to Snider in center. Irvin scored. The Dodgers and Giants were dead even again.

After the inning, Newcombe came to the Dodger dugout and claimed he was tired: tired of pitching and tired of listening to the foul epithets hurled at him by Leo Durocher, managing from the third base coach's box. Robinson snapped at him.

"Don't give me that tired shit," Robinson said. "Get out there and pitch."

But first there was the top of the eighth. After Furillo fanned, Reese and Snider singled. Reese went to third. Robinson was up. Maglie tried to keep Robinson from pulling the ball into the right field stands. But in working carefully, he wild-pitched a ball into the dirt, scoring Reese and sending Snider all the way to third. Durocher then ordered Robinson to be walked, hoping that the slow-footed Andy Pafko, batting next, would hit into a double play.

Pafko hit the ball hard, squarely at Bobby Thomson at third. The ball played Thomson, however. Snider scored when Pafko reached first. The official scorer awarded a hit.

Gil Hodges, who could never hit Maglie, popped up. But Billy Cox drilled another ball past Thomson as Robinson scored the third run of the inning. Dodger fans were delirious, particularly when

Newcombe set down the Giants in order in their half of the eighth. Now the Dodgers were three outs away from the pennant that had once seemed easily theirs. Newcombe was coasting. What could go wrong? The writers assigned to the game started toward the Dodger dugout as Larry Jansen pitched the top of the ninth and retired the Dodgers in order.

With three outs to go in the season, Durocher clapped his hands in the New York dugout, trying to rally his troops. "You've had some kind of year," he told his team. "You got nothing to be ashamed of. When you go off the field, hold your heads up high."

Minutes later, Dark whacked a ball toward first base. It took a low, skidding hop, glanced off Gil Hodges' glove, and rolled into short right field. Dark was on with a single and the Giants fans started to yell.

Don Mueller was up next. Mueller, seen here, was always a smart hitter, a thinking man's ballplayer, and a gifted batsman. He saw Hodges holding Dark on first, a meaningless maneuver since Dark's run wasn't important. Mueller, a left-handed hitter with a style similar Don Mattingly of a later generation, had all of the right side of the infield to aim at.

"What happened next," Mueller recalled years later, "was no accident."

Mueller placed a belt-high fastball from Newcombe exactly where he wanted it, just to Hodges' right. The ball streaked all the way out to right field. By the time Furillo could play the ball, Dark was on third and thirty thousand people were screaming. Across New York City, anyone near a radio or television came to a halt.

In the Dodger bullpen, Ralph Branca and Clem Labine hurriedly started to throw. Newcombe looked bewildered. Robinson came over to him as Monte Irvin, a power hitter, approached the plate.

"Two cheap hits," Robinson said. "You're all right."

"No, I ain't. I ain't all right."

Newcombe again said he was tired. But there was no move from Dressen. Newcombe looked at Irvin, then induced him to pop up to Gil Hodges. On his way back to the dugout, Irvin shattered his bat in anger. One out.

In the press box an announcement came across the loudspeaker. "All accredited writers should pick up press passes for tomorrow's World Series game at Ebbets Field. Passes will be distributed in the Dodger clubhouse until five P.M."

Down below, Whitey Lockman stepped in against Newcombe. On the radio, Russ Hodges was saying, "And now the action is set to resume…"

Lockman fouled off Newcombe's first pitch. Then Newcombe threw again. Lockman swung and the unbelieving Giant fans sprang to their feet. The ball soared over Billy Cox's head at third, landed fair several yards behind third, and caromed down into the left field corner. Andy Pafko chased it frantically, catching up with it and firing it back in to second, trying to keep Lockman out of scoring position. But that was hopeless. Lockman was already there.

Almost unnoticed in the pandemonium was Don Mueller, lying at third base, clutching his ankle and the bag. As he had sprinted toward the base, he had started to slide, changed his mind, and had tangled his spikes in the dirt. A tendon had popped in his right ankle.

Durocher signaled the trainer, Doc Bowman. Bowman darted out of the first base dugout toward third, passing Chuck Dressen, who was on his way to the mound. Newcombe was about to get his wish. He would leave the game. So would Mueller, his own part of the heroics finished for the season.

On the mound, a decision had to be made. Who would pitch to Bobby Thomson? Catcher Rube Walker suggested Labine, even though he had pitched the previous day. Pitching coach Clyde Sukeforth, out in the pen, had already indicated Branca. Meanwhile, at third base Rigney and three teammates were placing the injured Mueller on a stretcher. Clint Hartung had also been called over as a pinch runner.

"I wanted the big Texan," Durocher later recalled, "because I knew at the end of the game Newcombe would be coming for me. I wanted the biggest guy around."

Branca trudged in as Mueller started a journey to the hospital.

There was a brief discussion of whether or not to walk Thomson. He had, after all, hit 31 home runs that year and had battered the Dodgers all season. He had socked a homer off Branca as recently as two days earlier. But Dressen was not about to walk the winning run onto first base. In the same vein, he had not warmed up the Dodgers' most effective pitcher that year, Preacher Roe. Preach, Dressen would reveal later, was being saved "for Game One of the World Series."

Branca looked at Thomson, and the latter, Glasgow-born and the son of a carpenter, took a few practice swings. Russ Hodges described the next ninety seconds over WMCA Radio.

Bobby Thomson up there swinging.... He's had two out of three, a single and a double, and Billy Cox is playing him right on the third base line... One out, last of the ninth... Branca pitches and Bobby takes a strike call on the inside corner... Bobby hitting at .292... He's had a single and double and drove in the Giants' first run with a long fly to center... Brooklyn leads it 4-2.... Hartung down the line at third not taking any chances.... Lockman without too big a lead at second, but he'll be running like the wind if Thomson hits one... Branca throws...

There's a long drive... It's gonna be...
I BELIEVE....   THE GIANTS WIN THE PENNANT! THE GIANTS WIN THE PENNANT! THE GIANTS WIN THE PENNANT!... BOBBY THOMSON HITS INTO THE LOWER DECK OF THE LEFT FIELD STANDS!...
THE GIANTS WIN THE PEN- NANT AND THEY'RE GOING CRAZY!...
YAAAYH 0-0-0- 0!!!
3:57 P.M.

Complete bedlam! Players on the field! Leo jumping on Bobby's back as the hero rounded third. Giants mobbing Thomson at the plate, after he has completed leaping around the bases. Branca slinking off.

Robinson standing defiantly on the field, watching Thomson, making sure the Scot touched all the bases. Fans all over. The Giants swaggering triumphantly to the clubhouse, celebrating their victory noisily as the Dodgers listened in silence through the thin wall.

An hour later there were still hundreds of fans in the outfield, imploring Thomson to come out for one final bow. He did.

"Holy hell broke loose all over," Wes Westrum recalled as he thought back on the moment. "We couldn't believe what had happened. Several Giant players cracked heads against the roof of the dugout when we jumped up to see where the ball went."

"It was a real line drive home run," said Durocher, who used to complain about such short round-trippers. "In any other ballpark in the country, the left fielder would have come in a few steps to catch it."

"That's the first time," said Carl Erskine, the Dodger pitcher, who viewed things from a different angle, "that I've ever seen a big fat wallet flying into the grandstand."

The miracle that Arthur Daley said was necessary?

Well, there it was.

A believable finish to an unbelievable baseball season?

Absolutely not.

Perhaps Red Smith, writing a few hours after the game, had already established the proper perspective. Under the heading 1951: NEW YORK GIANTS 5, BROOKLYN DODGERS 4, he wrote:

"Now it is done. Now the story ends. And there is no way to tell it. The art of fiction is dead. Reality has strangled invention. Only the utterly impossible, the inexpressibly fantastic can ever be plausible again."

But it was over, and the Giants had won. They had won because they had come from far behind and because they had never given up. They had won because they were a very good ball club, every bit as good as the Dodgers. In the end, over the course of 157 games, they were one hit and one run better. And that made the difference.

Chapter 79   Three in a Row for Casey

"It is all falling indelibly into the past."

Don DeLillo, *Underworld*

Probably no single play in the history of any professional sport has been so discussed and analyzed as Bobby Thomson's home run.

Don DeLillo wrote a novel titled *Underworld* in 1997. The novel opens on the day of the fateful game, October 3, 1951. A boy named Cotter Martin sneaks into the Polo Grounds, not the easiest thing, to watch the game. There's a prologue titled, *Pafko at the Wall*, which was previously published on its own. In real life, the fate of the ball that Thomson hit has never been known. But in DeLillo's novel, Cotter Martin snares, or steals, the ball away from another fan and dashes home. Cotter's father steals the ball from his son and later sells it for thirty-two bucks and change.

Then the book drops Branca and Thomson and rambles along. It that touches upon many actual events including the Cuban Missile Crisis of a decade later.

Underworld is not an easy book, but it contains some great writing. Try this: "The cheesecake was smooth and lush," wrote Mr. DeLillo, "with the personality of a warm and well-to-do uncle who knows a hundred dirty jokes and will die of sexual exertions in the arms of his mistress."

More than half a century later, Joshua Prager, the distinguished writer for *The Wall Street Journal* gave us something new, although rumored for years.

In a fascinating book titled *The Echoing Green: The Untold Story of Bobby Thomson, Ralph Branca and the Shot Heard Round the World*, Prager wrote not only about the most famous home run in American baseball but also its aftershocks and about the conspiracy theory that surrounds it.

The key part of Prager's exhaustive inquiry: did the Giants know what the Dodger pitchers were going to throw before they threw it? Said in baser terms, were the Giants swiping signs?

Good question.

Prager, who first exposed the chicanery in 2001 for *The Wall Street Journal*, says, why yes, they did. Down the stretch, a tight cabal of Giants players and employees were stealing signs at the Polo Grounds. All that was involved was a telescope, a buzzer, an isolated bullpen catcher, and the fortuitous location of the windows in the Giants center field clubhouse.

From a center field office in the Polo Grounds, Giants coaches with a telescope could pilfer the signs to the pitcher. Though a system of buzzers, the message could be relayed to let the batter know what type of pitch was to be served next. The system was in place, according to Prager's account, during the last half of the season. The system was installed by an ordinary electrician, a gentleman who happened to be a Brooklyn fan.

Now another question.

Did Thomson know beforehand that Branca's second pitch would be a fastball?

Thomson answered no to Prager. The hitter's focus was on Branca and the pitch, not the sign.

Prager's book is remarkable and convincing. But of course, there are no specific rules in baseball about sign stealing. It's often called "gamesmanship" and is as old as the game.

In any case, Russ Hodges' call was that the Giants won the pennant, not that the Giants cheated and stole the pennant. Hodges' call was accurate.

"Even if Bobby knew what was coming, he had to hit it... Knowing the pitch doesn't always help," Branca said many years later in an interview in The New York *Times*.

The final score stands.

The Giants won the pennant.

Nothing that happened in the 1951 World Series could possibly have been anything but an anticlimax to baseball's most exciting season since 1908. But the Series, the sixth between the Yankees and the Giants, was played anyway.

The Giants carried their momentum to Yankee Stadium the next afternoon. On a high, the Giants behind Dave Koslo surprised the Yankees with a 5-1 win. Irvin was four-for-five and stole home against Allie Reynolds. Alvin Dark kicked in with a three-run homer.

But a day later, the Yankees came right back behind Eddie Lopat's five-hitter and won, 3-1.

On October 6, the action came back to the Polo Grounds, where the New York Giants worked their final bit of 1951 magic. Jim Hearn, pitching masterfully, held the Yankees scoreless into the bottom of the fifth. As the Giants nursed a 1-0 lead, Eddie Stanky walked. When he tried to steal second, Yogi Berra handled a pitchout perfectly and fired the ball to Phil Rizzuto covering second. The ball was there in plenty of time for a tag, but Stanky kicked the ball out of Rizzuto's glove with the expertise of an NFL punter. Phil was charged with an error, a play that Rizzuto kvetched about for decades. The break ignited a Giant five-run rally that carried the Polo Grounders to a 6-1 win.

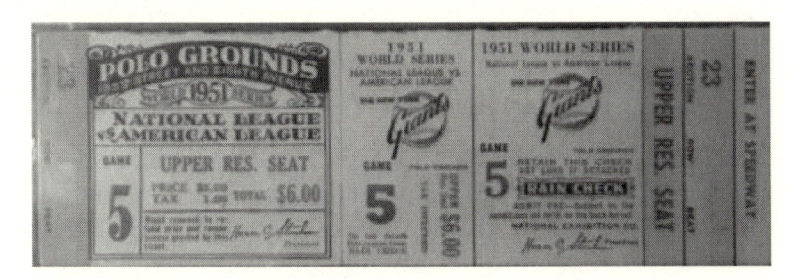

For a day the Yankees appeared to be in trouble. Then God cooperated and sent rain on October 7. The Yankees regrouped and grabbed the momentum. On October 8 Allie Reynolds pitched a complete game to tie the Series in Game Four. Joe DiMaggio homered with one on off Sal Maglie, the Yankee Clipper's final World Series home run. (His first had been in 1937.) Eddie Lopat was back in Game Five to torment the Giants with his array of junk. In the third inning Gil McDougald popped a grand slam into the upper deck of left field at the Polo Grounds. Rizzuto also homered (Yes, you read that right; Phil hit one in the 1942 World Series, also) as the Bronx Bombers swamped the Giants, 13-1.

Game Six was the end of it.

Vic Raschi held the Giants in check all day and brought a 4-1 lead to the ninth. Then the Giants attempted a final rally against Johnny Sain, their old friend from his Boston Braves days. When Sain couldn't get the side out, Casey Stengel brought little-used Bob Kuzava into the game. Never question Casey's wisdom. Kuzava, coming in with the bases loaded and none out, retired Irvin, Thomson, and Sal Yvars on consecutive outfield flies. Monte Irvin's outstanding regular-season play carried over into the World Series. He hit .458, tying a record with his 11 hits. But it wasn't enough.

The Yankees had another World Championship, their third in as many years and their last one with a magnificent player named Joe DiMaggio. But the Giants had the lingering memory of the most dramatic pennant victory in the history of American baseball.

A Coach's Reminiscence – Tom Yankus

HOW COULD YOU DO THAT?

In the summer of 1952, Ed Buckie was the coach of our St. Cyril's team in the Hartford Twilight League, but more importantly - in our eyes - he was also a scout for the New York Giants. Always on the prowl for likely "prospects," he seemed larger than life. To us eighteen-year-old players in a so-so league, Ed obviously had little time for non-prospects - until the day he invited me to a tryout at the Polo Grounds. New York City! The show! Me! The non-athletic, wild left-handed non-prospect!

On the day of the tryout, I was out of bed and ready to go three hours early. I kept pestering my dad to drive faster down the Merritt Parkway. Soon enough we were standing at the players' entrance of the sprawling, massive Polo Grounds. Then milling around the infield with the other players, I began to feel queasy. The gap between Hartford and New York City combined with the roar of LaGuardia's jets didn't help. I could be torched in my one-inning stint or I could have one of my wild moments with a floating strike zone.

Fortunately, as I warmed up, my fastball had life and sink and a touch of gitti-up. This might not be bad after all, but "bad" was an understatement, as line drive after line drive made it to the wall and beyond. It was especially embarrassing because several Giants scouts were staring at their shoes wondering if Ed Buckie had lost his mind.

Thankfully, the inning ended, and as I scooted to the clubhouse to get out of sight, my catcher caught up to me to admit that he had told all of the hitters what pitches were coming.

"I know most of these New York guys from our league, but I never seen youse before. Sorry."

"Thanks for sharing."

It was a long ride home, but at least I didn't quit the game. Catchers are good for something, after all.

Tom Yankus
Wallingford, CT
May 2018

(Editor's Note: Tom Yankus is currently a Special Advisor to the Wesleyan University baseball program, following fifty-two enormously successful years coaching baseball at Choate Rosemary Hall. Yankus attended Williams College, graduating in 1956 as president of his class. He has since been named to the Ephs' All-Time Baseball Team. After graduation, he was signed by the New York Yankees, with minor league stints in Montana, Washington and North Carolina. He also pitched in the prestigious Cape Cod League and served as manager of the Orleans Cardinals for nine seasons, coaching, among others, Todd Helton, Nomar Garciaparra and Frank Thomas. The Orleans Cardinals' annual Thomas Yankus Pitching award is named after him. In November 2017, he was inducted into the Cape Cod League Hall of Fame. An English teacher at Choate, he was inducted into the Choate Athletics Hall of Fame in 1996. In 2014, the school's varsity baseball field was named after him.)

Chapter 80   '52 and '53, The Bums Bounce Back

"What are you waitin' on, skip? Ah'm your man!"

Dusty Rhodes

The Miracle of Coogan's Bluff, as it was popularly known, was fresh in the minds of New York baseball fans the following year. Just as many Yankee fans looked unrealistically to Roger Maris for an encore in 1962, Giant and Dodger fans expected some fireworks in 1952. They got them, but of a different sort.

Eddie Stanky departed over the winter to take the managerial reins of the St. Louis Cardinals. Arriving were a pair of rookies: Hoyt Wilhelm, who, after hitting a home run in his first at-bat (his only homer in a twenty-one-year career), developed into the finest knuckleball pitcher ever, and Dusty Rhodes, a cheerful, muscular, shuffling Alabaman who had all the fielding ability of a fire hydrant. But he would amaze the world, and particularly his manager, with his prowess as a pinch hitter.

"Every time we needed a pinch hit to win a game," Durocher would say a few years later, "there was Dusty Rhodes to deliver it for us. Confident? The average fan may think a manager has to fight his men off when he's looking for a pinch hitter. Don't kid yourself. You look down the bench and more often than not every eye is averted. Not Dusty Rhodes. Dusty would always be up on his feet, at the far end of the dugout, hefting a bat. 'Ah'm your man,' he would call down. 'What are ya waitin' on, skip? Ah'm your man!'"

By June 1, however, Brooklyn took the league lead and held tenaciously to it. The Dodgers slumped in late July and the Giants drew closer, fueling again the public's expectations for a "second miracle." In early September the teams met for five straight games, as they frequently did, two in one park, three in the other. The Giants won the first two to shave the Dodgers' lead to four games. Every National League fan in New York was thinking alike.

Things turned ugly in the third game, played at the Polo Grounds. Hoyt Wilhelm hit Gil Hodges in the fifth inning, with the Dodgers leading 5-0. In retaliation, Hodges went hard into second base and cut open Bill Rigney's leg with his spikes. For the rest of the day, a beanball war ensued, with Larry Jansen eventually being bounced from the game. But the Dodgers won that game, 10-2, and won the next game in the series, 3-2. The Giants were six back. No miracle followed, perhaps because fate and Uncle Sam had messed things up.

Monte Irvin had broken his ankle in Denver in April during an exhibition game against Cleveland. Uncle Sam put the kibosh on the Giants a second time by drafting Willie the Wonder into the United States Army on May 29. True, Mays had only been hitting .236 when he left, but the Giants had been in first place. Upon Willie's departure, the team lost eight of ten and fell from the lead to stay.

It wasn't a good year for Leo, either. Following three separate dirt and shin-kicking episodes with umpires, Durocher was suspended three separate times while the Dodgers went on to win the pennant by four and a half games. Honestly, now, wouldn't Mays and Irvin have made five games difference over the course of the season?

There should be a key on the typewriters of those who write about such things which, with one tap, types out "But the Yankees won the World Series four games to - "

That's what happened, in seven games.

In 1953 the Boston Braves departed from their crumbling old stadium. A grand total of 281,278 fans trickled into Braves Field in 1952, sealing the loss of the franchise to Milwaukee. The move magically transformed the lowly Braves into a pennant contender. Early in the season, Milwaukee first baseman Joe Adcock hit the first home run ever hit in a League game into the Polo Grounds bleachers. The move to Milwaukee also put ideas in "The O'Malley's" head, as time would tell.

Roger Kahn once called the eight everyday players of the 1953 Dodgers - Hodges, Jim Gilliam, Reese, Cox, Furillo, Snider, Robinson, and Campanella - "the most gifted baseball team that has yet played." That goes a long way toward explaining how Brooklyn wired the field that year, winning the pennant by an easy thirteen games. Ignominiously, the Giants fell back to fifth midway through the year. There they stayed, as the fans quickly started to climb aboard Leo's back .

Chuck Dressen even had the temerity to tempt the baseball gods by reuttering his remark "The Giants is dead!" in mid-August. Dressen must have believed the old adage about lightning.

In August 1953, *The Sporting News* ran a full-page feature about a young pitcher named Ruben Gómez. "Giants Plucked a Peach in Puerto Rico," the article announced.

Gómez was a rookie with the Giants, having pitched extremely well in Puerto Rico, where he had been a teammate of Willie Mays. Now he was embarked on a streaky year, but he received help from pitching coach Freddie Fitzsimmons, especially with the slider. Cincinnati manager Rogers Hornsby, who had watched Gómez in a previous Caribbean Series, told Durocher that Gómez was the best pitcher he had seen from the region. Casey Stengel told the Yankees brass that they'd made a mistake by not signing Gómez earlier.

On Sunday, September 6, the Giants and Dodgers celebrated their beanball war of exactly one year earlier by starting another. The aforesaid rookie pitcher Ruben Gómez of the Giants was looking to make a mark in his first season. He made one when he plunked Carl Furillo, Durocher's least favorite Dodger, on the wrist. Furillo shook off the hit, did some pushing with the umpires and his manager and started for the mound. Both dugouts emptied, but nothing really happened. Furillo was finally talked into reporting to first base, against his lesser instincts.

Things had just started to simmer down when Durocher's rasping ever-irritating voice caught Furillo's ear. Furillo looked to the Giants' dugout and saw the skinny Durocher making threatening and uncomplimentary gestures. Then Durocher invited him into the dugout to discuss things.

Furillo accepted. Durocher charged out to greet him and one of the fiercest brawls in Giant-Dodger history was in progress, an impressive accomplishment considering some of the warfare of the McGraw era or the later 1930s.

Durocher and Furillo met head on. The benches and bullpens cleared for a second time and the entire teams met at Ground Zero.

Monte Irvin of the Giants and Gil Hodges of the Dodgers served as peacemakers and attempted to separate the two combatants. brawlers.

Author Lawrence Baldassaro, in a fine book titled, *Beyond DiMaggio*, recalled that various "accounts have Furillo clamping Durocher in a headlock as they grappled on the ground while others tried to separate them. One observer who did not try to break up the fight, according to Duke Snider, was umpire Babe Pinelli, who reportedly yelled, 'Kill him, Carl, kill him!' Fifty-three years later Dodger pitcher Carl Erskine confirmed Snider's assertion: 'Furillo had Leo on the ground and was choking him. I was on the perimeter as was Babe Pinelli. He was exclaiming 'Kill that SOB, kill him.' He then saw that I had heard him, so he went on, 'I mean it. That no good low life. I mean it.'"

The loser in the grand scuffle that followed was Furillo, who never landed a solid punch on Leo, but who injured a bone in his wrist, missing much of what remained of the season. ("Durocher was a dirty manager. He was a dirty player… I hated his guts," Furillo said many years later. Nonetheless Furillo led the league in batting at .344 and presided in right field as the Yankees beat Brooklyn's finest bunch of Dodgers yet again in the World Series. Billy Martin was the unlikely hitting star with 8 hits in 12 at bats.

By season's end, Gómez had gone 13-11, 3.40 with three shutouts. He earned 1953 major league All Rookie team honors. A few of the pieces were drifting into place for 1954.

Gómez was one of them.

Chapter 81   A Final Pennant

**"Joe Louis, Jascha Heifetz, Sammy Davis
and Nashua rolled into one."**

Leo Durocher describing Willie Mays

In 1954, the chemistry of the New York Giants changed with the return of Willie Mays from the U.S. Army and the addition of Johnny Antonelli to the pitching staff.

Lou Perini, the Braves owner, had signed Antonelli on June 29, 1948, by giving him an amount reported in excess of $50,000, the largest bonus in baseball history at the time. The figure reported in the press was probably hyped. The bonus probably inhibited Antonelli's development more than aided it.

The Braves were chasing a rare pennant in 1948. The size of Antonelli's bonus required them to keep him on the major league roster for at least two years. So the kid sat on the bench for months, an untried teenager with no experience under pressure, with resentment brewing every day from the veterans over how much money the club had thrown at an unproven young man.

In June 1949, Antonelli teamed with another kid, catcher Del Crandall, to form a battery of two nineteen-year olds. There followed a stint in the army.

By the time Antonelli was discharged in 1953, the Braves were in Milwaukee. When the All-Star Game rolled around, he already had an 8-4 record. But then, more bad luck. He contracted pneumonia. His strength ebbed and he ended the year 12-12. Then on February 1, 1954, the Braves made a monumental six-player swap with the New York Giants. Antonelli went to the Polo Grounds with pitcher Don Liddle, catcher Ebba St. Claire, infielder Billy Klaus, and $50,000 for outfielder Bobby Thomson and catcher Sammy Calderone. The trade of Bobby Thomson was perhaps one of the greatest *What-have-You-done-for-Me-lately?* transactions in baseball history.

But for Antonelli, as he later recalled later it, this was "the best break of my career."

In 1954 Antonelli led off the season with a decent 5-2 record. Then he found a groove and zipped off eight straight victories before the All Star Game. Eventually, Antonelli was the most effective pitcher in the league in 1954, posting 21 wins, which was really saying something, and a league-leading 2.30 ERA.

Maglie and Ruben Gómez had excellent years also, with 14 and 17 wins, respectively. Marv Grissom, picked up on waivers from the Red Sox the previous season, helped out in the bullpen with 19 saves.

But there was more than just pitching in 1954.

This team was a wrecking crew, much like the squads of the late 1940s. Their total of 186 home runs tied Brooklyn for the league lead. And early in the season they served notice that they were not to be defeated. On May 28 the Giants hit six home runs in one game as they walloped the Dodgers, 17-6, at the Polo Grounds. A week later they devastated the Cardinals, 13-8, in St. Louis. On July 11 they again hit six home runs in a game as they battered the Pirates, 13-7, in New York.

Then again, there was Sunday May 2 at Sportsman's Park in St. Louis.

Sunday, Sunday, Sunday!

The New York Giants were on the receiving end of, not a funny car or a late model dragster, but a one man wrecking crew in the form of a future Hall of Famer with a bat.

In the first game of a double header, Antonelli was pitching.

Stan Musial hit a home run in his second at bat after walking earlier. Then in the fifth inning, Musial's third at bat, The Man clubbed a home run over the pavilion in right field. In the eighth, with the score tied at 6-6 and two men in base, Musial sent a slider from Jim Hearn onto the roof of the aforesaid pavilion to nail down a 10-6 St. Louis victory. Both drives went out onto Grand Avenue.

The winning pitcher, also known as the last pitcher left standing in this event, was forty-one-year-old Al Brazle, a World War Two veteran who had played his first professional season in 1936. He had re-emerged after the war as a side-arm sinkerball pitcher.

Brazle added just the appropriate touch of surrealism to the day's events. He was tall, bony, and gaunt with a thin, leathery face. He had sunken cheeks, deep blue eyes and a thick shock of cottony white hair. His nickname was "Boots and Saddles" because he looked like a half-starved cowboy. More erudite Cardinal fans, and there were a few, thought he resembled the mythical Ichabod Crane of *The Legend of Sleepy Hollow*.

Then there was a second game.

The home team turned the lights on, presumably so Stan could see better. Again, Musial walked the first time up. The second time around, Musial blasted a ball to the deep cavern in right center, more than 400 feet away. It would have been at least a triple, or maybe an inside the park home run, but Willie Mays - always a killjoy when it came to long fly balls - ran it down and caught it.

Stan, however, was just getting warmed up. In his third at bat he hit another ball onto the busy pavilion roof, 394 feet from home plate over a forty foot screen. Then the next time, he straightened out one of Hoyt Wilhelm's knucklers, also to right center and also onto the roof.

The last time up, his 12th plate appearance of the day, Musial popped up.

Musial's final official stats for the day were eight at bats, five home runs, one single, nine RBI's, two walks and 21 total bases.

The Cardinals scored seventeen runs off Giants pitching. Know what? The Redbirds only gained a split of the doubleheader. The Giants hung up an eight spot in the fourth inning of the second game. Don Mueller had five hits and the day's outcome was not decided until Stan had popped up in his final at bat.

The Giants won 9-7.

"A bruising twin bill that kept 26,662 roaring fans in a dither for the better part of seven hours," John Drebinger breathlessly wrote in the New York *Times* the next day. Drebinger did not even take time to note the Devil's number, 666, nestled in the attendance figure. Seven hours of baseball, half in daylight, half under the lights. For the pitchers, this was shorter than a performance of *Die Gotterdammerung*, and nowhere nearly as funny.

The split left the Giants in fifth place. That was the bad news. The good news was they were only one game behind with a 9-8 record. The season was young and no one was breaking away. Yet.

As the season progressed, however, the hits continued to come from every direction for the New Yorkers.

Don Mueller would lead the league with 212 hits and would finish just three points behind Willie Mays for the batting championship, .345 to .342. Mays also hit 41 home runs. Hank Thompson, now installed at third upon Bobby Thomson's departure, hit 26. Rhodes destroyed the league with his pinch hits, batting .341 with 15 home runs.

Rhodes, also known as "The Colossus of Rhodes" in the tabloids, made the term "Chinese home run" a frequent one on the sports pages. Dusty had the happy faculty, while juiced up on bourbon, of whacking a ball just far enough into the friendly confines of the right field stands.

Durocher loved him. So did New York.

Against all this, the Dodgers finally faltered. Some said their spirit had been broken - temporarily, at least - by the Yankees. Billy Cox was benched in favor of pugnacious young Don Hoak.

Campanella, recovering from injuries, never got untracked. He hit .207. Pafko had departed to the Milwaukee Braves. Sandy Amoros was not a quality replacement, despite the incredible catch he would make against Yogi Berra in the 1956 World Series. Newcombe was a decent courteous man, but he was fighting the twin demons of alcohol and a fear of flying. He faded to 9-8.

At one point in July, the Dodgers closed to within two games of the league-leading Giants. But Brooklyn never could get in front. There was, inevitably, the big final series in September. The Dodgers won two out of three and seemed as if they would overtake New York at last. Then they left the Polo Grounds and dropped a doubleheader at Forbes Field in Pittsburgh to the lowly Bucs. A few days later, the Giants had a five-game lead. The Dodgers never came close again, finishing second.

There was one memorable Durocher touch to the pennant race.

Late in the year, when the Dodgers were flirting with the league lead, Carl Erskine of Brooklyn was ahead of the Giants, 5-4. The Giants loaded the bases with two outs, bringing up Wes Westrum, who was mired in a terrible slump.

"He (Westrum) was only playing," Durocher later recalled, "because we had no other catcher. The way he was going, he couldn't have hit me if I ran by slow and ducked a little bit."

Leo pulled his last catcher and sent Dusty Rhodes up to pinch-hit. Rhodes knocked the second pitch into center field to win the game.

Who would have caught if Rhodes had made an out? Leo never needed to provide an answer for that, but probably would have selected a "volunteer" from the end of his bench.

"I'd rather be in the tenth inning without a catcher than in the clubhouse with a loss," Leo said afterward. It was that type of year and this was Leo's type of philosophy. As Casey Stengel once said, or more than once actually, "What would you rather be: Good or lucky?"

Leo Durocher's 1954 New York Giants were the talk of the town.

They won the NL pennant by five games over the Brooklyn Dodgers. Gómez's best season in the majors helped: a 17-9 record and 2.88 ERA, fueled by four shutouts.

"I was in a groove most of that season," Gómez recalled many years later. "I established a friendship with Willie Mays and knew Don Liddle and Monte Irvin from winter ball. I was 13 when Irvin first came to Puerto Rico (with San Juan) so it was a joy being Monte's teammate in New York."

A Fan's Reminiscence – Dave Baines

I became a Giants fan in 1954 when I was eight. It was during the World Series when we lived in Rowayton, Connecticut and my mom would drive me after school over to the house of my friend, Chuck Kirkorian, to watch the series. He was a huge Giants fan and his family had a much better TV. Dusty Rhodes and Willie Mays became my two favorite players. The Giants went on to sweep Cleveland in four straight, and I thought they would be the kings of the National League forever, just like the Yankees usually were in the AL.

The next spring, in May 1955, for my 9th birthday, my parents gave me a complete NY Giants uniform – as I remember it, pure white with orange and black striping down the sides of the legs and the word *GIANTS* emblazoned across the front of the jersey in big black letters with orange trim. And, of course, there was the black ball cap with the orange *NY* above the bill. I felt like I looked just like Davey Williams, the Giants' second baseman, because that was my position in our pick-up games with all the kids from my 3rd grade class at Rowayton School. Then, to top it off, my parents, who were avid Dodger fans, got us tickets to a Saturday afternoon Dodgers – Giants game at the Polo Grounds a week or so past my May 18 birthday.

On game day we drove the 30 miles from Rowayton to the Polo Grounds. In the fourth inning, the Dodgers had runners on first and second with no outs. Jackie Robinson hit a line drive over Davey Williams' head which the runners thought would go into right field. But no – Davey leaped high in the air with his glove hand while the runners {Ed: Gil Hodges on 2nd, Carl Furillo on 1st} broke for the next base. The ball hit the top of the webbing of Williams' glove and fell toward the ground in front of him, but he managed to bend down and turn his glove up so that the pocket faced the sky, and he caught the ball! Davey then threw to Dark who was covering second to double up the runner, and then Alvin then threw to Lockman at first to triple up that runner who had broken for second base.

A triple play! I'll remember that play forever.

Lockman and catcher Wes Westrum each hit solo home runs for the Giants. I don't remember if Willie got a hit but he sure was smooth gliding through center field making every catch look easy. However, I do remember Duke Snider, the Dodgers center fielder getting a hit or two and Gil Hodges hitting a three run homer in the first inning which helped propel the "Bums" to victory. That year the Dodgers would also win the NL pennant and win their first World Series by beating the Yankees.

New York baseball during the 50's was the center of the baseball universe with all three teams winning pennants and the World Series and each having one of the three best center fielders in the major leagues – Willie, Mickey and The Duke. Unfortunately, that era came to an abrupt end after the 1957 season as the Giants and Dodgers each abandoned New York for the lure of the west coast.

>Dave Baines
>Naples, FL
>April 2018

Chapter 82   New York Four, Cleveland Nada

> **"They say anything can happen in a short series.
> I just didn't expect it to be that short."**
>
> **Al Lopez**

Something was conspicuously absent from the World Series in 1954: the New York Yankees. Casey Stengel had a fine squad as usual. They won 103 games and lost only 51, the best overall record of any of Casey's teams in the 1950's. In almost any other year, they would have won the pennant.

Instead, the Cleveland Indians with awesome pitching by Early Wynn, Bob Lemon, Mike (the Big Bear) Garcia, Bob Feller, Ray Narleski, Hal Newhouser, and Don Mossi, won 111 games. They had Larry Doby in center, Al Rosen at third, Bobby Avila at second, and Vic Wertz at first. They were heavily favored to knock off the Giants.

A dozen days after Rocky Marciano knocked out Ezzard Charles in the third round to retain his heavyweight championship at Yankee Stadium, Cleveland visited the Polo Grounds to open the World Series. Perry Como crooned *The Star Spangled Banner*. Bob Lemon started for the Tribe. Jack Brickhouse and Russ Hodges were the television announcers on NBC.

Sal Maglie opened for the Giants. Sal shaved Al Smith too close and hit him with a pitch to start the game.

Avila followed with a single. Two outs later, Big Vic Wertz, who would remember this day well, boomed a triple off the distant right field wall. Cleveland was up, 2-0.

In the Giants' third, Mueller and Hank Thompson drove in runs to tie the game. But Lemon, rising to the occasion, grew crustier as the day wore on. It was still a 2-2 tie in the top of the eighth when Doby walked and Rosen singled. Two on, none out. Wertz, who already had a triple and a pair of singles, came up. No way was Leo letting Wertz hit off Maglie, whom Wertz had had measured all day.

In came Don Liddle, the lefty who had come over to the Giants from the Braves in the Antonelli trade. Liddle had been an effective spot starter for Durocher all year.

Liddle made only one pitch that day, but in doing so secured his participation in baseball folklore. Wertz sat on a fastball and drove it in a long, fast arc to straightaway right center field. In any other ballpark it would have been a home run. With any other outfielder it would have been an extra-base hit.

But this was the Polo Grounds. This was Willie Mays. This was, "The Catch."

Mays was running by the time anyone looked at him, sprinting deep, straining, reaching, and hoping. Yet when the ball came down, there was Willie's glove, poised over his left shoulder. He caught the ball, spun, and rocketed the ball back toward civilization, losing his cap in the process. Just as Cox and the Dodgers had stared in disbelief in 1951, now it was the turn of the Cleveland Indians.

A thirty-two year old native New Yorker named Arnold Hano had picked this day to sit in the Polo Grounds bleachers to write about the game. As a younger man, Hano had worked as a copy boy at the New York *Daily News*. He established his sports background at that paper and eventually accompanied the *News* photographers to sporting events. As a nineteen-year-old, he wrote captions for the photographic shots that returned from ballparks to the newsroom.

Hano served in World War Two. After the war he returned to New York and began a career in commercial book publishing. In 1951 Hano debuted as a baseball author with a young adult novel, *The Big Out*.

The Big Out, indeed! Talk about being in the right place at the right time.

As a younger man, Hano had been sitting in the Ebbets Field press box when the famous third strike got away from Mickey Owen. Today, Hano was positioned perfectly in the bleachers to watch Willie Mays' iconic robbery of Vic Wertz's three mile long - okay, only maybe 465-foot - fly ball to center. Hano's report became a short non-fiction work titled *A Day In The Bleachers*.

Mays "whirled and threw," Hanno reported, "like some olden statue of a Greek javelin hurler. What an astonishing throw. This was the throw of a giant, the throw of a howitzer made human."

The catch that preceded the throw hadn't been bad, either.

"People talk about that catch and, I've said this many times," Mays said years later, that I've made better catches than that many times in regular season. But of course in my time, you didn't have a lot of television during the regular season. A lot of people didn't see me do a lot of things."

Marv Grissom relieved Liddle, who left secure in the knowledge that he had retired the one man he had to get: Wertz. He also announced such in the clubhouse after the game. Grissom retired the side and remained through the tenth. Then Dusty Rhodes hulked out of the Giants' dugout with two on and one out.

Rhodes lofted Bob Lemon's second pitch gently down the right field line. Outfielder Dave Pope came over to haul in the routine fly. But, ah. Suddenly Pope was fallible. He had his back to the fence and was out of room, right near the 257 FT sign. He lunged upward.

Gone!

The ball landed in the first row of the grandstand, then popped out and rolled tauntingly to his feet. Game One went to the Giants, 5-2.

Another day, another performance by Dusty the Great.

This time, to open Game Two, Al Smith smacked Johnny Antonelli's first offering into the seats, instead of being hit himself. In the fifth, along came Rhodes again, who pinch-hit for Irvin with runners on first and third. Early Wynn was pitching, so Rhodes was knocked down on his first pitch. There had been something about the home run the previous day that Wynn hadn't liked. The second pitch Rhodes lined into center field, tying the game. Seconds later, the Giants scored a second run. There it remained until the seventh when Rhodes faced Wynn again. Leo had left Dusty in to play left field, always an adventure. Rhodes remembered the knockdown of the fifth inning and gave Wynn his receipt, a long loud blast onto the right field roof.

The Series shifted to Cleveland for Game Three the next day. Game Three had a paid attendance of 71,555.

"Game 3 started with a distinct Latin-American flavor as far as the starting pitchers were concerned," reported *The Sporting News*. "Mike Garcia, the California-Mexican, opened against Gómez, Durocher's Puerto Rican."

It was a first of a kind. Both World Series starters were of Latin-American heritage. Gómez (who preferred the use of the accent in his name) and Garcia had a pre-game chat in Spanish. Garcia asked Rubén how his wife was doing and whether Rubén signed his winter contract. Important stuff like that which had a critical bearing on the game. Gómez, aware that Lefty Gomez (who didn't use the accent) had been 6-0 in the World Series with the Yankees, said he would add to the number of victories by pitchers so-named.

Brooklyn-born Danny Kaye, who had just finished filming *White Christmas* with Bing Crosby and Rosemary Clooney, George's aunt, sang the national anthem. Tris Speaker threw out the first pitch. Cleveland manager Al Lopez had his photo taken with Speaker, player-manager of the World Series champion 1920 Indians and Lou Boudreau, player-manager of the 1948 winners.

But nothing could change the tide of events.

The Giants nicked Mike Garcia for a run in the first. Then in the third, New York loaded the bases. Irvin was scheduled to hit. Again Durocher called on Rhodes. This time Dusty singled sharply to center, scoring Mueller and Mays. Seconds later, Durocher, who always knew when the other team was off-balance, ordered a suicide squeeze. Giant second baseman Davey Williams executed it perfectly, scoring Hank Thompson from third. The Giants led, 4-0. They would win, 5-2.

Cleveland manager Al Lopez had a choice to make for Game Four.

Facing elimination, he could use Bob Lemon with two days' rest, or aging Bob Feller with plenty of rest. Probably it didn't matter. Don Liddle, who had retired Vic Wertz so memorably three days earlier, started for New York. By this time, Cleveland was so demoralized that Durocher probably could have pitched. Nonetheless, there was genius to Leo's strategy: even if the Indians had gotten to Liddle, Leo was ready to come back in Game Five with a sharp, rested Antonelli.

Two Indian errors presented the Giants with a pair of runs in the second. Mays doubled home a run in the third. The Giants chased Bob Lemon with a series of singles in the fifth inning. Hal Newhouser relieved, but had no better luck. By the time the side was retired, the Giants had seven runs. The Indians attempted a comeback, but it was too late. Far too late. The final score was 7-4. The Giants had an improbable four-game sweep.

Leo, with his kind of club, had finally brought a World Championship to the Polo Grounds, the first in twenty-one years. Not since Adolfo Luque had hitched up his belt and retired the last three Washington Senators in the 1933 Series had the New York Giants come off the field as World Champions.

But champions they were.

How had the New York Giants, who had won 89 games during the regular season, dispatched the Indians so handily? Years later in 2004, (a date that would have seemed like science fiction in 1954) Johnny Antonelli gave an interview to the Boston Braves Historical Association and its members. He recalled the fact that the Indians and Giants trained near each other in Arizona and had played together 18 times during Spring Training, with the Giants usually coming out on top. Thus, many Giants pitchers were well acquainted with the Indians. It should have worked the other way, too, but it didn't.

To flip time in the other direction, nine years prior to 1954, on August 14, 1945, Japan ceased fighting in World War Two. V-J day prompted the most lavish ticker tape parade in New York City history. Revelers celebrating the Allied victory over Japan filled the air with cloth, feathers, hat trimmings, paper and confetti. That evening, street sweepers worked through the night to clean it up, only to have their efforts undone when the merriment continued the next morning. All told, merrymakers flung 5,438 tons of material on New York City's streets.

The 1954 parade honoring the New York Giants' National League pennant win was smaller, but as the first one to celebrate a local New York team, it set a precedent. The city in the future would welcome their championship teams a ticker tape extravaganza, something the Yankees had never received during their five straight pennants. Maybe it was because the Giants were Manhattan's team.

Farther south, Rubén Gómez received a hero's welcome when his Pan Am flight arrived in San Juan on October 11, 1954. He went to a reception hosted by Doña Felisa Rincón de Gautier, San Juan's mayor. Willie Mays arrived five days later to play for the 1954-55 Crabbers, considered by many, including future Dodger-Met-Yankee Don Zimmer, to be "the best winter league team ever assembled."

The 1954 Giants. Pitching. Defense. Strategy. The key substitution. The critical pinch hit. Then maybe a big home run, Mays or Rhodes or Thomson style.

Durocher had won it the old fashioned way and had given the proud old franchise another taste of glory. It was the fifth World Championship and the seventeenth pennant since the days of Jim Mutrie, the sharp-dressed man.

"Inside baseball" had won it. Somewhere the ghost of John McGraw had to be smiling. Then the year, which began with Bill Terry's election to the Hall of Fame, ended with Willie Mays being selected as the Most Valuable Player in the National League. It was the first of two MVPs for Mays, but his only one as a New York Giant.

There was a curious footnote, no pun intended to the season. "Musial," wrote George Vecsey in his wonderful biography, *Musial: An American Life*, "had a soft spot for the Giants. Many years earlier, Horace Stoneham… had learned that he and Musial had the same shoe size. Every time the two teams met, Stoneham would give The Man a pair of new shoes."

Footnote, indeed.

The 1954 World Champions

A Fan's Reminiscence – Gordon Taylor

Growing up on Long Island, trips to weekend Giants and Dodgers baseball games with my father were the most special of times. I have magical memories of sitting with him high in the stands - generally along the third base line - watching the games unfold, sharing the anticipation of the next pitch, the joy of a win, and the disappointment of a loss. When both teams decamped for California in the same year, I wept inconsolably.

Gordon Taylor
Fairfax, Virginia
June 2018

A Fan's Reminiscence – Don Scheck

I saw my first two major league baseball games at the Polo Grounds in 1956 when I was seven years old. My grandfather and I had first-row box seats on the third base side at both games. I have little recollection of the first one other than the final score, the Giants lost to the Braves 11-0, and what I believe were the polished brass fixtures on the railings in front of our seats.

The second game, on September 16, was more exciting because I saw Willie Mays hit a home run. It landed in the left field seats but, from where I was sitting, the ball sailed through the air across the sky as if it was headed for the Harlem River. Willie was my favorite player when I was growing up. I remember getting the chills watching him come up to bat when the games were on television. I have faithfully followed and rooted for the Giants for most of the years since seeing those games.

Don Scheck
Mountainhome, PA
March 2018

A Fan's Reminiscence – Bob Schwartz

In April 1957, I was in the second grade at PS 196, Forest Hills, Queens, New York. I was sitting at my desk when suddenly my father appeared in the classroom's doorway and motioned toward the teacher. They conversed for a few minutes and then Mrs. Stern, the teacher, told me to leave with my dad. He wouldn't tell me where we were going, but he had a big smile on his face so I figured that nothing bad had happened.

We got on the subway and arrived an hour later at the Polo Grounds. It was home opening day against the Phillies! He had started taking me to games the year before, but this was indeed something very special. How can you beat being at a ballgame with your dad, and being near Willie Mays, too?

We didn't know this would be the New York Giants' last home opener. Sadly, my dad, like many other Giants and Dodgers fans, gave up on baseball when the moves to San Francisco and Los Angeles were announced. I remained a loyal Giants fan, however, mainly because of Willie, and I continue to be a big fan to this very day.

In 2013, I sent plane tickets to my adult sons and we met up in San Francisco for the home opener that year. It wasn't exactly a surprise, but I did arrange for a scoreboard message, which was a surprise for them. I think I had succeeded in creating another great memory for all of us.

Bob Schwartz
Boca Raton, FL
April 2018

Chapter 83   Stalin, Hitler & O'Malley

**"The kids? I feel sorry for the kids.
But I haven't seen many of their fathers recently.**

**Horace Stoneham, explaining the move
to San Francisco**

Once the giddy glow of the 1954 championship had faded, there was nothing left but an inexorable drift downward. The Brooklyn Dodgers came back with a vengeance in 1955, winning the pennant. It seemed like a lost season from the start. A clubhouse fistfight between Willie Mays and Ruben Gómez set a noxious tone in spring training and the tone never improved. The Milwaukee Braves, with young sluggers like Joe Adcock, Hank Aaron, and Eddie Mathews, were the new heirs apparent in the National League.

In August Eddie Brannick celebrated his fiftieth anniversary with the Giants. He had arrived as McGraw's office boy in 1905 in the days of Mathewson and John T. Brush. He had stayed a half a century. Rarely did he see a complete game, as a secretary's duties included attending to gate receipts with the visiting club secretary while each game was in progress. More than a thousand New Yorkers attended a dinner given in Brannick's honor at the Waldolf Astoria.

At the Polo Grounds, things continued to fall apart. The Giants peddled Maglie to the Cleveland Indians at the end of the July for some much needed cash, removing a 9-5 pitcher from the rotation. Attendance nosedived. Morale at the ball park tanked as the attendance dropped to sixth in an eight team league. Willie Mays was almost the sole bright light for the Giants during the entire year. Mays flirted with Babe Ruth's home run pace of 1927 for several months. In the end, Willie hit 51, tying Johnny Mize's club record of 1947. Antonelli and Gómez had uneven years.

Sadly, the Polo Grounds became a less pleasant place to see a game, play a game or even sell a hot dog. The Harry M. Stevens company was still the concessionaire. HMS. The grouchy vendors - unhappy because their business was down - referred to their boss company as, "Hitler Mussolini and Stoneham."

What else do you need to know? There were even those accelerating stories about the neighborhood being "dangerous."

In the end, the Giants fell to third place, a distant 18.5 games behind a very strong Brooklyn club that would eventually win the only World Championship in that borough's history.

Giant fans had tolerated Leo Durocher when he was winning. Now in 1955, the romance was chilly. The fans began to turn on him. It was okay to be abrasive and obnoxious when one was on a roll, but the constant acidity wore thin when the team was heading toward the second division. The press turned on him, also. The clock started to tick tick tick tick on Leo's tenure.

The feelings were mutual. In late September Durocher resigned, but not without a weird event to mark his farewell. On September 25, 1955, Leo's last day as manager of the New York Giants, the Giants closed the season with a doubleheader against the Phillies.

New York won the first game, 5-2.

In the second game, Philadelphia nursed a 3-1 lead into the last of the ninth at the Polo Grounds. With Joey Amalfitano on second base and Whitey Lockman on first, batter Bobby Hoffman lined a ball to the Phillies shortstop, Ted Kazanski. Kazanski flipped the ball to Bobby Morgan, the second baseman, to double Amalfitano. Then Morgan threw to first before Lockman could return. Leo must have been muttering to himself as he took his final walk as a Giant manager to the center field clubhouse. His reign in John McGraw's old job had ended on the short end of a triple play.

As for the major "other" tenant of the Polo Grounds, the Football Giants, they were on their way out, also. Their final season and the ancient oval would be 1955. They would move to Yankee Stadium in 1956 where they would pick up some Yankee pixie dust and win an NFL Championship

Horace Stoneham hired Bill Rigney, a capable baseball man and a Stoneham favorite since the late 1940s, to replace Durocher. But the most capable hands in baseball are useless without the proper material.

Rigney tried, but in 1956 there was nothing to build upon. There was only Willie Mays, who was something special, but not enough. Even Willie's home run totals were down: "only" 36.

There were also dark clouds gathering for National League

baseball in New York City.

During the Dodgers' inevitable roll to the World Series in 1955 and 1956, Walter O'Malley had reached an agreement with the league that the Dodgers might play "six or seven home games" at Roosevelt Stadium in Jersey City, the now rickety park that had once been home to the Jersey City Giants.

It was O'Malley's first step in either trying to find a new stadium in the area for the Dodgers or, as is now much clearer in retrospect, leaving the city completely. The Dodgers would eventually play one game in Jersey City in 1956, then eight in 1957. To paraphrase a young Minnesotan, one didn't need a weatherman to know which way the wind was blowing.

The hot-wired Ruben Gómez just couldn't stay off the back pages of the *News* and the *Daily Mirror*. Ruben Gómez was not a bad guy when he was in control of himself, but a loose cannon when he wasn't. Gómez didn't always get into fights, but when he did, he picked the wrong ones.

Ruben Gómez, who had engaged in a fistfight with Willie Mays during spring training of 1955, then got into an even worse mess plunking huge Joe Adcock of the Milwaukee Braves in the ribs with a pitch in Milwaukee on July 17, 1956. Adcock had a history of serious injuries after being hit by pitches. He also claimed that Gómez had yelled at him on his way to first base. Gómez could be wild, and he was not averse to knocking batters down, as he evidenced with Carl Furillo of Brooklyn in 1953.

When Adcock charged the mound from the first base line, Gómez threw the ball at Adcock again, hitting him in the hip. Gómez, terrified, then fled to the Giants' clubhouse with the slower Adcock in hot pursuit. A few minutes later, Gómez attempted to re-emerge, brandishing an ice pick, according to some witnesses. Saner members of the team intervened and pinned him to the clubhouse floor.

There were other problems, too. Irvin had retired. Jansen was long gone and so was Koslo. No one had replaced them.

The farm system, lacking the financial support from gate attendance that both the Dodgers and Yankees had, wasn't coming up with stars. A young third baseman named Foster Castleman socked 14 home runs and split the position with a dynamic young athlete named Ossie Virgil, who was the first Dominican to play in the American major leagues. Basically a third baseman, Virgil played all positions except pitcher and center field.

After the 1955 season, August Busch in St. Louis had hired Frank Lane, noted for the frequency of his trades, as general manager. "Trader" Lane had previously been the G.M. of the Chicago White Sox for seven years. During that time, he made 241 trades. Some players suggested that Lane was pathological or worse, or made trades just for the thrill of it. In any case, Lane's mania for making trades coincided with the Giants' desire to make a big move.

So on June 14, 1956, a day before the trading deadline, the Cardinals and the Giants executed a whopper. Red Schoendienst, Dick Littlefield, Jackie Brandt, Bill Sarni and a player to be named later came to New York Giants in exchange for Al Dark, Ray Katt, Don Liddle and Whitey Lockman.

After the season ended, the Giants received Gordon Jones.

Driving to the ballpark in St. Louis that day, Red heard that he had been traded to the New York Giants. His wife Mary had been notified at home and said she "just about fell over" from the shock. Stan Musial called losing his friend to another team his "saddest day in baseball." The Schoendienst family had just moved into a new home and had no desire to relocate from St. Louis. So Red came to the Polo Grounds alone and not terribly happy. In his first game he hit a pinch-hit home run, but beyond that he was generally miserable.

Then there were the further embarrassments.

Sal Maglie was still in Cleveland, unhappily sitting on the bench at the outset of the 1956 season and probably muttering to himself. He even considered retirement. But something great in his personal life had kept him in baseball. After almost 15 years of childless marriage, Sal and his wife had adopted a son. The boy gave Maglie a new determination to continue his baseball career.

Enter a weird turn of fate.

Early in the 1956 season, the Cleveland club sold Sal Maglie to his old archenemies, the Brooklyn Dodgers, much to the horror of the Flatbush Faithful. In what may be the greatest bargain in baseball history, the Dodgers' astute general manager Buzzie Bavasi fleeced the Indians' Hank Greenberg. Brooklyn obtained Maglie for $100. A used car in 1956 America normally cost more.

So now Sal Maglie returned to Brooklyn in 1956.

The move was almost beyond comprehension. Yet it was a strange karmic payback for Durocher's defection to Manhattan in 1948. The Flatbush Faithful had hated no Giant more than Maglie. And now he had come over to their side. Well maybe, the fans decided, he wasn't so bad after all…as long as there was something left in that arm.

It was as if, wrote Jimmy Cannon in the New York *Journal-American,* "the Daughters of the Confederacy [were] building a monument to General Grant in Richmond."

And so it went.

The Barber, who was still knocking guys down, helped lead the Dodgers to their final Brooklyn pennant. There was plenty left in the arm. He won key game after key game. In one of those must-win late season contests Sal tossed a no-hitter, a night game in September against the Phutile-Again Phillies. In another he won the game that clinched a tie for the pennant. The Barber finished with a 13-5 won-lost record.

All the Giants fans could do was listen to the radio, sip warm Knickerbocker Beer from cans and think what might have been. Sal would even surface again in the World Series of 1956, winning the first game against Whitey Ford, 6-3. He pitched again in Game Five against Don Larsen. Sal pitched an excellent game. Larsen pitched perfectly.

(Not by coincidence, Maglie was the starting pitcher in two of the most famous games ever played: the Bobby Thomson home run game in 1951 and Larsen's World Series perfecto five years later. Maglie was one of the greatest 'big game' starters ever.)

The New York Giants team fell to sixth in 1956 early in the season and wallowed there. Worse, attendance plummeted to 629,297, less than half of what it had been in the giddy excesses of the postwar years. Without the influx of cash at the box office, the Giants were a team in big trouble.

The ultimate insult? In December, when the Giants obtained Jackie Robinson in a trade from the Dodgers, Robinson retired rather than report to his old rivals. Everyone understood.

You know much of the rest. You know how Walter O'Malley, "a truly devious man," in the words of Red Barber, connived and cajoled to move the Dodgers - the most profitable club in the league, blessed with the most fanatic fans - three thousand miles away from their birthplace.

You know how he schemed to bring the Giants along with him. You know how New York lost two of the city's three teams.

There were some vague attempts to induce the Giants to stay. The Polo Grounds was creaking after all those busy years, and the neighborhood outside, to put it kindly, was perceived to a war zone with muggers and gangbangers. Some of it allegedly spilled into the Polo Grounds.

"There were times," Lee Allen once remarked, "when the Giants couldn't guarantee their box-seat customers safety from armed robberies during night games." At the same time, Horace Stoneham started to complain about not being able to install pari-mutuel windows at his ball park.

While seeking a new stadium to replace the crumbling Polo Grounds, the Giants began to contemplate a move from New York, initially considering Metropolitan Stadium in Minneapolis - St. Paul, which was home to their top farm team, the Minneapolis Millers. Under the rules of the time, the Giants' ownership of the Millers gave them priority rights to a major league team in the area.

There was talk of Bill Terry buying the team and moving the Giants into Yankee Stadium as tenants of Del Webb and Dan Topping. There were also discussions about a huge domed stadium to be built for the Giants on stilts above Manhattan's West Sixties, between Eighth Avenue and the Hudson River. Residents of that area today will be pleased to know that those plans have been officially shelved. There was also a humbler plan to build a ball field for the Giants above Penn Station, where the current edition of Madison Square Garden now sits.

Robert Moses, who never missed an opportunity to bulldoze, proposed a multi-purpose stadium in Flushing, perhaps to house both National League clubs. And The O'Malley hatched a self-serving plan for New York City to condemn and buy a huge parcel of what was termed "slum land" at Atlantic and Flatbush Avenues near the Long Island Railroad terminus and then "sell" it to him dirt cheap.

There was another domed proposal designed by the renowned architect, Buckminster Fuller, ready to go for that area. Ironically, the area did eventually transform into a sports venue: the current Barclays Center was built to the south across the street from the Atlantic Terminal, in neighboring Pacific Park.

But nothing came of any of this.

At this time, San Francisco mayor George Christopher approached the Giants about moving to the City by the Bay. Despite objections from many shareholders, including Joan Whitney Payson, who later owned the Mets, majority owner Horace Stoneham entered into negotiations with San Francisco officials. At about the same time Walter O'Malley began courting the city of Los

Angeles. We use the term "city" loosely, but L.A. was indeed a growing population center, though it more closely resembled a giant sprawling suburb.

Then, during the 1957 season all these conversations became more serious. On May 28, 1957, the National League approved the move of the Brooklyn Dodgers and New York Giants baseball teams to Los Angeles and San Francisco if certain conditions were met. The National League informed O'Malley that he could only go to Los Angeles if he brought another team to the west coast with him. Travel expenses, after all. New York National League fans started to break into a sweat. As well they should have. The teams had permission, but now had to actually decide to make the moves.

On August 19, Horace Stoneham announced that his board of directors - yes, he had one - had voted to move the club to San Francisco. The single vote of dissent belonged to a minority stockholder named M. Donald Grant, who later ran the Mets into the ground under different circumstances. O'Malley had scheduled a similar press conference for the same day to make a similar announcement. O'Malley, who already had made his decision, cancelled his conference and claimed he was still studying the situation, suggesting that it was Stoneham who was engineering the exodus.

Brooklyn fans would not be fooled, however. An often-told joke made the rounds in the late 1950s. There were several variations, but it went like this: "If Stalin, Hitler and O'Malley are in a room and you have two bullets, who do you shoot?"

The answer, of course: "O'Malley, twice."

The bitterness did not subside over the ensuing half century. Many decades later, two Brooklyn-born columnists for The New York *Post*, Pete Hamill and Jack Newfield, sat down together and wrote a list of their ten most evil men of the Twentieth Century. Then they compared lists.

The only three names on both lists were the same: Stalin, Hitler and Walter O'Malley.

Reminiscence - Jerry Liebowitz

I inherited my loyalty to the New York Giants from my dad who owned a candy store in Englewood, N.J. which served as a debating site for Giants, Yankees and Dodger fans. The store was a member of the Chesterfield 3 to 1 Club. One of our customers was Bob Trocolor, a Baseball Giants scout and former New York Giants football player.

My dad took me to the Polo Grounds throughout the 1940's and early 50's. At my first game in 1943 I thought the Polo Grounds looked like a huge bathtub. I got to see Carl Hubbell pitch and Mel Ott bat. We were there for Ike Day, June 19, 1945 at which time I got Milton Berle's autograph on the back of my admission ticket. In 1947 I got Mel Ott's autograph on my game program. In 1948 Mickey McGowan, a pitcher who was up only long enough to have a cup of coffee, gave me a baseball. On the evening of September 9, 1948 I witnessed the Dodgers Rex Barney pitch a no hitter against the Giants. In 1954 I got an autograph from Ruben Gómez. Years later I became a friend of Willard Marshall and Bobby Thomson.

I saw 250-foot pop fly home runs bounce off the scoreboard in left field and many 475-foot fly balls to center field result in long outs. A great ballpark for weak pull hitters; power hitters to left and right center, not so good.

Unfortunately negative experiences began to occur. The neighborhood became threatening and dangerous. Kids demanded money to "watch your car." Failure to pay an acceptable amount resulted in a flat tire or the removal of a headlight or windshield wiper.

On July 4, 1950 a fan sitting in the stands was shot and killed by a kid on the roof of a building atop Coogan's Bluff. At that time my father decided that we would no longer attend night games. Given the rapid decrease in attendance from 1.1 million in 1954, when the Giants won the World Series, to a paltry 629,000 in 1956, it is easy to justify Horace Stoneham's decision to move the team to San Francisco.

Jerry Liebowitz
Ft. Lee, NJ
May 2018

(Editor's Note: Mr. Liebowitz has one of the largest private New York Giants memorabilia collections: thousands of photos, over 100 single signed Giants baseballs, Giants team signed baseballs from 1926, '36 '37, all of the '40s and '50s, plus hundreds of autographs, programs, yearbooks, advertising signs, eight exhibit card vending machines, baseball card sets, every issue of *Giants Jottings* published from 1936 through 1948, and books. Fifty-five items from his collection were exhibited in the Museum of the City of New York and some at the Sports Museum of America.)

Photo (Courtesy of Mr. Liebowitz): Mr. Liebowitz with one of the highlights of his collection: the original Bronze plaque awarded to John J. McGraw by the New York Baseball Writers Association in 1927 in honor of his 25 years as manager of the Giants.

A Reminiscence...

Sunday morning, June 3, 1962. I was nine years old. My dad was in the bathroom shaving.

"What would you like to do more than anything else in the world?" he asked.

I responded, "Go see Willie Mays and the Giants."

"Well, get yourself ready 'cause I have two tickets," he answered.

I was excited beyond belief. After a five-year absence the Giants had returned to the beloved Polo Grounds that weekend, and we were going! It was a gorgeous baseball day, warm, clear and dry. Ideal. We drove to the game in our green '54 Chevy from Scotch Plains, New Jersey, about 25 to 30 miles west of New York City. We crossed the George Washington Bridge to Manhattan. The Giants may have moved 3,000 miles away but it made no difference in my family's loyalty to the Black and Orange. We had been Giants fans dating back to my grandfather in the 1890's.

We sat in the upper deck behind home plate. After striking out in his first two at bats, Willie Mays hit a titanic home run deep off the roof façade in left-field which drove dad, me and the majority of the crowd wild. I was just so thrilled to have Mays and the Giants back, and to be in the Polo Grounds again, a place I just loved, I didn't care about much else. The electricity and energy in the ballpark that weekend was amazing. That was a special time, never to be repeated. We were fortunate to be there!

The Giants beat the newly minted Mets 6 to 1.

After the game we worked our way down to the field boxes and out onto the field. You could do that in those days. We walked to the base of the left-field wall at the 315-ft mark, right where Bobby Thomson's home run left the park in 1951. And then slowly, reluctantly, with shadows lengthening, we gradually headed toward the center-field exit under the massive clubhouse.

Dad saved my ticket stub from that day, seat 5. I'm looking at it today as I type.

> Rich Rodgers
> Phoenix, Arizona
> April 2018

{Editor's note: Dad chose a great date! The game was laden with future Hall of Famers: Giants Juan Marichal, Orlando Cepeda, Willie McCovey in addition to Mays, plus Richie Ashburn of the New York Mets, and ex-New York Giant Casey Stengel managing the Mets.}

Left to right: Eddie Logan (the last New York Giants Bat Boy), Rich Rodgers, and *The Giants of The Polo Grounds* author Noel Hynd in Surprise, Arizona, October 2018.

Endgame

> "It's an odd thing, but anyone who disappears is said to be seen in San Francisco."
>
> Oscar Wilde
> *The Picture of Dorian Gray* (1882)

The 1957 season felt like a season being played under water.

The headlines about the move overshadowed everything on the ball field. Willie Mays had another fine year at the plate and led the league in triples. Johnny Antonelli led the pitching staff in wins and led the league in losses.

In June of 1957, the St. Louis Cardinals offered to send several players to New York plus $750,000 for Willie Mays. "Trader" Frank Lane couldn't control himself again, though he had created his own gap in center field by trading 1955 Rookie of the Year Bill Virdon to Pittsburgh for Bobby Del Greco.

The Giants didn't bite at Lane's offer. Musial's old buddy from the Cardinals, however, did land on his feet. On June 15, 1957 the New York Giants traded Red Schoendienst to the World Series-bound Milwaukee Braves in exchange for Danny O'Connell, Ray Crone and Bobby Thomson, the latter coming home as a hero, at least for a while.

Thomson would never play for the team in San Francisco. He would be dealt again to the Cubs the following spring, then play for the Red Sox and have a sip of coffee with the Orioles in 1961 before retiring. When the Giants left New York, Thomson had more home runs for the team than any player other than Mel Ott. Willie Mays was one home run behind him, one he would soon hit for the team in San Francisco. Eventually, Mays would be considered by some as perhaps the greatest player of all time, or perhaps second only to Ruth.

Soon thereafter, the Brooklyn Dodgers and the New York Giants met for a final series at the Polo Grounds. The Dodgers won the first two, but the Giants won the third. Curt Barclay beat Don Drysdale,

3-2. A two-run home run by Hank Sauer, his 25th of the year, was the difference. The New York Giants won the lifetime series against the Brooklyn Dodgers, 650-606. The Giants had fifteen pennants and five World Championships in the modern era. The Dodgers had nine pennants and one World Series win. The balance would shift in the future.

Both teams were heading west, where the rivalry would continue and flourish. All of which, after seven and a half decades of baseball at a place known as the Polo Grounds, brought everyone to the bitter end.

For a final time, on September 29, 1957, the Giants fans settled into a game at the Polo Grounds. The Pirates came to bat in the second inning.

It was difficult to fathom. Just three years after a World Championship, the Giants were last in the National League in attendance. One could daydream. One could recollect.

Memories were everywhere...

Several city blocks away, in a fading apartment on West 116th Street, an old man in his late eighties flipped the pages of a personal scrapbook as he watched the game on television. His name was Frederick Engel. You remember him, of course, from long ago.

His hair was white. His health was fading, but the pictures in his scrapbook - the likenesses of Smilin' Mickey Welch, Orator Jim O'Rourke, and John Montgomery Ward - brought back his own memories.

Frederick Engel, called Freddy as a boy, had been the Giants' original mascot. But that was in a different time, way back seven decades earlier when his father, Nick Engel, operated the restaurant called The Old Home Plate. Back when men in tall hats and striped trousers watched the Giants play at 110th Street and Fifth Avenue, Freddy Engel had run messages from ballplayers to their lady friends. The scrapbook had been left to Engel by his father, who had died in 1897. For sixty years, the son had always cherished it.

Back at the ball park, Frank Thomas of the Pirates homered off Antonelli to lead off the second. Roberto Clemente followed with a double. Antonelli hit Johnny Powers with a pitch. Hardy Peterson singled to right field, scoring Clemente from second. Bob Friend, the Pirate pitcher, singled to score Powers.

By the fourth inning, Antonelli was gone. Young Curt Barclay was pitching. The Bucs were leading 6-1. As the game continued and as the Giants' deficit mounted, the mood of the crowd darkened. In the top of the sixth inning, Ray Crone relieved Barclay. During the bottom of the inning, Rigney, a kind wise man who sensed the angry menace of the crowd, advised his players to sprint for the clubhouse at the game's conclusion.

"I told Mays not to worry about his hat or his glove," Rigney later recalled, "but about his life."

Watching the game from the dugout along with the players (and pictured here), was a sixteen-year-old boy named Eddie Logan, Jr. Eddie was the last New York Giants' batboy. Black and orange blood flowed through his veins. Eddie's grandfather, Fred Logan, was employed in the Giants clubhouse in the late 1880s before later becoming clubhouse manager for both the Giants and Yankees in the 1920s. His father, Eddie Logan Sr., was the Giants' clubhouse manager in both New York and San Francisco.

Like Mays, Eddie received some good advice from a wise elder.

"Just before the last out, (Giants trainer) Doc Bowman said, 'Eddie, as soon as the last out is made, stay by me. Just stick by me. Take your cap off because we're going to run to the clubhouse. Be careful, because everybody is going to run on the field and the first thing they're going to want to do is steal your hat,'" Logan recalled many years later. "Sure enough, that's what happened. My father and grandfather were there all the time but they were never on the field. I was on the field for that one season."

{Author's note: Never underestimate a great batboy. Eddie Logan Jr. later became a Lt. Colonel in the United States Air Force.}

Stu Miller relieved Crone. Miller pitched the seventh and eighth. In the top half of the ninth, Ramon Monzant relieved Miller. Monzant was a young Venezuelan who was the fleetest man afoot on the pitching staff. Johnny Powers capped a perfect day at the plate by hitting a blast over the right field roof, the last homer to be served up by New York Giants pitching in the Polo Grounds.

In the bottom of the ninth, Friend retired the first batter, Don Mueller, to fly out to right. That brought up Willie Mays, who already had two hits. Fans put their anger aside long enough to give Willie a Standing O. They begged for Willie to hit one out, pop one just one last time.

"The crowd was cheering so loud I felt helpless," he said later. "I got a home run my first time at bat in the Polo Grounds, and I wanted to bow out with another."

It was not to be. Mays bounced out to Dick Groat, the Pirate shortstop.

Dusty Rhodes prolonged things for a few minutes working to a full count. Then he broke his bat and knocked a weak ground ball to Groat. The surlier elements of the crowd started hopping over fences before Groat's throw reached Frank Thomas at first base.

It was 4:35 P.M., around the same time on a September afternoon - give or take a half an hour - as Thomson had homered.

Ugliness followed.

A significant element of the crowd pillaged the once majestic old park. The players from both teams fled immediately toward the weather-beaten center field clubhouse, some in real fear for their lives.

The first of the vandals cut second base loose from its moorings and then tossed it to a partner in crime to escape the groundkeepers. Some security people attempted to save the other two bases but were unsuccessful. Small crowds stood over home plate (where Ott used to dig in) and the pitcher's rubber (where Mathewson used to throw), eventually prying up both and absconding with them.

Invaders tore up the green canvas screen behind home plate. The bullpen shelters were smashed and splintered into portable pieces. Nothing vulnerable was untouched or undamaged. Driven by indignation, sorrow, and rage, the marauders went after everything.

The 483-foot sign in the deepest part of the ballpark was bent in half before security guards secured it. Thousands of others dug up sod or dirt. The heavy wooden seats, sturdy and bolted down, proved too stubborn. The most sacrilegious of the looters stole the center field plaque honoring Eddie Grant, the former Giant infielder who died in World War One. The other plaques were stolen also.

None was ever seen again.

"Thousands of fans responded to the final melancholy out by chasing their California-bound idols to the clubhouse," wrote John Drebinger in The New York *Times*, "and carrying away everything on the field that could be moved. The mass pursuit was touched off by affection, excitement, nostalgia, curiosity and annoyance at the fact the team next year will represent San Francisco."

The image was that of a carcass being picked. It wasn't pretty. Some in the crowd chanted, "We want Stoneham, with a rope around his neck!"

"Only a witness to the Vandals' sacking of Rome in 455," wrote Steve Wulf in *Sports Illustrated*, many years later as he recalled the scene, "could do justice to a description of those frenzied minutes right after the game."

By quarter past 5 P.M, the darkness of evening approached. The pillaging subsided. Many fans congregated in front of the Giants' clubhouse. After taunting Stoneham, who was far away by this time, they pleaded to bid adieu personally to Willie Mays. Willie wisely declined to appear. Finally, turning angry again, the fans serenaded the Giants with some verses to the tune of *The Farmer in the Dell*:

"We hate to see you go,

"We hate to see you go,

"We hope to hell you never come back—

"We hate to see you go."

Really, it was horrible.

"I played my first major league game here in 1946," Bill Rigney said to reporters. "And I can't tell you what a thrill it's been for me to put on the uniform in the same clubhouse that Matty and McGraw and Terry and Ott occupied."

"I guess I'm dispossessed," said groundskeeper Matty Schwab, as he and his family gave up their apartment under the seats in left field.

By 5:30, a bittersweet calm had replaced the insanity on the field.

The Polo Grounds, what remained of it, was serene, though beaten up. Strains of *Auld Lang Syne*, drunkenly sung by the final guests who staggered out, echoed throughout.

On their way to the exit, Rigney and Giant vice-president Chub Feeney stopped to say goodbye to the members of the grounds crew who wouldn't be moving west to Seals Stadium.

Rigney told one of them, "I want to thank you guys for making this the best damn field..." Rigney began to one of them.

But he was too choked up to finish. He gave the man a hug and walked on. And he had been correct. It *had* been the best damned field.

Out on the diamond, with the crowd finally dispersed, between what remained of the first base line and the Giants' dugout, Bobby Thomson and his wife walked their daughter, five-year-old Nancy, to home plate. Her father recorded the scene with a home movie camera, the little girl happily circled the bases, shouting with happiness.

"Who knows?" said Bobby. "Maybe someday Nancy will have her own children. She can show them this movie and tell them about the home run that grandpa hit."

The old park would see major league baseball - or what occasionally passed for it - for two more years with the advent of the Mets in 1962 and 1963. At the time, a graceful ardent New York essayist named Murray Kempton would write in *Sport Magazine* that the return of National League baseball to the old Polo Grounds was "like the raising of a sunken cathedral, its place sacred in history and hallowed in memory."

Absolutely correct.

But that would be five years in the future.

Today, everyone was looking backward, not forward.

Writer Roger Angel, on assignment from *Holiday* magazine, and a longtime Giant fan, was there until the end.

"I didn't feel anything," he would later write. "Nothing at all. I guess I just couldn't believe it. But it's true, all right. The flags are down, the lights in the temple are out, and the Harlem River flows lonely to the seas."

On September 29 there were only memories. And ghosts. As the afternoon died and you glanced around the old ballpark, you could see them, the ghosts, the memories in the autumnal shadows that deepened minute to minute.

There was the young John J. McGraw arriving from Baltimore, exorcising the demons of Andrew Freedman.. Christy Mathewson on the mound, young, handsome, gracious and gifted. Fred Merkle missing second, Rube Marquard winning nineteen in a row....McGraw furious as the White Sox won the 1917 World Series.. Casey Stengel sitting on the bench with Mac, learning strategy... The men and women of Broadway. Cohan. Dauvray. Ida Schnall. Sinatra. Blossom Seeley.... FDR watching the World Series. Jimmy Walker. LaGuardia... Babe Ruth furiously barging into the Giant dressing room...

The ballpark as a backdrop of the racy wild limitless adventurous feel of Manhattan in the 1920s, when jazz was the soundtrack of the city and the liquor never stopped flowing despite Prohibition…the "constant flicker of men and women and machines," as F. Scott Fitzgerald wrote in *The Great Gatsby*…Bill Terry arriving from Louisiana. Then Carl Hubbell taking the mound with his bent left arm… Ott hitting 363 homers down the friendly right field line….

The international soccer.

The Gaelic soccer. Verdi. The crazy little midget racers.

The great boxing.

The college and pro football.

The war years of the 1940's… The dim-outs… Leo arriving belligerently from Brooklyn to take over his arch rivals and guide them to pennants… Sal Maglie with a game-day scowl that could scare the Devil himself… The crisp white home uniforms with the black caps and the orange NY… Willie the Wonder, the ballplayer of a lifetime…

Johnny Mize…

Bobby Thomson…

Monte Irvin…

Dauntless Danny Gardella….

White Lockman… Hank Thompson… Antonelli… Jansen… Dusty Rhodes…

The New York Giants weren't dead, as Chuck Dressen twice suggested.

It was worse. They were gone.

Eventually, police cleared everyone from the old park. Mrs. John McGraw, still clutching her now-wilting roses, walked down the aisle toward an exit. Jane Mathewson was still conspicuous in her absence. Fifty years ago, when Jane's husband played for the Giants, she and Christy lived on Coogan's Bluff. She could see the scoreboard from her apartment window. When Christy was pitching, she could put a roast in the oven in the seventh inning and be certain that her husband would be home for dinner. Today, she lived far away and chose not to come. Too painful.

Officially, Blanche McGraw was the last Giants fan to leave. She was helped to a car that would take her home to Pelham.

The gates clanked shut. They were padlocked.

"It would have broken John's heart," she said softly.

She was right. It would have.

The Polo Grounds

155th Street and Eighth Avenue
New York City
1911 - 1964

Requiescat in pace

Feedback

Readers can reach Noel Hynd at Nh1212f@yahoo.com. Readers are invited to communicate with any comments, observations or possible corrections. I'm happy to hear from you. Reviews on Amazon.com are greatly appreciated also.

Acknowledgements

Photographs

All photographs are either public domain or Creative Commons unless otherwise indicated. Sometimes the rights to specific prints have become muddled over the years. If an unknown photographer covered a ball game in 1942 and turned his work over to a newspaper that no longer exists, who owns the rights today, for example? Generally speaking, American photos from 1928 or before are now in the public domain, as are many in the decades that followed where rights were never claimed or renewed. Bowman baseball cards, for example, never renewed their copyrights. Some photographs are in the public domain in the United States because they were published in the United States between 1923 and 1977 without a copyright notice. Publicity shots of film stars, theater and tv stars baseball stars were frequently in this category. The most recent photo or illustration used here is from 1957, aside from photos [provided with personal anecdotes. I've done my best to track down rights and attribute them here. In the odd event that something here has been used without proper permission, please contact me at Nh1212f@yahoo.com.

The Boston Braves playing during spring training in The Choate School's Winter Ex, 1943 – Photograph courtesy of Choate Rosemary Hall Archives.

Artwork from the "Illustrated Schedule" of the 1887 New York Ball Club's season is in the Public Domain via United States Library of Congress. (page 511 or thereabouts.)

World Champion 1954 New York Giants is from the estate of a

former team member. Signatures are from the top row, left to right: "Paul Giel", "Joe Amalfitano", "Don Liddle", "Bill Gardner", "Al Worthington", "Foster Castleman", "J. McCall", Alex Konikowski," "Al Corwin", "Marv Grissom", "Ray Katt", "George Spencer", "Wes Westrum", "Jim Hearn". Second row is signed: "Ed Logan", "Hoyt Wilhelm", "Jim Rhodes", "Willie Mays", "Don Mueller", "Al Dark", "Monte Irwin", "Bill Taylor", "Bob Hofman", "Joe Garagiola", "Ruben Gomez". Bottom row is signed: "Johnny Antonelli", "Sal Maglie", "Whitey Lockman", "Larry Jansen", "Fred Fitzsimmons", "Leo Durocher", "Frank Shellenback", "Herman Franks", "Dave Williams" and "Hank Thompson".

Bibliography

Alexander, Charles C., *Ty Cobb*. New York: Oxford Univ. Press, 1984.
Allen, Lee. *The National League Story*. New York: Hill & Wang, 1961.
--. *The World Series*. New York: Putnam, 1969.
Appel, Marty, *Casey Stengel: Baseball's Greatest Character*, Doubleday, New York, 2017
Baldassaro, Lawrence, *Beyond DiMaggio*, U of Nebraska Press, Lincoln, Nebraska, 2011
Bevis, Charlie, *Sunday Baseball*, McFarland and Company, 2003
Cohen, Richard M., and David S. Neft. *The World Series*. New York: Macmillan, 1986.
Connor, Anthony J. *Voices from Cooperstown*. New York: Macmillan, 1982.
Creamer, Robert W. *Babe: The Legend Comes to Life*. New York: Simon & Schuster, 1974.
--. *Stengel: His Life and Times*. New York: Simon & Schuster, 1984.
Daley, Arthur. *Sports of the Times*. New York: Dutton, 1959.
Dickey, Glenn. *The History of the World Series Since 1903*. New York: Stein & Day, 1984.
Durocher, Leo. *Nice Guys Finish Last*. New York: Simon & Schuster, 1975.
Durso, Joseph. *The Days of Mr. McGraw*. Englewood Cliffs, N. J.: Prentice-Hall, 1969.
Einstein, Charles, ed. *The Baseball Reader*. New York: Harper & Row, 1980.

Fair, James, *Give Him To The Angels*, -, 1946 (Republished by Summersdale Publishers, 1997)
Fitzgerald, F. Scott, *The Great Gatsby*, Charles Scribner's, New York, 1925
Fleming, Gordon H. *The Dizziest Season.* New York: Morrow, 1984.
--. *The Unforgettable Season.* New York: Holt, Rinehart & Winston, 1981.
Frommer, Harvey. *New York City Baseball.* New York: Macmillan, 1980.
Gehrig, Eleanor, and Joseph Durso. *My Luke and I.* New York: Crowell, 1976.
Golenbock, Peter. *Bums: An Oral History of the Brooklyn Dodgers,* New York: Putnam, 1984.
Graham, Frank. *McGraw of the Giants.* New York: Putnam, 1944.
Goldstein, Richard. *Spartan Seasons.* New York: Macmillan, 1980. Honig, Donald. *The National League.* New York: Crown, 1983.
Heller, Peter, *In This Corner*, Da Capo Press, New York, 1994
Jennison, Christopher. *Wait 'Til Next Year.* New York: Norton, 1974.
Joyner, Ronnie. Hardball Legends and Journeymen, McFarland & Company, Jefferson, N.C. and London, 2012
Kahn, Roger. *The Boys of Summer.* New York: Harper & Row, 1972.
Kiernan, Thomas. *The Miracle at Coogan's Bluff.* New York: Crowell, 1975.
King, Joe. *The San Francisco Giants.* Englewood Cliffs, N. J.: Prentice-Hall, 1958.
Levine, Peter. *A. G. Spalding and the Rise of Baseball.* New York: Oxford Univ. Press, 1985.
- , Ellis Island to Ebbets Field. New York, Oxford, 1993
Lieb, Fred. *Baseball as I Have Known It.* New York: Coward, McCann & Geoghegan, 1977.
Mack, Connie. *My Sixty-six Years in the Big Leagues.* Philadelphia: Winston, 1950.
Mathewson, Christy. *Pitching in a Pinch.* New York: Putnam, 1912.
McGraw, John J. *My Thirty Years in Baseball.* New York: Boni & Liveright, 1923.
McGraw, Mrs. John J. *The Real McGraw.* New York: D. McKay, 1953.
Mead, William B. *Even the Browns.* New York: Contemporary Bks., 1978.
Meany, Tom. *Baseball's Greatest Teams.* New York: A. S. Barnes, 1949.
Morris, Lloyd. *Incredible New York.* New York: Random House, 1951.
Morris, Peter, A *Game of Inches: The Stories Behind the Innovations That Shaped Baseball*, Ivan Dee, Chicago, 2006, 2010

Neft, David, Cohen, Richard and Korch, Rick, in *The Complete History of Professional Football from 1892 to the Present,* St. Martin's, New York, 1994

The Ultimate Baseball Book. Okrent, Daniel, and Harris Lewine, eds. Boston: Houghton Mifflin, 1979.

Nelson, Kevin. *Baseball's Greatest Quotes.* New York: Simon & Schuster, 1982.

New York Giants Yearbook(s), Big League Books, New York, 1951-57

Peterson, Robert. *Only the Ball Was White.* Englewood Cliffs, N.J.: Prentice-Hall, 1970.

Reichler, Joseph L. *The Baseball Trade Register.* New York: Macmillan, 1984.

Ed., The Baseball Encyclopedia. New York: Macmillan, 1982, 1984.

Reidenbaugh, Lowell. *Cooperstown.* Norwalk, Conn.: Arlington House, 1986.

--. *Take Me Out to the Ball Park.* St. Louis: *The Sporting News,* 1983.

Ritter, Lawrence. *The Glory of Their Times.* New York: Macmillan, 1966.

Robinson, Ray, Matty: An American Hero, Oxford University Press, NY, 1993

Rust, Art, Jr., with Edna Rust. *Recollections of a Baseball Junkie.* New York: Morrow, 1985.

Seymour, Harold. *Baseball: The Early Years.* New York: Oxford Univ. Press, 1960.

Smith, Kenneth. *Baseball Hall of Fame.* New York: A. S. Barnes, 1952.

Smith, Robert. *World Series.* Garden City, New York: Doubleday, 1967.

Stein, Fred. *Under Coogan Bluff.* Glenshaw, Pa.: Chapter & Cask, 1978.

Stein, Fred, and Nick Peters. *Giants Diary.* Berkeley, Cal.: North Atlantic Books. 1987.

Threston, Christopher. *The Integration of Baseball in Philadelphia.* McFarland, Jefferson, N.C.

Thorn, John. *A Century of Baseball Lore. Hart Publishing* New York, 1983

---, *Baseball in the Garden of Eden: The Secret History of the Early Game,* Simon and Schuster, New York, 2012

Van Hyning, Thomas. E., *Puerto Rico's Winter League: A History of Major League Baseball's Launching Pad.* Jefferson, North Carolina: McFarland & Co., 1995.

--- *The Santurce Crabbers: Sixty Seasons of Puerto Rican Winter League Baseball.* Jefferson, North Carolina: McFarland & Co., 1999.

Weintraub, Robert, The Victory Season, Little Brown, Boston, 2013
Zang, David, *Fleet Walker's Divided Heart: The Life of Baseball's First Black Major Leaguer,* Legacy Audio Books, 2007

(Oddly enough, since the first edition of this book appeared in 1988, a few of the books above which I've consulted for this 2019 edition, cite this same book in their own bibliographies. I'm flattered.)

Periodicals and on Line Sources

Barra, Allen, *'Dempsey and Firpo: The Greatest American Sports Painting', The Atlantic,* Boston, Mass. April 2012
Slate.com
New York *Times,* New York *News,* Boston *Globe,* The Philadelphia *Inquirer, The Sporting New*s, The Brooklyn *Eagle, The Wall Street Journal,* The Chicago *Sun, Variety, The Morning Telegraph,* The Chicago *Sun.*
Wikipedia
The Ring Magazine
Baseball Almanac: Baseball History, Baseball Records and Baseball at www.baseball-almanac.com

http://www.baseballinwartime.com

I used Baseball Reference (https://www.baseball-reference.com) as my source for statistics. Thank you BB-Reffy for all those beautiful numbers.

Special Mention - SABR

I used SABR (Society for American Baseball Research) extensively. The site is https://sabr.org.
I gratefully acknowledge use of SABR's site and the work of countless SABR historians. I am specifically indebted to SABR's researchers on the following players, with the researcher acknowledged in parentheses after the player's name.
In random order: Sal Maglie (Judith Testa), Leo Durocher (Jeffrey Marlett), Bill Rigney (Alan Cohen), Rube Marquard (Joseph Wancho), John McGraw (Don Jensen), Christy Mathewson (Eddie Frierson), Bill Terry (Fred Stein), Willy Mays (John Saccoman), Monte Irvin (Larry Hogan), Danny Gardella (Charlie Weatherby), Danny Litwhiler (Glen

Vasey), Bobby Thomson (Jeff Findley), Hugh Mulcahy (C. Paul Rogers III), Sid Gordon (Ralph Berger), Jack 'Lucky' Lohrke (Andy Sturgill), Johnny Antonelli (Alexander Edelman), Jack Chesbro (Wayne McElreavy), Moonlight Graham (Jimmy Keenan), Mike "Pinky" Higgins (Mark Armour), Al Brazle (Gregory H. Wolf), Ruben Gomez (Thomas Van Hyning)

*

The original edition of The Giants of The Polo Grounds carried the following permissions, which are also included here. The author gratefully thanks the all concerned following for permission to reprint previously published material:

Harper & Row Publishers, Inc., for an excerpt from *For 2 Cents Plain by Harry Golden*. Copyright © 1959 by Harry Golden.
Random House, Inc., for permission to reprint material from *Ragtime*. Copyright © 1974, 1975 by E.L. Doctorow.
G.P. Putnam's Sons for permission to reprint material from *Summer of '42*. Copyright© 1971 by Herman Raucher.
Indiana University Press for "*Polo Grounds*" from *The Collected Poems of Rolfe Humphries*. Copyright© 1956 by Indiana University Press.
Mr. Ira Sadoff and *The New Yorker* for permission to reprint "*Autumn Elegy for the Giants.*" Copyright© 1986 by Ira Sadoff.
Mr. Joseph Durso for permission to reprint material from The Days of Mr. McGraw.
Copyright© 1969 by Joseph Durso.
Mr. Robert Creamer for permission to reprint material from *Babe: The Legend Comes to Life*. Copyright© 1974 by Robert W. Creamer.
William Morrow and Co., Inc., for permission to reprint material from *The Glory of Their Times*. Copyright© 1966 by Lawrence S. Ritter.

Hardcover edition published in 1988 by Doubleday.

Noel Hynd is the author of several highly successful political thrillers such as *Firebird* and *Flowers From Berlin* as well as several supernatural thrillers such as *Ghosts* and *Cemetery of Angels*. He is a graduate of the University of Pennsylvania and a former contributor to *Sports Illustrated*.

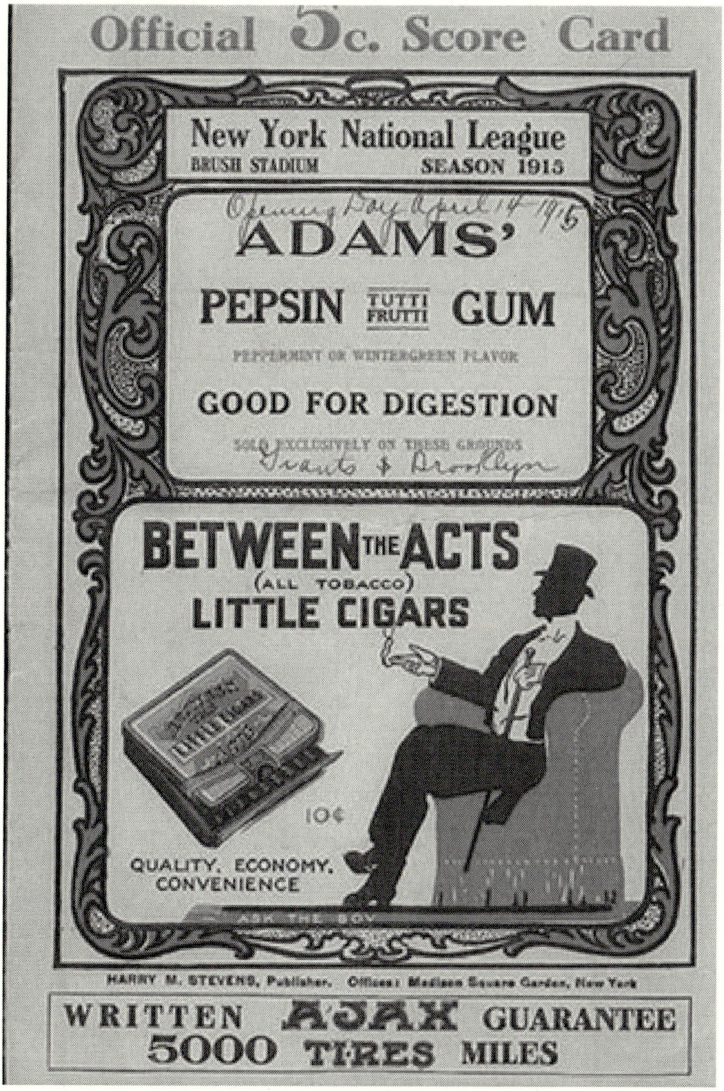
Official 5c. Score Card
New York National League
BRUSH STADIUM
SEASON 1915
Opening Day April 14 1915
ADAMS'
PEPSIN TUTTI FRUTTI GUM
PEPPERMINT OR WINTERGREEN FLAVOR
GOOD FOR DIGESTION
SOLD EXCLUSIVELY ON THESE GROUNDS
Giants & Brooklyn
BETWEEN THE ACTS
(ALL TOBACCO)
LITTLE CIGARS
10¢
QUALITY, ECONOMY, CONVENIENCE
ASK THE BOY
HARRY M. STEVENS, Publisher. Offices: Madison Square Garden, New York
WRITTEN AJAX GUARANTEE
5000 TIRES MILES

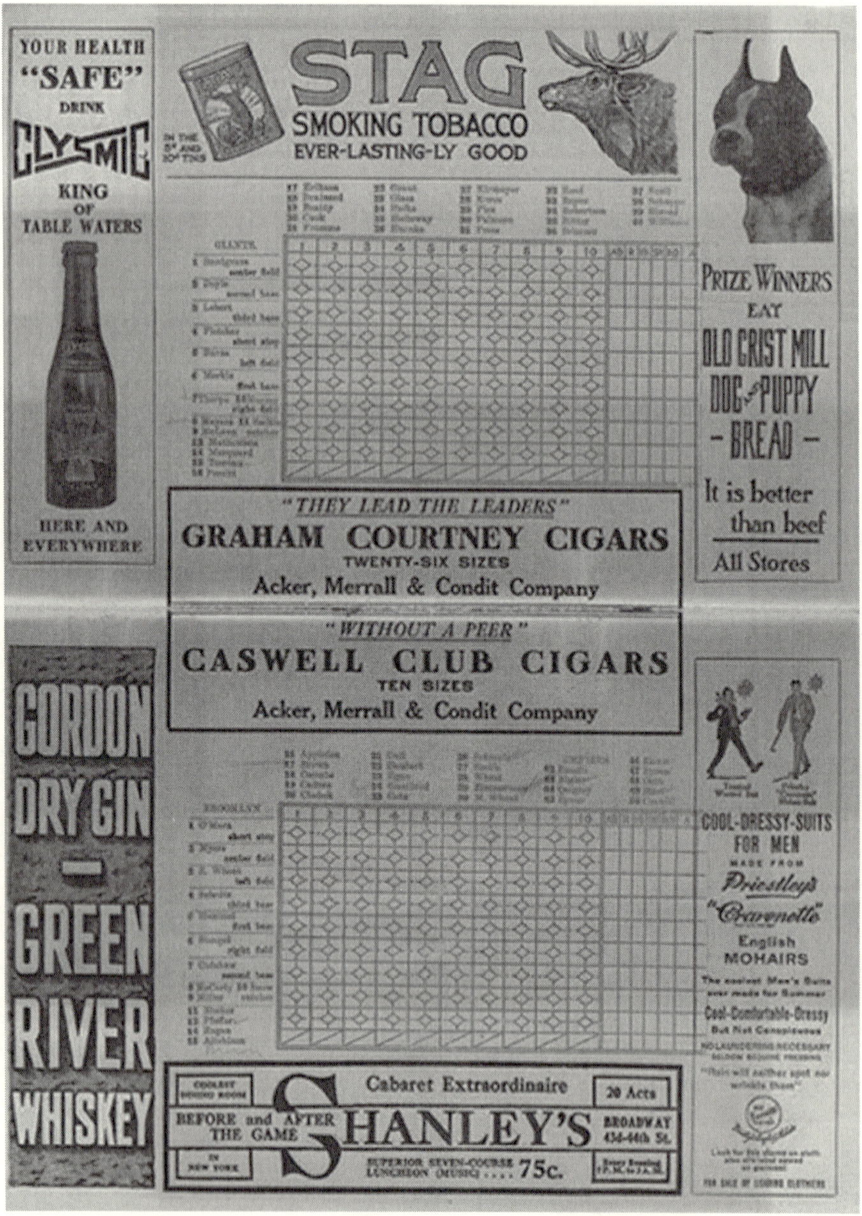
YOUR HEALTH
"SAFE"
DRINK
CLYSMIC
KING
OF
TABLE WATERS
HERE AND
EVERYWHERE
STAG
SMOKING TOBACCO
EVER-LASTING-LY GOOD
PRIZE WINNERS
EAT
OLD GRIST MILL
DOG & PUPPY
- BREAD -
It is better
than beef
All Stores
"THEY LEAD THE LEADERS"
GRAHAM COURTNEY CIGARS
TWENTY-SIX SIZES
Acker, Merrall & Condit Company
"WITHOUT A PEER"
CASWELL CLUB CIGARS
TEN SIZES
Acker, Merrall & Condit Company
GORDON
DRY GIN
GREEN
RIVER
WHISKEY
COOL-DRESSY-SUITS
FOR MEN
MADE FROM
Priestley's
"Cravenette"
English
MOHAIRS
Cool-Comfortable-Dressy
Cabaret Extraordinaire
20 Acts
BEFORE and AFTER THE GAME
SHANLEY'S
BROADWAY
75c.

Made in United States
North Haven, CT
23 February 2024